# contemporary issues in
# Language intervention

# contemporary issues in
# Language Intervention

**Editors**

**Jon Miller, Ph.D.**
Professor, Department of
   Communicative Disorders
University of Wisconsin
Madison, Wisconsin

**David E. Yoder, Ph.D.**
Walker Bascom Professor,
Department of Communicative
   Disorders
University of Wisconsin
Madison, Wisconsin

**Richard Schiefelbusch, Ph.D.**
University Distinguished Professor,
Department of Speech, Language and
   Hearing Science and Disorders
University of Kansas
Lawrence, Kansas

**1983**
ASHA Reports 12
THE AMERICAN SPEECH-LANGUAGE-HEARING ASSOCIATION
Rockville, Maryland

## General Information

The American Speech-Language-Hearing Association publishes ASHA Reports; ASHA Monographs; Asha; Journal of Speech and Hearing Disorders; Journal of Speech and Hearing Research; and Language, Speech, and Hearing Services in Schools

ASHA Reports publishes the proceedings of conferences on speech, hearing, and language, or related topics. The conferences are sponsored wholly or partly by the American Speech-Language-Hearing Association.

Manuscripts and related correspondence should be addressed to Theodore J. Glattke, Editor, ASHA Reports, Department of Speech and Hearing Sciences, University of Arizona, Tucson, Arizona 85721. ASHA Reports will consider only those manuscripts that are submitted exclusively to this publication and that have not been printed elsewhere.

ASHA Reports 12 is produced by B.C. Decker Inc., 3 Belmont Circle, Trenton, New Jersey 08618.

Copies of ASHA Reports 12 may be obtained by writing to ASHA Reports, American Speech-Language-Hearing Association, 10801 Rockville Pike, Rockville, Maryland 20852.

Contemporary Issues in Language Intervention          ISBN 0-910329-02-8

Library of Congress catalog card number          82-050935

Last digit is print number:     10    9    8    7    6    5    4    3    2    1

# CONTRIBUTORS

**ANTHONY S. BASHIR, Ph.D.**

Division of Hearing and Speech, The Children's Hospital Medical Center; Lecturer in Medicine, Harvard Medical School, Boston, Massachusetts
*Issues in Language Disorders: Considerations of Cause, Maintenance, and Change*

**ROBIN S. CHAPMAN, Ph.D.**

Department of Communicative Disorders, University of Wisconsin, Waisman Center on Mental Retardation and Human Development, Madison, Wisconsin
*Discussion: Part V: Deciding When to Intervene*

**JANIS M. COSTELLO, Ph.D.**

Professor, Speech and Language Pathology, University of California-Santa Barbara, Santa Barbara, California
*Generalization Across Settings: Language Intervention with Children*

**PAUL FLETCHER, Ph.D.**

Department of Linguistic Science, University of Reading, United Kingdom
*An Outsider's View of Language Intervention*

**LEE J. GRUENEWALD, Ph.D.**

Director, Department of Specialized Education Services, Madison Metropolitan School District, Madison, Wisconsin
*Language Intervention in the Multiple Contexts of the Public School Setting*

**NANCY HELM-ESTABROOKS, D.Sc.**

Chief, Audiology/Speech Pathology Section, Neurology Service, Boston Veterans Administration Medical Center; Assistant Professor of Neurology (Speech Pathology), Boston University School of Medicine, Boston, Massachusetts
*Language Intervention for Adults: Environmental Considerations*

**AUDREY L. HOLLAND, Ph.D.**

Professor of Speech, Research Assistant Professor of Psychiatry, University of Pittsburgh, Pittsburgh, Pennsylvania
*Language Intervention in Adults: What is it?*

**ROBERT HOEKENGA, M.S.**

Coordinator, Speech/Language Program, Department of Specialized Educational Services, Madison Metropolitan School District, Madison Wisconsin
*Language Intervention in the Multiple Contexts of the Public School Setting*

**DORIS J. JOHNSON, Ph.D.**

Professor of Learning Disabilities, Northwestern University, Evanston, Illinois
*Design for Individualization of Language Intervention Programs*

**JUDITH R. JOHNSTON, Ph.D.**

Assistant Professor, Department of Speech and Hearing Sciences, Indiana University, Bloomington, Indiana
*Discussion: Part I: What is Language Intervention: The Role of Theory*

**JAMES C. KEMP, Ph.D.**

Director, Speech-Language Pathology and Audiology, Variety Children's Hospital, Miami, Florida
*The Timing of Language Intervention for the Pediatric Population*

**SANDRA N. KLEINMAN, M.A., Ed.M.**

Department of Neurology, Division of Hearing and Speech, The Children's Hospital Medical Center, Boston, Massachusetts
*Issues in Language Disorders: Considerations of Cause, Maintenance, and Change*

ARLENE KRAAT, Ph.D.

Coordinator, Augmentative Communication Center, Queens College, Flushing, New York
*Intervention Issues in Non-Speech Communication*

KARL C. KUBAN, M.D.

The Children's Hospital Medical Center; Instructor, Department of Neurology, Harvard Medical School, Boston, Massachusetts
*Issues in Language Disorders: Considerations of Cause, Maintenance, and Change*

LEONARD L. LA POINTE, Ph.D.

Coordinator of Instruction, Audiology and Speech Pathology Service, Veterans Administration Medical Center, Gainesville, Florida; Adjunct Professor, Department of Speech, Department of Communicative Disorders, University of Florida, Gainesville, Florida
*Aphasia Intervention with Adults: Historical, Present, and Future Approaches*

LAURENCE B. LEONARD, Ph.D.

Department of Audiology and Speech Sciences, Purdue University, West Lafayette, Indiana
*Discussion: Part II: Defining the Boundaries of Language Disorders in Children*

MARK W. LIPSEY, Ph.D.

Associate Professor of Psychology, Claremont Graduate School, Claremont, California
*Program Evaluation for Speech and Hearing Services*

CHRISTY L. LUDLOW, Ph.D.

Research Speech Pathologist, Communicative Disorders Program, National Institute of Neurological and Communicative Disorders and Stroke, Bethesda, Maryland
*Identification and Assessment of Aphasic Patients for Language Intervention*

KATHLEEN LYNGAAS, M.S.

Program Support Teacher, Speech/Language, Department of Specialized Education Services, Madison Metropolitan School District, Madison, Wisconsin
*Language Intervention in the Multiple Contexts of Public School Setting*

JAMES E. McLEAN, Ph.D.

Senior Scientist, Bureau of Child Research, University of Kansas, Parsons, Kansas
*Historical Perspectives on the Content of Child Language Programs*

MALCOLM R. MCNEIL, Ph.D.

Associate Professor, Department of Communicative Disorders, University of Wisconsin, Madison, Wisconsin
*Discussion: Part IV: Moving from Assessment to Treatment*

LEIJA V. MCREYNOLDS, Ph.D.

Professor, Hearing and Speech Department, University of Kansas Medical Center, Kansas City, Kansas
*Discussion: Part VII: Evaluating Program Effectiveness*

JON F. MILLER, Ph.D.

Professor, Department of Communicative Disorders, University of Wisconsin, Madison, Wisconsin
*Identifying Children with Language Disorders and Describing Their Language Performance*

BARBARA NYBERG, M.S.

Program Support Teacher, Speech/Language Department of Specialized Educational Services, Madison Metropolitan School District, Madison, Wisconsin.
*Language Intervention in the Multiple Contexts of the Public School Setting*

NORMA S. REES, Ph.D.

Vice Chancellor for Academic Affairs, University of Wisconsin, Milwaukee, Wisconsin
*Language Intervention with Children*

JOHN C. ROSENBEK, Ph.D.

Audiology and Speech Pathology, William S. Middleton Memorial Veterans Administration Hospital, Madison, Wisconsin·
*Some Challenges for Clinical Aphasiologists*

ANNEBELLE SCAVUZZO, M.S.

Division of Hearing and Speech, The Children's Hospital Medical Center, Boston, Massachusetts
*Issued in Language Disorders: Considerations of Cause, Maintenance, and Change*

TERIS KIM SCHERY, Ph.D.

Associate Professor of Speech Pathology, California State University at Los Angeles, Los Angeles, California
*Program Evaluation for Speech and Hearing Services*

RICHARD L. SCHIEFELBUSCH,
Ph.D.

University Distinguished Professor, Department of Speech, Language and Hearing Science
and Disorders, University of Kansas, Lawrence,
Kansas
*Language Intervention in Children: What is it?*

GERALD M. SIEGEL, Ph.D.

Director, Center for Research in Human Learn-
ing, Professor, Department of Communication
Disorders, University of Minnesota, Min-
neapolis, Minnesota
*Discussion: Part VI: Intervention Context and
Setting: Where?*

LYNN S. SNYDER, Ph.D.

Assistant Professor, Department of Speech Pa-
thology and Audiology, University of Denver,
Denver Colorado
*From Assessment to Intervention: Problems and
Solutions*

ROBERT T. WERTZ, Ph.D.

Chief, Audiology and Speech Pathology, Veterans Administration Medical Center, Martinez,
California; Adjunct Professor of Speech, University of California, Santa Barbara, California; Adjunct Associate Professor, University of California, School of Medicine, Davis, California
*Language Intervention Context and Setting for the
Aphasic Adult: When?*

RONNIE B. WILBUR, Ph.D.

Associate Professor of Linguistics, Department
of Audiology and Speech Sciences, Purdue University, West Lafayette, Indiana
*Discussion: Part III: Where Do We Go From Here?*

DAVID E. YODER, Ph.D.

Walker Bascom Professor, Department of Com-
municative Disorders, University of Wisconsin,
Madison, Wisconsin
*Intervention Issues in Non-Speech Communication*

# PREFACE

The publication of this volume represents the culmination of five years of development, planning, writing, and editing. It was all started by Richard Schiefelbusch in 1977. At that time he recognized the need for a re-examination of the entire enterprise we call language intervention. Since 1977 the need for a reanalysis of our clinical practices in language has become even more acute. The concept of language and communication has continued to broaden, prompting an expanded conceptualization of deficit performance across clinical populations. Indeed, target populations thought to require intervention have also continued to expand to the point where teaching language and teaching communication skills are not viewed as distinct enterprises. In this volume, language intervention is examined in terms of its historical roots, its present forms, and its future course for all clinical populations, adult as well as children.

In 1980 the Executive Board of the American Speech-Language-Hearing Association established an ad hoc committee to organize a national conference on language intervention, which would result in publication of a proceedings. The charge to the committee was to cover all aspects of language intervention as it is practiced across settings, age, and disability groups—a task that was nearly impossible. The committee did, however, undertake the project with great enthusiasm, though it soon became apparent that the scope of the charge would lead to serious organizational problems. The first task was to select a committee that would represent various aspects of the enterprise, including geographic location, occupation, and primary population served. A committee was appointed by the Executive Board and assigned to the Vice President of Clinical Affairs, David Yoder, as the Board liaison. The committee consisted of Richard Schiefelbusch, Audrey Holland, Ronnie Wilbur, Lynn Snyder, James Kemp, Teris Schery, and Jon Miller as chairperson.

The committee first met in 1980 to formulate the conference organizing theme and to invite experts in the field to begin to develop their constributions to the volume. The committee agreed that the overall theme should be "Issues in Language Intervention," thereby providing a potential bridge between adult and child language intervention. Clearly, issues in one population are potential issues in other populations, and the habilitation of adult language bears comparison with the facilitation of child language. The conference and proceedings were organized around a series of general questions designed to provoke discussion of intervention issues from different perspectives. These issues, which are the major section headings of this book, include the following:

What is language intervention?
Who should receive language intervention?
Deciding how to carry out language intervention
Moving from assessment to intervention
When to begin and end language intervention
Where to conduct language intervention
Evaluating program effectiveness
The charge to the language professional

Experts were selected to write a paper for each of these topics reflecting the issues for the population with which they have clinical experience. The committee invited one expert to write on the issues of each topic area as it pertained to adult populations, and a second expert covered the issues as they relate to children. In addition, a contributor was assigned to each section with the difficult task of discussing the papers presented and providing additional insights and issues on the section topic.

After two years of searching for funding to support the Conference, it was held April 18–21, 1982, at the Boys Town Center, Boys Town, Nebraska. The Boys Town Institute on Communication Disorders in Children graciously hosted and cosponsored the event with ASHA. At this time we express our sincere appreciation to the numerous people who helped make the conference a success. Betty Jane Philips with her staff at the Boys Town Institute did a superb job of taking care of the local arrangements. Our thanks to Dr. Patrick Brookhouser and Father Robert Hupp for their sponsorship and use of the facilities. Thanks to the ASHA national office staff, Charles Diggs, Kathleen Griffin, and Frederick T. Spahr for their support and assistance throughout the project. We also express our appreciation to the 1980 and 1981 ASHA Executive Boards under the direction of Margaret Byrne and Alan Feldman for their support and confidence. Our thanks to B. C. Decker, Inc., Publisher, who in producing this volume for ASHA coordinated the copy editing, typesetting, and design and met a rigorous production schedule. And we especially extend our thanks and appreciation to the participants for contributing so much to make this volume possible.

JFM
DEY
RLS
July, 1982

# CONTENTS

# IV. Moving from Assessment to Intervention

# V. When to Begin and End Language Intervention

# VI. Where to Conduct Language Intervention

# PART I

# WHAT IS LANGUAGE INTERVENTION?

# 1

# LANGUAGE INTERVENTION IN ADULTS: WHAT IS IT?

*AUDREY L. HOLLAND*

The task of defining language intervention as it applies to adults might well give pause to some of us in clinical aphasiology who, at various times in our careers, have espoused numerous different theories, from programmed instruction to language pragmatics. But in truth, the multiple and varied faces of American clinical aphasiology in general reflect both the changing nature of the art as it has been influenced by our expanding knowledge, and the flexible willingness of its practitioners to try, in principled, responsible ways, to meet the varied needs of adults with language disorders.

This chapter is an attempt to build an extended operational definition of language intervention as it is currently practiced in the United States. The emphasis is on poststroke aphasic adults. However, as you shall see, language intervention has recently begun to be practiced in somewhat different forms with the demented and those with closed head injuries, in the patient with right hemisphere damage, and even with the normally aging who reside in institutions or in isolation from companionship where they suffer some loss of normal daily language interaction and its varied blessings. First, individual, direct aphasia treatment will be discussed; followed by counseling concerns of individual patients, groups, and families; and then, briefly,

treatment for other populations, that newer area about which much less is known.

At the end of the chapter is a brief answer to the question posed in the title: Language intervention: What is it? Hopefully, this definition will be narrow enough to be useful and broad enough to incorporate the multiple faces of language intervention in adults.

## DIRECT INDIVIDUAL TREATMENT

"Direct individual treatment" refers to approaches that attempt to improve the language and communication abilities of aphasic patients, as opposed to counseling and family therapy, which have indirect but nonetheless often critical effects on communication. Typically, individual aphasia treatment has been characterized as *stimulation*, which usually means intensive language bombardment of sensory input modalities; *programmed*, which usually means some concern with hierarchically arranged responsive tasks (often coupled with a pious hope that "good, Mrs. Jones" is a reinforcing consequent event); *traditional*, which usually means that it isn't quite so "stimulating" and its hierarchies and reinforcers are more haphazard; and *other*, which is anything else. Obviously, the typical categorization does not appear to be productive, for many of the present techniques do not fit neatly into it. In its place, we would suggest three alternative categories for direct treatment. These are:

1. didactic language treatment, that is, a frontal assault on a patient's missing or deficient language,

2. treatment that attempts to modify the processes that underlie language, and

3. treatment oriented toward developing new or alternative communication strategies in the face of, or even in spite of, language loss.

These categories, like the ones they replace, are not mutually exclusive. In addition, they are not necessarily incompatible. Often the good therapist will use all three. Nonetheless, their use is to some degree dictated by three clinical assumptions, often unstated. The first assumption has to do with the nature of aphasia itself. The second relates to the manner in which change in the aphasic condition occurs in the brain. The third concerns what the goals for aphasia treatment actually are. The next section is a discussion of the principles that appear to underlie the use of each type of treatment, and provides some illustrations of each of them from the clinical literature.

## DIDACTIC TREATMENT

Didactic treatment is historically the oldest approach to treating the aphasic patient and is usually what is meant by "traditional." It is also currently the most widely used approach in American clinical aphasiology. For example, Brookshire (personal communication) has reported that over 70 percent of the samples he analyzed in developing the Communicative Interaction Analysis System (CIAS) represents what he termed "point to" therapy, clearly a didactic approach. (Incidentally, "point to," a technique for improving comprehension, has a parallel form for teaching language production. The name of this treatment is "itsa" therapy.) The crucial underlying assumption of didactic treatment is that the damaged brain can be taught again its former role in using language. Treated recov-

ery is therefore mediated by the teaching process. As changes occur in applied education psychology and the technology of teaching, their applications to the aphasic patient also change. "Programmed" therapy is thus a didactic treatment. Nonetheless, the basic approach—learning the names of things—has not been altered much since Itard applied it to teaching language to the Wild Boy of Aveyron in the late eighteenth century.

Some assumptions about the nature of language loss in aphasia also seem to accompany the didactic approach to treatment. The majority—but far from all—of the research concerning the effectiveness of clinical techniques in a didactic mode does not distinguish the type of aphasia a patient might have. Instead it describes patients on the basis of degree of impairment in a particular language modality or compares pre- and post-treatment states of individual patients, again without consideration of the type of aphasia a given patient is displaying. This suggests that aphasia clinicians with a primary bias toward didactic approaches believe that aphasia is best described (at least for treatment) as a unitary disturbance of language, or at least that the aphasias are more alike than they are different. The reader is referred to Darley (1982) for a full explication of this point of view.

The majority of specific procedures are geared toward improving one or more of the language modalities by specifically and directly treating them. For example, therapy might concentrate on the specific behaviors of confrontation naming, reading, writing, or demonstration of comprehension by correctly "pointing to" or following commands similar to those on the Token Test. Therapy is often acontextual, that is, normal conversational context is seldom used or directly attended to in treatment. Stimuli are directed toward the most intact language modality; responses might require the use of less intact ones. "Deblocking," the name attached to this stimulus-response arrangement by Weigel and Beirwisch (1970), long preceded the advent of its name.

The ultimate goals of treatment seem to be related to educational assumptions and appear to be closely tied to estimates of over-all severity. That is, the didactically oriented clinician, starting usually with disordered comprehension, will attempt to rebuild as much language as the total time he or she has to spend with the aphasic patient.

The strengths of didactic treatment are simple and important. Primarily they afford the cleanest opportunity to provide replicable methods for others to use; they allow for careful gathering of pretreatment baseline and post-treatment, criterion-referenced data; and they can easily incorporate educational advances in their adaptation to clinical language intervention. For many quite specific problems in aphasia, such as re-establishing rudimentary comprehension, they are often direct and efficient. Finally, they provide an effective framework for careful hierarchical arrangement of stimuli and thus can shape language usage gradually. The most positive new uses of didactic approaches are related to these strengths, and the last big innovation was programming treatment.

An interesting recent example is the approach of Helm-Estabrooks, Fitzpatrick, and Barresi (1981) to retraining syntax in agrammatic aphasia patients—the Syntax Stimulation Program. Based on Gleason and colleagues' empirically derived hierarchy of difficulty for eight syntactic constructions (1975), and also using psycholinguistic data, they have shown how to use unmarked members of a semantic pair to teach the marked member.

Concerning efficacy of treatment, a study by Watamora and Sasanuma (1978) has advantageously used a didactic approach. In this study the authors used two bilingual aphasic subjects, equally impaired in both English and Japanese. Each patient was given therapy in one language, and subsequently tested in the other. Only the trained language improved. After this testing therapy was conducted in the second language and the gap was closed on subsequent testing. Thus each subject served as his own clinical control and in an ingenious fashion demonstrated the effectiveness of therapy, as well as contributing to a surprising insight on aided recovery in bilingual aphasic patients.

## PROCESS APPROACHES

Let us turn now to treatment that attempts to modify the processes that underlie language, rather than modifying modality-specific language itself. Schuell (1964) defined aphasia as a problem in language retrieval, as an impaired ability to gain access to language, rather than a language loss. Didactic approaches fit the conceptualization of aphasia as a loss of access to language.

Because retrieval of language and access to it are the focus, process approaches are far less closely tied to the words and grammatic structures that aphasic patients can or cannot use or comprehend than are didactic approaches. Process approaches are far more closely involved with developing new cortical routes and/or new perceptual mechanisms by which access to (intact) language can be gained. Process treatments assume that language is there, somewhere, but brain damage has interfered with its retrieval. In part, treatment consists of getting to the language. Underlying processes that have been the focus of treatment include attempts to develop increased auditory and visual perception, attempts to reorganize and reintegrate cortical function, attempts to improve memory for language, and attempts to involve the usually untapped language abilities of the right hemisphere in language. They are discussed in that order below.

### Sensory-Perceptual

Historically, Schuell's principles of intensive auditory stimulation, coupled with drill and training to redevelop what she called "reauditorization" in the aphasic patient, are the cornerstone for perceptual approaches to aphasia rehabilitation (1953). Systematic application of Schuell's principles, therefore, can be considered to represent a present-day sensory approach. Schuell herself viewed aphasia unidimensionally, suggesting that auditory-perceptual difficulties underlay the aphasic patient's multiplicity of language problems. Thus it is curious that her position regarding underlying problems has been more strongly influential in approaches to treatment that attempt to correlate the form of therapy to type of aphasia the patient is manifesting. Techniques designed to help the patient to reorganize and to monitor auditory input have been used primarily with patients designated as manifesting Wernicke's or mixed aphasia, in which auditory comprehension is poor. Auditory parameters that can be modified include rate of speech, insertion of pauses, manipulation of linguistic complexity, and/or redundancy of messages. In a typical paradigm, the training strategy developed by Salvatore (1979), pause time at constituent junctures in Token-Test-type commands was systematically lengthened and then shortened to approximate more and more normally paused speech. Training patients to reduce the volubility typical of some Wernicke's aphasia output and to begin to monitor their own output are other examples of auditory-perceptual approaches to aphasia treatment (Mysak and Guarino, 1981).

### Reorganizing and Reintegrating Cortical Function

Luria (1970) has suggested that for aphasia therapy to be successful, the clinician must arrange events in such a way that different cortical pathways are trained for language use or that the cortex is somehow reorganized, thereby establishing alternative routes for language use. Whether or not this actually happens in successful therapy is not yet open to scientific test, or course. Nonetheless, clinical approaches stemming from this rationale are increasingly visible in language treatment. Rosenbek (1978), for example, relies heavily on this approach for treating apraxia of speech. Increasing recognition of the utility of movement—even limb movement—to initiate speech-related activities is another example (Helm-Estabrooks, in press; Rosenbek, 1982).

An interesting aspect of reintegration approaches is that they sometimes involve activities that superficially appear to have little to do with the actual language used by aphasic patients. One of the most exciting of these approaches is that of Helm-Esta-

brooks, Fitzpatrick, and Barresi—Visual Action Therapy (in press), for globally aphasic patients. Designed to "reintegrate some of the conceptual systems necessary for linguistic performance," it is a totally silent program. Only after successful completion of the program are patients moved into treatment involving speech. Visual Action Therapy employs visual and gestural modes and uses a set of real and pictured objects that can be easily symbolized by a distinct gesture. The program has twelve steps, the earliest of which train matching of objects with life-size and then smaller drawings of them. Then manipulation of objects is trained, using action pictures and ultimately, pretended use of randomly selected members of the set. The next three steps train recognition and production of pantomimed gestures for each object. The final steps train the patient to produce a representational gesture to symbolize a hidden object. Two objects are shown, both are then hidden, and one is brought back into view. The patient is required to produce the gesture to symbolize the missing one, thus communicating gesturally.

Using this approach intensively with chronically global aphasic subjects, these authors have demonstrated significant improvement in BDAE auditory comprehension and in PICA gestural scores. The authors suggest that such training of alternative visual and gestural pathways possibly permits access to the intact linguistic knowledge of the global patient. This clearly places the technique in the cortical reintegration category.

### Memory for Language/Visual Imagery

Another process approach to aphasia treatment involves attempts to enrich the aphasic patient's often deficient memory skills, especially as they relate to memory for words. If aphasia is indeed partially a retrieval problem, then techniques that enhance retrieval and memory in normal individuals should be capable of being modified for effective improvement in the aphasic condition. Training "visual association" and visual imagery has long been a dominant technique for memory training, and the utility of such training for aphasic patients has recently been demonstrated by Gasparrini and Satz (1979). Aphasic patients were taught to remember paired associates with a visual mnemonic technique, as well as with a verbal mediation technique. The visual imagery technique was shown to be more effective, and in a subsequent experiment, shown also to be more effective than rote repetition with encouragement.

West (1979) has also provided systematic data on the positive effects of imaging stimuli for aphasia rehabilitation. She has also suggested that the use of action imagery, for example, concentrating clinical activities on verbs of motion, might facilitate right hemisphere processing of language, our next topic of consideration.

## Right Hemisphere Participation

(In this presentation, "right hemisphere" is used to refer to the nonlanguage dominant hemisphere). Long ago, Nielson (1946) suggested that what happened in aphasia recovery was that the intact right hemisphere was successful in assuming the language functions of the damaged left. That then untestable idea was almost laughable until the right hemisphere was "rediscovered" in relation to commissurized patients by Sperry's group in the mid-sixties. Now a large body of data suggests that in the brain damaged patient at least, the right hemisphere possesses some usually dormant language potential, particularly for comprehension, and possibly even for rudimentary speech. Thus involving the right hemisphere systematically in language activities has become a provocative clinical idea. The success of Melodic Intonation Therapy (Sparks, Helm, and Albert, 1974) is possibly attributable to its use of intonational activities on which language is superimposed, thus engaging the right hemisphere in the left hemisphere's typical business. A host of other possibilities for so engaging the right hemisphere, as yet unsubstantiated by clinical research, have been suggested. These include systematic left-

handed writing activities, using the left hand for holding objects to be named, and so on, not organized as alternatives for the right hemiplegic, but required for naming activities, regardless of hemiplegia; training on cognitive-linguistic tasks related to right hemisphere function, such as map-following and so on; or auditory stimulation tasks fed intensively to the left ear.

Before moving on to communicative strategy approaches, the third major form of direct treatment, a summary comment regarding process approaches is in order. Much new work is going on in this area, most of it in need of further experimental verification and expansion. The strengths of the approaches lie in their generalization possibilities; that is, shoring up underlying linguistic processes has its potential payoff beyond the linguistic content of the stimulus material. This necessitates measuring the effects of the approaches, not only on the tasks used clinically, but on untrained material and on language usage in everyday life.

## COMMUNICATION STRATEGY APPROACHES

A third direct approach to language intervention in aphasia involves the development of strategies for communicating despite the presence of aphasia. These basically make the same set of assumptions regarding the nature of aphasia as process approaches—that is, aphasia represents a condition of impaired access to language. In addition, they make a further assumption: Communicative competence, the rules by which one knows how to use language and nonverbal communicative forms, remains accessible in aphasic patients to some degree, regardless of language impairment.

Making fewer assumptions about how language recovery is effected than do the other two, communicative strategy approaches appear to make a fairly unquiet peace with the problems of aphasia. That is, the condition of aphasia, to some (usually significant) degree, is here to stay. Part of the task of the aphasia therapist is to help the patient to capitalize upon his knowledge of language and communication to get along communicatively in spite of aphasia.

It is hard to find a key word or phrase to describe explicitly what the fundamental mechanism in communicative strategy approaches is all about. But as "teaching" was related to approach one, and "reintegration" to approach two, "externalization" relates to this approach. The techniques usually involve making apparent and explicit to the aphasic patient a number of ways to solve communicative dilemmas, then observing which of those aspects of communicative behavior allow the patient to get his own messages across successfully. Next, the patient is systematically required to use the strategies in normal communicative interactions.

Whitney (1975) has described a series of compensatory activities for patients with comprehension losses that consist of training them to request of speakers that the speakers change their messages in ways that facilitate that particular patient's comprehension. Thus, if slowing down the message helps, the patient is required to request "slow down"; if repetition facilitates, the request becomes "repeat, please"; and so forth. For word retrieval problems, a survey of alternatives is made and the patient is trained to use those that have been shown empirically to be most effective for him. Word retrieval strategies include preceding utterance attempts with facilitating gestures, writing, consulting patient-generated and organized word lists, involving others in providing cues, and so forth.

Communicative strategy approaches typically but not exclusively emphasize conversational settings for treatment, and attempt to approximate the conditions that obtain in normal communicative transactions. While these principles have been in the literature since the work of Backus and colleagues (1947), they have most recently been heavily influenced by research in language pragmatics. Rather than stressing language attributes, such as names-of-things or syntax, communicative strategy approaches stress communicative acts, such as making requests, comments, informing, and so forth.

A particularly ingenious application is PACE therapy, developed by Davis and Wilcox (1981). PACE is a treatment technique that reshapes the interaction between the aphasic patient and his therapist to approximate natural dyadic communication. PACE stands for Promoting Aphasics' Communicative Effectiveness. There are four principles:

1. An exchange of new information is promoted.

2. The aphasic patient is free to, in fact encouraged to, explore the most effective communicative channel, such as gesture, writing, speaking, and so on.

3. Both therapist and patient send and receive information.

4. Feedback is simply the success of communicating, the characteristic feedback of normal communication.

PACE works like this: A set of unselected picture cards (usually limited to 10 or 15) is placed face-down between client and clinician. Alternatively, therapist and patient select a card and communicate, via whatever means, the content (even possibly the name of the object) of the card. If the patient selects a picture of, say, a boat, and communicates by whatever means (for example, writing, gesturing, or saying it), the adequacy of the communication is checked naturally by the clinician's response ("Oh, it's a boat."). Remember, the clinician really does not know what's on the card. Feedback, instead of being a "Good, Mrs. Jones," is of the kind applied to received messages in the real world.

How does such therapy differ from a didactic approach? First, while it is contrived, it approximates the give and take of everyday communication. Remember, therapist and patient alternate roles of sender and receiver. Second, it approximates normal communication by sending new information. (Language intervention is one of the few life situations in which one person usually knows in advance all of the answers to the questions he or she asks.) Third, it provides real feedback; if a message is correctly sent, it is correctly received. If not, totally naturally, the aphasic patient can judge how far off target he was by the therapist's response. In this way it provides constant data to the aphasic patient that allow him to judge what is the most effective communicative mode, and develops flexibility by providing and training alternatives.

PACE procedures can be expanded to include direction following (reproduction of simple patterns of circles and squares across a screen), reading and writing activities, and group interactions between aphasic patients or among patients and families.

In addition to these strategies, it is important to point out that techniques for augmenting verbal communication, such as Skelly and colleagues' use of Amerind for patients with apraxia of speech (1974), or the use of alternative communication systems, such as communication boards, comfortably can be listed among strategy approaches in aphasia.

It seems appropriate to conclude this section on direct treatment with some observations on the contributions of Wepman to this area of language intervention. Wepman began didactically to treat the deficient language of his aphasic patients. Always a man of flexibility and of generosity in sharing his notions of appropriate treatment with others, his last professional writings stressed the need for clinical attention to the thoughts and ideas that underlie communication (1972, 1976). Language (particularly speech), he pointed out, should be the "handmaiden" of the thought process, and direct attention to speech reversed this natural relationship by making speech the master of thought instead. As Martin (1981) recently cogently argued, Wepman's last contributions to language intervention legitimized communicative treatment concerns, for they are, at heart, thought-centered approaches.

## COUNSELING ASPECTS OF TREATMENT

Language intervention in aphasia simply cannot be described only by listing direct intervention techniques, regardless of how exhaustive the catalogue. This is because aphasia, occurring usually without warning to adults whose pretraumatic lifestyles and coping mechanisms encompass the full range of experience, is not merely a language problem. It is an interpersonal crisis with potentially serious ramifications for other family members, vocational alternatives, and finances (to list only a few). That counseling is an integral part of language intervention in aphasia can easily be demonstrated by observing that virtually no significant writer on aphasia treatment has failed to stress the importance of counseling in effective treatment for the problem. This feature is true, regardless of orientation toward direct treatment. Sarno ended her romance with programmed instruction in aphasia, not by saying that treatment was not effective (an interpretation made by others), but by urging that counseling was the more crucial feature of the clinical relationship (1970). Eisenson (1973) has never abandoned the belief. While the role of counseling in language intervention was out of vogue during the mid-sixties, and it was almost anachronistic or quaint to bring up the subject for a while, it was even practiced (perhaps closet-style) then, and has made a robust and hopefully lasting recovery.

It is not the intent here to describe techniques of counseling in aphasia, but rather simply to underscore the notion that an adequate definition of language intervention in adults simply must include counseling, possibly even assign to it a central role. It must also be added that recent conceptualizations of aphasia as an interpersonal problem have broadened the nature of counseling to include the aphasic family as well. Webster and Newhoff (1981) have provided a powerful model for such activities, as well as a strong rationale for them.

## TREATMENT FOR OTHER LANGUAGE DISORDERS IN ADULTS

It is virtually irresistible in 1982 to limit definitional remarks on language intervention in adults simply to aphasic patients. For a variety of reasons, four other groups of adults have come to the attention of clinical aphasiologists within the past few years. Three of these groups, patients with a variety of dementias, patients with right hemisphere brain damage, and patients with closed head injuries might legitimately be considered to have language disorders, albeit ones not comfortably handled by the term aphasia. The fourth group is hardly language disordered, but it has come to the attention of speech-language pathologists as they have worked with aphasic patients in geriatric centers and nursing homes. I speak of the normally aging who are living in communicatively impoverished environments. A description of language intervention in adults at this juncture must be broad enough to include these groups, even though it must be recognized that we are on far more unsteady ground in discussing them. A limited survey of methods for each group will follow, beginning with patients whose neurologic diseases produce general intellectual deterioration, including language dissolution. These patients have dementing conditions.

## DEMENTIA

As national attention has been increasingly focused upon the health and social problems of the aging, clinical aphasiology has become correspondingly aware first, that aphasia across the adult life span actually differs as a function of age and that more severe global aphasias and Wernicke's aphasia (for males at least) are disproportionately represented in older aphasia patients (Obler and associates, 1978; Harasymiw, Halper, and Sutherland, 1981). Second, it has become apparent that differential diagnosis of aphasia is often complicated in older patients by concomitant disorders of general intellectual deterioration, as well as by some (possibly superficial) overlap in the symptoms of dementia and aphasia. Halpern, Darley, and Brown (1973) were the first in the literature to call attention to these problems, and recently Wertz (1978) more fully elaborated upon them. Since the publication of Wertz's work, a rich and rapidly developing literature on the language of dementia has begun to emerge, most notably fueled by the contributions of Obler and Albert

(1981) and, directly in speech-language pathology, by the work of Bayles and Boone (1982).

The present focus remains upon description of dementing language at various levels of progression of the disorders. But at its very core, speech-language pathology is a fixing profession, and recently a few writers have begun to articulate a role for the speech-language pathologist in treatment of the dementing patient. Bayles, for example, has stressed the counseling role and has suggested a number of activities geared to retarding the rate at which language and cognitive skills might deteriorate (in press). It is not seriously entertained by anybody that speech-language intervention might "cure" dementia; nonetheless, skilled practitioners might perform an important palliative role in its management. It is our belief that explicit elaboration of useful techniques for working with demented patients and their families will be increasingly visible in the literature of the next decade.

## THE NORMALLY AGING

At the outset of this brief section, it is important to underscore that "normal aging" is just that, not a pathologic condition like the other problems that have been the focus of discussion in this chapter. However, the communicative environments in which a significant number of elderly Americans may find themselves, owing to deteriorating physical or social conditions, are pathologic. In a series of recent papers, Lubinski (1981a, 1981b) has outlined a broadened role for the speech-language pathologist in home health care agencies and in nursing homes. This broadened role, in addition to the more usual ones of staff education and diagnostic and clinical services to patients with true language and sensory disorders, includes direct manipulation and "refurbishing" of what Lubinski terms the "communication impaired environment" to foster more normal communication among the elderly inhabitants of institutions, to engage in patient advocacy, to increase the role of communication in reality orientation, and so forth. In a sense, Lubinski has suggested that an appropriate responsibility for the speech-language pathologist is the application of what we experts know about normal communication and what enhances it to that segment of the population whose life circumstances deny them access to it. Along with increasing involvement with demented patients, such work will surely increase within the next decade.

## PATIENTS WITH CLOSED HEAD INJURIES

Following World War II, when American clinical aphasiology really began to develop its roots, the majority of patients treated in the intensive rehabilitation centers necessitated by the war were young people who had suffered head injuries, usually of the penetrating, open type. A highly important change in the population served by language interventionists has occurred since that time. Today, the great majority of patients are older and have aphasias as a result of stroke. Even the younger head injured population (at least those of the post-Vietnam War period) has changed. More and more people suffer closed head injuries, the likely consequence of life in a high-speed society.

Work with today's head injured is no longer the "aphasia" treatment it used to be, but is becoming increasingly more holistic, more oriented to cognitive function generally. A major, but still-developing methodologic change is the result of differentiation between appropriate aphasia treatment after stroke of focal trauma and more general cognitive-language treatment following closed head injury, in which the well-known techniques are often inappropriate.

Rehabilitation of closed head injury is quintessentially interdisciplinary, and in the ideal world, includes the usual litany of rehabilitation specialists, usually augmented by an educational specialist. Speech-language pathologists, however, whether because they are willing to try anything or because they are traditionally gluttons for punishment, often have a very central role. Hagan (in press), working

within a model related to levels of cognitive functioning, describes a viable approach based on the following postulates:

1. Treatment is directed toward reorganization of cognitive processes, rather than toward modification of the abnormal consequences of the cognitive disorganization.

2. As cognitive processes become reorganized, there will be commensurate reorganization of phonologic, semantic, syntactic, and verbal reasoning abilities.

3. Reorganization of cognitive abilities follows a predictable and systematic hierarchical sequence in which the reacquisition and stabilization of lower level processes is necessary for emergence and stabilization of higher level ones.

4. Cognitive structure is maximized and behavioral responses become more organized when the treatment progresses sequentially from the patient's present level through higher levels.

5. Treatment stimuli should be presented through the patient's most intact modality and increased to other modalities only when increasing cognitive abilities allow him to deal with multiple stimuli.

6. Regardless of the level of treatment, manner of stimulus input is critical. Consequently, rate, amount, duration, and complexity of stimulus input must be manipulated in a manner consistent with the patient's cognitive abilities at any given time.

Hagan's comprehensive approach is possibly the most extensively developed approach currently available. Others are emerging, however, and in the future will perhaps articulate some different methodologic details. But it is doubtful if the coupling of cognition, memory, and language that is the essence of present-day work with closed head injuries will be broken. And it is this interweaving that distinguishes intervention for these problems from treatment for aphasia.

## PATIENTS WITH RIGHT (OR NONLANGUAGE DOMINANT) HEMISPHERE DAMAGE

It was suggested earlier in this chapter that a reconsideration of the functions of the right hemisphere had, and continues to have, an impact on aphasia rehabilitation. Another effect was that the professional community was forced to reconsider the general myth that suffering a right cerebral insult was tantamount to having "lucked out" cognitively, in terms of the behavioral aftermath. No one seriously believes this anymore. Although the effects of right hemisphere damage are perhaps more difficult to discern, or at least superficially are not as dramatic as the aphasic aftermath of damage to the language dominant hemisphere, they are nonetheless real. Visuospatial deficits, difficulty in interpretation of the context of human interaction, particularly of the cognitive-emotional interface, neglect of the left side of space, even language problems that Meyers (1979) characterizes as "difficulty in extracting critical bits of information, in seeing the relationships among them, or in reaching conclusions or drawing inferences based on those relationships"—these are only a few of the problems of patients who have suffered right hemisphere damage. And who is being called upon to work with such patients? Increasingly, speech-language pathologists are finding a place for them in their caseloads. As was true of the other problems described in this section, elaboration of effective techniques for use with right hemisphere damaged patients will have to be a feature of the next decade's work in language intervention.

## EFFICACY OF TREATMENT

The preceding section was much more speculative than was the section on aphasia. It tends to generate an uncomfortable feeling, as it probably would in most proper aphasiologists. The discomfort perhaps relates to a feature of language intervention in adults which is one of its most distinguished (and perhaps distinguishing) characteristics: the concern that this branch of speech-language pathology has shown regarding the efficacy of the treatment it renders. Clinical aphasiologists, as a group, are used to being questioned about the usefulness of their work, used to

producing data to demonstrate it, used to expecting their fellow-practitioners to do the same. But about these last few topics in this chapter, there have been little data to back us up. This situation will undoubtedly change, for the same spirit that infuses aphasia rehabilitation is apparent here as well.

Efficacy data in adult language intervention abounds. It exists on all levels, from the single-case designs La Pointe's work has legitimized (1978), to detailed case studies (Holland and Harris, 1965), to carefully-designed large-scale treatment comparisons, of which the study of Wertz and colleagues (1981) can serve as a technical model for the field. The efficacy of treatment is also reflected in the growing trend to treat aphasic patients years after the onset of treatment, when no claims about spontaneous recovery can possibly be made. Description of such treatment and appropriate pre- and post-treatment comparisons are a strong source of efficacy data. An example is the work of Rao and Koller (1982).

We apparently have enough assurance to begin to examine which treatment approaches work and which do not. By coupling a different approach to treatment, in this case, communication-centered group treatment, to quite chronic aphasia, Aten and colleagues (1982) recently demonstrated the validity of the approach. Brookshire's major clinical contributions are best illustrated by his experimental demonstrations of the relative usefulness of specific techniques that are commonly used in treatment. Brookshire and Nicholas' experimental data on the typical reinforcement paradigms encountered in treatment are beginning to convince clinicians of the futility of such activity (1978). That type of research, it is felt, could only be conducted in a profession that had a measure of confidence in itself. And Helm-Estabrooks, Naeser, and Kleefield (1980) have recently opened the door to examination of why some approaches work with some patients and not with others. Examination of failure, at least as crucial as examination of success, is a sign of professional maturity.

More than anyone else, it is necessary to thank Darley for his insistence on the collection of efficacy data. He has continually exhorted the profession and meticulously catalogued the emerging data (1972, 1977, 1979). He has begun to convince us, finally, that we are the responsible and effective profession that, down deep, he always knew we were.

## CONCLUSIONS, AND PERHAPS AN ANSWER TO THE QUESTION IN THE TITLE

This chapter has been sobering, as I said in the beginning, for it has required a great deal of self-examination. But more than that, it has been a great deal of fun. I am proud of American clinical aphasiology, and I think this chapter was a perfect place to let it show. I became aware about halfway through it that it afforded a wonderful opportunity for name-dropping. The chapter includes a fair sampling of the clinical workers who continually shape the profession. However, because the concentration was on language intervention in the United States, and on treatment rather than on assessment or on the more basic research that underlies it, many, many more names are missing. But in spite of the limited sampling of contributors to it, the vitality of language intervention with adults shows through.

So what is language intervention in adults? It is a multifaceted enterprise involving many and varied direct attempts to modify and to move back toward normal the disturbed communication that follows in the wake of a variety of calamities of the central nervous system. Further, language intervention with adults is counseling by sensitive practitioners who understand the multiplicity of effects that disruption of communication can bring. Language intervention is principled concern with the effectiveness of those activities, coupled with enough flexibility to change when methods fail or when research shows them to be ineffective. More simply stated: Language intervention is rolling up your sleeves, and doing whatever your principles, your training, your skill, your sensitivity, and finally, your patients themselves tell you needs to be done to make the communicative world a little more natural for them again.

## REFERENCES

Aten J, Caliguiri M, Holland A: The efficacy of functional communication therapy for chronic aphasic patients. J Speech Hear Dis 47(1): 93–96, 1982

Backus DL, Henry D, Clancy JW, Dunn H: In West R, Kennedy L, Carr, (eds): Aphasia in Adults. Ann Arbor: University of Michigan Press, 1947

Bayles K: Language and dementia. In Holland A (ed): Recent Advances in Language Pathology. San Diego: College Hill, in press

Bayles K, Boone DR: The potential of language tasks for identifying senile dementia. J Speech Hear Dis 47(2): 210–217, 1982

Brookshire RH, Nicholas L: Effects of clinician request and feedback behavior on responses of aphasic individuals in speech and language treatment sessions. In Brookshire RH (ed): Clinical Aphasiology Conference Proceedings. Minneapolis: BRK, 1978

Darley F: The efficacy of language rehabilitation in aphasia. J Speech Hear Dis 37(1): 3–21, 1972

Darley FL: A retrospective view: Aphasia. J Speech Hear Dis 42(2): 161–169, 1977

Darley FL: Treat or neglect. ASHA 21(8): 628–631, 1979

Darley FL: Aphasia. Philadelphia: WB Saunders Co, 1982

Davis A, Wilcox J: Incorporating parameters of natural conversation in aphasia treatment. In Chapey R (ed): Language Intervention Strategies in Adult Aphasia. Baltimore: Williams & Wilkins, 1981

Eisenson J: Adult Aphasia: Assessment and Treatment. Englewood Cliffs, NJ: Prentice Hall, Inc, 1973

Gasparrini B, Satz P: A treatment for memory problems in left hemisphere CVA patients. J Clin Neuropsychol 1(1): 1979

Gleason J, Goodglass H, Green E, et al: The retrieval of syntax in Broca's aphasia. Brain Lang 24(3): 1975

Hagan C: Language disorders secondary to closed head trauma: Diagnosis and treatment. In Holland A (ed): Recent Advances in Language Disorders. San Diego: College Hill, in press

Halpern H, Darley FL, Brown J: Differential language and neurological characteristics in cerebral involvement. J Speech Hear Dis 38(2): 162–173, 1973

Harasymiw S, Halpern A, Sutherland B: Sex, age and aphasia type. Brain Lang 12(1): 190–198, 1981

Helm-Estabrooks N, Fitzpatrick P, Barresi B: Responses of an agrammatic patient to a syntax stimulation program for aphasia. J Speech Hear Dis 46(4): 422–427, 1981

Helm-Estabrooks N, Fitzpatrick P, Barresi B: Visual action of therapy for global aphasia. J Speech Hear Dis, in press

Helm-Estabrooks N, Naeser M, Kleefield J: CT Scan localization and response to Melodic Intonation Therapy. Paper presented at a meeting of the Academy of Aphasia, 1980

Holland A, Harris A: Aphasia rehabilitation using programmed instruction: An intensive case history. In Sloan H, MacAulay B (eds): *Operant Procedures in Remedial Speech and Language*. Boston: Houghton Mifflin, 1968

LaPointe L: Aphasia therapy: Some principles and strategies for treatment. In Johns D (ed): *Clinical Management of Neurogenic Communicative Disorders*. Boston: Little Brown, 1978

Lubinski R: Environmental language intervention. In Chapey R (ed): *Language Intervention Strategies in Adult Aphasia*. Baltimore: Williams & Wilkins, 1981a

Lubinski R, Morrison E, Rigrodsky S: Perception of spoken communication by elderly chronically ill patients in an institutional setting. J Speech Hear Dis 46(4): 405–412, 1981b

Luria AR: *Traumatic Aphasia: Its Syndromes, Psychology and Treatment*. The Hague: Mouton, 1970

Martin D: An examination of Wepman's thought centered therapy. In Chapey R (ed): *Language Intervention Strategies in Adult Aphasia*. Baltimore: Williams & Wilkins, 1981

Meyers P: Profiles of communication deficits in patients with right cerebral hemisphere damage. In Brookshire R (ed): *Clinical Aphasiology Conference Proceedings*. Minneapolis: BRK, 1979

Mysak E, Guarino C: Self-adjusting therapy. In Chapey R (ed): *Language Intervention Strategies in Adult·Aphasia*. Baltimore: Williams & Wilkins, 1981

Nielson JM: *Agnosia, Apraxia, Aphasia: Their Values in Cerebral Localization*. New York: Hoeber, 1946

Obler L, Albert M: Language in the elderly aphasic and in the dementing patient. In Sarno MT (ed): *Acquired Aphasia*. New York: Academic Press, 1981

Obler L, Albert M, Goodglass H, et al: Aphasia type and aging. Brain Lang 6(1): 318–322, 1978

Rao P, Koller J: A total communication approach to aphasia treatment in three chronic aphasic adults. Paper presented at the 10th Annual Meeting of International Neuropsychology Society, 1982

Rosenbek J: Treating apraxia of speech. In Johns D (ed): *Clinical Management of Neurogenic Communicative Disorders*. Boston: Little Brown, 1978

Rosenbek J: Apraxia workshop. Presented at the Three Rivers Conference, Pittsburgh, Pa, 1982

Salvatore AJ: Training an aphasic adult to respond appropriately to spoken commands by fading pause duration within commands. In Brookshire RH (ed): *Clinical Aphasiology Conference Proceedings*. Minneapolis: BRK, 1978

Sarno M, Silverman M, Sands E: Speech therapy and language recovery in severe aphasia. J Speech Hear Dis 13(1): 607–623, 1970

Schuell H: Auditory impairment in aphasia: Significance and retraining techniques. J Speech Hear Dis 18(1): 14–21, 1953

Schuell H, Jenkins J, Jiminez-Pabon J: *Aphasia in Adults*. New York: Hoeber, 1964

Skelly M, Schinsky L, Smith R, Fust R: American Indian sign (Amerind) as a facilitator of verbalization for the oral-verbal apractic. J Speech Hear Dis 39(4): 445–456, 1974

Sparks R, Helm N, Albert M: Aphasia rehabilitation resulting from Melodic Intonation Therapy. Cortex 10(4): 303–316, 1974

Ulatowska H, Baker S: On a notion of markedness in linguistic systems: Application to aphasia. In Brookshire RH (ed): *Clinical Aphasiology Conference Proceedings*. Minneapolis: BRK, 1975

Watamori T, Sasanuma S: The recovery process of two English-Japanese bilingual speakers. Brain Lang 6(1): 127–140, 1978

Webster E, Newhoff M: Intervention with families of communicatively impaired adults. In Beasley D, Davis GA: *Aging: Communication Processes and Disorders*. New York: Grune & Stratton, 1981

Weigl E, Bierwisch M: Neuropsychology and linguistics: Topics of common research. Foundations Lang 6(1): 1–18, 1970

Wepman J: Aphasia Therapy: A new look. J Speech Hear Dis 37(2): 203–214, 1972

Wepman J: Aphasia: Language without thought to thought without language. ASHA 18(1): 131–136, 1976

Wertz RT, et al: Veteran's Administration cooperative study on aphasia: A comparison of individual and group treatment. J Speech Hear Dis 45(4): 1981

Wertz RT: Neuropathologies of speech and language: An introduction to patient management. In Johns D: *Clinical Management of Neurogenic Communication Disorders*. Boston: Little Brown, 1978

West J: Heightening the action imagery of materials used in aphasia treatment. In Brookshire R (ed): *Clinical Aphasiology Conference Proceedings*. Minneapolis: BRK, 1978

Whitney J: Developing aphasic compensatory strategies. Paper presented at a meeting of the American Speech and Hearing Association, Washington, DC, 1975

# 2

# LANGUAGE INTERVENTION IN CHILDREN: WHAT IS IT?

*RICHARD L. SCHIEFELBUSCH*

The term *language intervention* emerged during the late 1960s, but it seems to have an uncertain origin. The term *intervention* in a standard dictionary appears to be defined rather obliquely for our purposes. For instance, the American Collegiate Dictionary has only two definitional subparts that come close to the mark, but they require interpretive reflection. These sub-parts apply to the verb *to intervene* and not to the noun *intervention*. The first is, "To intervene . . . to occur incidentally so as to modify a result." The second is, "to come in, as something not belonging." Perhaps we might agree that the unknown technical writer who prepared those statements had a prescient flash of knowledge and stated what is best, as well as what is worst, about language intervention.

We could assume that the term intervention was selected and an elaborated meaning set was inferred to fit the functional requirements for those promoting language acquisition. Over a period of approximately 10 to 15 years the term language intervention has been applied so widely that we tend to assume that it has a standard meaning. All interventionists do not agree on the meaning or upon a common set of intervention procedures. So, at the beginning of this book it seems appropriate to discuss the term and the apparent intentions that unite us.

Intervention is an important concept for the helping disciplines. The term implies that professionals are competent to enter the lives of certain individuals to help them achieve a more desirable state. The term also implies that we are able to determine when and how we should intervene. Embedded in our assumption is the belief that under mandated circumstances intervention programs should be undertaken and, indeed, that the needy individual has the right to such intervention.

Intervention, then, denotes an act of assistance. As a concept for assistance it is more general than *training,* or *instruction,* or *therapy*. Clinical interventions should be both feasible and practical. Interventions from a scientific point of view should be efficient and should provide information to make subsequent interventions more effective. At the same time each intervention should be keyed, as much as possible, to the best interests of the child/client.

Increasingly, we study the intentions of the child so that the language we assess is functional to the child's reasons for communicating. This issue provides a focal purpose for intervening: to assist the child to develop the social/communicative competence for achieving both immediate and long-term purposes. Our efforts consequently do not culminate in ends, but rather represent means to the ends that are personal and individualized. As an act of good faith we should submit our own intentions for observation and consideration. Such acts lead us to establish better our own accountability to the child and the child's family and also to further our own professional competencies. In this fashion our professional ends and the long-term, personal ends of the client can become congruent. Our scientific systems must contribute to the humanistic ends of the clients and families we serve. That is our primary accountability. However, there is a second implied accountability in the term language intervention, and that is the responsibility for increasing our competence so that subsequent clients may be better served. Only through our competence can we bridge the value systems of scientific and humanistic accountability. This issue is addressed in a more limited perspective at the end of this chapter. But let us now consider how we may undertake to design language interventions.

## DESIGNING LANGUAGE INTERVENTIONS

Intervention procedures can be considered as an extension of a science of design. This assumption is difficult to comprehend and requires careful explanation. Perhaps as a starting point we might consider the role of design in architecture. Architectural scientists and artists seek to bring a synchrony among all parts of the visual and functional features of the ecology in which their creation must exist. To do this they must know a great deal about the parts of the environment in which their design is to appear. They must also know what the human participant perceives as synchronous and pleasing. They must create a unity among the physical and psychologic variables so that the completed creation is viewed with artistic and/or functional approval. Designing is the instrumental reality in this process of bringing unity and achievement out of the complex dissonance and confusion of parts and pieces.

## DESIGN

Design functions for physical or purely structural harmonizing differ from designs for activity systems. Thus, a building that looks impressive and esthetically appealing may have a poor design for human occupancy. The flow of events within the building and between the building and its surroundings may be constricting and the effects upon the participants distressing. The design should not simply produce a structure that looks good but also one that is functional. In other words, *the design should be functional for the persons it serves.*

In this sense, then, design must accommodate the purposes, the flow of movement, and the range of events that come from human usage. In analogous ways, educative designs may look good but may not actually serve the learner. One reason for this lack of functionality may be that we do not actually understand the human purposes to be served. So we may fashion the program design to be structurally complete and well organized but not good for human purposes.

Designs for educative processes have undergone major improvements in recent years because of computer assisted instruction (Atkinson, 1976; Glaser, 1976), systems analysis (Schiefelbusch, 1977), and behavior and cognitive learning theories (Carroll, 1976; Klahr, 1976). However, we have thus far been less effective in designing education to meet the long-term needs of learners. Apparently educational design must be keyed both to the learner's immediate purposes and long-term needs. In this discussion the learners are children and the designers are adults who have responsibilities for determining the needs and purposes of children. In most instances the designs, as well as the purposes to be served by the designs, become complicated by values and abstractions. In certain instances these value systems may produce dissonance in the educative design.

Perhaps we do not want a refined or scientific design for educative functions. In historic perspective, a powerful, tactical design for educational outcomes has been feared by some and generally distrusted by many more. The reasons for this are fairly obvious. If instruction becomes fully unified into a design that is universally applicable, it could be used alike by those of good and bad intentions, and the potentials for danger and distress would arise as easily as the potentials for human progress. In recent years we have seen that thoughtless incidents leading to unfortunate consequences in the application of "behavior modification" procedures in institutions, prisons, or other special environments have aroused great public indignation even though careful, objective observers might see the appropriate application of these tactics as a legitimate and perhaps highly instrumental part of human care systems. In many instances these same systems have greatly improved the environments for the residents or have enabled them to leave the institutions and to live more comfortably in society.

## MODELS

A distinction should be made between design and model; this distinction is necessary because we frequently use the word *model* in our intervention literature. We refer to the medical model, the developmental model, the remedial model, the cognitive model, the behavioral model, and even the incidental model. In most instances, what we label as a model is a loose integration of many elements and features, most of which we have not carefully analyzed and which we could not operationally specify. There may be nothing much wrong with such imprecise specification unless, of course, one should want to refine the "model."

Because language designs possibly can best be explained in relation to models or model building, we should look closely at models as useful formulations for intervention planning. Krauss (1979) explains that *model* is often used in two ways. First, the model can be used to explain the potential of the chimpanzee as an animal model

for the study of language (Rumbaugh, Savage-Rumbaugh, Gill, Warner, 1979). A range of animal models has been used to study various processes that could not be studied by using human subjects. The intention in using the animal model is to contribute ultimately to the well-being of humans, that is, their health, their environment, their longevity, their genetic limitations, and so forth. In the instance of Rumbaugh's model, of course, the intention is to contribute to our understanding of the language of the human child and to the development of his communication competencies.

A second way that model is used is to study a particular theory, such as a theory of cognition or learning. For instance, we encounter the phrase "a stochastic model for paired-associate learning." To be useful such a model must provide an explicit system for exploring the relationships and the effects of certain variables that are theoretically identified. The method of research used is often the manipulation of variables, usually single variables, so that rigorous testing can be pursued and the ultimate validity or truth of the hypothesis can be determined. Such painstaking studies provide a firm foundation in many areas of reliable knowledge. Also, this kind of model is extremely important in experimental research in areas of psychology, as well as biobehavioral, psychoacoustic, and neurophysiologic science.

There are essential prerequisites to model building and to research based upon models. One prerequisite is that we know a great deal about the phenomena involved in the model. This knowledge enables the scientist to develop an abstract facsimile of the system. The abstract replica should conform closely to the way the system actually works, and it is usually theory based. A model is useful if it accounts for the instrumental variables. We must be able to avoid the confounding of these variables unknowingly. In this sense some variables must be held constant while we manipulate one or more of the other variables. Also, our model must be sufficiently congruent with the theory that we can test out many research questions that apply to the theory. The ultimate purpose is to disprove, prove, or modify the theory into a more useful or potent form.

Models, as described here, cannot readily be used to develop intervention programs. Basic research provides much of the reliable knowledge that the clinician draws upon in the development of intervention programs. Instead, we might better use the concept of designing. For our purpose a design is a system of adequately elaborated functions that include the *environment* and the language *program* (both structure and function), the principal *operations*, and the *strategies* of language instruction. A design is not limited to a single theory. It is an empiric formulation that addresses an important, desired outcome. It should be organized so as to address in the most feasible way possible the how-to-do-it features that are functional to that outcome. Furthermore, these design functions must be sufficiently explicit that they can be objectively established, analyzed, and adjusted. The reason that a design for language intervention is so difficult to conceptualize is because it is dimensional and complex and because it functions as a total system. Nevertheless, we must break it down into functional parts before it can be comprehended as a whole. The discussion of language intervention designs should include a careful analysis of language structure and function. However, this analysis is included in the section of this book on language content.

## SUBSYSTEMS IN LANGUAGE INTERVENTION DESIGNING

This chapter considers the subsystems that exist naturally in language intervention designing: *environmental* designs, *strategic* designs, and *operational* designs.

## ENVIRONMENTAL DESIGNS

An environment as defined here is a comprehensive teaching context designed to support the instructional program of the child with a language delay or disorder. The environment should be flexible and functional, and it should be an inclusive arrangement for the operational and strategic systems that may serve as teaching procedures. The instructional environment should be the locus of learning and also the context for usage, often referred to as *generalization*. The learning environment may be a classroom or a school or clinic, or, in some instances, a home and a school, a clinic and a classroom, or other combinations of arrangements. Bronfenbrenner (1976) advocated multiple environmental designs in teaching children. This ecologic conceptualization of learning has led directly to environmental adequacy studies in which estimates of the effects of environments upon child development can be made. Because the purposes of language interventions vary it is likely that there will continue to be a range of environments in which language is taught. The selection or the creation of functional environments is a prominent feature of language design.

The environment in which language is taught may be constituted informally to offer the optimum amount of stimulation for the child along with numerous natural, incidental transactions that are functional for the child. A "play" school or preschool classroom arranged to optimize the communication interaction between the children and the teacher and among the children is an example of a language teaching environment. This type of environment has been described by Hart and Risley (1975) Ruder, Bunce, and Ruder (in press), and Rogers-Warren and Warren (1981).

Another environment might be the one-to-one design used in intensive task teaching for children who presumably need specific antecedent skills or skill components. This is probably the most frequent arrangement for language instruction. Clinics are easily arranged for direct or formal instruction. Such arrangements can be combined with a more "incidental" environment so that the skills taught directly can be integrated into social activities.

In addition to these two arrangements

there are environments where group play is maintained as a natural extension of the play of infancy and early childhood. Such environments are often combined with play activities within the home so that combinations of home/center functions are interactively maintained. The center may be used as a training site for the mother so that the synchrony of home and center can be optimized. Other environments are explained in the section on strategic designs.

An instructional environment should be functional to the language learning needs of the child. Natural environments provide adequately for most children, including many who are language impaired. However, for others the environment must be arranged to include "prosthetic" features that support certain social or physical limitations of the child. In this sense, what is natural for one child may not be natural for another. Consequently, individualized adjustments within an environment are essential to good design and can be enhanced by operational and strategic designs.

## STRATEGIC DESIGNS

There are many optional procedures in teaching language. These options include program issues, such as a decision to teach an alternative language system, or procedural issues, such as a decision to teach word imitation skills. Daily decisions influence the quality of teaching. Often these decisions bear on the individual differences and make programs of instruction adaptable to children. Language instruction should be adapted to utilize the functional strengths and capabilities of the child. We call those adaptive decisions *strategies*.

A strategy is the exercise of an option that may directly or indirectly facilitate instruction. Examples of *program* strategies are early intervention, nonspeech intervention, milieu intervention, developmental intervention, or functional (remedial) intervention. These program strategies represent options regarding alternative program designs for teaching a child or a group of children. They are broad, complex strategies that have become well established through both research applications and service usage. Within the complex program strategies are subsets that also produce optional decisions. Thus strategies may influence decisions at all levels of the intervention process. There are also *procedural* strategies for teaching direction following, phrase and sentence elaboration, vocabulary development, or short-term memory. One way to define a procedural strategy is to call it a systematic arrangement or pattern that increases the probability of achieving a desired outcome or achieving it more efficiently or both.

A strategy (either program or procedural) has bearing on an individual difference (age, impairment, or purpose) and outcomes. For instance, the decision to alter a wheelchair to allow better posture for conversation could be a strategy. Likewise, fitting a wheelchair with a communication board could be a strategy. Small group discussions could be a classroom strategy for teaching language usage skills. Teaching imitation prior to receptive skills and teaching receptive skills prior to expressive skills could be a strategy. An interesting feature of strategy is that its utility can be objectively assessed and its application can be subject to refinement.

**Early Intervention.** One compelling reason for early intervention is that many of the features of language, both structural and functional, are based upon antecedent experiences. Many handicapped children may not work their way through these experiential antecedents by the time they are expected to use formal language. In such cases their adult companions may not have functioned effectively as language transactors. Perhaps they fail to understand that the acquisitional history of the child, although out of phase, should include play activities and other reciprocal experiences that create functional communication and may lead to formal language in subsequent stages.

The rationale for early intervention is not simply to teach words and other linguistic features, but rather to teach communication skills on the way to formal language. Early intervention also may provide the child with concept training (functional use of objects and the meaning of actions) along with semantic correspondences to formal language (Bricker and Bricker, 1974). The child apparently thrives on an extensive amount of caregiver attention and mutual play.

Much of the strategy of early intervention is inherent in parent training and parent involvement in the intervention activities. The strategy is to work out infant-adult experiences that approximate those of normal adult-child relationships. This approximation may require alternative or augmentative patterns of play for communication training and symbol mapping. Usually the infant for whom early intervention is prescribed is at risk for speech, language, or communication development; and special transaction procedures may be required.

Observations of the natural behaviors of mothers of organismically impaired babies show that they do not learn as easily to socialize effectively with them as they do with normal babies. Perhaps, then, the social prerequisites to normal language may not evolve naturally and may require early intervention designed to synthesize the stimulation functions.

Fortunately, early assessment procedures are available for detection of risk conditions and for guiding the training program for parents (McDonald, 1980). A happy, positive relationship between mother and handicapped baby may depend upon early instruction by a professional specialist who can help the mother to achieve a positive, functional plan for early child care. If this can be achieved the specialist can coordinate his or her work with what is done at home to achieve developmental progress.

**Nonspeech Intervention.** As our knowledge of the functional uses of symbol systems has increased, the importance of alternative systems of symbolization has grown. Consequently, nonspeech intervention strategies have assumed a prominent place in intervention designs. This development in no way reduces the importance of speech in language and communication designs. Instead the nonspeech strategies open the way for language instruction for children who will not speak, who will speak at a later stage of development, or who will need nonspeech symbolization as a supplement to their total communication (Shane, 1980).

Nonspeech strategies offer the challenge of designing a special symbol set for the individual child, most often a child who is multiply handicapped, probably with severe auditory, motor, cognitive, or autistic impairments (Schiefelbusch, 1980). There is a range of logical issues involved in the nonspeech strategies, but the purpose here is to enter the strategy of developing individualized symbol systems for children who cannot use the audio-visual system functionally in talking. The use of a communication board, a sign system, or a lexic display system now is becoming more practical.

The advantages of a functional nonspeech system are apparent at all ages, but the possibilities seem dramatically urgent for small children who need a symbol system to learn the cognitive functions that better orient them to their environments and enable them to map the referential meanings of their expanding range of experience. The long delays that often characterize the nonverbal child are largely unnecessary. We now must formulate careful, definitive strategies for selecting and facilitating the development of functional systems for all children who have the capacity to learn them in their simplest forms.

**Milieu Intervention.** The milieu intervention strategy, developed by Hart and Rogers-Warren (1978), builds upon an incidental teaching model developed by Hart and Risley (1975). The milieu design involves preparation in three areas: (1) arranging the context to prompt the use of language, (2) assessing a child's current skill level to arrange for functional language usage, and (3) training adults to ensure that the child uses language functions frequently and that the language works for the child. These functions always interact in the milieu design whether in the home, the classroom, the ward, or the playroom.

In brief, the environment must be arranged to provide impetus and support for language usage. A variety of attractive materials and play activities should be available to the child on request. The adult mediates materials and activities so as to reinforce verbalizations and to demonstrate how language works to obtain desired ends for the child.

The strategy is designed to integrate aspects of both the training and the natural environments. It focuses on building high rates of spontaneous language in functional settings that include a variety of people, objects, and events, and on elaborating the topographic uses of language in an expanding range of contexts.

## OPERATIONAL DESIGNS

Operational designs denote the purposeful system that the language clinician manages in teaching a child. For instance, if language is taught in a preschool context, the operational design could include the organization of the room (including the placement of toys and materials), the arrangement of play and activity areas, the planned activity flow, the assessment procedures, the schedule, the grouping of children, the entry skills needed for membership in the program, the activity system or curriculum and instructional management, and other instructional tactics used by the clinician. However, these statements suggest that there are many parts and one cannot easily integrate many parts into an operational design. It is better to start with an operational design that is broken down into a limited number of functional parts. This involves the simple tactic of selecting the most functional categories and organizing the numerous smaller operational functions under them.

The main emphasis should be upon the procedures and the technology used in planning and maintaining the program. An operational system can be divided into five parts: (1) program planning, (2) program development, (3) program maintenance, (4) program evaluation, and (5) program generalization.

**Program Planning.** Planning requires information about the child that can be used to guide the child's entry into the program, to determine levels of functioning, and to establish objectives. The information can also be the basis for subsequent comparisons to determine progress. The information that planning is based upon should be distinguished from screening assessments, which may be used to select children who need a language intervention program. Such procedures are often referred to as detection and fall short of comprehensive planning. Assessments for program planning purposes should map out the child's functional language behavior and should be a first sampling in a series of samples that guide the language training program. The planning, of course, is also extended across the full span of training and provides for modifications as indicated by subsequent assessments.

Planning is the first phase of the training program and one that is functionally related to all the phases and operations that follow. It is keyed to initial assessments and continues into program development, program maintenance, program evaluation, and program generalization. The information for planning may be derived from standardized tests, developmental scales, nonstandardized tests, behavioral observations, and specialized diagnostic assessments.

**Program Development.** Program development is based upon some assumptions about the way language is used. For instance, one assumption may be that language is acquired or learned in a series of phases or stages. Thus the instructor can set down a sequential design of language units. The units could represent a practical curriculum that includes objectives that culminate from the sequential series of phases. The objectives are specified levels of language usage. The child who fits into this hypothetic program could be a child in any age range. The language program could be the sequential program that we think approximates that for a small child in a natural environment with the informal assistance of parents, other children, and friends. This program of activities sometimes has been designated as the developmental model (Ruder and Smith, 1974). The developmental model is based on the assumption that the sequence of language training should parallel the attainments of normal children.

However, others may build their curriculum to achieve functional outcomes for the child in relation to environmental contexts (a remedial model) (Guess, Sailor, Baer, 1974). The assumption used in remedial logic is that children who have not learned a functional language during the normal time range have probably developed inadequate social competencies. Consequently, functional skills need to be learned along with new language forms. The training sequences, then, should reflect pragmatic considerations, that is, the importance of specific language attainments for evoking favorable responses from the environment.

In any event, current language theory suggests that both language structure (content) and function (usage) should be taught. The language structure includes the words and the syntax of formal language. The functions include the codes of communicative behavior that are not embedded in the processing level of language. The functions are related to the context that gives the communicative event its intended meaning. In addition to formal language, then, program development includes pragmatic functions that determine the social competence features of language and communication. Simply stated, the child should learn functional communication skills.

**Program Maintenance.** The term program maintenance suggests that there are instructional procedures that help the intervener conduct the program effectively from start to finish (Schiefelbusch, 1981; Schiefelbusch, 1976). The procedures must be adaptable to levels and styles of language usage. Literally, the task is to motivate the children to participate actively and consistently in language learning activities. Consequently, a maintenance system must be adaptive, functional, and supportive. Because language events have great complexity, most systems of maintenance seem simplistic regardless of their

apparent usefulness in teaching complex language tasks.

McReynolds (1970) discusses a maintenance system under the heading of "Contingencies and Consequences in Speech Therapy." She is interested in consequent events that can be used with antecedent events (stimuli) to increase training efficiency. The reinforcer is an event subsequent to a response by the child which increases the rate of that response. It is combined as a teaching strategy with carefully programmed antecedent events (stimuli) that also have shaping properties for the child's language responses. Stimuli can be objects, pictures, facial expressions, instructions, or vocal modeling. The skillful utilization of antecedent and subsequent events comprises the primary basis of face-to-face language instruction. Teacher attention and selective use of social approval form the primary bases for both antecedent and consequent events.

Both the stimulus features of antecedent events and the response supporting features of subsequent events become part of the child's semantic orientations in learning language. Perhaps the clue to the child's semantic acquisitions is the way in which the child and the adult respond to each other and to the objects and actions in their shared environment. In the naturally occurring, reciprocal chain of events, the participants serve as each other's antecedent and subsequent events. In responding to the adults' visual and vocal acts, the child receives double exposure to his own receptive and expressive language functions. The child perceives language events, initiates language events, and receives reinforcing confirmation to both. The child knows that the clinician's responses are important to him and that his responses are important to the clinician. Both events in the chain have orienting and reinforcing effects. However, we have not yet established congruencies between social (pragmatic) functions and instructional procedures in teaching usage skills. Nevertheless, program maintenance can be improved by the way in which adults respond sensitively to the child during periods of language usage. Both the quality of the evoking stimuli and the sensitivity of response events appear to be highly similar to those used in creative parenting.

**Program Evaluation.**   Program evaluation should be combined with initial assessments done during the initial planning to form a functional evaluation system.* For instance, the intervener needs feedback on the short-term progress of the child, on the effectiveness of teaching procedures, and on the rate of correct responding (relative to criteria). The need for subtle changes in strategy can be indicated by immediate data feedback. Clinical hunches are useful because they may guide preliminary choices of procedure, but they cannot substitute for direct, objective information about the effects of instruction.

Simple, reliable procedures have been developed for charting and graphing behavior and for maintaining a cumulative record. Such records can show differences in performance dimensions under various instructional conditions. Along with procedures for recording behavior, strategies for using a variety of recorders have emerged. Parents, teaching aides, older children, and even children themselves have been trained to record events critical to the program.

Continuous probes are frequently used in language evaluation. For instance, the clinician may want to sample the child's performance before the training for that unit is begun. In that case the probe provides a specific baseline to use in proceeding with that unit. A probe can also be used to check on performance maintenance for phases that have been completed already. Probes may show the need to recycle to an earlier training phase to re-establish a performance unit that has been lost.

A typical probe involves sampling several words or phonemic units that have been taught or are soon to be taught. The responses can be charted and reviewed in relation to criteria or to anticipated progress. Probes usually are mini-replications

of the same units that have been, or will be, taught.

Frequent use of data descriptive of short-term effects allows for refining and improving procedures. Efficiencies developed in this way also can be described and built into subsequent programming.

Data collected for long-term evaluation are also extremely useful. These data may include tabulations of short-term data, serial probe evaluations, and periodic broader samplings of performance to compare with data derived in the initial evaluation. These data enable the clinician to develop major changes in the program or to substantiate the long-range design.

**Program      Generalization.**   Generalization may be any effective carry-over or transfer (in time or location) beyond the context of the training session. The common thread underlying all definitions is that generalization is an extension of a behavior to new circumstances. Generalization thus seems to be the key to understanding how taught language may be integrated by the child into a broad range of language uses.

Several salient issues have emerged from longitudinal observations of severely retarded adolescents and language delayed children receiving individualized language training. Apparently generalization to everyday language contexts does not occur until the learners successfully generalize across less complex, individual stimulus conditions (objects, trainers, and settings; Rogers-Warren and Warren, 1980). Results also have shown that generalization from training to natural environments is a function of the child's complement of language. The degree to which children use language is influenced by their existing repertoires (Hart and Risley, 1980). Generalization is also a function of the environmental opportunities for verbal expression (Hart and Rogers-Warren, 1978). Studies by Hart and Risley (1968, 1980) and by Warren, Rogers-Warren, Baer, and Guess (1980) have demonstrated that normal and language delayed children's use of newly learned language correlates highly with the frequency of opportunities to talk in a given setting. Also, if the newly trained language

---

*Program assessment as discussed here should not be confused with program evaluation as discussed in Chapters 15 and 16. The term as used here can also be designated as programming assessments.

is not functional for the child, generalization does not occur. In this case, function is determined by the extent to which language succeeds in mediating the behavior of others in the setting. Finally, generalization is facilitated by the degree of similarity (physical and behavioral) between the training environment and the generalization setting (Rincover and Koegel, 1975). In summary, when developmentally delayed children have something to say (a repertoire), a chance to say it (opportunity), a reason for saying it (function) in a familiar environment (similar to the one in which the response was first learned), they will generalize newly taught language. Rogers-Warren and Warren (in press) point out that these ideal conditions for generalization overlap remarkably well with the conditions available to normal children in the context of caregiver-child interactions. Generalization also seems to occur more readily in incidental (natural contextual) environments where the adult (clinician or teacher) adheres closely to the conditions summarized above.

## DISCUSSION

It is possible to project a simple schema of the information just presented, like the one below.

The importance of each of the designs in the diagram categories is apparent. *Environments* must be designed to provide arrangements for instruction. The different

environments may have both direct and indirect advantages. For instance, a classroom includes a number of peers, and a curriculum of academic and social activities and prereading and reading activities. These activities, together with the passage of time, offer extensive experiences for language learning, whereas a playroom is an unstructured, flexible arrangement for social language elaboration.

*Strategies* are flexible features of the intervention plan that enable the specialist to design for the individual differences of children. Strategies may be broad program designs that relate to age, disability, or purpose, or they may be more limited procedural functions. The important philosophic purpose of strategy designing is to adapt the language program to fit the child rather than requiring the impaired child to learn a standard program in a standard way.

*Operations* are also discussed in preceding sections. The power of the operational system is in the integration of the identified operations to produce a combined system of teaching. The simple, logical nature of the operations should not obscure their potential rigor and potency.

However, the three major components of the design, together with the subcomponents, do not suggest the immense complexity of the structure and functions involved. There is always the challenge that elegant designs can be created which will simplify this complexity. Simplicity is an objective in all designs—simplicity and

Table 2–1   DESIGNING FOR LANGUAGE INTERVENTION

| Environmental Designs | Strategic Designs | Operational Designs |
|---|---|---|
| Classroom | Early intervention | Program planning |
| Clinic | Nonspeech intervention | Program development |
| Home | Milieu intervention | Program maintenance |
| Playroom | Developmental intervention | Program evaluation |
| Special contexts | Functional intervention | Program generalization |
| (Environments may be used in combination. They are arranged here generally from formal to informal.) | (These strategies can be used to fit age, impairment, and purpose variables.) | (Operations may be used in any of the environments or for any strategy.) |

elegance. In the current state of knowledge, however, we do not yet know the simple keys and rules for teaching complex structures and functions, and so we let the complexity of the content to be taught confound our methods of teaching. Yet there are artists and scientists among us who have already contributed to these ends. In the past few years significant progress in the designs for teaching a first language has been made. We simply need to maintain the intensity of our efforts. But then, this chapter was not meant to describe *how to do it*, but simply to tell *what is it?*, as intervention relates to children.

## A POSTSCRIPT

The preceding is a general design for language intervention—a *what is it* statement. However, the reader may not agree with this version. The reader is encouraged to make his or her own design for language intervention based upon experiences, an analysis of the research literature, and a philosophy of human services. Perhaps the primary purpose of a design for language intervention is to provide order and purpose for the intervener. If so, we should each develop a design for our own professional use. Perhaps it should always be open to modification, and also we ourselves should expect to change in directions that are indicated. We may never achieve an optimal design, but we shall benefit from trying. If we do succeed in maintaining this effort, there is some assurance that our clients also will benefit.

Efforts to design and to maintain optimal environments for teaching language may establish contexts for sensitive exchanges between interveners and children with language problems. Ideally, we should all learn from these transactions.

The *strategies* that are selected may also provide strength for the design. They collate many clinical functions that have emerged from efforts to teach a wide range of children from profoundly and multiply handicapped to the mildly impaired and from early infancy throughout the life span of the individual. Also, strategies reflect

the logical assumption that teaching builds upon the evolving, developmental functions of children, as well as upon the functional relationships they must have with their environmental contexts.

Operations are built into virtually all teaching designs from computerized instruction to informal teaching. Instructional *operations* are a combination of behavioral, cognitive, developmental, and social research backgrounds. It is a system that will continue to evolve from the research of many basic and applied scientists.

## REFERENCES

Atkinson RC: Adaptive instructional systems: Some attempts to optimize the learning process. In Klahr D. (ed): *Cognition and Instruction*. Hillsdale, NJ: Lawrence Erlbaum Associates, 1976

Bricker W, Bricker DD: An early language training strategy. In Schiefelbusch, RL Lloyd LL (eds): *Language Perspectives—Acquisition, Retardation, and Intervention*. Baltimore: University Park Press, 1974

*Bronfenbrenner U*: Is Early Intervention Effective? A Report on Longitudinal Evaluations of Preschool Programs, vol II. DHEW Publication No (OHD) 76–30025, 1976

Carroll JB: Promoting language skills: The role of instruction. In Klahr D. (ed): *Cognition and Instruction*. Hillsdale, NJ: Lawrence Erlbaum, Associates, 1976

Glaser R: Cognitive psychology and instructional design. In Klahr D. (ed): *Cognition and Instruction*. Hillsdale, NJ: Lawrence Erlbaum Associates, 1976

Guess D, Sailor W, Baer DM: To teach language to retarded children. In Schiefelbusch, RL, Lloyd LL (eds): *Language Perspectives-Acquisition, Retardation, and Intervention*. Baltimore: University Park Press, 1974

Hart B: Pragmatics and language development. In Lahey, BB Kasden A (eds): *Advances in Clinical Child Psychology*, vol 3. New York: Plenum Press, 1980

Hart B, Risley T: Establishing the use of descriptive adjectives in the spontaneous speech of disadvantaged preschool children. J Appl Behav Anal 1:109–120, 1968

Hart B, Risley T: Incidental teaching of language in the preschool. J Appl Behav Anal 8:411–420, 1975

Hart B, Risley T: In vivo language intervention: Unanticipated general effects. J Appl Behav Anal 13:407–432, 1980

Hart B, Rogers-Warren A: A milieu approach to language teaching. In Schiefelbusch RL (ed): *Language Intervention Strategies*. Baltimore: University Park Press, 1978

Klahr D: *Cognition and Instruction*. Hillsdale, NJ: Lawrence Erlbaum Associates, 1976

Krauss RM: Communication models and communication behavior. In Schiefelbusch, RL, Hollis JH (eds): *Language Intervention from Ape to Child*. Baltimore: University Park Press, 1979

McDonald E: Early identification and treatment of children at risk for speech development. In Schiefelbusch RL (ed): *Nonspeech Language and Communication: Analysis and Intervention*. Baltimore: University Park Press, 1980

McReynolds L: Reinforcement procedures for establishing and maintaining echoic speech by a nonverbal child. In Spradlin, JE, Girardeau FL (eds): *Application of Functional Analysis to Speech and Hearing*. Monograph No. 14, American Speech and Hearing Association, 1970, pp. 60–66

Rincover A, Koegel RL: Setting generality and stimulus control in autistic children. J Appl Behav Anal 8:235–246, 1975

Rogers-Warren A, Warren SF: Mands for verbalization: Facilitating the display of newly trained language in children. Behav Mod 4:361–382, 1980

Rogers-Warren A, Warren SF: Form and function in language learning and generalization. Anal Interven Develop Dis 1:3–4, 1981

Rogers-Warren A, Warren SF: Pragmatics and generalization: Processes in language learning and remediation. In Schiefelbusch RL, Pickar J (eds): *Communicative Competence: Acquisition and Intervention*. Baltimore: University Park Press, in press

Ruder KF, Bunce B, Ruder C: Language intervention in a preschool/classroom setting. In McCormick L, Schiefelbusch RL (eds): *Introduction to Language Intervention*. Columbus, Ohio: Charles E. Merrill Publishing Co, in press

Ruder K, Smith M: Issues in language training. In Schiefelbusch RL, Lloyd LL (eds): *Language Perspectives—Acquisition, Retardation, and Intervention*. Baltimore: University Park Press, 1974

Rumbaugh DM, Savage-Rumbaugh ES, Gill TM, Warner HW: The chimpanzee as an animal model in language research. In Schiefelbusch RL, Hollis JH (eds): *Language Intervention from Ape to Child*. Baltimore: University Park Press, 1979

Schiefelbusch RL: Language training strategies for retarded children. In Sankar DV (ed): *Mental Health in Children*, vol III. Westbury, NY: PJD Publications, LTD, 1976

Schiefelbusch RL: Advances in school and classroom learning. In Hamerlynck LA (ed): *Behavioral Systems for the Developmentally Disabled. 1. School and Family Environments*. New York: Brunner-Mazel, 1977

Schiefelbusch RL (ed): *Nonspeech Language and Communication: Analysis and Intervention*. Baltimore: University Park Press, 1980

Schiefelbusch RL (ed): A philosophy of intervention. Anal Interven Develop Dis 1:3–4, 1981

Shane HC: Approaches to assessing the communication of nonoral persons. In Schiefelbusch RL, *Nonspeech Language and Communication: Analysis and Intervention*. Baltimore: University Park Press, 1980

Warren SF, Rogers-Warren A, Baer DM, Guess D. The assessment and facilitation of language generalization. In Sailor W, Wilcox B, Brown L (eds): *Methods of Instruction for Severely Handicapped Students*. Baltimore: Brooks Publishers, 1980

# 3

# INTERVENTION ISSUES IN NONSPEECH COMMUNICATION

*DAVID E. YODER*
*ARLENE KRAAT*

For the severely speech and language impaired person, many of the barriers that prevented active participation in the communication process in the past are now disappearing. Fortunately, our attitudes about communication are changing. We are transcending the era when not only was oral communication the standard, but there were also inflexible rules for what constituted appropriate oral communication. One has only to examine some of the earlier texts on the nature of "effective speaking" to realize how much our attitudes have changed and are changing. We are learning to acknowledge and respect the integrity of communication differences and variance.

At the present time, our clinical intervention model emphasizes the entire communication process. The speech-language pathologist is no longer obsessed with the need to have persons speak if the physiologic mechanisms to produce speech are nonfunctional or deviant. We have the option to *not* engage in frustrating and unproductive therapeutic efforts for severely disabled individuals for whom intelligible speech is not currenly or never will be a reality. We have become knowledgeable in the variety of ways in which a person can communicate (for example, natural gestures, facial expressions, body postures, sign systems, language boards, computerized devices), rather than just the ability to comprehend and produce spoken language. This is in sharp contrast to earlier clinical intervention procedures, which focused primarily on oral production and speech articulation. There is currently a genuine emphasis on the pragmatic aspects of language. Professionals continue to research the functions of language as well as the relationship of nonverbal behavior to the communication process. Current conceptions stress communication competence and acknowledge that speech is one aspect of this competence—but only one aspect of the communication process. This broader view of the nature of communication and the efficacy of various nonspeech communication systems has had a very dramatic effect on individuals with severe speech impairment or severe language disorders. It is also having an effect on our service delivery systems and professional expectations.

Recently there has been increased acceptance and implementation of augmentative nonspeech communication systems for the severely speech impaired and language disordered population. Apart from the more obvious example of the dysarthric cerebral palsied child, augmentative systems have been used with language delayed and language deviant children, including those who are cognitively impaired and autistic. We are witnessing the emergence of "total communication" programs, the use of Blissymbolics, Signed English, Amerind, syllable based systems along with a host of electronic and computerized communication devices.

To understand the clinical application and intervention issues in augmentative communication, it is important to be aware of the different ways in which these systems are currently being used. In one major application group, nonspeech systems are being successfully used as primary communication systems to augment insufficient production and reception skills. For example, a person with a severe dysarthria or apraxia may be actively communicating through one of these systems or augmenting his dysarthric speech when it is unintelligible to a listener. These systems also occasionally augment the understanding of spoken language, as when signed input or written communication might be used to facilitate comprehension abilities in an adult aphasic.

In a second group of severely impaired individuals, augmentative communication models are being utilized to allow more conventional speech and language to emerge. For example, in developing beginning communication with some impaired children and adults, it has been useful to rely heavily on visual materials, such as plastic forms, rebus pictures, and pictographic symbols. Sometimes gestures can accompany the input and substitute for, or accompany, the output. Autistic, severely intellectually retarded, or aphasic persons may be in the latter group. With many such individuals, these sign and symbol systems serve as a bridge to vocal speech understanding and use and may later be discontinued.

Other individuals may be maintained on these systems once representation skills are developed. The primary intervention task with this group of augmentative systems users is very different than it is with

those in the first group. Augmentative, nonspeech means are being used in conjunction with speech or without speech to establish symbolic behavior in these very impaired groups. While the prognosis for any person with more severe cognitive and language disability is extremely guarded, some of the success in cases in the literature through use of signs and other augmentative communication systems has been encouraging.

As we gain more experience and examine the information produced by the few interaction studies we have available (Harris, 1978; Beukelman and Yorkston, 1980, 1982; Calculator and Dollaghan, 1982; Kraat, 1981, 1982), we are troubled by some of our observations of how effectively these systems are being used. Granted, the level of communication that is possible with an augmented system is certainly greater than what is possible without such a system. Our interaction studies done in real environments, however, do not demonstrate as high a level of conversation and communication as we had expected. This is true not only for system users with developmental disabilities, but for adults with previously intact language systems as well. Augmented communication systems are not being used with the frequency that we would like, and when used, they are not generally employed to their maximum capacity or at the level we want to see achieved. This realization brings with it a need to re-examine our intervention, our expectations, and how we are going about applying augmentative systems in general. To correct this situation, we need to examine our observations of what is and is not going on relative to current use of augmentative systems, isolate some of the barriers we observe, and alter our intervention procedures in view of this information.

It seems apparent to us that part of the problem lies in the differences imposed on communication by these unique systems themselves. They are not just different vehicles that are comparable to speech. They are uniquely different systems with different capabilities and constraints. These differences and their effect on communication must be recognized if effective intervention procedures and goals are to be established. This is further confounded by the observation that users of systems and speaking persons in the environment do not bring the same experiences, abilities, and discourse strategies to the communication exchange. There is thus a need for very special intervention strategies to circumvent these differences. We must examine *how* we are teaching nonspeakers and *what* we are teaching them. We would suggest that strict adherence to a vocal communication development and use model may not be most appropriate for this population, if effective communication is our goal. We will explore some of these intervention concerns in the subsequent sections of this chapter.

## DIFFERENCES IMPOSED BY AUGMENTATIVE SYSTEMS

It has become increasingly obvious to those of us working with the nonspeaker and augmentative systems that nonspeech communication is not a direct substitute for vocal speech communication. There are many unique features as well as constraints within these systems. For example, the rate of communication is markedly reduced and vocabulary limitations are often imposed. These differences create very specific constraints on what is probable, what is profitable, and what is possible in a communication interaction. Limitations and differences embedded in augmentative systems not only affect the augmentative system user in terms of what the use is and is not capable of saying, but they also affect how the speakers will respond when communicating with the augmentative user. It is important that we understand how these system features affect the communication interaction of both parties, the message senders as well as the message receivers. With this knowledge, we have a better framework for approaching decisions regarding what intervention should be. For that reason, these features and their effect will be discussed in further detail here.

## REDUCED RATE OF COMMUNICATION

One of the major differences between augmentative and vocal communication is the rate of communication. Normal vocal communication occurs at a rate of approximately 126 to 172 words per minute (Foulds, 1980). Augmentative communication, in contrast, is extremely slow. The exact rate of communication that can be achieved varies, depending on the type of system used and the augmentative user's physical abilities. Potentially, signing systems afford us the nearest approximation to vocal speech. However, signing systems that literally translate English form into sign, such as Signing Exact English or Signed English, still fall short of vocal speech (Bellugi and Fischer, 1972; Mayberry, 1976). Aided communication systems, that is, those using an external, physical device, are extremely slow in comparison. Scanning type devices used with the most severely physically impaired may produce as few as two words per minute (Foulds, 1980). Direct selection type devices have reported rates of 6 to 25 words per minute (Foulds, 1980; Rosen and Goodenough-Trepagnier, 1981; Shane, 1980; Beukelman and Yorkston, 1977). Needless to say, the discrepancy between 2 or 25 words per minute, given an augmentative communication, and the 126 words per minute available in vocal speech is great. This imbalance in the rate of communication seriously affects the types of communication and the nature of the communication interactions that occur.

Observations and interaction studies of augmentative system use suggest that the reduced rate of communication has a particularly detrimental effect on communication for those persons using aided systems. Because of the huge discrepancy between vocal speech rates and aided communication forms, the vocal partner in any exchange has a definite advantage. He generally has the power, under the circumstances, to control the interaction. That is, when it will occur, how long it will be, how much the device user will be able to participate, and often even what the topics will be. In contrast, the user has difficulty getting into such a conversational imbalance, holding his turn, continuing conversation beyond one utterance, and terminating it when he wishes. The slower communicator also has difficulty getting conversational entry for the purposes of repairing communication breakdowns. In the few interaction studies that have been done with device users, it appears that these different communicators have fewer opportunities to communicate, communicate less frequently, and often are given but one utterance per turn (Harris, 1982; Beukelman and Yorkston, 1980, 1982; Kraat, 1981, 1982). This is in spite of the fact that some of these device users were previously competent vocal speakers, or had spelling and advanced language capabilities. This is illustrated by such communication samples taken from device use as 3770 words over a 2-week period (Beukelman and Yorkston, 1982); 112 utterances over a 10-hour period (Kraat, 1981); and 2053 words generated by a scan-printer user over a period of 3 months (Kraat, 1982). In comparison with vocal communication, these samples from device users show severely reduced amounts of communication. Not all of the blame for these sample sizes can be placed on rate alone. Other factors, such as mobility, contribute to this reduced amount of communication. A sizeable portion of this lack of communication and amount of communication, however, can be attributed to the slowness of aided communication, and the stress and time demands it places on the interactional process.

Another consequence of a slow rate of communication is seen in the types of communicative acts addressed to the device user. Often, the user is barraged with yes/no questions, questions that require a single word answer only, or utterances that do not expect or require participation from the user (Harris, 1982; Shane and Cohen, 1981; Kraat, 1981). This occurs in exchanges with augmentative users capable of responding at a more sophisticated level. Generally it stems from the vocal person's need for expediency or the lack of time available to converse at a higher level.

Again, the vocal person's behavior may not be exclusively the result of communication rate, but obviously this variable contributes greatly. It is important to understand the nature of the communications that are coming at the device user. It is within this context that they must learn to be effective communicators. It is not the same as what comes at another vocal speaker.

There are other instances when aided augmentative communication cannot meet the demands of "real conversational time." Events and shared referents go by too quickly. For example, in watching a hockey game on television, one might say "Great play," "Did you see that?", "Watch out!", and so on. Everyone sharing the game is also sharing in the action that is going on at the same time the vocal comment is made. It is particularly difficult for a device user to make the same comment in time and space. By the time a message such as "That was a great play" is completed, the referent is long gone. The utterance may then be ambiguous or inappropriate. This may also be the case when an aid user wants to make a comment that is humorous and time-dependent for effect.

In normal vocal conversation we use numerous pronouns and referents, such as that, here, and this, when the referent is clear from the preceding statement, or shared information. In the case of augmentative device use, the rate may be so reduced that considerable time may elapse between the preceding statement, or shared referent, and the response. Other conversational utterances may have intervened, or events occurred or disappeared that make the presuppositions and pronouns ambiguous or even misunderstood. To avoid miscommunication, the device user may not be able to use the same linguistic forms and usage styles that the vocal person can use in the same situation. Specific referents may have to be specified more often, and the user made aware of the reasons and need for these altered forms.

Conversational samples involving augmentative communicators also point to the rate factor as having an influence on what the device user says and doesn't say, as well as the manner in which something is said. Lengthy and elaborated communications may find the device user without a listener. Aided communication is not only an effort for the listener, it may also be effortful for the aid user. In looking at the types of speech acts generated by adult aid users, it is obvious that there is a high proportion of requests and giving of information (Beukelman and Yorkston, 1980; Lossing, 1981; Kraat, 1981). This may partly reflect their physical disability. However, it is also probable that essential needs are met by conversation, and less salient communication may be left unsaid. For example, comments such as "I bet Jane would love to come down to see the Song of Norway Festival" in the context of reading and advertisement, occur infrequently in augmented communication samples.

Slow rate also creates a need for efficiency in the utterances and communications of the augmentative communicator which is reflected in a variety of ways. For example, a user might produce an utterance in a telegraphic way, leaving out the syntactic and stylistic elements that are secondary to the message (for example, "Hook—back" rather than "There is a hook poking me in the back somewhere"). It is faster. In another situation, a device user might reduce the utterance to the least possible number of words, but produce it in a syntactic manner (for example, "I want a bath" as opposed to "If you have time later, could you give me a bath?"). In still other situations, a gesture, vocalization, or facial expression may be used in lieu of an aided system to effect quick communication with a familiar person. For example, a nonspeaker wishing to request that another person loosen his seatbelt might get the other person's attention by vocalizing, and then looking down at his waist. This is faster than spelling out the communication. Those using unaided communication means also switch modes for efficiency, even though the rate of communication using signs is greater. For example, pantomine or pointing may be used in place of a word-by-word construction for expediency. This certainly is not the pattern of vocal speakers.

In other situations, the need for effi-

ciency and rate leads to the use of prediction. It may be that the user generates a single word and has the listener expand it quickly. Or the impatient listener may jump ahead of the user and predict what word or though he believes the person wants to communicate. Obviously, if used effectively, these techniques can be helpful. Often, however, they are the source of communication breakdowns and misunderstandings, both in regard to content and the user's intentions.

## RESTRICTED SYMBOL SETS

As discussed, rate has a significant effect on the type and quality of interaction that occurs in aided communication use. Of equal, if not greater, importance is the presence of finite and restricted vocabulary sets that interfere with the effectiveness of our augmentative techniques. This includes both aided and unaided augmentative techniques.* These vocabulary limitations present special problems both for communication development and communication use.

An able-bodied, speaking 8-year-old has thousands of words available to him for expression. In hearing a new word or vernacular expression that has particular meaning and importance to him, such as Actavision, Dungeons and Dragons, PLO, or "Do you party?", he can immediately incorporate these into his productive vocabulary and explore how to use them, the effects of their use on various listeners, and where and when not to use them.

In contrast, augmentative communicators who do not have spelling abilities may have only 10, 40, or 100 vocabulary items available in their productive or receptive communication systems. If they are fortunate, they may have 250 vocabulary words, or in an exceptional case, 500-

---

*Aided techniques and systems refers to any device, either electronic or nonelectronic, used for communication purposes. Unaided techniques or systems refers to a nonexternal expressive mode, such as speech, manual signing, or gestures. See *ASHA*, August 1981.

to 600-word vocabularies. Additions of vocabulary as situations arise is far more difficult in this medium. In many cases, this
reduced vocabulary does not reflect the
user's knowledge of the world, or his representational abilities on a cognitive level.
Frequently, the nonspeaker is being asked
to communicate with a finite vocabulary set
that is below his needs and abilities. For
the physically disabled or ambulatory individual using an aided system, this finite
and restricted vocabulary set is often directly related to the user's lack of physical
ability, the limitations of the techniques
the user has available for accessing this vocabulary, the limitations involved in carrying around a large symbol dictionary, or all
three. It may also reflect visual or visual-
perceptual limitations of the user. Even
given multiple devices for varied codes and
situations, the limitations still exist. For
the person using signs or gestures, limitations in vocabulary may again be found in
physical limitations or the inability of those
in the environment to associate a new sign
or gesture with needed or new concepts
that the user wishes to code.

Regardless of the reasons for reduced
vocabulary access, the effects are pervasive and obvious. These augmentative
communication system users cannot say
what they want to, when they want, and
how they want to. It is very probable that
a nonspeaker, using an aided communication system, wanting to tell a peer that his
Dad got them tickets for a concert of the
Jackson Five, or that he just got a new an-
gel tail fish for his fish tank at home, or
that he thinks you are a creep or a turkey,
has no way to initiate and relay these
thoughts, except by emotion expressed in
body postures and facial expressions, altered vocalizations, or by looking at something in the room that has some association with the idea. Most likely his closed
vocabulary set does not have a symbol or
word that can assist him. The number of
possible entries is small in comparison
with the number of ideas and functions
that a user might want to code. It is difficult for these communications to occur in a
linguistic form at a prespelling level. Use
of advanced Blissymbolic strategies

(McNaughton and Kates, 1980) provides a
possible exception, in that vocabulary can
be expanded by combining various semantic notions. For example, a child may tell
another person that he had spaghetti for
dinner by indicating the symbol for food
and the symbol for long, thus expressing
"long food" to mean spaghetti.

It is important for us to examine how
limited symbol sets may impinge on the
nonspeaker's ability to learn language and
develop communicative use and competency. Recently one of us noticed a child of
about 3 looking out of the window at an
airport terminal as a small plane landed on
the runway. She excitedly said: "Get out
of here, airplane! . . . I said, get out of
here airplane! No . . . Go that way, airplane. . . . (plane maneuvers a turn) . . .
Not coming . . . here we go . . . here we
go!" One is struck by how such spontaneous communications do not occur with
those using signs and/or aided systems.
This is partly because only a limited vocabulary is available to them, and the decisions about what will be made available
(symbols or pictures on the device) are
often made by someone else—a parent or
a professional. It cannot just emerge spontaneously when they are ready to code an
idea.

In all probability, a sign user would
not communicate via signs in this same situation. Something that might be available
to him, such as "I see an airplane," is obvious. For the device user, whether or not
any linguistic communication will take
place depends on the symbols available to
him. In this case, the word "airplane" may
be accessible, and indicated. This is a far
cry from the utterances of the 3-year-old
child about the same situation and probably below the productive level and intent
of the user. Its use serves only as a topic or
a label. Expansion of that one symbol into
the intended meaning of the user depends
on the vocal listener in the interchange.

The illustration above is used to highlight the difficulties and limitations of the
nonspeaker in being able to code in a nonlinguistic or linguistic manner what the
user knows, wants to communicate about,
and with the intent he wishes to imply.

Content and form are severely restricted. Therefore, so is the ability to explore and play with language use in any extensive fashion. Even the number of opportunities for explaining productive communication is reduced. Functions of communicative attempts may be limited in number and type. For example, linguistic means for gaining attention, such as "Mommy," "Look," or "Hey" do not, in fact, get someone's attention in a nonspeech form as easily. These functions may need to be coded with tugging, pulling, fussing, pushing a switch to ring a bell, or engaging a light.

Because there are reduced linguistic capabilities available to the augmentative system user, the actions and capabilities of those interacting with this individual have serious consequences for the communicative exchanges that can and do occur. In many cases the user depends on the receiver to expand his communicative attempts. This must be done through a series of questions and shared knowledge. For example, being given the word "cold" without its referring to an ongoing event or ongoing topic places a huge burden on the receiver of that message to isolate the message and intent that is being conveyed. This may be as far from the clue word as "We got a new freezer," or "Aunt Judy can't come because the baby has a cold." This extensive need for listener expansion leads to communication breakdowns in some cases; to no communication in others; to the user accepting an approximation of what he intended as a communication in other instances. Because of the effort involved, and the odds against certain communication intents being completed, one has to question whether or not this lack of vocabulary has some relationship to one of our observed problems in communication system use, that of communication initiation by the user. Initiation of a variety of communication intents may be just too complicated, given the situation, and thus reserved only for the most salient communication interactions.

The need for interpretation and expansion on the part of the listener also appears to limit the number of interactants available to the device user. Some persons in the user's environment will not be able to communicate with the aided speaker at all, beyond social greetings and "talking at them." Others will be unable to communicate about certain topics because they do not share enough information with the user to expand on utterances made within a limited symbol repertoire. Consequently, less communication occurs with peers or people less familiar with the augmentative user and his symbol set. Instead, a communication dependency occurs between the device user and a set of caregivers, usually adults. The use strategies learned and developed within these dyads may or may not be useful to the augmentative user at later stages of development.

It is also important to note that the level of the speaking person's communication may be below the capabilities of the augmentative speaker because of limitations in productive output. A low level of productive communication, for example, a gesture or a single word utterance, may be responded to as if it marks the cognitive and understanding level of the user. We apparently use these signals to adjust or readjust our communication in speaking to young children or cognitively limited persons (Griffith and Robinson, 1980). Communication impairment often gives a false productive marker, and the augmentative device user is spoken down to, or utterances are not expanded or corrected to the level needed by the user (Shane and Cohen, 1981; Harris, 1982; Yoder and Calculator, 1981). Such observations bring into question whether or not developing nonspeakers on limited systems receive appropriate feedback to facilitate further learning.

The symbol system chosen for the person must provide a means of representing thoughts in a form that can be physically transmitted or presented to those with whom the person will be interacting.

For young children, as well as those functioning cognitively at sensorimotor stages V and VI, the selection and development of a symbol system and vocabulary are more important to communication effectiveness than is the specific augmentative technique. The symbol system and individual vocabulary selected will mark the success of the communication interaction for the person. Just as there is no one device for a person, there is no one symbol system for a person. What may have been determined as the most effective symbol system in the initial evaluation period may change over time because of developmental and environmental changes. The symbol and vocabulary selection process is therefore to be viewed as continuous and dynamic.

It is also important to view the selection and development of symbol system strategies in light of the multiple environments with which the person may interact. For example, what might be best suited for daily living and use at home or in the residential setting might not be best suited for the classroom or general social environments. For this reason it might serve the person's best interest to develop symbols and vocabularies to fit given environments. One family found it necessary to keep a symbol display and vocabulary board in the glove compartment of the car to carry on effective communication with their child while traveling. On the other hand, that same vocabulary display was not appropriate or useful at home or in school, and other symbols and vocabularies were selected and developed accordingly.

Some persons who are not physically handicapped may be greatly restricted by the use of physical displays such as communication boards and books. For these individuals it may be well to investigate the use of manual signing, formal gestures, or total communication, a communication system frequently used with hearing impaired and deaf individuals (Kopchik and Lloyd, 1976; Schaeffer, Musil, and Kollinzas, 1980). The basics of such systems as they relate to the hearing impaired are treated by Maestas y Moores and Moores 1980). However, it is important to point out that manual signing and total communication systems have been used effectively as augmentative systems with many severely cognitively and emo-

tionally handicapped children (Schaeffer, 1980). It is important to note that if a manual or total communication system is selected for a person as an expressive mode of communication, that person must have attained a cognitive functioning level of sensorimotor stage V or VI. One cannot expect a child to use Finger Spelling as a communication means until the person reaches the developmental level of approximately age 7. The choice of a specific signing system that is best suited to a given person may be a personal decision or one governed by what the community of signers within the family's community environment might be. On the other hand, learning a communication system will be difficult for many multiply handicapped persons, and our responsibility is to assist in making the task simple, while providing the most effective system possible.

Some advantages of the total communication system are its portability, its expediency, and in many cases, its less strenuous cognitive demands. Certainly the disadvantages of using the total communication system are that it has a limited audience and interactive availability. Unless there are a number of persons in the community who use sign language, the person may be using a communicatively restricted system. Other limitations are related to the need for good motor control (Shane and Wilbur, 1980). Communicating in sign language rules out using the hands for most ordinary purposes while signing, and the audience must be watching the message sender in order to receive the message. The latter is also a problem with users of communication boards: A receiver must be present and attentive to the communication board during the communication interaction.

There are a variety of symbol systems available which have been adapted to communication board use. These systems have been discussed in more detail by Vanderheiden and Harris-Vanderheiden (1976); Harris and Vanderheiden (1980); Clark and Woodcock (1976); Kates, McNaughton, and Silvermann (1977); and Musselwhite and St. Louis (1982). The professional team should keep the following considerations in mind when selecting the symbol system to be used with a given technique:

1. Is the symbol system and vocabulary compatible with the technique selected?

2. Does it allow for the greatest interaction with the fewest number of symbols? (Space is at a premium.)

3. Are the system and the vocabulary selected appropriate for the person's cognitive level, language comprehension skills, motor competency, and environmental demands?

4. Is the system dynamic, developmentally based, generative, and flexible to allow for the person's future growth and changes?

5. Is the system acceptable to the user, parents, caregivers, teachers, and those persons with whom the individual will interact most frequently? The most commonly used ones are photos, pictures and/or line drawings, Blissymbols, and traditional orthography (words, for example).

For young children and children functioning at low levels, pictures and photos may be the most appropriate elements. The child using a picture vocabulary system usually points to pictures that represent objects, ideas, or thoughts. For the young child who has been pointing to objects for communicative purposes, an appropriate transition is to have photos made of the objects the child has been using for interaction and have those mounted on a display for communication use. Subsequently, pictures from magazines or black-and-white line drawings may be substituted for the photos. The size of the pictures selected will, of course, depend upon the child's visual, motor, and perceptual skills. Size of pictures may also be determined by the number of picture symbols that have to be placed on the communication board display. Pictures are applicable to nearly all of the basic devices, except for the higher level independent devices that have some form of printout display. In any case, pictures are usually thought of as the easiest

system to implement with young children and mentally retarded persons. On the other hand, adolescent mentally retarded persons and adults with aphasia may become resentful when pictures are used, because they feel they are being treated as children. Age appropriate symbols are important.

In the last several years, Blissymbolics have become popular and useful for many nonspeaking persons, both normal and delayed cognitive functioning individuals (Harris and associates, 1975; Harris and associates, 1979; Kates, McNaughton, and Silvermann, 1977). Blissymbolics, like pictures, may be applicable to and used on all of the basic devices. Even some independent devices have a printout for Blissymbolics. The symbols may serve as a transitional system for the child who is not yet ready for traditional orthography but is in need of a more versatile system than pictures offer. Because of the linguistic nature of the Blissymbolic system, it has been found to facilitate the acquisition of language and has enhanced communication initiation and interactive skills (Harris and colleagues, 1979; Kates, McNaughton, and Silvermann, 1977).

Traditional orthography (TO) has been used on communication boards for years (McDonald and Schultz, 1976; Vicker, 1974). Because TO is the system used by able-bodied persons, it is often preferred by parents and teachers who want the affected person to appear and be as "unhandicapped" as possible. If TO is to be used, one must keep in mind that the person will be required to learn to read and spell before he can communicate effectively. It is well to keep in mind that the able-bodied person is not asked to acquire reading and spelling skills until long after he has mastered the skill of speech communication. TO is a skill that should certainly be learned by all persons who are cognitively able to do so.

The TO system can be applied to techniques at all levels of implementation. It is the most versatile of the systems, but the entry level for effective use is about 7 years developmentally (Clark and Woodcock, 1976).

## EXPRESSIVE MODES

Persons using augmentative systems may employ a variety of ways of expressing their messages, including linguistic and nonlinguistic forms of expression, such as gestures, nonelectronic and electronic/computerized devices, and vocalizations. Although these expressive modes provide the user with a significant means of communication, it is a different type of communication system than is available through vocal speech or handwriting. These augmentative forms have many unique features of output which need special consideration and recognition in developing intervention strategies.

Natural speech is generally universally understood. In contrast, symbols used in augmented forms of communication may not be as easily understood, and may place limitations on the communication interactions that can take place, in regard to both the nature and with whom they occur. This is particularly true in the use of formal signs and idiosyncratic gestures. These unaided forms vary in their decipherability to an untrained "listener."* Gestures referred to as emblems (Higginbotham and Yoder, 1982), such as a headshake "no," pointing to the location of an object, or indicating tiredness by closing the eyes and drooping head are relatively understandable to a large number of people. Idiosyncratic gestures, however, developed for use within a family, such as pointing to the knee to indicate "need," to the buttocks to indicate "but," and eyes rolled up to indicate "yes" are not easily understood without knowing the code. Still other, more formal signs require learning and memorization for use, for example, the sign in Signed English for "pain" or "wonderful." These differences reduce the number of interactants a nonspeaker can communicate with on that level.

Problems in symbol decipherability also exist in aided communication systems. Those systems using traditional orthography to convey communications isolate nonreading persons from the device user. This is particularly significant when these nonreaders are peers or younger children important to the communicator. Some of the more arbitrary symbols used in aided devices, such as / representing the, or nonpictographic Blissymbols, also make communication of these items difficult for those who do not read or know that particular symbol. Other vocabulary items may require knowledge of special symbol strategies. For example, interpretation of rebus symbols using a phonic or segmentation technique, or some Blissymbol strategies, may be confusing to unfamiliar message reviewers. Morningstar (1981) illustrates this in her excellent study of Blissymbolic communication with unfamiliar "listeners." These listeners, given the symbol for animal and then the letter "D," interpreted these items in a sequential manner, not in an integrated one. Her listeners attempted to guess a word beginning with D, rather than an animal that begins with the letter D, such as dog.

Electronic and computerized communication devices offer a variety of output media through which the person with limited speech capabilities can communicate expressively. These output models serve different communication needs and provide different communication capabilities (Vanderheiden, 1976; Harris and Vanderheiden, 1980; Kraat, in press). The specific outputs available in a user's aid may range from synthesized speech to video displays to hard copy printers. Nonelectronic communication devices generally convey communications by having the listener note selections as they are made by the nonspeaker, item by item. Obviously these outputs vary in what they require of a listener and the degree of overall independence they afford the user in communication. The specific outputs available to a nonspeaker will affect the types of communications he can easily have, and the communication needs that will be more easily met. A particular output may be relatively effective in face-to-

---

*Listener in this paper refers to a person who is the receiver of the intended message expressed by an augmentative communication system user.

face communication, but not effective from across the room or in a group conversation. Others have limitations in a noisy environment, for telephone use, for classroom use, or with peers who are physically unable to manipulate paper writing strips or position themselves so that they can view a printed output.

Observations also suggest that output type has an effect on communication interaction. For example, in a study done by Beukelman and Yorkston (1980) significant differences were found in the communicative functions accomplished by a printer versus a letterboard. These differences need to be studied further.

The unusualness of augmentative systems and devices in general can affect social approachability. Electronic and non-electronic aided systems must be looked at from this perspective. People are not accustomed to interacting and conversing with another person through a machine or board, in a one-to-one conversational setting. This factor may impinge on the number of communication opportunities that are made available to a given device user. It also implies that special use strategies may be needed to initiate new conversations and conversational partners. Machine to vocal communication may be less of a deterrent to children than adults, since children in general appear more adaptable to technology in the environment, for example, video games, electronic toys, robots, computer use in educational settings, and so on.

Communication is not only effected through linguistic symbols and their combinations. Meaning and intent are also conveyed through nonlinguistic means, such as paralinguistic features of vocal speech, and nonverbal behaviors. Recent research in the area of pragmatics has made us acutely aware of the contributions of these nonlinguistic modes and how they are used to convey a variety of communicative functions (Higginbotham and Yoder, 1982; Bedrosian, 1981). We use nonverbal features continuously, both as speakers and listeners, to convey meaning, to regulate conversation, to express attitudes and levels of intimacy, for exam-

ple. In intervention with the nonspeaking population, these communication modes and features need to be examined and addressed. A particular nonspeaker may have none of the conventional forms of nonlinguistic features available to him. Others may use distorted features and therefore convey a miscommunication; all may need to develop special means of conveying these intents, given their abilities and the unique augmentative system available to them.

In oral communication, we frequently use the paralinguistic features of stress, pause, intonation, or vocal quality changes to convey specific intents or to read intents of other speakers. Take the utterance "He did the laundry" as an example. Said in a regular fashion, it might simply represent a giving of information. By altering stress (for example, *He* did the laundry; or He *did* the laundry; or He did the *laundry*), the speaker can comment on either the unusualness of the situation or the speaker's feelings about "he" or the laundry. Use of an extended pause between He and the word did, or a slowly produced sentence might imply a reluctance to tell the listener an untruth, and so on. The same utterance said with rising intonation or a playful pitch pattern might convey humor, a victory, or that that was all he did. Oral speakers use these paralinguistic features with great frequency. these paralinguistic features with great frequency.

Use of paralinguistic features is often beyond the vocal capabilities of device users. Although some intents can be projected through increased loudness or some intonational contouring, more subtle implications have to be coded in a different manner. This might be done with underlining in written text, capitalizing, punctuating, prefacing a comment with the word joke, or by being explicit in the linguistic aspect, for example, "I finally got him to do the laundry!" Less complicated means may have to be provided for the beginning language learner. From the work of Dore (1975) and others, we know that young children can convey different acts at the single word level through the use of intonation.    For    example,    the    word "mama" can be used as a call, a label, or a request, depending on the paralinguistic features that accompany the utterance. This developmental use of prosody to indicate function is not available to the nonspeaker. It has been suggested that these functions might be expressed by noting a specific symbol and preceding or accompanying it with a gesture or eye gaze, such as raising of the eyebrows to convey a question (Blau, in press). It must be pointed out, however, that these codings of function may not be understood, except by those caregivers in the immediate environment.

Birdwhistell (1970) suggests that language in its natural occurrence as speech is never disembodied but is always manifested through multiple behaviors (synchronous). For example, what does the lowering of the voice "while" the eyes widen, "while" the brows raise, "while" an arm and finger move, "while" the head lowers, "while" a leg and foot shift, "while" the face flushes, have to do with what was said or left unsaid? How is this modified by the equally complex configurations of change that immediately precede and follow a statement? And how are all of the above changes in turn related to the similarly involved behavior of the other person or persons in the interaction?

We are often very clear about what a person said and meant but cannot tell precisely how he accomplished it or how we are able to accomplish our understanding of it.

What has all this to do with the person who uses an augmentative output? The interactional synchrony, as found in the normal speaker-listener dyad, is disrupted and perceptual difficulties are postulated. If this is so, and if it has been demonstrated that synchrony is important to a fully integrated behavior of communication, then we may be expecting a behavior that our severely neurologically impaired nonspeaking friends can never attain. While that may be a postulate still to be demonstrated relative to speech, what of nonspeech/augmented systems? If the visual stimulus is continuous, as is the case with manual signs and gestures,

rather than static, as it is with pictures, symbolics, and/or traditional orthography, is there a difference? Can visual stimuli bring about an interactional synchrony from the expressor of the message to receiver of that message visually as it does auditorally, accompanied by the abundant occurrences of related behaviors? These are questions we need to ask, and we are still far from the answers. Are these questions worthy of pursuing? We think so.

What level of message usage or communication level are we going to leave with our nonspeaking friends? We must get away from the parochial approach, which is sometimes a shackle, of the solely linguistic/verbal behavior view and include the nonverbal tenets of communication with our severely speech impaired friends. As we have not been bound exclusively to the linguistic verbal rules for learning and using communication systems, let us not stay exclusively with the verbal linguistic system for assessing and teaching communication systems to the severely speech impaired.

Conversation and dialogue are not just passing sentences back and forth. For example, the distance at which we seat ourselves from someone gives clues about what we have to exchange with each other. Seating ourselves in front or beside the person in the wheelchair gives a much different notion relative to the conversation that might take place than if we stand in front of the person who is seated. In the first place, it is difficult at best for a seated person to have eye contact with the standing person, especially if head control is a problem. Eye contact is much easier if we are on a similar physical plane. It is also easier for us to "read" each other's body movements when we are seated close to one another, as compared with one standing in front of the other.

Positioning ourselves in such a way as to observe facial expression is as important to the augmentative system user as it is to the speaking person. Information we exchange by means of the face, eyes, and body movement are very important for all of us in the maintenance of an interaction as well as the initiation and termination of one. For many motor disturbed persons, using kinesic behaviors for communicative exchange is difficult; however, because of its importance to communication we must explore ways of assisting the augmentative system user to employ nonverbal behaviors in their broadest and most efficient way (Higginbotham and Yoder, 1982).

## DEVELOPMENTAL CONSTRAINTS

Nonvocal persons, particularly those with developmental disabilities, often bring to augmentative system use well-established patterns of nonsystem communication, dependency, and limited physical and cognitive experiences. These patterns have a profound effect on what will be possible and what will occur when an augmentative system is implemented.

It must be recognized, in discussing intervention, that augmentative systems are introduced at widely varied ages, particularly with the nonspeaker who is developmentally disabled. Oral speech efforts and resistance to implementation of these augmentative systems often create a situation in which a system is first being introduced at the age of 8, or 14, or even 40. Obviously, the length of time a person is without a communication system affects their ability to utilize what is offered and the way training must be approached. Ideally, those children who have the best chance for normal development and who have the prerequisites for language would be given the opportunity to communicate via such systems at an early age, that is 18 to 24 months (Chapman and Miller, 1980; Shane and Bashir, 1980; Carlson, 1982).

Regardless of the age at which an augmentative system is introduced, it is important to be aware of the differences that occur because of nonspeech and the lack of physical ability prior to the introduction of such a system. Take the child who is physically disabled and nonspeaking since birth. Severe physical impairment can have a marked effect on cognitive development (Fieber, 1977; Morris, 1981; Harris and Vanderheiden, 1980).

These children often do not have enough controlled movement to really explore and interact with their environment, as physically able children do. Reflexes may interfere in the child's ability to see what is going on in his environment. Attempts to explore and grasp objects may be affected by an asymmetric tonic neck reflex (ATNR) pattern; in other instances, poor head and body control force the child to remain in a prone or supine position that does not give them the opportunity to observe what is going on in the environment. Reflex patterns may interfere with the child's attempts to react to events and persons in his environment. Something as simple as smiling or vocalizing, or looking at, or reaching out to may be beyond his capabilities. Mobility restrictions keep him from exploring things in the environment. These children cannot pull cans out of a closet; put keys into their mouth; touch the grass. They often cannot partake in reciprocal or imitative play, either in making sounds or imitating physical movements. In essence, life centers around restricted spaces and experiences. It is a tremendous effort even to take such a child to the supermarket. In general, nonspeakers have little opportunity to control, manipulate, regulate, or affect their environments. Life centers around physical care and routines.

It is also suggested that there may be a significant difference in the caregiver relationship because of nonspeech and/or physical disability (Calculator, 1980; Yoder and Calculator, 1981; Rees, 1982). These children are not able to do things that stimulate caregivers to give them continued interactive attention. Reflexes, involuntary facial grimaces, lack of controlled and readable responses all contribute to decreased social interaction. Yarrow and colleagues (1975) suggest that early cognitive and communication development can be significantly related to the level of social stimulation, intensity of expression of positive effect, active kinesthetic stimulation, and variety in the inanimate environment. This suggests that we must be attentive to issues from the first few months of life with the severely handicapped child, to assist in providing experiences that facilitate cognitive and communicative behavior.

In cases in which motor behaviors interfere with routine care, we find that caregivers may react negatively to the child. For example, feeding, bathing, dressing, and playing with the infant and young child are usually warm and rewarding for both the child and the caregiver. However, frustration and tension may replace these feelings when the caregiver is uncomfortable in dealing with the physically handicapped, nonspeaking child's erratic, involuntary, and spastic movements. Consequently, children may spend considerable time in physical environments that change infrequently, and in social environments that do not provide much touching, holding, hugging, or other physical contact.

These differences in experiences are of concern in approaching intervention with nonspeakers. There have not been enough studies to define the specific consequences and causal effects of some of these differences. It appears, however, that these children do come to the communication situation with a different base from which to develop. They come with limited experiences. Cognitive and language development are often backward. They have reduced opportunities and therefore poor development of interactive and communicative behaviors. Patterns of passivity may have been established in the environment. Needs are anticipated; there is little opportunity or ability to control events and others; the history of failure at interacting and attempting to communicate may be pervasive. There may be reduced stimulation and interaction from caregivers. They, too, have developed established patterns of relating to the nonspeaker by this time. The learned helplessness that is in evidence early on with the nonspeaking person is manifested by few or no initiations of requests and other early communicative intents.

It is into these interactive patterns and experiences that we introduce augmentative communication systems and expect the user to interact, initiate, and con-

trol his world through this new means of communication. Intervention with this population requires an understanding of the huge jumps we are asking both the augmentative aid user and caregivers or other interactants (such as teachers) to make. Most likely the nonspeaking communicator has been placed in a passive role for several months or years before intervention occurs. These individuals have learned ways of interacting and communication that reflect their abilities and situation. This usually consists of answering mostly yes/no questions, having their needs predicted and met, having others guess and expand on their gestural attempts, and so on. They have generally been in a respondent role, with the communication and experience burden placed on the other person. This may have been a pattern for 5 years, 14 years, or 30 years. We are then introducing an augmentative system, whether it be signing or an aided device, and expecting the nonspeaker to use this nonspeech system in a communicative manner very different from his learned and expected means of communication.

We must remember that these individuals have had very little of the exploration and interaction experience necessary to be active communicators. They are being asked to shift from a passive, respondent role to one of an initiator of conversations and topics. They are being asked to communicate functions that were not in their repertoire before; they may only have a basis for answering questions and making requests. They have to learn what to talk about, given these new options, and how to say it in this new medium. They have to recognize when to use their old modes of communication (for example, looking, fussing, gestures) and when to integrate and use the new one, and which one with whom, when. This is a sizeable and possibly an overwhelming task.

In addition, we are asking them to use this new and unusual system within environments that are not used to these systems and devices or means of communication. Thus vocal interactants often continue to use their old, overlearned patterns of talking to the nonspeaker and do not shift their expectations or style (Kraat, 1981; Calculator and Dollaghan, 1982; Harris, 1982). We are also asking the augmentative communicators to become active communicators with these new systems with few, if any, models available to them. The communication models they are familiar with, and that surround them, are vocal speakers, not nonspeech system users. Intervention with the nonspeaker must include recognition of these differences brought to the communication situation and incorporate these special behaviors and needs into a treatment intervention plan.

Adults with acquired nonspeech conditions do not bring a history of social, motor, and communication deprivation with them to the augmentative communication situation. They do, however, bring other factors to this new communication situation which need consideration in intervention. In particular, adults bring with them considerable knowledge about language and communicative competencies that are based on vocal speech models. These nonspeaking adults often try to translate the styles and devices used in vocal discourse into augmentative aid use. Because of the particular constraints and features found within these augmentative systems, such as rate, this mapping is ineffective. The same rules and strategies do not apply to this different way of communicating. Lengthy utterances to manipulate another person's behavior may no longer be viable; new conversational devices are needed to initiate conversation and hold one's place in discourse; intents previously conveyed by paralinguistic features of speech need to be actualized differently, and so on. Persons who have recently lost the ability to speak also bring with them the psychologic devastation of a tremendous loss in their lives. This is often confounded by newly acquired physical disabilities as well. One must be aware of the impact of these losses on the nonspeaker's acceptance and use of augmentative techniques.

The lack of mobility in many nonspeakers, both developmental and acquired, seriously affects the communication that occurs or does not occur. Mobility not only affects the experiences that one has or doesn't have, it also bears a relationship to whether or not one has experiences to talk about. Without mobility, interactants must often come to the nonspeaker in order for communication to occur. Speech output devices assist some in this respect, but without user mobility, they are also restricted in range. Situations and people the nonspeaker may want to converse about, or participate with, may be out of physical range.

## INTERACTION DIFFERENCES

Communication between vocal speakers and augmentative communication system users has many unique features, and it is not necessarily parallel to speech-to-speech communication interaction. While there are similarities between speech and nonspeech communication, there are many features of augmentative communication use which create special problems and needs, and the nonspeaker brings system constraints to any communication exchange. Some of these differences are outlined in Figure 3–1. These differences need to be understood in approaching intervention, since it is within this context and these limitations that the nonspeaking person attempts to learn to communicate.

It is interesting to note that some of our most successful augmentative system users alter, or break, conventional rules of form and discourse to circumvent these constraints. For example, they may use highly effective efficiency strategies in certain exchanges; they may use a high percentage of nonverbal elements to replace traditional linguistic forms; they maintain conversational place with a variety of devices, such as continuing communication use during interruptions; they have a unique way of coding a politeness marker, and so on. It is obvious that we need a

FIGURE 3–1   SPECIAL CONSIDERATIONS IN
AUGMENTATIVE COMMUNICATION USE

| Consideration | Effect |
|---|---|
| Limitations Imposed by the Augmentative Systems<br>Rate of Communication Exchange<br>Limited Vocabulary Sets<br>Unique Output Forms<br>Approachability | Rules of discourse and use are modified<br>Speaking persons dominate the communication exchange and often control the interaction<br>Augmentative communicator has less opportunity to interact and communicate<br>Speaking persons use many questions requiring yes/no response, one word response, or no response<br>System imposes limits on what can be communicated, where, and how<br>Increases demands on the listener<br>Reduced number of persons who can communicate with user<br>High percentage of miscommunications are probable<br>Need to develop use competencies not modeled in speech<br>Listener may not be able to receive nonverbal and linguistic information at the same time<br>Multi-modes of communication are necessarily used more frequently |
| Limitations Imposed by Physical Disability | Nonverbal aspects of communication are often limited, misinterpreted, or not understood<br>Limited experiences to talk about<br>Limited environment and number of interactants<br>Lack of developmental experiences in exploring environment<br>Interactants must frequently initiate contact with nonspeaker<br>Early caregiver/child interactions are different<br>Patterns of environmentally induced passivity and dependence may develop<br>Poor development of general interactive patterns |
| Limitations Imposed by Attitudes and Expectancies of Speaking Interactors | Fewer communication opportunities<br>Level of communication is frequently below the linguistic knowledge of the nonspeaker |
| Limitations Imposed by Lack of Intelligible Speech (Developmentally) | Reduced social development<br>Less communication interaction and usually a lower level of communication<br>History of communication failure<br>Established patterns of communication (for example, nonspeaker in a respondent role; caregivers predicting communication intents)<br>Reduced opportunity to explore language use, ask questions, get feedback regarding language form, content, and rule use |
| Limitations Imposed by Reduced or Lack of Communication Models in the Environment | With aided systems users, many oral language rules may be ineffective, or can not be used<br>Augmentative user has little modeling for how to effectively use aided systems<br>Speaking persons may react to communications via augmented systems as if they were "spoken". |

greater understanding of the particular strategies that can be used to convey effectively an intention, repair communication breakdowns, allow the user more communication and entry into conversation; that can assist them in gaining control in an exchange dominated by the more rapid, flexible speaker. Intervention must not only incorporate an understanding of the differences and constraints in communication with these systems, but must also specify user strategies to maximize the potentials and circumvent the difficulties.

At present, we have very little understanding of the effects of developmental nonspeech conditions on language development in general. We also have little information available regarding augmentative system use and language development in this population, outside of some preliminary studies by Montgomery and Hall (1980). Our intervention has been too recent, and the question is a very complex one. One might assume that, since many of these individuals with relatively normal cognition are observers and hearers of communication in the vocal world, they would develop adult language competency. There are many instances of adults with congenital cerebral palsy conditions in which augmentative spelling capabilities seem to provide them with the ability to participate competently, if not eloquently, in communication (Creech, 1982; Williams 1981).

However, an increasing number of language problems has been observed in nonspeaking individuals, some more obvious than others. We see limited understanding of vocabulary that they have not had experience with, problems in using syntax, difficulty in understanding idioms and subtle intents. Other observations include higher level language comprehension problems; difficulties in learning to read beyond a certain level; obvious problems in learning to spell, given systems with which to do it on and training. It may be that lack of productive experiences with language or experience with limited systems like those with restricted vocabulary sets or nonsyntactic strategies may in fact produce gaps in language develop-

ment and an understanding of language use. This does not mean to imply that these language limitations are not amenable to intervention. This experience and intervention may not have been provided or modeled. The issue is merely raised here in a question and reflects our concern that language, as well as communication intervention, be addressed with the nonspeaker. It is often the case, particularly with individuals who appear to exhibit intact comprehension and severe neuromuscular or apractic speech problems, that intervention solely addresses an effective, productive medium for communication.

Learning language form, content, and use is a formidable task for the physically able, speaking child. For the physically disabled nonspeaker, this task must be overwhelming. To complicate the issue further, we usually give these individuals systems with a limited vocabulary. What they know, learn, and can experiment with is restricted to the confines of these systems. Because of this, an augmentative system user may be forced by the situation to communicate an idea through very different and restricted content. For example, a child may want to ask that a parent buy a balloon. Given that there is no balloon in the immediate environment to refer to by looking at it, the child must try to use some available symbol content to express this idea. In this case, the aided speaker may have the symbol for "McDonald's" on his language display. The user must try to reference the content (balloon) through the symbol for "McDonald's," as there is shared knowledge with the listener that balloons were given away one day when they were together at McDonald's. Using "McDonald's" to express "balloon" certainly is not a competency required of normal speakers. This is used as an illustration here to make the reader aware of the different competencies that must be developed and are needed by the augmentative user. This is a complicated skill, and we know very little about how to teach it or what the prerequisites to learning it are.

Intervention with the augmentative communicator obviously involves some very special needs and concerns. Developing an understanding of language and communicative competency for spoken communication is but one of these. Superimposed on top of these requirements is a need to learn special kinds of ways to combine the inherent potentials of these systems with available content and form, and transpose these into effective communicative use.

## INTERVENTION STRATEGIES

Our discussion to this point has centered on major issues to be considered in establishing successful augmentative communication use with the severely speech impaired person. While the issues we are presenting in this section are no less crucial, we do want to call special attention to them.

### *VOCABULARY SELECTION*

Restricted vocabulary sets provided to nonspellers are critical in this population. The language available in a linguistic form provides the underpinning for communication and can make the difference between a successful communicator and a noncommunicator. Given a limited set, what symbols or signs should be provided, when, to code what functions? Although training can involve the use of any vocabulary item and form, 24-hour use of a system (particularly device use) may be more restricted to a core group of symbols. Some guidelines for initial system vocabulary selection have been provided by Fristoe and Lloyd (1980), Carlson (1981), Blau (in press), Musselwhite and St. Louis (1982), and Reichle, Williams and Ryan (1981). However, we have much study ahead of us before we can fully understand how to approach this restriction in the most effective manner for a wide variety of communicators and language abilities. What about the child whose comprehension of language far exceeds a 200-symbol

vocabulary? How can we most powerfully use this restricted repertoire, or make accessible multiple sets of vocabulary?

In the past we have often concentrated on increasing the number of symbols or vocabulary items in augmentative users, and have paid too little attention to the functions that the user can code with these items, or to how the nonspeaker is attempting to communicate using these items. It may be that the system user has been provided with vocabulary items that can easily be referenced in another manner or that have little salience and overall communicative value. One need but compare words such as "sock, bed, potty" to symbols representing "Yuk!, What?, No way" to see the differences in the types of communicative exchanges that are possible and probable. The former may lend themselves to labeling or answering questions. The latter, however, provide for different functions and levels of interactive communication. As the professional team is, in fact, making decisions about what will be available, and how it will be used and taught, much care and planning must be given to these decisions.

### *TEACHING FORM*

In intervention with augmentative systems, we must also re-examine the purposes and places of grammatic forms and perfect syntax. It is not that grammatic form does not have to be learned. What concerns us is the frequent preoccupation with form, rather than interaction and communication. Intervention goals following a normal language model may be concentrating on message creations like "Yesterday I went to see a movie," and "Saturday I went to see the Mets" when, in fact, the system user is not communicating at all effectively in his environment. It is a matter of emphasis on form over communication. Such an emphasis frequently leaves a nonspeaker, who already feels like a communication failure, with the notion that he must produce syntactically correct utterances in order to communicate. Communication can often be accomplished just as effectively and in a shorter time period by the effective use of multi-modes of communication or a reduced use of form. For example, "movie—yesterday."

## COMMUNICATION SYNCHRONY

Applying a communication orientation allows us to look beyond formal signs or symbol sets on a communication board, or the printed output of an electronic communication device. Communication also encompasses the nonverbal components of facial expression, body postures and tonus, natural pointing and eye gaze, movement away and toward people, and so on. Augmentative communicators who are the most effective communicators use all of these modes. The particular mode used at any given point depends on the message receiver, time factors, the availability of linguistic forms, and shared information. Augmentative communicators must select the most effective and efficient way of communicating at any given time. The following two examples illustrate the point:

V: "Halloween. What are you going to be?"
A: B. Man (Bliss/board user)
V: "Yeah, I could have guessed . . . Hey, you know they took Batman off the air?"
A: (Vocalizes, bangs fist, points in the direction of the bulletin board)
V: (Reads letter on the board from Joey and a friend protesting Batman going off the air.) "That's beautiful, Joe!"
(Kates, McNaughton, and Silvermann, 1977)

V: "What do you want?"
A. (Points to the ball)
V: "No, tell me with your board"
A: (Points to ball again)
V: "How can you tell me with your board?"
A: (Puts head down on laptray. No response)
(Harris, 1978)

The first example reflects a communication model and a nice blending of aided/unaided systems, as well as resourceful use of material in the shared environment. The second is indicative of viewing communication through linguistic parameters only.

Mixing of speech, aided systems, and gestural systems often affords the user the greatest amount of communication possible. A sign for "new house" accompanied by a distasteful facial grimace certainly relays a dislike. Pointing to a symbol for "Mommy" and shrugging the shoulders assists in communicating a question about Mommy, or that the person does not know where Mommy is. When a full linguistic code is not available and there are great efforts involved in indicating a message word by word, or letter by letter, these options need to be utilized.

## LITERACY SKILLS

As one of the most restrictive features in augmentative communication is the reduced available vocabulary, the importance of the acquisition of spelling or phoneme systems is increased. With this ability, or even a reduced spelling ability, greater communication potentials open up. Ideally, literacy in reading and spelling would be acquired as early as possible. (Obviously, spelling and reading are difficult for the speaking child.) A limited number of sight words can often be memorized and recognized, or even spelled. Fluency for the nonspeaker, however, is another matter. The orthographic rules in English are frequently inconsistent. Words are not necessarily spelled like other words that sound similar, nor are words that are spelled in a similar fashion pronounced alike. Take the words cough, bough, tough, through, though, and compare the pronunciation of "ough." Or, the words health and heal; the former is not pronounced "heelth."

The acquisition of reading and spelling skills by many developmentally nonspeaking persons is difficult. The reasons for this are not entirely clear. One would suspect that these difficulties are due to the person's inability to speak, in that reading and spelling require a degree of competency in the morpho-phonologic rule system between speech and print.

However, in reality, many anarthric individuals have gained reading and spelling abilities that represent adult competencies. The question that remains is *who* is having difficulty in acquiring these skills, and *how* best might we teach these much-needed abilities to the nonspeaker? Further research and study are needed in this area.

## CONVERSATIONAL STRATEGIES

Training must reflect unique and different ways of communicating, that effectively use augmentative communication media. We are only beginning to understand what these specific strategies might be. The need for efficiency certainly creates a need for both the listener and the augmentative speaker to develop special techniques for increasing the communication interchange. Special discourse strategies are needed in order that communicators might initiate conversations more easily, and maintain and extend those conversations. Special wording is needed to achieve certain communication acts and to reduce ambiguity.

Communication breakdown and miscommunications will occur more often in augmented communication. Since these speakers will find themselves on the giving and receiving end of a breakdown more frequently than other persons, special attention must be given to this area. Not only must the factors that create this breakdown be identified, but possible strategies within the capabilities of the user must be created to repair these miscommunications. (It is often observed that these persons let a communication breakdown go by because they do not know how to repair the situation in an unconventional way or because it takes too long to repair the breakdown.)

It is interesting to delineate some of the areas that have contributed to these breakdowns in communication samples. Frequently listeners will attempt to expand an utterance to save time in the exchange. They do not, however, verify with the augmentative user that that was, in fact, what was intended, and a miscommunication often occurs. Users may give a listener a miscue through some of their distorted postures or lack of facial expression. These nonverbal feedback systems may contribute to the wrong intent being placed on top of a written message, or serve as the basis for a misrepresentation in attempting to expand the user's utterance. Miscommunications are most frequently caused by limitations in what the augmentative user can code and say effectively.

Additional sources of difficulty are seen when individuals use a device or sign that is appropriate for familiar persons with people who are less familiar with it. In such situations, they need to recognize how these use strategies are inappropriate for particular contexts and listeners, and learn how to clarify these messages. Code switching is a critical skill that must be developed in an intervention program.

## INCREASING INTERACTANTS

Observations suggest that augmentative system users have a reduced number of interactants. Communication generally occurs less often with peers, younger children, and persons less familiar to the nonspeaker. We need to look more closely at why this is happening, and how we might assist the user to expand his communication opportunities. Sometimes the system itself makes this communication difficult, for example, with very restricted vocabulary sets, unfamiliar sign use, and so on. At other times, however, the lack of communication is related to the user's strategies or lack of strategies in these relatively new situations. For example, they may wait for the vocal person to take the initiative rather than explain their system to the vocal person and begin a conversation. At other times, users are attempting to approach the situation in manners that have served them in a family situation but which are not appropriate for other listeners and contexts. We observed an illustration of this in a nonspeaking ambulatory 20-year-old. He was very used to physically touching persons to let them know that he wanted to initiate a conversation, and he frequently used idiosyncratic gestures even though he had the ability to use an alphabet board. In approaching an unfamiliar listener, he used the same strategies that he used in familiar situations. This included tugging on a person's arm for attention and using nonunderstandable signs and vocalizations. The listener's first reaction was that of being attacked by a mad person. These actions on the part of the nonspeaker certainly didn't lend themselves to communication exchange in new situations.

## INCREASING EXPERIENCES

As communication development is viewed as inextricably intertwined with social and cognitive development, there is a need to provide the physically disabled person, in particular, with enriched experiences. Nonspeakers may not have experienced a multitude of events, objects, and consequences. They may never have been in the kitchen when a meal was being prepared; they may not have seen an umbrella used; they may never have, at the age of 8, experienced what grass feels like, or shaving cream. They may have also never been punished, reprimanded, or experienced refusal. It is unlikely that a physically disabled person has experienced "in" as a phenomenon, or what it feels like to move about in the air (as in being swung). Because of the nature of their deficits, additional attention must be given to the experiences that underlie language expression and understanding. This often requires a concerted effort by an interdisciplinary team and people in the environment.

Piaget (1964) postulated that throughout the sensorimotor period (0–21 months) motoric interaction and object manipulation are important for the development of symbolic representation and related cognitive skills that are prerequisites to the development and use of language. The exact nature of the relationships between these behaviors and the development of language is still under question; however, it is generally accepted that these experiences contribute to the development of communication readiness.

Intervention considerations with this population might include prespeech or preverbal intervention in an effort to facilitate the development of the underpinning of communication. Some of the procedures suggested for use with the physically disabled are outlined by Carlson (1982) and Wethered (1982).

## A RE-EXAMINATION OF INTERVENTION

How we view the teaching/intervention process of persons using augmentative communication systems is crucial to the user's success. In the past, intervention with the nonspeaker has often attempted to parallel the types of language intervention used with other communicatively impaired individuals. Given this reference point, training has often been focused around development of alternate symbol referents, which then are incorporated into the same linguistic communication used by others who are vocal speakers. It is becoming increasingly clear that we need to re-examine and re-evaluate this model in intervening with nonspeakers.

That is not to say that this model does not apply to the nonspeaker; much of it does. However, the model and the assumptions regarding that the nonspeaker needs to become an effective communicator present difficulties when embraced in their entirety without modifications. Augmentative communication systems present very real differences and contraints for the user. Several have been mentioned here. Others have been suggested by Bottorf and DePape (1982), Harris (1978, 1982), Fristoe and Lloyd (1980) and Musselwhite and St. Louis (1982).

In turn, these systems seem to generate very different types of utterances from speaking counterparts in conversational exchanges. These constraints and differences call into question the use of normal language models as the framework for intervention. What is effective in one communication medium may not, in fact, be effective in another. Our goal is to facilitate the most effective communication interactions possible for the nonspeaker. Therefore, it seems necessary and timely to define the apparent differences that are needed in our intervention to achieve effective augmentative system use. The following assumptions can be drawn from our studies and observations:

1. To be successful with augmentative systems, a user frequently needs to break down conventional linguistic rule usage.

2. Effective use of these systems requires the acquisition of a special set of communicative competencies in addition to those of the general community.

3. Training of vocal speakers in the environment (both in terms of how to interact with the augmentative user and in learning a set of special conversational strategies) is of equal importance.

4. Training of the severely speech impaired cannot focus exclusively on the verbal linguistic system. A broad communication orientation must be applied and the augmentative user must learn how to use paralinguistic behaviors whenever possible.

5. Special attention must be given to the cognitive and communication experiences provided for the person at risk for developing speech from birth.

6. Constraints within augmentative systems themselves affect the ultimate communication that is probable and possible. These various systems need to be examined individually to determine how to maximize communication potentials within each at various levels of implementation.

It is very probable that the poor use of augmentative systems and the reduced levels of communication that we are seeing with these systems are directly connected to our current intervention goals and procedures. We need to redefine these, based on our recognition of what is uniquely different about nonspeech com-

munication and what makes one speaker more effective than another. Concurrently, we also need to begin to define what "competency" and "effective use" might mean when applied to augmentative communication use. At present, we have only been alerted to the fact that these definitions are different for this population of communicators.

There is a wide variation in the communication needs and abilities of individuals who can use augmentative systems. For some, particularly those who are physically handicapped, it can be the difference between participating in the activities around them, or simply watching others act. For many multiply handicapped persons, an effective communication system will have a major impact on the personal, social, and educational process, as well as on future vocational considerations. For others, an appropriate communication system will permit them to communicate their needs systematically, and to express emotions in a manner understandable to others.

## REFERENCES

Bedrosian J: A sociolinguistic approach to communication skills: Assessment and treatment methodology for mentally retarded adults. Unpublished doctoral dissertation, University of Wisconsin-Madison, 1981

Bellugi U, Fischer S: A comparison of sign language and spoken language: Rate and grammatical mechanisms. Cognition 1:173–200, 1972

Beukelman D R, Yorkston K: A communication system for the severely dysarthric speaker with an intact language system. J Speech Hear Dis 42:265–270, 1977

Beukelman D, Yorkston K: Non-vocal communication—performance evaluation. Arch Phys Med Rehab 61:272–275, 1980

Beukelman D R, Yorkston K M: Communication interaction of adult communication augmentation system use. Topics Lang Dis 2:39–53, 1982

Birdwhistell R L: Kinesics and Context. Philadelphia: University of Pennsylvania Press, 1970

Blau A F: Vocabulary selection in augmentative communication: Where do we begin. In Winitz H (ed): For Clinicians By Clinicians: Language Disorders. Baltimore: University Park Press, in press

Bonvillian J D, Nelson K E, Rhyne J M: Sign language and autism. J Autism Develop Dis 11:125–138, 1982

Bottorf L, DePape D: Initiating communication systems for severely speech-impaired persons. Topics Lang Dis 2:55–71, 1982

Bruner J S: From communication to language: A psychological perspective. Cognition 3, 255–287, 1975

Calculator S: Modifications in the speech of group mothers interacting with pre-linguistic residents. Unpublished manuscript, University of Wisconsin-Madison, 1980

Calculator S, Dollaghan C: The use of communication boards in a residential setting: An evaluation. J Speech Hear Dis 47:281–287, 1982

Carlson F: A format for selecting vocabulary for the nonspeaking child. Lang Speech Hear Serv Schools 12:240–245, 1981

Carlson F: *Alternate Methods of Communication.* Danville, Ill: Interstate Printers, 1982

Chapman R S, Miller J F: Analyzing language and communication in the child. In Schiefelbusch R L (ed): *Nonspeech Language Intervention.* Baltimore: University Park Press, 1980

Clark C, Woodcock R: Graphic systems of communication. In Lloyd L (ed): *Communication Assessment and Intervention Strategies.* Baltimore: University Park Press, 1976

Cohen C G, Shane H C: An overview of augmentative communication. In Lass N J, McReynolds L V, Northern J L, Yoder D E (eds): *Speech, Language, and Hearing.* Philadelphia: W B Saunders, 1982

Cook A M, Preszler A M: Matching augmentative communication device characteristics to client's goals and skills. Available from Assistive Device Center, California State University, Sacramento, CA, 95819

Creech R D: Association, assimilation and memorization. In Montgomery J (ed): *The Assisted Communicator.* Phonic Ear, Inc, 1982

Dore J: Holophrases, speech acts and language universals. J Child Lang 2:21–40, 1975

Fieber N: Sensorimotor cognitive assessment and curriculum for the multihandicapped child. Working Papers in Developmental Disabilities, Meyer Children's Rehabilitation Institute, University of Nebraska Medical Center, 1977

Foulds R A: Communication rates for nonspeech expression as a function of manual tasks and linguistic constraints. Proceedings of International Conference on Rehabilitation Engineering, Toronto, Canada, June 1980

Fristoe M, Lloyd L: Planning an initial expressive sign lexicon for persons with severe communication impairment. J Speech Hear Dis 45:170–180, 1980

Griffith P L, Robinson J H: Influence of iconicity and phonological similarity on sign learning by mentally retarded children. Am J Ment Defic 85:291–298, 1980

Griffith P L, Robinson J H, Panagos J M: Perception of iconicity in american sign language by hearing and deaf subjects. J Speech Hear Dis 46:388–397, 1981

Harris D: Descriptive analysis of communicative interaction processes involving non-vocal severely physically handicapped children. Doctoral Dissertation, University of Wisconsin-Madison, 1978

Harris D: Communication interaction processes involving nonvocal physically handicapped children. Topics Lang Dis 2:21–37, 1982

Harris D, Brown W P, McKenzie P, Riener S, Scheibel C: Symbol communication for the mentally handicapped. Ment Retard 13 (1): 1975

Harris D, Lippert J, Yoder, D, Vanderheiden G: Blissymbols: An augmentative symbol communication system for nonvocal severely handicapped children. In York R, Edgar E (eds): *Teaching the Severely Handicapped,* vol 4. Columbus, Ohio: Special Press, 1979

Harris D, Vanderheiden G: Enhancing communicative interaction skills in nonvocal severely physically handicapped children. In Schiefelbusch R L (ed): *Nonspeech Language Intervention.* Baltimore: University Park Press, 1980.

Higginbotham D J, Yoder D E: Communication within natural conversational interaction: Implications for severe communicatively impaired persons. Topics Lang Dis 2:1–19, 1982

Hymes D: Introduction. In Cazden C, John V, Hymes D (eds): *Functions of Language in the Classroom.* New York: Teachers College Press, 1972

Hymes D: On communicative competence. In Pride J B, Holmes J (eds): *Sociolinguistics.* Baltimore: Penguin Books, 1972

Kates B, McNaughton S, Silvermann H: *Handbook for Instructors, Users, Parents, and Administrators.* Toronto, Ontario: Blissymbolic Communication Foundation, 1977

Kopchick G A, Lloyd L L: Total communication for the severely language impaired: A 24 hour approach. In Lloyd L L (ed): *Communication Assessment and Intervention Strategies.* Baltimore: University Park Press, 1976

Kraat A: The assessment/selection of augmentative systems. Proceedings of Research Planning Seminar in Augmentative Communication. Gothenberg, Sweden, 1981

Kraat A: Training augmentative communication use: Clinical and research issues. Proceedings of Research Planning Seminar in Augmentative Communication. Gothenburg, Sweden, 1981

Kraat A: Augmentative communication system use in structured and naturalistic contexts–a case study. Unpublished paper, 1981

Kraat A: Approaching electronic communication devices. In press

Kraat A: Communication form and function in scanning communication device use: Case study. Unpublished paper, 1982

Lewis M, Cherry L: Social behavior and language acquisition. In Lewis M and Rosenblum L (eds): *Interaction, Conversation, and the Development of Language.* New York: John Wiley and Sons, 1977

Lewis M, Rosenblum L (eds): *The Effect of the Infant on Its Caregiver.* New York: John Wiley and Sons, 1974

Lloyd L L: Unaided non-speech communication for severely handicapped individuals: An extensive bibliography. Educ Train Ment Retard 15:15–34, 1980

Lossing C A: A technique for the quantification of non-vocal communication performance by listeners. Unpublished Master's thesis, University of Washington, 1981

Maestas y Moores J, Moores D: Language training with the young deaf child. In Bricker D (ed): *Language Development and Intervention with the Exceptional Child*. San Francisco: Jossey-Bass, 1980

Mayberry R: If a chimp can learn sign language, surely my nonverbal client can too. ASHA 18:223–228, 1976

McDonald E T, Schultz A R: Communication boards for cerebral palsied children. Speech Hear Dis 38:73–88, 1973

McLean J, Snyder-McLean L: *A Transactional Approach to Early Language Training*. Columbus, Ohio: Charles E. Merrill, 1978

McNaughton S, Kates B: The application of blissymbolics. In Schiefelbusch R L (ed): *Nonspeech Language and Communication*. Baltimore, University Park Press, 1980

Meyers L F: The use of the phonic mirror HandiVoice with children under the developmental age of three. In Montgomery J (ed): *The Assisted Communicator*. Phonic Ear, Inc, 1982

Montgomery J, Hall P: Non-Oral Communication Center—1979–80. Project evaluation report: Results of a 3-Year study; Title IV—C, ESEA, Fountain Valley School District, 1980. Available from the State Department of Education, 721 Capitol Mall, Sacramento, CA 95812.

Morningstar D: Blissymbol communication: Comparison of interaction with naive vs. experienced listeners. Unpublished manuscript, University of Toronto, 1981

Morris S E: Communication/interaction development at mealtimes for the multiply handicapped child: Implications for the use of augmentative communication systems. Lang Speech Hear Schools 12:216–232, 1981

Musselwhite C R, St. Louis K W: *Communication Programming for the Severely Handicapped: Vocal and Non-Vocal Strategies*. Houston: College-Hill Press, 1982

Ochsman R, Chapanis A: The effects of 10 communication modes on the behavior of teams during cooperative problem-solving. Int J Man-Machine Studies 6:579–619, 1974

Piaget J: *The Origins of Intelligence in Children*. New York: Norton, 1964

Rabush D, Lloyd L, Gerdes M: *Communication enhancement* bibliography. Communication Outlook, Vols 3, 4, 1982

Rees N S: Book review of Fay W H, Schuler A L: *Emerging Language in Autistic Children*. In Appl Psycholing 3:81–83, 1982

Reichle J, Williams W, Ryan S: Selecting signs for the formulation of an augmentative communication modality. J Assoc Severely Handicapped 6:48–56, 1981

Reichle J E, Yoder D E: Communicative behavior for the severely and profoundly mentally retarded: Assessment and early stimulation strategies. In York R, Edgar E(eds): *Teaching the Severely Handicapped*, vol. 4. Columbus, Ohio: Special Press, 1979

Rosen M J, Goodenough-Trepagnier C: Factors affecting communication rate in non-vocal communication systems. Proceedings of the Fourth Annual Conference on Rehabilitation Engineering, Washington, DC, 1981

Schaeffer B: Spontaneous language through signed speech. In Schiefelbusch R L (ed): *Nonspeech Language Intervention*. Baltimore: University Park Press, 1980

Schaeffer B, Musil A, Kollinzas G: *Total Communication: A Signed Speech Program for Nonverbal Children*. Champaign, Ill: Research Press, 1980

Schuler A L, Baldwin M: Nonspeech communication and childhood autism. Lang Speech Hear Serv Schools 12:246–257, 1981

Shane H C: Approaches to communication training with the severely handicapped. In York R and Edgar E (eds): *Teaching the Severely Handicapped*. Columbus, Ohio: Special Press, 1979

Shane H C (ed): Non-speech communication: A position paper, Ad Hoc Committee on Communicative Processes for Non-Speaking Persons. ASHA 22:262–272, 1980

Shane H C: Approaches to assessing people who are nonspeaking. In Schiefelbusch R (ed): *Nonspeech Language Intervention*. Baltimore: University Park Press, 1980

Shane H C: Early decision making in augmentative communication system use. In Schiefelbush R, Bricker D (eds): *Early Language: Acquisition and Intervention*. Baltimore, University Park Press, 1980

Shane, H C, Bashir A S: Election criteria for the adoption of an augmentative communication system: Preliminary considerations. J Speech Hear Dis 45:408–414, 1980

Shane H C, Cohen C G: A discussion of communicative strategies and patterns by nonspeaking persons. Lang Speech Hear Serv Schools XII (4):205–210, 1981.

Shane H, Wilbur R: Potential for expressive signing based on motor control. Sign Lang Stud 29:331–347, 1980

Skelly M: *Amer-Ind Gestural Code*. New York: Elsevier Press, 1979

Vanderheiden G C: Synthesized speech as a communication mode for non-vocal severely handicapped individuals. Paper available from Trace Research and Development Center, University of Wisconsin-Madison, 1976

Vanderheiden G C: Augmentative modes of communication for the severely, speech- and motor-impaired. Clin Orthopaed Rel Res 148:70–86, 1980

Vanderheiden G, Grilley K: *Nonvocal Communication Techniques and Aids for the Severely Handicapped*. Baltimore: University Park Press, 1975

Vanderheiden G, Grilley K (eds): *Nonvocal Communication Techniques and Aids for the Severely Physically Handicapped*. Baltimore: University Park Press, 1976

Vanderheiden G, Harris-Vanderheiden D: Communication techniques and aids for the nonvocal severely physically handicapped. In Lloyd L (ed): *Communication Assessment and Intervention Strategies*. Baltimore: University Park Press, 1976

Vicker B: *Nonoral Communication System Project 1964–1973*. Iowa City: University of Iowa, Campus Stores, 1974

Wethered C E: Teacher-made response-contingent materials. In Greer J G, Anderson, R M, Odle J

(eds): *Strategies for Helping Severely and Multiply Handicapped Citizens*. Baltimore: University Park Press, 1982

Williams M B: What Emily Post never told me. Communic Outlook 3:, 1981

Yarrow L, Klein R, Lomonaco S, Morgan G: Cognitive and motivational development in early childhood. In Friedlander B, Sterrit G, Kirk G (eds): *Exceptional Infant*, vol 3. New York: Brunner-Mazel, 1975

Yoder D E: Communication systems for nonspeech children. *New Directions Excep Child* 2:, 1980

Yoder D E, Calculator S: Some perspectives on intervention strategies for persons with developmental disorders. J Autism Develop Dis 11 (1):, 1981

# DISCUSSION: PART I: WHAT IS LANGUAGE INTERVENTION? THE ROLE OF THEORY

*JUDITH R. JOHNSTON*

The topic before us is, What is language intervention? Chapters 1 through 3 provided stimulating answers to that question. What I found equally interesting, however, was the fact that they tried to answer the question at all. I want to focus my remarks on that point. In the process I will disagree a bit with Schiefelbusch, expand on Holland's comments, and reflect on the nature of our task together.

Let me begin with an inductive exercise. Imagine that you are participating in a concept discovery experiment in which you are to observe an event and decide whether or not it belongs to a selected class. You will be told only whether your judgments are correct; it will be up to you to infer the defining characteristics. Your friendly experimenter provides you with three initial positive instances to help establish the set:

1. A child and an adult are sitting at a small table. The child looks at two juxtaposed pictures portraying a person eating and a piece of candy. The adult says "eat candy." The child repeats the phrase. The adult says "good" and hands the child a plastic chip (Zwitman and Sonderman, 1979).

2. Two adults are conversing in a living room. One is a toy demonstrator (TD),

the other a mother. The TD gives the mother a new toy for her child to play with, explains how it may be used, then leaves (Levenstein, in press).

3. A young child is seated on the floor playing with an adult. The child drops a toy bus into a mailbox. The adult says "bus gone." The child pulls a lever and the bus reappears (Jeffree and colleagues, 1973).

Having provided this useful preliminary information, the experimenter then presents the first test item:

4. A parent sits alone in the kitchen reading a workbook that explains how to speak simply and talk about the same thing one's child is talking about (Hayes and Healy, 1979).

Do this event and the preceding ones belong to a single class? In fact, each of these scenarios represents a member of that set of events called *language intervention with children*, and is drawn directly from the current intervention literature. As I read this literature I am most impressed by its diversity: The direct recipient of the professional's efforts, the activity of the participants, the material context, and the immediate object of learning vary in almost every conceivable direction. The language used to talk about intervention events varies equally: *teach, reinforce, facilitate, motivate, illustrate,* and so on. The one thread that unifies these events is that they all were intended by some professional to promote language learning and use.

It is a perverse experimenter indeed who defines a set of observable events according to the intentions of one participant. What information could we add to our intervention scenarios that would reveal further similarities? Discussions of intervention programming frequently urge the professional to pay special attention to efficacy (for example, Connell and associates, 1977). Although we find great diversity among events *called* language intervention, there may be similarities among those events that actually *do* promote language learning and use. If the experimenter provided outcome data, such as "following a series of such events, the child used more N+V utterances than a matched control," and redefined the set so that it included only such effective events, would our inductive task be easier? Unfortunately, no. Each of these intervention scenarios is taken from an experimental study in which there was a significant treatment effect.

In a different context of argument, this fact is encouraging. Like Holland, I am relieved to find that language intervention is possible. It is indeed the mark of growing professional maturity that we have looked carefully and documented the results of our therapeutic efforts in ways that are replicable, objective, and convincing. But the fact that all of these treatment programs proved effective scarcely solves our definitional problem. Even if we pay attention only to those events that have been "proven effective," we meet diversity.

Perhaps we could improve our lot as experimental subjects if we could use comparative data. Common attributes may exist among those intervention events that *work best*. At this point, however, our experimenter balks. It turns out that there are few studies comparing the relative efficacy of two or more intervention methods (Leonard, 1981). More importantly, we need to define *best*. Is *fast* better? Is *functional* better? Is *cheap* better? These are not questions that can be answered by appeal to the "facts" of language intervention, even if they existed. These questions point to the underlying assumptions that guide investigations of relative efficacy . . . and the word *assumption* immediately challenges our *definitional* game.

At the very least, it is clear that any attempt to define language intervention must consider not only the intervention events, but the assumptions that shape those events. Holland has characterized the assumptions that determine various treatments of adult language disorders and the same could be done for the scenarios I have presented. If we admit these assumptions as data in our concept discovery task, however, we will continue to meet diversity.

The fundamental problem with the concept discovery metaphor is that there is no prevailing similarity among the various approaches to language intervention. To assume that there is, or should be, is wrong-headed. There is no single answer to the question What is language intervention? not because authorities disagree, not because we lack the necessary facts, not because there are many equally good therapy strategies, but exactly because theoretic frameworks differ (Perry, 1968). The question What is language intervention? can only be answered from within a theoretic model that addresses the nature of language, the nature of change, the nature of language disorders, and, by extension, the role of the interventionist. There will be as many definitions of language intervention as there are views on these points.

Part of my own definition of language intervention, for example, derives from the following assumptions: (1) that the human mind inherently seeks organizing principles, (2) that language behavior is generated from the knowledge of abstract rules, (3) that language rules are constructed by the knower based on an active analysis of linguistic events, (4) that new language behaviors reflect qualitative, self-regulated changes in the nature of abstract rules, and (5) that owing to imparments of attention, memory, and auditory perception, some children are ill equipped to discover linguistic rules. For such children, the interventionist serves as a facilitator whose activities present a body of linguistic data that is abnormally easy to analyze. To achieve this accessibility, he or she manipulates variables, such as the juxtaposition and proportional frequency of exemplars, the perceptual salience of key linguistic elements, the clarity of meaning-in-context, and the match between the focused-rule and the cognitive or linguistic resources of the child. Not wanting to do anyone else the injustice of a three sentence analysis, I will illustrate no further. I trust it is clear that each of my assumptions is disputable and that each has specific implications for my characterization of intervention practice.

To summarize thus far, any survey of language intervention programs reveals remarkable diversity, even if we consider only "effective" programs or "more effective" programs. This diversity stems in large part from differences in the theoretic assumptions that have shaped treatment approaches. There can thus be no single useful answer to the question What is language intervention? There must be many answers to this question, each formulated within a particular theoretic perspective. Assuming the validity of this argument, *our major challenge as language interventionists is to take theory seriously, that is, to accept the necessarily deductive nature of our definitional task and pursue it with energy and imagination.* What might this involve?

**Commitment to a Theory.** If it is true that language intervention can only be defined from within some theoretic perspective and that such definitions govern our practical activity, the interventionist has three response options. We can, like the proverbial ostrich, stick our heads in the sand and pretend that clinical practice has no theoretic motivation. Or we can continually redefine our roles as we vary our activities, echoing the tourist litany: "If this is Elmer, I must provide reinforcing consequent events." Or we can examine the assumptions implicit in intervention

practices, evaluate them, choose among them, and make them work for us. Commitment of the latter sort is to my mind the most constructive and reasonable response to the necessary link between practice and theory.

What constitutes a good theory? Certainly one that has strong empiric support and is countered by a minimum of fact. But other criteria are also important, for instance, the scope of the theory, its degree of refinement, and its ability to address the issues we believe are important. Such beliefs, of course, grow out of our life experience, our moral values, our epistemology, and even our metaphysics. Commitment to an intervention theory is thus a thoroughly personal statement. We should not be surprised to find that few professionals change their basic commitments.

(I might add here that I am all too aware that this discussion is itself an exercise in theory, namely metatheory. I obviously have committed myself to a particular view of the nature and value of theory, and I am sharing with you the assumptions and reasoning inherent in that view. This metatheory reflects my particular epistemologic stance, my experience with theories, the facts of theory as I know them, and so on. All of my arguments about language intervention theories could as easily be made about alternative theories of language intervention theories including Scheifelbusch's theory that "a design need not be theoretical. . . ." But this would require too many big words and draw us away from the topic of this book.)

**Explicit Reference to Theoretic Assumptions.** If it is true that theory guides practice and that particular versions of language intervention make sense only within specific theoretic contexts, we should explicate these frameworks for our colleagues and students. I was struck as I read the Schiefelbusch chapter by statements such as "skillful utilization of antecedent and subsequent events comprises the primary basis of face to face language intervention" (p. 22), or "participants serve as each other's antecedent and subsequent events" (p. 22), or "the common thread underlying all definitions is that generalization is an extension of a behavior to new circumstances" (p. 23). These statements reflect a particular view of language and language learning. Not only could I never make such assertions, it would never occur to me to do so. Schiefelbusch moves directly from his metatheoretic discussion of intervention design to descriptions of specific program attributes without explicit attention to mediating theories. I suspect that my version of a "behavior management" event would look quite different from Schiefelbusch's. I know I would describe it with different words. Our point of disagreement, however, would not be the intervention event nor the descriptive language but the theoretic model that underlies both.

If our absentee theories were to return from the mental suburbs they might do much to resolve senseless debates. A student of mine was recently trying to convince me of the importance of *reinforcement* in therapy. In desperation he asked the crucial question: "Do you *ever* give children M&Ms after they respond?" As I nodded yes, he smiled victoriously. "Then you *do* use reinforcement!" "Certainly not," I replied, and there began a long discussion of the difference between events and interpretations of events. This student had minunderstood the nature of our disagreement. For him, it was a matter of M&Ms; for me it was a matter of mechanisms of change. Notions such as *reinforcement, antecedent events, self-regulation,* or *functionality* are clearly constructs that assume particular theories. Discussion of intervention practice, it seems to me, is conducted most profitably when these assumptions are made explicit.

**Attention to Theory Coherence.** Language intervention theories by virtue of history and substance draw from previously existing theories of diverse sorts. There is no particular need for us to reinvent the wheel. If we are concerned with, for example, the nature of language, the mechanisms of change and the nature of language disorders, there is, for each of these issues, a rich empiric and theoretic tradition for us to build from. Our particu-

lar challenge is to construct a choerent whole out of the available materials. If the "arm" of our theory requires air pressure and our "motor" is electrical, we have a theory that can't work.

In this regard I am mystified by the union of behaviorist accounts of learning with structuralist accounts of knowledge that pervades our current intervention literature (Smith and colleagues, in press). If you assume that language knowledge consists of abstract rules that exist only in the mind of the knower, notions such as *reinforcement* or *stimulus* or *response* no longer have any explanatory force (Chomsky, 1959). When we advocate the use of "reinforcing consequent events" to effect "abstract rule formulation" we are not combining the best of two worlds. We are building a theory that can't work. By this I do not mean that children or adults won't profit from our intervention programs; they probably will. I mean that an incoherent theory lacks power to do the work of theories. More about that in a moment.

**Continual Re-evaluation of Theory.** Commitment to a theory depends in part on our initial assessment of its ability to account for empiric evidence. Such evaluation must continue for our theories to remain healthy. Theories do not thrive in an empiric vacuum. They are refined and reshaped as they confront facts.

My own assumptions about the relationship between conceptual development and lexical growth, for example, had led me to expect that language disordered children would use Experiencer-entailing verbs at abnormally high frequencies during the early language stages. If conceptual growth were the primary causal variable in predicate learning, the relatively advanced conceptual resources of this population should have enabled them to learn to express these developmentally advanced meanings in primitive forms. The fact that they do not (Leonard and colleagues, 1978; Johnston and colleagues, 1982) has redirected my attention to the importance of "perceivable meanings" in language learning. Verbs such as *know, hear, feel,* or *learn* may present a special challenge to young listeners because they refer to internal, nonobservable events. If nonlinguistic context provides the first keys to linguistic mapping, the language learner would find these verbs initially problematic—even if the requisite concepts were available. In this case, new research findings have led me to a more elaborated perspective on predicate learning with obvious implications for intervention practice.

Our challenge here is to pay honest attention to new or opposing views and the evidence that supports them. Sometimes these principles or facts will lead to theoretic refinements, other times to major restructurings. For example, I am currently working to understand the implications of information processing accounts of attention and memory. Thus far I have merely added constructs such as *limited capacity* and *automatization* to my existing model of intellect, but there may be a revolution brewing. Information processing theories emphasize quantitative and probabilistic aspects of mind, while my current view emphasizes the qualitative and logical. What I need to do next is identify the exact type of evidence that would require me to reformulate my notions of structural change in processing terms, then look for it. Neither step will be easy.

Thus far I have argued that the role of theory in language intervention is unavoidable, and that our best response to this fact is to take theory seriously. We do this insofar as we commit ourselves to a theory, make our theoretic assumptions explicit, pay attention to coherence, and re-evaluate our theories in the light of new evidence. I am convinced by the logic of this position and would hold it for logic's sake. I realize, however, that other interventionists may be more sensible, and so I wish to close my remarks with a brief discussion of the practical utility of theories.

## THE UTILITY OF THEORY

We are clinicians as well as scholars. As such our concern is that our clients acquire or regain proficiency in language for all the purposes it serves. Theories are vital tools in our therapeutic enterprise because they make us more creative and flexible clinicians. They work for us in at least two ways.

First, *theories raise new questions*. As I argued earlier, part of the impetus for change in intervention approaches is *external*, that is, we refine our strategies as we meet and study new facts. But impetus for change can also be *internal*, that is, we invent new approaches as they are suggested by theory. For example, if language learning is a rule induction process, what sorts of exemplars would facilitate linguistic analysis? If language growth is largely a process of self-regulated rule generalization, what should replace the M&M?

The possibilities for intervention programming far exceed the typical range, however diverse it may now seem. In this regard, I was struck by Holland's comment that the "didactic" school of aphasia treatment provided the "clearest opportunity" for hierarchic programming and gradual shaping of change. While it is true that members of this school have been the ones to focus on such issues, hierarchic programming seems equally compatible with a "cognitive process" or "communication strategies" approach. . Accidental conglomerates abound in the intervention literature. Theory suggests the points at which they can be creatively dissolved.

Second, *theories are the generative machinery for intervention events*. Psycholinguists argue that only the knowledge of abstract rules allows speakers to formulate the infinite range of utterances that language proficiency requires. This property of linguistic knowledge is referred to as *productivity*, or *creativity*. Clinical proficiency likewise requires an infinite range of intervention acts. If our knowledge of language intervention is abstract, or theoretic, in nature, we can be productive and creative therapists. No longer stuck with formulas, no longer hopeful imitators, we can use our intervention "rules" to generate activities that are thoroughly responsive to the client and the moment.

In sum, theories are not mere amusement for scholars, nor the unfortunate burden of reason; they are powerfully practical tools that serve our clinical endeavors.

## CONCLUSION

I began my discussion by pointing to great diversity in language intervention practice, and I have argued that this diversity is the inevitable result of differences in our perspectives on language, on mechanisms of human growth, and on the nature of language disorder. These theoretic differences make it impossible to provide a single answer to the question What is language intervention? Yet questions require a response. If we choose not to answer, how shall we respond? By sharing new facts, by pinpointing those key pieces of evidence that will promote theoretic growth, by clarifying assumptions. To my mind, this book will be useful to the degree that it furthers our various theory building efforts.

The catalyst for these remarks was a lecture given by W. Perry at the conference sponsored by the Lilly Foundation. I thank them both.

## REFERENCES

Chomsky N: Review of B. F. Skinner, *Verbal Behavior*, Language 35:26–57, 1959

Connell P, Spradlin J, McReynolds L: Some suggested criteria for evaluation of language programs. J Speech Hear Dis 42:563–567, 1977

Hayes S, Healy L: Parent training in language facilitation. Paper presented to the convention of the Canadian Speech and Hearing Association, Ottawa, 1979

Jeffree D, Wheldall K, Mittler P: Facilitating two-word utterances in two Down's syndrome boys. Am J Ment Defic 78:117–122, 1973

Johnston J, Kamhi A, McDonald J: Patterns of predicate use in language impaired children. Proceedings of the Second Symposium on Research in Child Language Disorders, University of Wisconsin at Madison, 1982.

Leonard L: Facilitating linguistic skills in children with specific language impairment. Appl Psycholing 2:89;-118, 1981

Leonard L, Steckol K, Schwartz R: Semantic relations and utterance length in child language. In Peng, F, von Raffler-Engel W (eds): *Language Acquisition and Developmental Kinesics*. Tokyo: University of Tokyo Press, 1978

Levenstein P: Implications of the transition period for early intervention. In Golinkoff R (ed): *From Prelinguistic to Linguistic Communication*. Hillsdale, NJ: Lawrence Earlbaum Associates, in press

Perry W: *Forms of Intellectual and Ethical Development in the College Years*. New York: Holt, Reinhart and Winston, 1968

Smith M, Ruder K, Stremel-Campbell K: An eclectic approach to language training: The case of past tense morphology. In Ruder K, Smith M (eds): *Developmental Language Intervention: Psycholinguistic Applications*. Baltimore: University Park Press, in press

Zwitman D, Sonderman J: A syntax program designed to present base linguistic structures to language disordered children. J Commun Dis 12:323–335, 1979

# PART II

# WHO SHOULD RECEIVE LANGUAGE INTERVENTION?

# 4

# IDENTIFYING CHILDREN WITH LANGUAGE DISORDERS AND DESCRIBING THEIR LANGUAGE PERFORMANCE

*JON F. MILLER*

Two assessment issues are of particular importance to intervention in children's language problems: how to find the children, and how to describe their problems. These problems of identification and description have traditionally been background themes in the literature on intervention. Their solution has been assumed as clinicians developed programs for children with particular etiologic characteristics. But intervention can only be as effective as our means for finding the children in a timely fashion in the first place, and the ways we choose to describe children's language will determine, in part, the content and the character of our intervention programs.

There are currently two broad approaches to assessment of child language disorders which offer different solutions to the problems of identification and description: (1) a traditional approach, governed by an etiologic model, in which children are first sorted out according to the condition thought to be the *cause* of the language disorder; and (2) a more recent approach, governed by developmental communication models, in which children are first sorted out by the *consequences,* or the presenting symptoms, of the language disor-

der. This contrast is not new. It is stated to focus attention on identification and description, which are independent notions.

The purpose of this chapter is to discuss each approach and the solutions that each offers, and to ask how each will help in intervention. How can we best find children for intervention? How can we best describe children's problems for intervention? The causal approach to identification is considered first, then the consequence approach.

## LOOKING AT CAUSES: PRIMARY ETIOLOGIC FACTORS AND LANGUAGE DISORDERS

The questions of how to find the children and how to describe their language become important at this time because research is beginning to demonstrate that traditional classification schemes for grouping language disordered populations are not sufficiently specific (Miller, 1982; Miller, Chapman, MacKenzie, 1981). Most of the research reported in the intervention literature on child language disorders has been governed by etiologic models, in which programs are constructed for children with specific disabilities that either directly cause language problems or are frequently associated with language delay or disorder. Language treatment programs abound for the mentally retarded, the sensorially impaired, the emotionally disturbed, the neurologically impaired, and the physically handicapped. Programs have also been constructed for children with linguistic deficits only, or linguistic deficits associated with learning disabilities. These children are distinguished by their lack of etiologic grouping; they are generally characterized by what they are not, rather than by positive performance descriptions.

Numerous subgroups have appeared within these etiologic categories based on subdiagnosis, such as Down's syndrome or severity of mental retardation. More frequently, multiple designators are used, including a primary etiologic factor (for example, mental retardation) with subdiagnosis including, for example, hearing status and a level of severity (moderate/severe/profound); developmental level expressed as chronologic age; or mental age and school status (early childhood, primary, or preacademic). The result can be language programs appearing for the severe and profoundly retarded, hearing impaired, preacademic child functioning in sensorimotor stage VI. Clearly, such descriptions reflect the organization of our health care and educational service delivery systems.

Two questions arise here. The first is whether there are specific linguistic outcomes associated with these etiologic factors, and further, whether we can identify expected language outcomes for factors presumed to affect language acquisition and use. The second question is, can language performance characteristics reveal organism integrity for cognitive, sensory, and physiologic processes prior to their appearance in nonlinguistic behaviors? The answers to these questions have important implications for the early identification of children at risk for language disorders, for the choice of dependent measures used to monitor change within treatment programs, and for the selection of parameters

used to describe research subjects that lead to straightforward generalization of the results.

## SPECIFIC LINGUISTIC OUTCOMES FOR VARIOUS ETIOLOGIC CONDITIONS ASSOCIATED WITH IMPAIRMENT OF LANGUAGE ACQUISITION AND USE

To understand the breadth of this question let us examine Table 4–1. Table 4–1 was constructed to compare the effects of various neuropsychologic, structural, physiologic, and environmental factors on language comprehension, language production, and the use of language for communication. It provides a format for comparative review of various etiologic factors wherein comprehension, production, and use may be independently affected. Beginning with the lefthand column, the major process factors are listed. In the next column the specific variables affecting language acquisition and use are listed for each process factor. Outcomes predicted for each of these variables can be read from left to right across the table for comprehension, production, and use, respectively. The numbers are consistent from left to right, referring to the same variable.

An examination of Table 4–1 reveals that a wide variety of problems affect language acquisition and use. While the table is not exhaustive, it shows that some nine conditions, each with several subcharacteristics, directly affect communication. Not all of these conditions result in the same communication deficits, even in the general categories used in the table. Speech motor control problems, for example, will directly affect production with intelligibility deficits of varying degrees of severity. Significant production limitations will result from respiratory control deficits, appearing as productive language delays, evidenced by short sentences with limited synthetic complexity. Lexical semantics in these cases, however, should not be affected. Such problems are frequently found in children with moderate to severe degrees of hypotonia, frequently associ-

**Table 4-1** VARIABLES IN LANGUAGE ACQUISITION AND USE

| | Variables Affecting Language Acquisition and Use | Effects Seen in Language Comprehension Reception | Effects Seen in Language Production (Expression) | Effects Seen in Use of Language For Communication |
|---|---|---|---|---|
| Neuropsychologic factors | 1. Cognitive development<br>2. Central processing<br>    Auditory<br>    Visual<br>    Perception/<br>    discrimination<br>3. (Speech) motor control<br>4. Attending, relating, motivation | 1. Delayed onset—slow development<br>2. Does not develop (severe) to delayed onset (minimal)—auditory—<br>3. Not affected<br>4. Does not develop to delayed onset, depending on severity | 1. Delayed onset—slow development<br>2. Does not develop (severe) to delayed onset (minimal)—auditory—<br>3. Not affected<br>4. Does not develop to delayed onset, depending on severity | 1. Delayed onset—slow development<br>2. Motor and motor vocal expression<br>3. Not affected<br>4. Disordered or nonexistent |
| Structural and physiologic factors | 1. Sensory<br>    Auditory<br>    Visual<br>    Acuity end<br>    Organ dysfunction<br>2. Craniofacial anomalies<br>3. Laryngeal anomalies | 1. Delayed onset (minimal to moderate)<br>2. Poor to fair in intelligibility (auditory)<br>3. Not affected | 1. Delayed onset—auditory<br>2. Intelligibility of speech related to structures affected and severity<br>3. Limited voicing; intensity, frequency, and quality disorders | 1. Motor and motor vocal expression<br>    Delayed onset (visual) minimal<br>2. Not affected<br>3. Motor and motor vocal expression |
| Environmental factors | 1. Social and Cultural<br>    SES<br>    Language and<br>    Dialect<br>2. Physical<br>    Experience<br>    Linguistic input (living situation) | 1. Delayed onset (bilingual home)<br>2. Delayed onset | 1. Delayed onset, dialect reflecting culture and community<br>2. Delayed onset | 1. Not affected<br>2. Delayed onset, few communication needs |

ated with Down's syndrome. Note that comprehension of language is not affected in deficits in speech motor control. Deficits in cognitive development, on the other hand, generally result in deficits in both comprehension and production, although both show variability relative to the level of cognitive development. Among sensory systems deficits, those in audition are more devastating for oral language than deficits in the visual system. Environmental factors—for example, limited exposure to language, limited stimuli, severe deprivation, or exposure to multiple languages—can all produce delays of varying degrees, proportional to the degree of environmental deficit.

The categories included in Table 4–1 do not reveal diverse outcomes for each condition. Most etiologic factors cause general delays in comprehension and production of language. At the level of specificity included in Table 4–1, primary etiologic agent will predict the existence of language and communication deficits, but not their specific characteristics. Etiologic labels can be useful in developing identification strategies in which the etiologic agent serves as an indicator of "at risk" status for communication development. At present, however, such early indicators are not sufficiently specific to be useful in determining prognosis: Either language performance can be diverse, or there is too little research to permit a prediction of linguistic outcome.

Within each etiologic category, multiple factors play a role in determining specific performance characteristics. The severity of the primary etiologic factor, the time of onset, and the age when a problem is identified are factors that can result in variable outcomes within a category. In addition, the primary etiologic factors frequently overlap, resulting in diverse language performance. Within each etiologic category, then, variable performance is to be expected relative to degree of deficit between comprehension and production processes, as well as among linguistic elements within processes, for example, syntax, lexicon, phonology, and pragmatics. Identifying the primary etiologic agent can predict an increased potential for language

deficits, serving as an "at risk" register for language disorders. Such a register is quite useful in the early identification of children requiring subsequent developmental monitoring. Language disorder is viewed as a result in this approach, in which cause is frequently attributed to the primary etiologic agent. As the primary indicator of "at risk" status, the etiologic agent will serve as a first-level screen in early identification leading to intervention. It will, however, miss many who will ultimately exhibit a variety of language disorders. How can we improve our strategies for finding children with disorders early in the developmental period?

## LOOKING AT CONSEQUENCES: ARE LANGUAGE AND COMMUNICATION BEHAVIOR SENSITIVE INDICATORS OF PROBLEM STATUS?

The primary identification strategy of the causal approach was to determine the etiologic factor; this hypothesis requires identification of the language deficit as the first step. To bring these contrasting views into focus, let us consider the problems of early identification when early intervention is a desirable goal.

Certain etiologic agents associated with language disorders, for example, genetic syndromes and physiologic deficits, are identifiable at birth or shortly thereafter. This is particularly true when degree of deficit is rather severe. For other conditions, language and communication serve as the first indications of possible problems. Mild and moderate forms of a number of primary etiologic factors, for example, mental retardation, hearing impairment, and central processing disorders, are identified only after the child's failure to develop language raises concerns about the child's integrity. Language and communication development serves in these cases as a particularly sensitive indicator of problem status. A focus on early language performance will lead to identification of mild to moderate language disorders associated with a variety of etiologic conditions, leading to early intervention, both medical and behavioral. This is certainly easier said than done. When significant deficits are evident, earliest identification is possible, and immediate intervention can be initiated. Less severe deficits must await developmental milestones as indicators of cognitive and physiologic integrity and proper environmental support. Given that there are significant numbers of children who evidence only language disorders, a focus on early identification is obviously the only means to achieve early identification and subsequent intervention.

## IDENTIFICATION: IS EARLY BETTER?

Recently reported successful early intervention programs (Schiefelbusch and Bricker, 1981) provide substantial motivation for establishing early identification networks. In recently reported programs we see effective interventions employed with normal middle class children (Fowler, 1981), low SES children of families identified as "at risk" for sociocultural retardation (Ramey and colleagues, 1981), and developmentally disabled children with conditions varying in severity (Kysela and colleagues, 1981). These programs demonstrate positive accelerated developmental change associated with training parents early in the child's life to interact positively and frequently with their children.

Fowler (1981) presents the only data available on the impact of language intervention initiated at different times in infancy. He reports that intervention begun at 3 months to 15 months results in immediate significant gains that continue to accelerate through the training period. Children whose training was initiated at 12 months continuing through 24 months show similar accelerated rates of development. These results demonstrate that intervention initiated at 12 months is as effective as when initiated at 3 months. It is possible that these effects may not be generalized to conditions in which basic parenting skills are suspect, however. The results of studies by Ramey and colleagues (1981) and

Thoman (1979) argue that early reciprocal interactions between mothers and their children are essential for fostering developmental growth and change. Intervention, to have maximal impact, should begin as soon as children are identified as having problems, the earlier the better.

Positive effects of early language intervention have been demonstrated with a variety of populations. No deleterious effects of early parent training programs on children have been reported. All children enrolled in these programs appear positively affected. While research in early intervention continues to provide improved strategies and identify processes associated with developmental change, findings to date can have an impact on existing service delivery systems.

## *A LOOK AT IDENTIFICATION STRATEGIES*

At the center of the health care service delivery system is the pediatric office. The pediatrician is likely to be the first professional to be in contact with the infant and family. The primary responsibility for the early identification and referral of children with known or suspected developmental delays can be said to rest with the pediatrician. There are a variety of neuropsychologic, psychologic, and environmental conditions associated with delayed communication development (see Table 4–1). The relationship of these conditions to the development of language skills is not well understood in all cases. With the identification of each condition, however, comes the expectation for significantly delayed communication development unless intervention is initiated. On the other hand, children identified early with delayed language development may be suffering significant physiologic, neuropsychologic, or environmental deficits. The child's communication behavior is a sensitive indicator of the integrity of the child and his environment.

While the importance of early identification is well recognized, the means to detect early developmental delay have

**Table 4-2  LANGUAGE ITEMS FROM THE DENVER DEVELOPMENTAL SCREENING TEST***

| Age At Which 50% Pass | Production | | | | | Comprehension | | | |
|---|---|---|---|---|---|---|---|---|---|
| | Phonology | Syntax | Semantics | Pragmatics | Phonology | Syntax | Semantics | Pragmatics |
| 1 month | Vocalizes not crying | | | | | | | |
| 2 months | Laughs Squeals | | | | | | | |
| 7 months | Mama or Dada Nonspecific Imitates speech sounds | | | Peek-a-boo (6) Pat-a-cake (9) | | | | |
| 10 months | | | Mama or Dada Specific | | | | | |
| 13 months | | | 3 words other than Mama or Dada | Indicates wants (re-quests) (12) | | | | |

| Age | | | | | |
|---|---|---|---|---|---|
| 17 months | | | | | Points to body part named (routine) |
| 20 months | Combines two different words | Names one picture | Interactive play (24) | | Follows two of three directions 1. *Give the block to mommy* 2. *Put the block on the table* 3. *Put the block on the floor* |
| 2 years, 6 months | Uses plurals | | | | |
| 2 years, 9 months | | | | Gives first and last name | |
| 3 years | | | | Compre-hends cold, tired, hungry Prepositions 3 colors | |
| 3 years, 9 months | | Defines 6 words | | | |

*From Miller, 1982.

emerged slowly. Significant improvements are being made in detecting problems at birth with the development of various high-risk registers. Various developmental scales are available, each evaluating a variety of behaviors emerging in infancy. Each scale includes some items evaluating communication. In most cases these scales do not include sufficient items to evaluate independently the child's developing skills in language comprehension, language production, and emerging conversational competence. More exhaustive developmental scales focusing on language employ formats that make them difficult to use in pediatric offices or too time-consuming for practical use.

One of the most widely used tests by pediatricians for screening developmental performance is the Denver Developmental Screening Test. In Table 4–2 the language items are listed by the specific aspect of language evaluated, phonology, syntax, semantics, and pragmatics in both comprehension and production. An examination of Table 4–2 reveals a number of significant gaps and deficiencies. In the items included, for example, little attention is paid to the sound system. The items evaluating comprehension do not begin until 17 months of age, wl.en the item is a frequent routine played by mothers and children. Such routines do not, however, provide sufficient evidence of linguistic understanding, given their frequency of occurrence, order of presentation, and potential nonlinguistic cues. Even the items at 20 months are questionable, since the child is required to understand only one word to comply with each direction and that is the last word in the stimulus string. The child, given the block, understands the implied action and gives the block back to mommy. The result is that children with significant problems in comprehension cannot be identified with this test until they are well over 2 years of age.

What is required is a set of items developed around time points when children are likely to visit pediatric offices for routine examination or immunization. These sets of items should be few in number and readily observable or easily elicited. Optimally, they could be administered in 5 to 10 minutes in conjunction with other routine tasks. Table 4–3 is a sample set of behaviors, derived from developmental research, which should be present at each point in time, birth to 1, 6, 12, 18, and 24 months. Where possible, the implications of absent performance for each item are included. Each age period represents an independent, criterion-referenced scale that is short but sufficiently detailed to recommend follow-up evaluation of language behavior or related characteristics.

Alternative strategies for data collection in the first two years of life involve parent diaries (Miller, 1981) and interview procedures (Snyder, Bates, and Bretherton, 1981). These procedures are somewhat useful as low-cost follow-up tools when performance on the criterion-referenced items is questionable or when few behaviors are directly observed. We have found one procedure particularly helpful in monitoring production from about 10 months through the second and third year of life; it has affectionately come to be known as "the refrigerator procedure."

In the refrigerator procedure we ask parents or caretakers to record a list of all the different words the child says over a week's time. The length of the recording time can be altered to suit the frequency with which the child talks and the degree of parent motivation. The procedure can also be used with older children with some training on sampling techniques, including choice of conversational context and activity. The name comes from the suggested recording method—taping a recording form on your refrigerator so that it's handy. The form includes two columns, one for the words and the other to record the meaning intended by the child in using the word, at least as best interpreted by the parent. While we are still experimenting with the procedures, results to date show agreement with tape-recorded speech samples (Miller, 1982). How far this procedure can be pushed is uncertain at the moment. Cost effective procedures that minimize the amount of time required to administer and score are essential requirements for useful early identification procedures.

Table 4–3  DEVELOPMENTAL AND CRITERION-REFERENCED SCALE
FOR IDENTIFICATION OF COMMUNICATION DEFICITS IN THE FIRST TWO
YEARS OF LIFE*

| Physiologic/Behavioral Indices of Problem Status at Birth | Implication or Potential Problem Area |
|---|---|
| Feeding problems | At risk for communication development |
| Weak cry | At risk for communication development |
| Congenital anomalies | At risk—developmental delay |
| Syndrome | At risk—developmental delay |
| Orofacial anomalies | Medical decisions surgery—timing |
| Laryngeal anomalies | Implications for speech motor control |
| Motor deficits—cerebral palsy | Implications for speech motor control |
| At risk—low birth weight | Long term follow-up |

### Behaviors that Should be Present at 6 Months

| | |
|---|---|
| COMPREHENSION | |
| Consistent orienting to sound | Hearing sensitivity |
| PRODUCTION | |
| Productive vocalization continues or increases | Hearing, or general developmental milestones |
| Syllable repetition (ba ba ba) | Speech mechanism or general developmental delay |
| Duration of cooing, singing, and babbling 203 sec | Speech mechanism |
| Variable intonation, both during crying and cooing | Speech mechanism |
| Voiced/voiceless contrast: /p/ vs. /b/ | Speech mechanism |
| Discrete tongue movements: /d/ /n/ /d/ | Speech mechanism or general delay |

### Behaviors that Should be Present at 12 Months

| | |
|---|---|
| Produces Ma-ma or Da-da, pet name referentially. Low frequency and intelligibility. Imitates speech sounds | Developmental delay, cognitive deficits, minimal hearing loss |

### Behaviors that Should be Present at 12 Months

| | |
|---|---|
| COMPREHENSION | |
| Understands his own name, or a name for present familiar person | Hearing or developmental delay |

### Use of Language for Communication

| | |
|---|---|
| Turn-taking vocalizations in communication games, peek-a-boo, pat-a-cake | |

(continued)

**Table 4–3**—*Continued*

| Behaviors that Should be Present at 18 Months | Implication or Potential Problem Area |
| --- | --- |
| COMPREHENSION | |
| Understands single words, names for objects within visual field | Developmental delay, hearing loss |
| PRODUCTION | |
| Few intelligible words | |
| Words frequently note familiar people and objects | |
| Frequency of vocalization increasing | |
| USE OF LANGUAGE FOR COMMUNICATION | |
| Requests, comments | Absence of intention to communicate |
| Rejects with motor and vocal or vocal behavior | |
| Hi and bye with gesture or vocal behavior | |

| Behavior that Should be Present at 24 Months | |
| --- | --- |
| COMPREHENSION | |
| Understands at least two words in an utterance, such as,"throw ball" indicating action object relation | Developmental delay |
| Also expresses single words, including action verbs and reference to absent objects | Specific communication delay |

| Behavior that Should be Present at 24 Months | |
| --- | --- |
| PRODUCTION | |
| Vocabulary increase to 20 words minimum | Developmental delay |
| Two-word utterances | |
| At least two intelligible utterances | Developmental delay |
| USE OF LANGUAGE FOR COMMUNICATION | |
| Request names, locations—"What's that," "Where's that" | Developmental delay |
| Uses words for multiple functions | |

*From Miller, 1982

Using parents as informants who record and report the child's behavior offers a potential productive solution.

The development and implementation of a scale like that presented in Table 4–3 is essential for identifying, monitoring, and following up communication development in children with known deficits and in those children in whom language deficits may be symptomatic of significant medical problems. At least as important is the early identification of a population of children who at age 3 evidence significant developmental delays in language and who have no other physiologic, neuropsychologic, or environmental deficits. This population has been estimated to be as high as 5 percent of children 3 years of age. At present there is no systematic way to identify them early in infancy. The major problem is to distinguish the children at the slow end of the developmental continuum from those whose rates of development will result in significant delays at 3 years of age.

This language delayed population, if it could be identified earlier, would be excellent cadidates for an intervention of the type described by Fowler and colleagues (1981). Based on documented effects of early intervention through parent training, prevention of these language delays appears to be a very real possibility.

## DESCRIPTION, TO WHAT END? COMMUNICATION, GENERALIZATION, OR RECORD FIGURATION

The word *describe*, according to Webster, means "to give an account of in words" or "to represent by a figure, model, or picture." Description is defined as "discourse intended to give a mental image of something experienced." Describing language performance then requires us to use language to talk about language. This paradox creates a complex problem for clinician and researcher alike. To create a mental image of children's abilities to create the proper mental images in a listener is rather like looking into a mirror with a mirror behind: an infinite regression of reciprocal images.

The need for detailed description of the language behavior of children with language disorders is not an issue. Clearly, the proper mental images must be invoked to communicate accurately. Characteristics of performance must be detailed to identify new instances and behavioral parameters for experimental manipulation and confirmation. Description, notes Tukey (1977), is the first step in scientific inquiry.

**Minimum Requirements for a Model of Language Description.** Using parameters of language behavior to define deficit performance requires a multidimensional view of language and a recognition of developmental growth and change. Developmental growth has both a horizontal and vertical dimension, where horizontal growth occurs within linguistic domains at each vertical developmental stage. The lexicon, for example, continues to expand, providing for expression of a variety of concepts within each level of development. This expanded lexicon improves flexibility and diversity of expression within the child's level of conceptual development. Communication is enriched in variety and achieves maximum utility even in the early states of development.

Horizontal development, as well as vertical development, marks linguistic change through the developmental period. Any model of description must keep these two notions distinct as potentially useful indicators of deficits performance. Without getting into the morass of what constitutes disordered performance, let us take up a model of description that, hopefully, will bring several issues into proper focus.

The goals of a model of description are several. The model should

1. deal with constructs that can be operationalized and measured;
2. lead to defining the parameters of disordered performance;
3. lead to identification strategies characterizing who is language disordered and defining what they are like;
4. provide for comparison of language processes with individual children as well as between children;
5. result in monitoring strategies, characterizing change within teaching programs or natural environment; and
6. define outcomes, characterizing performance expectations developmentally, as well as within linguistic contexts, and a variety of environments.

Lofty goals all, but are they achievable, and aren't they all tied to measurement? Indeed, at present proper description of language performance must be moved ahead *if* we are to improve communication about populations, generalize research findings, and reformulate population descriptions as a result of controlled research.

Within a discussion of language assessment, Miller (1978) posed a model of description to interpret the results of assessing multiple linguistic features across several processes. This model posed four major processes: *cognition*, measured nonverbally as an index of expected level of performance (see Miller, 1981; Miller,

Chapman, MacKenzie, 1981, for rationale); *comprehension* of language, involving both lexical and syntactic components; language *production*, including phonology, syntax, and semantics; and finally, *communication*, including functions, intentions, and interactions. Performance levels were measured in age level equivalents for each process, allowing comparison of performance across processes within children. Performance between children could also be compared with this model because standard units (age) were used for each process.

This basic model of description has proven useful in differentiating the language performance of mentally retarded children into several subgroups by their performance profiles (Miller, Chapman, MacKenzie, 1981). While the model is developmental, it provides a necessary window through which disordered performance can be judged. Children with acquired language disorders show deficits in both comprehension and production which must be judged relative to potential accompanying cognitive deficits. Their language performance, however, may deviate from that expected from normal children at the same developmental level (Miller, Campbell, Chapman, Weismer, in press). While the delay versus disordered controversy rages, disorders cannot be determined in the absence of a developmental descriptive model.

Four years later, this model retains its essential utility, though modifications would improve its accuracy and usefulness. The essential change is to move pragmatics into both comprehension and production, where it belongs. The original notion was to separate it for emphasis, but the result has been a potential for misinterpretation. In the next version we find the linguistic components listed within comprehension and production hierarchically. This model depicts each process of communication, comprehension, and production as independent and multidimensional. Each dimension within comprehension and production develops over time and is capable of independent measurement. While independent measurement is possible, each of

these domains interacts with the others to make up the language system. The relationships between domains must be substantial, and deficits in one must affect performance in another. Neither the developmental relationships nor the functional outcomes are well understood at this time. This model, to be maximally functional, will require considerable research effort.

The potential outcomes of this model are numerous:

1. Single domain, for example, productive phonology
2. Multiple domains, for example, phonology, syntax and semantics, pragmatics in production
3. Multiple processes, for example, comprehension of vocabulary, production of vocabulary
4. Multiple processes and multiple domains (the combinations here are endless when you add in variation and developmental level).

The model provides an hypothesis-generating mechanism that could add data to our descriptive process within the accumulation of research data.

## YARDSTICKS AND DATA

Cause and consequence approaches to finding children with language deficits and describing their performance have been discussed. Most of the discussion has been given to consequence approaches to our two major goals, finding and describing children, as extensions of the current etiologic categorization system. The two approaches provide unique perspectives on our goals and therefore unique contributions to potential solutions.

It should be fairly clear that each approach provides a piece of the solution but neither can stand alone. Etiologic factors can only provide general language performance predictions. In addition, whole populations of language disordered children fall outside the bounds of detection and description with this approach. Consequence approaches will fail to identify children at birth and through the early developmental period until developmental milestones are not achieved, even in children with known physiologic and neuropsychologic conditions resulting in language disorders. The issue is not which approach, but how rather, each individually contributes to the goals of finding and describing children with language disorders.

We have a problem of three-dimensional complexity: two approaches, cause and consequence, by two goals, finding the child and describing the child, by two objectives, evaluative criteria for finding children early and evaluative criteria for describing language disorders through the developmental period.

It appears that the time domain offers an organizing principle around which to pose a two-dimensional resolution to this complex problem.

Time will be used here to develop a longitudinal solution, considering both the entire developmental period and the time of identification as well. These two potentially independent chronologic varieties have significant consequences for language intervention, considering the old axiom, earlier is better, where intervention is concerned. Consider the following sequence:

1. Etiologic factor as primary identification system at birth for moderate and severe conditions of predictive significance. Add "at risk" characteristics, such as prematurity and low birth weight, and significant prenatal indicators, such as mother's ingestion of alcohol, educational level, and age, as factors indicating need for potential follow-up.

2. Developmental follow-up for "at risk" infants and others should follow the format set out in Table 4–3. Time frame could be extended. Failure to achieve any milestones requires further evaluation of language and other potential problems, for example, hearing and cognitive status.

3. At this point, because we have everyone alerted to monitoring development, we have identified all children with significant physiologic and genetic syndromes, have a list of definite maybes, and have begun to identify a number of children whose language is failing to keep pace with developmental expectations. In these latter cases we reverse the process and commence looking for causes; treatment for significant reversible medical conditions can alleviate the developmental deficit.

4. Decision point: We need some rules to decide who gets treatment when, what kind and where. Do we tune up mom or fix the child; at home, school, or clinic; one on one, small group, adult-child, child-child, and so on. This could be the topic of another entire discussion.

5. Children requiring description— invoke the new descriptive model. Description is invoked to determine if treatment is necessary, that is, more detailed data base, and further, to determine the nature and course of treatment. Here we invoke the decision rules. Children identified by etiologic factor will require follow-up with detailed evaluation to complete the description of performance required for individualized treatment program development.

## SUMMARY

The causal model is the classification system currently used in our systems of human services. This classification system does provide orientation as to general child characteristics and expectations for language performance. It has led to fragmented solutions to the problems of finding children with language disorders and describing the similarities and differences in their communication skills over time. Further, it leads experts on each etiologic factor to consider independent solutions to the problems of identification and description, such that the problem becomes that of identifying the etiologic agent rather than the language and communication characteristics of the group. Problems of treatment are then presumed to be specific to each etiologic group.

The consequence model looks good but requires better procedures and more normative data of several kinds to be fully functional: procedures allowing comparison across linguistic domains within and across processes; standards for data sampling; analysis; and interpretation.

In conclusion, all the fancy intervention programs, devices, kits, or tricks will not improve service delivery if we cannot document progress. Interventionists have traditionally looked to basic research on normal populations for ways to advance language development in deviant populations. It is time we began comparative studies across populations with deviant language to illuminate basic process characteristics. Baumeister (1967) called for studies of retarded children without comparison to normal controls, arguing that by definition the retarded children's learning rate is slower. What is interesting, he argued, is how specific learning characteristics differ across content and contexts within retarded populations. Individual differences need to be revisited.

Early intervention can be a highly productive framework for the design of experiments to document causal relationships identified in naturalistic, observational research. In the development of the science of language disorders, intervention, particularly early intervention, is no longer the stepchild of observational study but will become the cornerstone of scientific method in developmental research.

## REFERENCES

Baumeister A: Problems in comparative studies of mental retardates and normals. Am J Ment Defic 71(5): 869–875, 1967

Fowler W: A strategy for infant learning and developmental learning. In Schiefelbusch R, Bricker D. (eds): *Early Language Intervention*. Baltimore: University Park Press, 1981

Kysela G, Hillyard A, McDonald L, Ahlsten T: Early intervention: Design and evaluation. In Schiefelbusch R, Bricker D. (eds): *Early Language Intervention*. Baltimore: University Park Press, 1981

Miller J: Assessing language behavior: A developmental process approach. In Schiefelbusch R (ed): *The Basis of Language Intervention*. Baltimore: University Park Press, 1978

Miller J: *Assessing Language Production in Children: Experimental Procedures*. Baltimore: University Park Press, 1981

Miller J: The refrigerator and other diary procedures for monitoring early language development. Unpublished. University of Wisconsin, Madison, 1982

Miller JF: Early language intervention: When and how. In Lewis M, Taft L. (eds): *Developmental Disabilities in the Pre-school Child, Early Identification, Assessment and Intervention Strategies*, 1982

Miller J, Campbell T, Chapman R, Weismer S: The language behavior of children with acquired aphasia. In Holland A. (ed): *Recent Advances in Language Disorders*. San Diego: College Hill Press, in press

Miller J, Chapman R, MacKenzie H: Individual differences in the language acquisition of mentally retarded children. Paper presented at the 2nd International Congress for the Study of Child Language, University of British Columbia, Vancouver, BC, August 1981

Ramey C, Sparling J, Wasik B: Creating social environments to facilitate language development. In Schiefelbusch R, Bricker D (eds): *Early Language Intervention*. Baltimore: University Park Press, 1981

Schiefelbusch R, Bricker D (eds): *Early Language Intervention*. Baltimore University Park Press, 1981

Snyder L, Bates E, Bretherton I: Content and context in early lexical development. J Child Lang 8(3):565–582, 1981

Thoman E: Non-linguistic comminication as the prelude and context for language learning. In Schiefelbusch R, Bricker D. (eds): *Early Language Intervention*. Sturbridge, Massachusetts, May 1979

Tukey J: *Exploratory Data Analysis*. Reading, Mass: Addison-Wesley, 1977

# 5

# IDENTIFICATION AND ASSESSMENT OF APHASIC PATIENTS FOR LANGUAGE INTERVENTION

*CHRISTY L. LUDLOW*

As a member of the multidisciplinary team concerned with the treatment and rehabilitation of brain injured adults, the speech-language pathologist is usually asked to provide consultation on: first, whether the patient has a communication disorder (dysphasia, dyspraxia, dyslexia, dysgraphia); second, whether the patient could benefit from language intervention; and third, the expected prognosis for improvement of the disorder. For the purposes of planning language intervention services, the clinician will need to determine:

1. whether the patient has a speech/language disorder relative to normal functioning expected for the patient's age and previous communicative functioning;

2. whether the speech/language disorder is associated with a perceptual, motor, or cognitive disorder;

3. the characteristics of the patient's speech and language functioning, the patient's remaining skills, and the impairments treatment should focus on;

4. the environmental demands currently being made on the patient and those expected in the future;

5. the patient's beliefs and expecta-

tions regarding the disorder and his level of acceptance of various treatment goals;

6. the expectations for effecting change in the patient's speech and language functioning and his ability to meet environmental demands; and

7. the prognosis regarding the long-term outcome of the disorder, and whether the patient and family can expect eventual complete or partial recovery from the disorder.

This chapter covers the objectives of assessment, some of the techniques available, and new ones needed for conducting each type of assessment. It will not be concerned with speech disorders such as dysarthria or dyspraxia; these will only briefly be mentioned, with the focus remaining on aphasic language disturbances. Finally, this chapter will not provide a detailed review of the currently available tests for aphasia, but rather will focus on the principles to be considered when selecting various language tests for assessment purposes. Darley (1979) has provided an excellent review of commercially available tests. Further, since the ideal test to meet all objectives of assessment is not yet available, as will become apparent in this chapter, a combination of instruments must be used, depending upon the objectives of assessment. The principles are therefore more important for consideration at the present time.

## DETERMINATION OF SPEECH AND LANGUAGE FUNCTIONING RELATIVE TO NORMAL

The identification of those patients who are impaired in speech and language functioning relative to normal requires the use of standardized assessment techniques that have normative data for adults at different age ranges and with different educational backgrounds. Few tests for aphasia have such normative data. The Porch Index of Communicative Abilities (PICA) is the test with the most extensive normative data available and was found by Holland (1978) to be a valid indicator of a patient's overall level of ability. However, this test does not have norms for scores achieved by normal adults at different ages. Education levels may affect normal scores but do not affect the PICA scores of aphasic adults (Porch, 1967). Duffy, Keith, Shane, and Podraza (1976) reported that the PICA was accurate in 92 percent of the cases for differentiating between aphasic and non–brain-injured adults. Other tests with normative data for indicating when scores are in the impaired range are the Western Aphasia Battery (WAB) (Kertesz, 1979); the Neurosensory Center Comprehensive Examination for Aphasia (NCCEA) (Spreen and Benton, 1969); Communicative Abilities in Daily Living (CADL) (Holland, 1980); and more recently, The Boston Diagnostic Examination (BDAE) (Goodglass and Kaplan, 1972), with norms by Borod, Goodglass, and Kaplan (1980). Of these, three—the BDAE, WAB, and CADL—are commercially available, while the NCCEA must be ordered from the authors, and examiners must assemble their own testing materials, which weakens the applicability of norms from one center to another because of possible differences in materials. In general, data on normal subjects on aphasia tests are derived from very small numbers (less than 50), making these estimates of normal performance less applicable to different segments of the population.

The Western Aphasia Battery is a reduced version of the BDAE and was developed to screen for language impairment. The Communicative Abilities in Daily Living can also be used to screen for language impairment, although it is a measure of the ability of aphasic adults to perform communicative activities in everyday living and was carefully validated against observations of aphasic patients in their natural environments. As such, it is a valid measure of communicative impairment but not of degree of language dysfunction, for Holland has found that patients' deficits in language functioning are not always entirely consonant with their use of language in everyday functioning (Holland, 1980; 1982).

To summarize, when the purpose of assessment is only to determine whether the patient has a speech and language disorder, a test with normative data on both normal and aging adults which provides the criterion for determining whether a patient is impaired in speech and language should be used. Of those tests mentioned above, only the CADL has norms for different age levels.

Often criterion scores for identifying impairment must be derived either from percentile tables or tables providing the mean and standard deviation of scores in the normal population. To identify impairment with percentile scores, patients scoring at or below the fifth percentile can be termed impaired. If means and standard deviations are provided, then scores that are two standard deviations below the normal mean can be considered in the impaired range. Many clinicians find these criteria too rigid, particularly if a test is insensitive to mild impairment, allowing many patients with subtle impairments to be missed. Therefore, some advocate a criterion cut-off at the tenth percentile, or 1.5 standard deviations below the normal mean.

In many circumstances speech-language pathologists may need to develop their own normative data on the aphasia tests they are using for identifying when patients have aphasia. Most of the normal controls used in the development of normative data are non–brain-injured normal volunteers. Volunteers for research testing tend to be middle class and well educated. Such individuals would be inappropriate for comparison with poorly educated welfare recipients in an inner city hospital, for example. Further, the veteran population is quite different in its socioeconomic, ethic, and educational background and varies from one region to another in the country. Although gathering data for use in a specific population is time consuming, once the data are gathered, a "t" distribution can be computed for groups under 50 persons to determine the range of scores with a probability equal to or less than .05. As the number of cases increases, a Z distribution can be computed to identify scores more than two standard deviations from the normal mean.

The determination of whether a patient is impaired in language functioning is only a preliminary step and provides little information relevant to intervention planning. However, it may be necessary for court evidence in competency cases, for disability insurance coverage, or third party payment.

## DETERMINATION OF WHETHER THE SPEECH/LANGUAGE DISORDER IS SECONDARY TO SENSORY OR MOTOR DISTURBANCES

The measurement of an aphasic patient's hearing is an obvious first step that is all too frequently omitted. There is a high incidence of hearing loss, perhaps due to presbycusis, in the aphasic population (Karlin, Eisenson, Hirschenfang, and Miller, 1959; Miller, 1960; Terr, Goetzinger, and Konsey, 1958). A modified technique of using the descending approach to threshold has been found more reliable for assessing hearing in the aphasic population (Ludlow and Swisher, 1971).

Also to be considered following brain injury are hemianopias (visual field de-

fects), which are best determined by a neurophthalmologist and must be considered when there is evidence of a language disorder.

Apraxia of speech must be identified. A recent definition by Kent and Rosenbek (in press) seems most useful for differentiating this disorder from literal paraphasia and dysarthria. They include the following characteristics:

(1.) effortful, trial-and-error, groping articulatory movements and attempts at self correction;

(2.) dysprosody unrelieved by extended periods of normal rhythm, stress, and intonation;

(3.) error inconsistency on repeated productions of the same utterance elicited nontherapeutically; and

(4.) obvious difficulty initiating sentences. This disorder occurs in combination with aphasia more often than in isolation, and it can be further differentiated from aphasia on the PICA (Wertz, Rosenbek, and Collins, 1972) as well as on the Boston Diagnostic Aphasia Examination (Goodglass and Kaplan, 1972).

Dysarthria may also be present either as a lower motor neuron disorder or an upper motor neuron disturbance (Darley, Aronson, and Brown 1975). Oral peripheral movement strength and range of motion are important for determining the lower motor neuron integrity, while the rate, coordination, latency, and sequence of alternating and repeated oral and speech movements may be compromised in upper motor neuron disorders.

Cognitive, attention, and visuospatial disorders often accompany brain injury and can compromise a patient's performance on speech and language testing even though the patient does not have a specific language disorder. Disorientation, poor eye contact, and confusion should be identified. Although the patient may have a language disorder, these other symptoms of extensive brain injury may interfere with both the assessment of speech and language functioning and language intervention. Dementia, in the advanced stages, will interfere with a patient's ability to follow testing directions and perform many language tests, although he may show no expressive language deficits and can easily communicate thoughts, confusion, disorientation, and immediate needs. Anomia and frequent circumlocutions often accompany these disorders.

A neuropsychologic evaluation will help determine the extent of the patient's visuospatial deficits, memory disorder, and attention deficits. Thus assessment of aphasic patients is often a multidisciplinary team effort and not solely the concern of the speech-language pathologist, particularly when there is a need to determine the extent of confounding deficits. One caution, however: It is erroneous to expect patients with aphasia to score within the normal range on nonverbal tests of cognition. A language impaired patient should not be excluded from treatment on the basis of a lower score on the Raven's Matrices or the Performance Section of the Wechsler Adult Intelligence Scale. Not only will a severe language disorder interfere with the ability of a patient to take such a test, but left hemisphere damage may also affect other cognitive functions besides speech and language which are tapped by these tests (Basso and colleagues, 1981).

## ASSESSMENT OF LANGUAGE IMPAIRMENT BY MODALITY, LINGUISTIC SYSTEM, AND INFORMATION PROCESSING DEMANDS

Most aphasia tests have been constructed to examine by modality. This may be because of the characteristics of the various aphasia syndromes, which differ by the relative degrees of impairment found in different modalities. Weisenberg and McBride (1935) proposed the typology *expressive* and *receptive* aphasia based on the marked expressive language impairments found in Broca's aphasics with relatively good speech comprehension versus the fluent speech of Wernicke's aphasics with relatively poor understanding. Geschwind (1972) redefined the aphasia descriptions of Broca and Wernicke and proposed a brain organization underlying several syndromes (Geschwind, 1965). Goodglass and Kaplan (1972) developed the Boston Diagnostic Aphasia Examination according to his typology and provided excellent clinical descriptions of each type. Seven syndromes and the modality of greatest impairment for each are presented in Table 5–1. The BDAE and its abbreviated cousin, the Western Aphasia Battery, are the only aphasia tests that provide a clear-cut method of syndrome classification.

The distinguishing feature for each syndrome is the language modality that is impaired to the greatest degree. It should be remembered, however, that patients with the same syndrome pattern of language deficits may be impaired to different degrees. It is not the absolute amount of impairment on a particular test which is crucial for distinguishing between syndromes, but rather the pattern of different degrees of impairment across language modalities. Although a Broca's patient is more impaired in speech expression than auditory comprehension and the opposite is true for a Wernicke's aphasic, some patients with severe cases of Broca's aphasia may have greater impairments in auditory comprehension than those with a mild form of Wernicke's aphasia. This is a point of controversy in aphasiology.

There are two camps with different concepts of language breakdown in aphasia. One group, comprised of neurologists and neurolinguists, classifies all aphasic patients by syndrome and maintains that there are distinct differences between syndromes. This group has long asserted that the impairments of Broca's aphasics are primarily in expression and that these patients are minimally impaired in auditory comprehension. On the other hand, speech-language pathologists have long conceived of aphasia as a unitary disorder, with a patient's overall level of functioning being primarily related to the degree of impairment in auditory comprehension. Schuell's work best represents this view (Schuell, Jenkins, and Jimenez-Pabon, 1964). This latter view of speech-language pathologists may be a result of their intensive involvement with language testing and treatment of aphasic patients. Many ap-

Table 5–1  IMPAIRED LANGUAGE MODALITIES IN SEVEN SYNDROMES OF APHASIA

| Syndrome | Speech expression | | | Auditory Comprehension | | Reading | Writing | Repetition |
|---|---|---|---|---|---|---|---|---|
| | IMPAIRED FLUENCY | NAMING DISORDER | IMPAIRED SYNTAX | MILDLY IMPAIRED | MODERATELY TO SEVERELY IMPAIRED | | | |
| Broca's | + | + | ⊕ | + | + | + | + | + |
| Wernicke's | − | + | − | − | ⊕ | + | + | + |
| Anomic | − | ⊕ | − | + | − | + | + | − |
| Conductive | − | + | − | + | − | − | − | ⊕ |
| Transcortical sensory | − | + | − | − | ⊕ | + | + | − |
| Transcortical motor | ⊕ | + | − | + | − | − | + | − |
| Global aphasia | + | + | + | − | + | + | + | + |

Note: + = impaired; − = unimpaired; ⊕ = primary difficulty.

hasic patients may seem to have relatively good comprehension in general conversation but exhibit moderate impairment when their comprehension is tested with nonredundant material, such as the Token Test (DeRenzi and Vignolo, 1962). Also, from extensive dealings with aphasic patients in a one-to-one situation, the clinician gains a far greater understanding of the patient's level of functioning in each language modality. It may be, however, that both groups are partially correct in their view of aphasia. Neurolinguists are now finding that Broca's aphasics have deficits in language comprehension which mirror their expressive deficits when their comprehension skills are assessed in depth (Zurif, 1980). Further, although the degree of impairment of a patient's expressive and receptive deficits are highly related, speech pathologists are now using the BDAE and finding that there are patterns of deficits that differ between patients who have the same level of impairment. To determine whether patients are more impaired in one modality than in another, patients must be tested on equivalent subtests in different modalities. That is, a test of auditory comprehension must be scored on the same severity scale as a test of speech expression. Three aphasia tests provide this feature, the BDAE, the PICA, and the NCCEA. On each, either percentile scores or Z scores provide a method for comparing performance on different tests. However, the scales for subtests on each of these batteries were derived from scores obtained on large numbers of aphasic patients on each subtest. Thus the same score

of fiftieth percentile, for example, on the tests of speech expression or language comprehension means that 50 percent of the aphasic patients have scored below that level on each test. However, if all aphasic patients perform better on tests of language comprehension than on those of speech expression, the same score on these two tests would not be equivalent levels of function in absolute terms. Rather, a patient with equal percentile scores in comprehension and expression would actually have greater language comprehension skills than speech expression skills. To determine whether this is the case, we need to have tests normed on the basis of normal adults, providing percentile or Z scores relative to the functioning of normal adults on each test. The only aphasia tests that currently have this feature are the Neurosensory Center Comprehensive Test for Aphasia and the recent norms provided by Borod and colleagues (1980) on the BDAE.

Another obstacle preventing comparisons between language modalities is that none of the available tests assesses a patient's functioning in different modalities using the exact same language material. The PICA uses the same ten stimulus items in all subtests except one, but the linguistic information and complexity of the required responses differ enormously across subtests. Even the BDAE does not use the same linguistic material on tests in different modalities.

In Table 5–2, a two-dimensional model is provided to allow comparison of patients functioning in different modalities when the linguistic demands are the same.

Table 5–2  LANGUAGE MODALITIES AND LINGUISTIC SYSTEMS TO BE ASSESSED FOR COMPARISON OF APHASIC PATIENTS FUNCTIONING ACROSS MODALITIES WHEN THE SAME LINGUISTIC DEMANDS ARE MADE

|  | Phonetic | Phonologic | Lexic | Semantic | Syntactic |
|---|---|---|---|---|---|
|  | Comparison across linguistic systems →→→ | | | | |
| Auditory comprehension Speech repetition Language expression Reading comprehension Written expression | | Comparison across language modalities | | | |

On the rows, the five different language modalities previously found to be critical in syndrome classification are listed: auditory comprehension of language; speech repetition (imitation); speech expression; reading comprehension; and written expression. On the columns, five different linguistic systems are identified. In the phonetic area, the recognition of phones is assessed from discrimination curves when a specific acoustic attribute that distinguishes between two phones is varied. For example, by varying voice onset times the threshold for distinguishing between voice and unvoiced cognates, such as /p/ and /b/, can be determined. On the expressive side, voice onset times in speech can be measured from sound spectrograms. Phonologic information is concerned with the correct use of phonemes in language. A speech articulation test requiring phonemic contrasts with an analysis of phonemic substitutions (literal paraphasic errors) can be used for expressive testing, while the discrimination and identification of minimal phonemic pairs would be assessed as the receptive correlate. Lexical information can entail use of the nominative information and the recognition of word meanings. Semantic information can be regarded as the recognition of the meaning relationships between words and the correct usage of words in phrases to convey target meanings. Syntactic information is reflected by sentence construction using word order, different classes of words and morphophonemics, and comprehension of syntactic relationships in sentences. As represented by the vertical arrow in Table 5–2, within one linguistic system tests can be constructed to compare the patient's ability to process the same linguistic material for speech expression, repetition, comprehension, reading, and writing. For example, a large group of sentences could be developed which are equivalent in syntactic structure, vocabulary frequency, and length and are demonstrated to have equal degrees of difficulty for aphasic patients. These sentences could then be randomly assigned to six different test groups for use as tests of sentence comprehension, sentence repetition, sentence expression, sentence written production, sentence reading comprehension, and sentence copying. Thus linguistically equivalent subtests would be used across language modalities.

Table 5–2 also illustrates the ability to compare language functioning within the same modality but using different types of linguistic information. Neurolinguists have proposed that the different syndromes of aphasia may represent specific impairments in one type of linguistic information. That is, Broca's aphasics may have a primary impairment in processing syntactic information, regardless of the language modality it is assessed in. Conversely, Wernicke's aphasia may represent a primary impairment in processing of semantic information, as demonstrated by the paucity of specific information in these patients' speech and their poor language comprehension. The model of assessment presented in Table 5–2 would allow assessment of these issues. To determine whether patients have specific impairments in the recognition or expression of particular language information, language functioning within each modality can be assessed for different types of linguistic information. This model of assessment could address several issues regarding the nature of language breakdown in aphasia—information critical for the development of intervention strategies. If aphasic patients demonstrate different degrees of language functioning across modalities when the same language material is used, then treatment could focus on the modalities most impaired which are of importance to the patient. On the other hand, if patients demonstrate impairments only in particular language systems, then those may need attention during intervention.

There is another dimension of language functioning which has been largely neglected, but which could be important for treatment planning—information processing. Language is information, and like other information it is stored in the brain. Cognitive psychologists define four different types of information processing that are relevant to the breakdown of memory skills in various dementias (Weingartner, Caine, and Ebert 1979a, 1979b; Caine, Ebert, and

Weingartner, 1977) and may be relevant to verbal information processing in aphasia.

These four processes are recognition, recall, retrieval, and encoding. Different tasks using our knowledge of road signs can provide an illustration of these four processes. While driving, we all recognize correctly many nonverbal symbols, such as those for parking, stop, turn left, single lane overtake, and so on, and based on our stored information regarding their meaning, we interpret them. Subject's recall, retrieval, and encoding of the same signs can be assessed. To test recall, a subject is shown a sign, it is taken away, and then the subject is asked to draw it or describe it. If the subject has previously stored information of that symbol, his recall will be more accurate and rapid than if he had never seen it before. Another process is retrieval, in which subjects are asked to draw signs for parking, no passing, and so on from memory. There are some details that subjects may not remember, and overall their production on retrieval will be less accurate and slower than on recall. Also, the complexity of symbols and their frequency of use will affect both recall and retrieval. Finally, the process of encoding can be illustrated when subjects are given a set of directions and asked to represent them by drawing a sequence of road signs. To do this, subjects must select those meanings represented by signs, retrieve the signs from memory, order them correctly, and then reproduce each accurately. This process is more complex and can fail for many different reasons. However, by also examining a subject's recognition, recall, and retrieval of the same material, it can be determined whether the individual already has stored the necessary information, whether he can perceive it, whether his interpretation of the information is correct, and what is his ability to retrieve the signs in isolation. If these processes are intact and encoding fails, the relationships among the information elements and their correct ordering may be the difficulty.

The speech-language pathologist dealing with aphasic patients can observe these different levels of information processing and their relative intactness. The clinicians know how to assist patients in retrieving words they cannot encode spontaneously by cuing semantically or phonetically. Schuell and colleagues (1964) believed the major difficulty of aphasic patients was in retrieving language information still stored in their brains. This dichotomy between recognition and retrieval was also posited by linguists as the difference between language competence and language performance. The fact that aphasic patients can often recognize linguistic information which they cannot retrieve provides support for this notion.

What we would like to propose is that clinicians systematically examine aphasic patients' abilities to process the same linguistic information at these processing levels to determine whether all or only certain types of aphasic patients follow this continuum in their language breakdown. Although this continuum may not seem to hold in some syndromes, such as conductive aphasia and transcortical sensory aphasia, we may find it applicable when it is experimentally addressed across different processing tasks using the same linguistic material.

Table 5–3 summarizes a model of language assessment which combines various language processing skills with testing by language modalities and across linguistic systems. If there is a continuum of breakdown within patients across the various processing tasks, then a continuum of intervention strategies might be applicable to improving efficiency of performance, first on recall, followed by retrieval, and finally encoding.

We are currently assessing this model of language processing in the Vietnam Head Injury Study (VHIS). Over 500 veterans who sustained head injuries in Vietnam have agreed to participate in the study. Between 1967 and 1970 the neurosurgeons in the field maintained records on over 1100 veterans who received surgical treatment for head injury. The VHIS is an intensive multidisciplinary examination of their status 12 to 15 years following injury. Each participant receives a CT scan and extensive neurologic, physical, motor, neuropsychologic, audiologic, speech and

Table 5–3 LANGUAGE ASSESSMENT BATTERY BY MODALITY, LINGUISTIC
SYSTEM, AND INFORMATION PROCESSING CURRENTLY IN USE IN THE
VIETNAM HEAD INJURY STUDY

| LANGUAGE MODALITIES | INFORMATION PROCESSING TASKS | LINGUISTIC SYSTEMS | | | | |
|---|---|---|---|---|---|---|
| | | PHONETIC | PHONOLOGIC | LEXIC | SEMANTIC | SYNTACTIC |
| Language comprehension | Recognition | X | X | X | X | X |
| Speech repetition | Recall | | X | X | | X |
| Language expression | Retrieval | X | X | X | X | |
| | Encoding | | | X | X | X |
| Reading comprehension | Recognition | | X | X | X | X |
| Oral reading | Recall | | X | X | X | X |
| Written | Recall | | X | X | X | X |
| | Retrieval | | X | X | | |
| | Encoding | | X | X | X | X |

language, and behavioral examinations. The pattern of breakdown in the aphasic patients is being compared with that in nonaphasic patients with left hemisphere injuries, right-hemisphere-damaged nonaphasic controls, and controls without head injuries from the same units as our patients. By comparing the patterns of language breakdown in these various groups we hope to learn what is specific about language breakdown in aphasia.

## ASSESSMENTS OF THE PATIENT'S AND FAMILY'S BELIEFS, EXPECTATIONS, AND COMMUNICATIVE NEEDS

In the 1960s many authors placed an emphasis on the psychosocial needs of aphasic patients and the ramifications these may have for the language intervention process. Wepman (1968), Eisenson (1963), and Buck (1968) described the psychologic reactions of the patient and his family on the onset of aphasia. Webster and Newhoff (1981) reviewed the literature in this area and discussed how counseling techniques can be used by speech-language pathologists in their care of communicatively impaired adults and their families. Since speech-language pathologists are now contacted early in the course of

aphasia and often see the patient and his family at the bedside during acute care, it is increasingly important to be aware of the dynamics of the psychologic reactions the patient and his family may be going through immediately following the onset of aphasia. Figure 5–1 is a hypothetic model of the psychosocial process which may be exhibited by some patients and which, through interview techniques, the speech-language pathologist should probe for during assessment. If some of these factors are present, early intervention may need to take the form of counseling. The assessment of the patient's beliefs regarding his disability should precede much of the formal language testing. If a patient is undergoing acute anxiety, denial, or severe depression, the aphasia test results will be invalid and testing should be postponed until later.

The onset of most aphasias is usually sudden—there is no warning for this catastrophe. The initial reaction of the patient and family is often one of fear and extreme anxiety. All stroke patients experience fear and anger (Eisenson, 1967) when they find they are unable to respond as they formerly did or presently wish to. Bardach (1963) indicated that the way in which many patients deal with this threatening reality is by denial, which has the function of preventing the patient from becoming over-

**PSYCHO–BEHAVIORAL CHANGES FOLLOWING ONSET OF APHASIA**

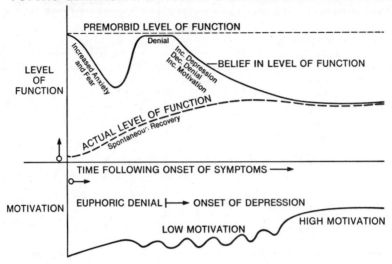

Figure 5–1. A model of the psychologic reactions of aphasic patients over time following the onset of aphasia.

whelmed by his tragedy. Such denial may be conscious or unconscious. This is an emotional reaction to the handicap and not the syndrome of either "anosognosia" or "asomatognosia" (Weinstein and Kahn, 1955; Kreindler and Fradis, 1968), which often occur subsequent to right hemisphere damage. Wepman (1968) described denial as the first observable state after the sudden onset of aphasia; however, he referred to this as "euphoria" and implied that it is unconscious. A probable theoretical explanation for the appearance of euphoric denial is available in Festinger's theory of cognitive dissonance (Festinger, 1957). The original framework of beliefs supporting the patient's self-value is contraindicated by the reality of the verbal and physical disability following brain damage. An attempt is made to reduce the dissonance between the two belief systems, to make the beliefs imposed upon the patient by reality more palatable. Thus the patient may cling to the old belief in order to reject the traumatic reality, and "euphoria" and denial may appear as the patient's first emotional reactions to his disability. He retains the belief that he is part of the normal population and does not alter his conceptions of his own ability to work and function as he has done before.

Both Bardach (1963) and Diller (1963) stressed the handicap induced by denial and the subsequent unrealistic goals of the patient in responding to treatment. The patient may not see the need to apply himself to tasks that are not relevant to him as a functioning normal member of society. If this state continues a patient may refuse to accept treatment and planning for rehabilitation. Wepman (1968) cautioned that intervention should not begin during this period of euphoria.

In most cases, the euphoric denial state is transient. As time goes on, the degree of denial may gradually lessen. As it does so, there may be a more or less corresponding increase in depression. Clinicians are often surprised by patients who at first were cooperative and happily went through initial testing showing only brief surprise when they can't perform tasks, but who later become angry and uncooperative during treatment. This depression is necessary as the patient reacts to the reality he is now facing. The periods of extreme outward depression may gradually lessen as the patient becomes more realistic and begins to adjust to the disability (Bardach, 1963). Although the state of depression may also disrupt the therapy process, most authors regard it as a more healthy stage

(Bardach 1963). However, both Wepman (1968) and Buck (1968) advised against therapy during severe bouts of depression.

Blackman (1950) observed that as a result of recurring defeats the patient experiences as he attempts to behave as he once did, he may often choose to avoid speaking. Wepman (1968), Buck (1968), and Biorn-Hansen (1957) indicated the crucial need for family counseling and education of hospital and professional staff on creating a rewarding social environment for the patient.

Many family members may go through the same emotional process as the patient but at different rates, often complicating the patient-family interactions. The necessary involvement of the family in adopting positive attitudes toward the patient to maintain the patient's motivation was emphasized by Malone (1969), Turn-bloom and Myers (1952), Biorn-Hansen (1957), Wepman (1968), and Buck (1968). During attempts to deal with reality, the patient develops negative attitudes and an altered self-concept which can interfere with motivation for rehabilitation. These detrimental attitudes should not be augmented by the family's negative attitudes toward the patient.

Attitudes toward aphasia have been shown to be alterable by the environment. First, with regard to the patient himself, Stoicheff (1960) found that aphasic patients subjected to discouraging instructions do significantly worse on language tasks than those who receive encouraging instructions. Beyond this, Stoicheff found that the aphasics who received discouraging instructions rated their performances more poorly than did those whose instructions were encouraging.

Buxbaum (1967) found that degree of nurturance of the wives of aphasics affected their appraisal of their husbands' speech disorder. Those wives who most readily adapted to the role shift of giving affection and care to their husbands underrated their husbands' deficits.

To summarize, then, the clinican's role in assessment, particularly for acute cases, is to determine the patient's beliefs regarding his language disorder, the fami-

ly's attitudes toward the patient, and the immediate environmental demands being made on the patient and his family. Early intervention may need to focus on resolving psychosocial problems and meeting environmental demands rather than on dealing directly with the language or communicative disorder.

## ASSESSMENT OF THE PROGNOSIS FOR LONG-TERM OUTCOME OF APHASIA AND THE PROBABLE EFFECTS OF INTERVENTION

The prognosis for recovery from aphasia is one of the first questions both the family and patient address to the physician and speech-language pathologist. For any family dealing with a catastrophic event, this information is of primary importance in meeting immediate financial and emotional needs. As the condition becomes chronic, the entire family must become involved in planning realistically to meet financial, logistic, and psychosocial demands. The speech pathologist is also responsible to the rehabilitation team, the primary physician, and the social worker for providing an estimate of the patient's future communicative status for decisions regarding the patient's living arrangements following acute care, and later, following rehabilitation. Providing an indication of the prognosis for recovery is therefore as much a professional responsibility as is language intervention. When the clinician provides no indication of the prognosis for recovery, the family and patient often assume that the objective of therapy is to "cure" the language disorder.

Many times the family and patients will not ask the clinician the prognosis. This is an indication that they are not yet ready to deal psychologically with the information; afraid that it might not be favorable, they do not ask. In such a situation, the clinician should not force such information on the family or patient, particularly if the outlook is negative. However, when a family member asks for the prognosis, the speech-language pathologist must be as explicit and clear as is possible to aid the family and patient to begin to deal realistically with the dramatic changes to be expected in their lives, financial status, and emotional responses to dealing with the catastrophe.

There has recently been a significant increase in the information available regarding the prognosis in aphasia. In the near future these data should become even more definitive, allowing the speech-language pathologist to assist the family and patient better in dealing with the disorder, both during the language intervention process and afterwards.

During the first weeks after onset of aphasia following stroke, brain functioning may be affected as a whole by neural shock (Brain, 1965; Luria, 1963). As edema and other factors subside, the physiologic healing process begins and there may be rapid resolution of deficits, particularly during the first eight weeks. The physiologic healing process may contribute to recovery for up to six months after onset. During this period of spontaneous recovery, the amount of change is greatest and includes both physiologic and language intervention effects. As time passes, the contribution of physiologic processes to recovery may decrease while the contribution of language intervention increases. In some cases recovery continues over many years. In an ongoing study of head injured Vietnam veterans, we have found quite a few patients who have a history of severe aphasia up to 5 to 7 years following injury and who then show a significant recovery over 2 or 3 years, with only very mild deficits on testing at 12 years following injury. Warren and Datta (1981) have reported a similar finding of speech restoration four and one-half years following head injury. The mechanisms for such recovery are elusive, however, and not likely to be physiologic. As Geschwind (1974) concluded: "Regeneration of transected nerve fibers certainly occurs in the peripheral nervous system, and may lead to some of the phenomena of aberrant regeneration which are rather difficult to explain. We continue to assume that this type of regeneration of the main body of the axon does not occur in the central nervous system in higher animals" (p. 483).

These cases of late recovery may not be relevant to patients with stroke, however, who are older and often have extensive cerebrovascular disease. We cannot rule out further recovery in aphasic patients many years after the onset, except in patients with very severe language dificits.

The Porch Index of Communicative Ability is the only test that has been demonstrated to predict the level of function following treatment (Porch, 1974). The validity of this predictive formula must be further evaluated with several different types of aphasic patients with different etiologic factors.

An overall score on the PICA is only an estimate of severity and does not indicate the types of dificits the patient will continue to exhibit following treatment. The patient's type of aphasia may be predictive of the degree of recovery as well as of the residual pattern of deficits. Global aphasic patients scoring at the twenty-fifth percentile or less on standardized aphasia tests have a poor prognosis for recovery (Schuell and colleagues, 1964; Sarno, Silverman, and Sands, 1970). When global aphasia persists past the third month postonset, the chances for total recovery are slim and the patient will likely continue to have moderate to severe deficits in most areas of language function. On the other hand, anomia has the best prognosis, and close to 50 percent of these patients may have function completely restored by one year postonset (Kertesz, 1979).

Two other syndromes that are relatively rare have a good prognosis for significant recovery: transcortical motor aphasia and conductive aphasia. Kertesz (1979) reports that of three transcortical aphasics, two became anomic and one completely recovered. The most dramatic recovery we have observed was in a patient with transcortical motor aphasia first examined at two months postonset, who completely recovered by four months postonset. Conductive aphasia also has a relatively good prognosis based on the Kertesz data. Five of eight cases completely resolved, while two became anomic and only one remained unchanged.

Patients with Broca's and Wernicke's

aphasia have more guarded prognoses. Wernicke's aphasics seem to have a moderate degree of recovery, with many becoming anomic, although Kertesz did not find any whose language disorder completely resolved. Broca's aphasics seem to have more mixed degrees of recovery. Several investigators have noted that the prognosis for a significant recovery is guarded (Schuell and colleagues, 1964, Vignolo, 1964; and Keenan and Brassel, 1974).

Ludlow (1977) reported on the patterns of recovery of Broca's and fluent aphasics during the first, second, and third months postonset while they were receiving treatment. The degree of recovery for the two groups differed substantially during this early postonset period. Recovery was greater in all areas, except speech repetition, for the fluent aphasics, while the Broca's aphasics had a slower rate of recovery that continued longer.

Although analyses for groups of aphasic patients have indicated some relationship between degree of recovery and age, sex, handedness, education, and type of cerebrovascular accident (see Chapter 13), none of these factors has good predictive power for recovery in individual aphasic patients. Thus they are of little use in providing the physician and family with prognostic information for any particular patient.

With the advent of CT scanning, the extent and location of brain lesions can be examined in relation to recovery from aphasia. Naeser, Hayward, Laughlin, and Zata (1981) examined the relationship between infarct size as measured by the number of 1 mm$^2$ pixels involved in the lesion and the type of aphasia, and found the lesions were greatest in size for global aphasics, less for mixed aphasics, still less for Broca's, less again for Wernicke's, and least for transcortical motor and conductive aphasics. Further, there was a significant overall correlation between severity of aphasia and lesion size in the 30 patients studied, based on CT scans performed at 2 months following stroke.

Other dimensions than the lesion size appear to be related to the severity and outcome of aphasia. Mohr (1973, 1976) found that patients with infarctions in Broca's region seem to have relatively dramatic recovery if the lesion is confined to the superficial layers of the grey matter without disruptions of the underlying brain. Other Broca's aphasics with relatively limited recovery usually had embolic infarctions of the upper division of the middle cerebral artery with lesions in Broca's region, including underlying structures such as the putamen, and some posterior extension. Naeser and colleagues, (1982) reported on nine cases of subcortical aphasia, indicating that in these cases it was the lesion location and not the size of lesion which was important to the severity of the resulting aphasia. All cases had involvement of the putamen and severity increased when there was involvement of the caudate as well.

In the Vietnam Head Injury Study, we have begun to notice a significant difference between the final residual deficits in head injured patients with similar types of aphasia, depending upon whether there is involvement of subcortical structures. Both of the following two cases have a residual Wernicke's aphasia; one has only mild residuals, while the other has a moderate impairment. In Case One there was extensive involvement of the angular gyrus and the supramarginal gyrus (Fig. 5–2). The lesion involves all of Wernicke's area, the anterior parietal, and the posterior temporal lobes. This was the patient with only mild deficits in comprehension and naming, a few verbal paraphasic errors, and only slightly reduced speech expression content. The second patient (Fig. 5–3) had a much smaller cortical lesion with no involvement of the supramarginal gyrus, angular gyrus, or Wernicke's area. However, there is involvement of the thalamus, anterior and posterior putamen, and globus pallidus, as well as the temporal lobe. This latter patient had a moderate aphasia with limited sentence comprehension, severe anomia, empty speech with frequent paraphasia errors, and severe reading and writing deficits. These are only two cases, and only preliminary results. Perhaps the depth of lesion and involvement of the basal ganglia and/or white mat-

Figure 5–2. CT scan of Case One, with only mild aphasia 12 years after a penetrating head injury.

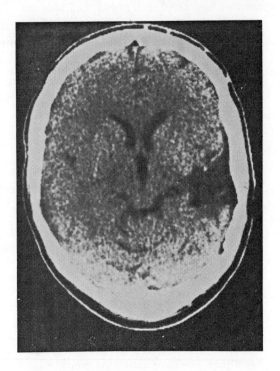

Figure 5–3. CT scan of Case Two, with moderate fluent aphasia 12 years after a penetrating head injury.

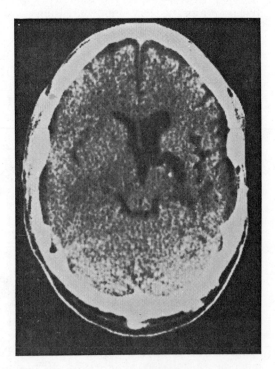

ter tracts are important to the prognosis for recovery.

It became obvious very early in our examination of these head injured veterans that the presence of bilateral damage is significant in the persistence of aphasia 12 years following injury. In the first 53 previously right-handed patients with left hemisphere damage, the percentage of residual aphasias differs greatly between the unilaterally and bilaterally injured groups. Of those with lesions confined to the left hemisphere, 3 of 21 cases, or 14 percent, exhibit aphasia, while in those with bilateral lesions, 10 of 32 cases, or 31 percent, exhibit aphasia.

In the CVA population, as the resolution of CT scanners improves, small deficits are appearing in the contralateral hemisphere which may be from subclinical infarcts (Ruben, personal communication). Given the impending development of nuclear magnetic resonance (NMR), which will soon replace CT scanning (Traveras, 1982), we will be able to determine the effects of cerebrovascular disease on anatomic structure. The extent of cerebrovascular disease and the presence of small bilateral infarcts may have prognostic significance for recovery from aphasia.

## SUMMARY

The main points in this review of the identification and assessment of aphasic adults are as follows.

First, identification, the determination of whether a patient has aphasia, and the determination of whether there are confounding deficits in sensory, perceptual, motor, and cognitive functioning, have been relatively well worked out. The necessary tools are currently available for this purpose.

Second, assessment, which involves the determination of the aphasic patient's intervention requirements, needs further development. Further testing procedures are needed for determining a patient's pattern of language breakdown, the particular linguistic information remaining intact in each modality, and the information processing skills of which a patient is capable.

Third, attention must be given to formalizing our assessment of the patient's psychosocial needs and those of his family. This should have a greater role in intervention decisions regarding when to initiate formal language assessment and direct treatment, particularly with the acute aphasic.

Finally, information is becoming available which is improving the understanding of the prognosis for recovery from aphasia. In the near future, the speech-language pathologist will be better able to estimate a patient's potential for language recovery with the aid of CT scanning and nuclear magnetic resonance in particular.

The assistance of Celia Bassich, Christine Fair, and Jeanette Rosenberg is gratefully acknowledged. A great deal is owed to Margaret S. Leslie for input regarding the psychosocial reactions of the patient and his family to aphasia.

## REFERENCES

Bardach JL: Psychological factors in hemiplegia. Paper presented at the American Physical Therapy Association, New York, 1963

Basso A, Capitani E, Luzzati C, Spinnler H: Intelligence and left hemisphere disease: The role of aphasia, apraxia and size of lesion. Brain 104: 721–734, 1981

Biorn-Hansen V: Social and emotional aspects of aphasia. J Speech Hear Dis 22:53–59, 1957

Blackman N: Group psychotherapy with aphasics. J Nerv Ment Dis 3:154–163, 1950

Borod JC, Goodglass H, Kaplan E: Normative data on the Boston Diagnostic Aphasia Examination, Parietal Lobe Battery, and the Boston Naming Test. J Clin Neuropsychol 2:209–216, 1980

Brain R: *Speech Disorders: Aphasia, Apraxia, and Agnosia*, 2nd ed. London: Butterworths, 1965

Buck M: *Dysphasia: Professional Guidance for Family and Patient*. Englewood Cliffs, NJ: Prentice Hall, 1968

Buxbaum J: Effect of nurturance on wives' appraisals of their marital satisfaction and the degree of their husband's aphasia. J Consult Psychol 31:240–243, 1967

Caine ED, Ebert MH, Weingartner H: An outline for the analysis of dementia: The memory disorder of Huntington's disease. Neurology (Minn) 27:1087–1092, 1977

Darley FL: *Evaluation of Appraisal Techniques in Speech and Language Pathology*. Reading, Mass: Addison-Wesley Publishing Co, 1979

Darley FL, Aronson AE, Brown JR: *Motor Speech Disorders*. Philadelphia WB Saunders Co, 1975

DeRenzi E, Vignolo L: The Token Test: A sensitive test to detect receptive disturbances in aphasics. Brain 85:665–678, 1962

Diller L: The problem of denial in rehabilitation. In Martin D, Downey J (eds): *Whither Diagnosis*. Boulder, Co: Pulver Press, 1963

Duffy JR, Keith RL, Shane H, Podraza BL: Performance of normal (non–brain-injured) adults on the Porch Index of Communicative Ability. In Brookshire RH (ed): *Clinical Aphasiology Conference Proceedings*. Minneapolis: BRK Publishers, 1976, pp 32–43

Eisenson J: Aphasic language modifications as a disruption of cultural verbal habits. ASHA 5:503–506, 1963

Eisenson J: Associated psychological problems of aphasic patients which interfere with vocational rehabilitation. Paper presented at the Workshop on the Vocational Rehabilitation Problems of the Patient with Aphasia, Western Michigan University, 1967

Festinger L: *A Theory at Cognitive Dissonance*. Chicago: Row, Peterson, 1957

Geschwind N: Disconnexion syndromes in animals and man. Brain 88:237–294, 1965

Geschwind N: Language and the brain. Sci Am 226:76–83, 1972

Geschwind N: Late changes in the nervous system: An overview. In Stein DG, Rosen JJ, Butters N (eds): *Plasticity and the Recovery of Function in the CNS*. New York: Academic Press, 1974, pp 467–508

Goodglass H, Kaplan E: *The Assessment of Aphasia and Related Disorders*. Philadelphia: Lea and Febiger, 1972

Holland AL: Estimates of aphasic patients' communicative performances in daily life (Contract No N01-NS-5-2317). Final Progress Report to the Communicative Disorders Program, National Institutes of Neurological and Communicative Disorders and Stroke. NIH DHHS, 1978

Holland AL: *Communicative abilities in daily living*. Baltimore: University Park Press, 1980

Holland AL: Observing functional communication of aphasic adults. J Speech Hear Dis 47:50–52, 1982

Karlin IW, Eisenson J, Hirschenfang S, Miller MH: A multievaluational study of aphasic and non-aphasic right hemiplegic patients. J Speech Hear Dis 24:369–379, 1959

Keenan SS, Brassel EG: A study of factors related to prognosis for individual aphasic patients. J Speech Hear Dis 39:257–269, 1974

Kent RD, Rosenbek JC: Acoustic patterns of apraxia of speech. J Speech Hear Res, in press

Kertesz A: *Aphasia and Associated Disorders: Taxonomy, Localization and Recovery*. New York: Grune & Stratton, 1979

Kreindler A, Fradis A: *Performance in Aphasia: A Neurodynamical Diagnostic and Psychological Study*. (Collection Neuropsychologia.) Paris: Gauthier-Villars, 1968

Ludlow CL: Recovery from aphasia: A foundation for treatment. In Sullivan M, Kommers MS (eds): *Rationale for Adult Aphasia Therapy*. Omaha: University of Nebraska Press, 1977, pp 98–134

Ludlow CL, Swisher LP: The audiometric evaluation of adult aphasics. J Speech Hear Res 14:535–543, 1971

Luria AR: *Restoration of Function After Brain Injury*. New York: Macmillan Co, 1963

Malone RL: Expressed attitudes of families of aphasics. J Speech Hear Dis 34:146–150, 1969

Miller MH: Audiologic evaluation of aphasic patients. J Speech Hear Dis 25:333–339, 1960

Mohr JP: Rapid amelioration of motor aphasia. Arch Neurol 28:77–82, 1973

Mohr JP: Broca's area and Broca's aphasia. In Whitaker H, Whitaker H (eds): Studies in Neurologistics, vol I. New York: Academic Press, 1976, pp 201–236

Naeser MA, Alexander MP, Helm-Estabrooks N, Levine HL, Laughlin SA, Geschwind N: Aphasia with predominantly subcortical lesion sites: Description of three capsular/putaminal aphasia syndromes. Arch Neurol 39:2–14, 1982

Naeser MA, Hayward RW, Laughlin SA, Zatz LM: Quantitative CT scan studies in aphasia. 1. Infarct size and CT numbers. Brain Lang 12:140–164, 1981

Porch BE: *Porch Index of Communicative Ability, vol I. Theory and Development*. Palo Alto, Calif: Consulting Psychologists Press, 1967

Porch BE, Wertz RT, Collins MJ: A statistical procedure for predicting recovery from aphasia. In Porch BE (ed): *Clinical Aphasiology Conference Proceedings*. New Orleans: Veterans Administration, 1974, pp 27–37

Sarno MT, Silverman M, Sands E: Speech therapy and language recovery in severe aphasia. J Speech Hear Res 13:609–623, 1970

Schuell H, Jenkins JJ, Jimenez-Pabon E: *Aphasia in Adults*. New York: Harper and Row, 1964

Spreen O, Benton AL: *Neurosensory Center Comprehensive Examination for Aphasia*, (rev ed) Victoria, BC: University of Victoria, 1969

Stoicheff ML: Motivating instructions and language performance of dysphasic subjects. J Speech Hear Res 3:75–85, 1960

Terr M, Goetzinger C, Konsey C: A study of hearing acuity in adult aphasic and cerebral palsied subjects. Arch Otolaryngal 67:447–455, 1958

Traveras J: Preliminary results on the application of nuclear magnetic resonance imaging. Special presentation to the National Advisory Neurological and Communicative Disorders and Stroke Council. NIH, Bethesda, Maryland, January 1982

Turnbloom M, Myers JS: Group discussion programs with the families of aphasic patients. J Speech Hear Dis 17:393–396, 1952

Vignolo LA: Evolution of aphasia and language rehabilitation: A retrospective exploratory study. Cortex 1:344–367, 1964

Warren RL, Datta KD: The return of speech four and one-half years post head injury. In Brookshire RH (ed): *Clinical Aphasiology: Proceedings of the Conference*. Brookshire, 1981, pp 301–308

Webster EJ, Newhoff M: Intervention with families of communicatively impaired adults. In Beasley DS, Davis GA (eds): *Aging: Communication Processes and Disorders*. New York: Grune & Stratton, 1981, pp 229–240

Weingartner H, Caine ED, Ebert MH: Imagery, encoding and the retrieval of information from memory: Some specific encoding retrieval changes in Huntington's disease. J Abnorm Psych 88:52–88, 1979

Weingartner H, Caine ED, Ebert MH: Encoding processes, learning and recall in Huntington's disease. Adv Neurol 23:215–225, 1979b

Weinstein ÉA, Kahn RL: *Denial of Illness*. Springfield, Mass: Charles C Thomas, 1955

Weisenberg TH, McBride KE: *Aphasia*. New York: Commonwealth Fund, 1935

Wepman JM: Aphasic therapy: Some "relative" comments and some purely personal prejudices. In Black JW, Jancosek EG (eds): *Proceedings of the Conference in Language Retraining for Aphasics*. Columbus, Ohio: Ohio State University, 1968

Wertz RT, Rosenbek JC, Collins MJ: Identification of apraxia of speech from PICA verbal tests and selected oral-verbal apraxia tests. In Wertz RT, Collins MJ (eds): *Clinical Aphasiology Conference Proceedings*. Madison, Wis: Veterans Administration, 1972, pp 175–190

Zurif EB: Language mechanisms: A neuropsychological perspective. Am Sci 68:305–311, 1980

# 6

# ISSUES IN LANGUAGE DISORDERS: CONSIDERATIONS OF CAUSE, MAINTENANCE, AND CHANGE

*ANTHONY S. BASHIR*
*KARL C. KUBAN*
*SANDRA N. KLEINMAN*
*ANNEBELLE SCAVUZZO*

Language disorders is a general term that designates a heterogeneous group of problems characterized by varying degrees and types of deficits in the comprehension, production, and use of language. The disorders are associated with a diverse group of developmental problems and medical conditions. The implications of developmental language disorders for future educational success have recently been the subject of study.

It is generally agreed that there exists a group of children who evidence normal hearing and normal aspects of nonverbal intelligence, but who have persistent problems in the acquisition and development of language. These children have been described as "congenital aphasics," "developmental aphasics," or "children with specific language learning disorders." Who are they? What are the causes of their disorders? What happens to them? The issues involved in answering these questions are the subjects of this chapter.

## DEVELOPMENTAL LANGUAGE DISORDERS: ISSUES IN CAUSE

Developmental language disorders are described in the following manner. The child shows evidence of slowed or altered acquisition of language structures; this is realized through an analysis of the child's utterances or by an analysis of performance profiles on test protocols. The child must demonstrate normal hearing and normal intelligence, that is, perform within one standard deviation of the mean on performance test measurements. The general nature of the child's affective system must be appropriate, with no major disruption in interactional patterns.

The above description, except for purposes of initial diagnosis, is of little value in the long run, since it does not address the processes of language acquisition in children with language disorders nor address issues of intervention. Neither does it address issues of similarities or differences in the acquisition of language between children with and those without impairment of language. Similarly, the description does not address issues related to differences across subgroups of children with language disorders of varying origins.

The study of etiologic factors must focus on the different influences of causal events on the processes involved in the development of language. Each underlying process may be regulated by a different maturational timetable. This is true in language acquisition, which is seen as a hierarchically learned set of abilities over time (Chomsky, 1969; Brown, 1973; Menyuk, 1977). There is reason to believe that different etiologic factors in language disorders may affect developmental rate, emergence of component processes, or both to different degrees and in various combinations. These quantitative differences in rate and variation, in turn, induce qualitative differences in the structure of behavior. The differences in performance profiles across different subgroups of language disordered children may not simply imply specific neurologic deficits per se. Differences in performance may also reflect the consequence of heterochronous timetables in development of component processes. Such differences are developmental in nature and the differences will be seen when we examine patterns of behavior across different domains of cognitive, linguistic, and affective adaptation.

The concept of heterochronism may be basic to our understanding of the late sequelae of early childhood language disorders. Gould (1977) argues that the time in which a morphologic characteristic emerges in ontogeny is as important to defining a species-typical feature as is the genetic potential for the appearance of that feature. As such, either the accelerated or delayed emergence of a particular feature is itself sufficient to induce variations in structure of the organism. This would be so even if the genetic basis for these features remains unaltered. Therefore, Gould argues that the isochrony or heterochrony of developmental clocks for distinctive characteristics induces variations in overt structure.

By analogy, we might pose the following questions. How does the presence of deviant linguistic strategies induce variations in the child's acquisition of new structures presented by the curriculum? What influences do time-displaced acquisitions or normal syntactic and morphologic rules have on the functioning of the child with a language disorder when this child is asked to participate in learning activities based on developmental readiness and presuppositions about the presence of certain linguistic knowledge? Aspects of these questions will be addressed in another part of this chapter. Answers to these and other questions will facilitate our understanding of the natural history of children with language disorders. Similarly, an understanding of the influence of etiologic factors will enhance our knowledge of differences in developmental rate and emergence of behaviors within a developmental timetable.

Numerous reasons exist for the study of etiologic agents. We are confronted daily with the prognostic problems involved with outcome in "high-risk babies." We all share a responsibility for prevention of catastrophic outcome. Our planning, design, and implementation of early intervention and therapeutic programs are based on amelioration, or "normalization," of outcome behaviors. It is true that our planning and subsequent treatment do not necessarily depend upon a knowledge of etiology per se, but rather, on an understanding of the cognitive and linguistic status of the child (Miller and colleagues, 1978).

However, knowledge of primary etiologic factors (whether these be perinatal events, structural dysgenesis, asymmetry of brain development, effects of subsequent neurotrophic disease, other encephalopathies, central nervous system trauma, or genetic or biochemical alteration) allows us to postulate mechanisms to explain overt behavior. While this statement may appear to reflect an extreme biologic deterministic position, it is not intended to do so. Rather, it is an approach to examine how changes in the central nervous system give rise to alteration in rate and eventual emergence of behaviors within an interactional context. We start with the a priori assumption that the linguistic and psychologic measures by which language disorders are defined are not represented specifically in brain structures. The measures are intended to examine manifestations of underlying component processes. Information about primary etiologic agent is important, not because there is necessarily a one-to-one correspondence between specific causes of language disorders and their behavioral manifestations, but because the various causes may influence differently the ability of the brain to recover from damage (plasticity) or influence the rate or eventual emergence of component processes. Such variations and limitations, in turn, will induce structural differences in the development and organization of behavior.

## ISSUES IN NEUROPLASTICITY

Developmental plasticity continues to be the focus of debate (Gollin, 1981). Rudel (1978) provides an extensive review of issues in neuroplasticity. Based on her work and that of others the following issues merit consideration when discussing issues in neuroplasticity: the relationship of outcomes and the age of onset of lesion (Kennard, 1938, 1942); the relationship of age at the time of damage and the age at the time of testing for the ability to perform complex tasks (Goldman, 1979); the relationship of sex differences and experience on recovery (Goldman, 1977); the relationship of future functional abilities of areas of the brain usurped in the recovery process and the neural requirements for reorganization of behavior (Goldman, 1977, 1979); and the differences in neuronal growth patterns after damage (Schneider, 1977, 1979).

The work of Goldman suggests that central lesions may provoke developmental problems that emerge subsequent to a clinically silent period. Since behaviors mediated by specific brain areas may not emerge normally until a later developmental stage, identification of injuries to these areas may not be discerned until the behavior is expected or required. Alternatively, early in life the behaviors associated with a given brain area may be successfully mediated by other brain structures capable of similar function. As task complexity increases, the ability of the usurped area to support that level of task complexity decreases.

This idea is seen in the work of Hurt and Teuber (cited by Rudel, 1978) on later recovery of visual field and linguistic skills in younger and older men with penetrating brain injuries. The younger men, under 26 years of age, recovered visual field and language abilities to a greater degree than did those over 26. However, the recovery in all groups was greater in the domain of visual field deficits than in the recovery of language. Rudel uses Vygotsky's notion—that the more complex the task the less recovery of function—to explain the report of Hurt and Teuber. It is specifically the ideas of late emerging abilities and the eventual achievement of complex tasks that are critical to our understanding of children with language disorders.

## ISSUES OF CENTRAL NERVOUS SYSTEM DAMAGE

While not all language impairment is due to central nervous system damage, the work of Rudel and Denckla (1974) and the recent work of Johnston and colleagues (1981) suggest that in some language impaired children unilateral or bilateral hemispheric dysfunction may be present. The ability to sustain language function following complete removal of the left hemisphere in older children and adults has been established (Basser, 1962; Milner, 1974). The ability to mediate language, however, is not developed equally in both hemispheres (Dennis and Kohn, 1975; Dennis, 1980). Zaidel (1979), in a summary of his work, suggests that the right hemisphere has the ability to mediate lexic and some syntactic comprehension. In adults, both right and left hemispheres show activity during speech. Using electrical mapping methods, Penfield and Roberts (1959) have shown that speech can be elicited by stimulation of either the right or left hemispheres. Recent work by Larsen and colleagues (1978) and Lasser and colleagues (1978), in which they measured blood flow rates in various brain regions, provides evidence that regional activation occurs in both hemispheres during automatic speech. While we continue to focus on the unique properties of the right and left hemisphere functions in language, Wolff (1977) reminds us that "the developmental analysis of interhemispheric cooperation and competition may be as critical to an understanding of brain behavior relationships as the study of lateralized function *per se*" (p. 12).

Most studies note that early left hemisphere lesions are not sufficient to account for permanent language deficits; this is supported by the observation that left hemisphere infarcts do not lead to a greater incidence of permanent language disorders than do right hemisphere infarcts (Basser, 1962). Although Basser's original study has been criticized, Annette's (1973) more recent study did not find a significant difference in the incidence of language disorders among those children who develop their infarcts at less than 13 months of age when left hemiplegics were compared with right hemiplegics. Woods and Teuber (1978), reporting on a series of 65 children who suffered unilateral cerebral infarcts, include only 1 case that presented at less than 18 months. However, Woods and Carey (1979) note that among 11 patients studied for left hemispheric infarcts incurred during the perinatal period, none had specific language deficits, although as a group they were mildly impaired intellectually. The controversy concerning the differences in effects of early and late hemispheric lesions on language development has been summarized by Ludlow (1980) and Kinsbourne (1979).

Although most studies suggest that early left hemisphere lesions are insufficient to account for permanent language deficits, Rankin and associates (1981), in a study of language in right and left hemiplegics, reported different rates of acquisition of speech favor'ng left hemiplegics. Left hemiplegics performed better for tasks involving production, vocabulary, comprehension, syntactic comprehension, and formulation.

In a study of speech and language abilities of 318 children with cerebral palsy (Bashir, 1968), specific language disorders were found to be present in 49 of the 318 children; this small number of cases probably reflected the use of a conservative definition of language disorder. No significant difference was found in the frequency of language disorders among children with different types of cerebral palsy. When the children with congential spastic hemiplegia and language disorders were considered, the occurrence of language disorders in congenital right spastic hemiplegics did not differ significantly from that in congenital left spastic hemiplegics.

For this group of children, a prediction of language disorder on the basis of laterality of involvement or on the type of cerebral palsy was not warranted. What appeared to be important with regard to language disorders in this group of cerebral palsied children was the presence of bilateral alteration of the central nervous system without regard to manifest laterality of motor involvement. The basis for this supposition was found in an examination of the perinatal histories of those children with language impairment and cerebral palsy. Thirty-nine of 44 children either had anoxia or were born prematurely. The majority of congenital cerebral palsied children with a language disorder had histories of perinatal events that are presumed to have a bilateral effect on the central nervous system. This was true even if the motor manifestations of the central nervous system alterations were unilateral.

Other studies have implicated anoxia producing events as important antecedents in the history of children presenting with specific language disorders (Goldstein and colleagues, 1958; Rutherford and Perlstein, 1963; Ehrlich, 1973). These studies and others support the notion that bihemispheric compromise is a basis for developmental language disorders. Support for this hypothesis is derived also from pathologic studies (Landau and colleagues, 1960; Gilles, 1982) and from recent studies of the neurologic status of some children with specific language disorders (Johnston and colleagues, 1981). Furthermore, acquired aphasia of childhood has been associated with bihemispheric convulsive disorders in some children (Worster-Draught, 1964, 1971; Landau and Kleffner, 1957; Gascon and colleagues, 1973).

Application of brain electrical mapping (BEAM), a method for extending the clinical use of the electroencephalogram and evoked potential data (Duffy and associates, 1979), provides further support for the effects of bihemispheric involvement. In a series of studies of dyslexic boys and normal controls using BEAM methodology, Duffy and his coinvestigators have shown that aberrant physiology in the dyslexic boys was not restricted to a single locus. Rather, four discrete regions of differences involving both hemispheres, left more than right, were present in the children with dyslexia when compared with normal controls (Duffy and colleagues, 1980a,b).

In summary, it appears that bihemispheric dysfunction underlies central nervous system based developmental language disorders. This may occur as a consequence of direct damage to both hemispheres or damage to one hemisphere when associated with physiologic dysfunction of the contralateral side. We suggest that bihemispheric dysfunction restricts the brain's plasticity and interferes with the mediation of language functions, otherwise potentially available with strictly unilateral damage.

The importance of the continued study of primary etiologic agent has been argued. We have chosen to select two etiologic conditions to review briefly: prematurity and sex chromosome abnormalities.

## ISSUES IN PREMATURITY OF BIRTH

As previously indicated, studies have implicated anoxia producing events as po-tentially important etiologic factors in developmental language disorders. With the advent of the modern intensive care nursery, the incidence of asphyxia is relatively low. Nonetheless, recent reports and our own clinical experience suggest that very low birth weight infants, while usually spared major neurologic deficits, evidence an increased incidence of language disorders.

The current era in neonatal care has been characterized by a marked increase in the number of very low birth weight infants who survive the neonatal period. Between 1947 and 1968, 40 to 51 percent of infants weighing between 1000 and 1500 gm survived, in comparison with present survival rates of up to 90 percent (Lubchenko and associates, 1972; Francis-Williams and Davies, 1974; Stewart and Reynolds, 1974; Hack and colleagues, 1979). Similarly, infants born weighing between 500 to 1000 gm now have improved survival rates of 50 to 60 percent (Stewart and Reynolds, 1974; Schreiner and colleagues, 1980).

Long-term morbidity rates for premature infants changed dramatically during the same time period. Early studies reported that abnormalities such as cerebral palsy and mental retardation occurred in the majority of surviving infants (Lubchenco and associates, 1972; Drillien, 1961, 1972). The incidence of such outcomes was 48 percent in the early 1970s (Fitzhardinge, 1980), and at the present time is approximately 15 to 25 percent (Stewart and Reynolds, 1974; Hack and colleagues, 1979; Fitzhardinge, 1980). In recent years, increased attention has focused on more subtle yet still disabling handicaps, including deficits in hearing, vision, speech, language, and learning disorders (Fitzhardinge, 1980; Fitzhardinge and Ramsay, 1973; Dunn and colleagues, 1980; Kitchen and colleagues, 1980; Saint-Anne Dargassis, 1977).

Specifically, studies examining the speech and language skills of children born at less than 36 weeks' gestation or children with very low birth weights report the presence of differences in communicative abilities when these children are compared with normal controls. Follow-up studies of premature infants conducted in the early 1960s found that the attainment of developmental milestones occurred later in life when the premature children were compared with normal controls. In addition, these children had a significantly higher incidence of communicative disorders (Kastein and Fowler, 1959; Rabinovitch and associates, 1961).

In a study of oral language performance skills of 51 premature children and 55 controls, deHirsch and colleagues (1964) concluded that the premature children performed significantly below their controls on measures of mean length of utterance, number of words used, verbal definitions, sentence elaboration, single word understanding, and word-finding abilities. They concluded, however, that the differences noted in language functioning resulted from the premature infant's "lingering neurophysiologic immaturity." This conclusion implies that as the premature infant develops, neurophysiologic immaturity will resolve and the differences noted in the child's speech and language behaviors will normalize. The idea that the differences in the acquisition of speech and language abilities of premature children reflects a delay, rather than a deficit, is seen in the results of the Collaborative Perinatal Project of the National Institute of Neurological and Communicative Disorders and Stroke (Lassman and associates, 1980). This study of premature children (defined as less than 36 weeks' gestation or weighing less than 2500 gm) suggested that the children did not have significant speech and language deficits and concluded that "a majority of prematures . . . eventually reached developmental levels that are within normal limits" (p. 319).

In contrast, the results of other studies indicate that the outcome for speech and language development in the premature child is different from that of normal children (Pape and colleagues, 1978; Shiddhaye and colleagues, 1972; Calame and colleagues, 1976). For example, Ehrlich and associates (1973) noted prominent dysfunction in word-finding abilities and memory for sentences, as well as speech

sound production deficits among a group of 5-year-old children who had high-risk neonatal histories. These deficits occurred primarily in children with histories of respiratory distress syndrome, with birth weights less than 2500 gm, and with shortened gestational age.

Fitzhardinge and Ramsay (1973) noted increased problems in communication abilities in a cohort of 32 premature infants. The disorders, including persistence of infantile articulation, immaturity of vocabulary, and reduced language skills, were seen in 17 of the children; only 10 of these children had normal intelligence. Eleven of the 17 children had deficits that persisted into the school years.

The results of recent studies emphasize that the problems of the premature child may persist through the school years and are seen as specific learning disabilities (Fitzhardinge, 1980; Fitzhardinge and Ramsay, 1973; Kitchen and associates, 1980). Fitzhardinge (1980), in a study of 65 children whose birth weights were less than 1500 gm, noted that among the children who had finished 1 year of school, 45 percent were failing consistently a major subject or required special classes in school. Among children with an intelligence quotient between 100 and 115, 33 percent were having learning disabilities. Kitchen and colleagues (1980) reported on an 8-year follow-up study of 158 infants whose birth weights were between 1000 and 1500 gm and who were born between 1966 and 1970. In this study, 26 percent of the children had reading accuracy or comprehension of at least one year below grade appropriate levels. While these studies of school performance among children with birth weights less than 1500 gm do not address the issue of the relationship between disorders of speech and language and later school failure, there are clear indications that children with early disruption in language acquisition are at risk for later school failure (Strominger and Bashir, 1977; Aram and Nation, 1980).

As previously noted, with the advent of the modern intensive care nursery the incidence of asphyxia is relatively low. On the other hand, subependymal and intraventricular hemorrhage (SEH-IVH) occurs in 40 percent of babies born with a gestational age of less than 34 weeks. However, of these infants, 30 percent are asymptomatic (Ahmann and colleagues, 1980; Volpe, 1977; Lazzara and colleagues, 1980; Bejar and colleagues, 1980; Krishnamoorthy and colleagues, 1979). The overall mortality rate in infants with SEH-IVH is 25 to 50 percent, and among survivors 25 to 75 percent have neurologic sequelae, including hydrocephalus (Hambleton and Wigglesworth, 1976; Bejar and associates, 1980; Krishnamoorthy and associates, 1979).

The source of SEH-IVH in very low birth weight babies is the germinal matrix, from which centrifugal migration of glia and, to a lesser extent, neuronal cells occurs. Although SEH-IVH may be either unilateral or bilateral, brains that are thought to have a unilateral site on CT scan or ultrasound may demonstrate contralateral petechial hemorrhages on pathologic study. In addition, bilateral vasoconstriction may occur with unilateral SEH. Clearly, the long-term developmental effects of hemorrhage in the germinal matrix are not known, although permanent bilateral cytoarchitectonic changes may occur secondary to disruption of glial migration. The study of this "new generation" of babies will provide us with important information on etiologic factors and the developmental disorders of language.

## SEX CHROMOSOME ANOMALIES

The study of the relationship that exists between sex chromosome aneuploids in males (XXY boys) and females (XXX girls) and aspects of development has revealed the presence of specific language disorders (Walzer and associates, 1978; Graham, 1981). Following the original report of Walzer and colleagues (1978), extensive study of the XXY boys during the early school years revealed persistent problems in certain aspects of comprehension and oral language formulation abilities (Graham, 1981; Graham and colleagues,

1981; Walzer and colleagues, 1982). Receptive language skills were age appropriate for the XXY boys, but problems in the comprehension of complex syntax was below age expectation. Significant differences between the control group and the XXY boys were found in the ability to follow directions with increasing numbers of critical units. Expressive language abilities were relatively more impaired than receptive abilities. Problems in the appropriate use of syntax and in word-finding abilities and problems in narrative organization were documented. In addition, the XXY group evidenced reduced abilities in phonic knowledge, word analysis skills, oral reading achievement, and spelling abilities.

The possibility that pathologic variations in sex chromosome complements may be associated with specific developmental language disorders and changes in the central nervous system is raised when the XXY data are considered in light of the findings of Silbert and associates (1977) on older patients with Turner's syndrome (XO). These patients did not evidence language problems but rather problems in visual spatial abilities. Variations in male and female performance are emerging as potentially important variables in language impairment (Strominger, 1982). Consideration of these issues is important not only for prognosis but for the appreciation of differences in outcome.

## DEVELOPMENTAL LANGUAGE DISORDERS: ISSUES IN WHO

The question of who is to be called language disordered occasions extensive debate (Leonard, 1972). On the basis of research, groups of children are defined who demonstrate deviant patterns of production strategies (Menyuk, 1964; Lee, 1966), time displaced acquisition of normal syntactic or morphologic structures (Moorhead and Ingram, 1973; Johnston and Schery, 1976); and reduced frequency of use of structures (Leonard, 1972). These findings are of interest when compared with the findings of Thomas and Walmsley

(1976) in their study of individuals with learning disabilities. They indicate that their 10- to 16-year-old students evidenced either delayed or attenuated linguistic development within a normal progression or evidenced aberrant development. For individuals with learning disabilities, difficulties in comprehension (Wiig and Semel, 1976) or production (Vogel, 1974; Wiig and Semel, 1976), alteration in naming and retrieval abilities (Denckla and Rudel, 1976; Wolf, 1979), or reduced rate of naming (Wiig and associates, 1982) are but a few of the persistent problems in language abilities. The relationship between language knowledge and production has given rise to a reformulation of the problem of dyslexia that emphasizes a verbal deficit hypothesis as opposed to a perceptual causative hypothesis (Velluntino, 1977). The extensive research findings supporting this reformulation are presented in Velluntino (1977) and need not be reviewed here. Similarly, Johnston (1982) has presented a review and critique of research in language disordered children, and the reader is referred to her work for its clear presentation of the issues.

The point to be made in this chapter is the similarity between findings in language disorders and learning disabilities. This is true when follow-up studies and classification system are considered. Are we speaking about a group of children who, by virtue of time and learning context, are called by different names but who in reality evidence a continuum of deficits in language learning? We believe the answer to be yes. Problems in language use and naming abilities have been shown to be valid predictors of subsequent problems in reading and writing (deHirsch and Jansky, 1972). It should come as no surprise, then, that some preschool language impaired children subsequently develop problems in the acquisition of the language arts curricula.

Longitudinal studies of children with language disorders have focused on case reports (Berry, 1968; Weiner, 1974; Rawson, 1968) or follow-up studies of children with preschool speech and language problems (Griffiths, 1966; deAjuriaguerra and colleagues, 1976; Garvey and Gordon, 1973; Sheridan and Peckham, 1975). These studies indicated the presence of persistent problems in school learning experienced by some of the preschool language impaired children. In a follow-up study, Hall and Tomblin (1978) determined that 50 percent of their language impaired subjects continued to exhibit communication problems in adulthood. Only 1 of the 18 speech impaired individuals had persistent problems. Persistent, chronic problems in the acquisition of reading and writing characterize some children with preschool language problems (Strominger and Bashir, 1977; Wolpaw, Nation, and Aram, 1977; Aram and Nation, 1980; King and colleagues, 1982). The results of the Collaborative Perinatal Project (Lassman and associates, 1980) implicate early failure in language acquisition in later problems with reading and writing. Children who evidenced problems on the three-year language protocol were two to three times more likely to fail on the written communication section of the eight-year protocol.

Menyuk (1981) has considered three positions on the relationship between the development of oral language processes and written language processing. From her study she concludes:

". . . the possible nature of the difficulty in oral language development will affect the nature of the reading problem in particular children. Some children may be delayed in the development of semantic-syntactic structures or both. They will, therefore, have difficulty in reading structures that are unavailable to them. Other children will have difficulty in assessing or realizing semantic syntactic structures or both, although these structures are available to them. They, therefore, will consistently have difficulty reading. Still other children have difficulty in integrating and recalling relations over conversations or stories. . . . The above are only some of the possible relationships that might exist. . . ." (p. 63).

Menyuk's summary is of interest because it notes the interrelationship between aspects of oral language and written language, a position earlier stressed by Johnson and Myklebust (1974). We hypothesize, then, that outcomes for language impaired children will differ as a function of the underlying disorders inherent in the child's linguistic and cognitive systems.

## DEVELOPMENTAL LANGUAGE DISORDERS; ISSUES IN HETEROGENEITY

Clinical experience and recent research findings suggest that children with language disorders do not represent a homogeneous group of patients with a single outcome. Johnson and Myklebust (1974) stressed this point in their early work. For example, using factor analytic approaches, Aram and Nation (1975) defined six patterns of language impairment. Heterogeneity of disorders also characterizes the classification studies of dyslexia (Mattis and associates, 1975; Denckla, 1979). Strominger (1982), in a follow-up study of 38 preschool children with language disorders, has successfully used the categories specified by Denckla to classify those children who evidenced persistent problems in oral language and reading. This is most promising, because Strominger used a protocol that was different in detail from that used by Denckla.

Our clinical experience to date suggests that four major groups of children presenting with preschool impairment of language are at risk for later school difficulty. Briefly these are: (1) children who present with mixed receptive and expressive disorders; these are revealed as varying problems in the comprehension of single words and the comprehension of differing sentence structures, especially complex or embedded structures; they also demonstrate varying problems in production; (2) children who present with oral language formulation problems consisting of deficits in the production of syntax, regulation of morphologic rules, dysnomia, problems in the organization and maintenance of narrative or storytelling abilities, and differences in verbal response between solicited and unsolicited speaking situations; (3) children who present with dysnomia

but without specific problems in the production of syntax or morphology, but who may also demonstrate problems in narrative organization and maintenance and who have difficulty in storytelling; and (4) children with phonologic disorders associated with problems in the voluntary patterning and sequencing of oral movements for purposes of speech sound production. Within each of these major groups we believe there are subgroups yet to be formally determined.

We cannot as yet predict those who will succeed and those who will encounter difficulty in reading. Case by case management and follow-up are necessary to ensure appropriate therapy and effective use of adaptive and modified curriculum. Similarly, we cannot as yet predict type and degree of reading problem, although differences are seen on a case by case basis. Aram and Nation (1980) express concern about the possibility of replication as a consequence of the specific protocol used to establish their groups. The particular test battery and the population from which the research samples are drawn may determine and potentially limit our view of language disorders (Stark and Tallal, 1981; Luick and associates, 1982). Careful design of prospective, longitudinal studies will enhance our ability to determine and clarify the reality of various kinds of language disorders in children. We can hope for future improvement in our prognostic abilities with regard to type and degree of subsequent problems in read and written language. Clearly, we are only beginning to understand the diversity of patterns that represent language disorders in children and their implications.

## DEVELOPMENTAL LANGUAGE DISORDERS: ISSUES IN NATURAL HISTORY

Cazden states that "language poses multiple problems for education because it is both curriculum content and learning environment, both the object of knowledge and a medium through which other knowledge is acquired" (p. 135). This position is germane to our understanding of preschool language problems that extend into the school years, causing the child to remain at risk for experiencing problems or failure in learning. The planning of educational curricula assumes the learner's ability to access his or her theory of how language operates (Mattingly, 1972). It is under this assumption that all children, including language disordered children, enter school.

Clinical experience has shaped the perspective from which we view the interdependence between language acquisition and the academic achievement of children with language disorders. These children gain language competence to different levels and at varying rates, which may or may not be synchronous with the demands of the elementary, middle, or high school curricula. In fact, the asynchrony of language acquisition and academic learning becomes important in both the maintenance of or onset of other language and/or learning disabilities. Either outcome is reflected in the ability or inability of these same children to demonstrate successful learning of other language based information (for example, social studies, health, geography, reading, math, and so on).

Our clinical experience also suggests that children with language disorders will "look differently" as a function of the contexts of learning, the inherent demands placed on the child by the curriculum and the assumptions made about the child as learner. From time to time the child will seem suddenly even more severely involved. This is especially true during the transition from third to fourth grade when "learning to read becomes reading to learn." Basic prerequisites of automatization and fast application of skills, the requirement of self-imposed organizational strategies, and the management of multiples, such as, multisyllabic words, multiple word meanings, and coreferences, must be met. The vocabulary assumed present and available in the child forms the basis for the increased demands for understanding various content subjects. This is a potential problem for children who may show reduction in the rate of growth of vocabulary as

well as in their overall naming and retrieval strategies (Wolf, 1979).

As the curriculum content changes and the style and methods of the teacher change in relationship to the learner, so do the assumptions about the knowledge and skills of the learner. The child with language problems continues to be "at risk" for failure in school. In many instances these factors will cause a seemingly abated disorder to resurface again and again in different ways. In others, that which was previously camouflaged now becomes apparent; for example, the child who has mastered basic skills now demonstrates comprehension problems in reading (Kleinman and Scavuzzo, 1981). For instance, the transitions from kindergarten to first grade, from third to fourth grade, and from fifth to sixth grade appear to be particularly difficult. Each grade shift assumes that the child can apply, extend, and elaborate previously acquired skills, strategies, and information.

The child is expected to adapt to changes in classroom behavior expectations as well as changes in the curriculum. The crisis for the child is precipitated by many factors. Among these are the following: a marked increase in new vocabulary; increased length and complexity of sentence structures; changes in text composition; problems of story organization; increased demands for oral and written production; demands for the application of information during problem-solving; requirements for increased speed of performance; and demands for self-directed, independent work habits. Additional changes occur in teacher style and expectations about the learner. The cumulative effect of these factors will create new problems for the child with language disorders.

The manifestation of the disorder changes, and so do the services provided for the child. The language disordered child who has demonstrated early problems in language acquisition may either have received speech and language therapy or have been placed in a preschool program. The child enters school and the services of the speech and language pathologist are continued. As time goes by the child may evidence problems in the acquisition of appropriate strategies to break the code in reading and the child *becomes* a remedial reader. Subsequent failure in written language, handwriting, reading comprehension, and so on yields to a new label of "learning disabilities," and the services of yet another group of professionals are added. Therefore, although the surface aspects of the original speech/language problems seem to abate, other service providers will be responsible for the child. The child is seen as having "new problems." Finally, persistent problems in the acquisition of decoding strategies will distance the child from other aspects of the curriculum. Problems in comprehension begin to surface. A debate occurs about retention of the child, and in light of the child's already fragile image, the child is promoted with psychologic counseling added to the program (Kleinman and Scavuzzo, 1981).

As the child and the manifestations of the child's problems change over time, so do our perspectives on the child's needs. The perspectives require us to develop and continually reassess our programs of intervention. Insights into the child's needs require that treatment programs be coordinated with the adaptive and modified curricula that are provided for the child. If we are to meet effectively the needs of children and young adults with language disorders, we must expect the continuous nature of their disabilities and provide effective models of intervention, planning, and cooperation with educators and families. Advocacy on behalf of individuals with language disorders is essential.

## SUMMARY

This chapter has considered some issues specific to cause, maintenance, and change in developmental language disorders of childhood. Developmental language disorders are regarded as a heterogeneous group of problems with potentially different outcomes. In reviewing issues in cause, we have noted that different etiologic factors in language disorders may affect developmental rate, emergence of component processes, or both to different degrees and in various combinations. Different causes may influence the ability of the central nervous system to recover from damage or influence the rate or emergence of various abilities.

We have briefly reviewed issues in central nervous system damage and commented on prematurity of birth and sex chromosome anomalies as they relate to developmental language disorders. We have stressed the importance of similar findings in developmental language disorders and learning disabilities, emphasizing that a continuum of deficits exists for some preschool language impaired children who later evidence learning disabilities.

Outcomes for language impaired children appear to differ as a function of the underlying disorders inherent in the child's linguistic and cognitive systems. Children with language impairments "look differently" over time. The changing outlook for children with language disorders reflects the interaction among the child, the demands of the curricula, and assumptions made about the child's ability to apply, extend, and elaborate previously acquired skills, strategies, and information.

## REFERENCES

Ahmann PA, Lazzara A, Dykes FS, Brann AW Jr, Schwartz FJ: Intraventricular hemorrhage in the high risk preterm infant: Incidence and outcome. Ann Neurol 7:118–124, 1980

Annett M: Laterality of childhood hemiplegia and the growth of speech and intelligence. Cortex 9:4–39, 1973

Aram DM, Natton JE: Preschool language disorders and subsequent language and academic difficulties. J Communic Dis 13:159–170, 1980

Baker L, Cantwell DP, Mattison RE: Behavior problems in children with pure speech disorders and in children with combined speech and language disorders. J Abnorm Child Psychol 8:245–256, 1980

Bashir AS: Etiologic agents associated with communication disorders in 418 children with known central nervous system dysfunction. Doctoral dissertation, Department of Communication Disorders, School of Speech, Northwestern University, Evanston, Illinois 1968

Basser LS: Hemiplegia of early onset and the faculty of speech, with special reference to the effects of hemispherectomy. Brain 85:427–460, 1962

Bejar, R, Curbelo V, Coen RW, Leopold G, Hames H, Gluck L: Diagnosis of intraventricular and intracerebral hemorrhages by ultrasound studies of an infant's brain through the fontanelles and sutures. Pediatrics 66:661–673, 1980

Brown JW, Hacaen H: Lateralization and language representation. Neurology 26:183–189, 1976

Brown R: A First Language—The Early Stages. Cambridge, Mass: Harvard University Press, 1973

Bryan T, Donahue M, Pearl R: Learning disabled children's communicative competence and social relationships. In Language, Learning and Reading Disabilities: A New Decade. Preliminary Proceedings of an Interdisciplinary Conference. Department of Communication Arts and Sciences, Queens College of The City University of New York, 1981, pp 67–77

Calame A, Reymond-Goni I, Maherzi M, Roulet M, Marchand C, Prod'hom LS: Psychological and neurodevelopment outcome of high risk newborn infants. Helvet Paediat Acta 31:287–297, 1976

Cantwell D, Baker L: Psychiatric disorders in children with speech and language retardation. Arch Gen Psychiat 34:583–591, 1977

Cazden CB: Problems for education: Language as curriculum content and learning environment. Daedalus 102(3): 135–148, 1973

Chomsky L: The Acquisition of Syntax in Children from 5 to 10. Cambridge, Mass: MIT Press, 1968

deAjuriaguerra J, Jaeggi A, Guignaro F, Kocher F, Mauard M, Roth S, Schmidt E: The development and prognosis of dysphasia in children. Morehead D, Morehead A (eds): In Normal and Deficient Child Language. Baltimore: University Park Press, 1976, pp 345–385

deHirsch K, Jansky J: Predicting Reading Failure. New York: Harper and Row, 1962

deHirsch K, Jansky J, Langford WS: The oral language performance of premature children and controls. Speech Hear Dis 29:60–69, 1964

Denckla MB: Childhood learning disabilities. In Hekman KM, Valenstein E (eds): Clinical Neuropsychology. New York: Oxford University Press, 1979, pp 535–573

Denckla MB, Rudel RG: Naming of object-drawings by dyslexic and other learning disabled children. Brain Lang 3:1–5, 1976

Dennis M: Capacity and strategy for syntactic comprehension after left or right hemidecortication: Left hemisphere superiority. Brain Lang 10:282–317, 1980

Dennis M, Kohn B: Comprehension of syntax in infantile hemiplegics after cerebral hemidecortication: Left hemisphere superiority. Brain Lang 2:472–482, 1975

Drillien CM: The incidence of mental and physical handicaps in school-age children of very low birthweight. Pediatrics 27:452–464, 1961

Drillien CM: Abnormal neurologic signs in the first year of life in low-birthweight infants: Possible prognostic significance. Development Med Child Neurol 14:575–584, 1972

Duffy FH, Burchfiel JL, Lombroso CT: Brain electrical activity mapping (BEAM): A new method for extending the clinical utility of EEG and evoked potential data. Ann Neurol 5:309–321, 1979

Duffy FH, Denckla MB, Bartels PH, Sandini G: Dyslexia: Regional differences in brain electrical activity by topographic mapping. Ann Neurol 7:412–420, 1980a

Duffy FH, Denckla MB, Bartels PH, Sandini G, Kiessling LS: Dyslexia: Automated diagnosis by computerized classification of brain electrical activity. Ann Neurol 7:421–428, 1980b

Dunn HG, Chrichton JU, Grunae RVE, McBurney AK, McCormick AQ, Robertson AM, Schulzer M: Neurological, psychological and educational sequelae of low birth weight. Brain Develop 2:57–67, 1980

Ehrlich CH, Shapiro E, Kimball B, Huttner M: Communication skills in five-year-old children with high risk neonatal histories. J Speech Hear Res 16:522–529, 1973

Fitzhardinge P: Current outcome: ICU populations in neonatal neurological assessment and outcome. 77th Ross Conference on Pediatric Research. Columbus, Ohio: Ross Laboratories, 1980, pp 1–5

Fitzhardinge PM, Ramsay M: The improving outlook for the small prematurely born infant. Development Med Child Neurol 15:447–459, 1973

Francis-Williams J, Davies PA: Very low birth weight with later intelligence. Development Med Child Neurol 16:709–728, 1974

Galaburda AM, Kemper TL: Cytoarchitectonic abnormalities in developmental dyslexia: A case study. Ann Neurol 6:94–100, 1979

Garvey M, Gordon N: A follow-up study of children with disorders of speech development. Brit J Dis Communic 8:17–28, 1973

Gascon G, Victor D, Lombroso CT, Goodglass H: Language disorder, convulsive disorder, and electroencephalographic abnormalities. Arch Neurol 28:156–162, 1973

Geschwind N: Anatomical foundations of language and dominance. In Ludlow CL, Doran-Quine ME (eds): The Neurological Basis of Language Disorders in Children: Methods and Directions for Research. US Department of Health, Education and Welfare. NINCDS Monograph No 2, 1979, pp 55–86

Gilles F: Personal communication, 1982

Goldman PS: Age, sex and experience as related to the neural basis of cognitive development. In Buchwald NA, Brazier MAB (eds): Brain Mechanisms in Mental Retardation. New York: Academic Press, 1975, pp 379–392

Goldman PS: Development and plasticity of frontal association cortex in the infahuman primate. In Ludlow LL, Doran-Quine ME (eds): The Neurological Basis of Language Disorders in Children: Methods and Directions for Research. US Departmetn of Health, Education and Welfare. NINCDS Monograph No 2, 1979, pp 1–16

Goldstein RM, Landau WM, Kleffner FR: Neurologic assessment of some deaf and aphasic children. Ann Oto-Rhino-Laryngo 67:468–479, 1958

Gould SJ: *Ontogeny and Phylogeny*. Cambridge, Mass: Belknap Press, 1977

Graham JM: Communicative skills of XXY boys. Doctoral dissertation, School of Hygiene and Public Health, Johns Hopkins University, 1981

Graham JM, Bashir AS, Walzer S, Stark RE, Gerald PS: Communication skills among unselected XXY boys. Ped Res 15:562, 1981

Griffiths CPS: A follow-up study of children with disorders of speech. Brit J Dis Communic 4:46–56, 1969

Hack M, Fanaroff AA, Merkatz IR: The low birth weight infant—evaluation of a changing outlook. New Engl J Med 301:1162–1165, 1979

Hall P, Tomblin B: A follow-up study of children with articulation and language disorders. J Speech Hear Dis 43:227–241, 1978

Hambleton G, Wigglesworth JS: Origin of intraventricular hemorrhage in the preterm infant. Arch Dis Child 51:651–659, 1976

Hier DB, Lemay M, Rosenberger PB, Perlo VP: Developmental dyslexia evidence for a subgroup with a reversal of cerebral asymmetry. Arch Neurol 35:90–92, 1978

Johnson DJ, Myklebust HR: *Learning Disabilities: Educational Principles and Practices*. New York: Grune & Stratton, 1974

Johnston JR: Disordered child. In Lass NA, McReynolds LV, Northearn JL, Yoder DE (eds): *Speech, Language and Hearing*, vol II. *Pathologies of Speech and Language*. Philadelphia: WB Saunders Co, 1982

Johnston J, Schery T: The use of grammatical morphemes by children with communication disorders. In Morehead D, Morehead A (eds): *Normal and Deficient Child Language*. Baltimore: University Park Press, 1976

Johnston RB, Stark RE, Mellits ED, Tallal P: Neurological status of language impaired and normal children. Ann Neurol 10:159–163, 1981

Kastein S, Fowler EP: Language development among survivors of premature birth. Arch Otolaryngol 69:131–135, 1959

Kennard MA: Reorganization of motor function in the cerebral cortex of monkeys deprived of motor and premotor areas in infancy. J Neurophysiol 1:477–496, 1938

Kennard MA: Cortical reorganization of motor function. Arch Neurol Psychiat 48:227–240, 1942

King RR, Jones C, Lasky E: In retrospect: A fifteen-year follow-up report of speech-language disordered children. Language, Speech Hear Serv Schools 13:24–32, 1982

Kinsbourne M: Language lateralization and development disorders. In Ludlow LL, Doran-Quine ME (eds): *The Neurological Bases of Language Disorders in Children: Methods and Directions for Research*. NIH Publication No 79–440, August 1979, pp 99–107

Kitchen WH, Ryan MM, Richards A, McDougall AB, Billson FA, Keir EH, Naylor, FD: A longitudinal study of very low birth weight infants. IV: An overview performance at eight years of age. Development Med Child Neurol 22:172–188, 1980

Kleinman SN, Scavuzzo A: Snowballs and Band-Aids for Pentimento. Seminar, American Speech and Hearing Association, Los Angeles, California, November 1981

Krishnamoorthy KS, Shannon DCE, Delong GR, Todres ID, Davis KR: Neurologic sequelae in the survivors of neonatal intraventricular hemorrhage. Pediatrics 64:233–241, 1979

Landau W, Goldstein R, Kleffner F: Congenital aphasia: A clinicopathologic study. Neurology 10:915–921, 1960

Landau WM and Kleffner FR: Syndrome of acquired aphasia with convulsive disorder in children. Neurology 7:523–530, 1957

Larsen B, Skinhøj E, Lasser NA: Variations in regional cortical blood flow in the right and left hemisphere during automatic speech. Brain 101:193–209, 1978

Lasser NA, Inguar DH, Skinhøj E: Brain function and blood flow. Scientific American 239:62–71, 1978

Lassman FM, Fisch RO, Vetter DK, LaBenz ES: Early correlates of speech, language and hearing: The Collaborative Perinatal Project of the National Institute of Neurological and Communicative Disorders and Stroke. Littleton, Mass: PSG Publishing Co, 1980

Lazzara A, Ahmann P, Dykes F, Brann, AW, Schwartz J: Clinical predictability of intraventricular hemorrhage in preterm infants. Pediatrics 65:30–34, 1980

Lee L: Developmental sentence types: A method for comparing normal and deviant syntactic development. J Speech Hear Dis 31:311–330, 1966

Leonard L: What is deviant language? J Speech Hear Res 37:427–446, 1972

Lubchenco LO, Delivoria-Papadopoulos M, Butterfield LJ, French JH, Metcalf D, Hix IE Jr, Kanick J, Downs M, Freeland MA: Long-term follow-up studies of prematurely born infants. I. Relationship of handicaps to nursery routines. J Pediat 80:501–508, 1972

Ludlow CL: Children's language disorders: Recent research advances. Ann Neurol 7:497–507, 1980

Luick AH, Agronowitz A, Kirk SA, Busby R: Profiles of children with severe oral language disorders. J Speech Hear Dis 47:88–92, 1982

Mattis S, French JH, Rapia I: Dyslexia in children and young adults: Three independent neuro-psychological syndromes. Development Med Child Neurol 17:150–163, 1975

Mattison RE, Cantwell DP, Baker L: Behavior problems in children with speech and language retardation. Child Psychiat Human Develop 10:246–257, 1980

Menyuk P: Comparison of grammar of children with functionally deviant and normal speech. J Speech Hear Res 7:109–121, 1964

Menyuk P: *Language and Maturation*. Cambridge, Mass: MIT Press, 1977

Menyuk P: Syntactic competence and reading. In *Language, Learning and Reading Disabilities: A New Decade*. Preliminary Proceedings of an Interdisciplinary Conference. Department of Communication Arts and Sciences, Queens College of the City University of New York, 1981, pp 48–66

Miller J, Chapman R, Bedrosian J: Defining developmentally disabled subjects for research: The relationship between etiology, cognitive development and language and communicative performance. New Zealand Speech Therapists' Journal, 1978

Milner B: Sparing of language after unilateral brain damage. Neuroscience Research Program Bulletin 12:213–217, 1974

Morehead DM, Ingram D: The development of base syntax in normal and linguistically deviant children. J Speech Hear Res 16:330–352, 1973

Pape KE, Buncie RJ, Ashby S, Fitzhardinge PM: The status at two years of low-birth-weight infants born in 1974 with birth weights of less than 1001 gm. J Pediat 92:253–260, 1978

Rabinovitch R, Bibace R, Caplan H: Sequelae of prematurity: Psychological test findings. Canad Med Assoc 84:822–824, 1961

Rankin JM, Aram DM, Horwitz SJ: Language ability in right and left hemiplegic children. Brain Lang 14:292–306, 1981

Rawson MB: Developmental Language Disability: Adult Accomplishments of Dyslexic Boys. Baltimore: Johns Hopkins Press, 1968

Rudel RG: Neuroplasticity: Implications for development and education. In Chall JS, Mirsky AF (eds): Education and the Brain. Chicago: The University of Chicago Press, 1978, pp 169–307

Rudel RG, Denckla MB: Relation of forward and backward digit repetition to neurological impairment in children with learning disabilities. Neuropsychologia 12:109–118, 1974

Rutherford DR, Perlstein MA: Etiologic factors associated with hearing loss and language disorders in children with cerebral palsy. A report to the thirty-ninth Annual Convention of the American Speech and Hearing Association. Chicago, Illinois, November 3–6, 1963

Saint-Anne Dargassies S: Long-term neurological follow-up of 286 truly premature infants: I. Neurological sequelae. Development Med Child Neurol 19:462–478, 1977

Schneider GE: Growth of abnormal neural connections following focal brain lesions: Constraining factors and functional effects in neurosurgical treatment. In Sweet WH, Obrador S, Martin-Rodriguez JG (eds): Psychiatry, Pain and Epilepsy. Baltimore: University Park Press, 1977, pp 5–26

Schneider GE: Is it really better to have your brain lesion early? A revision of the "Kennard Principle." Neuropsychologia, 1979

Schreiner RL, Kisling JA, Evans GM, Phillips S, Lemons JA, Gesham EL: Improved survival of ventilated neonates with modern intensive care. Pediatrics 66:985–987, 1980

Sheridan MD, Peckham C: Follow-up at 11 years of children who had marked speech defects at 7 years. Child Care, Health Develop 1:157–166, 1975

Shiddhaye S, Shah PM, Udani PM: Physical growth

and development of pre-term children during the first five years of life: Longitudinal study. Indian Pediat 9:282–289, 1972

Silbert AR, Wolff PH, Lilienthal J: Spatial and temporal processing in patients with Turner's syndrome. Behavior Genetics 7:11–21, 1977

Stark RE, Tallal P: Selection of children with specific language deficits. J Speech Hear Dis 46:114–122, 1981

Stewart AL, Reynolds EO: Improved prognosis for infants of very low birth weight. Pediatrics 34:724–735, 1974

Strominger A: A follow-up study of reading and linguistic abilities in language delayed children. Doctoral dissertation, Boston University, Boston, Massachusetts, 1982

Strominger A, Bashir A: A nine-year follow-up of language disordered children. Paper presented at the American Speech and Hearing Association Meeting, Chicago, 1977

Thomas EK, Walmsley SA: Some evidence of continuing linguistic acquisition in learning disabled adolescents. A paper presented at the International Federation of Learning Disabilities, Montreal, Canada, 1976

Vellutino FR: Alternative conceptualizations of dyslexia: Evidence in support of a verbal-deficit hypothesis. Harvard Educ Rev 47:334–354, 1977

Vogel SA: Syntactic Abilities of Normal and Dyslexic Children. Baltimore: University Park Press, 1975

Volpe JJ: Neonatal intracranial hemorrhage: Pathophysiology, neuropathology, and clinical features. Clin Perinatol 4:77–102, 1977

Walzer S, Graham JM, Bashir AS, Silbert AR: Preliminary observations on language and learning in XXY boys. In press

Walzer S, Wolff, PH, Bowen D, Silbert AR, Bashir AS, Gerold PS, Richmond JB: A method for the longitudinal study of behavioral development in infants and children: The early development of XXY boys. J Child Psychol Psychiat 19:213–229, 1978

Weiner P: A language-delayed child at adolescence. J Speech Hear Dis 39:202–212, 1974

Wiig E, Semel E: Language Disabilities in Children and Adolescents. Columbus, Ohio: Charles E. Merrill Publishing Co, 1976

Wiig EH, Semel EM, Nystrom LA: Comparison of rapid naming disabled and academically achieving eight-year-olds. Language, Speech Hear Serv Schools 13:11–22, 1982

Wolf M: The relationship of disorders of word-finding and reading in children and aphasics. Doctoral dissertation, Harvard University School of Education, Cambridge, Mass, 1979

Wolff PH: Maturational factors in behavioral development. In McMillan MF, Henao S (eds): Child Psychiatry: Treatment and Reserach. New York: Mazel, 1977, pp 1–22

Wolpaw T, Nation JE, Aram DM: Developmental language disorders: A follow-up study. Illinois Speech Hear J 12:14–18, 1979

Woods BT, Carey S: Language deficits after apparent

clinical recovery from childhood aphasia. Ann Neurol 6:405–409, 1979

Woods BT, Teuber HL: Changing patterns of childhood aphasia. Ann Neurol 3:273–280, 1978

Worster-Drought C: An unusual form of acquired aphasia in children. Folia Phoniatria 16:223–227, 1964

Zaidel E: The split and half brains as models of congenital language disability. In Ludlow LL, Doran-Quine ME (eds): *The Neurological Basis of Language Disorders in Children: Methods and Directions for Research*. US Department of Health, Education and Welfare. NINCDS Monograph No 2, 1979, pp 55–86

# DISCUSSION: PART II: DEFINING THE BOUNDARIES OF LANGUAGE DISORDERS IN CHILDREN

## LAURENCE B. LEONARD

My comments on Chapters 4 through 6 will be concerned with two principal topics. First, I shall discuss some considerations involved in dividing language disordered children into clinically useful subgroups. Next, I will provide a few comments concerning certain subgroups of children whose status with regard to language intervention is often unclear.

### THE NATURE OF SUBGROUPS

Given the findings from the follow-up studies reviewed by Bashir in Chapter 6, it is clear that children experiencing language learning difficulties must be identified at the earliest age possible. At the same time, the heterogeneity seen in this group of children makes it unlikely that, following identification, all language disordered children can be treated the same. In short, it appears necessary to find ways to subdivide children according to characteristics or variables that have clinical relevance.

In Chapter 4 Miller has noted two approaches that can be used in this regard. One approach is based on an etiological model "in which children are first sorted according to the condition thought to be the *cause* of the language disorder." The other approach is based on developmental communication models "in which children are first sorted by the *consequences,* or the presenting symptoms, of the language disorder." Neither of these models is fully developed. With regard to the first model, we still have little idea of the etiologic factors involved in many cases of language disorders. With regard to the second model, because of the explosion of research in child language it seems that we are continually changing our views concerning which linguistic and communicative features best reflect the consequences or presenting symptoms of a language disorder. Given the incomplete status of these models, I cannot resist the urge to propose a third model, one that can be used in conjunction with, though it is not dependent upon, the other models. Although children were my concern when I initially thought about this model, it may also be relevant to adults with aphasia. In this model, which I will term the "intervention-linked" model, children are sorted according to characteristics that have a bearing on the choice of language intervention procedures to use with a child.

It is clear that we are a long way from knowing just which characteristics these are. However, such information can be obtained, and I would therefore like to outline some of the steps that will be required to make this intervention-linked model operative. Let us begin with an example from the area of lexical facilitation in preschool-aged children. We might first study a large number of children ranging in age, say, from 2.4 to 4.0, in expressive lexicon size from 20 to 60 words, in comprehension scores from well below age level to age level, and in nonverbal IQ from 70 to 100. These variables, among others, can serve as pretreatment variables in the analysis discussed below. The particular variables selected for consideration might be based on hypotheses concerning the nature of language disorders, the factors important in treatment, or both. Thus characteristics derived from the etiologic and consequence models can (but need not) serve as input data for this model.

These children could be randomly assigned to one of two lexical training procedures, for example, one in which the clinician selects the words and referents and has the child imitate; the other in which the child selects the referents and the clinician models the appropriate words without requesting the child to respond. The data could then be examined in the same general manner as recently employed by Friedman and Friedman (1980). The children's lexical gains could be tested for aptitude × treatment interactions, using those pretreatment variables—such as IQ, lexicon size, comprehension score, and so on—that prove to have a linear relationship with lexical gain. This test can indicate which of the pretreatment variables show significantly different regression slopes for the two intervention procedures. For each of these pretreatment variables, the scores above which or below which one or the other intervention procedure is more effective can be determined. For example, the clinician-initiated imitation procedure might be found to be more effective for children with IQs below 80 and expressive lexicons below 30 words.

The next step would involve comparative studies in which, for each intervention procedure, the performance of children showing the same characteristics as those for whom the procedure was found more

effective would be compared with the performance of children showing characteristics that were associated with only moderate success with the procedure. Thus the issue of whether or not certain child characteristics are predictive of success with a particular procedure can be tested on an a priori basis.

Up to this point we would have information suggesting that certain intervention procedures are successful with children showing particular sets of characteristics. Yet many children will not precisely fit these sets of characteristics. Therefore, to maximize clinical utility, we need to know whether a given procedure can be about as effective with a child exhibiting, say, a lexicon of 35 words as with one having a lexicon of just under 30 words. This calls for additional comparative studies that attempt to determine the degree to which children can vary on a particular characteristic before the intervention procedure proves no better than others. Finally, it may also be the case that slight variations in the intervention procedure may not alter its effectiveness with children showing particular characteristics. For example, an imitation procedure that allows the child to choose the referents may be as appropriate for children with IQs below 80 as an imitation procedure in which the clinician selects the referents. To answer such questions, studies involving either between-subjects comparisons or within-subjects comparisons alternating treatment designs might be employed.

From these comments, it is no doubt clear that a great deal of work is required before we can sort children according to characteristics that have a bearing on the choice of language intervention procedures. However, I would like to note a couple of advantages that this approach might offer. The first might be best explained using an example. We often hear ourselves say "the earlier the intervention the better." However, the decision to intervene is not always so easy. Let us consider this decision process for each of the three models under discussion, the etiologic and consequence models described by Miller in Chapter 5 and the in-

Table 1  DESCRIPTIVE DATA FOR THREE CHILDREN

| Child | Chronologic Age | Expressive Lexicon | Number of Communicative Functions | Language Comprehension Age | Nonverbal IQ | Hearing | Birth and Medical History |
|-------|-----------------|--------------------|-----------------------------------|----------------------------|--------------|---------|---------------------------|
| A | 2.4 | 30 words | 10 | 1.8 | 95 | Normal | Unremarkable |
| B | 3.0 | 30 words | 12 | 2.2 | 95 | Normal | Unremarkable |
| C | 3.8 | 30 words | 12 | 2.4 | 75 | Normal | Unremarkable |

tervention-linked model just discussed. In Table 1, three hypothetic children are described. When examined from the perspective of the etiologic model, none of the children exhibit any of the high-risk characteristics that would have permitted a classification at the outset. It is possible that Child C might be regarded as showing a language deficit associated with mild mental retardation, although this would be a judgment made on a post hoc basis. Child B could probably qualify for the classification of specific language impairment, given the criteria of Stark and Tallal (1981). However, those who have come to expect such an impairment to be associated with bilateral damage to the brain, as discussed by Bashir in Chapter 7, might be unwilling to classify this child in this way, given only the information provided. Given the child's unremarkable birth and medical history, I suspect that many of these individuals would favor the view that this child is an essentially normal child who is unusually slow in language development. I am relatively confident that this position would be taken for the case of Child A.

When the children are examined from the perspective of the consequence model, Child C and even Child B present us with little difficulty. That is, their language abilities are significantly below those expected for their chronologic age, and enough information has been obtained on them to develop a profile of relative strengths and weaknesses. However, Child A is more problematic. Although we are able to develop a profile of the child's abilities, it is not clear that the degree of the child's deficit warrants the term "language disordered." I suspect that clinicians are divided in their recommendations when faced with a child of this type. The most likely recommendation is for the parents to enroll the child in a preschool "so he/she can interact with other children," or to enroll the child in a low structure language intervention program involving a group format. Some clinicians might prefer to recommend only a reevaluation in a few months, to be certain of the appropriateness of intervention.

To examine the children from the perspective of the third model, the intervention-linked model, we must of course assume that steps have been taken toward determining which characteristics seem to predict success with particular intervention procedures. With this in mind, it would seem that the model could accommodate Child B and Child C with little difficulty. But the same was true for the consequence model. The intervention-linked model would be particularly helpful, though, in the case of Child A. Although it is true that this model provides no more information than the consequence model with regard to whether or not Child A is truly language disordered, it may enable us to match the child up with a particular intervention procedure that had been found to facilitate similar children's linguistic skills beyond levels expected by maturation alone. With the knowledge that there is a procedure that has an excellent chance of aiding the child, clinicians and parents may be less likely to adopt a "let's wait and see" attitude. To repeat, this model does not tell us anything more about whether a child is language disordered, but it might provide us with more information concerning the likely outcome of intervention if a child who falls in this gray area is seen for treatment.

There is a second advantage associated with the intervention-linked model. The development of this model can serve as an impetus to conduct more research on the nature and effectiveness of language intervention. Such work is in short supply and any additional information we can provide in this crucial area would be valuable, regardless of the motivating force behind our gathering it. In fact I can imagine a situation in which, in the development of this model, a particular intervention procedure is shown to be lacking in its ability to sort children into subgroups but is found to be effective in facilitating the linguistic skills of children in general. Thus, although the model may not have been advanced, our efforts will have resulted in a new tool to use in helping handicapped children become better communicators.

## THE APPROPRIATENESS OF LANGUAGE INTERVENTION FOR CERTAIN SUBGROUPS

I now wish to discuss the status of certain subgroups of children with regard to the appropriateness of language intervention. This discussion will entail a basic question asked about each of these subgroups, an answer to the question, and a few remarks concerning the reasons for the answer and why the question was important to ask in the first place.

**Children with No Apparent Cognition-Language Gap.** Should children with nonlinguistic cognitive deficits of the same magnitude as their language deficits be viewed as appropriate candidates for language intervention, even when circumstances do not allow for the child to receive intervention for the nonlinguistic deficiencies? Yes. Although most clinicians would probably argue that children of this type should be enrolled in intervention programs that offer assistance in a variety of developmental areas, I am not sure that they would expect language treatment to be very successful if it occurred without attention to these other areas. This feeling has probably been reinforced by the recent Piagetian oriented literature in which a number of parallels between linguistic and nonlinguistic cognitive abilities have been reported. However, a close inspection of this literature reveals a number of individual cases in which the linguistic, rather than the nonlinguistic, counterpart of a presumably related pair of abilities proves to be the more developed ability in the child. Similar findings have been reported for mentally retarded children. Different proposals have been offered as possible explanations for such findings. For example, Greenwald and Leonard (1979) have suggested that the relationship between communicative and cognitive ability in retarded children may weaken with increasing chronologic age. Miller, Chapman, and Bedrosian (1977) have proposed that an extended period of time at a particular cognitive level may allow certain linguistic skills to surpass their presumed nonlinguistic counterparts. Aside from calling into question the causal role played by nonlinguistic cognitive abilities, evidence of this type raises the possibility that language ability can be facilitated through intervention to a point at which it surpasses the level of the child's other abilities. Thus, although a more global intervention program may be the most appropriate for the group of children just described, it would appear that attempts to facilitate these children's linguistic abilities need not await the availability of such a program.

**Children with Auditory Perceptual Deficits.** Should children with auditory perceptual deficits be included in language intervention rather than, say, a training approach designed to improve their auditory perceptual skills? Here I am referring to children exhibiting a language deficit who also perform poorly on those auditory perceptual tasks that are not themselves tasks of metalinguistic ability. In any case, the response to the question is the same. Yes. I have noted elsewhere (Leonard, 1979; 1982) the difficulty I have had in finding a correspondence between the pattern of auditory perceptual problems reported for these children (for example, Tallal and Stark, 1980) and the speech and language characteristics they exhibit. Also the latter too often resemble the characteristics seen in the speech of younger normal children, for which auditory perceptual explanations are not involved. These observations, as well as the still unknown effects on language of perceptual training, allow me to answer the question in a straightforward manner. At this point in time we have no choice but to include these children in language intervention rather than in perceptual training programs.

**Children with Developmental Apraxia.** Should children with developmental apraxia be included as a subgroup of language disordered children? Yes, although this should not be taken to mean that the children's apraxic problems should be ignored. First, children diagnosed as developmentally apraxic typically exhibit language problems that transcend problems with phonology (Rosenbek and Wertz,

1972). There is evidence that some of these language problems cannot be attributed, even indirectly, to the apraxia, such as difficulty with third person singular morphemes in spite of accurate plural and possessive morpheme usage (Ekelman, 1981). Yet on more than one occasion I have heard clinicians refer to otherwise language impaired children as apraxic, the intent being that such children constitute a distinct subgroup requiring a different type of intervention. I am not entirely clear about the precise nature of remediation for apraxia, but it seems to me that a training approach involving the selection of syllables, words, and phrases strictly on the basis of sound production considerations would meet only some of the child's needs. At the very least, supplementary language intervention seems appropriate for such children.

The second consideration is that many of the phonologic limitations observed in the speech of apraxic children are seen as well in the speech of other groups of language disordered children as well as in the speech of younger normal children. Consonant omissions, metathesis in multisyllabic words, and difficulty with fricatives and consonant clusters are not unique to children with apraxia. Therefore, even if some of these phonologic difficulties are attributable to an apraxia in a given child, this is not to say that all of them are linked to the apraxia. Thus, while some aspects of the child's phonology might be best facilitated by an approach that emphasizes production, other aspects might best be taught through a language oriented approach, such as teaching the use of sounds to achieve lexical contrast.

## SUMMARY

Rather than review the points raised in the preceding chapters, I have attempted to expand upon them by providing a few remarks of my own. Although the specific topics selected by each of us were based primarily on personal preference and a belief that they had relevance to clini-

cal practice, one can nonetheless see several common themes running through the chapters. Regardless of whether the focus is on language disordered children or on adults with aphasia, there seems to be a common recognition of the heterogeneity within these clinical groups in which, along with cases fitting the classic definition of the disorder, we find cases that do not so easily fit the mold. For each of these clinical populations great importance is placed on identifying meaningful subgroups. Finally, there is a recognition that for adults who incur cerebral insult as well as for slowly developing children, early assessment and intervention may be necessary to maximize the likelihood of a successful outcome. It is hoped that the varied directions in which we have taken these common themes will stimulate thinking and serve as a basis for a number of clinical research efforts in the mid-1980s.

## REFERENCES

Ekelman B: Syntactic findings in developmental verbal apraxia. Paper presented to American Speech-Language-Hearing Association, Los Angeles, 1981

Friedman P, Friedman K: Accounting for individual differences when comparing the effectiveness of remedial language teaching methods. Appl Psycholing 1:127–150, 1980

Greenwald C, Leonard L: Communicative and sensorimotor development of Down's syndrome children. Am J Ment Defic 84:296–303, 1979

Leonard L: Language impairment in children. Merrill-Palmer Quart 25:205–232, 1979

Leonard L: Phonological deficits in children with developmental language impairment. Brain Lang 16:73–86, 1982

Miller J, Chapman R, Bedrosian J: Defining developmentally disabled subjects for research. Paper presented at the Boston University Conference on Language Development, Boston, 1977

Rosenbek J, Wertz R: A review of fifty cases of developmental apraxia of speech. Lang Speech Hear Serv 3:23–33, 1972

Stark R, Tallal P: Selection of children with specific language deficits. J Speech Hear Dis 46:114–122, 1981

Tallal P, Stark R: Speech perception of language-delayed children. In Yeni-Komshian G, Kavanaugh J, Ferguson C (eds); Child Phonology, vol 2 Perception. New York: Academic Press, 1980

**Part III** _____

# DECIDING HOW TO CARRY OUT LANGUAGE INTERVENTION: HISTORICAL, PRESENT AND FUTURE PERSPECTIVES

# 7

## HISTORICAL PERSPECTIVES ON THE CONTENT OF CHILD LANGUAGE PROGRAMS

*JAMES E. MCLEAN*

An awareness of the history of the content of child language treatment programs in the discipline of speech-language-hearing would seem to be important for us at this particular point in our discipline's development. In an effort to foster this awareness, this chapter concentrates on the Gestalt of what we, as clinicians, have been doing in the name of this discipline as we have approached language problems of children over the past thirty to forty years. Such an approach seems particularly appropriate in this context because it submits our clinical practices to accountability measures that will evaluate our overall effectiveness as an academic discipline. Instead of maintaining us in our more traditional historical postures in which we canonize various leaders, it will bring us to judge the effectiveness by which our overall discipline has gathered relevant knowledge and translated it into applied clinical programs in this extremely important area. A broader historical perspective on our clinical content and procedures in child language will also allow us to identify the steps we must take as an academic discipline to alter any deficiencies we might see in the processes reflected therein.

Some academicians among us may blanch at the notion of judging our academic discipline's overall effectiveness at the level of our consensus on clinical practices in child language. But it is only through such a process that we can effectively measure and judge the *balance* that we have attained as we sum the products of the many and varied professional roles that are subsumed in this discipline. Many of us still believe in the old-fashioned notion that the speech-language-hearing discipline exists to serve eventual clinical ends realized at the level of people who have speech, language, or hearing problems.

### RELATIONSHIP OF CLINICAL PRACTICES TO THEORY

It might be advisable to state some assumptions about what the analysis of clinical practices should tell us about our discipline. First, it would seem that any set of goals and procedures that purports to represent a discipline's clinical treatment of child language necessarily emanates from a *theoretic* model of child language which includes some consideration of three rather basic questions:

1. What are the human behaviors that constitute child language?

2. What are the human experiences and learning processes that account for the attainment of these behaviors?

3. What are the biologic, psychologic, and environmental factors that act as constraints to the realization of these processes or behaviors?

The way in which a discipline answers these questions sets up its theoretic model and determines *what* its practitioners teach as language and *how* they attempt to teach it to their clients. In essence, then, the clinical practices of a discipline can be used to infer the consensus or dominant theoretic model represented within that discipline. The clinical practices of the speech-language-hearing discipline will clearly show that we have answered these three questions in very different ways at different times in our history.

If we analyze the three questions above, we can see that they are interactional in that the answer to one question necessarily has some effect on the other two. Most interestingly, however, we shall see that each of these questions has, at various times, been considered independently from the others, and this concentration on only one of them at certain times in our history has had a profound impact on our model for clinical practices. By tracking the historical trends of our clinical practices, we should also have an accounting of the consensus theoretic model of child language which has existed in our discipline over a period of time.

## PRIOR TO 1960

We are all aware of the fact that the history of this discipline in the United States effectively began in the 1930s as programs in "speech correction" were installed in a few major universities in the country and its practitioners moved into clinical roles in schools and university clinics. In these early days and for almost three decades thereafter, the focus of this discipline clearly was, as its name speech correction implied, speech. Child language in those days was represented primarily in a category of disorder called "delayed speech." To be sure, clinicians of that time were aware of language systems as

real entities separate from speech; speech correctionists' approaches to language, however, were exclusively as speech.

It is important to note that even though the discipline as a whole reviewed speech as the behaviors of language, our clinical practices reflected two important dimensions in that perspective. These dimensions related to the way we answered questions about the *learning processes* needed to acquire speech, and the way we answered questions about possible *constraints* to speech behavior or speech acquisition.

**Psychologic and Educational Dimensions.** The dimension of our discipline which had emerged from clinical and experimental psychology and from speech-arts education focused attention on the functional experiences and processes that accounted for speech acquisition. These procedures reflected a strong predilection for "learning by doing," and speech (and language) therapy consisted of a wide array of vocal modeling and textual control of talking behaviors. The materials of those early days included books of poems and speech improvement exercises, such as *Speech and Play* (Finley, 1940), *Better Speech and Better Reading* (Schoolfield, 1937), and *Sounds for Little Folks* (Stoddard, 1940). The Bryngleson and Glaspey (1941) *Speech Improvement Cards* were much in evidence and the local dime store was forever out of stock on *Little Golden Dictionaries*. Clearly, we as clinicians were concentrating on evoking speech, and, while our most dominant targets were articulatory, we also thought it important to target language forms at the levels of vocabulary, prosody, and traditional grammar for those children deficient in these areas. This approach reflected the functional learning-theory bases of the day: bases focused on simple stimulus-response and trial and error principles articulated by Hull (1943) and the habituation constructs espoused by Spence (1956).

With such perspectives, however, the clinicians of the 1940s and 1950s were hard-put to apply these procedures to children who had not attained speech. When confronted with nontalking clients, they would put down their speech improvement books and stimulus pictures and, rather desperately, attempt to stimulate lower levels of "speech" by targeting babbling and vocal play. When such functional approaches did not work, early clinicians would turn gratefully to that dimension of our model which dealt with identifying the constraints to the acquisition of speech.

**Medically Oriented Dimension.** This constraint identification dimension was supported primarily by those early members of our discipline who came into speech correction with orientations that were more medical than psychologic or educational. This medically directed dimension of the model was also focused on speech, but it was more concerned with the biologic constraints that interfered with speech learning. It was this dimension of our disciplinary model that set some precedents for our clinical practices with children which had some profound effects on the basic clinical roles that we have been willing and able to accept—effects that have only recently been overcome.

The early views of the constraints to speech (and thus to language) acquisition were appropriately focused on the brain and its role in the production of both the motor and semantic elements of language. Since speech was the hallmark of an intact brain and neurologic system, absence of speech was obviously an indication that the brain and neurologic system were *not* intact. While we will look at this assumption and its implications again later in this chapter, it is of primary importance here to acknowledge the effect of this perspective in the earlier days of our discipline.

In those days, the "organic" view of speech and language was both powerful and pervasive in its effect on our clinical practices with children. This view of the basic organicity of speech (and thus language) set the stage for the discipline rather systematically and consistently to *exclude* speech deficient children from its clinical purview. Speech clinicians, for example, heeded West's (1937) advice that they not waste their time on "aments"

(mentally retarded). The medically oriented model encouraged them to exclude from their rolls handicapped young children who had not yet attained levels of development adequate for speech. The organicity principles were also extended to exclude certain other "medical" problems, such as emotionally disturbed children, from speech correction programs. Interestingly, for organically involved children who could at least vocalize, speech therapy services were still available. Thus cerebral palsied and severely hearing impaired children were served. Note, however, that even for these children, the target was still *speech*. Anything *less* than speech was not tolerated well at all by the speech therapist. (And we are still wondering—"what's in a name?")

**Summary of the Pre-Sixties.** In summary, it seems clear from our clinical practices with children prior to about 1960 that our discipline generated a clinical model that reflected certain specific answers to the questions posed early in this chapter. Clearly, the *behaviors of language* were considered to be speech and various speech forms. Just as clearly, our discipline's model considered functional processes, such as imitation, trial and error learning, and habituation, as the keystones to the processes by which speech behavior was acquired. However, functional approaches were deemed unlikely to overcome the organic or biologic constraints known to affect speech or speech acquisition of children.

Thus our clinical targets in those early days were related to speech. Our clinical procedures were concentrated on vocal, pictorial, and textual stimuli to evoke and habituate speech of various forms and levels. Finally, our clinical model reflected a view that organic factors that militated against speech were constraints that could not be overcome by our functional methods, and thus, when such constraints were in evidence, the affected child should be excluded from the service domain of speech correctionists and should depend on medicine for treatment. Such a model of both the nature of our clinical services and the children who could benefit from them remained dominant for almost 30 years.

## 1960–1970

The theoretic antecedents of the clinical changes that occurred in the decade of the sixties emerged in literature of the late 1950s. There were two such antecedents, and they related to two of the three questions posed early in this chapter. Specifically, psycholinguistic theory altered our traditional answer to the question of what behaviors constituted language. Concomitantly, behavioral psychology trends altered our answers to the question about the processes necessary to attain these behaviors. These theories emerged in our knowledge base almost simultaneously. Each had its independent effects, and each too had its interactional effects on our model of child language, and thus on the clinical services that such a model permitted.

**Generative Grammar Models.** Chomsky's (1957, 1965) "generative grammar" theories filled an immense void in the clinician's theoretic model. They set the stage for clinicians to begin to separate "language" from speech. Although in retrospect Chomsky's model seems to have been less than ideal for our true understanding of language and language behavior, it was nevertheless an important event for us. Even though the generative grammar model still reflected the primacy of the *speech* mode for language, it did suggest some new taxonomies for clinical models. It got us beyond the phoneme as a clinical preoccupation and also allowed us to quantify deficits in language through application of syntactic measures.

Besides reinforcing our speech bias, however, Chomsky's (1957) model further reinforced our previous notions about the irrevocability of organic constraints to speech—and, now to language. His hypothesis regarding the "innateness" of a syntax-directed "language acquisition device" further solidified our previous positions that excluded certain handicapped children from speech-language therapy.

It seems important to note that while

Chomsky's theories altered our answer to the question about the behaviors that constitute language without diverting us from our basic orientation toward speech, and, in addition, reinforced our previous positions on constraints to speech and language, they did not intrinsically alter or add to our most basic notions about the processes needed to attain speech-language behaviors. If we were to continue to function as treatment providers in this general domain, we still had to believe that functional arrangements of modeling and evocation of speech production in the forms prescribed by grammar rules could be productive for children who did not yet reflect them in their speech repertoire. Thus, although clinicians maintained their overall exclusionary practices for nonspeaking children, they followed their historical educational procedures in targeting the newer forms of language structure through imitation and reward despite Chomsky's views that there could be no impact on these forms through functional means.

**Radical Behavioral Models.** It is difficult to imagine that when the last chapter of this history is finally written, the fact that functional behaviorism emerged in this field at the same time as did generative grammar will not be viewed as one of the more important coincidences that has occurred in an academic discipline. While the radical behavioral theories of Skinner (1953, 1957) have not provided the complete solution to all clinical problems in speech-language any more than Chomsky's have, it is disturbing to contemplate what might have happened to clinical efforts for severely language deficient children had they not been available to counter some of the effects of Chomsky's model. For Skinner's model radically altered our perceptions about the functional treatment processes that might facilitate the acquisition of speech-language behavior. In fact, it altered our perspectives about our clinical procedures so powerfully that it reduced our willingness to accept our historical views of the absoluteness of certain constraints to the development of language. Radical behaviorism thus began to alter our views about the severely handicapped children who could be considered appropriate for our clinical services.

It seems patently clear that it was these Skinnerian revisions of our notions about functional treatments that could effect changes in speech-language behaviors which initiated our clinical acceptance of mentally retarded, autistic, and similarly severely speech-language deficient children. The behavioral data that had been generated by Skinner's followers in their work with severely damaged and deviant people completely altered our previous perspectives about the various constraints to speech and language. As a result, our clinical model of over 30 years was dramatically changed and we began to target "functional" language responses with child populations we had heretofore ignored.

We shall see, in the changes that occurred in the following decade, that our reactions to both Chomsky and Skinner were probably too great and, to some degree, too precipitous. Yet it is impossible to judge how we might have been prepared to consider today's important changes had we not been moved from our traditional postures by the impact of these two nearly incompatible forces.

Ironically, neither the Skinnerian nor the Chomskian theories jarred us from our traditional views on speech as the mode of language in any immediate sense. Although our later moves to alternative modes in the 1970s certainly have antecedents in Skinnerian theory, the most immediate applications of both grammar and behavioral theories in the 1960s were still focused on speech behavior.

**Summary of the Sixties.** The decade of the 1960s brought important changes in the clinical practices of the speech-language-hearing discipline. Certainly, the effects that functional behaviorism produced were critical to our discipline's emergence as a broader based educational resource. When we became philosophically and procedurally ready to accept children in etiologic categories previously considered to produce pervasive constraints to speech, we had made a major break with our history. We should note here, however, that the move to treat these populations heretofore excluded from our services was not as extensive then as it has become today. In the 1960s we were still largely targeting speech modes, and our retarded clients were generally those in the mild to moderate ranges of retardation. Still, it was a significant move, and certainly it prepared the way for greater moves in the next decade.

The alterations in our clinical perspectives which came from linguistics were also most significant. Although, in retrospect, the specific theories that precipitated this move have not been maintained, in that Chomsky's abstract grammar systems have been supplanted by systems and taxonomies of far more breadth and depth, the move to language considerations beyond speech and the phoneme was important. In the same way that behaviorism set up a dynamic process of change in our model, generative grammar theories prepared us to move into the semantics and pragmatics perspectives that direct our applied models today.

Most basically, we had broken away from the limited focus of articulation and stuttering of 30 years' duration and had prepared ourselves for including language in our clinical model. It was a momentous period in our history and we should savor it.

## 1970–1980

If the events of the 1960s are worthy of savoring, the events of the 1970s should beget ecstasy. There seems little question that this past decade has seen changes of enormous importance to our discipline's clinical model. Our model of child language has been enhanced exponentially rather than linearly, and the effects of such enhancement should yield further changes in all elements of our clinical philosophies and practices.

**Overview of the Seventies.** While the events of the seventies primarily had an impact on our identification of the behaviors that constitute language—the first of our model-determining questions—they also had important interactional effects on the other two questions relating to the processes that accounted for these behaviors and the various constraints to these processes or behaviors. As the perspectives on language as a multidimensional behavior that included meaning, social function, and linguistic structure were established and their specifics made clear, it became obvious, that our perspectives on the functional experiences and processes that accounted for these many dimensions had to be modified to keep pace. Thus in the late 1970s the model in clinical language began to reflect a view that language behavior, and the processes that account for that behavior, had to attain some complementary forms and levels if we were to attain the validity levels necessary to a model in child language.

**Need for Complementary Relationships Among Model Elements.** As we have noted previously, the three questions about language which are used to generate our clinical model have often been pursued independently of one another. We might thus have concentrated on the behaviors that constituted language at one time; the experiences and processes that accounted for these behaviors at another time; and the constraints to the development of these behaviors or processes at still another time. We might also have answered any one of these questions in a way that represented a totally different theoretic system than did the answer to another of the questions. For example, behaviorists answered the question about necessary experiences and processes needed to account for language in ways that were quite different from the way Chomsky answered the same question. Behaviorists posited stimulus-response-reinforcement processes as adequate to attain language, while Chomsky opted for an "innate predisposition toward syntax" as the means to a language end. Yet when the behaviorists began to treat persons with language problems, many of them used their behavioral procedures to target Chomsky's descriptions of language. Thus, for example, Gray and Ryan (1973) used rigorously behavioral techniques to teach generative grammar response forms. Even

more telling, Carrier (1974) moved to a nonspeech mode by using symbol forms similar to those used by Premack (1970) in his work with a chimpanzee. Carrier then used rigorous behavioral techniques to train his mentally retarded subjects to use these symbols as a language form. The final language form that Carrier targeted, however, was that of Chomsky's generative grammar, and seven-element syntactic strings with the plastic language form were the final goal of his behavioral program.

Thus many brilliant researchers and clinicians were somewhat victimized by the fact that our model often reflected answers to our three model questions which were theoretically different and often incompatible. Obviously, if people at the level of Gray, Ryan, and Carrier were vulnerable, the rest of us stood little chance.

The point of all of this discussion is to set the stage for a full appreciation of both the need for, and the impact of, the events of the 1970s. It is important for us to recognize the voids that existed in our clinical model at the beginning of that decade and thus to understand both the magnitude and the function of both the semantic and pragmatics revisionism that occurred in the period being analyzed. It is also important for us to appreciate the fact that the events of the seventies were getting us close to full compatibility among the three necessary elements of our clinical model. This compatibility will be discussed further later in this chapter.

**Substance of the 1970s.** Beginning as it did with the "semantic revolution" fueled by the research of such people as Bloom (1970), Schlesinger (1971), Bowerman (1973), and Slobin (1973), and ending with the "pragmatics revolution" attributable most notably to the research of Bates and her colleagues (1976, 1979) and the philosophic work of Austin (1963) and Dore (1975) which preceded their work, the decade of the 1970s should logically be called revolutionary. By both expanding our perspectives about the behaviors that constitute language and describing the natural learning experiences and processes that seem to account for these behaviors, the substantive data that became available in the 1970s not only solidified the gains made in the 1960s but extended them in important ways. The knowledge base made available in the area of child language in the 1970s will not only bring about profound changes in the basic academic fabric of our discipline, but it will also bring about profound changes in its clinical service system as well. Both of these changes will be logistically and intellectually taxing.

Conceptualizations about language behaviors at the close of the 1970s reflected the belief that the linguistic structure of children's utterances was *multidetermined* by dual needs to "*mean*" and to have some *social effect*. Obviously, such a belief represented another exponential leap in an element of our model and was destined to have important effects on other elements of it as well. For example, treatment procedures designed to train grammatic structures clearly had to be radically altered to accommodate the notion that such structures were multidetermined by both semantic needs and social performance needs. Also, previous adult notions about what constituted the "functional utterances" that had become the coin of the realm in radical behavior programs had to be altered. "Want drink" and "go bathroom" were obviously pale representations of the functions of truly normalized child language. If previous notions about what constituted functional language forms were altered, what would this do to the procedures designed to evoke the previously targeted forms noted above? Obviously, there was some rethinking to do.

In addition, new conceptualizations about language behavior and the processes that accounted for it raised anew the issues about what psychologic, environmental, and biologic constraints militated against such a complex behavioral system. Since most of these newer conceptualizations had come from research that tracked and analyzed the first language learning of *normally developing* children, what were the implications for handicapped children of varying types and levels of involvement?

Since the decade we are discussing is in the recent past, it is obvious that the issues raised above are still awaiting final resolution, and we will cover some of them later in the section on Future Implications. Suffice it now to look carefully at the "state of the art" model that existed at the close of the 1970s and to draw some conclusions about our clinical model and its implementation at this point in time.

At the close of the 1970s and the beginning of the 1980s it seems clear that our answer to the question about what constitutes language behaviors reflects a body of knowledge that is both substantively and philosophically rich. For example, if we can consider language as having meaning content, social instrumentality, and a predefined, culturally specific structure, we are a long, long way from where we started with vocabulary and grammar goals. If we can further consider language as most basically *communicative*, and thus targetable in various *modes*, we are far beyond previous perspectives that brought us to deny communication therapy to children who did not have speech. Going even further, if we can consider communication as a continuum of ever-escalating signals that begin with gaze and motoric actions on objects and caregivers, move to gestures, and then into conventionalized signal systems in several modes, we have advanced quite a bit from our previous abilities to identify and target valid communicative behaviors at prespeech and prelinguistic levels. These advances obviously have important implications for our clinical management of both developmentally disabled children, very young children, and children with severe motoric handicaps.

Our discipline's child language programs today are beginning to reflect the conceptualizations outlined above. The clinicians in our field are moving rapidly to take advantage of this. They have been deprived of adequate and logical substantive models for a long time, and they are both anxious and willing to work to deserve the modification of their title to speech-*language* clinicians.

It is obvious that most of our previous *procedural* models are not adequate to meet the demands of our new *content* models. Wide-ranging changes are needed and there are significant design and logistic obstacles to the attainment of these changes.

The data appear persuasive in their indications that many of the response forms now being targeted as communicative depend heavily on contextual information to make the bases of both their *form* and their *function* clear to child learners. Such indications are reflected in the fact that our basic clinic-based model is being modified the better to meet the individualized needs of various clients. To be sure, a 7-year-old who requires articulation changes, added vocabulary, and syntactic refinement might still be well served by our traditional clinical service contexts. Many severely language deficient children now included in our caseloads, however, cannot be adequately served by our traditional isolated clinical contexts for treatment. Moves to service models that are more representative of a child's full environment are becoming more and more prevalent. In consequence, moves to include other people who are significant in a child's environment as vital participants in the experiences of communication and language acquisition are much in evidence in both clinical practices and in research. Also well represented in the clinical work of the late 1970s onward is our awareness that communication and language are social and that the treatment processes must reflect this dimension of sociability.

On a procedural and program content level, it seems clear that the initial reductionist models of abstract "rule-systems" for language have not proven to be adequate as *operational* models for clinical designs. The models of Chomsky (1965) in syntax; Katz and Fodor (1963) in semantics; and Jakobson, Fant, and Halle (1952) in phonology all *under-represent* the variables that must be represented in clinical goals. Thus the trend is obviously away from the isolated training of idealized forms of surface linguistic structures and toward the training of classes of communicative responses in the conditions of their appropriate contextual occurrence and their social use.

Similarly, in the development of training procedures the reductionist Skinnerian paradigm (Skinner, 1953, 1957) seems inadequate to represent all of the variables and realities involved in the production of particular communicative functions and linguistic forms. The most obvious problem here is the behaviorist's insistence that only immediately *observable* antecedents and consequences be considered in the identification of controlling variables for linguistic responses. Since recent research (for example, that of Bates, 1976; Bowerman, 1973; and Olson, 1970) clearly suggests multiple control of communicative utterances by private, internal states of communicative intent, desired semantic intent, and audience induced events, it seems more and more apparent that the current functional analysis of behavior model is not adequate to operationalize all of the variables inherent in clinical work in child language. It thus appears that the problem with the current behavioral paradigm is very much like those problems we have seen with the idealized linguistic paradigms. It simply *under-represents* the actual variables involved in the process by which people generate differential linguistic utterances. In the difficult clinical endeavors we face, we cannot continue to ignore important variables because they are not accommodated by a specific model that we have used in the past. Instead, models must be reworked and enriched to represent better the variables that empiric efforts and revised theories identify. We have accomplished this enrichment in the linguistic domains. It's now time to carry this enrichment into the behavioral domains as well.

It does seem apparent that today's communicative perspectives still maintain the basic optimism that also characterizes functional behaviorism. Clinicians still appear to believe that nonintrusive, educational procedures can effect changes in communicative and linguistic behaviors. Similarly, clinicians seem still to maintain the goals of being systematic and data-based in their clinical work. Yet, by moving into paradigmatic representations of both the cognitive and social variables in communication and language, current clinical approaches move considerably beyond the relatively gross relationships that can be mapped by the current behavioral constructs, which, as we have noted, consider only immediately observable, external antecedent and consequent controlling stimuli.

If we can expand the current behavioral perspectives on antecedent and consequential controls to include multiple controlling stimuli, some of which might exist as internal states of the speaker, we will be better able to design the contexts for language teaching that will facilitate the acquisition of well-formed and socially valid communicative behaviors. It is a formidable task and obviously a somewhat dangerous one. It will be important for us to ensure the validity of hypothesized internal events by seeking observable behaviors that will confirm them.

In the most basic ways, then, current clinical procedures seem to be becoming well focused on the treatment variables that are directed toward the processes and experiences basic to the acquisition of the many dimensions that have come to be considered functional in child language behavior. As these procedurally directed changes have been made, it would appear that they in turn have had considerable impact on our perceptions about the various factors that can interfere with language acquisition. The basic treatment model available today seems most impressive in its overall breadth and depth. Yet it is also clear that this most pervasive model has not yet been tested at all adequately to measure the degree to which it can overcome the most severe of the conditions that constrain language development which we see in some of our current clinical populations. While our substance is rich and our procedures gaining in texture and detail, we are still far from attaining a clinical practice model in child language that we can be sure is adequate to the clinical tasks before us. This need for further testing and refinement will shape the next decade.

The failure to overcome all of the handicapping conditions manifest among clinical constituencies seems always to be the fuel for the continued drive toward new answers and new applications within our discipline's model. Today we do not yet know how our new models will hold up under the assault of autism, severe mental retardation, and other formidable constraints to the development of human communication systems. We do not yet know either how the normal language systems might be systematically simplified to ensure minimal levels of communication forms and functions among seriously handicapped children. Certainly we have not yet been able to specify adequately those biologic conditions that will militate against gains made with even this most comprehensive treatment model.

Clinically, we seem to be well situated for an enthusiastic test of our current models. As this clinical test proceeds over the next few years, we must be alert for data that point the way to further modifications of our model and our clinical practices.

## IMPLICATIONS FOR THE FUTURE

Many of the implications for the future of this discipline are made clear by the basic substance of today's theoretic model for clinical practice with child language problems. As we have noted previously, our broadened perspectives about the many dimensions of language have radically altered our clinical targets, our clinical procedures, and our clinical contexts. These changes in our basic language model have also radically expanded our most basic role perceptions as clinicians have accepted child populations that were previously excluded from our clinic rolls. In addition, our discipline now seems totally ensconced in a broader educational posture than ever before. Many elements of our public school clinical arm are very close to attaining the more pervasive environmental treatment contexts needed for severely language impaired children. There are, however, still too many of our more traditional "clean" speech clinics, clinics "uncontaminated" by retarded or autistic clients. There are also far too many good in-service clinicians who are handicapped by dated models and inadequate knowledge of these newer substantive bases.

It seems fairly certain that our activities in the immediate future must assure refinement of these significantly altered perceptions of child language through intensive and pervasive clinical applications. Service delivery models must be considerably more viable than they have traditionally been. Multidisciplinary treatment programs that include teachers and parents will need to be encouraged. Even further, speech-language clinicians will need to expand their treatment target repertoires to include social and cognitive behavioral repertoires that might precede language behaviors by a considerable amount of time. All of these implications will have a direct impact on the clinician, and we must concentrate intensive efforts on enabling and implementing these needed changes.

The demands of the future that have been identified by the current model would also seem to be a productive context which to look at the Gestalt of our disciplinary history and make some judgments about the patterns that are apparent in those patterns. It would seem that some introspection about those patterns might be extremely productive for our future planning in this discipline. For example, we have seen considerable change in our most basic child language models over the past 30 years. It seems important to identify some of the motivations and the mechanisms that have fueled these changes. Could we have done it better? Can we see elements of our discipline that have been particularly conducive to change; and conversely, can we identify factors in our discipline that have attenuated change? Can we use this brief review of our historical model trends in child language to identify voids that might remain in our current model? It would seem to me that we can at least begin to consider such questions.

## MOTIVATIONS AND MECHANICS OF CHANGE

Although change is the expectation in any academic discipline, there are differential pressures for change among various disciplines. It would seem difficult to deny the selective effects that our clinical service presence has on the speech and hearing discipline. While speech-language-hearing substance commands respectful audiences in many other related behavioral disciplines, it is our own clinical consumer who comprises the greatest constituency for our research and didactic products. Our discipline often appears either to forget, ignore, or deny this fact.

A clinical constituency does not preclude basic research or relatively esoteric interests within the speech-language-hearing discipline. It does, however, insist that the discipline, on balance, provide a substantive base adequate for those members who are on line with clinical cases. In that context, it seems appropriate to reiterate Norma Reese's request to the 1980 ASHA convention that we make sure to ask the "big questions" about human communication products and the processes that are involved in their attainment.

It would seem obvious to anyone who has examined the events of the past 20 years that we have seemed overly dependent on the research of other behavioral disciplines to alter our clinical model. Although many members of our discipline have made highly significant contributions to our body of knowledge, it appears that it has been the basic research efforts in developmental psychology and developmental psycholinguistic research which have most basically made possible our quantum leaps in child language model building. This seems particularly disturbing when we can also see that basic research in our discipline has actually grown at a tremendous rate during this same period. The topics of our basic research, however, seem guided more by some unwritten commitment to electromechanical instrumentation and, ironically, a continued preoccupation with speech rather than with a broadly based and in-depth interest in the communicative behaviors that enable the most basic social compacts of human beings.

While it is beyond the scope of this chapter to develop this point fully, it would seem important to consider the implications for the future of our discipline which might be extrapolated from an analysis of the content of ASHA's primary research journal and a consideration of the fact that we had to depend on developmental psychologists to tell us that young children's communicative behaviors functioned to establish "joint attention and joint action routines" between them and their primary caregivers (Bruner, 1975). While wishing only to seek balance and not to denigrate any research efforts, this writer would suggest that, since our current perspectives imply that children do not talk just to create syntax or to receive M&Ms, we should also emphasize that neither do they talk just to create vocal-onset times.

It does seem clear, then, that we must work diligently to alter the perception, which now seems to permeate our discipline, that the psychosocial variables of human communication are a "soft" scientific area. The dependence on other disciplines that can be seen in our recent history must be reversed by our commitment to basic research into the broadest dimensions of normal and disordered communicative processes. Concomitantly, our applied research efforts must be rigorously structured to demonstrate the adequacy of our clinical practices to effect important changes in the communicative performances of a wide range of clients.

## CONTINUING VOIDS IN OUR MODEL FOR CHILD LANGUAGE

If, as suggested above, we can mobilize our discipline for a basic and applied research initiative in the area of child language, we should seek direction for this effort by analyzing what our current, enhanced model still lacks for total clinical adequacy. What elements of the model have not been recently scrutinized and acted upon in our most recent period of revisionism?

Current analysis would suggest that more precise identification of the factors that function as *constraints* to language (or communicative) acquisition is the element in our model which is now most in need of

rigorous clinical and research attention. Despite the fact that our perceptions of these constraining factors have been considerably altered by the optimism engendered by the overall functional analysis of behavioral techniques, we have not yet examined the effectiveness of our altered clinical models and procedures against these inhibiting conditions.

Obviously, this writer is not one who would insist that no clinical model should be applied until research data fully document its effectiveness. Rather, it would seem that it is totally appropriate for us to apply the richest clinical procedures that we can design on the basis of current knowledge, for it is in the application of these "best" models that we can begin to identify both their areas of adequacy and their areas of relative inadequacy.

It is clear, however, that we cannot be lulled into complacency by the greatly enhanced clinical practices that recent knowledge has generated. Instead, while we can revel in the logic and the richness of these new practices, we must also be willing to specify their shortcomings. We must be willing to assure our practitioners and our clients that they will be protected from expectations that go beyond current capabilities. To do this, we must subject current clinical models to rigorous tests against the most carefully specified and discriminated biologic, psychologic, and environmental conditions among our clients. Only such research will reveal the additional knowledge and clinical revisions that will enable our effective treatment of all human communicative deficits.

It is time that this discipline took on the big clinical questions. No other discipline can do it as well. No other discipline would be so well served by such efforts.

## SUMMARY

A review of the viability and accommodation of this discipline's clinical practices in child language over the past 30 years is encouraging overall. While our early biases and relative substantive myopias should be viewed with alarm, our rapid clinical responsiveness to the major substantive changes of the past 20 years should be viewed with some pride. Our current idealized clinical state of the art seems very close to the leading edge of the knowledge base upon which it depends.

While our discipline has clearly attempted to develop a substantive base adequate to support clinical practices in child language, it does seem to have been overly dependent on the basic research of other behavioral disciplines in the fleshing-out of this model. It would seem that we have been relatively narrow in our definitions of "good science" and thus have missed broad areas of clinically important substance— substance for which we are both philosophically and intellectually well prepared to pursue.

It is ironic that it might well be the area of clinical attention to severe child language problems, which it historically rejected, that can provide the infant discipline of "speech correction" with the intellectual perspectives, the psychologic momentum, and the social and ethical pressures that can transform it into a major force among behavioral disciplines in academe.

## REFERENCES

Austin JL: *How to Do Things with Words*. Cambridge: Oxford University Press, 1963

Bates E: *Language and Context*. New York: Academic Press, 1976

Bates E, Benigni L, Bretherton I, Camaioni L, Volterra V: *The Emergence of Symbols: Cognition and Communication in Infancy*. New York: Academic Press, 1979

Bloom L: *Language Development: Form and Function in Emerging Grammars*. Cambridge: M.I.T. Press, 1970

Bowerman M: *Learning to Talk: A Cross-linguistic Comparison of Early Syntactic Development, with Special Reference to Finnish*. London: Cambridge University Press, 1973

Bruner JS: The ontogenesis of speech acts. *J Child Lang* 2:1–19, 1975

Bryngleson B, Glaspey E: *Speech Improvement Cards*. Chicago: Scott, Foresman and Co, 1941

Carrier J: Application of functional analysis and a non-speech response mode to teaching language. American Speech and Hearing Association Monograph No. 18, Washington, DC: 1974

Chomsky N: *Syntactic Structures*. The Hague: Mouton, 1957

Comsky N: *Aspects of the Theory of Syntax*. Cambridge: M.I.T. Press, 1965

Dore J: Holophrases, speech acts and language universals. 2:21–40, 1975

Finley G: *Speech and Play*. Magnolia (Mass): Expression Co, 1940

Gray B, Ryan B: *A Language Program for the Non-language Child*. Champaign, Ill: Research Press, 1973

Hull CL: *Principles of Behavior*. New York: Appleton-Century, 1943

Jakobson R, Fant CGM, Halle M: *Preliminaries to Speech Analysis*. Cambridge: M.I.T. Press, 1952

Katz JJ, Fodor FD: The structure of semantic theory. Language 39:170–210, 1963

Olson D: Language and thought: Aspects of a cognitive theory of semantics. Psycholog Rev 77:257–73, 1970

Premack D: A functional analysis of language. Experiment Anal Behav 14:107–125, 1970

Reese N: Presidential address at the Annual Convention of the American Speech and Hearing Association, Detroit, 1980

Schlesinger IM: Production of utterances and language acquisition. In Slobin D (ed): *The Ontogenesis of Grammar*. New York: Academic Press, 1971

Schoolfield LD: *Better Speech and Better Reading*. Magnolia (Mass): Expression Co, 1937

Skinner BF: *Science and Human Behavior*. New York: Macmillan Co, 1953

Skinner BF: *Verbal Behavior*. New York: Appleton-Century-Crofts, 1957

Slobin DI: Cognitive prerequisites for the development of grammar. In Slobin DI, Ferguson C (eds): *Studies of Child Language Development*. New York: Holt, Rinehart and Winston, 1973

Spence KW: *Behavior Theory and Conditioning*. New Haven: Yale University Press 1956

Stoddard CB: *Sounds for Little Folks*. Magnolia (Mass): Expression Co, 1940

West R, Kennedy L, Carr A: *The Rehabilitation of Speech*. New York: Harper, 1937

# 8

# APHASIA INTERVENTION WITH ADULTS: HISTORICAL, PRESENT, AND FUTURE APPROACHES

*LEONARD L. LAPOINTE*

## HISTORICAL ASPECTS OF APHASIA

Since ancient times humans have been taken aback and fascinated by the peculiar and convoluted utterances that fell from the mouths of their brain-struck companions. The peculiar and confusing disorder that came to be known as "aphasia" has proven to be fertile ground for bemused scholars who seemed to be in the grasp of an evolving obsession to record it, label it, rename it, sort it, resort it, categorize it, argue about it, and generally regard it as a weird and wonderful subject to study.

But the idea that shattered language can and should be mended, that is, that it can be darned instead of damned, is all too recent. What seems a very logical and appropriate attitude today was either ignored or accorded low priority by all but a few generations of scholars and healers. Not until this very century—as Carl Sagan would say "the last few ticks on the cosmic clock"—has anything other than a few cursory gestures been directed toward rehabilitation of those with aphasia. This chapter focuses on rehabilitative efforts and approaches to alleviate or circumvent this acquired disruption of language in adults, approaches that *have been,* approaches that *are now,* and approaches that *may well be.* The temptation toward hyperexuberant flights of speculation about what the future holds will be tempered by a firm grasp of the stagnation and disappointments of the past.

## SPIRITS, GODS, AND HUMORS

To establish the proper foundation for an understanding of contemporary approaches to the treatment of aphasia, it is helpful to sketch the development of some ancient ideas about the interconnection of brain, language, neuropathology, and the subsequent disarray of language. We can assume that since the dawn of man, when terrified primates huddled in dark caves, wondering what on earth to do with their evenings, the emerging faculty of language has been susceptible to disruption or loss. A wayward claw, a misthrown rock, a clumsy fall down a ravine after a binge on overripe berries in the hospitality cave all had the potential to inflict massive brain injury to the Cro-Magnon, and to compromise language. These causes, plus the clandestine small explosions inside the head *created* communication loss and reaffirmed the dependence of language on the integrity of the nervous system.

The first recorded reference to the nervous system, according to McHenry in *Garrison's History of Neurology* (1969), was in an Egyptian papyrus composed about 3500 B.C. The word "brain" was first used in this papyrus along with a description of its coverings and the fluid beneath them. This was the era during which diseases were thought to be caused by demons, disfavor of the celestial Gods, or spirits. Tiu, the evil spirit of headache, was thought to roam about wreaking random havoc, and in one description of an attack it is recorded:

Headache roameth over the desert, blowing like the wind. Flashing like lightning, it is loosed above and below. . . . This man it has struck and . . . like one bereft of reason he is broken. . . . Like a wild ass . . . his eyes are full of cloud. . . . Headache, whose course like the dread windstorm none knoweth . . . None knoweth its full time or its bond. (McHenry, 1969, p. 6)

This, of course, provided ample reason to stay in after dark. This also was the age of mysticism and superstition, which surrounded everything concerned with breakdowns of functions of the body. The celestial gods or the gods of Olympus were believed to inflict or avert disease at their whim.

The Golden Age of Greece was responsible for many changes in Western thought, and the area of disease and affliction was no exception. Science and the arts occupied such minds as those of Pericles, Socrates, Plato, Diabetes, and Sophocles, and the healers were represented by Hippocrates, whose revolutionary writings provide a firm anchor for many aspects of contemporary medicine. Not everything Hippocrates believed has stood the test of time, though. The pathology of this period was based largely on the concepts of the humors; that is, that disease was caused by the wrong combinations of four liquids: blood, phlegm, black bile, and yellow bile. Hippocrates also believed that the arteries contained air, a conclusion apparently

based on their state of emptiness in dead goats. However, the Hippocratic treatise *On the Sacred Diseases*, written about 400 B.C., was remarkable in that it disavowed the superstitions associated with epilepsy and other brain disease, and for the first time in history assigned the brain an exclusive role in mental functions.

"I am of the opinion," said Hippocrates, "that the brain exercises the greatest power in man. [It is] the messenger to the understanding and that from nothing else come joys, delights, laughter and sports, and sorrows, griefs, despondency, and lamentations. And by this, in an especial manner we acquire wisdom, and knowledge, and see and hear, and know what are good, what are sweet, and what unsavory" (Riese, 1959, p. 78).

## EVOLUTION OF BRAIN-LANGUAGE RELATIONSHIP

It was during this time as well that the unique relationship between speech and the brain was emerging. In his aphorisms on apoplexy (the old name for stroke) Hippocrates observed that ". . . persons in good health are suddenly seized with pains in the head, and straightway are laid down speechless. . . ." (McHenry, 1969, p. 11).

In *Epidemics* he describes hemiplegia and loss of speech in what McHenry calls probably the first written description of aphasia, although the speech description— "the tongue unable to articulate . . . her speech was delirious . . . speech was indistinct . . ." (McHenry, 1969, p. 11)—could be either aphasia, motor speech impairment, or the language of hallucination.

Centuries passed without any appreciable advance in understanding language dysfunction and its relationship to the brain. Six hundred years after Hippocrates, the influential work of Galen (A.D. 131–201) furthered the science of neuroanatomy, particularly our knowledge of the cerebral ventricles and some of the cranial nerves, but even with the passing of six centureis, the basic physiology of the nervous system was thought to be based on the action of animal spirits within the ventricles (Meyer, 1971). After Galen's considerable contributions to neuroanatomy, an even greater void opened in the march of knowledge. The remarkable feature of this relative vaccuum is that it spanned 15 centuries and encompassed even the Renaissance with its remarkable flourish of knowledge. da Vinci made some contributions to neuroanatomy, but apparently the great masters of the Renaissance were too busy redecorating ceilings and drawing crude helicopters to pay much attention to the brain and disorders of speech.

## PRIMEVAL TREATMENTS OF NEUROGENIC DISORDERS

### ALCHEMY, POLYPHARMACY, CASHEWS

During the time from Galen until approximately the seventeenth century, some of the very first specific treatment suggestions for neurogenic disturbances appeared. The prevailing principles of treatment were alchemy, richly laced with imagination, and polypharmacy—the practice of creating treatment concoctions by combining vast arrays of roots, herbs, liquids, and selected rodent parts. For nearly a thousand years patients with brain damage were fed, massaged, and impacted with combinations of ingredients such as crow feathers, wine, berries, and essence of turtle.

One of the first very specific recommendations for the treatment of aphasia is found in the *History of Medicine* by Mettler (1974). It was noted that "cashew (Anacardium), recommended for practically all psychiatric and neural afflictions, especially aphasia."

### CAUTERY, LEECHES, CUPPING

Other treatments commonly used for a wide variety of disorders, including those that affected the nervous system, were the use of leeches, cautery, and a practice called cupping. The practice of leeching for the purification and local abstraction of blood was carried on for generations, as was cautery.

The principles of cautery are still used today, as in cauterization to minimize bleeding during surgery. But earlier, less sophisticated devices, such as tongs and heated coals, were used. Practitioners were cautious, as we read in a book entitled *Ancient Therapeutic Arts* (Brookbank, 1954, p. 120): "If cautery is applied to the skull the application must be gentle, so as not to risk roasting the brain or shriveling its membranes."

Cupping involved the use of suction cups with small incisions beneath them to produce slow bleeding and rid the offending area of its disease. For example, for brain diseases, bilateral cupping of the temples was a treatment of choice. The temples were not the only locations chosen for cupping. Some practitioners moved lower in the central nervous system and did some work on the spinal cord.

Most of these medieval treatments of applying cautery and blisters and such were pressed into the neck to stimulate what was thought to be a sluggish tongue. As Critchley has pointed out (1970), it is difficult to explain how most of the healers of the seventeenth and eighteenth centuries could have overlooked or misinterpreted such features as use of the wrong words, recurrent utterances, the inability to read or even comprehend words, and particularly, as Critchley has stated, "the striking phenomenon of a prolix torrent of gibberish" (p. 54).

## CLASSICAL PERIOD

The classical period in the history of aphasia is generally recognized as encompassing the latter part of the nineteenth century, the so-called aphasia explosion of the 1800s. Prior to 1800, however, important descriptions of the disorder can be found. Some of these descriptions were of literary figures or celebrities, such as Jonathan Swift and Dr. Samuel Johnson.

Written after he had recovered somewhat, Dr. Samuel Johnson's personal account of his aphasia is striking. It illustrates
the moment of stroke, subsequent aphasia
characterized by verbal formulation impairment and agraphia, and a somewhat
dubious treatment.

About three in the morning . . . I awak-
ened . . . and sat up. . . . I felt a confusion and
indistinctness in my head which lasted, I suppose about a half a minute. . . . Soon after I
perceived that I had suffered a paralytic stroke
and that my speech was taken from me. . . . My
organs were so obstructed that I could say "no"
but scarely say "yes." . . . I had no pain . . . I
put myself in violent motion . . . but all was in
vain. I then wrote to Mr. Allen. . . . In penning
this note I had some difficulty, my hand, I know
not how or why made wrong letters. . . . Dr.
Heberden and Dr. Brocklesby were called. . . .
They put a blister upon my back, and two from
my ear to my throat . . . before night I began to
speak with some freedom, which has been increasing ever since. . . . (Critchley, 1970, p. 75)

One of the earliest references to a
more contemporary approach to language
rehabilitation is buried in the early descriptive literature on alexia. A German
physician named Johann Schmidt described in 1673 the nature of alexia in a
patient and said, "The patient never recovered from Alexia despite tutoring." A
second case, on a more optimistic note, was
reported to have responded to tutoring. No
specific details were given as to what constituted the "tutoring" in these cases, but
we may infer that this approach was a little
closer to contemporary treatments than
many of the earlier attempts.

Another early reference to re-education in aphasia, as documented by Licht
(1975), concerned the efforts of Thomas
Hun in 1851. Hun saw a 35-year-old blacksmith who had recently lost his speech following a stroke. Hun recommended exercises in reading, spelling, and repeating
words, and in reporting his success he gave
credit to the patient's wife, who apparently
had done most of the training. The loss of
speech suffered by the blacksmith was
called "aphemia" and "amnesia nervalis,"
two popular expressions of the time.

## GREAT APHASIA EPIDEMIC OF THE 1800S

Joynt has indicated that prior to the
nineteenth century the brain was looked
upon as "kind of an amorphous gruel" without specific functions assigned to different
areas (1975, p. 40). Though a little exagge-
rated, that generalization is essentially correct. If relatively little regard was paid to
brain and language in the previous thousands of years, the 1800s saw attention to
aphasia emerge with "almost explosive
suddenness" (Riese, 1947).

It was almost as though a great epi-
demic of aphasia swept Europe and
focused attention on the disorder. Not the
least of the contributors to this explosion
was Franz Joseph Gall. As with many of us,
Gall is remembered most vividly for his
excesses, and therefore he is associated
with phrenology, that pseudoscience of at-
tributing character and behavioral traits to
bumps on the skull. His very legitimate
contributions to our understanding of brain
and behavior nearly get lost in the shuffle.
But Gall, and subsequently the French
physicians Bouillaud and his son-in-law
Auburtin, did more to advance the hypothesis that speech and language were lo-
calized in the frontal lobes of the brain than
all of their predecessors.

Paul Broca gets most of the credit for
associating the "seat of articulate language"
with the left cerebral hemisphere following
his two famous case presentations at the
Paris Anthropological Society which rock-
ed medical and philosophic circles in Europe and spawned theoretic and termi-
nologic controversy that continues to this
day. Thus 1861, the year of Broca's first
advancement of Bouillaud and Auburtin's
views, serves as a convenient historic
milestone and is perhaps the most remembered date in the history of aphasiology.
Karl Wernicke, who contributed much to
our understanding of comprehension impairment in 1874, and a host of others began diligently studying the disorder on the
wards and in the laboratories.

These giants instigated an interest in
aphasia that resulted in an unprecedented
number of case studies, position papers,

and theoretic ruminations. There is no denying that the 40 years from 1860 to the turn of the century are among the most important in the history of the disorder.

But most of the interest at this time, as in some quarters today, was a trancelike preoccupation with the weird and fascinating symptomatology of the disorder. There appeared to be much greater interest in aphasia, the disorder, than in aphasics, the unfortunate people who suffered from it. Unfortunately in many camps that attitude persists.

## RISE OF REHABILITATION

As you can see, seeds of interest in rehabilitation were scattered sparingly prior to the 1900s. Some concern for preservation and restoration of function can be seen in early writings about how to manage loss of movement and weakness subsequent to neurologic disease. Licht (1975) notes that a Swiss physician named Frenkel formulated in 1889 what may be the core of rehabilitative medicine. Frenkel suggested that in chronic neurologic disease the fundamental methodology of rehabilitation consisted of daily sessions of active attempts by a patient to correct subnormal function by voluntary repetition. In this hint we see the skeleton of strategies not only for the restoration of physical function, but for dealing with communication impairment as well.

## C. K. MILLS

An important early contributor to the philosophy of a systematic program of restoration of language was the Philadelphia neurologist, C. K. Mills. He outlined, in a 1904 article in the *Journal of the American Medical Association,* an advocacy paper with an abundance of very specific training exercises and suggestions. Mills' contribution often gets overlooked in the aphasia literature, and though his methods were largely substantiated by anecdote and case report, we read Mills and recognize scraps of many contemproary approaches. Mills

anticipates the excitement surrounding the birth several generations later of "neurolinguistics" by focusing treatment on form class. Says Mills: "In connection with a study of his reacquisition of language, particular attention was paid to the degree in which he regained different parts of speech" (1904, p. 1941).

Mills' contributions were many. He suggested prognostic indicators; advocated a phonetic placement approach using what he termed the physiologic alphabet of J. Wyllie; associated sounds and letters with objects; attacked semantic-lexical deficit with dictionary drills; and in general prescribed a systematic and progressive course of training that had differential emphasis across modality and across aphasia type.

Mills also anticipated the fresh air of pragmatics that was to blow through language intervention years later. He noted the facilitating effect of using pragmatically appropriate and emotionally meaningful stimulus items when he suggested one of his patients could always "pick out words which had evidently been unusually familiar to him, . . . for example, the words whiskey, brandy, and beer in the hospital diet list were at once recognized" (p. 1946).

## WORLD WARS I AND II

The world wars did much to advance the thesis of rehabilitation of brain injured patients. Because of World War I aphasia was much more readily recognized and became a good deal more prevalent. Prior to 1917, 90 to 96 percent of the soldiers who suffered penetrating head injuries died. But improved transportation and surgical techniques and the creation of hospitals whose exclusive purpose was the treatment of the brain injured changed this. Aphasia was no longer considered an academic problem, though most of the emphasis at this time was on the constellation of problems associated with brain damage and still not narrowed in any significant degree to aphasia.

This changed a great deal with the contribution of Weisenberg and McBride

(1934) and with World War II. The devastation across Europe and the Pacific produced thousands of brain injured patients, and in the United States remedial efforts gained momentum. During World War II, the Surgeon General of the United States Army set up centers for training aphasic patients, and Joseph Wepman, one of the fathers of clinical aphasiology, was chosen to coordinate these centers. In considerable detail, Wepman described the organization of an aphasia center and offered guidelines for the organization of therapy for aphasia (Wepman, 1947).

## INFLUENCES OF A NEW PROFESSION

Wepman was one of the first of many to exert the influence of the fledgling profession of speech pathology and aphasiology.

One of the first articles in our journals which was devoted to aphasia treatment was written by Ollie Backus and published in the *Journal of Speech and Hearing Disorders* in 1945, entitled "The Rehabilitation of Aphasic Veterans." Backus was a visionary in more than one area of communication impairment, and about aphasia she wrote, "In the case of soldiers disabled by aphasia, the responsibility for rehabilitation rests with speech pathologists and speech therapists" (p. 149).

She advocated that the treatment constitute an intensive program that required attendance from 5 to 7 hours a day. She and her colleague Vivian Mowat Sheehan studied aphasia therapy that included both individual and group instruction with such activities as group singing, creative dramatics, club meetings, and social activities.

Awakening interest is evident in several early postwar articles on aphasia. In a doctoral dissertation completed at the University of Wisconsin in 1942 and subsequently published in the *Journal of Speech Disorders*, Anderson described clinical and linguistic findings in 18 cases of aphasia studied from the viewpoint of a speech pathologist (Anderson, 1945). Jon Eisenson also catalogued his impressions of his experiences in working with aphasic soldiers (Eisenson, 1947). The perplexities of aphasia led him to remark, "Aphasic patients and especially young aphasics, whose disturbances are related to traumatic head injuries, are an inconsistent and unconventional lot, who show little evidence of what the textbooks indicate their behavior ought to be as a result of their injuries" (p. 290).

At about this time the influence of speech pathologists in the Veterans Administration and in nongovernmental rehabilitation clinics began to be felt as well. Many people were involved in this gathering momentum, not the least of whom were Martha Taylor in New York; Hildred Schuell, who performed inspired and meticulous work at the Minneapolis VA Hospital, and Frederic Darley at the Mayo Clinic.

As Sarno has pointed out (1975), the techniques and materials used in treatment in those days were similar to and often borrowed from those employed in the elementary classroom. Methods associated with second language and literacy teaching were often used. In most cases these materials were adapted to adult interests. Since naming deficit is ubiquitous in aphasia and crosses all aphasia types, tasks, drills, and practice sessions reflected a good deal of attention to object and picture naming and the confrontation of vast stacks of flashcards. The mixed parentage of our new profession, arising as it did from the genes of both psychology and education, afforded some of the best approaches and influences from each of these disciplines. It also contributed to a horrible and persisting identity crisis, especially when aphasiologists are forced to exist with the philosophies and approaches of diagnosis/prognosis/treatment found in the medical model. We struggle with the identity problems forced upon us by our mixed and recent roots to this day. As is true of other orphans and waifs, this has contributed to a hard-knock life, but it certainly has not precluded progress.

A comforting fact should be that more mature professions, such as medicine, trace their roots back to Hippocrates and Galen and have had centuries of retrospection to progress, refine their procedures, and bury their leeches. We, quite to the contrary, are new kids on the block and trace our roots only to the time of Herbert Hoover and Al Capone (LaPointe, 1977). As John Keats said, "Time, that aged nurse, rocks us to patience" (1818).

## CONTEMPORARY APPROACHES

Contemporary approaches to aphasia treatment are an outgrowth and amalgamation of models perpetuated in the fields of education, psychology, and medicine. Approaches that reflect these models have been refined, blended, and pruned by the relatively new profession of speech/language pathology, but very little new has been added.

### NONBEHAVIORAL TREATMENTS

Management and comfort of the person with aphasia come from a variety of sources. In the early stages of an evolving or newly resolved CVA, medical and surgical intervention are paramount because the condition is often life-threatening. The extent of aphasia may be influenced by the medical-surgical treatments of choice. Anticoagulant therapy is often considered, particularly in evolving infarction or in the face of hypertensive disease. Vasodilators to produce increased blood flow and adrenocorticosteroids to reduce edema are frequently used as well. Unfortunately, two cold, hard facts about cerebral tissue that differentiate it from other body tissues stand out all too clearly. One is that neurons do not regenerate. As Schmidt has stated (1968), we are born with a full complement. Neurons also require a continuous supply of nutrients in the form of oxygen and glucose in the blood, and cease to function normally if deprived of either of these for more than a few minutes. Though some aggressive recent microsurgical techniques can reverse trends in ischemic disease, in the face of fully destroyed brain cells, function may be permanently dis-

rupted. Functional readjustment may take place in remaining healthy tissue, however, and as we well know, with a favorable environment and competent help, restitution and reorganization of function may proceed on an orderly and predictable course.

### BEHAVIORAL MODELS, PHILOSOPHIES, BIASES

Contemporary approaches to the restitution and reorganization of communication constitute a veritable cornucopia of strategies. As Sarno has stated (1981), literally hundreds of specific techniques are cited in the literature, and aphasia therapy is rarely identical in two treatment settings. Yet common threads exist which usually can be traced back to the philosophic and theoretic underpinnings of the dispenser. Some rationale or model is evident in most treatment methods, and for the most part these have fallen into two primary categories, depending on whether the aphasia is viewed as interference with access to language or loss of language competence. These two primary approaches have been called the stimulation-facilitation and the programmed-operant methods (Darley, 1975).

Though predominant, these are not the only rationales guiding management of aphasia. Others include psycholinguistics, cybernetic, modality, cognitive, and preventive orientations; all of these have been reviewed elsewhere (LaPointe, 1978).

### STIMULATION-FACILITATION

Perhaps the most prevalent form of aphasia therapy in the United States is stimulation-facilitation, an outgrowth of the concepts fathered by Joseph Wepman and nurtured and refined by Hildred Schuell. This approach can be observed in clinics from Providence to Portland and from Marquette to Key West.

As outlined elsewhere (LaPointe, 1978), proponents of this approach

(Schuell, Jenkins, and Jiminéz-Pabón, 1964) view the goal of language therapy as not so much to re-educate the aphasic patient but rather to stimulate disrupted processes to function at maximum levels.

Intensive and repeated sensory stimulation, with focus on the auditory channel, is characteristic of this approach. In fact, this emphasis on input has been termed *auditory bombardment*, since Schuell believed that disrupted auditory retention and comprehension skills were the underlying culprits in most aphasic deficits.

Specific treatment suggestions include the following:

1. Intensive auditory stimulation
2. Varied, abundant, and meaningful clinical material
3. Repetitive sensory stimulation and repetitive sensory stimulation
4. High patient response rates
5. Avoidance of forced responses and struggle
6. Avoidance of correcting defective responses
7. Making the stimulus adequate

After analysis of the nature of the aphasic person's defective response, the clinician has a variety of options for manipulating the stimulus to make it adequate. These include altering loudness, length, associational strength, and duration of stimuli; prompting and cueing; repetition; gapping; fading; altering tempo and pace; and changing the selection of input mode combinations.

Schuell abhorred rigidity in treatment and suggested that if the method leaves the patient behind or if the patient progressed faster than the method, the method must be changed. She recognized and advocated often, that there is no room for rigidity in clinical practice. Perhaps that is one of the reasons why her concepts remain relevant while some others appear somewhat dated.

## PROGRAMMED-OPERANT

Behavioristic, or programmed-operant, approaches to intervention view language rehabilitation more as an educative or reteaching process. The experimental analysis of behavior and principles of operant conditioning provide the basis for this approach. The chronology of the major steps can be found in many sources, but Brookshire (1967) and Holland (1972) have presented them as lucidly as anyone. Programmed-operant methods were at their peak in the sixties and seventies and for some reason appeared to be strangely correlated with the crest of popularity of the Beatles. At any rate, both have left their legacy, and in fact behaviorists have not disbanded but have left us principles and strategies that permeate language intervention.

## BASE-10 PROGRAMMED STIMULATION

In recent years an amalgamation of principles from both the programmed-operant and stimulation-facilitation schools has been incorporated into a system of therapy called programmed-stimulation (LaPointe, 1978). This strategy of organizing intervention features clearly defined tasks, baseline performance measurement, session-by-session progress plotting, and the flexibility to incorporate a rich array of stimulation procedures designed to encourage many responses from aphasic patients. With our particular variety of the programmed-stimulation approach, speech and language performance can be converted to a graphic display of progress (or lack of it) in percentages over ten treatment sessions. This approach to treatment has been adequately addressed in other sources (LaPointe, 1978) and need be only briefly mentioned here. This approach, and other attempts to add a degree of organization to the therapeutic process, does not obviate the need for counseling, providing realistic hope, being a source of information and emotional support, communicating with related professionals, and all the other humanistic details that constitute the sum of efficient and compassionate patient management. In the past, however, much aphasia management has been long on rapport, warmth, support, and coffee consumption, but short on the planning and drudgery necessary to remove specific language barriers. Some might argue that in the past few years we have seen more "trends away from structured treatment," but certainly trends away from structure cannot mean abandonment of systems that aid us in getting a firm grasp of our goals, enhance therapeutic planning, organize what transpires in a therapy session, and document change in a person's communication performance.

## THEME VARIATIONS

A rich array of contemporary variations on the theme of aphasia intervention is evident in recent literature. We read about and are influenced by such concepts as PACE therapy, pragmatics, and incorporation of parameters of natural discourse in treatment; thought-centered therapy; related strategies of divergent semantic therapy which attempt to resist more firmly the separation of cognition from language; self-adjusting therapy and systems of self-cueing; psychosociolinguistic and environmental systems of intervention; melodic intonation therapy; and many other innovative and inherently sensible strategies of refinement of our treatment form, content, and medium. Many of these approaches are reviewed in greater detail in the books of Sarno (1981), Chapey (1981), and Darley (1982).

## ORACLES AND PROPHECY: WINGS AND WAVES OF THE FUTURE

What does the future hold for aphasia treatment? We don't know. Certainly the area of *neurodiagnostics* is undergoing a technologic revolution. Positron emission computed tomography, xenon and regional blood flow studies, and the remarkable contributions of CT scan technology have contriubted mightily to answering the riddle of "Lesion, lesion, where is the lesion?" and to an even greater understanding of brain and behavior correlates.

But with a few exceptions, the technology of aphasia *treatment* is still a Model A in a space shuttle world. The materials that a present day aphasia clinician takes into the clinic room for treatment are not much different from those that were set before the aphasic patient by the starch-collared French physicians in the 1880s. We absolutely must explore (and some aphasiologists are) the vast potential of the creative application of existing computer hardware and software science, and the contributions of other breakthroughs in instrumental assistance to our traditional behavior treatment approaches. It's about time.

We welcome as well any contributions from neuropharmacology, biochemistry, and basic neuroscience. It is unlikely that breakthroughs in these areas will eradicate neuropathology or make our services unnecessary in the near future, but we would welcome anything that would augment or enhance our efforts.

Of course these are not the only approaches to aphasia rehabilitation to have been tried. Many have gone unmentioned. This is simply one person's view of what has been done to try to unravel this enigma so that we can help these people get on with loving and learning and living.

No doubt we will continue to learn slowly and build on the past as we have done. The impressive contemporary thinker from the University of Colorado, Kenneth Boulding, has written essays on "Human Knowledge as a Special System" (1981) and has expressed optimism about the potential of human discovery. He says that estimates have been made that only 10 percent of the brain is used, even by academics, and that the information potential of the human brain, with 10 billion neurons capable of being on or off and assuming different states, would be $2^{10,000,000,000}$ (2 to the 10 trillionth). This is a very large number. If we could write it at one digit per second, it would take 90 years to complete it. It's hard not to believe, therefore, that the potential for structure of this extraordinary organization, and for solving some of our enigmatic problems in aphasia, is very large, and that it is extremely improbable that we have even approached its boundary.

## REFERENCES

Anderson JO: Eighteen cases of aphasia studied from the viewpoint of a speech pathologist. J Speech Dis 10:9, 1945

Backus O: The rehabilitation of aphasic veterans. J. Speech Dis 10:149, 1945

Boulding K: Human knowledge as a special system. Behavioral Sci 26:93, 1981

Brookbank W: *Ancient Therapeutic Arts*. London: W. Heinemann Books, 1954

Brookshire RH: Speech pathology and the experimental analysis of behavior. J. Speech Hear Dis 32:215, 1967

Chapey R: *Language Intervention Strategies in Adult Aphasia*. Baltimore: Williams & Wilkins, 1981

Critchley M: *Aphasiology and Other Aspects of Language*. London: Arnold, Ltd, 1970

Darley FL: Treatment of acquired aphasia. Adv Neurol 7:111, 1975

Darley FL: *Aphasia*. Philadelphia: WB Saunder Co, 1982

Eisenson J: Aphasics: Observations and tentative conclusions. J Speech Dis 12:290, 1947

Holland A: Case studies in aphasia rehabilitation. J Speech Hear Dis 37:3, 1972

Joynt RJ: *Reading, Perception and Language*. Baltimore: York Press, 1975

Keats J: *Endymion*. London, 1818, 1. 705

LaPointe LL: What the speech pathologist expects from the neurologist. In *Clinical Aphasiology Conference Procedings*. Minneapolis: BRK Press, 1977, pp 5–9

LaPointe LL: Aphasia therapy: Some principles and strategies for treatment. In *Clinical Management of Neurogenic Communication Disorders*. Boston: Little, Brown, 1978

Licht S: *Stroke and Its Rehabilitation*. New Haven, Conn: E. Licht, Publishers, 1975

McHenry LC: *Garrison's History of Neurology*. Springfield, Ill: Charles C Thomas, 1969

Mettler CC: *History of Medicine*. Philadelphia: Blakiston, 1947

Meyer A: *Historical Aspects of Cerebral Anatomy*. London: Oxford University Press, 1971

Mills CK: Treatment of aphasia by training. J Am Med Assoc 42:1940, 1904

Riese W: The early history of aphasia. Bull Hist Med 23:322, 1947

Riese W: *History of Neurology*. New York: MD Publications, Inc, 1959

Sarno MT: Disorders of communication in stroke. In *Stroke and Its Rehabilitation*. New Haven, Conn: E. Licht, Publishers 1975, pp 380–408

Sarno MT: *Acquired Aphasia*. New York: Academic Press, 1981

Schmidt R: Neurological dysfunctions. In *Dysphasia: Professional Guidance for Family and Patient*. Englewood Cliffs, NJ: Prentice-Hall, Inc, 1968, pp 1–17

Schuell H, Jenkins J, Jiminéz-Pabón E: *Aphasia in Adults*. New York: Harper and Row, 1964

Weisenberg T, McBride K: *Aphasia: A Clinical and Psychological Study*. New York: Hafner Publishers, 1934

Wepman J: The organization of therapy for aphasia. I. The inpatient treatment center. *J Speech Dis* 12:407, 1947

# DISCUSSION: PART III: WHERE DO WE GO FROM HERE?

*RONNIE B. WILBUR*

Isaac Asimov once remarked that in order to predict the future for his science fiction stories, he relied heavily on what was going on around him in the present. In the same vein, a survey of ongoing research in the field of linguistics may provide some indication of future directions for research in language acquisition and language development. The chapters of McLean and La Pointe have provided historical perspectives on the past and present of language intervention goals and techniques with children and with adult aphasics (if, indeed, work with this latter group can appropriately be called "language intervention" at all). Emphasis entirely on speech eventually gave way to a primary focus on the phoneme. Then, as new developments occurred in linguistics, "language" came into the intervention setting. In many ways, intervention techniques and perspectives have paralleled various linguistic developments (see, for example, Wilbur [1977] for a discussion of how this parallelism has affected the teaching of English to hearing impaired children), and it is on this parallelism that I base many of my predictions and speculations about the future.

The advent of transformational generative grammar engendered certain changes in perspective on language development and intervention. Aside from Chomsky's (1957) innatist view, which contrasted sharply with the empiricist-behavioral view in vogue at the time, transformational grammar reinforced a general lack of interest and concern for the very young child with possible language difficulties. Transformational grammar focused heavily on the syntactic structure of related sentences; therefore, children who had not yet progressed to the two-word stage (at least) were largely ignored (especially by researchers, as therapists were still interested in pronunciation and could work even at the one-word stage), because syntax does not clearly come into play at the one-word stage. Braine's (1963) pivot grammar may be seen as an attempt to write a formal syntactic grammar for the child at the two-word stage. With much older children, several acquisition studies revealed a general tendency for certain transformations to be acquired before others (Menyuk, 1963, 1964; Brown and Hanlon, 1970, among others), suggesting that certain structures/transformations ought to be taught/trained before others in intervention or educational settings.

Many difficulties arose. It was not obvious, for example, how a normal child progressed from the pivot-open grammar to the full-blown transformational grammar, and therefore also not obvious how to assist a child in therapy in doing so. Further, a close examination of the data from the two-word stage revealed that the words did not in general obey the definitions of "pivot" and "open," thus creating problems in writing the grammars (Bloom, 1970; Bowerman, 1973). Using developments in linguistic semantics, such as Fillmore's (1968) case grammar, Bloom (1970) looked at the two-word stage in terms of the semantic relations the two words expressed, rather than the word order and possible grammatic relations (such as subject, direct object, indirect object) that might be expressed. Thus Bloom suggested that the child chose specific things from the environment to express and put those words into a sequence without regard for the requirements of the adult transformational rules. Going one step further, in 1973 Bloom suggested that a single-word utterance might be the child's choice to express an entire sentence, the rest of which is omitted because of performance factors such as breath control and memory span. Although this latter view was eventually abandoned, it gave new respectability to the child at the one-word stage. Researchers moved further away from transformational grammar as a theory of language acquisition and began investigating the comprehension and production capabilities of the child at the one-word stage. For a review, see Chapter 13 in Clark and Clark (1977).

The study of the one-word stage raised questions about the effects of cognitive development (Bates, 1976a, 1976b; Bates and colleagues, 1979, among others) and the role of environment in acquisition (again the work of Bates has been instrumental, but see also Bateson, 1975; Cross, 1977; Dore, 1974; Snow, 1972, 1977; Snow and Ferguson, 1977). Working within the framework of linguistic pragmatics, particularly the work of Grice (1975) and Searle (1969), researchers focused on gestures, vocalizations, and other kinds of behaviors (back channel nodding, eye contact) which might signal communicative intent. Certain of these nonverbal behaviors made it possible to study the prelinguistic child, pushing the developmental scale back

even further. The precursors to turn-taking and conversational interaction 'were identified in early adult-child interactions such as peek-a-boo and routines ("Say thank you to the nice lady") (Thomas, 1979; Gleason, 1982).

With older children, much of the recent research has focused on units larger than sentences, utilizing story grammars (Mandler, 1978; Stein and Glenn, 1979), text analysis (Kintsch, 1977; Rumelhart, 1977), or frameworks for the general comprehension of connected prose (Clark, 1977; Kintsch and Kozminsky, 1977, Just and Carpenter, 1977). To the extent that conversations involve less narrative and more turn-taking, story and text grammars must be supplemented by more fine-grained analyses, such as those of Haviland and Clark (1974), Gordon and Lakoff (1971), Sacks, Schegloff, and Jefferson (1974), Keenan (1977), Keenan and Schieffelin (1976), and Ochs and Schieffelin (1979).

A major side effect of this willingness to look at aspects of communication other than formal structure was the added benefit for language intervention of increasing acceptance of various forms of nonspeech language forms, such as symbol systems and signs (for an overview, see Schiefelbusch, 1980). The net result has been an increased distinction between language and speech, and a broadening of the interests of interventionists to the point where such traditional educational domains as reading and writing now appear to be potential domains for "language intervention."

When one looks at the future of language intervention, a number of predictions seem fairly safe. The "whole person" approach will probably be maintained, with its interest in larger communicative purposes and intents, its emphasis on language rather than merely speech, and its continued appreciation of the value of augmentative systems to speech. What then, do I see as the gap?

One obvious omission from the content of the chapters in this and other sections is that of syntax. With the focus on the larger domain of communication, the more formal, and perhaps to some less interesting, structure of language itself appears to have been dwarfed. The development of syntax in children and its related disorders have not been carefully and fully explored. This is in part owing to a backlash arising from the inadequacies of transformational descriptions of language. Whatever the causes, however, the fact remains that those children and adults who need intervention at a higher syntactic level present a problematic situation, because there is a significant lack of understanding of how pragmatics and syntax relate.

A major area of controversy in linguistics during the late 1960s and early 1970s was the nature of the relationship between syntax and semantics (an overview of the history is given in Newmeyer, 1980). One side, the interpretive semantics group led by Chomsky, sought to maintain a separation between semantics and "autonomous syntax," evolving transformational grammar into lexicalist grammar. The other side, the generative semantics group led by Lakoff, McCawley, and Ross, argued for an interdependence of semantics and syntax, and for the relevance of presuppositions, logic, and semantic representations to linguistic analysis. They expanded their concept of those forms requiring grammatic analysis to include what were traditionally called "pragmatic" concerns (see Sadock, [1969] for an argument that the relative status of speaker and hearer must be represented in deep structure to account for the ungrammaticality of German sentences with mixed polite and familiar pronoun forms). From the generative side of this controversy emerged the speech act research of Searle (1969) and Sadock (1970, 1972, 1974), and the conversational research of Grice (1975) and Gordon and Lakoff (1971).

On the interpretive side, continued research into the syntactic structure of language has overhauled the face of transformational grammar. It may come as a surprise to many that within transformational grammar as Chomsky now conceives it, there are no longer any transformations (see Newmeyer [1980] for a general discussion). Looking at the major transformations

that had been identified for English, Chomsky (1977) noted that movement of constituents appeared to be the central role of most of them. The remaining functions (deletion, insertion, and so on) seemed to be consequences of the movement itself. Focusing then on the movement function, by 1976 Chomsky had only two transformations—move Noun Phrase and move Wh-word. By 1977, those two had been collapsed into a single rule. The remaining details are handled by sets of filters and constraints on the surface form (rather than by rules that operate on the deep structure or intermediate forms) and are articulated as his theory of government and binding (Chomsky, 1981).

The demise of transformations takes the "transformational" out of "transformational generative grammar," but it still leaves a generative theory, one in which an infinite set of sentences is produced (or better, related) by a smaller, finite set of principles. Still working under this assumption, several other researchers (Gazdar and Pullum, 1981; Klein and Sag, 1981; Stucky, 1981) are expanding the complexity and function of phrase-structure rules into what they call "generalized phrase-structure grammar," which appears to be highly promising.

There have been numerous syntactic theories developed outside of the generative framework as well. Volume 13 of *Syntax and Semantics*, "Current Approaches to Syntax" (Moravcsik and Wirth, 1980), contains twelve chapters outlining different theories of syntax, only one of which (trace theory) is clearly identifiable as related to Chomsky's. Two of these, tagmemics and stratificational grammar, trace their origins to the middle 1960s (Pike, 1964; Lamb, 1966). Others have received varying degrees of attention in the past decade: Relational grammar and functional grammar have been highlighted by special sessions and volumes in the Chicago Linguistic Society series; Montague grammar is pursued in several major linguistics departments; while corepresentational grammar, daughter-dependency grammar, equational grammar, and role and reference grammar are still relatively new.

Another volume of the *Syntax and Semantics* series, "Discourse and Syntax" (Givón, 1979a), includes several efforts to more specifically relate pragmatic and syntactic concerns. In one chapter, Givón discusses the historical development of languages and how syntax (and morphology) arise from more general communicative interactions. Givón outlines a theoretic model for this development and then shows how this perspective allows a profitable comparison of pidgins versus creoles, unplanned versus planned (informal versus formal) discourse, and child versus adult communication.

Essentially, Givón views discourse as the source of syntax. The communicative mode contains two extreme poles, the pragmatic mode and the syntactic mode. Every human language has both extremes, as well as intermediate properties. Pragmatics gives rise to syntax, which leads to the development of grammatic morphology, which then decays by phonologic reduction, leaving unmarked discourse again. Languages seem to cycle around creating syntactic and morphologic markings and then losing them again.

The pragmatic mode is characterized by a topic-comment structure, loose conjunction of elements, a slow rate of delivery using several intonation contours, word order that reflects a basic principle of old information before new information, a ratio of about one-to-one of verbs to nouns in discourse, semantically simple verbs, little or no grammatic morphology, and the focus of new information marked with prominent intonation-stress. By contrast, the syntactic mode is characterized by a subject-predicate structure, more complex subordination, a faster rate of delivery with several structures under a single intonation contour, word order that reflects semantic cases more than pragmatic-topicality relations, a larger ratio of nouns to verbs, semantically complex verbs (causatives, for example), extensive use of grammatic morphology, and similar intonation-stress but with less functional importance (Givón, 1979b).

The pragmatic mode tends to be utilized in situations of communicative stress.

For example, speakers in a pidgin speaking community are thrown together without a fully developed common language, but most nonetheless communicate with each other. Similarly, the child has no established mode of communication with the people around him, especially at the earliest stages. In these situations, the pragmatic mode is used. The pragmatic mode is also used when there is a lack of a common pragmatic background. The speakers of a pidgin community generally come from different cultural and racial backgrounds and thus share few of the general pragmatic presuppositions that provide the basis for effective communication. The child also lacks this background. Again, the pragmatic mode is used. Another characteristic of pragmatic mode situations is that the communication involves topics that are immediate, obvious, and nonremote. That is, they are within the context of the here-and-now, for both pidgin speakers and children. The pidgin community evolves into a Creole community, one in which the Creole language is fully developed and contains a more complex syntactic mode. As the child develops, the shift in communicative mode is from totally pragmatic toward the gradual acquisition of the syntactic mode, so that the mature adult controls a range of modes from the fully pragmatic to the fully syntactic. The extreme syntactic mode is best represented by the complex, educated language used to write a formal paper. There is no time pressure on the reader (presumably) to decode the message, so that complicated structures can be used which the reader can go over if necessary for comprehension. In face-to-face communication, the listener hears the message and it is gone. To get a message across, complex structures with several embeddings are best avoided.

In a similar vein, Hopper (1979) discusses the relationship between syntax and discourse in the context of the structure of stories. He discusses the characteristics that distinguish foreground information, which is the actual story line of the narrative, and background information, which supports the story with additional material but does not further the main story line.

Foregrounded material is sequenced such that the events in the story follow each other in the same order as they occur in the real world. It is unusual for new information to be introduced as the subject of the sentence; as Givón (1979b), Li and Thompson (1976), and Keenan (1976) have indicated, sentence subjects tend to be topics that represent old information and are highly presuppositional. New material is more likely to be introduced in the predicate of a sentence; many languages have a tendency to put the new information as close to the end of the sentence as possible. In foregrounded material, the verbs tend to be punctual (an event at a point in time), rather than durative (an event continuing over a period ot time) or iterative (an event repeated several times in a period of time). Further, the verbs in foregrounded material tend to have a perfective aspect (that is, completed by the time of some reference event), while backgrounded verbs of the durative/stative/iterative type tend to be imperfect. Thus, in stories, discourse factors affect the choice of syntactic structure, subject, verb tense and aspect, and clause order.

A final example of the relationship between pragmatics and syntax comes from a paper on dative movement in English by Erteschik-Shir (1979). The author defines a pragmatic characteristic "dominance" in the following way: "A constituent C of a sentence S is dominant in S if and only if the speaker intends to direct the attention of his hearer to the intension (meaning or semantic content) of C by uttering S." This definition represents a significant departure from previous types of definitions in syntax in that it does not refer to the internal phrase structure or categories (Noun Phrase, Verb, and so on) in sentences but rather to the intention of the speaker and its desired effect on the listener. Erteschik-Shir demonstrates that the dominance relations that hold in a particular sentence will determine when that sentence can be used appropriately in discourse, which transformations (in the old style of transformational grammar) will apply to that sentence, which determiners and pronouns can occur in that sentence, and what the

sentential stress of that sentence will be.

Erteschik-Shir's test for dominance is to determine what sentences can appropriately follow the sentence in question. Thus the sentences "John said that Mary kissed Bill" and "John thought that Mary kissed Bill" can be appropriately followed by sentences that somehow focus on Mary, such as "That's a lie, she didn't" or "That's true, she did." But a similar sentence, "John mumbled that Mary kissed Bill," is less appropriately followed by a sentence concerning Mary and more appropriately followed by a sentence concerning John.

With syntactic choices so heavily dependent on pragmatic factors, it is hard to maintain a model of language in which syntax is completely autonomous (as argued by Chomsky since 1957). Givón (1979b) concludes that "syntax cannot be understood or explained without references to both its evolution ex-discourse and the communicative parameters and principles that govern both its rise out of the pragmatic mode and its selective use along the register scale of human communication. Therefore, the . . . extreme position, that of the transformational-generative orthodoxy, seems even more untenable."

Which of the alternative theories (if any) will eventually dominate is a prediction that my crystal ball does not allow me to make. What is clear is that developments in linguistics will continue, changing our perspective on language as they come and go. The future of language acquisition research and language intervention techniques lies, to some degree, in the present of linguistics. Major research questions, such as the nature of comprehension (Chapman, 1981) and the decisions concerning who, when, where, and how discussed elsewhere in this volume, are critically dependent on a better understanding of the *what*, the nature of the language that is acquired.

## REFERENCES

Bates E: *Language and Context: The acquisition of pragmatics*. New York: Academic Press, 1976a
Bates E: Pragmatics and sociolinguistics in child lan-

guage. In Morehead D, Morehead A (eds): *Normal and Deficient Language*. Baltimore: University Park Press, 1976b

Bates E, Benigni L, Bretherton I, Camaioni L, Volterra V: *The Emergence of Symbols: Cognition and Communication in Infancy*. New York: Academic Press, 1979

Bateson M: Mother-infant exchanges: The epigenesis of conversational interaction. In Aronson D, Rieber R (eds): *Developmental Psycholinguistics and Communication Disorders*. Ann NY Acad Sci 263:101–113, 1975

Bloom L: *Language Development: Form and function in Emerging Grammar*. Cambridge: MIT Press, 1970

Bloom L: *One Word at a Time: The Use of Single Word Utterances Before Syntax*. The Hague: Mouton, 1973

Bowerman M: *Learning to Talk: A Cross-linguistic Study of Early Syntactic Development, with Special Reference to Finnish*. Cambridge, England: Cambridge University Press, 1973

Braine M: The ontogeny of English phrase structure: The first phase. *Language* 39:1–13, 1963

Brown R, and Hanlon C: Derivational complexity and order of acquisition in child speech. In Hayes J (ed): *Cognition and the Development of Language*. New York: John Wiley and Sons, 1970

Chapman R: What about comprehension? Proceedings from the Second Wisconsin Symposium on Research in Child Language Disorders, pp 116–129, Dept of Commun Disord, Univ of Wisconsin, Madison, 1981

Chomsky N: *Syntactic Structures*. The Hague: Mouton, 1957

Chomsky N: On Wh-Movement. In Culicover P, Wasow T, Akamaijan A (eds): *Formal Syntax*. New York: Academic Press, 1977

Chomsky N: *Lectures on Government and Binding*. Dordrecht, Holland: Foris Publications, 1981

Clark H: Inference in comprehension. In LaBerge D, Samuels S (eds): *Basic Processes in Reading: Perception and Comprehension*. Hillsdale, NJ: Lawrence Erlbaum Associates, 1977

Clark H, Clark E: *Psychology and Language: An Introduction to Psycholinguistics*. New York: Harcourt Brace Jovanovich, 1977

Cross T: Mother's speech adjustments: The contributions of selected child listener variables. In Ferguson C, Snow C (eds): *Talking to Children: Language Input and Acquisition*. Cambridge: Cambridge University Press, 1977

Dore J: A pragmatic description of early language development. J Psycholing Res 3:343–350, 1974

Erteschik-Shir N: Discourse constraints on dative movement. In Givón T (ed): *Discourse and Syntax. Syntax and Semantics*, vol 12. New York: Academic Press, 1979

Fillmore C: The case for case. In Bach E, Harms R (eds): *Universals in Linguistic Theory*. New York: Holt Rinehart and Winston, 1968

Gazdar G, Pullum G: Subcategorization, constituent order, and the notion "head." Presented at the Fifty-sixth Annual Meeting, Linguistic Society of America, New York, 1981

Givón T (ed): *Discourse and Syntax. Syntax and Semantics*, vol 12. New York: Academic Press, 1979a

Givón T: From discourse to syntax: Grammar as a processing strategy. In Givón T (ed): *Discourse and Syntax*, vol. 12. New York: Academic Press, 1979b

Gleason J: When language interaction breaks down. Presented at the Fifth Annual Language Awareness Conference, Brown University, Providence, RI, 1982

Gordon D, Lakoff G: Conversational postulates. Chicago Ling Soc 7:63–84, 1971

Grice H: Logic and conversation. In Cole P, Morgan J (eds): *Syntax and Semantics*, vol 3. New York: Academic Press, 1975

Haviland S, Clark H: What's new? Acquiring new information as a process in comprehension. J Verb Learn Verb Behav 13:512–521, 1974

Hopper P: Aspect and foregrounding in discourse. In Givón T (ed): *Discourse and Syntax*. New York: Academic Press, 1979

Just M, Carperter P (eds): *Cognitive Processes in Comprehension*. Hillsdale, NJ: Lawrence Erlbaum Associates, 1977

Keenan E: Toward a universal definition of subject. In Li C (ed): *Subject and Topic*. New York: Academic Press, 1976

Keenan EO: Making it last: Uses of repetition in children's discourse. In Ervin-Tripp S, Mitchell-Kernan C (eds): *Child Discourse*. New York: Academic Press, 1977

Keenan E, Schieffelin B: Topic as a discourse notion: A study of topic in the conversations of children and adults. In Li C (ed): *Subject and Topic*. New York: Academic Press, 1976

Kintsch W: On comprehending stories. In Just M, Carpenter P (eds): *Cognitive Processes in Comprehension*. Hillsdale, NJ: Lawrence Erlbaum Associates, 1977

Kintsch W, Kozminsky E: Summarizing stories after reading and listening. J Educ Psychol 69: 491–499, 1977

Klein E, Sag I: Semantic type and control. Presented at the Fifty-sixth Annual Meeting, Linguistic Society of America, New York, 1981

Lamb S: *Outline of Stratificational Linguistics*. New York: Harcourt Brace Jovanovich, 1966

Li C, Thompson S: Subject and topic: A new typology for language. In Li C (ed): *Subject and Topic*. New York: Academic Press, 1976

Mandler J: A code in the node: The use of story scheme in retrieval. Discourse Proc 1:14–35, 1978

Menyuk P: Syntactic structures in the language of children. Child Develop 34:407–422, 1963

Menyuk P: Syntactic rules used by children from preschool through first grade. Child Develop 35:533–546, 1964

Moravcsik E, Wirth J: *Current Approaches to Syntax. Syntax and Semantics*, vol 13. New York: Academic Press, 1980

Newmeyer F: *Linguistic Theory in America: The First Quarter-century of Transformational Generative Grammar*. New York: Academic Press, 1980

Ochs E, Schieffelin B: *Developmental Pragmatics*. New York: Academic Press, 1979

Pike K: Discourse analysis and tagmeme matrices. Oceanic Ling 3:5–25, 1964

Rumelhart D: Understanding and summarizing brief stories. In LaBerge D, Samuels S (eds): *Basic Processes in Reading: Perception and comprehension*. Hillsdale, NJ: Lawrence Erlbaum Associates, 1977

Sacks H, Schegloff E, Jefferson G: A simplest systematics for the organization of turn-taking for conversation. Language 50:696–735, 1974

Sadock J: Hypersentences. Papers Ling 1:283–370, 1969

Sadock J: Whimperatives. In Sadock J, Vanek A (eds): *Studies Presented to Robert B. Lees by His Students*. Edmonton: Linguistic Research Inc, 1970

Sadock, J: Speech act idioms. Chicago Ling Soc 8:329–339, 1972

Sadock, J: *Toward a Linguistic Theory of Speech Acts*. New York: Academic Press, 1974

Schiefelbusch R (ed): *Nonspeech Language and Communication*. Baltimore: University Park Press, 1980

Searle J: *Speech Acts*. Cambridge, England: Cambridge University Press, 1969

Snow C: Mother's speech to children learning language. Child Develop 43: 549–565, 1972

Snow C: The development of conversation between mothers and babies. J Child Lang 4:1–22, 1977

Snow C, Ferguson C (eds): *Talking to Children: Language Input and Acquisition*. Cambridge, England: Cambridge University Press, 1977

Stein N, Glenn C: An analysis of story comprehension in elementary school children. In Freedle R (ed): *New Directions in Discourse Processing*. Hillsdale, NJ: Ablex, 1979

Stucky S: Linear order and case marking. Presented at the Fifty-sixth Annual Meeting, Linguistic Society of America, New York, 1981

Thomas E: It's all routine: A redefinition of routines as a central factor in language acquisition. Presented at the Fourth Annual Boston University Conference on Language Development, Boston, 1979

Wilbur R: A pragmatic explanation of deaf children's difficulty with several syntactic structures of English. Volta Rev 79:85–92, 1977

# PART IV _____

# MOVING FROM ASSESSMENT TO INTERVENTION

# 9

# FROM ASSESSMENT TO INTERVENTION: PROBLEMS AND SOLUTIONS

*LYNN S. SNYDER*

Language assessment can be regarded as the speech and language pathologist's contribution to time and motion efficiency studies. In a limited amount of time, we sample selected oral, written, and gestural language behaviors that allow us to estimate an individual's typical performance, determine whether it will meet his communicative needs, and identify some major aspects of language to which any necessary intervention efforts might be addressed.

The secret of the great efficiency and relative success of our language assessment seems to be related to a number of factors. First, motivated by linguistic and psycholinguistic theory supported by empiric study, the language behaviors that we sample are considered representative of language processing and production. Second, these selected language behaviors tend to be robust behaviors that occur reliably among all individuals. Third, these behaviors typically seem to possess some concurrent and predictive validity. There seems to be a relationship between performance in these aspects of language and the ability to communicate linguistically now and at some future point. Lastly, the standardization and normalization of measurement instruments allow us to determine reliably whether an individual's performance is significantly discrepant from that of his peers.

Thus language assessment is a relatively efficient and economical process that provides data that can be used in planning subsequent intervention.

An important question, however, is how one makes the leap from assessment to intervention. Language assessment samples only a subset of psycholinguistic processes. Consequently, we need to determine the individual's proficiency with other aspects of language and where his skills lie on the continuum of intermediate steps between one major language achievement and the next. In addition, it is critical to determine the individual's style or way of performing and of learning language. In this way we can choose the most effective intervention strategies for the individual. Thus programming language intervention requires that we determine the content of the intervention program and the strategies to be elicited during its course.

Of course we determine intervention strategies and content throughout the treatment course. However, we tend to devote more of our time to these goals at the outset, when we are less familiar with the individual client and his needs. This notion of continuing assessment during the course of intervention has been called diagnostic therapy, diagnostic teaching, and clinical teaching (Lerner, 1977). The concentrated efforts that we make in diagnostic teaching at the outset of intervention seem to provide a bridge between assessment and intervention.

When we evaluate the way in which the speech and language pathologist makes the transition from assessment to intervention, we are faced with two major questions:

1. Do current language assessment practices truly sample the *critical* and *representative* aspects of language?

2. Have current diagnostic teaching efforts been successful at uncovering the individual's language learning style?

Thus we must question our determination of the relevant content of language assessment and our ability to discern individual language performance and learning styles. This chapter addresses each of these issues, acknowledging our achievements and identifying problems and areas for research and development.

## CONTENT OF CURRENT ASSESSMENT PRACTICES

Language assessment is a remarkably efficient and effective procedure whose efficiency partially derives from its ability to sample robust and relevant behaviors. These behaviors are often considered to be those mobilized for oral and written communication. Consequently, the impairment or delayed development of these behaviors tends to have a negative effect on linguistic communication. The content of oral language assessment has traditionally included the measurement of the individual's ability to comprehend and produce single vocabulary words, syntactic structures, morphologic forms and markers, and relevant phonologic distinctions under a variety of conditions. In addition, the individual's ability to recall a wide variety of types of language stimuli in sequential and in free order is often assessed (Nation and Aram, 1977; Byrne, 1978).

The assessment of written language has typically examined the individual's reading, spelling, and written composition skills. Reading assessment has looked at the individual's word attack skills, and silent and oral reading for words, sentences, and paragraphs (Hammill and Bartel, 1977; Harris and Sipay, 1975; Johnson and Myklebust, 1967). The assessment of spelling examines the individual's ability to spell phonetically regular and irregular words in written and oral form (Frith, 1981; Johnson and Myklebust, 1967; Larsen and Hammill, 1982). Our assessment of written composition has examined productivity, syntax and morphology, and the level of the ideation expressed (Hammill and Larsen, 1978; Myklebust, 1965).

This seemingly comprehensive list of language skills is assessed during early and middle childhood and adulthood with both standardized and informal descriptive measures (Bloom and Lahey, 1978; Launer and Lahey, 1981). Our assessments, however, seem to fall short of our goal of representative sampling in two ways. First, there are critical language processing and production skills that we fail to sample. Second, some of our standardized measures are poorly constructed, presenting the listener and reader with nontypical language stimuli and measuring the least important information. The net effect of these shortcomings has been our limited ability to meet adequately the assessment and intervention needs of the greater proportion of school-aged and adolescent language disordered children and some language disordered adults. It is much like solving a puzzle when some pieces are missing, or when those you have belong to another puzzle.

## THE MISSING PIECES

Those aspects of oral and written language which we have failed to sample seem to fall under the semantic and syntactic components of language, the pragmatic or functional aspects of communicative language, and the processing and production of narrative discourse.

**Lexical Semantics.** An individual's ability to comprehend and produce single words, the entries of one's lexicon, has long been the core of systematic language assessment (Nation and Aram, 1977). The preferred method of determining an individual's lexical skills has been to assess his comprehension of the direct denotative meaning of a word, for example, using the *Peabody Picture Vocabulary Test-R* (Lloyd and Lloyd, 1981), the *Ammons Full Range Picture Vocabulary Test* (Ammons and Ammons, 1948), or subtests and items from more comprehensive language batteries for adults and children, and also to assess his production during a confrontation naming task, using, for example, the *Boston Naming Test* (Kaplan, 1976), the *One Word Expressive Vocabulary Test* (Gardner, 1980), or similar subtests from comprehensive assessment batteries.

The lexicon, however, contains more information than the phonologic shape of the word and its primary meaning (Fillmore, 1971). It also contains information about the multiple meanings that each word may take or its polysemy. It is precisely this aspect of lexical semantics that we have failed to assess.

Historically, language disordered children (Johnson and Myklebust, 1967; Strauss and Lehtinen, 1947; Wiig and Semel, 1976) and adults (Goldstein and Scheerer, 1941) have been described as concrete in their concepts and understanding of words and phrases. Their concreteness may be partially attributable to their difficulty in acquiring the more abstract semantic features of word meanings. Another portion of their lack of abstract attitude may be attributable to their difficulty in handling polysemous words (Wiig and Semel, 1976). We often observe their concreteness in their difficulty comprehending puns, metaphors, and proverbs (Johnson and Myklebust, 1967; Wiig and Semel, 1976). Such linguistic operations rely upon the listener's knowledge of polysemous words in order to be successful. Thus language disordered children often fail to understand how a clock can have hands or a bed can have a foot. Language impaired adults may also sustain similar problems with lexical processing.

Consequently, it is important that we not only assess the individual's ability to comprehend polysemous words but also focus our remedial efforts in that direction when necessary. At this time, there are few standardized measures that tap the oral language and reading comprehension of polysemous words. *The Word Test* (Jorgensen, Barrett, Huisingh, Zachman, 1981) is one such measure, but certainly more are needed, particularly as part of our more comprehensive assessment batteries. It seems important to know whether language impaired individuals can deal with this aspect of the flexibility of language.

**Advanced Syntactic Forms.** Our ability to assess the syntactic comprehension and production of school-aged children and adolescents does not seem to be particularly well developed. It appears that most standardized measures exclusively devoted to the estimation of children's syntactic abilities come to a dead stop at the 8 year level. Some recently developed measures, for example, the *Test of Language Development* (TOLD) (Newcomer and Hammill, 1977), *Test of Adolescent Language* (TOAL) (Hammil, Brown, Larsen, Wiederholt, 1980), the *Clinical Evaluation of Language Function* (CELF) (Wiig and Semel, 1981), and the *Screening Test of Adolescent Language* (STAL) (Prather, Breecher, Stafford, Wallace, 1980), extend beyond that age range. However, apart from the Listening/Grammar subtest of the TOAL (Hammill and colleagues, 1980), a particularly robust way of assessing the comprehension and production of advanced syntactic forms, for example, those described by Chomsky (1969), has yet to be developed.

This seems to be a tremendous oversight. These syntactic forms clearly distinguish school-aged youngsters with underlying language deficits from their normal peers (Byrne, 1981). And we have known about them for some time. Carol Chomsky's work was first published almost thirteen years ago. The speech and language pathologists in school settings have indicated that this is a crying need, particularly in these times when school districts or state guidelines or both often require them to demonstrate a *statistically significant* discrepancy in the language disordered child's performance from his normal peers. This is nearly impossible when few standardized measures extend into this age range.

Our ability to assess the reading comprehension of advanced syntactic forms has been similarly limited. Few reading measures have systematically controlled the syntactic complexity of single sentence items or have included appropriate foils to tap the reader's understanding of advanced forms. La Pointe and Horner's (1979) reading comprehension assessment for language impaired adults is a nice exception. Surprisingly, the TOAL (Hammil and colleagues, 1980) does not select as advanced or representative syntactic forms for its syntactic reading comprehension component as for its listening comprehension component. Older notions and methods of deriving readability levels based upon the sentence length may have constrained these items. The need, however, remains. Syntactic abilities have been implicated in a number of youngsters who have difficulty with written language (Fry, Johnson, Muehl, 1970; Vogel, 1975). Researchers (Vellutino, 1982) have resorted to using the more complex items selected from the *Test of Syntactic Abilities* (TSA) (Quigley, Steinkamp, Power, Jones, 1978), a measure devised for hearing impaired children.

We encounter similar problems when we attempt to assess the syntactic complexity of sentences written by older children. At this time, the T-unit analysis (Hunt, 1965) and a corresponding metric, the syntactic density score (Golub and Kidder, 1974), are the only *discriminating* means of assessing the level of *clausal* development of written language in older children and adults. This measure is particularly sensitive to systematic differences in syntactic complexity, even discriminating among adults (Hunt, 1970) at various levels. While the *Picture Story Language Test* (PSLT) (Myklebust, 1965) may contain a measure of written syntax, it is largely confined to the global characteristics of general word order, the individual's application of morphologic markers, and the mechanics of

written language: capitalization and punctuation. Although the PSLT has served us well, clinicians do need more information about the complexity of the syntax produced. The T-unit analysis serves this purpose admirably. Clinicians can even program their microprocessor to perform the analysis for them (Golub and Kidder, 1974).

While the T-unit and syntactic density score have been around for quite some time, few clinicians seem to know about it or use it. They seem to be under the influence of the Madison Avenue effect: The analysis has never been packaged or marketed! Found in a juried nonspeech and language pathology publication, this measure and its psychometric information are readily available to the professional interested in the syntactic complexity of productive written language. Our ability to assess the syntax of written language in children and adults would be considerably enhanced if we were to utilize this resource.

In sum, our language assessment procedures must be broadened to include the assessment of advanced syntactic structures in both oral and written language. This information will not only allow us to identify the syntactic deficits of older language disordered youngsters more accurately, it will also help us program more comprehensive and effective language intervention.

**Pragmatic Skills.** The psycholinguistic research of the seventies has made an important contribution to our conceptualization of language. It brought our attention to the pragmatic, or functional, aspects of language. In addition to considering the structures used in communicative language, we began to consider the functions that utterances assumed (Austin, 1962; Parisi and Antinucci, 1979; Searle, 1969) and the ways in which conversation was structured and conducted (Grice, 1975; Schegloff, 1968). We no longer analyzed sentences in an isolated fashion. Rather, we began to consider the relationship between the sentence and the context or situation in which it was used, to determine how the speaker intended it to be taken. As Bates (1976) so aptly put it, pragmatics is concerned with the use of language in a context. Consequently our concern for the language disordered individual not only included his proficiency with language structures but also his ability to mobilize those language structures for communication and to understand them when they were mobilized by other speakers. In a sense our concern extended from linguistic performance to the broader issue of communicative competence.

Research on the pragmatic aspects of adult communication has demonstrated that one syntactic form can serve many functions depending upon the contextual constraints. For example, the declarative sentence, "My, it's warm in here," can be interpreted as a request for someone to open a window, a joking complaint about a too-efficient air conditioner, or a humorous acknowledgment of a disagreement. Conversely, a single function may be carried out by more than one type of syntactic form (Wollner, 1978). For example, requests can be made with both declarative and interrogative sentence forms, alternately using modals, contrastive stress, the conditional mood, and other syntactic devices.

In addition, conversations appear to be conducted in particular ways and are constrained by a predictable set of rules or conversational postulates (Grice, 1975). Speakers are polite to one another, tell each other the truth, and try to share relevant and sufficient information with one another. While they may not always succeed in complying with all of these conversational postulates, they try to comply and assume that their partner will do the same (Clark and Clark, 1977).

At this time, a standardized measure is available which can be used to assess pragmatic aspects of adult language. The *Communicative Activities of Daily Living* (CADL) (Holland, 1980) broadens the scope of our assessment of adult language.

Children acquire these aspects of pragmatic or communicative competence. From their early limited repertoires of functions expressed by language (Bates, 1976; Carter, 1975), they develop large functional repertoires by their late pre-school years (Dore, 1977, 1979; Ervin-Tripp, 1977). They seem to develop conversational skills less quickly. In their early preschool years, they repeat words and utterances or use sound play to maintain or keep conversations going (Keenan, 1974, 1977). Also they often need more than one conversational turn to complete the production of their message (Keenan, 1977). It seems that youngsters do not completely master conversational rules until middle childhood. In addition, some aspects of conversational skills continue to show developmental gains throughout late childhood, for example, the ability to request message clarification observed in the normal subjects studied by Donohue, Pearl, and Bryan (1980).

We might wonder whether pragmatic skills are a critical or relevant concern for language assessment in children. There is mounting evidence to suggest that some language disordered children sustain deficits in their functional communication. Some—but not all—language disordered youngsters have difficulty producing a variety of language functions (Geller and Wollner, 1976) and indirect requests (Prinz, 1977). In addition, some children have difficulty systematically varying their request forms with the age of the listener (Messick and Newhoff, 1979) and revising their utterances for the listener (Gallagher and Darnton, 1978; Hoar, 1977). Although older language impaired children may be active conversational participants, they are less assertive than their normal peers (Donohue, Pearl, Bryan, 1980). Thus there seem to be a number of children whose functional language skills will require assessment.

In recent years, informal, descriptive assessment techniques have emerged which can be used to assess children's functional communication. These include the Chapman (1980), Coggins and Carpenter (1981), McLean and Snyder-McLean (1978), and Becker and Silverstein (1982) approaches, among others. The informal assessment of children's conversational competence can be performed with the Bates and Johnston (1977) method. While these approaches are helpful, we also need standardized measures that will allow us to sample and compare a child's performance with that of a group of peers.

Thus we need some standardized measures of children's pragmatic skills. They will offer us a more accurate and efficient way of sampling and measuring children's ability to mobilize their language skills for effective communication.

**Constructive Comprehension Processes.** Although all of these language skills are important and relevant aspects of language performance, there seems to be none so critical as constructive comprehension processes in oral and written language. These processes include listening and reading comprehension for narratives—particularly discourse narratives—and the ability to draw inferences. In other words, these are processes that allow the individual to go beyond the sentence level to comprehend the way in which sentences relate to one another and to the narrative as a whole.

Narratives, particularly story narratives, are an important source of an individual's daily exposure to language and world knowledge. Storybooks are read to children daily, stories are told to them, stories are played out on the television and movie screens, and youngsters are expected to learn to read stories. Adults have a similar exposure to stories. In addition, jokes and anecdotes often take the narrative form. Individuals, then, spend a great proportion of their time listening to narrative discourse.

Narrative discourse processing is thought to be a constructive comprehension process (Spiro, 1980). Listeners and readers actively construct an interpretation of what they have heard or read. They use their knowledge of the world, or schemata, their knowledge of language, and of narratives themselves as "scaffolding" (Anderson, Spiro, Anderson, 1978) upon which they build their understanding. Listeners do not listen for each piece of information conveyed sentence by sentence and gradually add the meanings to derive an understanding of the narrative. Rather, they seem to obtain an initial understanding of the theme or major events of the story. They use this information and their knowledge of language and narrative structure to set up expectations and to organize and interpret the information that is yet to come.

Typically, listeners' and readers' understanding of narratives does not reflect all of the detailed information contained in the story (Kintsch, 1977), nor is it necessarily accurate in its detail or order. Rather, listeners and readers seem to comprehend the "gist" or main ideas of the story (Kintsch, 1974). The more world knowledge or background information that a listener or reader has about the events or topics of the narrative, the more information he will be able to understand and remember (Schank and Abelson, 1977; Thorndyke, 1977). In addition, the more well structured a narrative is or the more closely it conforms to our understanding of how stories are structured and sequenced, the more of the story the listener or reader will be likely to understand (Kintsch, 1977; Mandler and Johnson, 1977; Thorndyke, 1977).

Listeners' and readers' active construction of the meaning of narratives is a very powerful process. It is so powerful that when they are faced with a story that does not conform to our Western notions of story structure, for example, Indian folk tales and myths or scrambled stories, they rearrange, construct, and understand the stories in terms of their notions of Western tales (Bartlett, 1932; Kintsch and Greene, 1978; Kintsch, Mandel, Kosminsky, 1977). This type of constructive processing occurs whether the story is heard (Stein and Glenn, 1979), read (Kintsch, 1974), seen in a series of pictures (Polson, Kintsch, Kintsch, Premack, 1979), or viewed on film (Baggett, 1979).

Adults engage in these comprehension processes easily and use them to handle narratives of varying length and complexity. Children gradually acquire this skill. They develop the ability to get the main idea or gist of the story, interpret its logical sequence, and understand an increasing number of details (Baker and Stein, 1978). While these types of constructive comprehension seem to begin developing during the child's preschool years (Polson and colleagues, 1979), they continue to develop and make their greatest strides during the elementary school years (Baker and Stein, 1978: Stein and Glenn, 1979).

There is evidence that some school-aged language and learning disabled children have difficulty processing discourse narratives. Weaver and Dickenson (1979) read Stein and Glenn's (1979) stories to reading disabled children and compared their mean performance to that of Stein and Glenn's sample. Examining the number of story grammar categories recalled, they found no significant differences between the groups. However, their reading disabled sample was rather heterogeneous, containing youngsters with both high and low verbal WISC-R IQs. When they conducted a within-group analysis of their reading disabled subjects, they found significant differences between their "high verbal" and "low verbal" poor readers. The poor readers with high verbal ability recalled significantly more ideas than those with low verbal ability.

Recently, Graybeal (1981) compared the ability of matched normal and language impaired children to recall stories read to them. At the outset of the study, she assessed the language abilities of each language impaired child to ensure that the child had the vocabulary and syntactic processing skills necessary to understand the stories. Each child was read and asked to recall two stories whose episode structure was based upon Mandler and Johnson's model for story grammars (1977). Graybeal found that the language impaired children recalled significantly fewer ideas than their normal peers.

One might infer, however, that the language and learning disabled subjects in these studies performed more poorly because their language production deficits may have limited their output in the retell paradigm. However, Snyder, Haas, and Becker's (1982) comparison of the discourse processing of normal and language and learning disabled sixth graders controlled for production deficits, using a probe recall question technique. Even under this condition, the language and learning disabled youngsters recalled significantly less information than did their age mates. Thus the literature seems to offer some support for the notion that language disordered children may sustain deficits in this aspect of constructive comprehension processes.

Listeners and readers also engage in one other type of constructive comprehension process. They go beyond the information explicitly stated in the narrative to draw inferences. They derive and understand information that is not explicitly stated or given in the spoken or written narrative. They can do this by making lexical inferences (Sordon, 1979). More often they do this intersententially or between sentences or over the course of whole episodes in a story (Johnson and Smith, 1981). Take for example, this sentence pair used by Haviland and Clark (1974):

Horace got some picnic supplies out of the trunk.
The beer was warm.

To understand this sequence of sentences the listener must draw the inference that Horace included beer in his picnic supplies. This information, however, was never explicitly stated.

Similarly, take the following sentence pair used by Keenan and Kintsch (1974):

A burning cigarette was carelessly discarded.
The fire destroyed many acres of virgin forest.

This sequence of sentences is understood by inferring that the discarded cigarette caused the fire. Again, however, this information is never explicitly stated.

Listeners and readers seem to draw those inferences that are relevant to the story's progress and are necessary for accurate comprehension of the narrative (Hildyard and Olson, 1978). Such inferences establish events, their causes, characters' actions, responses, and motivations (Warren, Nicholas, Trabasso, 1979). Inferences place an additional processing load on the listener or reader (Keenan, McKoon, 1974; Keenan and Kintsch, 1974; Haviland and

Clark, 1974), requiring additional processing time. On the other hand, since the individual is actvely engaged in using his internal knowledge to draw the inference, the inferred information tends to be processed as deeply as information explicitly stated (Kintsch, Keenan, McKoon, 1974).

Adults typically engage in this type of constructive processing, and children as young as preschoolers are observed to make "local" or intersentential inferences. Young children can answer questions about inferred information (Kail, Chi, Ingram, Danner, 1977; Paris and Upton, 1976). They can also make transitive inferences (Bryant and Trabasso, 1971; Riley and Trabasso, 1974; Trabasso, 1975) and inferences about antecedent states, causes, and outcomes in familiar events (Gelman, Bullock, Meck, 1980). Young children, however, have greater difficulty drawing "global" inferences or those in which premises are widely separated, for example, occurring in earlier episodes in a story. Adults draw these inferences with ease (Just and Carpenter, 1981). Children do not seem to engage in this level of processing as easily and seem to develop the skill during their elementary school years (Johnson and Smith, 1981).

We currently know very little about the inferential abilities of language impaired adults. Some beginning efforts with language disordered and learning disabled children, however, indicate that they are deficient in this aspect of constructive comprehension. Weaver and Dickenson (1979) examined the constructive comprehension processes of reading disabled children, using Stein and Glenn's (1979) stimuli. They found that the youngsters with written language disorders drew fewer inferences than the normal children tested by Stein and Glenn (1979).

Ellis-Weismer (1981) compared the inferential abilities of language disordered and two groups of normal children matched for nonverbal cognitive abilities and for comprehension, respectively. She looked at their ability to draw spatial and causal inferences presented verbally and pictorially, and found that the language

disordered children performed much like the younger, normal subjects, with similar language comprehension skills on both the verbal and pictorial conditions. They performed worse than their cognitively similar peers on both conditions, but similar for explicitly stated information on the pictorial conditions. Thus the language disordered children seemed to be deficient in their inferential abilities.

Lastly, Snyder, Haas, and Becker (1982) compared the ability of matched normal and language and learning disabled sixth graders to draw inferences from three schema-based narratives. Using probe questions to elicit evidence of their subjects' inferential skills, they assessed the ability to draw spatial, causal, world knowledge, and social motivation inferences. The analysis of their findings revealed that their language and learning disabled subjects were less adept at drawing inferences than their normal peers. They seemed to have particular difficulty drawing spatial, world knowledge, and social motivational inferences.

Taken together, these studies provide some early evidence for deficient constructive comprehension processing in language disabled children. In light of the pervasive nature of this processing and its central role in daily language comprehension activities, it is important that we assess all aspects in language impaired children and adults—particularly in school-aged children.

Just as a listener's knowledge of story and event structures and language help him construct an understanding of narratives, this knowledge also helps the speaker structure his discourse narrative. Consequently, the story grammars that reflect an individual's knowledge of story structure can also be considered as valid expectations for the structure of oral and written narratives that are not part of a recall paradigm.

Research has only begun in this area. Glenn, C. and Stein, N. (in press) have begun to document young children's development of written narratives. Snyder, Downey and Kintsch (in preparation) and

Miller and Snyder (in preparation) have begun studies comparing the oral and written narrative discourse of matched normal and language and learning disabled children. These studies not only examine the structure or story grammars that underlie narrative discourse but also the cohesion of the text (Halliday and Hasan, 1976). When we learn more about the outcomes of this and similar research, its relevance and stability, we can determine whether this will be an appropriate approach to use in assessment.

In summary, although constructive comprehension processing is a central aspect of linguistic processing, we fail to assess it systematically. Our assessment tools fail to control test stimuli adequately for the number and structure of episodes within and across stories and the number and types of inferences they contain. In fact, many of our measures of listening and reading comprehension are poorly structured and tell us about the least important aspects of narrative discourse processing.

## THE WRONG PIECES

Standardized measures and subtests that assess listening and reading comprehension for paragraphs have been around for a very long time. Recent characterizations of comprehension processes and the investigations that have tested their psychologic reality have radically changed our ideas about how the process occurs and the core aspects of listener and reader interpretation or understanding. These notions have led educators and cognitive psychologists to question the relevance of what we are measuring in our reading and listening comprehension tests and with readability formulas.

**Reading and Listening Comprehension Tests.** Most silent reading comprehension tests and tests of listening comprehension are structured in similar ways. The individual being tested is requested to read or listen to a paragraph read to him. He is then asked to answer a series of questions that probe for his recall of the mate-

rial. The stimuli at the early grade levels often consists of story narratives. Nonfiction expository narratives tend to characterize subsequent material.

Recent advances in the study of narrative discourse processing have contributed some data that are relevant to our evaluation of listening and reading comprehension tests. The first important finding is that well-formed story narratives seem to have an underlying structure or grammar. These story grammars (Mandler and Johnson, 1977; Rumelhardt, 1980; Stein and Glenn, 1979) contain categories based on action theory. They are motivated by the actions, responses, goals, and considerations of the protagonist, the major characters, or both. Thus story grammars postulate that stories consist of one or more episodes. Episodes are structured so that they often contain a number of underlying categories. Reviewing the Stein and Glenn (1979) categories, which are representative of this avenue of study, we find that they have postulated the following set of major story grammar categories:

*Setting:* information that introduces the main characters, the protagonist, and the time and place in which the event is taking place

*Initiating Event:* a complication, mental or physical, or event that induces the main character to act

*Internal Response:* the protagonist's thoughts, feelings, or interpretation elicited by the initiating event

*Attempt:* the actions that the protagonist takes to change the complicating situation

*Consequence:* the events or states that result from the protagonist's attempt

*Reaction:* any affective or evaluative response by the protagonist to the preceding events.

An examination of many of the paragraph stories contained in our standardized reading and listening comprehension tests suggests that many of them are poorly structured. As Bruce (1978) pointed out, many of the materials prepared for children beginning to read are often little more than sentence strings. Conflicts and goals, critical elements of story structure, are notably absent. Other stories are so poorly structured that the identity of the protagonist changes in the middle of the story, never to re-emerge (Snyder and Johnston, 1980).

Likewise, the expository paragraphs contained in many standardized listening and reading comprehension tests are often poorly structured. Expository narratives are expected to contain a topic, gist, or problem statement at the outset. New information often needs to be defined and the solution to the problem or its history reported. A number of paragraphs from some of our standardized tests lack topic or problem statements. Rather, they contain a string of factual statements from which the listener or reader must infer the underlying theme.

We would never assess language impaired children and adults by asking them to comprehend syntactic items that are ungrammatical. Yet we often try to assess listening and reading comprehension with "ungrammatical" stories.

**Readability.** The traditional and preferred method of controlling the difficulty of reading material contained in tests—whether paragraphs or sentences—has been to ascertain its readability. Readability can be determined in a number of ways, for example, those proposed by Fry (1970), Harris and Sipay (1975), and Lorge (1968). Although the numerical formulae differ, the various methodologies seem to possess some common characteristics. They all use tabulations of the number of words or syllables and sentences contained in the selection. Typically, the longer the selection and/or the sentences it contains, the less readable it is.

Recent research in constructive comprehension processes, however, suggests that readability metrics are, in fact, very poor predictors of a reader's speed and accuracy (Kintsch and Vipond, 1979; Kintsch and Miller, 1979; Miller and Kintsch, 1980). Rather, the underlying structure and coherence of the text and its relation to the reader's prior knowledge strategies predict readability and reading time. In fact, they yield multiple correlations between .8 and .9 in most experiments (see Kintsch and Vipond, 1979, for a more comprehensive review; Miller and Kintsch, 1980). Thus how well the underlying story in expository grammar is structured, how well it is connected logically and causally, and the familiarity of the topic to the reader predict readability, and they do so with far greater success than those metrics that count words and sentences. Consequently, short, poorly structured paragraphs on obscure topics can be more difficult to read than longer, well-formed stories. Yet our readability formulae indicate the converse.

Unfortunately, all of our standardized reading measures seem to use formulae methods to determine readability. The information they give us, then, may be less than accurate and, at the very least, less than helpful.

**The Hole in Our Puzzle.** Many of the areas of linguistic processing and production we have just considered share a common denominator: The greatest strides in their development are made during the elementary school years. They represent the later aspects of language acquisition. We have observed that our ability to assess these skills has been limited by content areas that remain unassessed and measurement tools that are poorly structured and possibly inaccurate. The effect of these limitations is reflected by our difficulty in meeting the assessment and intervention needs of school-aged and adolescent language disordered children. Some of these children simply fall between the cracks in our system because we do not have the tools with which to identify their problems adequately. Others are shortchanged because we do not know how to sequence or direct our intervention to meet their needs. Consequently, it is critical that we begin to devise language assessment tools and techniques that can sample and accurately evaluate these areas of linguistic processing and production.

## STRATEGIES OF LEARNING AND LEARNING LANGUAGE

In trying to make the transition from assessment to intervention, we need to determine the content that the language impaired or delayed individual needs to learn. However, we also need to determine how it is that he learns, particularly how he learns language. This vital information helps us choose more effective ways of presenting stimuli and the strategies that we will facilitate during the course of intervention. Consequently, we need to determine how the individual allocates his resources and his ability to activate different language learning processes.

## *RESOURCE ALLOCATION: HOW THE PIECES FIT AND WORK*

Our assessment of the content of language processing and production gives us some insight into some of the resources of the language impaired individual. The results of systematic assessment of his language strengths and weaknesses allows us to infer those skills that are more intact than others and that can be mobilized for successful compensation.

We have frequently used the results of task analysis to provide us with this information. We carefully analyze the input, processing, and output characteristics of test items on which individuals succeed and fail. From these data we make inferences about those skills that the individual has available. When using a traditional model, the modality characteristics—visual versus auditory—the number of modalities, or the processes required by the task might be relevant descriptors of the individual's performance. A logical outcome of this model would suggest a series of conditions, such as modality and processing level, that would limit or constrain his ability to perform. This approach, however, does not account for an individual's ability to perform a specific task in one context and fail at that same task in another.

Recently, clinicians have begun to use interactive models, for example, Rumelhardt (1976) and Norman (1976), and to adapt them to the needs of speech and language pathology (Lemme and Daves, 1980). These models deal with levels of processing—perceptual versus conceptual—and the drain they make on a limited capacity single resource system. These characterizations take a somewhat different look at human performance. They often include aspects of two models: the data and resource limiting models and the dual processing models.

Focusing on the problem posed by man's ability to successfully perform two activities simultaneously in some instances and not others, Norman and Bobrow (1975) examined the effect of data versus resource factors on human performance. They suggested that the human processing system had a fund of *resources* or processing capability available to it. To use a metaphor, it is much like a savings account with a fixed balance. The account's balance could be likened to the resources one can bring to any task or set of tasks. If one sets out to perform two activities at once, the demands of each may drain all of the resources available. When all of the resources are depleted and more are needed, the individual will fail to complete the task or do it well. For example, if one had $20 worth of resources deposited in his resource bank account, he could deploy it as necessary. The task of typing a letter might require $10 worth of resources, while chatting to the budget director about next year's salaries might require $17 worth of resources. One could begin to perform both tasks simultaneously, gradually drawing one's resources out of the bank. However, at some point the individual would run out of resources and no longer be able to do both tasks at once. Norman and Bobrow called this *resource limited* processing. Task performance is impeded because all of the available processing resources have been depleted or allocated. If, however, a kind uncle had deposited $50 in the resource account, the individual could continue to perofrm both tasks simultaneously. The presence of additional resources would allow the individual to complete the task. In this way we see the operation of the factor of resource limits.

Human performance can suffer interference of a different type. It would be constrained by the operation of data limits. To return to our banking metaphor: Imagine that the goal of the salary conversation with the budget director was to convince him to reassign duties and boost existing salaries instead of hiring an additional staff member. The crux of the argument must hinge on the cost-effectiveness of such a plan, since that is an administrative requirement for such a massive reorganization. Unfortunately, the records were not kept very well and there were no data or figures that could be used to demonstrate costs and cost-effectiveness. No matter how many resources the individual could allocate to the task of persuading the director of his plan, he would never be able to complete the task because he is *data limited*. Thus the human processing system can perform two tasks at once when they are both within the system's resource *and data limits*. Conversely, performance may fail under the constraints of data limits or processing limits.

Use of this model has caused some difficulty in determining those tasks that will place an individual into resource constraints and those that will not. To deal with this, some of the more eclectic views have also included notions derived from dual processing models.

Dual processing models, for example, those of Posner and Snyder (1975), Schneider and Shiffrin (1977a), and Shiffrin and Schneider (1977b), have suggested that there may be two different types of processing that make quantitatively different drains on resources. They suggest that there is an automatic, inhibitionless, well-learned mode of processing. This mode, called *automatic processing*, makes few drains on the system's resources. And it can occur in parallel with other kinds of resources.

On the other hand, there are tasks that require processing that is not highly overlearned, that demand our conscious attention, and are under our direct control. This mode, called *controlled processing*, is usually serial in nature and makes high demands on the system's resources.

To return to our earlier banking metaphor and the tasks of typing and talking, consider the possibility that typing has become such an overlearned skill that it requires only $2 of one's processing resources. The conversation with the budget director, however, still requires $17 worth of resources. Given the original $20 balance of resources in the bank account, one will be able to stay within one's limits and the two tasks can be performed at once. The system can perform two tasks simultaneously when one is performed in the automatic mode.

Such models of attention or effort are particularly well suited to explaining our success at producing speech while simultaneously formulating messages. Articulatory programs are considered to be highly overlearned and automatic. Consequently they can occur in parallel with other conceptual operations, such as message formulation, which require more conscious control. Dual processing models have been troubled by experiments that suggest that performance in one task may actually *improve* when another has been added. For example, Long (1977) found that subjects could discriminate noverbal signals better when the signals were presented together than when they were presented in isolation. Consequently, some researchers have turned to multiple resource models, for example Kuehn with Snyder (1981) and Polson and Friedman (in press).

The multiple resource model (Navon and Gopher, 1979) suggests that the human processing system contains many mechanisms, each of which has its own set of resources with its own limits. A task may require the operation of several mechanisms. Different tasks may require the operation of different mechanisms. Further, the environmental context and the subject's skills may change the nature of the mechanisms needed to complete the task.

To return to our banking metaphor, and problem, the tasks of typing and talking require two different production mechanisms: digital or finger articulation or production and language processing and production. Because each uses a different mechanism, with a different bank account of resources, one can execute both tasks at the same time. However, they both may also need to use the same program storage mechanism containing $10 of resources in its bank account. Because typing only makes a $5 withdrawal and language production a $4.50 withdrawal, one can do the two simultaneously. However, a slip of the tongue error may occur despite a balance of 50¢ in the motor program storage account. What happened? The bank may have charged the account $1 to cover the cost of the transactions. In other words, the coordination of the two activities (withdrawing two different types of programs) may also cost resources. On the other hand, if the problem tasks were playing a musical instrument and tapping one's foot, the foot tapping may require $2.50 worth of programs, while the playing may require $7 worth of the $10 account of programs. The $1 service charge should still be in effect. However, not only can the system retrieve both programs, but the novice may also perform better when a foot tapping program is retrieved (Navon and Gopher, 1979). The programs may be stored in such a way that if the bank retrieves one, it automatically retrieves the other. If only one is required, it may take an extra transaction to separate them. Consequently, when a customer wants both programs, the bank levies only a single service charge and the individual can stay within his resource limits for that mechanism's account. Thus a multiple resource model suggests that the different mechanisms required for performance have their own separate resource pools. They do not draw successively from a single, generic pool of resources.

These conceptualizations of human performance, particularly the more recent multiple resource model, can be used to view the inconsistencies of the performance of the language impaired individual. They allow us to predict more accurately those intervention strategies and language content that will facilitate an individual's performance and those that will

constrain it. Too often we are left to wonder at the many inconsistencies we observe in the performance of language impaired individuals. Fortunately, Lemme and Daves (1980), Kuehn with Snyder (1981), Stark (1981), and others have begun to apply these notions to the performance of language impaired individuals in both assessment and intervention. These recent efforts have helped us visualize how parts of our puzzle fit together.

## LANGUAGE LEARNING STRATEGIES: THE PAPERBACK ANSWER KEY

Determining the language impaired individual's pattern of resource allocation tells us about one aspect of his performance. It neglects to identify another aspect: the strategies that he can use and/or prefers to use in learning language. This information seems to be critical in planning language intervention. The ability to facilitate strategies that can or have worked well for the individual can only improve the efficiency and effectiveness of our intervention.

The most comprehensive characterization of language learning strategies is that put forward by MacWhinney (1975, 1978, 1980). MacWhinney's research has identified three major strategies that account for the acquisition of syntax (1981) and morphophonology (1975, 1978). These strategies include rote, analogy and combination.

The first language learning strategy proposed by MacWhinney is *rote*. Rote refers to the memorization of the target structure as a whole. This fixed-order holistic memorization involves committing a morphologically marked word to memory long before the child understands the morphologic marking system. This is observed in children's early use of irregular forms. Rote also involves committing word strings or whole sentences to memory although the child cannot productively use those forms. MacWhinney (1981) cites (among other evidence) Clark's (1977) report of a child's use of I *could easily do that* when *could* was absent from the child's productive repertoire.

As clinicians we have made heavy use of this strategy, modeling forms for imitation. However, recognizing that memory resources limit its effectiveness for exclusive use, we often prefer to elicit more analytic strategies. On the other hand, rote items can be processed automatically, placing little drain on one's resources. Consequently those language items that require little analysis themselves are acquired with this mechanism. They include many non-propositional items, for example, greetings and conversational closers, and fixed form items, such as clichés and metaphors.

Too many sentences and morphologically marked forms and lengthy sentences make it difficult for us to learn language entirely by rote. Also, neologisms and developmental errors suggest that rote is not a sufficient explanation of language learning. These notions led MacWhinney to postulate a second strategy: analogy. Analogy in syntactic acquisition refers to the ability to recall immediately an item or items in memory that contains an implicit pattern and to use that item or item set to extract the pattern and apply it to a new item. An example cited by MacWhinney (1980) was Leopold's (1949) report of when his wife told their daughter, Hildegarde, that when she went away on a trip, *You won't see Papa for a long, long time*. When Hildegarde had returned, she remarked, *I was in Milwaukee. You did not see me for a long, long time*. Languages that are subject to many exceptions tend to elicit a greater use of analogy (MacWhinney, 1978). By contrast, we find this intermediate strategy quickly replaced by the combination strategy in more regular systems.

Combination is the final major strategy posited by MacWhinney. In syntactic learning it refers to the formation of principles or rules from words and patterns that may contain a number of complexities and irregularities. In other words, the individual has figured out the rule when the pattern demonstrating its application is not very apparent. For example, MacWhinney (1981) cites Klima and Bellugi's (1967) report of *I not hurt him* and *Ask me if I not made mistake*, which suggests that the positioning of a negative is not learned by rote and may reflect more than analogy which sets up the immediate pattern with an obligatory *do*, for example, *I did not hurt him*, and *Ask me if I did not make a mistake*.

At the present time, we do not seem to make very systematic use of our knowledge of these language learning strategies in planning intervention. We often assume that the individual uses or has used rote imitation to learn language. The presentation of our language stimuli often takes on an anologic form. We present immediate, repeated patterns. From that point, we assume that the individual will somehow develop the combinatorial strategy that allows him to use the target rule productively. In addition, we do not use this information to analyze the individual's errors. Consequently we do not know how to discern where he is in the language learning process. It makes a great deal of difference whether a child's syntactic error is one produced from analogy or combination. If it is produced from combination, the child is much more advanced in the language learning process. Thus we need to explore this information more fully. It can only enhance the effectiveness of our intervention.

## SOLVING THE PUZZLE

At the outset, we likened the problem of making the transition from assessment to intervention to solving a puzzle. Success in solving puzzles seems to require that we have all of the pieces. In addition, we need to have *only* the correct pieces. It takes time and effort to identify and discard the wrong pieces. Further, we need to be able to conceptualize how the pieces fit together and operate as a whole. The puzzle is not really solved unless it fits together and works. Lastly, we can always profit from an answer key; it can reduce the amount of time one spends on problem-solving maneuvers.

Our evaluation of these requirements indicated that, although we have a majority of the pieces to our puzzle, some large pieces are still missing. In addition, we also have a number of pieces from other puzzles, and we waste a great deal of time and effort learning that they do not meet our needs. Fortunately, we discovered that we have become rather good at conceptualizing how the puzzle fits together and works. We are increasingly less likely to confront language impaired individuals with tasks that will frustrate them. Lastly, an answer key is available to help us solve the puzzle. We have yet to consult it often enough, and so a certain proportion of the solution process is left to chance. On the other hand, we cannot rely on any answer key too heavily. We may wind up solving the puzzle by remembering the solution (Platt and MacWhinney, 1979). The individual differences of the language impaired population are such that the solution for one puzzle may not apply to another.

Sometimes we seem to solve our puzzles, despite the missing pieces, incorrect pieces, and inefficient use of the answer key. Some puzzles are just easier to solve. We have all of the pieces to other puzzles, and, just as in some of our solutions to the Rubik's Cube, we may also have been helped by an element of chance.

## REFERENCES

Ammons RB, Ammons HS: *Full-range Picture Vocabulary Test*. Palo Alto, Calif: Psychological Test Specialists, 1948

Anderson RC, Spiro RJ, Anderson MC: Schemata as scaffolding for the representation of information in connected discourse. Am Educa Res J 15:433–440, 1978.

Austin J: How to do things with words. Cambridge: Cambridge University Press, 1962

Baggett, P: Structurally equivalent stories in movies and text and the effect of medium or recall. *J Verb Learn Verb Behav*, 18:333–356, 1979

Baker L, Stein M: The development of prose comprehension skills. Technical Report No. 102, Center for the Study of Reading, Champaign-Urbana, Illinois, 1978

Bartlett FC: *Remembering: A Study in Experimental and Social Psychology*. Cambridge: Cambridge University Press, 1932

Bates E: *Language and Context: Studies in the Acquisition of Pragmatics*. New York: Academic Press, 1976

Bates E, Johnston J: Pragmatics in normal and deficient child language. Short course presented to the American Speech and Hearing Association Convention, Chicago, November 1977

Becker LB, Silverstein J: Directives in client-clinician discourse: Scoring and reliability. Paper presented to American Speech and Hearing Association South Central Regional Conference, Colorado, 1982

Bloom L, Lakey M: *Language Development and Language Disorders*. New York: John Wiley and Sons, 1978

Bruce B: What makes a good story? Language Arts 55:460–466, 1975

Bryant P, Trabasso T: Transitive inferences and memory in young children. Nature 232:456–458, 1971

Byrne B: Deficient syntactic control in poor readers: Is a weak phonetic memory code responsible? Appl Psycholing 2:201–212, 1981

Byrne MC: Appraisal of child language acquisition. In Darley FL, Spriestersback DC (eds.): *Diagnostic Methods in Speech Pathology*. N.Y.: Harper and Row, 1978

Carter A: The transformation of sensorimotor morphemes into words: A case study of the development of "more" and "mine." J Child Lang 2:233–250, 1975

Chapman RS: Exploring children's communicative intents. In Miller JF: *Assessing Language Production in Children*, Baltimore: University Park Press, 1980

Chomsky CS: *The Acquisition of Syntax in Children from 5 to 10*. Cambridge, Mass: MIT Press, 1969

Clark H, Clark E: *Psychology and Language*. New York: Harcourt, Brace and Jovanovich, 1977

Clark R: What's the use of imitation? J Child Lang 4:341–358, 1977

Coggins TE, Carpenter RL: The communicative intention inventory: A system for observing and coding children's early intentional communication. Appl Psycholing 2:235–252, 1981

Donohue M, Pearl R, Bryan T: Learning disabled children's conversational competence: Responses to inadequate messages. Appl Psycholing 1:387–404, 1980

Dore J: Oh them Sheriff. In Ervin-Tripp S, Mitchell-Kerman C (eds): *Child Discourse*. New York: Academic Press, 1977

Dore J: What's so conceptual about the acquisition of linguistic structures? J Child Lang 6:129–138, 1979

Ellis-Weismer S: Constructive comprehension processes exhibited by language impaired children. Unpublished doctoral dissertation, Indiana University, 1981

Ervin-Tripp S: Wait for me, roller skate! In Ervin-Tripp S, Mitchell-Kerman C (eds): *Child Discourse*. New York: Academic Press, 1977

Fillmore CJ: Types of lexical information. In Steinberg DD, Jakobovits LA (eds): *Semantics: An Interdisciplinary Reader in Philosophy, Linguistics and Psychology*. Cambridge: Cambridge University Press, 1971

Frith U (ed): *Cognitive Processes in Spelling*. New York: Academic Press, 1981

Fry MA, Johnson CS, Muehl S: Oral language production in relation to reading achievement among select second graders. In Bakker DJ, Satz P (eds): *Specific Reading Disability: Advances in Theory and Method*. Rotterdam: Rotterdam University Press, 1970

Gallagher T, Darnton B: Conversational aspects of the speech of language disordered children: Revision behaviors. J Speech Hear Res 21:118–135, 1978

Gardner R: *One-Word Expressive Vocabulary Test*. Novato, California: Academic Therapy Publications, 1980

Geller E, Wollner S: A preliminary investigation of the communicative competence of three linguistically impaired children. Paper presented at the New York State Speech and Hearing Association, Grossingers, 1976

Gelman R, Bullock M, Meck F: Preschoolers' understanding of simple object transformations. *Child Development*, 51, 1980

Glenn C, Stein N: Syntactic structure and real world themes in stories generated by children. Champaign-Urbana, Ill: Center for the Study of Reading, 1980

Goldstein K, Scheerer M: Abstract and concrete behavior. Psychol Monog 53:110–130, 1941

Golub L, Kidder C: Syntactic density and the computer. Elem Eng 51:1128–1131, 1974

Graybeal CM: Memory for stories in language-impaired children. Appl Psycholing 2:169–283, 1981

Grice HP: Logic and conversation. In Cole P, Morgan JL (eds): *Syntax and Semantics: Speech Acts*. New York: Academic Press, 1975

Halliday MAK, Hasan: *The Cohesion of English*. London: Longmans Ltd, 1976

Hammill DD, Bartel N: *Teaching Children with Learning and Behavioral Problems*. Boston: Allyn and Bacon, 1977

Hammil DD, Brown VL, Larsen SC, Wiederholt J: *Test of Adolescent Language*. Austin, Texas: Pro-Ed, 1980

Hammill DD, Larsen SC: *Test of Written Language*. Austin, Texas: Pro-Ed, 1978

Harris AJ, Sipay ER: *How to Increase Reading Skills*, 2nd ed. New York: David McKay Co, 1975

Haviland SE, Clark HH: What's new? Acquiring new information as a process in comprehension. J Verb Learn Verb Behav 13:515–521, 1974

Hildyard A, Olson DR: Memory and inference in the comprehension of oral and written discourse. Discourse Proc 1:91–117, 1978

Hoar N: Paraphrase capabilities of language impaired children. Paper presented at Second Annual Boston University Conference on Language Development, October 1977

Holland AL: *Communicative Activities of Daily Living*. Baltimore: University Park Press, 1980

Hunt KW: Grammatical structures written at three grade levels. National Council of Teachers of English, No 3, 1965

Hunt KW: Syntactic maturity in school children and adults. Monographs of the Society for Research in Child Development, 35, February 1970

Johnson DJ, Myklebust HR: *Learning Disabilities:*

*Educational Principles and Remedial Approaches*. New York: Grune and Stratton, 1967

Johnson H, Smith L: Children's inferential abilities in the context of reading to understand. Child Develop 52:1216–1223, 1981

Jorgensen C, Barrett M, Husingh R, Zachman Z: *The Word Test*. Moline, Ill: Lingui Systems Inc, 1981

Just M, Carpenter P (eds): *Cognitive Processes in Comprehension*. Hillsdale, NJ: Lawrence Erlbaum Associates, 1977

Just M, Carpenter P: Toward a theory of reading comprehension: Models based on eye fixation. Psycholog Rev 1981

Kail R, Chi M, Ingram A, Danner F: Constructive aspects of children's reading comprehension. Child Develop 48:684–688, 1977

Kaplan E: *The Boston Naming Test*. Boston: Boston University Press, 1976

Keenan, EO: Conversational competence in children. J Child Lang 1:163–184, 1974

Keenan E: Making it last. In Ervin-Tripp S, Mitchell-Kerman C (eds): *Child Discourse*. New York: Academic Press, 1977

Keenan JM, Kintsch W: The identification of explicitly and implicitly presented information. In Kintsch W: *The Representation of Meaning in Memory*. Hillsdale, NJ: Lawrence Erlbaum Associates, 1974

Kintsch W: *The Representation of Meaning in Memory*. Hillsdale, NJ: Lawrence Erlbaum Associates, 1974

Kintsch W: On comprehending stories. In Just M, Carpenter P (eds): *Cognitive Processes in Comprehension*. Hillsdale, NJ: Lawrence Erlbaum Associates, 1977

Kintsch W, Greene E: The role of culture-specific schemata in the comprehension and recall of stories. Discourse Proc 1:1–13, 1978

Kintsch W, Mandel TS, Kozminsky E: Summarizing scrambled stories. Mem Cognition 5:547–552, 1977

Kintsch W, Vipond D: Reading comprehension and readability in educational practice and psychological theory. In Nillson L (ed): *Memory Processes and Problems*. Hillsdale, NJ: Lawrence Erlbaum Associates, 1979

Klima E, Bellugi U: Syntactic regularities in the speech of children. In Lyons J, Wales R (eds): *Psycholinguistics Papers: The Proceedings of the 1966 Edinburgh Conference*. Edinburgh: Edinburgh University Press, 1967

Kuehn DP, Snyder L: Speech production and cognition. Paper presented at University of Kansas Conference, Kansas City, 1981

La Pointe L, Horner J: *Reading Comprehension for Aphasia*. Tigard, Ore: CC Publications, 1979

Lemme M, Daves NH: Information processing: Behavioral and neurological correlates and clinical implications. Paper presented to American Speech and Hearing Association Convention, Detroit, 1980

Larsen SC, Hammill DD: *Test of Written Spelling*. Austin, Texas: Pro-Ed, 1982

Launer PB, Lahey M: Passages: From the fifties to the

eighties in language assessment. Topics Lang Dis 1:11–30, 1981

Leopold WF: *Speech Development of a Bilingual Child: A Linguist's Record* (4 vols). Evanston, Ill: Northwestern University Press, 1949

Lerner JW: *Children with Learning Disabilities*, 2nd ed. Boston: Houghton Mifflin Co, 1977

Lloyd LM, Lloyd LM: *Peabody picture vocabulary test—revised*. Circle Pines, Minn: American Guidance Services, 1981

Long J: Contextual assimilation and its effect on the division of attention between nonverbal signals. Quart J Exper Psychol 29:397–414, 1977

Lorge I: *The Lorge Formula for Estimating Difficulty of Reading Material*. New York: Columbia University Press, 1959

MacWhinney B: Rules, rote and analogy in morphological formations in Hungarian children. J Child Lang 2:65–77, 1975

MacWhinney B: The acquisition of morphophonology. Monographs Soc Child Develop 43:1–2, 1978

MacWhinney B: Levels of syntactic acquisition. In Kuczaj S (ed): *Language Development: Syntax and Semantics*. Hillsdale, NJ: Lawrence Erlbaum Associates, 1980

Mandler JJ, Johnson NS: Remembrance of things parsed: Story structure and recall. Cognitive Psychol 9:111–151, 1977

McKoon G, Keenan J: Response latencies to explicit and implicit statements. In Kintsch W: *The Representation of Meaning in Memory*. Hillsdale, NJ: Lawrence Erlbaum Associates, 1974

McLean J, Snyder-McLean L: *A Transactional Approach to Early Language Training*. Columbus, Ohio: Charles E. Merrill, 1978

Messick C, Newhoff, M: Request form: Does the language-delayed child consider the listener? Paper presented to American Speech and Hearing Association, Atlanta, 1979

Miller J, Kintsch W: Readability and recall of short prose passage. J Exper Psychol: Human Learn Mem 1980

Miller N, Snyder L: The oral and written discourse of language and learning disabled children. Manuscript, 1982

Myklebust HR: *Picture Story Language Test*. New York: Grune and Stratton, 1965

Nation JE, Aram DM: *Diagnosis of Speech and Language Disorders*. St. Louis: CV Mosby Co, 1977

Navon S, Gopher D: On the economy of the human processing system. Psycholog Rev 86:214–255, 1979

Newcomer P, Hammill DD: *Test of Language Development*. Austin, Texas: Empiric Press, 1977

Norman D, Bobrow D: On data-limited and resource-limited processes. Cognitive Psychol 7:44–64, 1975

Norman D: *Memory and Attention*, 2nd ed. New York: John Wiley and Sons, 1976

Paris S, Upton L: Children's memory for inferential relationships in prose. Child Development 47:660–668, 1976

Parisi D, Antinucci F: *Essentials of a Grammar*.

Translated by E. Bates. New York: Academic Press, 1979

Platt C, MacWhinney B: Solving a problem vs. remembering the solution. Paper presented at the Conference on Language Development, Boston University, Boston 1979

Polson D, Kintsch E, Kintsch W, Premack D: Children's comprehension and memory for stores. J Experi Child Psychol, 28:379–403, 1979

Polson M, Friedman A, Gaskill S: Competition for left hemisphere resources: Right hemisphere superiority at abstract verbal processing. Brain Lang in press

Posner M, Synder C: Attention and cognitive control. In Solso RL (ed): *Information Processing and Cognition: The Loyola Symposium*. Hillsdale, NJ: Lawrence Erlbaum Associates, 1975

Prather EM, Breecher SN, Stafford ML, Wallace EM: *Screening Test of Adolescent Language*. Seattle: University of Washington Press, 1980

Prinz P: The comprehension and production of requests in language disordered children. Paper presented at Second Annual Boston University Conference on Language Development, Boston, October 1977

Quigley S, Steinkamp MW, Power DJ, Jones BW: *Test of Syntactic Abilities*. Portland, Ore: Dormac, Inc, 1978

Riley C, Trabasso T: Comparatives, logical structures, and encoding in a transitive inference task. J Exper Child Psychol 17:187–203, 1974

Rumelhardt D: Toward an interactive model of reading. Technical Report #56, Center for Human Information Processing, 1976

Rumelhardt DE: Schemata: The building blocks of cognition. In Spiro RJ, Bruco BC, Brewer WF (eds): *Theoretical Issues in Reading Comprehension*. Hillsdale, NJ: Lawrence Erlbaum Associates, 1980

Schank RC, Abelson RP: *Scripts, Plans, Goals and Understanding*. Hillsdale, NJ: Lawrence Erlbaum Associates, 1977

Schegloff E: Sequencing in conversational openings. Am Anthropol 70, 1968

Schneider W, Shiffrin R: Controlled and automatic human information processing. I. Detection, search and attention. Psycholog Rev 84:1–66, 1977

Searle JR: *Speech Acts: An Essay in Philosophy of Language*. Cambridge: Cambridge University Press, 1969

Shiffrin R, Schneider W: Controlled and automatic human information processing. II. Perceptual learning, automatic attending, and general theory. Psycholog Rev 84:127–190, 1977

Snyder L, Downey D, Kintsch E: The discourse narratives of normal and reading disabled children. Manuscript, 1982

Snyder L, Haas C, Becker LBB: Discourse processing in normal and language and learning disabled children. Manuscript, 1982

Snyder L, Johnston J: Cognition and reading in normal and language/learning disabled children. Short course presented to American Speech and Hearing Association Convention, Detroit, 1980

Sordon S: The development of lexical inferences in children. Unpublished doctoral dissertation, Northwestern University, 1979

Spiro, RJ: Constructive processes in prose comprehension and recall. In Spiro RJ, Bruce BC, Brewer WF (eds): *Theoretical Issues in Reading Comprehension*. Hillsdale, NJ: Lawrence Erlbaum Associates, 1980

Stark J: Reading: What needs to be assessed? Topics Lang Dis 1:87–94, 1981

Stein N, Glenn C: An analysis of story comprehension in elementary school children. In Freedle R (ed): *New Directions in Discourse Processing*. Hillsdale, NJ: ABLEX, 1979

Strauss AS, Lehtinen L: *The Psychology and Education of the Brain Injured Children*. New York: Grune and Stratton, 1947

Thorndyke P: Cognitive structures in comprehension and memory of discourse. Cognitive Psychol 9:77–110, 1977

Trabasso T: Representation, memory and reasoning: How do we make transitive inferences? In Pick A (ed): *Minnesota Symposium on Child Psychology*, vol. 9. Minneapolis: University of Minnesota Press, 1975

Vellutino FR: Personal communication, 1982

Vogel SA: *Syntactic Abilities in Normal and Dyslexic Children*. Baltimore: University Park Press 1975

Warren W, Nicholas D, Trabasso T: Event chains in understanding inferences and narratives. In Freedle R (ed): *New Directions in Discourse Processing*. Hillsdale, NJ: ABLEX, 1979

Weaver R, Dickenson D: Story comprehension and recall in dyslexic students. Bull Orton Soc 29:157–171, 1979

Wiig EH, Semel EM: *Clinical Evaluation of Language Function*. Columbus, Ohio: Charles E. Merrill Co, 1981

Wiig EH, Semel EM: *Language Disabilities in Children and Adolescents*. Columbus, Ohio: Charles E. Merrill Co, 1976

Wollner S: Communicative competence and language disorders: Issues and directions. Working Papers Speech Hear Sci 3:1–14, 1978

# 10

# DESIGN FOR INDIVIDUALIZATION OF LANGUAGE INTERVENTION PROGRAMS

*DORIS J. JOHNSON*

A design for an individualized program of language intervention requires the integration of at least two major bodies of knowledge. First, one needs to understand patterns of language and cognitive development in normal children. Second, one needs to understand the handicapping conditions that may prevent a child from learning or performing in the expected manner (Myklebust, 1954).

The rationale for understanding normal development is obvious. This knowledge provides the clinician with guidelines for assessment and for determining whether the individual deviates significantly from others of similar age and mental ability. Secondly, developmental sequences can provide the clinician with general directions for remediation in several areas of language, including semantics, syntax, phonology, and language usage (Bloom, 1980; Cazden, 1972; Lee, Koeingsknecht, and Mulhern, 1974; Schiefelbusch, 1978).

Equally important, however, is the need for an intensive study of the atypical learner to determine more about the problems that may be present and to investigate processes that may be interfering with the acquisition and use of language (deHirsch,

Jansky, and Langford, 1966; Johnson, 1977; Keith, 1981; Wren, 1980). Unlike professionals in the fields of psycholinguistics and developmental psychology who study normal children in whom all systems are intact, those whose task it is to evaluate and teach atypical learners must be prepared to work with children in whom all systems are not "go." For example, the professional who attempts to study syntactic development in a cerebral palsied nonverbal child or an apraxic youngster who can say only a few sounds must be prepared to alter various forms of input and output to find out what a child knows. Similarly, the psychologist who attempts to investigate intellectual functions of handicapped children will need to select carefully tests that do not involve the impaired systems (such as oral expressive language, perceptual-motor functions). Note, for example, the range of intellectual functions of the preschool children as listed in Table 10–1.

Rarely does a language problem exist in isolation. Often children have a variety of nonverbal cognitive deficits, perceptual-motor disorders, and symbolic problems (Johnson, 1968; Johnson, 1980; McGrady, 1964; Orton, 1937; Wren, 1980). Thus a comprehensive study that includes an as-

**165**

Table 10-1   PERFORMANCE OF PRESCHOOL LEARNING DISABLED CHILDREN
ON TESTS OF MENTAL ABILITY

| Test | Subject #1 | Subject #2 | Subject #3 | Subject #4 |
|------|-----------|-----------|-----------|-----------|
| Columbia | 98 | 100 | 98 | 116 |
| Hiskey | 95 | 72 | 77 | 125 |
| WPPSI-P | 112 | 82 | 78 | 126 |
| WPPSI-V | 65 | 102 | 80 | 111 |
| Peabody | 83 | 78 | 102 | 116 |
| Goodenough | 79 | 65 | 89 | 116 |

sessment of intellectual functions, nonverbal cognitive behaviors, and a host of verbal and nonverbal symbolic processes should be conducted to provide for the child's total needs (Johnson, Blalock, and Nesbitt, 1978). In addition, we strongly recommend periods of diagnostic teaching to determine the forms of stimulation, cuing techniques, media, instructions, and reinforcement that facilitate learning. These comprehensive studies provide the clinician with information about intact processes as well as those that are impaired. The intact systems may be used to help children acquire rules, principles, and skills they have difficulty learning. For example, some students with language disorders make better progress in oral syntax by using the visual verbal system (for example, reading). They perceive, retain, and abstract rules through the eye that they are unable to acquire through the ear. If, on the other hand, the child also has a severe reading disorder, the clinician will need to explore other forms of stimulation. Thus we analyze the total pattern of *intra-organismic* strategies that are available for learning.

Several theoretic constructs guide our studies of children. Each of these is used in the analysis of various subsystems or oral language, reading, written language, mathematics, and other forms of symbolic behavior.

## INPUT-INTEGRATION-OUTPUT-FEEDBACK

The first schema pertains to information processing theory and provides the

basis for asking several diagnostic questions. The first question is, Are there any problems at the level *input?* Is the message getting through clearly? For example, when one hears a 20-year-old with residual language problems ask, "Would you please be more pacific—I didn't get the jiff of that?" one might wonder whether she can perceive the differences between the words, whether she understands the meaning, whether she can repeat them correctly, and whether she is aware of her own mistakes. This woman's problem was primarily at the level of perception but she also had some difficulty with comprehension. When she was asked to perform on various receptive language tests in which she was asked to point to a picture that went with the target word, she often asked the examiner to repeat the word. Frequently she asked, "Did you say _____?" The young woman had no hearing loss but had a long history of school problems.

The level of *integration* refers to the acquisition of meaning. The echolalic child and the word caller demonstrate good input and output skills but they have little or no integration. In recent studies Blalock (1977) and Cicci (1978) reported that preschool learning disabled children appeared to use language that was not well integrated with experience. For example, Cicci stated that some of the children who were asked to pantomime objects and tell what they were doing did not always have a good "action-verbal match." Blalock found that normal children were more internally consistent in their verbalization and actions on a prediction task. These findings would suggest that the clinician be very careful in planning remediation lest the children repeat words and sentences without understanding. We have long emphasized the need for simultaneous presentation of words and experience when teaching language impaired children (Johnson and Myklebust, 1967).

In terms of *output*, we want to know whether there are problems of retrieval, production, or other aspects of performance which prevent the individual from conveying what he knows. Many preschool children have multiple output disorders; therefore, the clinician may need to be aware of the ways in which word retrieval problems interfere with oral syntax. For example, a 5-year-old boy frequently made errors because of difficulty in recalling nouns. Hence he would say, "I see—I see—a sitting" (instead of chair) or "I see a drinking" (for cup).

Finally, the clinician should note whether children are aware of their errors. While many youngsters are aware of the fact that they are not performing at the level of expectancy, recent research suggests that many language and learning disabled students are unable to detect their mistakes (Johnson, 1980). Several years ago we suggested that the first step in the remediation for written language disorders is to help the student detect errors (Johnson and Myklebust, 1967).

Each of the above questions is asked with regard to all symbol systems, including spoken language, reading, writing, and mathematics. As all of the data are tabulated the clinician may be able to determine whether there are generalized deficits or whether there are discrepancies in ability. For example one might note whether there are generalized problems of word retrieval or whether the problems are limited to spoken language, in which case the printed word might be used in remediation. Or, to cite another example, a 17-year-old who was still having difficulty repeating words such as "dominoes, hospital, and spaghetti" could perceive the differences between patterns such as "dominoes and donomoes" both auditorially and visually; he could point to the one that was said by the examiner; he also knew that he was not saying the words correctly (mon-

itoring) and he improved in his oral production when the printed words were presented in the following manner: "dom in o." The goal of the analysis is to determine not only what is "down" but what is "up," that is, to ascertain which avenues are available for instruction.

## LEVEL OF DISTURBANCE— HIERARCHY OF EXPERIENCE

The diagnostic questions that derive from this construct are used in conjunction with the material discussed above. Myklebust refers to this schema as the hierarchy of experience (1960). As each symbol system is studied, efforts are made to determine whether the problem occurs at the level of attention, perception, imagery (memory), symbolization, or conceptualization. We wish to emphasize that these processes are studied not in isolation, such as memory for digits, unrelated words, or sounds. Rather, the processes are studied in relation to an area of academic achievement or language. For instance, assumptions regarding reading (a visual *verbal* system) cannot be made from studying visual *nonverbal* behaviors, such as memory for designs or pictures. Rather, memory for meaningful printed words would be analyzed in the diagnostic process. In remediation it is not assumed that training in sequential memory for digits or unrelated words will aid a child with the sequence of sounds in words or the sequence of words in sentences. While various auditory memory tests may be given to children during the course of the evaluation, the results are used for the study of memory strategies. An example of how processes might be used to study various aspects of morphology is shown in Figure 10–1.

## SEMIAUTONOMOUS SYSTEM

Another theoretic schema that is useful in diagnosis and remediation is the semiautonomous system proposed by Hebb (1963). In essence this concept suggests that the brain is composed of systems

1. Auditory Perception
    "Do these sound the same?"—boy, boys;
    jump, jumped.
    "Do these sound the same?"—The boy
    jumped, The boys jumped.
2. Auditory Comprehension
    "Do these mean the same thing?"—cat, cats;
    the cats eat; the cat eats.
    "Show me the boy; show me the boys."
    "Show me the blocks are piled; Show me the
    blocks are unpiled."
3. Auditory Repetition
    "Say these after me"—boy, boys; the boy
    jumped; the boys jumped. (Single words,
    phrases, sentences, questions)
4. Spontaneous Oral Production
    From actions, pictures, or experiences
    attempt to elicit the correct form (e.g.,
    hold up one boy doll figure—and then 2—
    then manipulate the doll figures and
    attempt to elicit a sentence).
    Increase complexity of picture or setting and
    attempt to determine percentage of
    correct usage.
3. Visual Perception
    "Do these words look the same?" boy, boys;
    jumps, jump.
    "Do these sentences look the same?" The
    boy jumps; the boys jump.
6. Visual Comprehension
    "Do these mean the same?"
    "Match the pictures with the sentences or
    questions." The boy jumped; the boys
    jumped.
7. Auditory-Visual Recognition
    "Point to: boy, boys."
    "Point to: the boy jumps; the boys jump."

8. Visual to Auditory Verbal Production
    "Read these: boy, boys; the boy jumps; the
    boys jump."
9. Visual-Motor Imitation
    "Copy these words and sentences."
10. Spontaneous Written Production
    From actions, sentence completion, pictures,
    etc., attempt to have the student write
    grammatically correct sentences.
    Increase complexity of setting and ask the
    child to write stories. Note percentage of
    correct usage and rule patterns.
    Note random vs. systematic errors and
    automaticity.
11. Application of Rule in Novel Situations
    Nonsense pictures and nonsense words (oral
    and/or written)
    "Here is a wug; here are two

    _____."
    "This wug is troppy; this one is troppier;
    this one is _____."
12. Comprehension of Morphology at an Explicit
    Level
    "Show me the part of the word that means
    more than one: boy, boys."
13. Verbal Expression of Meaning of Morphology
    "If I add an s to a word such as cat, what does
    it do?"
14. Monitoring of Other Production-Auditory
    "Listen—tell me whether this sounds
    correct; the boys is jumping."
15. Self-Monitoring—Auditory
    "Did you say that correctly?" (tape-recorded)
16. Monitoring of Other Productions—Visual
    "Look—see if you can find any mistakes: The
    boy are jumping."

Figure 10–1. Tasks for studying levels of rule acquisition and application.

that may operate semi-independently or together. Tasks may be arranged to ascertain whether children can process information via one sensory system (intra), through two systems (inter), or through multisensory systems (Birch and Belmont, 1964; Ettlinger, 1967; Johnson and Myklebust, 1967). Birch and Belmont found that poor readers had difficulty integrating certain visual-spatial patterns with auditory-temporal patterns. While their work was criticized somewhat by Bryant (1968) and others because they did not control for intrasensory learning, other projects they conducted did involve the study of both intra- and intersensory learning.

The language clinician and other educators should be conscious of the number of sensory systems that are involved in various tasks. For example, certain phonemic discrimination tasks that include a comparison of words involve only the auditory system; others that require the child to point to pictures require intersensory functions. Similarly, tasks that require children to name pictures require visual interpretation as well as auditory-motor responses. Thus when a child fails, follow-up tasks may be needed to determine the source of the problem.

The remediation question from this theory pertains to the combination of sensory inputs that facilitate learning. Typically, periods of diagnostic teaching are needed to answer this question. For example, in teaching a child a new syntactic structure one might note whether the child needs to experience the actions (for example, hop; hopped), whether pictures aid comprehension and production, whether auditory modeling is useful, and/or whether printed sentences aid comprehension and production. Although auditory verbal behavior is normally acquired before reading and writing, at times one might use a higher level to aid the lower. To cite another example, some youngsters with severe oral apraxia have been taught to speak by using printed symbols (Johnson and Myklebust, 1967). In some instances we began with "iconic" letters that served as a guide to the motor pattern (for example, l—raise your tongue; o—make your lips look like this).

As clinicians consider alternative communication systems for the severely language impaired, it is important to remember that some symbols can remain present for inspection. Whereas spoken language, speech reading, signing, and finger spelling are all "here and gone" after the message is produced, the printed word can be reviewed and matched with objects. Printed words also can be used to help children remember a sound or a word in a sentence. Students also can be taught to monitor their production by listening to tape recordings of themselves while they are looking at the printed material. Finally, at the upper age levels we have found reading to be useful in helping students to think inferentially. Some could not grasp the idea of inference by listening, but through reading they learned that some answers are actually *in* the lines whereas others are *between* the lines. One must think about the merely possible and look beyond the information given.

## LANGUAGE AND THOUGHT

It is more than a little presumptuous even to begin to address questions regarding interrelationships between language and thought, since philosophers, linguists, psychologists, and others have grappled with these issues for years. Furthermore, many of the previous topics in this chapter pertain to some aspects of cognition and verbal behavior. It should be emphasized, however, that clinicians frequently must decide whether to spend time on thinking skills per se or whether to help children acquire, organize, and use symbols to convey what they know. In many instances there is no clear dichotomy, but consider the following illustrations.

A 6-year-old is given a large colored picture of a house on fire and is asked to tell what is happening. His response was "Oh, look—they're having a birthday party—see the packages." He apparently responded only to the flames above the house and to two red-and-white-striped doorposts that vaguely resembled packages. In this instance, there were no problems with the forms of language, but what he said had little to do with the referent. Hence, the remediation focus was on guiding the boy's looking, reducing impulsive responses, helping him to see logical relations between objects and events, and monitoring his verbal responses.

In contrast, a 15-year-old was asked to write something about "running" shortly after the Olympics. He wrote, "The distanse you want run is determine by your health, age and determined you are to runned that distance. Your health is probably main factor in running if bad health you should take easy on the running because get a heart attack when running hard." Here the boy seems to have a clear understanding of the topic and many issues surrounding it, but he cannot use an elaborated verbal code effectively. In this case the focus of remediation was on the organization of words in sentences, grammatic rules, and on monitoring of verbal errors. In this case reading was very beneficial in helping him to acquire syntactic rules.

Not all cases are so clear-cut; usually problems occur concomitantly and there is a need to combine instruction on thinking and language. The following case illustrates that need. An 8-year-old was asked to tell what was happening in a picture in which a waitress was taking an order from a family in a restaurant. His response was, "The lady—the nurse—is writing—she talk to people." Although this boy had average ability on many nonverbal tests of intelligence, he had marked difficulty with both nonverbal conceptualization and language. Therefore he needed extensive training in thinking. In the example above it seemed that he had problems with the selection of criterial attributes that define an individual as a nurse. It was his assumption that anyone who wore a white pointed hat was a nurse, irrespective of other attributes, such as the type of work, setting, and so on. His problems were similar to those described many years ago by Strauss and Lehtinen (1947) and by Lewis, Strauss, and Lehtinen (1960). His attention to details interfered with the acquisition of concepts and with the appropriate verbal label. Thus, in remediation, activities and materials were provided which helped him acquire the concept of nurse and waitress. Multiple positive and negative instances were needed to help him acquire meanings. Neither definitions nor single explanations are sufficient, for they may lead to nothing more than empty verbalization (Johnson and Myklebust, 1967).

To individualize instruction clinicians should be prepared to probe below surface-level responses. For instance, children frequently are asked to tell how two things are alike (for example, cat and dog; knee and elbow). While we never use the test item per se for specific probes, we want to know several things when the student fails: (1) Is there a problem with comprehension of the task and did the child know that a superordinate term was expected?; (2) is there a problem with retrieval of the superordinate term?; (3) is there a problem with verbal comprehension? (show me animals): (4) can the child sort and classify objects, pictures, and so on with no verbal stimulation?; and (5) can the child hold a mental set on a series of items?

Throughout the intervention program, clinicians should be aware of the types of tasks and responses expected from normal children. Some of the curricular objectives for a Piagetian program can be very useful. Kamii (1971) has an excellent sequence of activities which can be used to assess various aspects of physical, logical, and social knowledge. Lavatelli (1971) also

includes examples of syntactic patterns that are needed to express various forms of knowledge (such as seriation and conservation). As emphasized throughout this chapter, tasks must be considered with regard to each child's combinations of strengths and weaknesses. In her study of conceptualization (1977), Blalock carefully controlled tasks so that she could study prediction, verbal expression, verbal comprehension, and discrimination of the attributes necessary to complete the task. Similarly, Stone (1980) studied adolescents in our diagnostic clinic using a Piagetian formal operations task. He found that some students had problems in cognition, whereas others were good thinkers but they had problems with verbal expression. In a study of the conceptual structure of measurement of length, James (1972) found that the learning disabled children had the concept but they gave more ambiguous verbal responses than did their normal peers. When designing tasks and analyzing performance of atypical learners, the processes and factors illustrated in Figure 10–2 can be useful.

## FORMS OF REPRESENTATIONAL BEHAVIOR

Several pioneers in the field of language disorders noted that children with verbal deficits had problems with other forms of symbolic behavior. For example, Myklebust (1954) reported that aphasic children frequently had difficulty with play and pretend behavior. Eisenson (1972) also noted that aphasics needed help with several aspects of representational behavior, including picture interpretation and gesture. In recent years, research studies have corroborated these clinical observations (Cicci, 1978; Cable, 1981; Sigel, 1972). That these problems might occur concomitantly is in keeping with the theory of Piaget and Inhelder (1969), who suggest that language is but one form of representational behavior that develops early in life. Along with language development, one can also observe symbolic play, drawing, pantomime, and gesture, all of which require a

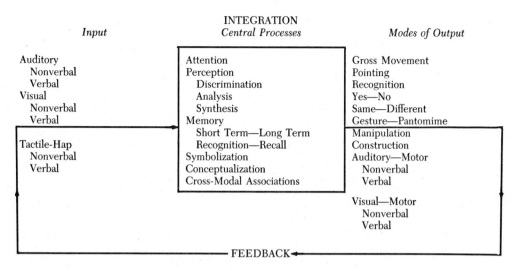

Figure 10–2. A plan for systems and task analysis.

certain amount of distancing from the real object or event (Sigel, 1972). While verbal symbols are among the most arbitrary, all forms of representation involve knowledge that something stands for something else.

During normal growth and development many processes develop together which permit the child to perceive and mentally "image" objects or actions, and to label them. In addition, perceptual-motor systems develop, so children have the vehicle to demonstrate what they know. In essence, sensorimotor development is used both for the acquisition of knowledge and for the perceptual-motor schemas necessary to express knowledge. If children have developmental imbalances, one or more aspects of representational behavior may not progress normally. Therefore a systems analysis is needed to see what is required in the intervention program.

Cicci (1978) designed a series of tasks to study pretend behavior, drawing, picture interpretation, and pantomime among language impaired children. Throughout each investigation she attempted to determine whether the children had difficulty with some aspect or reception or production of the symbol. In the area of pantomime, she asked the children to (1) pantomime to a verbal command, (2) tell what the examiner was doing when pantomim-

ing, (3) identify the object that went with the pantomime (for example, cup for drinking), (4) imitate the action, (5) match real objects with photographs and line drawings, and (6) show how the real object is used. She found significant differences between the normal and language impaired children on the first two tasks, but there were no differences on the pantomime-photograph match. She reported that the language impaired children imitated the movements but their actions were not as refined as those of the normal children. All children played equally well with the real objects.

For individualization of remediation one would need to look at the performance of each child on each set of tasks. While the study of groups is important for research, clinicians need to analyze each case.

Other forms of symbolic behavior must be studied among older children and adolescents. Based on findings in several language impaired children followed over 20 years, it is evident that remediation for higher levels of symbolic behavior often will be needed (Johnson, 1980). Many children with oral language problems will have reading, written language, and mathematics problems (deHirsch, Jansky, and Langford, 1966; Johnson and Myklebust, 1966). In addition, most have difficulty with foreign languages. A great deal depends upon how the language is taught; some students were unable to master conversational foreign language but managed to acquire some reading skills. Music also is an interesting symbol system to explore with language and learning disabled children. The same schema discussed earlier are used to analyze each child's performance. Some children have excellent ability to play an instrument by ear but they cannot read the notes. Others cannot manage visuospatial relations for certain instruments, such as a guitar or a trombone, but they do quite well on a piano or a clarinet where there is a specific finger placement.

Finally, one cannot overlook the importance of nonverbal communication as a form of representation. We have long been concerned about children who have problems with social perception and have noted that some were unable to interpret facial expressions, body language, proxemics and other behaviors that convey meaning. In our clinical work we emphasized the need to note whether the child perceives the differences between certain postures, distances, and facial expressions; then we noted whether the child understood the significance of these features. Eisenberg and Smith (1971) provide a very good review of research in nonverbal communication.

Other researchers who are interested in social perception emphasize verbal interactions (Bryan, 1978, 1979; Bryan and Bryan, 1978). Future research in pragmatics probably should incorporate detailed investigations of both verbal and nonverbal behaviors. In addition, some consideration should be given to the number of messages that any individual is capable of handling. Eisenberg and Smith (1971) point out that during any communication situation an individual responds to a host of both verbal and nonverbal cues, including facial expression, posture, voice set, tactile cues, and space. In her book on verbal and nonverbal language development, Wood (1976) provides teachers with research data and examples to show the growth of communicative competence in young children.

## STRATEGIES, PLANS AND ORGANIZATION

Considerable research in cognitive psychology and learning disabilities has been devoted to strategy selection and usage. Investigators are interested in *how* children try to solve problems as well as in the solutions. The findings have enhanced our understanding of both normal and atypical learners. For example, in the area of memory, we are interested in knowing which strategies children select and try to use when asked to recall a series of digits, unrelated words, sentences, pictures, and so on. As indicated previously, these data are not used for generalized memory training; rather, the goal is to help children select and use efficient strategies to accomplish tasks. It appears as though certain learning disabled children do not have limited memory capacities; rather, they have faulty strategy selection and usage. To illustrate, Newman (1980) studied a group of school-aged normal and learning disabled children performing a series of memory tasks. In the first condition she randomly organized pictures and asked children to recall as many as they could. In the second condition the pictures were preorganized into semantic groups, such as foods and clothing. In the third condition children were provided with verbal labels for the categories—that is, when presented with pictures they were told that there were groups of fruits, vegetables, and so forth. While there were differences between the groups on all three tasks, some of the most significant were on the second condition. Apparently the learning disabled children failed to use the verbal knowledge they had in order to recall the pictures. They might not have taken the time to ask themselves questions such as, "What would be the best way to try to remember this material?" Throughout the intervention programs, the clinician needs to *externalize* such questions until children *internalize* strategies for themselves. Thus, rather than focusing on serial memory per se, one asks, "what are some ways I can use to try to remember telephone numbers, directions, and so on?" Older children can be included in the decision-making process so they can see how rehearsal might be best for some tasks but classification might be better for others. Other strategies, such as writing or visualization, also might be tried. The goal is to make the child an independent learner.

Many language and learning disabled children often are reported to be disorganized in their behavior and in their approach to tasks. Currently, in our young adult program we find that many have difficulty on the job because of the lack of organization and systematic approach to work. At the preschool level, Cicci (1978) reported that normal children seemed to have a better "plan" in mind on her pantomime and drawing tests than did the language impaired children. They were more goal-directed and they seemed prepared to follow a set sequence.

These and other findings suggest that the clinician needs to help children develop "schemas" (Kagan, 1971) or "blueprints" for various types of tasks. Rather than simply modeling, the teacher should think about how to help the children hold both nonverbal and verbal plans in mind. For example, our clinical work and research indicates that children need to have plans in mind for giving definitions. Often they know the meanings of words but they do not have appropriate definitional forms, although these do change with age. They also need plans for describing objects, for telling how two objects are alike, plans for telling stories from pictures (Podhajski, 1980), for carrying on a conversation and the numerous other verbal activities. Cazden (1971) suggests a wide range of objectives for young children. She includes skills such as narration, description, explanations, and predictions. She also emphasizes the use of language for affective purposes and for verbal mediation.

## ACTIVITY AND AUTONOMY

In keeping with our interests in problem-solving we have long been interested in children's exploratory behavior and curiosity. At times it has appeared that some language and learning disabled children were rather passive. These observations were confirmed in one study of preschoolers on haptic perception tasks. The hands of the children were video-taped while they were exploring (feeling) various familiar and unfamiliar objects. Whereas the normal children actively felt all distinctive features, edges, and surfaces, some of the atypical learners simply pressed or squeezed the objects. This led us to conclude that some disturbances or delays in perceptual development resulted from a lack of exploration. Further evidence of this problem was reported by Cable (1978), who analyzed various types of play behavior and found that learning disabled preschool boys engaged in less sustained exploratory play than their normal age mates. Thus it seems that clinicians need to guide the child's exploration, looking, and questioning behavior to foster learning.

Some of these observations would suggest that atypical learners show fewer autonomous behaviors than normal children. Banta (1970) defines autonomy as "self-regulating behaviors that facilitate effective problem-solving." It includes curiosity, exploration, persistence, resistance to distraction, control of impulse, reflectivity, analytic perceptual processes, and innovative behavior. He has developed a series of tests that can be used by clinicians who are interested in these areas of learning.

## RULE APPLICATION AND METALINGUISTIC AWARENESS

Considerable attention has been devoted to the concepts of "metacognition" and "metalinguistics" by linguists and psychologists. In essence, these concepts suggest that older children learn to reflect on their own performance and that they acquire conscious control of their learning processes. Some of the issues discussed in previous sections are related to metacognition. For example, the development of strategies and schemas involves conscious control over one's thinking and performance.

With regard to linguistic awareness, we have been particularly interested in the knowledge children have about language as they enter school and begin to read. Liberman and colleagues (1974) reported that poor readers are often deficient in their ability to segment words into syllables and phonemes. Liberman feels that in order for children to read they must have some knowledge about how sentences and words can be segmented. We also have found that poor readers are less adept than good readers in their ability to analyze words and to manipulate sounds (Johnson and Hook, 1978). This was particularly evident on "secret language" (pig Latin) tasks. Every normal reader learned the task but none of the poor readers could.

Often metalinguistic skills are tested by having children perform some activity with nonsense words. For example, the Berry-Talbott test requires the children to complete sentences with the appropriate grammatic form (This wug is troppy; this one is_____; this one is the _____). Several studies from our center, including those with young adults, indicate that the language and learning disabled students have significant problems with these tasks. Myklebust also found that the test which best discriminated normal and atypical learners was the reading of nonsense words. This task requires children to apply rules in novel situations. Clinically, we see many children who are capable of reading lists of words with short vowels but who cannot read any nonsense words containing the same phoneme-grapheme patterns. In remediation, we avoid work with nonsense words until children have acquired some ability to use rules with real words. Ultimately, however, some work on auditory analysis, segmenting, and rule application is necessary for the children to attack new words and to spell.

language impaired individuals. The program of remediation depends on the nature of the problems that are identified. While much of this discussion focused on the study of children in an intensive one-to-one study, it is equally important to observe children in various settings whenever possible. In order to see how children use language across contexts they must be observed with adults, peers, parents, and others, because these are the best times to study knowledge application and interaction. Group sessions are useful for gathering data, for formulating hypotheses about the nature of the disorder, for instruction, and for evaluation. However, the overall program should contain a balance between group and individual work, and between work on subskills and communication. Just as the physical education teacher prepares children for the world of games by doing exercises and subroutines, so also we need to see how children deviate in the "communication game" and try to provide for their specific needs.

The *scope* of the program will vary with the severity and number of problems; clearly we are dealing with a heterogeneous population. *Intensity* of the program will be determined by the facilities in the school and community and by the number of professionals working with the children. It is of the utmost importance to coordinate efforts among the classroom teacher, parents, other specialists, and the speech-language clinician. Finally, our longitudinal studies indicate that many students have persistent disorders and that they may need help periodically throughout high school and even into the college years. Although many have made significant gains, there may be residuals of the disorders. Thus, whenever assistance is needed, we hope that services will be available in the community.

## SUMMARY AND GENERAL ISSUES IN PROGRAM PLANNING

The purpose of this chapter has been to define some of the problems that clinicians should anticipate when working with

## REFERENCES

Banta T: Tests for the evaluation of early childhood education: The Cincinnati autonomy test battery (CATB). In Helmuth J (ed): *Cognitive Studies*, vol I. New York: Brunner/Mazel, 1970
Berlin L, Blank M, Rose S: The language of instruc-

tion: The hidden complexities. Topics Lang Dis 1:47–59, 1980

Birch H, Belmont L: Auditory-visual integration in normal and retarded readers. Am J Orthopsychiat 34:851–861, 1964

Blalock J: A study of conceptualization and related abilities in learning disabled and normal preschool children. Unpublished doctoral dissertation, Northwestern University, Evanston, Illinois 1977

Blank M: Teaching Learning in the Preschool: A Dialogue Approach. Columbus, Ohio: Charles E. Merrill, 1973

Bloom L: Language development, language disorders, and learning disabilities: LD. Bul Orton Soc 30:115–133, 1980

Bryan T: Verbal interactions and social relationships of learning disabled children in the classroom. J Learn Dis 11:107–115, 1978

Bryan T: Communication competence in reading and learning disabilities. Bul Orton Soc 29:172–188, 1979

Bryan T, Bryan J: Social interaction of learning disabled children. Learn Dis Quart 1:33–38, 1978

Bryant P: Comments on the design of development studies of cross-modal matching and cross-modal transfer. Cortex 4:128–137, 1968

Cable B: A study of play behavior in normal and learning disabled preschool boys. Unpublished doctoral dissertation, Northwestern University, Evanston, Illinois, 1981

Cazden C: Evaluation of learning in preschool education: Early language development. In Formative and Summative Evaluation of Student Learning. New York: McGraw-Hill, 1971

Cazden C: Child Language and Education. New York: Holt, Rinehart and Winston, Inc, 1972

deHirsch K: Interactions between educational therapist and child. Bul Orton Soc 27:88–101, 1977

deHirsch K, Jansky J: Patterning and organizational deficits in children with language and learning disabilities. Bul Orton Soc 30:227–239, 1980

deHirsch K, Jansky J, Langford W: Predicting Reading Failure. New York: Harper & Row, 1966

Eisenberg A, Smith R: Nonverbal Communication. New York: Bobbs-Merrill, 1971

Ettlinger G: Analysis of cross-modal effects and their relationship to language. In Millikan C, Darley F (eds): Brain Mechanisms Underlying Speech and Language. New York: Grune & Stratton, 1967

Groshong C: Ambiguity detection and the use of verbal context for disambiguation by language disabled and normal learning children. Unpublished doctoral dissertation, Northwestern University, Evanston, Illinois, 1980

Hebb D: The semi-autonomous process: Its nature and nuture. Am Psychol 18:16, 1963

James K: A study of the conceptual structure of measurement of length in normal and learning disabled children. Unpublished doctoral dissertation, Northwestern University, Evanston, Illinois, 1972

Johnson D: The language continuum. Bul Orton Soc 28:1–11, 1968

Johnson D: Psycho-educational evaluation of children with learning disabilities: Study of auditory processes. In Learning Disabilities and Related Disorders. Chicago: Yearbook Medical Publishers, 1977

Johnson D: Process deficits in learning disabled children and implications for reading. In Resnick L, Weaver P (eds): Theory and Practice of Early Reading. Hillsdale, NJ: Lawrence Erlbaum Associates, 1979

Johnson D: Persistent auditory disorders in young dyslexic adults. Bul Orton Soc 30:268–276, 1980

Johnson D: Factors to consider in programming for children with language disorders. Topics Lang Learn Dis July, 13–27, 1981

Johnson D, Blalock J, Nesbitt J: Adolescents with learning disabilities: Perspectives from an educational clinic. Learn Dis Quarterly 1:34–36, 1978

Johnson D, Hook P: Reading disabilities: Problems of rule acquisition and linguistic awareness. In Myklebust H (ed): Progress in Learning Disabilities, vol IV. New York: Grune & Stratton, 1978

Johnson D, Myklebust H: Dyslexia in childhood. In Learning Disorders, vol I. Seattle: Special Child Publications, 1962

Johnson D, Myklebust H: Learning Disabilities: Educational Principles and Practices. New York: Grune & Stratton, 1967

Kagan J: Understanding Children: Behavior, Motives, and Thought. New York: Harcourt, Brace, Jovanovich, Inc, 1971

Kamii C: Evaluation of learning in preschool education: Socio-emotional, perceptual-motor, and cognitive development. In Bloom B, Hastings J, Madaus G (eds): Handbook on Formative and Summative Evaluation of Student Learning. New York: McGraw-Hill, 1971

Keith RW: Central Auditory and Language Disorders in Children. Houston: College-Hill Press, 1981

Lavatelli C: Language training in early childhood education. Urbana, Ill: University of Illinois Press, 1971

Lee L, Koenigsknecht R, Mulhern S: Interactive language development teaching. Evanston, Ill: Northwestern University Press, 1974

Lewis R, Strauss A, Lehtinen L: The Other Child. New York: Grune & Stratton, 1960

Liberman I, Shankweiler D, Fischer F, Carter B: Explicit syllable and phoneme segmentation in the young child. J Exp Child Psych 18:201–212, 1974

Luria A: Language and Cognition. New York: John Wiley & Sons, 1981

McGrady H: Verbal and nonverbal functions in school children with speech and language disorders. Unpublished doctoral dissertation, Northwestern University, Evanston, Illinois, 1964

Myklebust H: Auditory Disorders in Children. New York: Grune & Stratton, 1954

Myklebust H: Psychology of Deafness. New York: Grune & Stratton, 1960

Orton S: Reading, Writing and Speech Problems in Children. New York: Grune & Stratton, 1937

Piaget J, Inhelder E: The Psychology of the Child. New York: Basic Books, 1969

Pistono K: Certain aspects of problem-solving abilities of learning disabled and normal 6- to 7-year-old boys as reflected in external cue incorporation of a memory task. Unpublished doctoral dissertation, Northwestern University, Evanston, Illinois, 1980

Podhajski B: Picture arrangement and selected narrative language skills in learning disabled and normal seven year old children. Unpublished doctoral dissertation, Northwestern University, Evanston, Illinois, 1980

Schiefelbusch R: *Bases of Language Intervention*. Baltimore: University Park Press, 1978

Sigel I: Language of the disadvantaged: The distancing hypothesis. In Lavatelli C (ed): *Language Training in Early Childhood Education*. ERIC, 1972

Speckman N: An investigation of the dyadic, verbal problem-solving communication abilities of learning disabled and normal children. Unpublished doctoral dissertation, Northwestern University, Evanston, Illinois, 1977

Stone CA: Adolescent cognitive development: Implications for learning disabilities. Bul Orton Soc 30:79–93, 1980

Strauss A, Lehtinen L: *Psychopathology of the Brain-Injured Child*. New York: Grune & Stratton, 1947

Wing C: Language processes and levels: A matrix. Lang-Speech Hear Serv Schools 13, 1:2–10, 1982

Wood B: *Children and Communication: Verbal and Nonverbal Language Development*. New Jersey: Prentice-Hall, Inc, 1976

Wren C: The relationship of auditory and cognitive processes to syntactic patterns of learning disabled and normal children. Unpublished doctoral dissertation, Northwestern University, Evanston, Illinois, 1980

# DISCUSSION: PART IV: FROM ASSESSMENT TO TREATMENT

*MALCOLM R. MCNEIL*

Instead of commenting directly on the well-formulated and well-written chapters of Drs. Snyder and Johnson, I will share some of my concerns for transforming test data into treatment paradigms. These concerns address several points in each chapter, but I will not attempt to make direct parallels. Although my orientation in this discussion is drawn heavily from an adult perspective, I believe the same issues are of concern for children as well.

The first issue is to decide *why* we assess or test in the first place. When posed in the interrogative form, the standard responses include (1) to detect or confirm a suspected problem, (2) for differential diagnosis distinguishing other disorders from the one under consideration, (3) to classify within a disorder group, (4) to determine site of lesion, (5) to specify the degree or severity of involvement, (6) to establish a prognosis or a candidacy for treatment, (7) to specify more precisely the treatment focus, (8) to measure any change that accompanies treatment, no treatment (maturation), or the exacerbation of the original etiologic factor, or (9) as criteria for treatment termination. In one form or another, then, the responses to this *why* indicate that tests are used primarily to *predict*. They detect that there either is or is not a problem present and predict that there is a relationship between the observed behav-

iors that brought the patient to seek assessment, and a logical explanation for those behaviors (a type of confirmation). They predict that the behaviors fit one complex or subcomplex and not others, and (in the case of adults with aphasia) they predict that there is high probability of an underlying physiologic malfunction (a lesion) that is causing the problem. They predict that treatment may be effective for one and probably less effective for others, or that continued treatment is not likely to be either of any further value or cost-effective. Some tests are even said to predict successful intervention strategies. For a tool to have predictive validity for any of these purposes, it must necessarily have not only *established* construct, content, and concurrent validity, but its administration and performance evaluation system must also be specified with such precision and clarity that it can be reliably scored and the same performance can be obtained on repeated test administrations. In order for these stringent, requisite conditions to be met, individualized and "informal" assessment procedures cannot be substituted for *psychometrically sound tools** that not only

---

*The term psychometric has come to mean more than just the application of numbers to behaviors. The term refers to all aspects of the development of standardized, valid, and reliable tests (Cronbach, 1970).

take years of experimentation to develop, but are open for experimental scrutiny from our professional colleagues. These psychometric requirements must be met for unstructured-observational assessments as well as formal structured-elicited assessment procedures.†

What do we need to know about the patient to begin treatment? Drs. Johnson and Snyder have given us an excellent variety of factors to consider, and these are, in my opinion, of equal concern for adult aphasics as for language disordered children. Many investigators, including myself (Muma and McNeil, 1981) have speculated about some psycho-socio-linguistic factors that, at least on the surface, appear to be candidates for influencing treatment. These factors also appear to be relevant for both language disordered children and adults with aphasia. The psycho-socio-linguistic factors include, for example, such cognitive elements as (1) cognitive distancing; (2) cognitive tempo; (3) Bruner's enactive, iconic, and symbolic processing; (4) analytic versus synthetic style of thinking; (5) restricted perceptual salience; (6) rule versus nonrule governed learning strategies; and (7) categorization and mediation skills. Also included are such linguistic factors as flexibility with word and referent relationships, flexibility with linguistic form and function relationships, and the ability to profit from linguistic and referential contexts. To these factors one might also add the myriad psychologic, physiologic, and information processing factors that have been shown to be of substantial, if not predominant, concern in explaining many of the language disorders demonstrated in adults with brain damage

(McNeil, 1982). These include such factors as (1) visual and auditory perceptual disorders; (2) motor disorders, such as apraxia of speech; (3) primary short term memory problems; (4) psychologic depression or lability of emotions; (5) increased performance time; (6) increased sensory thresholds; (7) increased inertia in excitation and inhibition processes; and (8) increased variability on tasks (possibly due to disordered attentional processes).

In the face of these treatment concerns, a more basic question emerges, namely; Does labeling someone aphasic or language delayed or disordered based on *any* test predict these treatment variables? Does labeling an aphasic, a conduction aphasic, a Broca aphasic, or any other type predict *any* of these treatment-influencing factors? Unfortunately, the answer at this time in our professional history is almost assuredly no. This is not to say that labeling an aphasic a "Broca" does not predict several important treatment variables. Helm-Estabrooks and associates (1981) have in fact demonstrated that some treatment variables can be predicted from the classification category to which they belong. Nonetheless, in the wake of that resounding "no," it seems to me that we are left with several options for basing treatment on assessment. The first option is to assess everything believed to be important or influential to our treatment. This must of course be done with standardized,* psychometrically sound tests, enabling us to make valid and reliable predictions relative to treatment decisions.† To accomplish

---

†It has been assumed that there are behaviors important to language intervention which are not amenable to measurement via elicited techniques. The assessment of pragmatic skills often ranks high among those behaviors that require observation in natural settings for their valid measurement. The development of the communication assessment in daily living (Holland, 1980) is a forthright attempt to modify this assumption. It is stressed here, however, that *all* elicited or observed behaviors are psychometrically accountable.

---

*"Standardized" in this context does not refer only to the collection of normative data. It also refers to such test control factors as specifying the administration and scoring procedures, the establishment of internal consistency of the test, as well as such factors as the physical characteristics of the test stimuli and the environment in which the test is administered.

†I am continually amazed by clinicians who will readily reject a study for its lack of experimental control on many dimensions as an unreliable or irreproducible finding, but will even more readily devise an assessment tool or procedure (often on the spot) for an individual patient and have enough confidence in the result to design treatment based on it and even charge the patient for these services.

this, each patient would be assessed over an extended time period during which they would change by virtue of maturation. However, the minimally required 50 to 100 hours of pretreatment assessment doesn't appear to be a likely or feasible choice for most clinicians or patients.

A second option is to treat as we do now, with little or no data on these treatment-influencing variables, and tenuously assume that their effect is inconsequential to our major treatment focus. A third option is not to treat at all until we can confidently make more valid predictions based on more efficient assessment procedures. Indeed, it might be found that some tools will predict more than one factor and thus reduce formal assessment time. Further research may demonstrate that certain of these factors would be expected to add little or nothing to the treatment process and therefore may be eliminated from consideration without sacrificing either efficiency or effectiveness.

None of these options (that is, to test everything, don't test anything, continue as we have in the past, or stop treating until we can efficiently test that which is important to test) seem particularly appealing. However, a careful consideration of two alternative approaches may be of value in the resolution of the major difficulties we now have in applying data derived from assessment to treatment. The first is to concentrate all our resources on test development. This effort would necessarily be directed toward cognitive, linguistic, communicative, and physiologic abilities and disabilities. Nothing that makes an ounce of sense can be disregarded until it has been demonstrated to be of little or no value in the treatment process. While this is the only way to reach the goal of predicting, the initial response to this is likely to be puzzlement because we don't yet know which variables are important for treatment. Therefore, to develop a test or assessment procedure prior to this knowledge is likely to be as inefficient as past procedures. This necessitates another alternative. This second alternative is to encourage treatment, essentially let progress occur as it has in test development, but

organize every so-called treatment‡ program into a research paradigm with the intent of evaluating and sharing the results of each intervention experience. Through this approach (which admittedly is generally time-consuming and possibly scientifically and practically expensive), treatment-influencing factors can be isolated and their potency defined. This approach would require little change in practice but would require a rather substantial change in attitude. Doing in therapy what is reasonable but untested cannot be considered efficacious. Likewise, ignoring the many treatment-influencing factors that the literature suggests should affect the efficiency and effectiveness of treatment cannot be considered efficacious. It seems to me that until we can equip ourselves with those treatment data that identify the most potent treatment-influencing variables, and until these factors are incorporated into psychometrically sound assessment tools and procedures that will predict, a priori, for whom the factor is operable, we will continue to treat by trial and error. While trial and error intervention is a monumental improvement over intervention without assessment, it is not yet time for complacency about our ability to monitor and change strategies if they are ineffective or if improvement levels off. Only through valid and reliable pretreatment predictions can we, who are responsible for the management of language disorders, take our place among (or possibly stand alone as) the respected health care delivery professionals. Prediction of treatment-influencing factors is one goal for which we must consistently strive.

---

‡This implies that we ought to *stop pretending* that we are doing things in the treatment arena which change behavior when such a priori evidence is unavailable. The definition of treatment in speech pathology implies that there is a benefit or positive effect to be expected with the intervention and not simply the manipulation of behavior. The term treatment should therefore not be used in cases in which a high probability of benefit cannot be predicted or in which a term such as intervention is more appropriate, as is often the case with many procedures used by most speech and language pathologists.

## REFERENCES

Cronbach LJ: *Essentials of Psychological Testing.* New York: Harper and Row, Publishers, 1970

Helm-Estabrooks N, Fitzpatrick P, Barresi B: Response of an agrammatic patient to a syntax stimulation program for aphasia. J Speech Hear Dis 46:422–427, 1981

Holland AL: *Communicative Abilities in Daily Living: A Test of Functional Communication for Aphasic Adults.* Baltimore: University Park Press, 1980

McNeil MR: The nature of aphasia in adults. In Lass NJ, McReynolds L, Northern J, Yoder D: *Speech, Language and Hearing,* vol II. *Pathologies of Speech and Language.* Philadelphia: WB Saunders Co, 1982

Muma JR, McNeil MR: Intervention in aphasia: Psycho-sociolinguistic perspectives. In Chapey R (ed): *Language Intervention Strategies in Adult Aphasia.* Baltimore: Williams & Wilkins, 1981

# PART V

# WHEN TO BEGIN AND END LANGUAGE INTERVENTION

# 11

# THE TIMING OF LANGUAGE INTERVENTION FOR THE PEDIATRIC POPULATION

*JAMES C. KEMP*

The purpose of this chapter is to discuss two timing decision processes that generally receive little attention: the timing decision process of when to accept a child into a language intervention context, and when to release a child from a language intervention context. The discussion of the first timing decision process is limited to one aspect of the process, which is the use or nonuse of a referential metric (quantitative standard) to which language behaviors are referenced (compared) so judgments of normalcy or deviancy can be determined. The discussion of the second timing decision process is concerned with several aspects of the process and is therefore broader in scope. Both discussions are concerned with oral language as it is acquired by the first language learner, with language intervention context being defined as that context wherein a speech-language pathologist directly intervenes by conducting therapy with the child and/or the family.

## TIMING DECISION PROCESS: WHEN TO ACCEPT A CHILD INTO A LANGUAGE INTERVENTION CONTEXT

There has been little discussion in the literature on this subject. Marge (1972) noted that "most scholars agree that it is important to apply interventional techniques as early as possible. . . ." He further noted that early intervention can be considered preventive and that intervention at the preschool-age level would be less complicated and present fewer problems than would intervention at the school-age level. Menyuk (1975) addressed the question of when to intervene by drawing conclusions from two theoretic positions: behavior modification theory and cognitive theory. The conclusion based on the former was that "behavior modification takes place naturally from birth. We can, however, control the environment in much better ways than naturally exist and, therefore, intervention should take place at any time, the earlier the better, with any individual or group of individuals." The conclusion based on cognitive theory was stated as follows: "Intervention should take place when development deviates markedly from the norm. The degree of deivation requiring intervention remains an open question. However, the earlier one intervenes, the better the prognosis for normal development."

Both Marge and Menyuk assume that the decision process of when to accept a child into a language intervention context is tantamount to the decision process of

183

identifying a child who has a language difference. However, in the practical world,
this is not the case. For example, one need
only compare the various state educational
guidelines to observe that not all children
identified as having language differences
are equally accepted into language intervention contexts. Many children identified as having language differences do not
receive special assistance until the differences are documented to be "differences that make a difference." Documentation varies, depending upon the
philosophic orientation of those who provide the context, upon the monies and
personnel available, upon the level of
awareness of consumer groups, and upon
how language or language learning is defined. It appears that the last variable has
made the timing decision much more
complex than that inferred by Marge and
Menyuk, and that the complexity is directly related to the modifications that
have occurred over the past two decades
in the operational definition of language or
language learning.

## SYNTACTICALLY BASED THEORIES AND THE TIMING DECISION PROCESS

When the syntactically based theories
(for example, Chomsky, 1965; McNeill,
1970; Slobin, 1971) were prevalent, language learning was defined primarily in
terms of form: morphology and syntax.
Language was viewed as the principal
means by which interpersonal communication was realized. It was presumed that the
ability to produce well-formed phrases was
a prerequisite for effective communication. Children younger than 24 months of
age, the age at which initial phrase production is developmentally expected, were not
commonly considered as candidates for a
language intervention program. With children older than 24 months, the timing decision process of when to accept a child into
a language intervention context consistently included chronologic age (CA) as
the referential metric.

Standardized tests, formal assessment
protocols, and sequences of normal language development used to sample morphology and syntax, based on norms referenced to CA, were employed. The referential aspect of the timing decision process was rather uncomplicated. It consisted of determining some sort of composite
language age (LA), comparing that with the
child's CA, and then determining whether
the LA-CA gap, if any, was of a magnitude
to warrant acceptance into a language intervention context. The relevance of the
magnitude of the LA-CA gap seemed to
vary, depending on numerous factors.

If the child also had a speech articulation problem, the speech problem was considered separately from the child's language status. The timing decision of when
the child should be accepted into an articulation management program was evaluated, in part, by comparing the child's articulation pattern with a normative scale of
articulation development referenced to
CA.

## SEMANTICALLY BASED THEORIES AND THE TIMING DECISION PROCESS

The semantically based theories (for
example, McCawley, 1971; Clark, 1973;
Bowerman, 1973), being concerned with
content of language, quickly precipitated
an interest in the function of language, that
is, pragmatics. The work of individuals
such as Bloom (1970), Brown (1973), Dore
(1974), Halliday (1975), Bates (1976), and
Bowerman (1976) emphasized the necessity of including semantics and pragmatics in
any treatise that attempted to explain first
language learning. Clinical implications resulting from the relative emergence of content and function over form were provided
initially by Bloom and Lahey (1978),
McLean and Snyder-McLean (1978), Miller (1978), Muma (1978), and Prutting
(1979).

At about this same time, clinical research was being directed toward the notion that aspects of speech needed to be

included in operational definitions of language learning. Clinical application of phonologic theories conceptualized by Chomsky and Halle (1968), Crocker (1969), and Compton (1970) were being provided by McReynolds and Engmann (1975), Shriberg and Kwiatkowski (1980), and Ingram (1981a).

In a little more than a decade, the operational definition of language learning was significantly modified. It changed from having two linguistic patterns of organization (morphology and syntax) to having five linguistic patterns of organization (phonology, morphology, syntax, semantics, and pragmatics). The modifications in the operational definition of language learning fostered changes in the perceived relationship between language and communication and in the constancy of usage of CA as the referential metric.

The extension of the operational definition of language learning by the inclusion of semantics and pragmatics confused the distinction that existed between language and communication when language was defined only in terms of morphology and syntax. The importance of the child's expression of relationships between people and things in the environment and his use of effective and efficient productions to relate to individuals in the environment was emphasized. Language learning became to be viewed less as the *means* for attaining communicative competence and more as the *process* of attaining communicative competence. This reconceptualization of the relationship between language learning and communication essentially had the effect of not limiting language learning to the verbal child. Infants, young children, and retarded children who do not verbalize exhibit communicative behaviors that can be categorized according to semantic and pragmatic taxonomies. Whether such categorization is indicative of language learning is open to debate (Cromer, 1981). Nonetheless, preverbal children who do not exhibit or are delayed in exhibiting communicative intentions are being considered as candidates for acceptance into early language intervention contexts (Herber and

colleagues, 1972; Bricker and Bricker, 1974; Hart and Rogers-Warren, 1978; Fowler and Swenson, 1979; Bricker and Schiefelbusch, 1981).

In essence, the effect on the timing decision process of including semantics and pragmatics in the prevailing operational definition of language learning is twofold. First, the notion of a language intervention context becomes rather broad. It is no longer limited to a situation wherein a child is assisted in acquiring the linguistic patterns of organization of a language. It now seems to include those situations wherein a child may be assisted in acquiring the social, affective, cognitive, and prelinguistic behaviors deemed necessary for, or related to, to later linguistic acquisition. Second, as a criterion for acceptance into a language intervention context, CA has been somewhat negated. A child of any age who is suspected of having a communicative or language problem or both is a possible candidate for some type of "language intervention."

Because of the need to assess the child's semantic intents and pragmatic functions, clinical analysis of the child's language learning abilities is currently focusing more on the child's production (expressive behavior) than on comprehension (receptive behavior). The result of this shift of fucus is that standardized tests indexed directly to CA are being used less frequently, while developmental scales and criterion-referenced procedures indexed indirectly to CA are being used more frequently. CA, as the referential metric, has assumed variable emphasis.

For example, after a child's development of patterns of linguistic organization (morphology, syntax, semantics, pragmatics) has been assessed, and they have been compared one to another (intralinguistic referencing), one of three courses of action may be taken. First, if development indicates relatively uniform acquisition across the patterns of linguistic organization and if the status of development is somewhat equivalent to the child's CA, then the child is usually considered to be learning language normally. Second, if development indicates relatively uniform acquisition across the patterns of linguistic organization but the status of linguistic development is below the child's CA, then the child may be considered to be language delayed. Third, if development indicates significant differences in acquisition within a pattern of linguistic organization, or an asynchronism of acquisition among the patterns, or both, and if development of at least one of the patterns of linguistic organization is at or near CA level, then the child may be considered to be language disordered or deviant. This variable emphasis of the referential metric CA appears to be the current modus operandi in most clinical settings. The effects of this variable are discussed as follows.

One effect is that variable emphasis of the metric CA allows for the distinction between language delay and language disorder. The ongoing discussion in the literature about whether the language learning of a child with a language problem deviates from normal development or is delayed in comparison with normal development has not yet been helpful clinically (see, for example, Menyuk, 1964; Leonard, 1972; Morehead and Ingram, 1973; Freedman and Carpenter, 1976; Johnston and Schery, 1976; Leonard and colleagues, 1976; Snyder, 1976). The attempt to distinguish between a language delay and a language disorder is clinically relevant because of the therapeutic importance this distinction assumes when one is trying to discern etiologic factors, to determine the need for assistive consultations, and to plan initial intervention strategies.

Another effect of the variable emphasis of the referential metric CA is that it allows for clinical flexibility in the timing decision process of when to accept an identified mentally retarded child into a language intervention context. When CA is used as the referential metric, the majority of mentally retarded children can be viewed as candidates for a language intervention program. In these instances, the goal of intervention is not to facilitate language performance level to CA level, but rather to facilitate the rate of language acquisition to a greater degree than previously, to expand the child's linguistic performance from the oral language area into the gestural or graphic language areas, or both. When intralinquistic referencing is used, some mentally retarded children are not considered candidates for a language intervention program because their patterns of linguistic organization are relatively similar, while others are considered candidates because their acquisition of patterns of linguistic organization are different and/or asynchronous. In either of these instances, the referential metric CA has been subjugated to intralinguistic referencing.

Another effect of the variable emphasis of the referential metric CA has to do with judging the qualitative significance of quantitative differences. Crystal and colleagues (1976), in an attempt to come to terms with the problem of significance, noted that when judgments are to be made about age scores on measures of language, specifically syntax, the age score should be considered as a mean with a range of $\pm$ six months. There appear to be two clinical problems with this scheme. First, it doesn't seem clinically logical that the $\pm$ six months quantification should hold across the entire childhood age range. The qualitative significance of a 9-month language difference for a 24-month-old child should be greater than that of a 9-month difference for a 48-month-old child in that the prognosis for normal language development would probably be poorer for the 24-month-old than it would for the 48-month-old. Second, the $\pm$ six months scheme has been generalized clinically from those instances when CA is used as the referential metric to those instances when reference is primarily made intralinguistically. Given the current state of knowledge about individual rates of acquisition of the patterns of linguistic organization, this may be an invalid generalization.

## COGNITIVELY BASED THEORIES AND THE TIMING DECISION PROCESS

The present variable emphasis of the referential metric CA as one aspect of the timing decision process of when to accept a child into a language intervention context may be subjected to closer scrutiny in the future because of implications being derived from the relatively recent resurgence of cognitive theories of language learning, particularly those subsumed under the rubric cognitive hypothesis (Bowerman, 1974; Cromer, 1976; Bates and associates, 1977). It appears that all three forms of the cognitive hypothesis (strong, weak, correlated) suggest that nonverbal mental age (MA) is probably a potent indicator for judging rate of prelinguistic and early linguistic development. Miller (1981a) notes that " . . . data to date clearly support MA as the general pacesetter for language acquisition. As a result, we cannot judge performance status as deficit unless we have measures of non-verbal mental age." This relatively recent accentuation of the non-verbal MA as " . . . the interpretive basis . . ." (Miller, 1981b) or referential metric for determining when a child should be accepted into a language intervention context may have significant clinical implications.

At present, however, it must be emphasized that the determination of the non-verbal MA as the metric of choice has not yet been achieved. The limited supportive research is based primarily on normally developing children between the ages of approximately 6 and 24 months (for example, Bates and colleagues, 1977; Corrigan, 1978; Miller and colleagues, 1980) and on retarded populations (Kahn, 1975; Greenwald and Leonard, 1979; Lobato and colleagues, 1981). Moreover, there is some evidence that certain normally developing children under 24 months of age and certain retarded children functioning at or below the preoperational period have lexic and syntactic skills in advance of those expected based on their MAs (Miller and associates, 1978; Cromer, 1981; Ingram, 1981b). Furthermore, if cognition is viewed, especially in the older child, as being composed of factors such as selective attention, perceptual organization, mnemonic strategies, imagery, problem evaluation, and social patterning, then it appears implausible to assume that factors such as these can be tapped by procedures designed to yield a nonverbal MA and that the nonverbal MA will be the valid metric indicating rate of acquisition across all patterns of linguistic organization. In sum, there is essentially no empiric evidence to substantiate the supposition that the referential metric nonverbal MA is valid for nonretarded children older than 24 months.

## CLINICAL DILEMMA: WHEN TO ACCEPT A CHILD INTO A LANGUAGE INTERVENTION CONTEXT

In certain contexts, such as some public school settings, where regulations specify that standardized tests and/or "recognized" sequences of normative development must be used, CA will probably—at least for the immediate future—continue to be used as the referential metric in the timing decision process of when to accept a child into a language intervention context. However, because of the continuing ramifications of PL 94–142, these school systems will need to reconsider their regulations. Children younger than 2 years who are developmentally delayed or retarded are already possible candidates for language intervention programs, and children younger than 3 years who are suspected of having communication/language problems will soon be eligible for consideration. The referential metric CA is essentially useless for these children, and other referencing procedures will be needed. In other settings, where there is some flexibility, careful consideration should be given to the procedures used when referencing the timing decision process of when a child should be accepted into a language intervention context. Some possible guidelines follow. These guidelines are subject to debate regarding their conceptual foundations, practical application, and interventional implications; however, they serve as a starting point for clinical investigation in the area of referencing as it relates to the timing decision process.

**Children Younger Than Two Years.** First, with children younger than 24 months, it appears reasonable to use the referential metric nonverbal MA as the metric of choice. Estimates of nonverbal MA/nonverbal cognitive level can be obtained using adaptations of developmental scales, such as the California First-Year Mental Scale (Bayley, 1933), the Cattell Infant Intelligence Scale (Cattell, 1947), the Bayley Scales of Infant Development (Bayley, 1969), the Griffiths Mental Scales (Griffiths, 1970), and the Ordinal Scales of Psychological Development (Uzgiris and Hunt, 1975).

The process would be to assess the child's development of each pattern of prelinguistic/linguistic development (phonologic, morphologic, syntactic, semantic, pragmatic) using sequences of normal development indexed to CA, and then quantitatively compare the CA level of each pattern of organization with the child's MA. If a CA-MA gap exists in one or more patterns and the gap is considered to be significant, it is concluded that the child is not developing communication/language normally and the timing decision is to accept the child into an early language intervention context. The obvious problem in this procedure is judging the significance of the CA-MA gap. Of the few language programs that employ procedures similar to the one outlined above, only one—the Interactive Communication Diagnosis Project being developed at Louisiana State University (Miller, 1981)—specifies qualitative significance. In that project, the ± six months criterion specified by Crystal and colleagues (1976) is employed. That means that if a child's CA-MA gap in one or more patterns of organization is greater than six months, the resulting timing decision is to accept the child into an early language intervention context. The advisability of using this criterion, as mentioned previously, is open to question. However, the Interactive Communication Diagnosis Project at least confronted the problem.

**Nonretarded Children Older than 2 Years.** As noted elsewhere in this chapter, the use of CA as the referential metric of choice with nonretarded children older than 2 years is quite variable; and the use of nonverbal MA as the referential metric of choice with nonretarded children older than 2 years has not yet been substantiated as a valid procedure. Thus it appears that the most plausible timing decision process for children older than 24 months who have not been identified as mentally retarded would be to use intralinguistic-only referencing. In such a procedure, the evaluation of the child's language development is made by comparing only the levels of patterns of linguistic organization, one to another. Of course, the levels of development of each pattern of linguistic organization are determined by normative data indexed to CA, but the important difference is that neither CA nor nonverbal MA is used as the referential metric. The qualitative significance of quantitative differences thus becomes the gap or gaps existing among the levels of patterns of linguistic organization. While the qualitative significance of any quantitative gap is still open to individual interpretation, the probability of over- or underestimating this significance appears to be reduced, because only linguistic variables are being considered.

One implication of employing intralinguistic-only referencing with nonretarded children older than 24 months is that those children who do exhibit a language problem would most likely be considered language disordered instead of language delayed. Hopefully, this subtle difference in labeling will have an impact on interventional approaches. Children identified via intralinguistic-only referencing will demonstrate differences within a pattern of linguistic organization or asynchronisms across the patterns of linguistic organization. Because of this, the causal factors that may account for these abnormalities in language learning may be investigated with more zeal than they have been to date. Moreover, emphasis might be redirected to the assessment of language comprehension as it integrates with language production (Swisher and Aten, 1981). These abnormalities of language learning may also suggest assistive consultations that would not have been otherwise considered. In addition, such abnormalities would ideally precipitate formulation of language intervention strategies that would attend to the specific remediation of the particular areas of difficuly presented by the "language disordered" child, rather than attending to the general stimulation of the overall language lag presented by the "language delayed" child.

**Mentally Retarded Children Functioning Above 2 Years.** The use of the nonverbal MA as the referential metric with mentally retarded children seems to have been researched mainly with moderately or severely retarded populations. Thus, at present, the use of the nonverbal MA as the referential metric of choice with retarded children who are cognitively functioning at a level greater than 24 months must reflect a sense of prudence. One way this prudence can be demonstrated is to base the timing decision process of when to accept a mentally retarded child into a language intervention context on two referencing procedures: intralinguistic referencing and nonverbal MA metric referencing. If a retarded child does not evidence a language disorder via intralinguistic referencing and does not evidence a language delay via nonverbal MA metric referencing, then that child would not be considered a candidate for a language intervention program. If, however, the retarded child evidences a language disorder (intralinguistic referencing) with or without an accompanying language delay (nonverbal MA metric referencing), then the most prudent timing decision would be to accept that retarded child into a language intervention context on a trial basis.

Estimates of nonverbal MA can be obtained using the Arthur Adaptation of the Leiter International Performance Scale (Arthur, 1952), the Columbia Mental Maturity Scale (Burgemeister and colleagues, 1953), the Coloured Progressive Matrices (Raven, 1960), the Hiskey-Nebraska Test of Learning Aptitude (Hiskey, 1966), and the performance scales from the Weschler

Intelligence Scale for Children (Weschler, 1949) or the Weschler Preschool and Primary Scale of Intelligence (Weschler, 1963).

## PHONOLOGY AND THE TIMING DECISION PROCESS

The inclusion of phonology in the prevailing operational definition of language learning has resulted in a specific timing decision process issue. Because the current definition of language learning stresses the synergistic relationship among the patterns of linguistic organization, it seems paradoxic to reference a child's level of phonologic development to a level of normal phonologic development indexed to CA. Instead, it appears reasonable to reference the child's level of phonologic development to those developmental levels the child exhibits in the other patterns of linguistic organization, specifically, morphology, syntax, and semantics. The work of Shriner and associates (1969), McNutt and Keenan (1970), and Winitz (1975) gives tentative and limited support to this method of referencing. However, research addressed specifically to this paradox has not been conducted.

## RESEARCH IMPLICATION

There is a need for comparable research to determine the most effective referential procedure as it relates to the timing decision process. At present most research methodologies employ either CA or the linguistic referent MLU as the referential standard. It seems justifiable at this point in the search for knowledge that nonverbal MA be used, in addition to one or both of the other referential standards (CA, MLU), when the research design demands referencing to a standard.

Also, it appears reasonable to use cross-domain research designs, as proposed by Johnston (1982). The use of cross-linguistic-domain paradigms should assist in determining the validity of the nonverbal MA as the metric of choice for each pattern of linguistic organization as it synergistically relates to another.

## TIMING DECISION PROCESS: WHEN TO DISCHARGE A CHILD FROM A LANGUAGE INTERVENTION CONTEXT

The timing decision process of when to discharge a child from a language intervention context has received even less attention than has the timing decision process of when to accept a child into a language intervention context. Clinically, the use of an objective, systematic timing decision process designed to discharge a child from a language intervention context appears limited.

It appears limited to those children whose acceptance was based on referencing to CA. That is, children who were accepted into a language intervention context because their performance on standardized tests, assessment protocols, and sequences of normal language development indicated that they were functioning below their CA with respect to one or more patterns of linguistic organization are frequently discharged from the language intervention context when their performance on the same or similar measures indicates they are functioning at or near CA level with respect to those same patterns of linguistic organization.

There are several difficulties with such a timing decision process. First, since there are few formal measures of semantic and pragmatic performance available, it is probable that the use of the referential metric CA for discharge purposes results in the dismissal of children whose phonologic, morphologic, and syntactic performance is at or near CA level but whose semantic and/or pragmatic performance may not be. Second, the use of the referential metric CA is not applicable to those children who were accepted into a language intervention context because of language problems secondary to mental retardation. Consequently, the discharge of mentally retarded children from a lan-

guage intervention context appears to be a dichotomized process. Either the child is discharged when the learning curve data obtained from one or more very structured language tasks suggest further learning will not take place, or when it is subjectively determined that the child is no longer benefiting from predetermined language stimulation experiences. Third, a timing decision process based on CA tends to be retrospective. It is a process that takes place after the fact, that is, after language intervention has been going on for a period of time. This tends to perpetuate a rather static and narrow perspective of language intervention and, in some instances, tends to perpetuate the use of interventional procedures designed to "teach to the tests." Fourth, the use of the referential metric CA in the timing decision process of when to discharge a child from a language intervention context can, in some instances, result in the release of a child for exogenous reasons. Some nonretarded children, for example, those who have an intractable seizure disorder, will not acquire language skills commensurate with their CA regardless of the amount of time spent in a language intervention context. If CA is used as the referential metric in the discharge process, intervention for these children is often protracted. When this occurs, the child may be discharged because of exogenous factors: the parents' decision that intervention is no longer effecting changes, the child's decision that further participation is no longer helpful, the cessation of funding by third party sources, and so on. Discharge due to exogenous factors reflects poorly on the design of the interventional program.

The difficulties encountered when the discharge timing decision process is based on retrospective CA referencing may be reduced if the timing decision process is based instead on prospective intralinguistic only referencing. Miller and Yoder (1974), when presenting an interventional strategy for retarded children, specified several criteria to guide program development. One criterion was as follows: "A program must be based on a realistic set of communication exit behaviors. Here we base the terminal behavior on linguistic needs which a given child may have, dependent upon the living and educational environment as well as developmental abilities." The critical intents in this criterion are that the exit behaviors are not referenced to CA; the exit behaviors must be realistically related to the child's activities of daily living; they must be prospective, that is, specified early in the design of the interventional program; and they must be attainable considering the child's cognitive, physical, social, and emotional status.

## THE TIMING DECISION PROCESS: FOUR STAGES

The timing decision process of when to discharge a child from a language intervention context appears to be more effective and efficient if it begins as soon as the child is accepted into a language intervention context, continues while the child progresses through the interventional program, and ends when the child leaves the language intervention context for the last time. Such a prospective timing decision process has four stages: (1) initial determination of general exit behaviors; (2) periodic review to determine specific exit behaviors; (3) evaluation of specific exit behaviors as they exist outside the language intervention context; and, (4) exit counseling.

**Stage One—Initial Determination of General Discharge Behaviors.** The initial determination of general discharge behaviors depends upon the prognostic statement made as a result of the initial assessment procedure(s). In formulating the prognostic statement, which is an essential part of the assessment protocol (Nation and Aram, 1977), a number of predictions need to be made. Three pertinent predictions follow as exemplars.

1. PREDICTING THE MODES OF LANGUAGE COMPREHENSION AND PRODUCTION. For most children, the primary modes of language comprehension will be auditory and visual. However, some children (for example, those with severe hearing impairments and those with auditory-verbal agnosia) may need to rely primarily on the visual mode. Others, such as deaf-blind children, will need to rely solely on the haptic and olfactory modes. For most children, the primary mode of language production will be verbal. However, some children (such as, those with severe hearing impairments or those with speech apraxia) may need to rely primarily on one or more nonverbal modes. Consequently, some children may be required to learn an augmentative communication method involving speech reading systems, manual systems, and/or communicative prosthetic systems. Furthermore, the systems the child needs to learn may be additive. For example, a young child with speech apraxia may first produce language via a manual sign system but, as intervention proceeds, may add or substitute a communicative prosthesis.

The predictive responsibility is to attempt to determine what mode(s) of comprehension and/or production the child will probably be able to use, the prerequisite behaviors the child needs in order to comprehend and/or produce language via these modes, and any augmentative systems required. If the prediction involves the use of augmentative systems, the decision-making strategies presented by Shane (1979, 1981) and Shane and Bashir (1980) should be consulted.

2. PREDICTING LEVELS OF PATTERNS OF LINGUISTIC ORGANIZATION. While most children who present with a language delay or language disorder will need to acquire relatively similar performance levels across the patterns of linquistic organization, this is not so for every child. For example, a child who is assessed as having a speech apraxia and for whom a manual system or communicative prosthesis has been selected will not be able to attain and may not need relatively equal levels of expressive performance across the patterns of linguistic organization. Such a child will have a low level of expressive phonologic organization and may not need to have a level of expressive syntactic organization comparable to the levels of expressive semantic and pragmatic organization. It may be inefficient to require a level of syntactic organization comparable to the levels of se-

mantic and pragmatic organization if, in everyday situations, the child produces telegraphic, yet communicative, output via the manual sign system or communicative prosthesis.

The predictive responsibility is to attempt to determine if the child needs relatively similar levels of performance across the patterns of linguistic organization.

3. PREDICTING THE EFFECTS OF THE CHILD'S ECOLOGIC STATUS.   Not every child who presents with a language disorder or language delay should, in the process of language remediation, be expected to acquire standard American English (for example, Feter, 1977; Labov, 1970). Children from families who are bilingual, from families where black English is the prevalent dialect, or from families who are at the lower end of the socioeconomic scale may not even need to learn to code-switch. Some parents want their children to communicate in standard American English for educational and economic reasons. Other parents do not. In some schools in certain sections of major cities and in certain regions of the country, instruction is not conducted in standard American English.

The predictive responsibility is to determine what the child's present communicative dialect is expected to be, what the parents' and child's foreseeable expectations are relative to linguistic usage, and what role code-switching may play in the child's future academic and social environments. Facilitation of language development does not necessarily mean facilitation to standard American English.

The purpose of the preceding discussion is to emphasize that a useful prognostic statement must be based on a set of predictions. Of course, in addition to the three predictions discussed, other predictions must be made and should consider factors such as the child's medical status, physical abilities, emotional set, personality type, the parents' attitudes, the language contexts available, and so on. If the formulation of predictions leading to a prognostic statement is conducted in a systematic fashion, the prognostic statement should include specification of general exit behaviors.

**Stage Two—Periodic Review to Determine Specific Exit Behaviors.** Usually the assessment procedure(s) does/do not answer all the questions posed regarding the child's language problem. Often the assessment results serve to suggest areas for further investigation as part of the interventional process. Consequently, the prognostic statement—including the general exit behaviors—should be considered tentative. In addition, language intervention is generally a long-term process. Moreover, it is an active process wherein the child's behaviors and the clinician's judgements change over time. It therefore becomes necessary to periodically review the set of general exit behaviors so they may be refined or modified. This refinement of the initial set of general exit behaviors increases the probability that the final set of specific exit behaviors will be attainable, communicatively realistic, and pertinent to the child's activities of daily living.

**Stage Three—Evaluation of Specific Discharge Behaviors Outside the Language Intervention Context.**   When the child, in the language intervention context, attains a specific discharge behavior within a pattern of linguistic organization or across the patterns of linguistic organization, it is then necessary to evaluate whether the child is able to demonstrate this discharge behavior outside the language intervention context. The attainment of a specific discharge behavior in a language intervention context may be quantitatively or qualitatively determined, depending on the particular orientation of the language intervention program. Also, even if the language intervention context was a group setting, was based on a transactional approach (McLean and Snyder-McLean, 1978), or followed a natural milieu orientation (for example, MacDonald, 1976; Hart and Rogers-Warren, 1978; Muma, 1978), evaluation of the child's use of the discharge behaviors in other settings pertinent to the child's activities of daily living is necessary. Also, since the clinician is a critical element (discriminative stimulus) within the language intervention context, the clinician should not be present in the evaluative settings.

Evaluation of a specific discharge behavior can be accomplished by having significant others (parent, teacher, supervisor, and so on) observe and report on the child's use of the behavior. The significant others will require written instructions and precise reporting forms on which to code their observations. The form must be simple yet informative. An exact behavioral definition of the discharge behavior, along with examples, has to be provided. The form also must be devised so that a method of coding can be applied when the discharge behavior is used appropriately in an obligatory context, is not used appropriately in an obligatory context, and is not used at all in obligatory context. Observation/recording should take place across different contexts over a specified period of time.

The information obtained regarding the child's use or nonuse of the discharge behavior in contexts other than that of language intervention determines the course of future interventional procedures. If the child evidences appropriate use of the discharge behavior in other contexts, that behavior is considered to be generalized and is no longer an interventional target. If the child does not evidence appropriate use of the discharge behavior in other contexts, specific generalization procedures will need to be instituted.

When all of the specific discharge behaviors determined for a child are appropriately used by that child in other contexts, then the timing decision process of when to discharge the child from a language intervention context should progress to stage four.

**Stage Four—Discharge Counseling.** Not every child who demonstrates all the specific discharge behaviors in contexts other than the language intervention context will be comprehending and producing language normally. However, if a timing decision process for discharging, similar to the one outlined in this section, is followed, each child should be as effective a communicator as he needs to be for his activities of daily living.

If the parent has been an integral part of the language intervention process, discharge counseling will probably be a review of what has transpired. If the parent has not been an integral part of the process, it becomes important to review the course of language intervention, cite the reasons for the child's successes, and explain the child's limitations—if any—that preclude further language intervention. The parent should be informed that if significant changes occur which alter the child's communicative effectiveness, the possibility of resumption of intervention is a reasonable subject for discussion.

The timing decision process of when to discharge a child from a language intervention context must receive more attention than it has to date. There are numerous implications of releasing a child prematurely or prolonging a child's intervention when it is no longer effective, involving ethical, educational, emotional, and monetary considerations.

## SUMMARY

The purpose of this chapter was to focus attention on two timing decision processes. The discussion of each timing decision process was approached from a relatively narrow perspective: the use or nonuse of a referential metric in the timing decision process of when to accept a child into a language intervention context, and the use of a prospective, predictive strategy in the timing decision process of when to discharge a child from a language intervention context. The purpose of this chapter will be realized if the notions presented herein foster discussion and generate hypotheses for future clinical research in the area of timing decisions.

## REFERENCES

Authur G: *The Arthur Adaptation of the Leiter International Performance Scale*. Washington, DC: Psychological Service Center Press, 1952

Bates E: Pragmatics and sociolinguistics in child language. In *Normal and Deficient Child Language*. Baltimore: University Park Press, 1976, pp 411–463

Bates E, Benigni L, Bretherton I, Camaioni L, Volterra V: From gesture to the first word: On cognitive and social prerequisites. In *Interaction, Conversation, and the Development of Language*. New York: John Wiley and Sons, 1977, pp 247–308

Bayley N: *The California First Year Mental Scale*. Berkeley: University of California Press, 1933

Bayley N: *Bayley Scales of Infant Development*. New York: Psychological Corporation, 1969

Bloom L: *Language Development: Form and Function in Emerging Grammars*. Cambridge, Mass: MIT Press, 1970

Bloom L, Lahey M: *Language Development and Language Disorders*. New York: John Wiley and Sons, 1978

Bowerman M: *Early Syntactic Development*. Cambridge, Mass: Cambridge University Press, 1973

Bowerman M: Discussion summary—development of concepts underlying language. In *Language Perspectives: Acquisition, Retardation, and Intervention*. Baltimore: University Park Press, 1974, pp 191–209

Bowerman M: Semantic factors in the acquisition of rules for word use and sentence construction. In *Normal and Deficient Child Language*. Baltimore: University Park Press, 1976, pp 99–179

Bricker W, Bricker D: An early language training strategy. In *Language Perspectives: Acquisition, Retardation, and Intervention*. Baltimore: University Park Press, 1974, pp 431–468

Bricker D, Schiefelbusch R: Major themes—an epilogue. In *Early Language: Acquisition and Intervention*. Baltimore: University Park Press, 1981, pp 576–586

Brown R: *A First Language*. Cambridge, Mass: Harvard University Press, 1973

Burgemeister B, Blum L, Lorge L: *Columbia Mental Maturity Scale*. New York: Harcourt Brace Jovanovich, Inc, 1953

Cattell P: *The Measurement of Intelligence in Infants and Young Children*. New York: The Psychological Corporation, 1947

Chomsky N: *Aspects of the Theory of Syntax*. Cambridge, Mass: MIT Press, 1965

Chomsky N, Halle M: *The Sound Patterns of English*. New York: Harper and Row, 1968

Clark E: What's in a word? On the child's acquisition of semantics in his first language. In *Cognitive Development and the Acquisition of Language*. New York: Academic Press, Inc, 1973, pp 65–110

Compton A: Generative studies of children's phonological disorders. J Speech Hear Dis 35: 315–339, 1970

Corrigan R: Language development as related to stage 6 object permanence development. J Child Lang 5:173–189, 1978

Crocker J: A phonological model of children's articulation competence. J Speech Hear Dis 34: 203–213, 1969

Cromer R: The cognitive hypothesis of language acquisition for child language deficiency. In *Normal and Deficient Child Language*. Baltimore: University Park Press, 1976, pp 283–333

Cromer R: Reconceptualizing language acquisition and cognitive development. In *Early Language: Acquisition and Intervention*. Baltimore: University Park Press, 1981, pp 51–138

Crystal D, Fletcher P, Gorman M: *The Grammatical Analysis of Language Disability*. London: Edward Arnold, 1976

Dore J: A pragmatic description of early language development. J Psycholing Res 3:343–350, 1974

Feter I: *Social Dialects: Differences Versus Disorders*. Rockville, Md: American Speech-Language-Hearing Association, 1977

Fowler W, Swenson A: The influence of early language stimulation on development: Four studies. Genetic Psych Monog 100:73–109, 1979

Freedman P, Carpenter R: Semantic relations used by normal and language-impaired children at stage I. J Speech Hear Res 19:784–795, 1976

Greenwald C, Leonard L: Communicative and sensori-motor development of Down's syndrome children. Am J Ment Defic 84:296–303, 1979

Griffiths R: *The Abilities of Young Children*. London: University of London Press, 1970

Halliday M: *Learning How to Mean: Explorations in the Development of Language*. London: Edward Arnold, 1975

Hart B, Rogers-Warren A: A milieu approach to teaching language. In *Language Intervention Strategies*. Baltimore: University Park Press, 1978, pp 193–236

Heber R, Garber H, Harrington S, Hoffman C: *Rehabilitation of Families at Risk for Mental Retardation: Progress Report*. Madison: Rehabilitation Research·and Training Center in Mental Retardation, University of Wisconsin, 1972

Hiskey M: *Hiskey-Nebraska Test of Learning Aptitude*. Lincoln, Neb: University of Nebraska Press, 1966

Ingram D: *Procedures for Phonological Analysis of Children's Language*. Baltimore: University Park Press, 1981a

Ingram D: The transition from early symbols to syntax. In *Early Language: Acquisition and Intervention*. Baltimore: University Park Press, 1981b, pp 260–286

Johnston J: The language disordered child. In *Speech, Language, and Hearing: Pathologies of Speech and Language*, vol II Philadelphia: WB Saunders Co, 1982, pp 780–801

Johnston J, Schery T: The use of grammatical morphemes by children with communication disorders. In *Normal and Deficient Child Language*. Baltimore: University Park Press, 1976, pp 239–258

Kahn J: Relationship of Piaget's sensorimotor period to language acquisition of profoundly retarded children. Am J Ment Defic 79:640–643, 1975

Labov W: The logic of nonstandard English. In *Twentieth Annual Round Table*. Washington: Georgetown University Press, 1970, pp 1–39

Leonard L: What is deviant language? J Speech Hear Dis 37:427–447, 1972

Leonard L, Bolders J, Miller J: An examination of the semantic relations reflected in the language usage of normal and language disordered children. J. Speech Hear Res 19:371–392, 1976

Lobato D, Barrera R, Feldman R: Sensorimotor functioning and prelinguistic communication of severely and profoundly retarded individuals. Am J Ment Defic 85:489–496, 1981

MacDonald J: Environmental language intervention: Programs for establishing initial communication in handicapped children. In *Language Materials and Curriculum Management for the Handicapped Learner*. Columbus: Charles E. Merrill, 1976, pp 163–194

Marge M: The problem of management and corrective education. In *Principles of Childhood Language Disabilities*. New York: Appleton-Century-Crofts, 1972, pp 297–313

McCawley J: Meaning and the description of languages. In *Readings in the Philosophy of Language*. Englewood Cliffs, NJ: Prentice Hall, Inc, 1971, pp 533–548

McLean J, Snyder-McLean L: *A Transactional Approach to Early Language Training*. Columbus: Charles E. Merrill, 1978

McNeill D: *The Acquisition of Language: The Study of Developmental Psycholinguistics*. New York: Harper and Row, 1970

McNutt J, Keenan R: Comment on "the relationship between articulatory deficits and syntax in speech defective children." J Speech Hear Res 13:666–667, 1970

McReyonlds L, Engmann D: *Distinctive Feature Analysis of Misarticulations*. Baltimore: University Park Press, 1975

Menyuk P: Comparison of grammars of children with functionally deviant and normal speech. J Speech Hear Res 7:109–121, 1964

Menyuk P: Children with language problems: What's the problem? In *Developmental Psycholinguistics: Theory and Applications*. Washington: Georgetown University Press, 1975, pp 129–144

Miller J: Assessing children's language behavior: A developmental process approach. In *Basis of Language Intervention*. Baltimore: University Park Press, 1978, pp 269–318

Miller J: Early psycholinguistic acquisition: Summary chapter. In *Early Language: Acquisition and Intervention*. Baltimore: University Park Press, 1981a, pp 331–337

Miller J: *Assessing Language Production in Children*. Baltimore: University Park Press, 1981b

Miller J, Chapman R, Bedrosian, J: Defining developmentally disabled subjects for research: the relationship between etiology, cognitive development, and communicative performance. New Zealand Sp Ther 33:2, 1978

Miller J, Chapman R, Branston M, Reichle J: Language comprehension in sensorimotor stages V and VI. J Speech Hear Res 23:284–311, 1980

Miller J, Yoder D: An otogenetic language teaching strategy for retarded children. In *Language Perspectives—Acquisition, Retardation, and Intervention*. Baltimore: University Park Press, 1974, pp 505–528

Miller P: *Interactive Communication Diagnosis*. New Orleans: Louisiana State University Medical Center, 1981

Morehead D, Ingram D: The development of base syntax in normal and linguistically deviant children. J Speech Hear Res 16:330–352, 1973

Muma J: *Language Handbook: Concepts, Assessment, Intervention*. Englewood Cliffs, NJ: Prentice-Hall, Inc, 1978

Nation J, Aram D: *Diagnosis of Speech and Language Disorders*. Saint Louis: The CV Mosby Company, 1977

Prutting C: Process /pra/ses/n: the action of moving forward progressively from one point to another on the way to completion. J Speech Hear Dis 44:3–30, 1979

Raven J: *Guide to Using the Coloured Progressive Matrices (Sets A, Ab, B)*. London: HK Lewis, 1960

Shane H: Approaches to assessing people who are nonspeaking. In *Nonspeech Language Intervention, Acquisition and Intervention*. Baltimore: University Park Press, 1979, pp 197–224

Shane H: Decision making in early augmentative communication system use. In *Early Language: Acquisition and Intervention*. Baltimore: University Park Press, 1981, pp 389–426

Shane H, Bashir A: Election criteria for determining candidacy for an augmentative communication system: Preliminary considerations. J Speech Hear Dis 45:408–414, 1980

Shriberg L, Kwiatkowski J: *Natural Process Analysis: A Procedure for Phonological Analysis of Continuous Speech Smaples*. New York: John Wiley and Sons, 1980

Shriner T, Holloway, M, Daniloff R: The relationship between articulatory deficits and syntax in speech defective children. J Speech Hear Dis 12:319–325, 1969

Slobin D: *Psycholinguistics*. Glenview, Ill: Scott, Foresman and Company, 1971

Snyder L: The early presuppositions and performatives of normal and language disabled children. Papers Reports Child Lang Dev 12:221–229, 1976

Swisher L, Aten J: Assessing comprehension of spoken language: A multifaceted task. Topics Lang Dis 1:75–86, 1981

Uzgiris I, Hunt J: *Assessment in Infancy: Ordinal Scales of Psychological Development*. Urbana, Ill: University of Illinois Press, 1975

Weschler D: *Manual for the Weschler Intelligence Scale for Children*. New York: The Psychological Corporation, 1949

Weschler D: *Weschler Preschool and Primary Scale of Intelligence*. New York: The Psychological Corporation, 1963

Winitz H: *From Syllable to Conversation*. Baltimore: University Park Press, 1975

# 12

# LANGUAGE INTERVENTION CONTEXT AND SETTING FOR THE APHASIC ADULT: WHEN?

*ROBERT T. WERTZ*

Attempts to improve the effectiveness and efficiency of language rehabilitation for aphasic adults prompt a search for the most opportune time to intervene with treatment. That search is guided by two assumptions. First, one must assume that the treatment administered is efficacious. Evidence mounts to indicate it is. Second, one assumes that intervention at one point in time will be more beneficial than at another. Support for the second assumption is elusive, and it tends to slip through one's grasp when filtered through when is best for whom, what is best when, where is best when, and why is treatment best when. Although not conclusive, the data to date indicate that early intervention, before two months postonset, is better than later intervention. However, the critical interval has not been specified precisely, and the belief that early is better than late tends to shatter when assailed by questions of who, what, where, and why. This chapter reviews what we know about when to intervene with treatment for aphasic adults; filters what we know about when to intervene through a mesh of the variables that might influence this choice; and suggests a means for specifying the critical interval more precisely.

A color-enhanced transmission electron micrograph of melt-spun neodymium-iron having 7.5 KOe coercivity recently appeared as part of an advertisement. It seems there has been a need in the industrial world for low-cost, high-performance permanent magnets. Discoveries in the General Motors Research Laboratories show promise of meeting this challenge by the application of new preparation techniques that determine *when* to employ the appropriate quench rate for fusing solidified alloys.

There has been a similar need in the treatment of aphasic adults to determine when—the critical interval—intervention with language therapy is most efficacious. Recent discoveries in neurology, neuropsychology, neurolinguistics, and speech pathology have brought us only a few steps closer to meeting this challenge than we were when Broca described the speech of Tan. It seems that what has been good for General Motors has not necessarily been good for aphasic patients.

The title of this chapter implies two assumptions. First, one assumes intervention with language therapy for aphasic adults is indeed efficacious in improving communication ability. Second, intervention with language therapy is more efficacious at one point in time than at another. However, complications arise to challenge the assumptions, especially the question of *when,* if one considers—and one should—the questions addressed in other chapters—the *who,* the *what,* the *where,* and, to complete our borrowing from the fourth estate, the *why.* For example, one must ask not only *when,* but *when* for *whom.* The answer will probably bifurcate into ambiguity. The best *when* for one *whom* may not be the best *when* for another.

In this chapter the quest for an answer to *when* has been organized into a silhouette: robust up front, cinched at the waist, slightly exploded toward the end, and trimmed at the ankle. First, those influences that must be considered if one is to determine when is the best time to treat aphasic adults will be briefly considered. Second, by way of cinching, variables will be discarded and we will focus on specific reports that seem to provide the best data available on when to intervene with treatment. Third, expansion will occur in considering why we intervene and how intervention at one time may differ from that at another time. Finally the silhouette will be trimmed with suggestions for means that may tell us when treatment is most efficacious.

## INFLUENCES ON WHEN TREATMENT IS EFFECTIVE

We know something, though not enough, about those things that must be considered if one seeks an answer to the question of when treatment should be offered. However, one must first be convinced that treatment is, in fact, efficacious. Just because a disorder exists does not mean there is an effective treatment for it. Fortunately, with regard to aphasia, more and more information is accruing to indicate that language therapy is an effective treatment, at least for most patients.

### *DOES THERAPY WORK?*

Evidence mounts for an affirmative answer to the question Darley (1972) posed: "Is language therapy for the aphasic

adult efficacious?" However, the latest evidence, like its predecessors, is not unassailable. The recent reports are plagued by the same problems that weakened the reports of the past. No one has compared the performance of randomly assigned treated patients with that of randomly assigned untreated patients. All "no treatment" groups can be questioned about selection bias, be it geographic; no treatment available; lack of interest; monetary; or because the patients were "overlooked." Thus treatment effects interact with spontaneous recovery in the treated groups, and spontaneous recovery interacts with selection bias in the untreated groups. Further, few clinics see enough patients to control the numerous variables believed to influence a patient's response to treatment. Sample size therefore becomes a problem. Even multicenter collaboration results in difficulty acquiring an adequate sample if the necessary selection criteria are imposed to control variables. Unfortunately, the "clean" studies are almost reduced to reporting, "Half of the patients improved, and the other one did not." Difficulties in conducting aphasia treatment studies are listed tersely, but accurately, in an editorial in *Lancet* (1977).

Another approach to demonstrating aphasia therapy's effectiveness is the single subject design. Such studies are sprinkled throughout the literature, and most indicate that the treatment administered to the patient reported resulted in improved performance. Negative results are rare in published single case reports. Holland (1975) has requested that both positive and negative results be shared. We make enough of our own mistakes; it would help if we could avoid those made by our colleagues.

Darley (1972) discovered less than a dozen treatment studies. In the decade since his review, over 20 additional efforts have found their way into the literature. Most, not all, indicate treatment for the adult aphasic patient is efficacious. The "data to date" are listed in Table 12–1.

Some of the positive results (Basso and colleagues, 1979) are unqualified testimony that treatment works. Others (Holland, 1980), while not initially designed as a treatment study, support the theory that

**Table 12–1**  REPORTS ON THE EFFICACY OF LANGUAGE THERAPY FOR ADULT
APHASIC PATIENTS

| Positive Results | Qualified Positive Results | Negative Results |
|---|---|---|
| Aronson et al (1956) | Marks et al (1957) | Kertesz and McCabe (1977) |
| Aten et al (1982) | Shewan and Kertesz (1981) | Levita (1978) |
| Beyn and Shokhor-Trotskaya (1966) | Vignolo (1964) | Ludlow (1973) |
| Broida (1977) | Wertz et al (1981) | Sands (1977) |
| Butfield and Zangwill (1946) | | Sarno et al (1970) |
| Deal and Deal (1978) | | |
| Eisenson (1949) | | |
| Frazier and Ingham (1920) | | |
| Gloning et al (1976) | | |
| Hagen (1973) | | |
| Holland (1980) | | |
| Meikle et al (1979) | | |
| Pizzamiglio et al (1976) | | |
| Sands et al (1969) | | |
| Sarno and Levita (1981) | | |
| Sarno and Levita (1979) | | |
| Sarno et al (1970) | | |
| Schuell et al (1964) | | |
| Smith (1972) | | |
| Weisenberg and McBride (1935) | | |
| Wepman (1951) | | |

treatment is efficacious. Some of the qualified positive results (Wertz and colleagues, 1981) make assumptions about the duration of spontaneous recovery, and others (Vignolo, 1964) set conditions that must be met—intervention must occur by two months postonset and continue for approximately six months. Some of the negative results (Sands, 1977) have limited their look at treatment's efficacy to a specific period, for example, during the first month postonset. Others (Levita, 1978) are internally inconsistent, for example, patients are reported to enter the study by three months after onset, but the tabled data report a range of two to plus four months postonset. Still others (Kertesz and McCabe, 1977), are retrospective views of data that one wishes had been controlled in a prospective design.

Nevertheless, while *the* treatment study has not been reported, we can change our earlier optimistic speculation to qualified certainty. Treatment appears to help most, but not all, aphasic patients. Benson (1969) the conscientious critic has become Benson (1979) the careful advocate. He concludes that "language therapy has a demonstrated effectiveness in the treatment of aphasia" (p. 189).

## WHEN FOR WHOM

Aphasic adults become that way for different reasons, at different ages, with different severity, and so on. Determining when to intervene with treatment may be more appropriate for one patient with a specific set of biographic, medical, and behavioral characteristics than for another patient with a different set of these characteristics. Any attempt to solve the mystery of when to treat must include evaluation of the clues residing in the variables believed to influence response to treatment.

These variables, reviewed extensively by Darley (1972, 1975), are believed to have either a positive or a negative effect on a patient's response to treatment. Recent evidence solidifies some of the earlier assumptions, but it shatters others. Some of the early "facts" have fallen. They appear today as decrepit leftovers sealed in the sarcophagi of their extinct virtues. Let us examine a few.

Younger aphasic patients have been reported by some researchers to improve more than older aphasic patients (Eisenson, 1949; Wepman, 1951; Vignolo, 1964; Sands and colleagues, 1969; Marshall, Tompkins, Phillips, in press). Not so, say others (Culton, 1969; Sarno and Levita, 1971; Smith, 1972; Keenan and Brassell, 1974; Messerli and colleagues, 1976; Rose and colleagues, 1976; Deal and Deal, 1978; Basso and colleagues, 1979; Porch and colleagues, 1980; Hartman, 1981). Still others qualify their findings. Gloning and colleagues (1976) report older patients improve less than younger patients but only when the older patient displays other negative factors. Kertesz and McCabe (1977) observed that younger patients make more gains early after onset than do older patients. Sands (1977) observed that age had no influence on a patient's response to treatment but that it may be important in a patient's prognosis. Does age have an influence on improvement? The data are debatable. Does age have an influence on when treatment intervention should occur? The answer is elusive.

Does a patient's education have an influence on improvement? The debate continues. Eisenson (1949) says yes, patients with more education have a poorer prognosis. Gloning and colleagues (1976) also say yes, but they answer differently. Poor school results have a negative effect on improvement. Most (Wepman, 1951; Sarno and colleagues, 1970; Smith, 1972) report no consistent influence of education on improvement.

A similar set of conflicting answers exists regarding the influence of intelligence on improvement in aphasic patients. Eisenson (1949) views above average intelligence as a disadvantage if one becomes aphasic. Wepman (1951) and Messerli and colleagues (1976) observe that patients with higher intelligence have a better outcome than patients with lower intelligence.

A final biographic variable that has received some interest is occupational status. Most (Sarno and colleagues 1970; Smith, 1972; Keenan and Brassell, 1974) observe that how a patient earned his living prior to onset has no significant influence on his prognosis for improvement once he becomes aphasic. Others disagree about the influence of employment at the time one becomes aphasic. Sarno and Levita (1971) observed that patients who were working when they became aphasic improved more than those not employed. Marshall and colleagues (in press) found no influence on improvement exerted by employment at the time of onset of aphasia.

Several medical variables—etiology, size of the lesion, location of the lesion, and health postonset—are reported to influence whether and how much aphasia improves. These must be considered because they may have an influence on when treatment might help.

What causes the aphasia may influence whether and when it improves. Patients who sustain closed head trauma are reported to have a better prognosis than those who suffer a CVA or penetrating head trauma (Alajouanine and colleagues, 1957; Eisenson, 1964; Luria, 1963). This seems to be true of acquired aphasia in children as well as acquired aphasia in adults (van Dongen and Loonen, 1976). Kertesz and McCabe (1977) and Kertesz (1979) reported that six of seven traumatic cases displayed significant recovery within the first three months after onset. Their vascular cases showed slower improvement, up to three or more years postonset. Glosser and colleagues (1982) suggest that aphasia resulting from a subcortical hemorrhage has a longer recovery pattern compared with aphasia subsequent to cortical involvement. Eisenson (1964) points out that aphasia following multiple CVAs results in a poorer prognosis than aphasia following a single CVA.

Where the damage occurs and the extent of the damage influence improve-ment. Yarnell and colleagues (1976) sum-marize data indicating that size, location, and number of lesions correlate with the amount of language recovery. A large le-sion, many small lesions combined with one large lesion, and bilateral lesions all forecast a poor prognosis for improvement in language. Eisenson (1964) agrees. He also observes that single lesions that spare the temporo-parietal region forecast the best future for language improvement.

Most (Eisenson, 1949; 1964; Ander-son and colleagues, 1970) agree that pa-tients in better physical condition with no sensory deficits have a more favorable prognosis for improved language than those who are ill and display significant sensory deficits.

Behavioral variables are linked to medical variables. For example, severity and type of aphasia probably relate to the size and location of the lesion. However, because these do not surface until patients are immersed in a psychometric marinade, and because they change over time, they will be considered separately from the medical influences.

Severity of aphasia forecasts the fu-ture. Almost everyone who has investigat-ed agrees that the less severely affected patient has more potential for ultimate re-covery (Basso and colleagues, 1979; But-field and Zangwill, 1946; Gloning and col-leagues, 1976; Hartman, 1981; Keenan and Brassell, 1974; Kertesz and McCabe; 1977; Messerli and colleagues, 1976; Sands and colleagues, 1969; Sarno and Levita, 1971, 1979; Schuell and colleagues, 1964; Wep-man, 1951). Kertesz (1979) cautions that one must separate amount of improvement from final outcome. For example, severely affected patients may improve more than milder patients, but the more severely af-fected patient does not attain the eventual language skills that the patient with a milder affliction does.

Type of aphasia and what it predicts about improvement are controversial. Ker-tesz and McCabe (1977) reported anomic and conduction types have the best prog-nosis for recovery. However, Broca's and Wernicke's types also make significant

gains. Kertesz and McCabe's global pa-tients, while experiencing a lot of change, never approximate very useful language skills. Lomas and Kertesz (1978) report similar observations. Conversely, Prins and colleagues (1978) found no difference in recovery among types. Similarly, Basso and colleagues (1979) found no differences between fluent and nonfluent types in their treatment study. Thus the influence of type of aphasia remains debatable. Part of the controversy is probably fueled by the different typing systems employed and by when the patient is typed. For example, a fluent versus nonfluent dichotomy col-lapses the more numerous systems em-ployed by Goodglass and Kaplan (1972) and Kertesz (1979). Further, Kertesz and Mc-Cabe (1977) observed a good deal of migra-tion among types—patients who were one type close to onset may evolve into another type in subsequent months. Therefore, the Broca's aphasic patient who has evolved from global aphasia may not have the po-tential for improvement that a patient who begins as a Broca's aphasic patient has.

A final variable remains: time post-onset. Because it is the main question ad-dressed in this chapter, a more elaborate discussion comes later. Briefly, the closer a patient is to onset, the better his prognosis with or without treatment. Differences of opinion occur when one asks, "How close to onset?" Opinions become more varied if the phrases "spontaneous recovery" and "treatment intervention" are added to the discussion. Again, these questions are cov-ered later. But most researchers (Deal and Deal, 1978; Butfield and Zangwill, 1946; Vignolo, 1964; Basso and colleagues, 1979; Kertesz and McCabe, 1977) report poten-tial for change is greater prior to six months postonset than later. Wepman (1951) ex-tends the period up to one year postonset, and Marks and colleagues (1957) noted im-provement in some patients after the first year. Further, some of the personal ac-counts of aphasia (Moss, 1972; Dahlberg and Jaffee, 1977) describe changes that oc-cur well into the future. Nevertheless, most patients seem to experience most of their return of language skills within the first six months postonset.

Table 12–2  SELECTED VARIABLES SUGGESTED TO HAVE AN INFLUENCE ON IMPROVEMENT IN APHASIA

| Variable | Status |
|---|---|
| Age | ? |
| Education | ? |
| Premorbid intelligence | ? |
| Occupational status | ? |
| Etiologic factor | + |
| Size of lesion | + |
| Localization | + |
| Health | + |
| Severity | + |
| Type of aphasia | ? |
| Time postonset | + |

Note: + = agreement, ? = conflicting reports

Other variables that influence improvement in aphasia probably exist: handedness, sex, social milieu, and so on. Those described above are listed in Table 12–2 along with what the literature implies about their potency. The problem with these, as Vignolo (1964) observed, is that they do not simply exist, they coexist. Marshall and colleagues (in press) point out that no single variable can predict improvement or the lack of it. They combined three—age, time postonset, and number of treatment sessions—in their multiple regression formula to predict a patient's response to treatment. If one is considering using variables as a ticket to treatment, Darley's (1979) advice is sage: "No single negative factor is so uniformly potent as to justify excluding a patient from at least a trial of therapy" (p. 629). But, because the variables influence improvement in aphasia, and, more specifically, because they may influence when to intervene with treatment, they must be considered.

## WHAT WORKS WHEN

"What should this treatment be?" Darley (1979) began his editorial. His answer was, "It should be intensive; provided early after onset; prolonged enough to deliver maximum impact; programmed to fit the individual's profile of capacities

and incapacities; appropriately graduated in difficulty, its effects measured regularly and appropriate adjustments made" (p. 629). Has it? Not always. If not, is outcome affected? Probably. If it is not what it should be, or even if it is what it should be, does this influence when is the best time to intervene with it? We do not know.

Improvement in aphasia may be influenced by what is done—the kind of treatment; how improvement is measured; the tests used; what is evolving spontaneously—the pattern of recovery; and when intervention occurs. For example, Ludlow (1973) observed that treatment had no influence on the recovery of syntax during the first three months after onset. Aten and colleagues (1982) observed that group treatment improved Communicative Abilities in Daily Living (CADL) scores in chronic aphasic patients—mean time postonset was 97.9 months—but there was no significant change in *Porch Index of Communicative Ability* (PICA) scores.

One *what* may be more appropriate at one point in time than at another. Attempts to determine the critical interval for intervention may be masked by the wrong what. There are reports in the literature on how language deficits improve. Should one treat a behavior that is evolving spontaneously? Will improvement be accelerated or impeded? Is one what more appropriate for a given whom? Reason would suggest an affirmative answer. But there are a lot of whats. How does one select? Benson (1979) suggests the next step beyond determining that treatment works is determining what works for whom.

Should a specific type of treatment be selected at a specific point in time? Should treatment ride on those behaviors that are improving or should it ignore them to tangle with the hard-core residuals that improve slowly or not at all unless treated?

Basso and colleagues (1979) observed that improvement in four language modalities—comprehension, reading, speaking, writing—followed a consistent trend not only across aphasic types but also across treated and untreated patients. While comprehension improved more than expression in both treated and untreated patients, the treated patients improved more. Treatment, they conclude, accelerates the natural course of recovery. Hagen (1973) found no significant difference between his treated and untreated groups on tasks requiring auditory comprehension, auditory retention, visual comprehension, and visual motor skills. Significant differences between groups occurred on tasks of reading comprehension, language formulation, speech production, spelling, and arithmetic. Should Basso and colleagues (1979) have ignored treating those skills that improved spontaneously in Hagen's (1973) patients? Should Hagen have treated everything Basso and colleagues did, thereby accelerating the natural course of recovery? We do not know.

Most researchers (Vignolo, 1964; Kenin and Swisher, 1972; Lebrun, 1976; Prins and colleagues, 1978) agree that comprehension improves more than expression. Sarno and Levita (1981) report that their global aphasic patients made the most improvement on comprehension tasks and the least on tasks requiring propositional speech. Lomas and Kertesz (1978) qualify their results. Patients with good comprehension made equal improvement on all language tasks. Patients with severe auditory comprehension deficits made more improvement on auditory comprehension and imitation tasks than on other language tasks. Kenin and Swisher (1972) also noted significant improvement on imitative tasks. So, should we have patients who cannot understand and who cannot repeat do a lot of listening and repetition? Probably, we do. And, conversely, should we have those who understand and repeat pretty well do something else? Again, we probably do. Most clinicians follow the dictate of Schuell and colleagues (1964) to intervene where the patient has some success. Whether this is what we should do or whether we do it at the right time, we do not know. Rosenbek (1979) suggested this earlier in his essay on non—wash-and-wear podiatry.

Certainly, we do not lack for something to do. Many do more than just think about, talk about, and study aphasia. Some do something about aphasia, and the result

has been an explosion in treatment techniques. There are a variety of things to do in a variety of situations offered by a variety of people. A recent book (Chapey, 1981) contains at least 13 different specific types of treatment, and these barely scratch the literature's surface. Therapy has come out of the individual clinic session into group settings (Aten and colleagues, 1982; Wertz and colleagues, 1981) and into the patient's home (Greenberg, 1973). Treatment is being administered efficaciously by nonprofessionals (Meikle and colleagues, 1979; Shewan and Kertesz, 1981).

There are reports on what works for what. For example, Beyn and Shokhor-Trotskaya (1966) report a method for preventing agrammatism in patients treated early after onset. We know that some whats accomplish specific purposes, and other whats do not. For example, Wiegel-Crump (1976) report programmed treatment improved agrammatism in her patients but group conversation did not. But we do not know enough about what we do most often. Rosenbek (1979) reviewed four of our cherished clinical beliefs and concluded that the rapid rush of change sweeps us downstream before we have mapped where we have been. He suggests that some of the treatment harbors for weathering the patient's linguistic storm may be safe, and some may be rocky. To keep from going aground, he suggests the waters be tested with more than a tentative toe.

What does all this have to do with when to intervene? Maybe nothing, but probably a lot. Sanity guides some decisions. Few place acute patients in maintenance groups. These are usually reserved for those we believe have profited maximally from what we have to offer. But it is a rare report, supported by data, that recommends, as Helm (1978) did, that a specific type of treatment works best at a specific point after onset—melodic intonation therapy is more appropriate for patients before six months after onset. Equally rare is a report like that of Helm and Benson (1978), which recommended that one type of treatment is more appropriate before other types of treatment—visual action therapy for global aphasic patients should precede other types of treatment. These clinical gems are prized, in part, because of their rarity. One would like to see them devalued by flooding the market.

## WHEN FOR WHERE

In Chapter 14 Helm-Estabrooks elaborates on where aphasic patients are, and probably should be treated. She lists the acute care facility, the chronic care facility, the rehabilitation center, and the patient's home. She answers the question of where with "where the patient is." The purpose of this chapter is not to add to her elaborate review, but we would do well to pause to consider how the where might influence when treatment should be offered. The pause will be filled with geographic considerations—hospital or home—and context considerations—individual or group session.

Clinic rooms can be disorienting. Sitting across the table, the clinician's right hand is the patient's left. What is right-side-up for the clinician is upside-down for the patient. One could get the notion that it is all done with mirrors. A quick reading of the literature indicates that there are other places to conduct treatment than in the therapy room. Buck (1968) observes that the patient is stimulated more and has less need for language in a good home environment than in any clinical facility. Holland (1982) testifies to the richness of patients' communication in natural settings which does not occur—perhaps is not permitted—in more traditional environs. Gessner (1966) suggests home is best. So, should aphasia therapists become itinerant? Not necessarily. However, they should, as Holland (1969) suggests, arrange opportunities for language performance outside as well as inside the aphasia clinic.

Does where a patient resides influence his improvement? Sarno and colleagues (1970) found no difference in language performance between inpatients and outpatients. Where a patient resides may influence whether he is treated or not. In the VA Cooperative Study (Wertz and colleagues, 1981), the most frequent reason for dropping out of treatment was geographic. Patients either tired of the long trip to obtain therapy, or they tired of remaining inpatients in order to receive treatment.

Should treatment be offered in acute care settings? Sands (1977) found no difference between treated and untreated groups seen prior to one month postonset. But this was "traditional" treatment. Perhaps there is a more appropriate treatment for acute patients that would make a difference. And perhaps that difference is not measured by our traditional tests.

Some patients do not have a choice about where to receive treatment. Where they are is where they are going to be. Holland (1978) reported that institutionalized aphasic patients display lower *CADL* scores than noninstitutionalized patients. Should we spring those patients from confinement? We probably cannot. Or should we rush into the institutions to treat because the inhabitants need it more, and should we do it early before "institutional behavior," whatever that may be, takes hold? It is an idea worth considering.

Home or hospital? The choice is not always ours, or the patient's. Aphasic patients at home may be like Willa Cather's Archbishop, who "sat in the middle of his own consciousness, none of his former states of mind . . . lost or outgrown. They were all within reach of his hand, and all comprehensible." We all do better when surrounded by our own stuff. Treatment's task is to recognize this and assist the aphasic patient to communicate about that stuff when it is out of reach. Most of that assistance will occur, whether we or the patient like it or not, in our clinics.

In our clinics, is one context, individual or group, better than the other? The answer is probably that each has advantages and disadvantages. Unfortunately, the decision is often made by the number of patients divided by the number of staff, or by time after onset. Large caseloads generate a lot of group therapy, and even when staff meet the demand, group members have usually migrated there from individual treatment. Sometimes group treatment is a means of deferring a decision to terminate treatment. It should be none of the above.

We know something, though not enough, about the efficacy of individual treatment. Those who toiled in the VA Cooperative Study (Wertz and colleagues, 1981) observed that individual treatment resulted in more gains on the measures administered than did group treatment. Significant differences between individual and group therapy were few, and the treatments were radically different—individual therapy consisted of stimulus-response language manipulation and group treatment consisted of discussion with no direct manipulation of language. Other researchers (Chenven, 1953; Basso and colleagues, 1979; Wepman, 1951) offered both individual and group treatment, but only Chenven compared results. His aphasic patients who received a combination of individual and group treatment made more gains than patients receiving only individual treatment.

Group treatment is not without its problems. The content of the treatment and the severity of the patients in the group need attention. Too often, group treatment is fractionated into mini-individual sessions with each group member, while the rest of the attendants sit and observe. This could be done as effectively in our waiting rooms. Further, the very severely affected patient in a group session receives little more than confirmation of the severity of his condition.

Group treatment may have its advantages. These have been pointed out by the best sources available, the patient and his family. An analysis of treatment dropouts in the VA Cooperative Study (Wertz and colleagues, 1981) failed to reach statistical significance, but it was headed there. It seems that more severely affected patients tended to drop out of group therapy and more mildly affected patients tended to drop out of individual therapy. Again, this comparison was not significant, but our patients may have been attempting to tell us something. A similar suggestion comes from Knox (1971), who observed his wife migrate through different treatments in different settings. He relates, "In the

cloistered and causal atmosphere of the therapist's workroom the patient may rise to heights that are very encouraging to the therapist and quite satisfying to the patient. But it remains a question whether the patient will make an equally good showing . . . under the social pressures of the group" (p. 71). When a patient is ready, he should be exposed to what only a group can provide. Knox lists several benefits of group therapy: It minimizes the feeling of isolation, provides the motivation of competition, satisfies the gregarious urge, satisfies the need for praise, satisfies the need for understanding, and diminishes fear.

Where patients are seen has an influence on when one might intervene with treatment. Some of the wheres we can control; some we cannot. We cannot intervene until a patient surfaces, and where he has been or where he is might influence intervention. A good home environment is probably the best place for an aphasic patient to abide, but it is unlikely that the bulk of his treatment will be administered there, or for that matter, should be administered there. We do have some control over whether to place a patient in individual or group treatment or a combination of the two. The decision should be based on what is likely to benefit the patient and not on the size of our caseload or the patient's time postonset. The best time to intervene with group treatment is when the patient can tolerate and profit from it.

## WHEN TO INTERVENE

Lest we forget, the primary purpose of this chapter is to examine when treatment is most efficacious for adult aphasic patients. Some of the variables that may influence when to treat have been sifted. We will pass over the literature that indicates morning sessions are better than afternoon (Marshall and colleagues, 1980; Tompkins and colleagues, 1980); before exercise is better than after exercise (Marshall and King, 1973), and after relaxation is better than after no relaxation (Marshall and Watts, 1976). Further, those exceptional patients, like the one reported by Warren and Datta (1981) who regained speech four and one-half years postonset, will not be considered. Instead, the focus will be on what the literature tells us about when treatment intervention is most efficacious. Two stops along the way are necessary. First, we must pause to consider this thing called "spontaneous recovery," and second, we must take a respite to view the amount and intensity of treatment that is offered when one intervenes.

## SPONTANEOUS RECOVERY

We talk a lot about spontaneous recovery but are not very precise in defining what it is or how long it lasts (Darley, 1972). Nevertheless, we assume it contaminates studies on efficacy of treatment. Is improvement the result of spontaneous recovery, the treatment administered, or both? We do not know, but we want to.

The spontaneous recovery we are interested in is improvement in language believed to result from physiologic restitution during some period postonset. The aphasic patient improves regardless—perhaps in spite of—of what is done or not done for him. Is this true? Most researchers (Culton, 1969; Vignolo, 1964; Hagen, 1973; Sands, 1977; Kertesz and McCabe, 1977; Lomas and Kertesz, 1978; Basso and colleagues, 1979; Hartman, 1981) say yes. Hartman observed significant improvement in *PICA* scores in 41 of 44 untreated patients tested prior to 14 days postonset and again between 27 and 30 days postonset. In fact, 14 of her patients made significant change between the first and second week postonset. Sands (1977) noted significant improvement in both her treated and untreated groups tested first by one month postonset and later by two months postonset. Spontaneous recovery, whatever it is, appears to occur.

The duration of spontaneous recovery is debatable. Culton (1969) limited its duration to two months postonset. While change continued to occur during the next month, change on his measures was not significant. Vignolo (1964) set the limit at two months postonset, and Eisenson (1964) and Sarno and colleagues (1970) stretch the duration to three months. More liberal reports come from Butfield and Zangwill (1946), Godfrey and Douglas (1959), Luria (1963), and Marks and colleagues (1957). All place the boundary of spontaneous recovery at six months postonset.

Thus spontaneous recovery occurs, but its limits are believed to range from two to six months postonset. There is a need to stress the qualifier "significant." Spontaneous recovery may continue beyond six months, but its continuance does not appear to be significant, at least on the measures we have used to determine it. Its occurrence and duration influence the decision of when to intervene with treatment. Should treatment intervention wait until spontaneous recovery runs its course? Or should one intervene during the period of spontaneous recovery and ride on any boost it may give? The evidence to support an answer leans toward the latter, but it does not take a giant step in that direction.

## AMOUNT AND INTENSITY OF TREATMENT

How much of this treatment shoud we give? Do the amount and intensity of treatment influence when it is offered? More specifically, does a lot of treatment at the wrong point in time override, or at least counteract, intervening at the wrong point in time? Conversely, does less treatment at the right point in time result in more improvement than more treatment at the wrong point in time? Again, we do not know. But we have an inkling. Probably the best solution is the right amount of treatment at the right point in time. But that is not how things have been or are today.

The literature on amount and intensity of treatment for adult aphasic patients makes one irrefutable point. The amount and intensity of treatment vary. Treatment varies in amount among studies—Wepman's (1951) patients received 6 hours a day, 5 days a week for up to 18 months, while some of Vignolo's (1964) patients received only 1 session a week. It varies within studies—some of Butfield's and Zangwill's (1946) patients received a total of 5 sessions and others received up to 290 sessions. In other reports, treatment may be intense but vary in duration. Sands and colleagues (1969) tell us that treatment was given daily but its duration ranged among patients from two weeks to two years and eight months.

Three recent treatment studies have been fairly consistent in the amount of treatment offered. Basso and colleagues (1979) administered at least three individual sessions each week to patients in their treated group, but most received four sessions a week. Those who did not receive at least six months of treatment were excluded from the study. The VA Cooperative Study (Wertz and colleagues, 1981) required 8 hours of treatment each week for both individually and group-treated patients. This continued for 44 weeks or until a patient dropped out of the study. Sarno and Levita (1979) experienced a time-postonset influence on the amount and intensity of treatment. During the first three months postonset, most of their group were inpatients and received three to five sessions a week. By six months postonset, all patients had been discharged from the hospital, and the number of treatment sessions began to vary. However, the global aphasic patients continued to receive daily treatment. At the end of the first year postonset, all patients were receiving one to three sessions a week.

Some believe the amount and duration of treatment influence improvement. Rose and colleagues (1976) reported that the number of treatment sessions correlated positively with the amount of improvement their patients made. Leischner (1976) observed that patients treated for less than two weeks had a poorer outcome than those treated for more than two weeks. Vignolo (1964) reported that patients who were treated for more than six months made significantly more gains than patients treated for less than six months. Significant trend analyses, looking at change between 4 and 48 weeks postonset,

led Wertz and colleagues (1981) to conclude that patients receiving longer treatment improved more than patients receiving treatment for a shorter time.

Thus the amount and intensity of treatment have varied in the reported studies, but in those that have been able to examine the influence, more seems to be better. Not one reported study has been able to disentangle the potential interaction between amount of treatment and when it was offered.

## WHEN? THE DATA TO DATE

Like the recent occurrence in the heavens, syzygy does not exist in the literature on when to intervene with therapy for the adult aphasic patient. Most reports line up, but not all. The balance seems to tip toward advocating early intervention. The evidence for and against ranges from clinical experience to statistical significance. Most of the reports did not control for the influence of when, but because, in the patients studied, there was a range in the number of months postonset, some investigators could take a retrospective look at the influence exerted by when treatment occurred. A few reports do permit a more controlled look at when treatment is most effective. Others indicate that treatment works (Smith, 1972; Broida, 1977) or does not work (Sarno and colleagues (1970) with patients many months postonset.

We can begin with a demonstration that most aphasic patients do improve over time, referring to data from the VA Cooperative Study (Wertz and colleagues, 1981). Because all patients began treatment at four weeks postonset, we can say nothing about the influence of when treatment occurs on improvement. Nevertheless, these data will anchor the fact that treatment works.

Figure 12–1 shows change in the PICA Overall percentile score for individually treated patients, Group A, and group-treated patients, Group B. The cohorts fractionate the sample by indicating how long each cohort was treated. For example, the 4–15-week cohort received 11

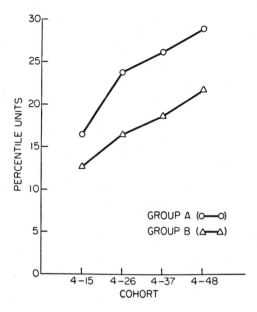

Figure 12–1. Mean *PICA* Overall percentile change scores for group A, individual treatment, and group B, group treatment, in each cohort. Cohorts indicate the number of weeks treatment was administered, for example, the 4–15-week cohort received 11 weeks of treatment, between 4 and 15 weeks postonset. (After Wertz et al, 1981).

weeks of treatment, between 4 weeks and 15 weeks postonset; and the 4–26-week cohort received 22 weeks of treatment, between 4 and 26 weeks postonset; and so on. The fact that individually treated patients made more gains than group-treated patients is not important for our purposes here. More important is the fact that patients in both groups made significant improvement, and improvement was greater in patients treated longer.

Figure 12–2 shows when improvement occurred. Most improvement in all cohorts occurred during the first 11 weeks of treatment. However, in longer cohorts, our patients continued to improve beyond the first 11 weeks. If we have any statement to make about the efficacy of treatment, it is based on the continued significant improvement made by patients in the 37 and 48-week cohorts after 26 weeks postonset, a period when significant spontaneous recovery is believed by conservative estimates to have ceased.

Finally, Figure 12–3 shows what hap-

pened to individuals hidden in our groups. Almost all patients improved, and a sizeable number made marked improvement—defined as a 21 or more percentile change in their *PICA* Overall percentile score. More patients who were treated longer made more improvement than patients who were treated for a shorter period.

These data make two points. First, treated patients improve. If they did not, the question of when to treat would not need asking. Second, treated patients continue to improve over a long period of time, ours at least up until we stopped looking at almost one year postonset. The first point has been documented in the early pages of this chapter. The second has a direct bearing on when to intervene and relates to the earlier discussion on amount and intensity of the treatment offered. When may be important only if viewed in the context of how long. Vignolo (1964) suggests that treatment should begin before six months postonset, but treatment after six months

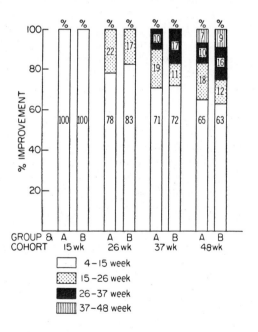

Figure 12–2. Percent of total improvement obtained during each treatment period by group A, individual treatment, and group B, group treatment, on the *PICA* Overall percentile score. (After Wertz et al, 1981.)

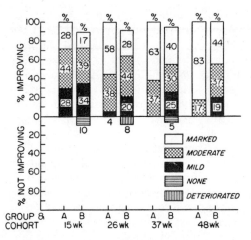

Figure 12–3. Percentage of patients in group A, individual treatment, and group B, group treatment, who improved, did not improve, or deteriorated on the *PICA* Overall percentile score. (After Wertz et al, 1981.)

may be all right if it lasts for at least six months. Hanson and Cicciarelli (1978) observed that it took their patients almost nine months of treatment to achieve maximum performance. Sarno and Levita (1981) document that their treated global aphasic patients who began treatment at three months postonset made the greatest gains between the sixth and twelfth months postonset. So a correct when may be obscured by an incorrect long enough.

Clinical suggestions to intervene early or later are based on a knowledge of patients and a knowledge of the literature. Buck (1968) suggests that biweekly contacts with the patient's family during the first month to six weeks postonset should take precedence over frequent appointments with the patient. Once treatment begins, Buck recommends that it be daily for approximately one month and drop back to weekly during the next month. How long the treatment should last, he concludes, can only be answered by the patient. However, Buck recommends reevaluations every two or three months throughout the first two years after onset. Wepman (1972) counsels that early intervention may be harmful. He believes early treatment may convince the patient that improvement will be rapid, as it is in the early days, but when spontaneous recovery

has run its course, the patient is devastated by the slow progress made with residual language deficits. Wepman reasons that the patient has learned to believe treatment is responsible for the early, rapid gains, and when things slow down, he feels treatment has lost its magic and may reject it. If one follows Wepman's advice, treatment is delayed until spontaneous recovery ends; two, three, or six months postonset, depending on which of the spontaneous recovery reports one accepts.

Conversely, Eisenson's (1949) clinical experience prompts him to advocate early intervention. The sooner treatment begins, he advises, the better a patient's prognosis for improved language. Similarly, Holland (1969) and Darley (1972) advocate early intervention, during the period of spontaneous recovery, because they believe spontaneous recovery can facilitate language therapy. We can conclude that advice based on clinical experience and knowledge of the literature lacks unanimity.

There is some literature that may appear to support clinical patience. Sands (1977) found no significant differences between her treated and untreated groups at one month postonset. Does this suggest one should not treat during the first month after onset? Ludlow (1973) observed no significant differences between treated and untreated patients at the end of three months postonset. Does this suggest one should not treat until four months after onset? Levita (1978) observed no significant differences between treated patients who received eight weeks of therapy beginning at three months postonset and an untreated group when he compared performance at five months postonset. Does this suggest one should not treat until five months after onset?

Each of these studies suggests only one thing. Each did not find differences between treated and untreated patients at the point in time when they looked. Each is important, because each provides a piece to the puzzle of when to intervene with treatment. None tells us that early intervention, before one, three, or five months should be avoided. All suggest we need to keep looking, but in a different way. None of these studies tells us the ultimate effects of early intervention. For example, what would Sands' (1977) results have been if she had studied three groups: all identified within a few days postonset, but one not treated for three months, one treated for three months, and one not treated during the first month but treated for the next two months? Perhaps the influence of treatment prior to one month postonset is not apparent until several months postonset. Blocking on time periods is a way of finding out.

The retrospective data that do not permit some careful control on time are useful, but they only entice, they do not answer. Wepman (1951) provided information about treatment before and after the first year postonset. His patients treated before 12 months had elapsed made more gains than those treated after 1 year. Butfield and Zangwill (1946) honed the period of observation further. Forty percent of their patients who were eventually rated "much improved" began treatment before six months postonset and can be compared with 22 percent of the "much improved" group who began treatment after six months postonset. Sands and colleagues (1969) looked inside four months postonset. Their patients who began treatment between two weeks and two months postonset made approximately 10 percent more gain on the *Functional Communication Profile* than patients who began treatment after four months postonset. Do these data support early intervention? Not necessarily. How much of the improvement in the early groups resulted from spontaneous recovery, and how much resulted from the treatment? More specifically, did the early groups improve more because they were treated early? We do not know.

I have found only three reports designed to look at when treatment is most efficacious. All are retrospective, at least in part, and none employed random assignment of patients to the groups studied. Still, they represent the best information available about when treatment may be most efficacious. Dabul and Hanson (1975) compared patients treated early after onset, between 13 and 34 days, with patients treated later after onset, between 7 and 147 months. The mean duration of treatment was 8 months for the early group and 13 months for the late group. Both groups significantly improved during the treatment trial when pre- and post-treatment *PICA* Overall Scores were compared. The early group showed significantly more improvement than the late group. All patients were tested three times: at entry, after six months of treatment, and at the termination of treatment. Both groups displayed significant improvement when the first test was compared with the third. Changes between test one and two and between test one and three indicated the early group improved more than the late group. Were the group differences the result of early intervention? Perhaps, but maybe not. When the second test was compared with the third, no significant difference was noted between groups. Test one, for the early group, was administered at approximately one month postonset, and test two was administered at approximately seven months postonset. Did the greater improvement in the early group, during their first to seventh month postonset, result from early intervention, or did it result from spontaneous recovery that may have occurred during the period the early patients were studied? We do not know.

Basso and colleagues (1979) conducted an efficacy of treatment study, discussed earlier. They analyzed four variables: time after onset, type of aphasia (fluent versus nonfluent), severity, and rehabilitation (treatment versus no treatment). All but type of aphasia turned out to be significant. Patients examined later after onset made less gains than patients examined earlier. More severely affected patients improved less, on the scale used, than less severely affected patients. Treated patients made more gains than untreated patients. Because they blocked on time postonset, and because they studied both treated and untreated patients, their data can provide some information about when treatment intervention may be most

Table 12–3   INFLUENCE OF TREATMENT AND TIME POSTONSET ON
IMPROVEMENT IN APHASIC PATIENTS

| Measure | Time Postonset at Entry | | | | | |
| --- | --- | --- | --- | --- | --- | --- |
| | <2 MPO | | 2–6 MPO | | >6 MPO | |
| | T | UT | T | UT | T | UT |
| | (%) | | (%) | | (%) | |
| Auditory verbal comprehension | 88 | 50 | 65 | 48 | 50 | 15 |
| Reading | 79 | 50 | 64 | 31 | 27 | 23 |
| Oral expression | 59 | 32 | 39 | 9 | 27 | 4 |
| Writing | 54 | 36 | 36 | 11 | 19 | 0 |
| All measures combined | 70 | 42 | 51 | 25 | 31 | 11 |

Note:
   T = treated, UT = unreated.
   Data indicate the percentage of patients improving in each group during the time period examined.
   This table is based on data from Basso A, et al, 1979.

efficacious. To obtain this information, one must manipulate the Basso (1979) data. Results of this manipulation are shown in Table 12–3.

The reported data separate treated and untreated patients and block on three time periods: evaluated before two months postonset, between two and six months, and after six months. All patients were reevaluated a second time, six months after the first. In addition, the results are reported in the number of patients, in each time period in each group—treated or untreated—that improved and that did not improve. Further, patients were separated by type of aphasia and by severity. In Table 12–3, severity and type of aphasia are combined. Also, because we know only how many patients improved and how many did not, the percentages have been calculated of patients improving in each group— treated and untreated—during each time period—entered the study before two months postonset, entered between two and six months postonset, and entered after six months postonset. Therefore, we can discuss the percentage of patients in each group who improved and the influence of time postonset on improvement, but we cannot determine how much patients improved. Nevertheless, these data permit us to look at the influence of early intervention and to differentiate between spontaneous recovery and treatment effect.

There is a remarkable order in the data of Basso and colleagues (1979). A greater percentage of the patients seen early after onset improve on all measures than patients seen later after onset, whether they were treated or not. However, a greater percentage of the patients in the treated group improve than patients in the untreated group regardless of the time period examined. Does early intervention with treatment have an effect that outruns spontaneous recovery? The data indicate it does. More patients who enter treatment early after onset, before two months have elapsed, improve than patients who enter treatment later, between two and six months postonset or after six months postonset, and more of the early treated patients improve than the early untreated patients. The data seem to argue favorably for early intervention.

Finally, Deal and Deal (1981) contribute additional information to support early intervention. They present data on five groups of patients: Group I, treatment begun during the first month postonset; group II, treatment begun during the second month postonset; group III, treatment begun during the third month postonset; group IV, treatment begun during the fourth to seventh months postonset; and

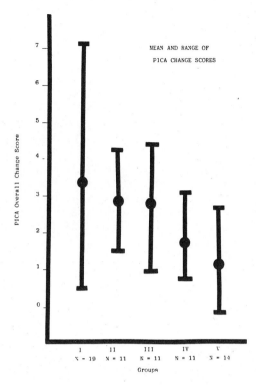

MEAN AND RANGE OF
PICA CHANGE SCORES

PICA Overall Change Score

I
N = 19

II
N = 11

III
N = 11

IV
N = 11

V
N = 14

Groups

Figure 12–4. Mean and range of change scores on the *PICA* Overall raw score for group I, began treatment during the first month postonset; group II, began during the second month; group III, began during the third month; group IV, began between the fourth and seventh months; and group V, received no treatment. (After Deal and Deal, 1981.)

group V, patients were not treated. Groups I–IV received at least two months of treatment, and the number of sessions ranged from 27 to 312 across groups. The mean number of sessions ranged from a low of 90 in group II to a high of 114 in group III. Patients were tested with the *PICA* when they began treatment and again when they ended treatment. Group V patients were tested first during one to two months after onset and later at 12 months postonset. Deal and Deal (1981) asked, "Does time postonset have an influence on treatment?" Their answer is shown in Figure 12–4.

Using an analysis of covariance—intial severity was the covariant—Deal and Deal observed that improvement in group I patients did not differ significantly from that

in group II patients, but group I patients displayed significantly more improvement than those in groups III, IV, and V. Group II patients were not significantly different from those in group III, but they displayed significantly more improvement than those in groups IV and V. Group III patients did not differ significantly from those in group IV, but they made significantly more improvement than those in group V. Group IV patients did not differ significantly from those in group V. Thus treatment had its effect: All but the late treated group improved more than the untreated group. There also appears to be an advantage in early treatment. Group I patients, those treated before one month postonset, improved more than those in groups III and IV, those treated after three months postonset. The advantage in the early intervention group cannot be explained solely by spontaneous recovery, because early treatment outran the spontaneous recovery noted in the untreated group. So the answer to Deal and Deal's question, does time postonset have an influence on treatment, is apparently yes.

## SUMMARY

When is the most efficacious time to intervene with treatment for the aphasic adult? The data to answer this question are sparse, but the best are beginning to pinpoint a time that is better than others. Basso and colleagues (1979) and Deal and Deal (1981) indicate that early intervention is most efficacious. Patients who begin treatment prior to two months postonset have a better chance of improving than those who begin after two months postonset. The gains made by beginning before two months postonset transcend improvement that results from spontaneous recovery. The amount and intensity of the treatment offered probably have an effect on the amount of improvement made. Similarly, the duration of treatment, especially for severely affected patients (Sarno and Levita, 1981), has an influence. While an unassailable study has not been conducted, we can conclude that the data to date indicate the best *when* is before two months postonset, especially if the treatment offered is intense and lasts at least six months, and probably longer for the severely affected patient.

## WHY INTERVENE WITH TREATMENT?

What is this treatment designed to accomplish? It is designed to improve an aphasic patient's communicative ability. Is that all? No, it also should assist a patient in compensating for those deficits that remain, and if compensation is not possible, it should assist a patient in living, as best he can, with a devastating disability. So treatment at one point in time might differ from treatment at another point in time? Probably.

Sarno (1981) recognized that language therapy for aphasic adults has different purposes at different points along the path postonset. She observed that for some, treatment need not extend beyond two or three weeks of language exercises, providing information, and counseling. For others, treatment may continue in some form for the remainder of their days—individual, group, or variations of the two. Most patients, Sarno suggests, fall somewhere in between.

We arrived independently (Sarno, 1981; Wertz, in press) at a similar analogy. She likens the aphasic patient's reaction to his condition to the Kübler-Ross (1969) discussion of death and dying. Sarno suggests that an aphasic patient may pass through three stages. The first, depression and denial, is characterized by withdrawal, lethargy, and unrealistic plans. The patient is stalling for time. Treatment during this stage may reduce depression by distracting the patient and acting as a substitute for the work he can no longer do. In the second stage, anger, the patient acts out verbally (to whatever extent he can) and nonverbally what has been internalized in stage one. "I'm mad as hell, and I can't talk about it anymore." The artificial larynx provides "instant argument" for the laryngec-

tomized patient, and the aphasic patient's few emerging words provide a means of fighting back against imposition. "Goddamit! Get off my waufus!" is speech, and it certainly carries its message. And, it should be encouraged. Folsom (1968) testified about the value of anger in combating depression. The third stage, adaptation, lasts the longest, perhaps for the remainder of the patient's life. During this period, the patient mobilizes. He inventories strengths and deficits, and he utilizes the strengths to compensate for the deficits. Treatment in the third stage focuses on helping the patient take stock and suggesting which goods may move the best and the fastest.

And what does all of this have to do with when to intervene? It indicates that there are different needs at different times. The course of managing aphasia has been likened to the temporal aspects of managing terminal illness (Wertz, in press). I do not imply that aphasic patients are terminal, no more than we all are. Most aphasic patients are aphasic for a long time. I do imply that the management of aphasia might have something in common with the management of terminal illness. That implication is shown in Figure 12–5.

The management of aphasia, like the management of terminal illness, may result in a cure-care conundrum. Terminally ill patients are not curable. If they are, they are misdiagnosed. However, medicine, at least for a time, seeks a cure for the terminal patient. During that period, doctors bring to bear all of their talents to preserve the patient's life. Preservation is the greatest value, and the pain and the expense preservation require are secondary. However, at some point, the value changes from preservation of life to quality of the life that remains. During this period, alleviation of pain is sought, radical and expensive surgical intervention is avoided, and withdrawal of uncomfortable support systems is instituted.

Similarly, in the management of aphasia, our values may change over time. Sarno (1981) observes that most aphasic patients do not "recover." I agree. Many aphasic patients "improve," but they do not

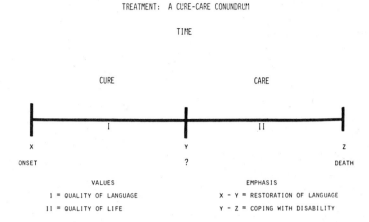

Figure 12–5. Indication of how the values emphasized in aphasia therapy may change over time. (After Wertz, in press.)

"recover." Complete recovery is rare. If it does occur, it is evident hours or a few days after onset. We rarely see these patients, or if we do, our contact with them is fleeting. Aphasia that continues for more than a few weeks is aphasia that is going to continue for the rest of the patient's life. Should "complete recovery" occur beyond several weeks postonset, it is the patient who identifies it. Aphasic patients consider themselves "recovered" only if they return to their premorbid level of language competence. Few do.

The cure-care conundrum presented by persisting aphasia may be avoided by realizing that values during the management of aphasia will probably change. Initially, we, and most patients, seek to regain linguistic skills. This period begins shortly after onset and continues indefinitely, depending on the patient—his response to treatment; severity of condition; and so on; but most importantly, his preference. During this period (I in Figure 12–5) our greatest value is the quality of language. We, and the patient, do our best to restore what we can. We ignore expense and we ignore hardships. We counsel that he remain an inpatient when he would be more comfortable at home, if going home would put him out of treatment's reach. We place him in front of our stimuli when he may be more comfortable doing something else. We beat down anything that may erode our val-

ue, restoration of language. At some point, our value changes. The continued pains do not justify the gains, at least the way we measure them. We switch to emphasizing the quality of the patient's life (II in Figure 12–5). Emphasis is placed on coping with disability. We spring the patient from inpatient status, or we lessen the frequency of the long trips to treatment. We suggest the patient abide where he does best, usually his home, and we suggest he do what he does best, usually not stimulus-response, individual aphasia treatment. We should do this gradually, and we should do it thoroughly. As much effort should go into assisting a patient to fill his days outside of treatment as went into filling his days in treatment. We leave the door to treatment open. A phone call, a re-evaluation visit, a maintenance group, a stroke club should be handy if a patient or those close to him feel a need to reach.

How long do these periods last? When does one value change to another? The answer is not six months postonset or Tuesday. The answer comes from the patient after he sifts, as best he can, the counsel we give him. For some, an attempt to restore language may be eliminated entirely, even if we advise it should not be. For some, life is changed little by aphasia, and what is changed can be accommodated. For others, an attempt to restore language continues indefinitely. Though aspirations change and ultimate outcome shrinks, there may be a need to continue seeking those elusive words. For all, assistance in coping with disability must be offered as an alternative at some point in time.

Thus we lean toward before two months postonset as the best time to intervene with treatment designed to restore language. But there is another when to consider: when to emphasize coping with disability. The critical interval for the latter may not be critical. Certainly, it does not appear until we know how much and what kind of disability will remain to be coped with. Nevertheless, clinicians must be ready to intervene with treatment that assists their patients in living with aphasia's residuals, because that when is when the patient decides, and it could be Tuesday.

## HOW TO DETERMINE WHEN?

Even though there is increasing evidence to indicate that early intervention, before two months, is best, we continue to seek facts that withstand the onslaught of scientific skepticism. One wonders why aphasiologists do this more than anyone else. But we do. Our tools are few. We study aphasia with group designs and with single case designs. Both have their advantages and their shortcomings, which have been listed elsewhere (Wertz and Rosenbek, 1978). I feel that one approach is better than the other to determine when treatment is most effective.

### SINGLE CASE DESIGN

The single case, or single subject, design can tell us a lot, but it cannot tell us when treatment is most effective. We can employ a single case design, even during the period of spontaneous recovery, to determine whether treatment works, but single case designs are confounded by time and will not tell us whether the treatment that worked during the period studied would have worked better or not as well at another time. Of course, one can use single case designs with multiple replications,

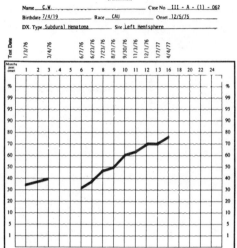

Figure 12–6. *PICA* aphasia recovery curve for C. W. showing change over time during periods of treatment (T) and no treatment (NT). (After Rosenbek et al, 1977.)

but after two of these, one has a group study.

The patient shown in Figure 12–6 is an example of how time confounds a single case design's answer to when treatment is efficacious. C.W. has been reported elsewhere (Rosenbek and colleagues, 1977), but he illustrates the point. A few weeks before Christmas in 1975, this gentleman took a wrong turn on a nocturnal trip to the bathroom, fell down a flight of stairs, and suffered a left hemisphere subdural hematoma that rendered him aphasic. He was evaluated in another clinic at one month postonset, and again at three months postonset. His *PICA* Overall percentile was 35 at the first evaluation and 39 at the second. C.W. returned home and received no treatment during the next three months. We met him six months after onset. *PICA* Overall performance had slipped to the thirty-second percentile. It took two weeks to work out the logistics necessary to provide therapy, because C.W. lived 250 miles from our clinic. He and his family agreed to a series of treatment periods that involved a month of treatment requiring him to be an inpatient, followed by a month of vacation at home. Three intensive months of treatment were interspersed with two months of no treatment. We followed up with two re-evaluations one and four months after treatment.

We obtained another *PICA* at the beginning of treatment. Overall performance had edged up to the thirty-seventh percentile. Following the first month of therapy, his *PICA* Overall had risen to the forty-fifth percentile. After a month of vacation, performance was at the fiftieth percentile. The next month of treatment resulted in a gain that reached the sixtieth percentile. C.W. went home and returned for his final treatment one month later. *PICA* performance was at the sixty-fifth percentile when he began his last month with us and at the seventhieth percentile when he ended it. Re-evaluation one month after treatment showed performance at the seventy-first percentile, and re-evaluation four months after treatment showed performance at the seventy-fifth percentile. Thus three months of intensive treatment alternated with two months of no treatment resulted in a gain of 28 percentile units in C.W.'s *PICA* Overall performance. This change occurred during the sixth to twelfth months after onset and indicates the efficacy of the treatment administered or that spontaneous recovery continued for 12 months in this patient. His lack of change during the first six months postonset prompted us to believe the gain resulted from treatment. Do the data indicate the best time to intervene with C.W. was after six months postonset? They do not.

We only know that C.W. improved during the period we studied him. We do not know whether he would have improved more, less, or not at all if we had intervened earlier or later or, possibly but not probably, not at all. His greatest gains followed the treatment periods, but he also made obvious change during the no treatment periods. Whether the latter resulted from the home treatment programs we gave him or from generalization of treatment effects, we do not know. Whether the time period we intervened was the best *when* for C.W., we do not know either. The single case design does not tell us.

Innovations with the single case design by LaPointe (1980) and Matthews and LaPointe (1981) which employ the quarter intersect procedure for predicting a patient's future performance may improve our ability to determine when treatment is most effective with individual patients. Collection of several baseline data points permits plotting a trend envelope that predicts the range of performance that can be expected in subsequent sessions. The extent that a patient falls within or exceeds his trend envelope at different points in time as he progresses through therapy may bracket the boundaries of the most efficacious when. However, even with this approach, we do not know whether treatment that shows little progress at one point in time was necessary for the patient to progress at another point in time, or whether the earlier treatment could have been eliminated. Nevertheless, the quarter intersect procedure has promise for helping us test different time periods with single cases. What we learn from one case may guide construction of the next single case design in a series of multiple replications.

## GROUP DESIGNS

When several patients are gathered in a search for determining when is the best time to intervene with treatment, the probability of finding an answer increases. Group designs are expensive; they take time to conduct; they require more aphasic patients than most single clinics see; and, to answer the question of when to intervene, they may be challenged on ethical grounds. But they provide the best means for determining when.

The second Veterans Administration Cooperative Study on Aphasia, currently in progress, will shed some light on determining when treatment works best. The design is shown in Figure 12–7. All patients enter the study between 2 and 24 weeks postonset. All meet most of the rigid selection criteria employed in the first VA Cooperative Study. Time postonset has been relaxed to obtain a sufficient sample, and its influence will be examined in analy-

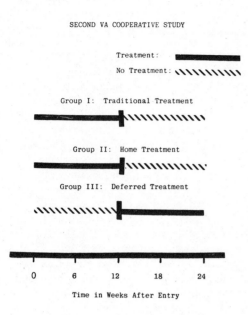

SECOND VA COOPERATIVE STUDY

Treatment:

No Treatment:

Group I:  Traditional Treatment

Group II:  Home Treatment

Group III:  Deferred Treatment

0        6       12       18       24

Time in Weeks After Entry

Figure 12–7. Design of the second Veterans Administration Cooperative Study on Aphasia showing periods of treatment and no treatment for each group.

ses of covariance. Patients, who meet selection criteria are assigned randomly to one of three treatment groups: group I, traditional, individual treatment by a speech pathologist during the first 12 weeks after entry followed by 12 weeks of no treatment; group II, home treatment by a family member or volunteer who administers a treatment program developed by a speech pathologist for the first 12 weeks and no treatment during the next 12 weeks; and group III, deferred treatment for the first 12 weeks after entry followed by traditional, individual treatment by a speech pathologist during the next 12 weeks. All patients receive an evaluation with a battery of measures at entry and at 6, 12, 18, and 24 weeks after entry. Comparison of performance by group III patients at 6 and 12 weeks after entry with performance by patients in groups I and II should provide information about the influence of early intervention. Further, comparison of group III with groups I and II at 18 and 24 weeks after entry should indicate whether the advantage of early intervention, if one exists, can be made up by interving later.

Not bad, but not good enough. Early versus late intervention was only one question posed by the second VA Cooperative Study. It was not *the* question. Results on when to intervene may be washed out by a number of uncontrolled variables. For example, time at entry varies from 2 weeks to 24 weeks. The analysis of covariance will permit some control, but we will not learn what we really want to know about when to intervene. If there are enough patients to block on time periods early after onset—for example, patients entering each group before four weeks postonset—we will do so. But even in this multicenter trial, sample size will be small because we employ rigid selection criteria. Further, the treatment period is intense, 8 to 10 hours a week, but it only lasts 12 weeks. The study does have an advantage previous efforts did not: It is prospective, and patients are assigned randomly to groups.

So, while the second VA Cooperative effort is a step in the right direction, it is not a giant one. What is needed? To answer the question when treatment is most effective, we need an effort that asks that single question. Rigid selection criteria that control variables believed to influence change in aphasia are necessary, as is random assignment to groups. Blocking on time periods postonset—before one month, between one and two months, and so on up to at least six months postonset—is essential. And the treatment period must be at least 6 months, preferably 12 months. Will such a study be done? Probably not. Too many patients are needed, and too many ethical objections exist. The required sample size could be obtained in a large, multicenter trial that continues for years. The ethical objections are another matter. Because treatment exists, many believe it is improper to withhold it. The data to date, though qualified by selection bias, imply that treatment is efficacious, and it is most efficacious if done early, before two months postonset. Only one thing would combat the ethical argument and facts, and that is a few well-controlled negative results. Without scientific support, we have a tool to answer the question when treatment is most effective—the group study that blocks on time periods and assigns patients randomly to treated and untreated periods—but no place to dig.

## CONCLUSIONS

It was necessary for this chapter to invade several of the other domains addressed in this book. To determine when one should intervene with treatment, one must demonstrate that treatment is worth offering. The evidence suggests it is. To evaluate the influence of intervening at one time and not another, one must determine that conditions in both periods are similar. This requires a look at who is treated, what the treatment is, where the treatment is done, and why the treatment is offered. Evidence exists to permit evaluation of each of these influences on when treatment works best.

The primary purpose of this chapter was to examine when treatment for aphasic adults should occur. The evidence on when, though not abundant, indicates early postonset, before two months, is the best time. Does that mean if you miss it, forget it? Not at all. The positive results reported for treated patients who started therapy after two months postonset, some over a year postonset, suggest a paraphrase of Helm-Estabrooks' conclusion on where treatment should occur. When does one treat? Whenever the aphasic patient seeks it. Though the linguistic improvement may be less than it may have been earlier, though the content of the treatment may differ from that employed at another point in time, when is when the aphasic patient surfaces. Unlike Gerturde Stein's observation of her birthplace, Oakland, California, "there is no there there," there is a when when, even though it may not be the best when. What we do at some inopportune when may be treatment that is not called treatment, but it may be the best treatment we do.

Determining when to intervene is important, and the importance may transcend just picking the best time to achieve the greatest linguistic gains. Most of our patients, regardless of when they come to us, arrive with external constraints that are not totally imposed by their disorder. Monetary and bureaucratic conditions also impose restrictions. Savings and insurance may limit the amount and length of time our patients are our patients. Similarly, regulations may limit how much and how long a patient remains eligible for our services. Many patients have only so many bullets in their arsenal. Should these be fired early in a burst, or should they be fired in volleys only when appropriate targets appear? The data indicate early in a burst, but we need to become certain.

There are ways of finding out. We have used single case and group designs to learn what we know, and what we know is not pelf. Our knowledge has been honestly acquired by toil in the clinical trenches. But we have a way to go. The single case design will probably not take us very far in determining when to intervene with treatment. A group design that blocks on time periods and assigns patients randomly to periods of treatment and no treatment is the best conveyance. But the road is littered with the ruts of expense and time and the potholes of ethical objections. Perhaps this is just as well. Too much information about aphasia based on group results may be too much information. Group studies talk about "the" aphasic patient. We never see these. Ours are always "a" patient.

"Professor Plum did it with a lead pipe in the conservatory." So goes a popular table game, and so goes aphasia therapy. Like the game, we collect evidence, some of it spurious, to determine who, what, and where. We also take our chances deciding when to pick the whom, the what, and the where. As in the game, we pay little attention to motive, the why, but it is the why that must take us out from under the shelter of what group data tell us about when to treat, because the why is specific for each patient.

Aphasia therapy has something in common with some countries, and this is the demand placed on those seeking to enter. There are strong, arrogant, merciless, crippling regulations, pitiless interests; a fear for the patient who does not represent a mass, the individual who does not match a specific card in treatment's computer, a code of conformity, a set of symptoms. Therapy has little room for the solitary reprobates. These patients cannot enter, and if they do, they may not be permitted to leave. There is no passport, no visa, to cross the frontier of treatment's tyranny. This has an effect on when treatment should be offered. We know a little about the group that meets treatment's mold, but we know almost nothing about individuals who do not. They must queue up and wait while they are prodded with psychometric tradition, and the time in line may carry them beyond the critical interval when treatment works the best.

Even for the representative aphasic patient, we cannot accept a Manichaean approach that dictates one point in time is good to intervene and another is bad. The data to date point the way, but they do not guarantee arrival. To determine *when* to treat, we must continue to pass the specific variables—the *who,* the *what,* the *where,* and the *why*—through a temporal sieve. Perhaps from the siftings will emerge evidence that establishes the best *when,* the critical interval.

## REFERENCES

Alajouanine T, Castaigne P, Lhermitte F, Escourolle R, de Ribancourt B: Etude de 43 cas d'aphasie post traumatique. Encephale 46:1–45, 1957

Anderson T, Bourestom N, Greenberg F: Rehabilitation predictors in completed stroke: Final report. American Rehabilitation Foundation Minneapolis, 1970

Aronson M, Shatin L, Cook J: Socio-psychotherapeutic approach to the treatment of aphasia. J Speech Hear Dis 21:325–364, 1956

Aten JL, Caligiuri MP, Holland AL: The efficacy of functional communication therapy for chronic aphasic patients. J Speech Hear Dis 47:93–95, 1982

Basso A, Capitani E, Vignolo L: Influence of rehabilitation on language skills in aphasic patients: A controlled study. Arch Neurol 36:190–196, 1979

Benson DF: Aphasia rehabilitation. Arch Neurol 36:187–189, 1979

Beyn E, Shokhor-Trotskaya M: The preventive method of speech rehabilitation in aphasia. Cortex 2:96–108, 1966

Broida H: Language therapy effects in long term aphasia. Arch Phys Med Rehabil 58:248–253, 1977

Buck M: *Dysphasia: Professional Guidance for Family and Patient.* Englewood Cliffs, NJ: Prentice-Hall, Inc, 1968

Butfield E, Zangwill O: Re-education in aphasia: A review of 70 cases. J Neurol Neurosurg Psychiat 9:75–79, 1946

Chapey R: *Language Intervention Strategies in Adult Aphasia.* Baltimore: Williams & Wilkins, 1981

Chenven H: Effects of group therapy upon language recovery in predominantly expressive aphasic patients. Doctoral dissertation, New York University, 1953

Culton G: Spontaneous recovery from aphasia. J Speech Hear Res 12:825–832, 1969

Dabul B, Hanson WR: The amount of language improvement in adult aphasics related to early and late treatment. Paper presented to the American Speech and Hearing Association, Washington DC, 1975

Dahlberg C, Jaffee J: *Stroke: A Physician's Personal Account.* New York: WW Norton, 1977

Darley F: The efficacy of language rehabilitation in aphasia. J Speech Hear Dis 37:3–21, 1972

Darley F: Treatment of acquired aphasia. In Friedlander W (ed): *Advances in Neurology,* vol 7. *Current Review of Higher Nervous System Dysfunction.* New York: Raven Press, 1975, pp 111–146.

Darley F: Treat or neglect? Asha 21:628–631, 1979

Deal JL, Deal LA: Efficacy of aphasia rehabilitation: Preliminary results. In Brookshire RH (ed): *Clinical Aphasiology: Proceedings of the Conference.* Minneapolis: BRK Publishers, 1978, pp 66–77

Deal JL, Deal LA: Aphasia rehabilitation: Influence of time postonset. Paper presented to the American Speech-Language Hearing Association, Los Angeles, California, 1981

Editorial: Prognosis in aphasia. *Lancet* II:24, 1977

Eisenson J: Prognostic factors related to language rehabilitation in aphasic patients. J Speech Hear Dis 14:262–264, 1949

Eisenson J: A point of view as to the nature of the disorder and factors that determine prognosis for recovery. Int J Neurol 4:287–295, 1964

Folsom JC: Reality orientation for the elderly mental patient. J Geriatr Psychiat 1:291–298, 1968

Frazier C, Ingham S: A review of the effects of gunshot wounds of the head. Arch Neurol Psychiat 3:17–40, 1920

Gessner J: Home rehabilitation of the stroke patient. Maryland J Med 15:105–107, 1966

Gloning K, Trappl R, Heiss WD, Quatember R: Prognosis and speech therapy in aphasia. In Lebrun Y, Hoops R (eds): *Neurolinguistics 4: Recovery in Aphasics.* Amsterdam: Swets and Zeitlinger, 1976, pp 57–64.

Glosser G, Kaplan E, Lo Verme S: Longitudinal neuropsychological report of aphasia following left-subcortical hemorrhage. Brain Lang 15:95–116, 1982

Godfrey CM, Douglas E: The recovery process in aphasia. Can Med Assoc J 80:618–624, 1959

Goodglass H, Kaplan E: *The Assessment of Aphasia and Related Disorders*. Philadelphia: Lea and Febiger, 1972

Greenberg S: Speech therapy for the severely impaired homebound aphasic patient. Paper presented to the Conference on Clinical Aphasiology, Albuquerque, New Mexico, 1973

Hagen E: Communication abilities in hemiplegia: Effect of speech therapy. Arch Phys Med Rehabil 54:454–463, 1973

Hanson WR, Cicciarelli AW: The time, amount and pattern of language improvement in adult aphasics. Brit J Dis Commun 13:59–63, 1978

Hartman J: Measurement of early spontaneous recovery from aphasia with stroke. Ann Neurol 9:89–91, 1981

Helm NA: Criteria for selecting aphasia patients for melodic intonation therapy. Paper presented to the American Academy for the Advancement of Science, Washington, DC, 1978

Helm NA, Benson DF: Visual action therapy for global aphasia. Paper presented to the Academy of Aphasia, Chicago, Illinois, 1978

Holland AL: Some current trends in aphasia rehabilitation. *ASHA* 11:3–7, 1969

Holland AL: The effectiveness of treatment in aphasia. In Brookshire RH (ed): *Clinical Aphasiology: Proceedings of the Conference*. Minneapolis: BRK Publishers, 1975, pp 1–27.

Holland AL: Factors affecting functional communication skills of aphasic and non-aphasic individuals. Paper presented to the American Speech and Hearing Association, San Francisco, California, 1978

Holland AL: The usefulness of treatment for aphasia: A serendipitous study. In Brookshire RH (ed): *Clinical Aphasiology: Proceedings of the Conference*. Minneapolis: BRK Publishers, 1980, pp 240–247

Holland AL: Observing functional communication of aphasic adults. J Speech Hear Dis 47:50–56, 1982

Keenan J, Brassell E: A study of factors related to prognosis for individual aphasic patients. J Speech Hear Dis 39:257–269, 1974

Kenin M, Swisher L: A study of pattern of recovery in aphasia. Cortex 8:56–68, 1972

Kertesz A: *Aphasia and Associated Disorders: Taxonomy, Localization, and Recovery*. New York: Grune and Stratton, 1979

Kertesz A, McCabe P: Recovery patterns and prognosis in aphasia. Brain 100:1–18, 1977

Knox DR: *Portrait of Aphasia*. Detroit: Wayne State University Press, 1971

Kübler-Ross E: *On Death and Dying*. New York: Macmillan Publishing Co., Inc, 1969

La Pointe LL: Quantification and accountability in aphasia therapy. Commun Dis: A Audio J Contin Educ 5: 1980

Lebrun Y: Recovery in polyglot aphasics. In Lebrun Y, Hoops R (eds): *Neurolinguistics 4: Recovery in Aphasics*. Amsterdam: Swets and Zeitlinger, 1976, pp 96–108

Leischner A: Aptitude of aphasics for language treatment. In Lebrun L, Hoops R (eds): *Neurolinguistics 4: Recovery in Aphasics*. Amsterdam: Swets and Zeitlinger, 1976, pp 112–123

Levita E: Effects of speech therapy on aphasics responses to the functional communication profile. Percep Motor Skills 47:151–154, 1978

Lomas J, Kertesz A: Patterns of spontaneous recovery in aphasic groups: A study of adult stroke patients. Brain Lang 5:388–401, 1978

Ludlow CL: The recovery of syntax in aphasia. Paper presented to the Academy of. Aphasia, Albuquerque, New Mexico, 1973

Luria AR: *Restoration of Function After Brain Injury*. New York: Macmillan Publishing Co, Inc, 1963

Marks M, Taylor M, Rusk HA: Rehabilitation of the aphasic patient: A summary of three years experience in a rehabilitation setting. Arch Phys Med Rehabil 38:219–226, 1957

Marshall RC, King PS: Effects of fatigue produced by isokinetic exercise on the communication ability of aphasic adults. J Speech Hear Res 16:222–230, 1973

Marshall RC, Tompkins CA, Phillips DS: Effects of scheduling on the communicative assessment of aphasic patients. J Commun Dis 13:105–114, 1980

Marshall RC, Tompkins CA, Phillips DS: Improvement in treated aphasia: Examination of selected prognostic factors. *Folia Phoniatrica*, in press

Marshall RC, Watts MT: Relaxation training: Effects on the communicative ability of aphasic adults. Arch Phys Med Rehabil 57:464–467, 1976

Matthews BAJ, La Pointe LL: Determining rate of change and predicting performance levels in aphasia therapy. In Brookshire RH (ed): *Clinical Aphasiology: Proceedings of the Conference*. Minneapolis: BRK Publishers, 1981, pp 17–25

Meikle M, Wechsler E, Tupper A, Benenson M, Butler J, Mulhall D, Stern G: Comparative trial of volunteer and professional treatments of dysphasia after stroke. Brit Med J 2:87–89, 1979

Messerli P, Tiscot A, Rodriguez J: Recovery from aphasia: Some factors of prognosis. In Lebrun Y, Hoops R (eds): *Neurolinguistics 4: Recovery in Aphasics*. Amsterdam: Swets and Zeitlinger, 1976, pp 124–135

Moss C: *Recovery with Aphasia: The Aftermath of My Stroke*. Urbana: University of Illinois Press, 1972

Pizzamiglio L, Appicciafuoco A, Razzano C: Recovery of comprehension in aphasic patients. In Lebrun Y, Hoops R (eds): *Neurolinguistics 4: Recovery in Aphasics*. Amsterdam: Swets and Zeitlinger, 1976, pp 163–167

Porch BE, Collins MJ, Wertz RT, Friden T: Statistical prediction of change in aphasia. J Speech Hear Res 23:312–322, 1980

Prins R, Snow C, Wagenaar E: Recovery from aphasia: Spontaneous speech versus language comprehension. Brain Lang 6:192–211, 1978

Rose C, Boby V, Capildeo R: A retrospective survey of speech disorders following stroke, with particular reference to the value of speech therapy. In

Lebrun Y, Hoops R (eds): *Neurolinguistics 4: Recovery in Aphasics*. Amsterdam: Swets and Zeitlinger, 1976, pp 189–197

Rosenbek JC: Wrinkled feet. In Brookshire RH (ed): *Clinical Aphasiology: Proceedings of the Conference*. Minneapolis: BRK Publishers, 1979, pp 163–175

Rosenbek JC, Green EF, Flynn M, Wertz RT, Collins M: Anomia: A clinical experiment. In Brookshire RH (ed): *Clinical Aphasiology: Proceedings of the Conference*. Minneapolis: BRK Publishers, 1977, pp 103–111

Sands ES: Early initiation of speech and language therapy and degree of language recovery in adult aphasics. Doctoral dissertation, New York University, 1977

Sands E, Sarno M, Shankweiler D: Long-term assessment of language function in aphasia due to stroke. Arch Phys Med Rehabil 50:202–206, 1969

Sarno MT: Recovery and rehabilitation in aphasia. In Sarno MT (ed): *Acquired Aphasia*. New York: Academic Press, 1981, pp 485–529

Sarno MT, Levita E: Natural course of recovery in severe aphasia. Arch Phys Med Rehabil 52:175–179, 1971

Sarno MT, Levita E: Recovery in aphasia during the first year post stroke. Stroke 10:663–670, 1979

Sarno MT, Levita E: Some observations on the nature of recovery in global aphasia. Brain Lang 13:1–12, 1981

Sarno M, Silverman M, Levita E: Psychosocial factors and recovery in geriatric patients with severe aphasia. J Am Geriatr Soc 18:405–409, 1970

Sarno M, Silverman M, Sands M: Speech therapy and language recovery in severe aphasia. J Speech Hear Res 13:607–623, 1970

Schuell H, Jenkins JJ, Jiménez-Pabón E: *Aphasia in Adults: Diagnosis, Prognosis, and Treatment*. New York: Hoeber Medical Division, Harper & Row, 1964

Shewan CM, Kertesz A: Language therapy and recovery from aphasia. Paper presented to the Academy of Aphasia, London, Ontario, 1981

Smith A: Diagnosis, intelligence, and rehabilitation of chronic aphasics: Final report. Ann Arbor, Mich: Department of Physical Medicine and Rehabilitation, University of Michigan, 1972

Struggling with aphasia. Med World News 10:37–40, 1969

Tompkins CA, Marshall RC, Phillips DS: Aphasic patients in a rehabilitation program: Scheduling speech and language services. Arch Phys Med Rehabil 61:252–254, 1980

van Dongen HR, Loonen MCB: Neurological factors related to prognosis of acquired aphasia in childhood. In Lebrun Y, Hoops R (eds): *Neurolinguistics 4: Recovery in Aphasics*. Amsterdam: Swets and Zeitlinger, 1976, pp 210–215.

Vignolo L: Evolution of aphasia and language rehabilitation: A retrospective study. Cortex 1:344–367, 1964

Warren RL, Datta KD: The return of speech four and one-half years post head injury. In Brookshire RH (ed): *Clinical Aphasiology: Proceedings of the Conference*. Minneapolis: BRK Publishers, 1981, pp 301–308

Weisenberg T, McBride K: *Aphasia: A Clinical and Psychological Study*. New York: Commonwealth Fund, 1935

Wepman J: *Recovery from Aphasia*. New York: Ronald Press, 1951

Wepman J: Aphasia therapy. A new look. J Speech Hear Dis 37:203–214, 1972

Wertz RT: A philosophy of aphasia therapy: Some things patients have not said but you can hear if you look. Commun Dis: J Contin Educ in press

Wertz RT, Collins MJ, Weiss D, Kurtzke JF, et al: Veterans Administration cooperative study on aphasia: A comparison of individual and group treatment. J Speech Hear Res 24:580–594, 1981

Wertz RT, Rosenbek JC: Group designs for the study of aphasia. In Brookshire RH (ed): *Clinical Aphasiology: Proceedings of the Conference*. Minneapolis: BRK Publishers, 1978, pp 1–10

Wiegel-Crump C: Agrammatism and aphasia. In Lebrun Y, Hoops R (eds): *Neurolinguistics 4: Recovery in Aphasics*. Amsterdam: Swets and Zeitlinger, 1976, pp 243–253

Yarnell P, Monroe P, Sobel L: Aphasia outcome in stroke: A clinical neuroradiological correlation. Stroke 7:514–522, 1976

# DISCUSSION: PART V: DECIDING WHEN TO INTERVENE

*ROBIN S. CHAPMAN*

When should language intervention take place? This question, simple on its face, proved to be an important focus of discussion at the National Conference. It is a question that Congress and many states are answering with specific legislation; that insurance companies are ruling on in making third-party payments; and that clients are deciding in seeking, continuing, or leaving therapy.

At the most general level, many clinicians agree on an answer: *Intervention should take place when there is a problem to which specialists in communicative disorders can offer a solution*. What should count as the problem and what should count as a solution, however, provoke lively debate. The issues underlying each of these two debates are the focus of this discussion.

## WHAT COUNTS AS THE PROBLEM?

Both Kemp's and Wertz's chapters reveal the general tendency among clinicians to identify clients on the basis of test results. Significant difference from the normal population's performance on a test is the admission ticket to therapy or a research project. Tests are based on particular models of what can go wrong, however,

and many versions of what can go wrong are implicit in the testing choices of investigators. All may be right some of the time; none of them is right all of the time.

The choice of measure and of comparison groups reveals many variations in the implicit model of communicative disorders adopted. Different versions of delay models, and of difference models, are discussed in various chapters in this volume, and the need for a third, event-based model for use in decision-making has become evident. Here some of the characteristics—and differences in detail—are summarized for each of the three models in turn: delay, difference, and communicative event.

One consequence of the discovery that normal children learn many aspects of their language in a predictable, invariant sequence has been to ask whether the language disordered children, different from their age peers, are nonetheless similar to younger normal children in the order of their acquisition of language structure, meanings, and uses. Is a child's pattern of omission of grammatical morphemes, for example, consistent with the developmental facts of early and late acquired morphemes? Is the order of acquisition over time similar to the order shown by normal children? That is, does the child's language resemble that of younger normal children, or is it different in some way that may illuminate the cause of the child's problems?

The delay-difference question can be asked about any aspect of language developing in a sequential fashion in normal children. Such sequences have been identified for language production in the acquisition of speech sounds; the orders in which the syntax of sentence negation, yes-no questions, Wh-questions, and tag-questions develop; the order of complex sentence acquisition; the sequence of mastery of the fourteen grammatical morphemes in obligatory contexts; the orders of emergence of different semantic roles expressed in one-word speech, different meanings of early negation, and the different semantic roles queried in Wh-questions; the order of emerging interpropositional relations; the emergence of early communicative intents; and the emergence of different ways to request action.

When the delay-difference question is asked about any single aspect of developing language it can be fairly easily answered; and most often, the answer has been that the group of children studied appears delayed, rather than different, in the pattern of acquisition of a syntactic, semantic, or pragmatic sequence. In contrast, tests of the regression hypothesis in adult aphasics—the hypothesis that language is lost in the inverse order of acquisition—have supported a difference model. Adult performance does not resemble, for any given aspect of language, that of a young normal child.

The issue of characterizing children's language problems can become more complex in two ways. First, the degree of delay in acquisition of some particular sequence can be compared against a standard: for example, the child's cognitive level of functioning, measured by nonverbal tests; or an overall index of syntactic development, such as mean length of utterance in morphemes (MLU). One can then ask whether the child's delayed performance is nonetheless commensurate with expectations for his cognitive or his overall level of syntactic production—or not. For example, hearing impaired children's acquisition of the fourteen grammatical morphemes may be delayed, but the delay may be much

greater than one would expect on the basis of either cognitive measures or an overall index of syntactic development. Some investigators would continue to call this sort of delay a delay; others would call it a difference.

In his discussion of when to intervene in a child's language development, Kemp explicitly adopts a "difference" rather than a "delay" model for language disordered children. He proposes that, unless a child is under age 2, he should be accepted for language intervention therapy if, and only if, one aspect of the communication system is lagging behind other aspects. His is a radical proposal, but it can better be understood in light of the model of disorders he has implicitly adopted and his view of intervention. The children that he would accept in therapy may be delayed in the sense that order of development of any given sequence is the normal order, slowed down; but they must also meet the criterion of asynchronous language development. Children with simple across-the-board delay in language development would be candidates, in Kemp's view, for a language stimulation program but not for language intervention narrowly defined. Kemp commented that he was surprised by the willingness of most participants in the National Conference to view almost any activity affecting the child's environment as language intervention. He chose to confine the term to the activities peculiar to speech-language pathologists, rather than including the activities of parents, peers, good classroom teachers, or language teachers in a classroom. This view of intervention as a special bag of tricks and techniques would understandably limit the children and adults to whom one applied it.

## COMPARING LINGUISTIC SKILLS WITH ONE ANOTHER: IS SYNCHRONY THE NORM?

A second way in which the issue of identifying children who are language delayed can become complicated is in comparing the rate of acquisition of one sequential aspect of language development with another: to ask whether the child's development is synchronous or asynchronous. Does the development of grammatical morpheme mastery occur in tandem with the expected aspects of sentence structure emergence? Does the emerging sequence of expression of interpropositional relations occur concomitantly with the expected developments of complex sentence construction? Or more generally, do the child's production skills parallel his comprehension skills, or is one far in advance of the other? Are pragmatic skills commensurate with syntactic skills? And so forth.

Although each aspect of developing language may itself show a normal or delayed pattern of acquisition, the asynchrony between aspects may lead investigators to apply a "different," rather than a "delayed" label to the child. Thus children regarded as delayed by investigators who have studied only single aspects of the children's language may, with equal truth, be labeled different when additional measures are made.

Kemp believes that most language disordered children will meet his criterion of asynchronous development, and that asynchrony is anomalous, or different, from the normal development pattern. There are at least three problems in the adoption of Kemp's Asynchronous Development Decision Rule. First, other researchers believe that a large proportion of language disordered children would be excluded from intervention (in a broad sense of the activity) if asynchrony in development were insisted on. Second, the failure to consider language functioning in relation to cognitive level in children older than 2 years would make it impossible to identify mentally retarded children who were further delayed (but not asynchronously) in language skills.

Third, there is little evidence to support this underlying assumption of such a model: that language development is synchronous across its different aspects. Intralinguistic variation in normal development has received little study. One needs to know what the normal variation in comprehension skills, compared with production skills, might be; what the normal variation in MLU stage of morpheme acquisition might be; what the normal range of variation in pragmatic skills, compared with semantic comprehension or production, might be.

There is reason to argue that different subsystems of language are linked to different clusters of causal variables, and hence can show differential rates of development. For example, phonologic development in mentally retarded children can often be nearer expectations for chronologic age than other aspects of language skill. Delay or idiosyncratic development of the phonologic system in cognitively normal children can occur independently of other aspects of the language system. Maturation of the speech motor control system, and the uses that are acquired, can proceed on a different timetable than cognitive growth.

Children's semantic development, in contrast, appears to reflect nonverbally measured cognitive development in large part. Cognitive measures contribute predictive power over and beyond age and mean length of utterance, in the preoperational period, for semantic but not syntactic aspects of development. Frequency of use of different complex sentence structures, in contrast, is better predicted by the children's mean length of utterance than by either age or Piagetian cognitive tasks. These are not surprising findings— that measures of acquired knowledge are closely related to the meanings expressed in children's speech, and that a general index of the complexity of children's speech is more closely related to the relatively invariant sequence in which structural solutions are being achieved by the child. Their implication, however, runs counter to a view that language acquisition is all of a piece. Phonologic, semantic, and syntactic development in children's talking can diverge, as the variables causally linked with each diverge.

Similarly, children's comprehension and production skills can diverge. Extreme examples can occur: the cerebral palsied child who understands but cannot speak, who has not yet had access to an augmentative communication system of some kind; the autistic child who can repeat syntactically complex utterances at the same time that comprehension is at an early single-word level. Among normal children, most researchers have expected comprehension and production skills to develop at the same pace; some have assumed that the linguistic competence acquired by the child entails similar development in the two domains, because the same competence underlies both. A closer view, however, suggests that there are performance skills peculiar to each modality as well. What the child must learn to do as a listener, and what he must learn to do as a speaker, are not identical. To the extent that listening and speaking tasks differ, they need not be acquired at the same time.

Studies of individual differences in children's acquisition patterns reveal other points at which asynchrony among linguistic milestones could occur as part of a particular normal pattern of development. Among the individual differences (hence, sources of variability) in language acquisition which have been identified or proposed are the following: rate of syntactic development; interpretability of child speech (word versus intonation babies, intelligibility); differences in syntactic patterns acquired first; differences in semantic content of speech; and differences in pragmatic characteristics of the speaker. Individual differences in syntactic acquisition proposed include analytic versus synthetic approaches to early speech (one word versus multiword early utterances); nominal versus pronominal early sentence patterns; greater noun phrase elaboration in precocious talkers; occurrence of word order errors and invented grammatical patterns versus no such occurrences; few versus frequent presyntactic forms; differing syntactic connectives to express similar meanings in complex sentences; and regular versus irregular past tense mastery first. Semantic differences proposed include a preference for idiosyncratic semantically based sentence patterns and referential versus expressive early vocabulary. Pragmatic differences proposed include the child's readiness to speak, given a degree of comprehension; the use of elaborated versus restricted codes; and the use of language for imaginative play versus no such use.

Some of these proposed differences will, of course, prove to be developmental rather than individual differences. Many of the others may reflect the variation in children's environments: What are the novel aspects of the situations they find themselves in, and what are the usual characteristics? The first is likely to affect what children talk about; the second, what they understand or assume as listeners. Further, the way these events are coded by speakers in the child's environment will affect what the child understands and says. Consistent morphemic encoding of meaning will be easier to grasp, all else being equal, than phrase or word order cues. The word or morpheme used consistently for a given meaning by the other significant speakers in the child's environment is likely to be the form the child adopts. A child who is eager to speak may exploit his available vocabulary to a greater extent than a child who is not as interested in verbal interaction. The sheer amount of linguistic input varies from child to child, as does its interpretability in the situation. The growth of a child's comprehension vocabulary will depend on input factors different from those influencing his spoken syntax. Whether these individual differences among children are ultimately traced to differences in input, or differences in the children's social and cognitive styles, the point remains for the purpose of this discussion: Departures from the idealized account of synchronous language development in language disordered children may be no more unusual than the same departures in normal children's development. It will be necessary to study the same processes in normal and disordered children, and to set aside the assumption that all language characteristics of a child are deviant simply because we have found one tested dimension of difference.

## THE COMMUNICATIVE EVENT: ANOTHER MODEL FOR IDENTIFYING PROBLEMS

This review suggests that we have much to learn before we can carry out complete assessments of children's language skills and before we can confidently apply criteria of intralinguistic variation to the identification of language delayed children. What is to be done while we wait for the millennium? I believe it is important to entertain a third perspective in identifying the adults and children who are candidates for language therapy: that of whether they are encountering difficulty in the communicative events that make up their world. Here the focus is on identifying breakdowns in the interactive communicative event: Are the participants having problems? Is the parent concerned that the child is not babbling back, or doesn't seem to understand? Does the speaker get his meaning across, or give up? Do the participants share a common set of expectations?

In Shakespeare's *Julius Caesar* there is a scene, shortly after the murder of Caesar, in which Cinna the poet is encountered wandering at night and charged to give an account of himself to the Roman citizens. The first citizen demands to know "What is your name?"; the second, "Whither are you going"; the third, "Where do you dwell?" and the fourth, "Are you a bachelor or a married man?" The citizens then give Cinna prudent advice on how to answer: "Answer every man direct"; "Ay, and briefly"; "Ay, and wisely"; "Ay, and truly, you were best." The reader may recognize these in their more modern version as the Gricean postulates for cooperative conversation: Be relevant, brief, informative, and sincere. Cinna, unfortunately, ignores the advice on conversational contributions and begins a rambling monologue; the crowd tears him to pieces. Although the cost of a communicative breakdown is not ordinarily one's life, it can have serious consequences. The point of this story is that we should ask whether our procedures for identifying language disordered or delayed children and adults will pick out the Cinnas: those for whom the communicative consequences will be troublesome or severe. Attention to communicative success and failure in the real world may offer a more valid and reliable guide to those most in need of services.

## WHAT COUNTS AS THE SOLUTION?

This same focus on the communicative event is useful to remember in evaluating our intervention therapies: Will they save our clients from the Roman citizens? A certain pessimism with respect to cure has been a recurrent theme in this volume: Improvements could be demonstrated, but neither aphasiologists nor child language clinicians believed that they had "cured" their clients. Problems would resurface as the adult encountered new situations or heightened stress or as the child encountered these and the tasks of his new developmental level. It is important, then, to view the success of therapy from the client's perspective, rather than look at a test result or an expectation of cure. The important question is, has the client benefited?

There has been much discussion on the question of whether certain therapies have been experimentally demonstrated to work. Some object that the goal of showing that any therapy works for any member of the group—as in the aphasia studies—is shortsighted. The research needs to be directed to the question of which therapy works best for which individuals. Most conference participants agreed, but pointed out the difficulties of doing so given the shifting baselines of spontaneous recovery in adults and ongoing development in children. Less was said about how gains were to be measured, although current practice is to use test measures only indirectly related to language use. It is here, again, that the perspective of the client should be introduced: Will our therapies save our clients from the Roman citizens—at least part of the time?

The preparation of this manuscript was supported in part by the facilities of the Waisman Center on Mental Retardation and Human Development, Core Research Grant No. 2-P30-HD-03352-14, NICHD, NIH; by the Department of Communicative Disorders, University of Wisconsin-Madison; and by the joint sponsors of the National Conference, Boys Town, and the American Speech-Hearing-Language Association.

# WHERE TO CONDUCT LANGUAGE INTERVENTION?

# 13

## LANGUAGE INTERVENTION FOR ADULTS: ENVIRONMENTAL CONSIDERATIONS

*NANCY HELM-ESTABROOKS*

In 1906 Shephard Ivory Franz, an American physician with a keen interest in aphasia, described in detail the re-education of one aphasic patient. At the beginning of that report Franz stated, "It should be noted that the patient was not insane although he was brought for treatment to a hospital for the insane."

Another approach to the care of aphasic patients in the early twentieth century was simply to put them to bed at home. Confined to bed, they often died of medical complications, such as pulmonary emboli, associated with prolonged periods of immobility.

For aphasic patients today the options of care are notably improved. Not only has aphasia, as a disorder, figuratively come out of the closet, but aphasic individuals now literally may be out of bed within the first 24 to 48 hours following onset because of the lower mortality rate associated with early mobilization (St. Luke's Hospital Data, 1979; Anderson, 1980). The rehabilitation of aphasic individuals, however, continues to present a major challenge to health care professionals. The American Speech-Language-Hearing Association es-timates that there are two million aphasic adults in the United States today. According to Brust, Shafer, Richter, and Bruum (1976), of the approximately 400,000 new stroke patients a year, as many as 21 percent, or 84,000, will be aphasic in the early stages after their stroke. For 8.4 percent, or 10,000, the aphasia will still be severe 4 to 12 weeks following onset.

Aphasia rehabilitation therefore is of great concern to our profession. *Where* that rehabilitation takes place is the topic of this chapter.

### VARIABLES AFFECTING APHASIC REHABILITATION DECISIONS

Several variables may determine the patient's needs and options for aphasia rehabilitation. Among these are: etiologic agent, nature and severity of the aphasia, sex, age, vocational status, and geographic location of the patient. These variables are generally interdependent, that is, no single variable determines the patient's rehabilitation course.

## ETIOLOGIC AGENTS IN APHASIA

Stroke is the most common cause of aphasia, defined here as an acquired language disturbance uncomplicated by cognitive disorders, such as memory loss and disorientation regarding time and place. For this reason, this chapter refers to stroke-related aphasia, with the recognition that aphasia also may result from traumatic head injury, tumors, infection, or degenerative diseases. In patients with the latter disorders, the course of recovery and the rehabilitative needs, approaches, and potential will differ from those of the aphasic stroke patient and should be discussed separately.

Strokes may be thrombotic, embolic, or hemorrhagic in nature. According to Obler and associates (1980), thrombotic strokes are linked strongly to frontal lobe lesion localization, while embolic strokes are distributed quite evenly in the frontal, parietal, and temporal lobes. This is interesting because nonfluent aphasias, such as Broca's aphasia, tend to be associated with anterior or frontal lobe lesions, while fluent aphasias, such as Wernicke's and anomic aphasia, are associated with temporal and parietal lobe lesions (Naeser and Hayward, 1978). Recent evidence from CT (computerized axial tomographic) scan studies indicates that subcortical, putaminal, or thalamic hemorrhages may produce a unique aphasic syndrome characterized by fluent, paraphasic speech, mild anomia, normal repetitions, and nearly intact auditory comprehension. Unlike patients with other types of fluent aphasia, the putaminal/thalamic patient will have right hemiplegia. In addition, attentional deficits, right neglect, lack of concern, and perseveration may make long-term outcome less favorable than that expected in victims of embolic/thrombotic strokes involving cerebral cortex (Albert and associates, 1981).

Thus the cause of the stroke and the site of the brain lesion may predict aphasia type and concomitant deficits. These in turn may predict the patient's need for a rehabilitation program.

## NATURE AND SEVERITY OF APHASIA

Both the nature and the severity of the aphasia will influence decisions regarding the rehabilitation plan for specific patients. For example, Wernicke's aphasia, which is associated with temporal lobe lesions, is characterized by fluent, linguistically disordered output with poor auditory comprehension but without concomitant hemiparesis. The patient has no physical signs of stroke, yet his speech does not make sense and he does not understand what is being said. If the aphasia is not recognized as such, the Wernicke's patient might be misdiagnosed as psychotic (Benson, 1973). If the physician correctly diagnoses Wernicke's aphasia but does not "believe in" language therapy, the patient may be sent home following the medical work-up, because he is unlikely to require physical rehabilitation. If the physician recommends language therapy but these services are not available within commuting distance, the patient may be sent to an inpatient rehabilitation facility. If, for either personal or financial reasons, the patient is unable to enter such a facility, then he may remain at home, untreated, despite a devastating communication disorder.

A patient with a nonfluent aphasia is likely to fare better. These aphasias are associated with frontal lobe involvement and hemiparesis, that is, weakness on one side of the body, usually the right (Albert and associates, 1981). The reduction of speech output and obvious motor signs contribute to an easy diagnosis of aphasia. In addition to requiring physical therapy, the patient may require therapy relating to the activities of daily living, such as dressing and grooming, so that referral to a full-service rehabilitation facility is more likely for the nonfluent patient. Furthermore, because this patient will require a variety of therapies, there is a greater chance that third party funding will pay for inpatient rehabilitation.

Mildly aphasic patients of any type may be considered "too good" for language therapy despite evidence that even a mild impairment may prevent resumption of former employment (Kertesz and McCabe, 1977). These patients often must refer themselves in order to receive treatment.

## GENDER AND AGE

In a discussion of aphasia rehabilitation two variables, gender and age, are best discussed together. According to Anderson (1980), women are slightly less prone to strokes than men. Women also are less likely to have thrombotic strokes, which, as stated above, are associated with anterior, nonfluent aphasias (Obler and associates, 1980). Instead of nonfluent aphasias women predominantly have "mixed" aphasias. On the basis of Sarno's observation that severely nonfluent aphasic patients are more likely to be referred to rehabilitation centers (Sarno and Levita, 1981), we can conclude that men have a better chance of referral on the basis of aphasia type.

Men, however, tend to have temporal lesions associated with emboli as they grow older, so that a greater incidence of Wernicke's aphasia is seen with advancing age in men. This tendency does not occur in women. Among older patients, therefore, women may be referred for language therapy more often than men because they are less fluent.

In addition to the contribution made by age and gender to prediction of aphasia type, these variables have some practical implications for the rehabilitation planning. Although this is rapidly changing, women in the United States are less likely than men to be employed outside the home. To whatever degree that there is less need for full communication skills within the home setting, women may be denied aphasia rehabilitation. Furthermore, companies may underwrite extensive rehabilitation programs for high-level employees, but women tend to hold lower positions in the marketplace, although the United States Department of Labor reports a threefold increase in the number of women in managerial positions since 1960.

Another disadvantage for women seeking aphasia rehabilitation is the fact that they are unlikely to have served in the armed forces. This excludes them from the free-to-the-patient rehabilitative services offered by the Veterans Administration. Women have no substitute for this major source of aphasia rehabilitation. Finally, aphasic persons over 62 years of age are eligible for Medicare, which pays for some rehabilitation services. Aphasic persons under 62 must rely on health insurance such as Blue Cross/Blue Shield, welfare-type funding such as Medicaid, or their own personal finances.

## GEOGRAPHICAL LOCATION

In 1979, Basso, Capitani, and Vignolo reported the results of a long-term treatment versus no-treatment study. They were able to compare the recovery patterns of 162 treated patients and 119 untreated patients because the latter group was unable, primarily for geographic reasons, to travel to treatment centers.

In the United States only patients in the most remote regions are more than 1 or 2 hours' traveling time from a comprehensive rehabilitation center (Anderson, 1980). With regard to outpatient therapy, however, this distance may adversely influence the therapy schedule, particularly where winter weather is a problem.

## TODAY'S APHASIA REHABILITATION OPTIONS WITH HISTORICAL PERSPECTIVE

The options for aphasia rehabilitation have improved steadily in the United States since Mills (1904) reported the case of a patient who treated himself at home with help from his secretary and suggestions from Mills. In this section today's options are discussed, along with some historical perspective.

## THE ACUTE CARE FACILITY

As stated earlier, the aphasic patient today is very likely to be admitted to an

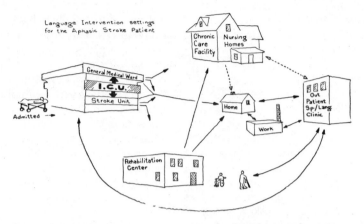

Figure 13–1. Language intervention settings for the aphasic stroke patient.

acute care facility for medical examination and a series of tests, such as CT scan and other localizing and diagnostic procedures (see Figure 13–1). If a speech/language pathologist is available, the patient may be referred for an aphasia examination early in the hospitalization. In hospitals such as St. Luke's in New Bedford, Massachusetts, patients are admitted to the Stroke Program directly from the admitting room unless they require intensive care. Once enrolled in the stroke program they are seen within 24 hours by clinicians from all the rehabilitative disciplines, including speech/language pathology. At this stage the patient may not be a candidate for formal language testing, but informal assessments are performed and aphasia therapy is instituted. While this thearpy may be informal or unstructured, it is no less therapeutic. Typically, the nursing staff is informed of the patient's communicative assets and deficits and every possible approach is taken to maximize successful communication. This, in turn, may minimize negative reactions such as frustration, withdrawal, depression, and rage. At the same time family members and other significant persons are informed of the present nature of the patient's language disorder and advised on optimal approaches to communication.

Chester and Egoff (1974) found that many people, including clinicians, give aphasic patients nonverbal negative messages, such as speaking of the patient in the third person, walking past without speaking, and using unnecessarily loud voices. Thus the earliest form of aphasia therapy may be to modify the behavior of the caretakers and significant others so that the patient can use his residual communication skills. Goodkin (1969) showed that when the verbal behavior of their spouses was modified, long-term aphasic patients increased their verbal output.

According to Sands and Sullivan (1977), more structured approaches to aphasia therapy also can be implemented in the acute care setting. These investigators treated patients with 45-minute sessions of programmed therapy beginning the first 3 to 10 days after onset of aphasia.

In hospitals without stroke programs the speech/language pathologist must educate staff members throughout the facility, but especially those on the medical wards. In our experience, nurses are among our best referral sources and are often highly cooperative regarding suggestions for management (Helm-Estabrooks, Chiavaras, in press). Very often the nursing staff may issue a cry for help with a severely aphasic patient who is not able to communicate basic needs. One way we help the nurses communicate with severely affected patients is to affix words and pictures for "yes" and "no" to the arms of the wheelchair for the patient to grab in response to questions.

In-service lectures are important to aphasia therapy in any setting, but especially within the acute care facility where patients are likely to be most severely impaired. Anyone who comes into contact with aphasic patients should be aware of the general nature of the disorder and of the many ways besides speaking that one can use to communicate, for example, writing, pantomiming, pointing, head nodding. Even a restricted verbal stereotypy can be used to communicate when it is given the appropriate intonational and emotional contours and volume changes. If hospital employees and others are aware of and explore all the possible means of communication, the patient will benefit and rehabilitation will have begun. Because the length of acute care hospitalization is likely to be brief, however, more formal language therapy may begin following discharge from such a facility.

## POST-ACUTE CARE FACILITIES

Following acute care hospitalization the patient may be discharged to either (1) a rehabilitation center, (2) a chronic care facility, or (3) home/halfway house. Let us then consider these three possible environments vis-à-vis aphasia rehabilitation.

**The Rehabilitation Center.** Before World War II very few aphasic patients in the United States could expect to receive any kind of language therapy unless they were fortunate enough to come under the care of a few pioneers, such as the aforementioned Shephard Ivory Franz, Charles Mills, or Mills' student Theodore Weisenberg and his colleague Katherine McBride (1935).

With World War II came a great increase in the number of head injuries, many of which caused aphasia along with physical impairments (Amos, 1948). To care for these patients, inpatient rehabilitation centers were established by the army and the Veterans Administration. Such clinicians as Ollie Backus, John Eisenson, Vivian Sheehan, and Joseph Wepman were recruited to help treat the large number of patients. Several units, housing approximately 20 noncommissioned men (according to Sheehan, 1949,

officers lived in separate quarters) were designed to provide intensive rehabilitation, including occupational and physical therapy, classroom instruction in school subjects such as math, and individual and group language therapy.

The speech/language pathologists were part of a multidisciplinary team that included neurologists and former teachers who became language retraining instructors. In the VA centers the speech/language pathologists were clinical psychologists who worked with the language retraining instructors, under the general supervision of neurologists, in providing various formal and group language therapy experiences (Amos, 1948).

Following World War II, civilian rehabilitation centers, such as the Institute of Rehabilitation Medicine in Chicago, the University of Michigan Aphasia Clinic, and the New York University Medical Center were established. At the same time some of the Veterans Administration aphasia units began to treat nontraumatic aphasic stroke patients. Among these are the aphasia sections of the Minneapolis and Boston Veterans Administration Medical Centers. All of these programs have made considerable contributions to the study and treatment of aphasia under such aphasiologists as Mildred Schuell, Martha Taylor Sarno, Aaron Smith, Frederick Darley, Harold Goodglass, and Edith Kaplan. The inpatient rehabilitation center has allowed us to examine aphasic patients in detail, develop aphasia tests, delineate aphasic syndromes and related behaviors, and conduct controlled studies of aphasic therapy. Because of the work carried out by these and similar centers, aphasia therapy is now considered to be an essential part of the stroke rehabilitation programs. Today virtually all rehabilitation centers offer speech/language therapy on a daily or twice daily schedule. Depending upon the physical layout of the center and the patients' mobility, aphasic patients are either brought to the speech/language pathology department or seen at bedside or in a room on the ward. As a general rule, the fancier the facility, the more likely it is that the speech/language pathology department will be separate from the patients' living quarters. This situation is not necessarily the best in terms of assessing the patient's communication needs and the effects of treatment. In therapy rooms we tend to administer standardized language tests and, as Holland (1980) has pointed out, "language and communication are not necessarily isomorphic." She stresses the need to investigate the relationship between language impairment and communication in natural contexts. While a rehabilitation ward is not the most stimulating context, it provides more opportunities for the patient to engage in a variety of communicative acts than does the therapy room, where certain predictable and limited interactions take place between the patient and the language clinician (Brookshire and colleagues, 1978).

A few aphasia tests have attempted to assess the aphasic patient's potential for daily communication. Holland's (1980) Communicative Abilities in Daily Living is one such test. Another is Sarno's Functional Communication Profile (1969), which partially relies on observation of, rather than interaction with, the patient in natural settings.

Some aphasia rehabilitation units, for example, that at the Boston VA Medical Center, are old-fashioned enough to have the speech/language pathology offices interspersed with the patient's rooms. This allows us to assess the patients' communication skills from 8:00 A.M. to 4:30 P.M. during everyday activities, such as eating, grooming, and interaction with other patients and staff in the hallway and in the TV room where smoking is allowed. The word gets around quickly when a severely aphasic patient first asks for a match, thus reinforcing the clinician and the generalizing effects of the treatment program in addition to whatever value such communicative successes may have for the patient. One might conjecture that, given the increased evidence that aphasia test scores may not tell us all there is to know about the patient's communication skills, the old-fashioned integrated rehabilitation unit may become the model for the future.

Depending upon the available finan-cial resources, the aphasic patient may spend at least a month at a comprehensive rehabilitation center following discharge from the acute care hospital. From the rehabilitation center the patient either will go home or to a chronic care facility, such as a nursing home. This latter option will be explored next.

**The Chronic Care Facility.** Ideally, the aphasic patient returns home following treatment at an acute care or rehabilitation hospital. If the patient cannot be cared for or cannot care for himself at home, admission to a chronic care facility may be the only option. This is not necessarily the end of the line. The conditions that prohibit the patient from returning home at any point in time may change. For a majority of patients, however, admission to a chronic care facility is the end of the line.

According to Lubinski (1981), at least 3.3 percent of the patients in nursing home settings have aphasia, while as many as 32 percent have various kinds of communication problems. Of the 292 nursing homes surveyed by Lubinski, Chapey, and Salzberg (cited in Lubinski, 1981), only 3 percent of the facilities that responded provided full-time speech/language pathology services, while 27 percent provided part-time services. Another 24 percent said they referred patients outside of the nursing home. One might assume that many of the homes that failed to respond also failed to provide or to refer patients for speech/language services.

Patients in VA chronic care domiciliaries, on the other hand, often are seen by speech/language pathologists from affiliated medical centers.

Lubinski (1981) described the environment of the typical nursing home as one in which there are few opportunities, places, or motivation for meaningful communication. She sees the role of the speech/language pathologist in these situations as being that of an educator to the other staff members and administration, and a stimulator to the patients. She says that older people will communicate if there is a reason to communicate and that the speech/language pathologist can bring patients and staff together in such a way that the potential for communication will improve.

Certainly the communicative needs of the aphasic patient under chronic care may be somewhat more limited than those of the aphasic individual in the community. These needs are no less real or relevant to the quality of life, however, and they are equally worthy of our professional attention. One solution for chronic care facilities with small numbers of aphasic patients may be to contract with private practitioners or clinics which can provide services according to need.

Earlier it was suggested that circumstances occasionally change, thereby allowing an aphasic patient to leave a chronic care facility and return home. One such patient was seen at the Boston VA Medical Center. This patient was unable to go home after his stroke because he could not verbalize beyond the syllable "ba" and therefore could not effectively use the telephone. His wife worked outside the home and was afraid to leave him alone without a link to the outside world. After almost a year in the nursing home he was readmitted to the VA with pneumonia and was once again referred to us. During the re-evaluation period we made a deal with his wife. If we could help him to speak, she would take him home. He was subsequently successfully treated with melodic intonation therapy (Albert, Sparks, and Helm, 1973) and went home, where he functioned well enough to stay alone.

**The Home.** The functional abilities of aphasic patients who return home range from little capacity for self-care to the ability to carry out all of their former activities. Most patients fall somewhere in between and are capable of all self-care and some but not all of the more complex activities of their preaphasic life. Earlier we cited Kertesz and McCabe (1977), who found that even mild aphasia may preclude resumption of employment. In addition to language problems many aphasic patients may have motor deficits that interfere with former employment skills, and/or related medical problems, such as heart disease, that dictate early retirement.

The rehabilitation challenge is much greater for the younger, employed aphasic patient than for the older, retired patient. Very little data exist as to employment patterns following onset of stroke and aphasia (Helm, 1980). One of the few such reports is that of Hatfield and Zangwill (1975) in which they describe four English patients with severe aphasia. Two patients had hemiparesis and nonfluent verbal output. Two were nonparetic but had fluent paraphasic output and auditory comprehension deficit. Of the four, three were resettled into new jobs, one as an assistant storekeeper, one as an assistant chef and one as a manager in a glass factory. The fourth patient, at age 60 with fluent aphasia, returned to his position as a laboratory technician. Five years later he was asked to stay on beyond retirement age. All four patients received speech therapy on a regular basis before and after returning to work, with the full approval of their employers.

Hatfield and Zangwill also found a notable dissociation between the patients' linguistic capacity and their ability to undertake skilled work. These linguistic deficits also appear not to have interfered with the patients' ability to interact and communicate successfully with their fellow employees and customers. Similarly, Holland (1982) recently reported that 39 of 40 aphasic patients studied at home had more communicative successes than failures despite Porch Index of Communication Ability scores that ranged from 8.13 to 14.23 out of a possible 16.0 points.

Opportunities for assessing functional communication skills of the type sampled by Holland are not readily available to speech/language pathologists who see patients in clinics and hospitals. For those who specialize in home care, however, the opportunities are ample, although the patient confined to home is often severely aphasic.

According to Hester (1981), of the approximately 2,616 certified home health agencies in the United States, 1,287, or 49 percent, offer speech/language pathology services. Added to those services are those offered by private practitioners. The 1981 survey by Chapey, Chwat, Gurland, and Peiras found that 33 percent of the 481 private practitioners who responded saw patients in their homes. An average of 9.65 hours per week of their time was spent in home care.

One alternative to visiting patients in the home is to use the telephone as a means of conducting therapy. Much of the research into telephone therapy has been stimulated by Gwenyth Vaughn at the Birmingham VA Medical Center. Our own experience using this method with two moderately aphasic patients has been very positive. Following hospital discharge one patient returned home to another state and one local patient was unable to reach an outpatient clinic because of transportation problems. Each had been evaluated and then introduced as inpatients to a formal therapy program for improving grammatic output (Helm-Estabrooks, 1981). Both were sent home with stimulus pictures for the program in a ring binder notebook. At a predetermined time each day the clinician telephoned the patient, who was ready with the notebook. After a short, informal conversation, the structured program was introduced with the clinician providing the verbal stimuli and the patient responding appropriately. One patient was reevaluated over the phone when the program was completed. A new program then was introduced, using the mail as well as the telephone. In this manner, patients have the advantages of the more stimulating home setting and daily language therapy.

A different approach to home care was taken by Greenberg (1970). She trained family members to carry out programs of therapy with eight homebound, severely aphasic patients. The patient and family assistant met with Greenberg once weekly to discuss the work and adjust the three therapy programs designed to teach numbers, names of objects, and body part recognition. Greenberg observed each patient in the home at least once. Comparisons of pre- and post-therapy test results showed that significant improvement was made by all eight patients.

Patients who are not homebound and live in an urban setting may take advantage of outpatient speech/language services provided by hospitals and medical centers, free standing and privately owned clinicis, and universities. In addition, meetings of the Stroke Club International, which now has affiliates in most major cities, offer aphasic patients an opportunity for informal exchange. These and similar group experiences often provide the optimal milieu for aphasic patients to express their frustrations, fears, hopes, and concerns. Some speech/language pathology departments, like ours, continue to offer patients group experiences after formal therapy is terminated. Our patients form car pools and then phone each other about travel arrangements and conditions before the drive into Boston. Once in the group, which is run by a speech/language pathologist and a social worker, they drink coffee and discuss such topics as depression, family problems, alcohol abuse, and the state of the world.

At the Fort Howard VA Ria Basili has a "lunch group." Once a week she has lunch in a small private dining room with a few patients no longer receiving formal language therapy. On a typical day they discussed what one patient would buy his wife for her birthday, how he would get to the store, pay for the present, and so on. Another patient volunteered to help him out. In addition, with Dr. Basili's guidance, two of the patients had recently begun work with the hospital newsletter. They assisted in mimeographing. These patients may no longer have been receiving formal language therapy, as we like to define our programs, but they were continuing to receive communication therapy of the highest order. Neither type is a substitute for the other, of course, nor should one be ignored in favor of the other.

## THE GENERAL ENVIRONMENT FOR APHASIA REHABILITATION

Simply stated, aphasia rehabilitation should take place wherever the aphasic individual finds himself. If we, as speech/language pathologists, cannot be where the patient is, then we must educate everyone who comes in contact with the patient as to the nature of aphasia and how best to communicate with those having this disorder. Furthermore, our patients have to be freed from our direct care and taught to maximize their own communicative potential in any environment.

Perhaps, conversely, the families or patients have something to teach us about aphasic communication skills. A unique study by Helmick, Watamari, and Palmer (1976) found that spouses of aphasic patients "overestimated" the patients' level of communicative competency, that is, they said the patient communicated at a higher level than their PICA scores indicated. This was seen as "positive bias on the part of the spouse" (p. 241). Perhaps another interpretation is that spouses know something about the patients that aphasia tests do not. Holland's recent study (1982) is a giant step in the direction of finding out what families may have known all along, that is, that aphasic individuals often have a good level of functional communication.

Holland's patients employed a rich variety of compensatory strategies, many of them nonverbal. Unfortunately, many speech/language pathologists regard successful verbalization as the only indication of a successful rehabilitation program. Beyond reactions to being called "the speech teacher," many of us have probably never been overly concerned with our professional titles. If one becomes what one calls oneself, however, perhaps aphasia therapists should start calling themselves "communication specialists." Were that to happen, it might drive aphasia rehabilitation beyond the walls of the therapy room where only certain restricted types of communication take place.

At a 1981 aphasia conference in Rotterdam we described a treatment program that trains patients to produce representational gestures (Helm-Estabrooks, Fitzpatrick, and Barresi, 1982). During that course Voinescu, a clinician from Bucharest, asked how well visual action therapy generalized to everyday life. While we had good post-VAT gains on standardized aphasia tests, we did not have hard evidence regarding the generalization of gesturing to more functional situations. Voinescu knows about the functional communication skills of his aphasic patients because, although he works in a clinic, he takes his patients to cafés and shops as part of their therapy.

Many of us trained in the United States, unfortunately, have been taught to maintain such distance from our patients that we do not get close enough to see them as whole human beings. Not too long ago I made an exception to the "rules of distance" and accepted a luncheon invitation from an inpatient. He had had a "successful" course of therapy and was about to go home to another state. Among the words he had regained during therapy was "coffee." After we had finished our entreé the waitress approached us but failed to ask the key question to elicit this high probability word. Instead of asking (as I had in therapy) "What would you like to drink?" she said, "Would you like coffee?" My patient didn't say "yes" and he didn't say "no." Instead he went into a prolonged word-finding struggle while I squirmed. After a full two minutes of agony, he finally blurted out "Sanka." I was ashamed to realize I never knew he drank only Sanka. Instead I had simply assumed that what I saw in his cup during meals on the ward was regular coffee.

Once again, we are not suggesting that formal therapies be replaced by socialization. The challenge, instead, is to combine structured methods, administered in formal treatment rooms, with functional approaches carried out in the patient's natural setting, whether that be a hospital ward, a rehabilitation center, a nursing home, a private home, or a job site. While we cannot be with our aphasic patients in each of these environments, we can teach them and those around them that each successful communicative exchange is a therapeutic victory, no matter what form it takes or where it takes place.

## REFERENCES

Albert M, Goodglass HJ, Helm NJ, Rubens AD, Alexander M: *Clinical Aspects of Dysphasia*. New York, Wein: Springer-Verlag, 1981

Albert ML, Sparks RW, Helm NA: Melodic intonation therapy for aphasia. *Arch Neurol* 29: 130–131, 1973

Amos ML: Speech rehabilitation for veterans. Quart J Speech 34:76–79, 1948.

Anderson JP. Rehabilitation of the patient with completed stroke. In *Cerebrovascular Survey Report for Joint Council Subcommittee on Cerebrovascular Disease*. National Institute of Neurological and Communication Disorders and Stroke, January 1980

Basso A, Capitani E, Vignolo L: Influence of rehabilitation on language skills in aphasic patients. Arch Neurol 36:190–196, 1979

Benson DF: Psychiatric aspects of aphasia. Brit J Psychiat 123:555–556, 1973

Brookshire R, Nichols L, Krueger K, Redmond K: The clinical interaction analysis system: A system for observational recording of aphasia treatment. J Speech Hear Dis 43:437–446, 1978

Brust JC, Shafer SO, Richter RW, Bruum B: Aphasia in acute stroke. Stroke 7:2, 1976

Chapey R, Chwat S, Gurland G, Pieras G: Perspectives in private practices: A nationwide survey. AHSA 23:335–342, 1981

Chester SL, Egoff DF: Non-verbal communication and aphasia therapy, Rehab Lit 8:231–233, 1974

Franz SI: The reeducation of an aphasic. J Philo Psychol Sci Methods 2:23, 589–597, 1906

Goodkin R: A procedure for training spouses to improve functional speech of aphasic patients. Proceedings of the 77th Annual Convention of the APA, 1969, pp 765–766.

Greenberg S: Speech therapy for the severely impaired homebound aphasic patient. Abstract Summary of Doctoral Dissertation, University of Pittsburgh, 1970

Hatfield FM, Zangwill OL: Occupational resettlement in aphasia. Scand J Rehab Med 7:57–60, 1975

Helm NA: Acquired aphasia: Implications for vocation. Paper presented at Workshop of National Scope: Stroke Rehabilitation for Rehabilitation Counselors. Sponsored by Hofstra University and U.S. Department of Education, Long Island, May 1980

Helm-Estabrooks N: *Helm Elicited Language Program for Syntax Stimulation*. Austin: Exceptional Resources, 1981

Helm-Estabrooks N, Chiavaras J: Management of aphasia stroke patients. In Shanks (ed): *Management of Patients with Communicative Disorders*. San Diego: College Hill Press, in press

Helm-Estabrooks N, Fitzpartick P, Barresi B: Visual action therapy for global aphasia. J Speech Hear Dis 47:4, 1982

Helmick JW, Watamari TS, Palmer JM: Spouses' understanding of the communication disabilities of aphasic patients. J Speech Hear Dis 41:238–243, 1976

Hester EJ: The status of speech-language pathology in the home health setting. ASHA 23:155–162, 1981

Holland AL: *Communicative Activities in Daily Living, A Manual*. Baltimore: University Park Press, 1980

Holland AL: Observing functional communication of aphasic adults. J Speech Hear Dis 47:50–56, 1982

Kertesz A, McCabe P. Recovery patterns and prognosis in aphasia. Brain 100:1–18, 1977

Lubinski R: Speech, language and auditory programs in home health care agencies and nursing homes. In Beasley DT, Davis A (eds): *Aging Communication Processes and Disorders*. San Diego: College Hill Press, 1981

Mills CM: Treatment of aphasia by training. JAMA 43:1940–1949, 1904

Naeser MA, Hayward KW: Lesion localization in aphasia with cranial computed tomography and the Boston Diagnostic Aphasia Exam. Neurology 28:545–551, 1978

Obler L, Albert M, Caplan L, Mohr J, Geer D: Stroke type, aphasia type, sex differences and aging. Paper presented at the Academy of Aphasia, Bass River, Massachusetts, October 1980

St. Luke's Hospital Stroke Program: *A Practical Approach to Care of the Acute Stroke Patient in a Community Hospital Setting*. Mortality and Morbidity Data, New Bedford, Massachusetts, 1979

Sands E, Sullivan R. Early initiation of speech therapy and recovery from aphasia. Paper presented at the ASHA Convention, Chicago, 1977

Sarno MT: *The Functional Communication Profile, Manual of Directions*. New York Institute of Rehabilitation Medicine, New York University Medical Center, 1969

Sheehan VM: Rehabilitation of aphasics in any army hospital. J Speech Hear Dis 11:149–157, 1949

Vaughn G: Remote machine-assisted treatment and evaluation. VA Grant, 1979–1982

Weisenberg JS, McBride K: *Aphasia: A Clinical and Psychological Study*. New York: The Commonwealth Fund, 1935

# 14

## LANGUAGE INTERVENTION IN THE MULTIPLE CONTEXTS OF THE PUBLIC SCHOOL SETTING

*KATHLEEN LYNGAAS*
*BARBARA NYBERG*
*ROBERT HOEKENGA*
*LEE J. GRUENEWALD*

Camelot is a legendary kingdom. It is the best of all possible worlds; it is the ideal for which we strive. Although residents of other kingdoms may have viewed life in Camelot as ideal, Arthur and Guinevere were fully aware of problems that roiled beneath the surface—such problems as defense spending, the legal boundaries of the kingdom and personality clashes among the knights.

So, too, in the small piece of the world known as Madison Metropolitan School District, the setting for this discussion. Located in the south central portion of the state, Madison, with a population of approximately 170,000 persons, is the home of the University of Wisconsin and is the state capital. It has been described as "among the twelve most beautiful cities in America, the good life in America . . . . the ideal city."

This chapter focuses on the "ideal program" toward which we strive—our personal version of Camelot. It also deals with the reality of what we are doing, given constraints of budget, reductions in staff, and unresolved issues that the staff and administration are committed to resolving. Although we may not have achieved Camelot yet, our educational decisions are based on:

1. broad philosophic constructs about education;

2. an administrative structure that not only permits information to permeate from the top down to language clinicians in the field, but also functions as a vehicle to permit information from the field to reach top administration;

3. the premise that assessment and programming are ongoing and interrelated;

4. an integrated educational program with options for all students; and

5. the belief that communicative competency is one of the goals of the entire educational system.

From these district-wide and broadly based beliefs, it is then possible to generate more specific beliefs regarding language intervention to design a service delivery model and to implement language programming based on individual student needs. The speech and language clinician who works in an educational setting must design assessment and intervention strategies based on sound educational principles directly related to the student's functioning in the contexts of the school setting. It is our hope that this chapter will assist you in exploring the relevant issues related to language assessment/programming in the public school setting.

## SCHOOL DISTRICT'S PHILOSOPHY OF AN INTEGRATED PROGRAM AND ASSESSMENT OF STUDENTS

The education of all children in a public school setting is the underlying philosophic principle from which programs and services are developed and implemented. This principle becomes a reality through the continuous development of one instructional program with options for all students. It is the responsibility of educators to accept the challenge of developing and implementing educational programs and support services that will provide the opportunity for all students to interact and communicate with one another in an integrated heterogeneous environment.

There are several major themes to be considered in developing effective integrated education.

1. A comprehensive and flexible range of service options that will provide appropriate educational services to the full spectrum of students. The spectrum encompasses all students with a variety of learning styles and abilities.

2. Systems of support to the regular educator designed to help teach and manage students with a wide range of individual differences, thereby preventing undue labeling and segregation of students

3. Close working relationships with the community and its agencies to prepare the community to receive and understand persons with varying abilities

4. Close working relationships with parents of students to ensure that appropriate and meaningful interventions are provided to the student and his family

5. Evaluation mechanisms for describing and measuring positive student changes as the primary intended outcome of all programs and services

The themes for the development of an integrated instructional program are translated into practice through the following (Gruenewald and Schroeder, 1979):

1. Strong support by the local Board of Education. The Board of Education must view itself as having responsibility for the education of all children, including provision of necessary support services to meet the students' needs within a heterogeneous educational environment.

2. Strong support from the regular education programs and recognition of the indirect and direct benefits to regular education students

3. Strong support from parents for mandates to include all children in the educational program

4. The exploding knowledge base and technology in education, medicine, and social sciences which provides solutions to the educational needs of handicapped students

5. Excellent instructional leadership in meeting the needs of students in terms of the best match of their learning style to a program style, rather than segregation through labeling

6. Excellent leadership in administrative personnel in both special education and regular education.

The degree of integration of handicapped students depends heavily upon the availability at the school of a variety of support services. It is the implementation of the concept of integrated programs and support services which makes it feasible for many handicapped students to attend regular schools and participate meaningfully in normal heterogeneous environments. In Wisconsin, speech and language is designated as an exceptional education program, as are other categorical programs. This classification imposes certain constraints and necessitates that the speech and language clinician adopt many roles, which will be described later in this chapter. The cooperative working relationships that must be developed and maintained are a natural extension of implementing an interdisciplinary team assessment/programming model.

## ASSESSMENT

An underlying strength of any public school integrated instructional program is its beliefs about assessment in identifying individual educational needs of students. *The function of assessment is to aid in instructional decision-making, and it must be based on the knowledge of the interaction between the educational needs of the individual and the educational expectations of the program.* Assessment must be an ongoing process of asking and answering the question "How does a student learn?" and "Under what conditions does the student learn best?"

Tull (1981) believes that the assessment process is an "ongoing integral part of the instructional program and that it must look equally at student learning, program evaluation and teacher effectiveness in educational/environmental expectations. Assessment must be for the purpose of increasing student learning" (p. 124).

It is crucial that an interdisciplinary team of professionals be involved in the assessment and program planning. This team approach is a departure from the time when a specialist most often unilaterally determined the identification and placement of a student. Particular expertise in the area of the individual discipline must be recognized; however, the compartmentalizing of services must be avoided. The team must be able to pool their resources based on actual, not perceived, competencies of team members so that the needs of the student can be met more effectively and efficiently. The assessment/programming process should allow for ongoing interaction among team members (ASHA, 1982). The Madison Metropolitan School District is philosophically committed to a building-based assessment/programming team. Some school districts employ diagnostic teams; however, it is our belief that one cannot separate assessment from programming. Therefore, the same team members continue to interact beyond the initial assessment.

Assessment cannot be done in a vacuum. Making decisions about a student's future demands the gathering of information about the student's functioning in multiple environments, such as home, community, classroom, and other aspects of the school environment.

Strategies to gather this information may include observation, interview, formal and informal testing, as well as diagnostic teaching strategies within instructional and social contexts. The information gathered must be analyzed, synthesized, and interpreted to develop hypotheses that will lead to further questions and intervention strategies. Within this process, the student's communicative and cognitive behaviors must be assessed in meaningful and relevant situations leading to programming that is functional for the student in his particular situation.

## SPEECH AND LANGUAGE PROGRAM POSITION

The program position of speech and language clinicians must be congruent with the broad philosophic construct of a district's beliefs concerning an integrated instructional program and assessment of student's individual educational needs. Speech and language clinicians should be committed to an educational model concerned with the "total individual" rather than clinical aspects of speech and language development alone. Language comprehension and production are the foundation for later success in academic achievement. Longitudinal research has demonstrated the relationship between early language competency and academic success as well as the relationship between oral and written language (ASHA, 1982; Loban, 1976). For this reason, early intervention for language impaired students with normal intellectual abilities should be provided.

The development of language and cognitive skills must be the province of all staff within the educational environment. The development of communicative competency to the best of their ability is a goal for all students in the educational system.

The speech and language clinician is a member of the assessment/programming team that works to achieve that goal. Language is more than a powerful tool for communication—it is an essential tool for reasoning and all learning.

Language is also more than a communication code system. The content (semantics) and function (pragmatics) aspects of communication are as important as structure (morphology, syntax). Of equal concern is the way in which the communication message is received, understood, and used (comprehension, processing). The acquisition of both language and speech is a developmental process. It normally proceeds from comprehension to production, from simple object naming to abstract problem-solving.

Precursors to oral language have been identified in the language acquisition literature (Kahn, 1975; Prutting, 1979). They include object permanency, means/end relationships, symbolic representation, and motor and vocal imitation. Structured activities to facilitate the development of these precursors must be included in the student's daily classroom activities. In order for language to be used meaningfully, it must become functional.

It is our belief that cognitive abilities cannot be directly taught, but structured experiences can be provided which will aid in concept development and generalization of concepts to new situations. The development of language and cognition are intertwined. Although there can be cognition without language, communication is limited without cognition (Inhelder and Piaget, 1964; Bloom, 1973; Bruner, 1975). In this sense, an individual's language system reflects his level of cognitive functioning. There are three possible interrelationships between language and cognitive functioning.

First, as a general rule students will acquire language behavior commensurate with, but not in excess of, their cognitive abilities (Miller, 1978).

Thus if a student's language ability and cognitive ability are approximately equal, even if they are below his chronologic age, that student does not exhibit a significant delay or disorder in language. The development of communicative competence as described by Gruenewald, Schroeder, and Yoder (1982) continues to be a program objective for those students just as it is a program objective for all students in our educational system. The speech and language clinician is a member of the assessment/programming team whose goal is the development of communicative competence.

A second possibility is that the student's language system appears to be better than his cognitive performance would warrant. It can be hypothesized that "a strong auditory modality resulting in good language production skills is coupled with weaker cognitive development" (Kellman, Flood, Yoder, 1977). This hypothesis seems substantiated by observations of a better social than academic use of language and specific difficulties academically in the general areas of comprehension and verbal reasoning. The language deficit is usually not apparent when the student is talking with peers or adults in social settings.

A third possibility is that the student's language performance will fall below his cognitive performance. This suggests there is a developmental delay or disorder in language. The degree of language delay or disorder is determined by the gap between cognitive level and level of language achievement in either comprehension or production.

The speech and language clinician provides direct programming when a student demonstrates a significant disorder or delay in the acquisition of speech and/or language skills in relationship to his cognitive skill acquisition. This may include students who are unable to use an oral communication system.

Consultation with parents and teachers is necessary to determine the match/mismatch among curricular expectations, teaching style, and response modes in the environments in which a student is expected to function.

There are multiply handicapped students who may never achieve symbolic function or for whom, because of their age, it is impractical to delay teaching communication strategies. In these instances, the assessment/programming team may decide to teach communication strategies that enable the student to function in his everyday environments. It is important that parents and teachers recognize that these communication strategies will most likely remain situation-specific. They should not be interpreted as ensuring readiness for a more generalized language system. The speech and language clinician, as a member of the assessment/programming team, helps to determine when, what, and how to teach these communication skills. The primary responsibility for teaching the vocabulary and developing communicative competence for these multiply handicapped severely retarded students rests with the classroom teacher for the following reasons: (1) there is no significant discrepancy between the student's language and cognitive performance; (2) these students need to be taught in the most functional way possible in view of their difficulty generalizing across environments; (3) the environmental approach ensures longitudinal programming.

Likewise, many severely retarded and/or multiply handicapped students may never develop oral communication because of cognitive or physical disabilities or both. The decision to initiate an augmented communication system is made by the assessment–programming team, of which the speech and language clinician is a member. Primary responsibility for developing communicative competency with an augmented communication system, once it is designed and implemented, is shared by the interdisciplinary team but ultimately rests with the student's classroom teacher. The primary educational need for these students is to develop a communication system; the focus of instruction must be on teaching functional communication skills.

Based on our clinical experience, there is an optimum time for learning specific language skills. This optimum intervention time is less related to a student's chronologic age than to his position in the cognitive continuum (Prutting, 1979). Recent research in psycholinguistics and neuropsychology suggests that there may be physiologic as well as cognitive reasons for optimum intervention times (Epstein, 1978; Arlin, 1975). Students who exhibit a severe primary disability in speech and language should receive programming in self-contained integrated classrooms staffed by teams of speech and language clinicians in conjunction with other appropriate regular or exceptional education staff. Differentiated staffing patterns are necessary to ensure quality speech and language programming for specific communicatively handicapped populations within the school district. Given the wide range of motor, sensory, and cognitive handicaps, coupled with the wide age range (0–21), it is unlikely that all clinicians would have equal expertise and interest in all areas.

The next section describes some of the roles adopted by speech and language clinicians within the individual school setting. The roles may vary, depending on the needs of the school population; however, the previously discussed philosophy always permeates program implementation whether the clinician is working with language disordered students in regular or special education.

## ROLE IN INTEGRATED PROGRAMMING

The speech and language clinician and the classroom teacher are members of the assessment/programming team responsible for the development and implementation of the individual education plan of the language disordered student. Additional support staff become part of that assessment/programming team when the student's needs warrant their intervention. In the context of the assessment/programming team, the speech and language clinician provides information about normal language acquisition and cognitive development and also analyzes the individual student's language system, in terms of both comprehension and production. The team examines curriculum materials, the language of instruction, and the cognitive prerequisites of the task. This analysis of teacher language, student language, and concepts involved in the instructional task enables the team to determine if there is a match/mismatch between the student's language system and the task expectations (Pollak and Gruenewald, 1978). In the case of a mismatch, the team determines how to modify either the teacher expectations, the language of instruction, or the materials in order for the student to achieve success.

At the same time, the clinician provides direct remediation of the student's language disability either in the context of the classroom and the ongoing instruction or in specially scheduled practice times that utilize classroom content and materials. Language intervention cannot be done in a vacuum; the materials used must be functional for the student and must relate to learning expectations in his broader environment. The only way for the clinician to be aware of this curricular content is to spend time in the classroom. It is also the only way to ensure generalization of specific language skills to everyday use. Team teaching situations provide opportunities for capitalization of "teachable moments" and for bridging from direct intervention experiences to everyday function.

The clinician's presence in the classroom also provides opportunities to analyze the student's use of language in peer interactions, which may differ significantly from his use of language in an academic context.

A review of research (Loban, 1976) has demonstrated that children with an intact language system develop better reading, writing, and speaking skills earlier than children with delayed/disordered language skills. The student with delayed/disordered language does not ever achieve the same level of success in language arts (Loban, 1976). Our clinical experience has demonstrated that the language disordered student is less and less able to achieve as the demands of the curriculum become more complex and abstract. Indeed, research suggests that language disordered students don't necessarily "catch up;" rather, they continue to have communication problems throughout adolescence and adulthood. Follow-up studies document continued

difficulty in syntactic, pragmatic, and other oral and written aspects of language (ASHA, 1982).

It is our belief that optimum times for learning language occur and that these times or stages must be capitalized on for maximum success (Loban, 1976; Epstein, 1978). Learning occurs most effectively when the student has reached a psychosocial, cognitive, and physical state of readiness to learn. This stage of readiness is not effectively predicted by the student's chronologic age, and most efforts directed toward instruction prior to his achieving cognitive readiness are lost.

The frequency of direct involvement of the language clinician depends upon the severity of the language disability of the students in the classroom. For some students the language disorder is the primary disability and early intervention must be provided in a self-contained integrated classroom staffed by a speech and language clinician functioning as a full-time teacher.

Other students exhibit a less serious disorder in language or may have another handicapping condition that is the primary factor preventing effective learning. For these students the clinician acts as a member of the programming team, providing both consultation to the classroom teacher and direct programming for the student on a resource basis as needed.

There is still another group of students who have no significant disability or handicapping condition in language. They may have received direct speech and language programming in the recent past, or the classroom teacher may wish the support of the speech and language clinician in task analysis of curriculum and the student's language or cognitive system. In these instances, the speech and language clinician acts as a consultant in the context of the assessment/programming team, providing information and support as needed but not on an ongoing or direct basis.

**Unresolved Issue.** Speech and language clinicians are subject to the constraints inherent in interdisciplinary programming. Perhaps the greatest obstacle of all is the need to evolve efficient interdisciplinary collaboration. Both special education and regular education teachers, while believing in a team approach, find it difficult to accept this in practice. The concepts articulated in legislation that calls for the intergration of the individual professional's objectives in various disciplines into an individualized education plan are yet to be fully realized.

## ROLE IN ASSESSMENT

Assessment is an ongoing process. It is based on the task analyses and modifications which occur in the context of programming and ultimately describe the student as a learner. In this context, the assessment/programming team members continually modify program objectives as more information becomes known about the student's needs and learning style. In other instances, teachers may become concerned about a student's academic achievement, or another area of development, and may wish to involve other professionals in a more careful assessment of a student.

## BUILDING TEAM

In Madison, every elementary, middle, and high school has an interdisciplinary team known as the building team, to which referrals are made. The building-based speech and language clinician is a member of this team, as are the school principal, psychologist, social worker, and other regular or special education teachers who work with any given student. Individual buildings further expand their building team resources by tapping the school nurse, occupational and physical therapy staff, audiology services staff, parents, student advocates, and others, depending upon the needs of the student under discussion. The building team acts as a problem-solving body to deal with individual student needs, or groups of students' needs, in any area of development. Students are referred to the building team by parents, teachers, and other school personnel as well as by outside agencies. The assessment function of the building team is

limited to screening. observations, interviews, and intervention designed by other professionals but carried out by the classroom teacher. It is important that the speech and language clinician be involved in the initial referral level of assessment. Regular classroom teachers, parents, and other specialists are not always aware of the importance of language skills to successful learning. Some academic problems are manifestations of language problems. In many instances, suggestions for modifications of classroom management, environment, or curriculum are sufficient to enable the student to function productively within his regular education classroom without further support.

## INTERDISCIPLINARY TEAM

In other instances, a disability area is suspected, a need for further assessment is determined, and a referral to special education is made. At this point an interdisciplinary team is formed, composed of a trained professional in each area of suspected disability. The speech and language clinician becomes a member of the interdisciplinary team only when speech and/or language is a suspected disability and handicapping condition. The building team's assessment activities will have generated questions that help to focus the assessment of the speech and language clinician as well as other members of the assessment team.

The speech and language clinician provides information about the students' language system and synthesizes that language information with language information from other disciplines. This information must be gathered from the students' functional use of language in academic and social settings as well as formal and informal assessment procedures obtained in one-to-one settings. The outcome of this assessment is a description of the student as a learner, documentation of eligibility for categorical program placement, and understanding of how the student's language system will impede or facilitate learning. For children whose handicapping condition involves a communicative disorder, the speech and language clinician must be a participant in the development and review of individual education programs. This begins the assessment/programming cycle all over again.

**Unresolved Issue.** The building-based speech and language clinician is often used both as a member of the building team and as a member of the inter-disciplinary assessment/programming team to sort out language/communication factors from other factors inhibiting academic success. Thus the speech and language clinician is involved in many more student-based assessments and program decisions at both the building level and the interdisciplinary team formal level than either teachers of other exceptional education programs or support service personnel. This is more than a time management problem; it reflects the quandary of speech and language clinicians being regarded as both a building resource and as teachers in an exceptional education program.

## ROLE IN ADMINISTRATION

In Madison, the Department of Specialized Educational Services consists of a Director and several Coordinators of categorical programs. Each coordinator is responsible for the administration and evaluation of the program(s) assigned, as well as direct supervision of the staff assigned to the categorical program(s). Figure 14–1 depicts the interactive relationships between administration and staff. In order to realize the goals of an integrated program, information must flow from the "top down" as well as from the "bottom up." This vehicle of information exchange underlies the principles of shared decision-making.

In addition, each coordinator has appointed several Program Support Teachers whose duties are delineated in Wisconsin State Statutes (1978), Chapter 115. The coordinator of the Speech and Language Program and the Speech and Language Program Support Teachers constitute the management team. There are presently

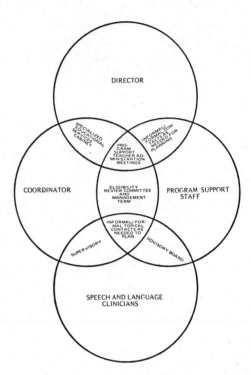

Figure 14–1. Administrative Structure and Relationships.

two PSTs assigned to the Speech and Language Program in Madison.

The purpose of the PST is to assist the special education administrative and instructional personnel in the development and implementation of the program. The program support teacher provides consulting services to the regular education teacher for those children with exceptional education needs enrolled in regular education classrooms. The program support teacher(s) are responsible to the director or program supervisor, or both.

The primary responsibility of the program support teacher focuses upon services to children with exceptional education needs and to special education and regular education teachers in the areas of assessment and intervention strategies, classroom management, curriculum development, instructional methods, educational assessment, and modification of instructional materials and equipment.

Another administrative vehicle used by management teams in special education is the Eligibility Review Committee (ERC). The ERC includes the coordinator of the program and the program support teachers; its purpose is to review the findings of the interdisciplinary teams when language is the student's documented area of disability. The ERC applies categorical program criteria to establish eligibility of the student for program placement. It may also make programming suggestions to the team. If the ERC does not agree with the findings of the interdisciplinary team, it may request clarification, additional information, or the elimination of discrepancies in assessment information. In addition, the Speech and Language Program Support Teachers serve as consultants to the Eligibility Review Committees of other categorical programs, such as Learning Disabilities, Hearing Impaired, Mental Retardation, and Early Childhood.

The Speech and Language Program also uses an advisory board to act as liaison between the clinicians and the administration. Its membership is composed of the PSTs and a representative cross-section of practicing clinicians, that is, representatives from early childhood through high school settings, resource programs and self-contained classes, experienced clinicians as well as newly hired ones.

**Unresolved Issues.** First, although the program support professionals' primary responsibility is to act as support/advocate for other teachers and individual students, they are often viewed by their peers as supervisory personnel. When this occurs, the effectiveness of program support teachers is severely reduced; they cannot supervise or make administrative decisions by their role definition and they are not able to solve problems effectively at a student level when they are viewed as administrators.

Second, the role of the program support teacher is broadly defined by state statute. Further definition is provided by individual coordinators and the director of special education. Therefore, role expectations for program support teachers across categorical programs varies considerably.

The expectations of building administrators frequently differ from the coordinator's expectation of the program support teacher. Since the role itself is a relatively new special education phenomenon, time and experience may help to resolve the problems.

## ROLE IN IN-SERVICE TRAINING

Continuing professional growth and development are necessary in the well-rounded educational program. Staff development may be fostered through both external and internal sources.

Madison is in a unique position because of its proximity to the University of Wisconsin, Department of Communicative Disorders. Madison clinicians are able to participate in University course offerings and research projects and can serve as cooperating teachers in the University's teacher training program. Also, the University faculty frequently participate in in-service programs for the school district.

Another unique component of Madison's staff development is the Teacher's Exchange. This is a resource center where teachers with a particular area of interest or expertise offer courses for continuing education credits to other teachers and support staff in the school district. These courses may be offered during the summer or after school hours. Language clinicians frequently enroll in those courses involving academic curricula. At other times, the instructor may be a language clinician. Recent course offerings include language sample analysis, the use of barrier games to teach specific syntactical patterns or content vocabulary, the development of language and cognitive skills, and modifications of the High/Scope philosophy with language disordered students (Weikaert 1971).

An in-service calendar is developed by the management team for continuing education of the speech and language staff. This usually occurs one-half day per month. The workshop topics are frequently generated by the staff. Speakers may include faculty from the University, representatives from outside agencies, the program support staff or other language clinicians who wish to share a specific area of expertise with their colleagues.

From time to time, task forces are established by the coordinator of the Speech and Language Program to practice problem-solving around specific issues. These groups usually meet for discussion, do research, generate a product, disseminate their information to the groups of professionals, and disband when task is completed. Recent task forces have generated position papers concerning the service delivery and philosophy of Speech and Language Program, report writing, and the role of the speech and language clinician in programming for students using non-standard English dialect. Projects have also included the development of cognitive assessment tasks, prelinguistic assessment, and materials to be used for high school programming.

All language clinicians are responsible for sharing information regarding normal language acquisition with the parents and teachers with whom they work. In addition, they provide consultation services to teachers and parents regarding modifications to be made in communication expectations in the environment. This usually is done with reference to specific language-disordered students.

**Unresolved Issue.** Administrators often view speech and language clinicians as a resource for delivering new instructional strategies to the teaching staff. The time required for sharing their clinical expertise with staff and for planning is not always recognized. In an era of budget reductions, administrators frequently reduce allocations because language therapists do not teach curriculum content ("reading and math").

As the range of students in any given school broadens, and in keeping with the district philosophy of building-based teams and decentralized programming for handicapped students, it becomes more important that quality in-service continue to be available. Quality programming must transcend fiscal constraints.

## SERVICE DELIVERY

The service delivery plan is based on the district's philosophic constructs of integrated programming, ongoing assessment, and the concepts inherent in the speech and language philosophy. There are two components of the Speech and Language Program: direct therapy and consultation.

**Direct Therapy.** Although rules and regulations vary among states, direct therapy is defined by the Wisconsin Department of Public Instruction Rules and Regulations (Chapter 115, 1978). An interdisciplinary team may recommend direct speech/language intervention when it determines that a student exhibits a disability in learning, a handicapping condition in speech and language. Following a multidisciplinary team evaluation and prior to enrollment, diagnostic data and recommendations are submitted to the Speech and Language Eligibility Review Committee. It is the responsibility of the professionally trained speech and language clinician, as a member of the assessment team, to make the decision that the delay or disorder has a significant influence on the student's academic, social, and/or emotional growth.

Three levels of direct intervention are available: (1) resource; (2) consultation with resource; and (3) self-contained integrated.

In resource programming, the speech and language clinician works with the student on a regular basis for remediation of identified needs. This level of programming is frequently used for speech pathology cases or instances in which other staff responsible for the student's education program do not need to be actively involved in the therapeutic process.

In consultation with resource programming, the student is most often served in the context of his regular or special education classroom. This often takes the form of team planning and teaching. The clinician may also see students individually or in small groups on a regular or intermittent basis. In this way, language is most likely to affect the student's total education program.

Self-contained classrooms are cur-

Table 14–1   ELIGIBILITY FOR DIRECT LANGUAGE PROGRAMMING

| Eligible | Not Eligible |
|---|---|
| 1. Students who demonstrate significant delay or disorder in the comprehension and/or production of oral language occurring in one or more of the following areas: content, structure, or function<br><br>2. Students who demonstrate a mismatch between language development and cognitive development; specifically, when the level of language performance is significantly less than would be expected when compared with cognitive performance | 1. Students who demonstrate a match between achieved cognitive development and achieved language development even though this achievement is less than would be expected considering the student's chronologic age<br><br>2. Students who have not achieved symbolic function<br><br>3. Students whose speech and language problems are the result of the lack of desire to communicate within the school environment rather than the inability to communicate<br><br>4. Students whose speech/language problems are not evident in all environments<br><br>5. Students who are fluent in a language other than English and whose speech and language problems are the result of second language learning.<br><br>6. Students whose speech and language problems reflect different environmental, cultural, or dialectical influences<br><br>7. Students whose speech and language problems are the result of inconsistent curriculum methodology and instructional approaches<br><br>8. Students whose speech and language problems are the result of environmental expectations that are superior to developmental norms |

rently provided only for 5- and 6-year old students whose primary exceptional education needs are speech and language. Both optional classrooms for 5- and 6-year-old students are team taught by classroom teachers with various professional training backgrounds and a speech and language clinician.

All three levels of programming described may provide individual small or large group therapy. The frequency and group size are determined by the professional judgment of the speech and language clinician and are documented in the Individual Education Plan (IEP).

The statements in Table 14–1 are used to determine eligibility for direct language programming (resource, consultation with resource, or self-contained integrated)

Similar criteria (eligible/not eligible statements) have also been delineated for speech pathology cases: articulation disorders, voice disorders, and stuttering.

## CONSULTATION

Students are eligible for consultation when an official referral to the speech and language program has been made and the speech and language clinician has been a member of the assessment team. Specific goals for the consultation and its duration for up to three years are outlined as part of the multidisciplinary team report. *Students eligible for consultation programming do not have a* significant *disability and handicapping condition in speech and language*. However, the curriculum and language of instruction must be modified to match the student's cognitive or language system. In other instances, the student may have been enrolled in direct therapy in the past and needs monitoring or is just beginning to have difficulty and needs monitoring.

Because the Wisconsin Department of Public Instruction currently does not recognize this component of the speech and language program, it is the responsibility of each clinician to support requests for consultation, knowing that direct therapy case load demands have first priority. The speech and language program support teachers will work with each clinician upon request to develop time management strategies that will facilitate access to consultation for students, programs and staff. Time management strategies may include setting priorities with the building team in regard to building needs, block scheduling of time available for consultation, flexible use of available time, and rotation of such services among staff requesting consultation time for their students/programs.

There are several types of consultation.

### Type I: Post-Program Consultation

The intent of the recommendation is to assess and monitor the student's current speech and language performance, to document continued speech and language progress, or to ensure that the student's speech and language needs can continue to be met in his current educational placement. The frequency of contact will not exceed an average of two times per semester.

### Type II: Student Directed Consultation

The intent of the recommendation is to support the individual student's success when his educational program is primarily the responsibility of another special or regular education teacher and when that student's speech and language system *is not significantly delayed or disordered*. This support occurs during instructional programming provided by that regular or special education teacher. The frequency of

contact will not exceed an average of two times per month.

### Type III: Teacher or Program Directed Consultation

The intent of the recommendation for Type III consultation is to aid in modifying the regular or special education program in terms of classroom expectations, task content, presentation style, and so on to more closely match the speech and language needs and learning style of the language disabled student when that student's speech and language system is not significantly delayed or disordered. The frequency of contact may not exceed one to two times per week. This type of consultation is dricted most often to the classroom teacher, although individual students may be discussed. The objectives/strategies modeled by the clinician are carried out in his or her absence.

1. It may be necessary for the clinician to have intermittent direct contact with various students in the context of all levels of consultation to identify changing student needs and determine new strategies.

**Unresolved Issues.** Middle school and high school students have been identified and enrolled in the speech and language program. However, the direct service model used most effectively in elementary schools may not be appropriate at the secondary level. Secondary programs are influenced by the number of teachers involved with each individual student, the changing academic structure of many middle schools, scheduling problems, and the nature of instructional patterns in special education classrooms. This topic needs further exploration by the secondary school clinicians to identify optimum service delivery models and to develop consistency.

2. Another professional concern is appropriate programming for students whose primary handicap is a severe language disorder. The Madison Metropolitan School District currently provides self-contained speech and language classes only for 5- and 6-year-olds. Continued exploration of the possibility of self-contained language program options for older students is needed.

3. The current Wisconsin Depart-

ment of Public Instruction guidelines recommend 15 to 30 students as the mini-
mum-maximum caseload for a full-time
speech and language clinician. Coupled
with the question of numbers of students
served are the questions of number of different schools the students are served in,
the number of program types and levels
(that is, regular education, special education, primary, intermediate, middle,
high), the number of teachers involved, severity of the speech and language disability, and the need for the speech and
language program to link with the student's
total education program. The number and
frequency of joint planning/decision-mak-
ing meetings of staff necessary for program
implementation is a major variable in determining the relative weight of a caseload
(Class list). Numbers alone do not tell the
whole story. The workload is greatly influenced by the frequency of new referrals,
the number of re-evaluations, and the demand for consultation within a given building. With current fiscal status suggesting
further staff reductions, it is becoming
more difficult to meet the needs of students
who are already identified as having problems. Systematic, consistent strategies for
service delivery reductions must be developed in keeping with our philosophy.

4. Most clinicians have an appropriate
background in normal development of cognitive and linguistic skills, but it is presumptuous to assume that all clinicians
have equal familiarity with all aspects of
curriculum demands from preschool to
high school. It is also difficult to be equally
familiar with all methods of augmented
communication systems and the wide
range of developmental disabilities associated with exceptional educational speech
and language needs. This implies a need
for differentiated staffing as well as for continuing staff development to meet professional needs.

5. Historically, the language clinician
has provided both direct and consultative
service to children designated variously as
special needs, Title I, culturally different/
disadvantaged. Owing to legal and fiscal
constraints, this service is no longer readily
available for teachers and students. The
limited time available for consultation services has been consumed by more seriously handicapped students. We have
not yet mastered the art of true consultation; that is, we do not move into a classroom for a brief period and move out, leaving our skills and knowledge behind with
the classroom teacher.

6. Before program evaluation can be
accomplished, data being collected which
accurately describes the many facets of the
speech and language clinician's role must
be analyzed. The use of consistent criteria
for direct therapy and consultation will facilitate this procedure and ensure that the
data are valid.

## SUMMARY

The speech/language program gains
vitality through the professional curiosity,
growth, and commitment of its staff and
administration. Our present perspective is
based on a wide body of research and clinical practice with a diverse language disordered population, accumulated over the
last twenty years.

Language intervention is a vital component of the handicapped student's integrated program. The role of the speech and
language clinician, as a member of the interdisciplinary assessment/programming
team, varies depending upon the needs of
the student.

The role of the interdisciplinary as-
sessment/programming team is crucial to
the development and maintenance of an
effective integrated program.

An integrated program for handicapped students will not be realized unless
there is philosophic congruence between
the professional disciplines and the school
district's educational goals in serving handicapped students.

Research and clinical practice do not
remain static; they are dynamic and ever-
changing processes. Therefore it is important that the speech/language clinician's
role continue to reflect the influence of current research and high standards of professional practice.

Ah, Camelot . . .

# REFERENCES

American Speech Language and Hearing Association: *Position Statement on Language Learning Disorders*. Ad Hoc Committee, Lee Gruenewald, Chairman, ASHA, 1982, in press

Arlin P: Cognitive development in adulthood: A fifth stage? Develop Psych 11: 1975

Bloom L: *One Word at a Time*. The Hague: Mouton & Co, 1973

Bruner JS: From communication to language—a psychological perspective. Cognition 3:255–287 1975

Epstein H: Growth spurts during brain development and implications for educational policy and practice. *Education and the Brain*. Chicago. 77th Yearbook of National Society for Study of Education, 1978

Gruenewald L, Schroeder J: Integration of handicapped students in public schools. Paris: Organization for Economic Cooperation and Development. February 1979

Gruenewald L, Schroeder J, Yoder D: Considerations for curriculum development and implementation. In Campbell B, Baldwin V (eds): *Severely Handicapped Hearing Impaired Students*. Baltimore: Paul H. Brookes Publishing Co, 1982

Inhelder B, Piaget J: *The Early Growth of Logic in the Child*. New York: WW Norton and Co, 1964

Kahn J: Relationship of Piaget's sensorimotor period to language acquisition of profoundly retarded kids. Am J Ment Defic 79(6):640–643, 1975

Kellman M, Flood C, Yoder D: Language Assessment Tasks, September 1977

Loban W: *Language Development*. No 18, National Council of Teachers of English, Urbana, Illinois, 1976

Miller J: Identifying language disabilities in the retarded child. 7(4):27–44, 1978

Nyberg B, Alexander M: Piaget language: Analyze new territory. Madison Metropolitan School District, 1977

Pollak S, Gruenewald L: Assessment of language interaction in academic tasks: A process. University of Wisconsin-Madison: Midwest IGE Services, 1978

Prutting C, Process: The action of moving forward progressively from one point to another on the way to completion. JSHD XLIV: 3–30, 1979

Rules Implementing Subchapter IV of Chapter 115, Wisconsin Statutes, Wisconsin Department of Public Instruction, 1978

Tull D: Assessment of learning disabilities. Sem Speech, Lang Hear 2(2): May, 1981

Weikart R, Adcock McC: *The Cognitively Oriented Curriculum*. Publications Department, National Association for the Education of Young Children, Washington, DC: 1971

# DISCUSSION: PART VI: INTERVENTION CONTEXT AND SETTING: WHERE?

*GERALD M. SIEGEL*

I won't attempt to summarize the chapters by Gruenewald and Helm-Estabrooks, nor will I add a third paper to this section. Rather, I will focus on a number of issues these authors have raised, and will pursue them beyond the bounds of their formal presentations.

## LANGUAGE INTERVENTION IN THE SCHOOLS

Lee Gruenewald described the philosophy, structure, and procedures that guide speech and language services for children in the Madison, Wisconsin, Metropolitan School District. It is evident from his discussion that times have changed and that the role of the speech and language specialist has changed. Some of these changes represent new insights into how our profession should operate in the schools. It seems to me that others are responses and accommodations to new mandates that have been thrust upon the profession by external social and legal forces. Since change is neither intrinsically good or bad, it is important that we examine the evolving nature of our professional practice in the schools and try to determine what we should applaud and what .we should possibly view with alarm. We must of course be responsive to the need for change, but we must also be willing to be contentious when, in our professional judgment, the changes do not best serve the children.

The major difference I perceived between traditional practices of clinicians in the schools and those described by Gruenewald is the extent to which the therapist is now functioning as a consultant and a teacher of teachers, rather than in direct contact with children. In the system described by Gruenewald, the clinician is part of an assessment and programming team and is a major source of information about normal language and cognitive acquisition. The clinician also functions in the classroom and acts as a consultant to the classroom teacher on matters ranging from a consideration of the performance of a particular child to the development of curricular materials for the classroom. In addition, the clinician, along with other professionals in the school, is part of a building team that acts as a problem-solving body to deal with individual student needs, or groups of students' needs, in any area of development. The clinician is also involved in growth and development for other professionals and, in general, is involved in a variety of consultative activities, in addition to providing direct therapy for some of the children.

I sense that the model presented by Gruenewald is increasingly coming to represent the role of the speech and language clinician in many school environments. It reminds me of the evolution of my own primary function from a researcher, collecting data and working in the laboratory, to a "research administrator" who counsels students about research design, data analysis, and interpretation of data, with less and less direct exposure to the conduct of the research. I can understand the pressures that have led to these changes. The populations currently served by language and speech therapists are severely handicapped and require lengthy, painstaking work from the therapist. There simply isn't enough time to see each of these children for extensive, direct contact. Classroom teachers do indeed have much more time with the children than clinicians can typically manage, and the classroom is an important environment, one of the significant places where speech and language skills truly matter. Still, it is not obvious to me that the skills our clinicians so laboriously acquire are readily transmitted to classroom teachers or paraprofessionals. The specific, close examination of the child's performance and the variability in that performance must be lost to the clinician who does not have continuous, direct contact with the child. The intensity of the programming becomes muted, I fear, as these levels are interpolated between clinician and child. And, I admit, I am concerned that attention to the group, and to "the whole child," may take precedence over the single child's specific speech and language needs. My concern comes in part out of my own history. It was not so many years ago that therapists in New York were struggling to be freed from the responsibility to perform general "speech improvement" in the classrooms, so that they could get on with the more serious business of therapy. Are we, by embracing these "new" roles, not drifting back to those nebulous sorts of programs?

I frankly do not know the answer to the many problems that emerge from our social and legal responsibility to provide maximum service with minimal resources. The consulting role is one approach. From time to time I have thought that another might be to teach by modeling, by having the clinician work intensively with a small number of children, in a clinic within the school, so that classroom teachers could observe the clinician doing his or her best work with a variety of problems and levels of disorder. The clinician would not pretend to see every child who needs help, but would see children with a variety of problems. There would still be general consultation and education of other school personnel, but the core of the clinician's efforts would be to run a model clinic that others would observe. This model clinic need not be confined to the therapy room. It could demonstrate the combination of individual therapy, group work, and classroom management, but it would demonstrate therapy at its most effective, for at least some children. I am not at all confident such a plan would be feasible—or legal. I am concerned, however, that we not confuse practical realities with ideal goals. If we are forced to change our roles because of legal mandates and excessive demands on our time, we must, of course, cope as well as we can, but we should not be lulled into thinking that we have elected these roles. To do so would dull the force of our advocacy for the children, and for our profession.

In perhaps somewhat the same vein, I was struck with the tiers of bureaucracy in the school system. The clinicians' judgments are passed through so many levels of evaluation and corroboration that I had the sense that the speech and language therapist was not trusted to make his or her own professional judgments without an elaborate system of checks. The assessment and programming team and the building team and the Eligibility Review Committee all confer on the clinician's judgments about the status and needs of a language handicapped child. Gruenewald refers to this as "shared decision making." I admit, I yearn rather nostalgically for the time when the school clinician was regarded as the local expert in language, with responsibility for designing programs for children, who would, when it was deemed necessary, seek out the advice and counsel of other professionals. Again, the ERCs and PSTs and Building and Assessment Teams all seem to stand between the clinician and the child. I can recall urging school clinicians in the past to visit classrooms, to talk with school administrators, to consult with teachers, *as necessary*. By mandating so many levels of formal interaction, I fear the clinician has been forced to sacrifice professional independence.

I have two further comments about the intervention environment described by Gruenewald. First, I am frankly envious of the close relationship between the schools and the University programs. It is clear that the needs of the Madison schools influence the academic programs at the University of Wisconsin, and that practices in the schools bear the imprint of research and theorizing emanating from the University. There is collaboration in program development in both environments, and shared participation in research and data gathering.

My second point does not apply particularly to the Madison schools, but it was raised in Gruenewald's chapter and should be examined for its broad implications. Gruenewald defined language delay or disorder in a way that juxtaposes language and cognition. He stated that if a student's language ability and his cognitive ability are approximately equal, even if they are below his chronologic age, that student does not exhibit a significant delay or disorder in language. There are similar statements in the literature. This view of language disorders suggests that a developmentally retarded child of 8, whose tested cognitive and language skills are at, say, the 4-year age level, would not be regarded as having a language deficit because language and cognition are commensurate. One implication of this definition is that the child would be defined as outside the framework of language therapy, and that strikes me as unfortunate, though other school resources might be available for such a child. I frankly cannot imagine thinking of an 8-year-old

who has a 4-year gap in language skills as not having a language problem, regardless of his other abilities.

The insistence that language is disordered or delayed only when it is significantly below the child's cognitive level is based on a questionable view of the relationship between these two constructs, "language" and "cognition." It is instructive to examine the assumptions that underlie that view. First, it must be assumed that language and cognition are separable and distinct. Second, it is assumed that cognition and language form a natural sequence, with development in cognitive areas preceding those in language. Third, it is assumed that this sequence is causal and that the cognitive accomplishments not only precede language, but are also prerequisites for language acquisition. Finally, the relationship is one-way: Cognition sets the stage for language; language is not regarded as promoting cognition.

I would like to submit that this construction of the relationship between language and cognition is surely not the only possible one, is not a necessary one, and is not a useful view to hold. Language is a construct, devised by theorists. Definitions of language have changed radically over the years, as theories of language have yielded to the influence of behaviorism, mentalism, psycholinguistics, and so on. Similarly, our ideas about the nature of cognition are determined by currently held views about mental processes. These constructs are human inventions. Language and cognition are separable and distinct if we define them in that way, but it makes little sense to me to define language in a way that obscures its use as a powerful cognitive tool. Language is not only a medium for communication. It is also a way of organizing knowledge, of knowing the world, of clarifying differences and relationships.

In practical terms, the way we learn about a child's language and cognitive levels is by administering tests that go under the proper labels. These tests are derivatives of the basic constructs and may themselves be conceptually very far from those constructs. Language tests often have content that overlaps with tests of cognition. It is commonplace that the same test items are sometimes regarded as cognitive, and elsewhere as linguistic, and still elsewhere as perceptual. The decision that a child's "language" and "cognition" are commensurate is based on assessments over performance domains that are very likely overlapping, at least to some degree. It strikes me that this view is very reminiscent of older arguments about the relationship of language and intelligence—arguments that were eventually abandoned because they proved logically unsound.

Even if it is possible to devise procedures that operationally distinguish "language" from "cognition," it does not follow that the two must be related in a one-way causal stream. The relationship is not likely to be so simple. Cognition influences language development, but language, in turn, affects the child's knowledge of the world. When one argues that cognition is a necessary prerequisite for language, does it follow that every specific linguistic structure has a correspondingly unique cognitive underpinning? Is it the level of general cognitive or intellectual status that is at issue, or is it the particular cognitive underpinning? I cannot imagine that we know the precise cognitions that underlie all of the components that comprise language adequacy.

In summary, I would hesitate to espouse a definition of language disorder that requires a discrepancy between linguistic and cognitive achievement. In the course of describing and assessing a child's linguistic achievement, I can well imagine that attention would be paid to the child's level of cognitive understanding. There is no formula, however, that indicates that in every instance cognition precedes language and must be taught independent of and prior to corresponding language skills. Finally, I can scarcely imagine any significantly retarded child who would not also have a serious language problem, and I would be very cautious about defining language in a way that might exclude such a youngster from consideration as disordered or delayed in language.

## LANGUAGE INTERVENTION FOR ADULTS

From Nancy Helm-Estabrooks' chapter I learned that even with respect to the prospects for aphasia therapy, circumstances often conspire to make it less likely that women will receive therapy than will men, except among older patients. It was arresting to learn what factors, and accidents, determine whether or not a patient will receive needed speech and language services. In this regard, society seems to have organized its resources more appropriately in the case of children, who almost universally become the responsibility of the public schools. As I read Estabrooks' chapter I wondered whether the time might not come when the public schools would take even further initiatives and serve as the resource to help the aged as well as children—a true commitment to life-span service.

Clinicians working with aphasic patients also serve the dual role of therapist and consultant, as was true in the schools described by Gruenewald. Spouses, nurses, and hospital personnel can be recruited early by the aphasia therapist to observe the patient's performance, to respond to the patient in appropriate ways, and to set up situations that will encourage and promote successful communication. For Helm-Estabrooks, the beginnings of aphasia assessment and therapy are in the patient's immediate surroundings. Informal assessment and therapy begin at once, with less constraint, it seemed, than may be encountered in the schools. The important similarity between the school and hospital environments is the role the clinician can play in marshaling the intelligent help of the larger professional community in organizing supportive programs for the patient.

When I worked at the Parsons State Hospital and Training Center for retarded children, I recall my colleague, Joe Spradlin, wryly noting how assiduously most institutions for the retarded placed barriers between the patients and the professional staff. Therapists, administrators, and teachers tend to huddle in special buildings where the children come for appointed instruction and then depart, leaving the professional staff in splendid isolation. I was struck by Helm-Estabrooks' comment that the same is true in many adult treatment units: "As a general rule, the fancier the facility the more likely that the speech-language pathology department will be separate from the patients' living quarters." Helm-Estabrooks' comment that the old-fashioned, integrated rehabilitation unit may become the model for new facilities was strikingly similar to Gruenewald's concern that therapy not be confined to the therapy room in the schools, and that language instruction become the responsibility of the entire educational community.

In her concluding remarks, Helm-Estabrooks reminds us that the arena for language therapy is wherever the patient is to be found, and that for many patients the proper goal is successful communication, however that is accomplished, rather than successful verbalization. She cites Holland's observation that frequently the family of an aphasic individual regards him as less handicapped than would be predicted by formal test scores. The family, it seems, is using a different standard to evaluate the patient. Language, we are reminded, is not communication. There are similar reminders now appearing in the child language literature, and this seems consistent with the increasing emphasis on pragmatics in child language.

I should like to add one caveat. Just as language is not communication, neither is functional communication language. I say this only because there has been a tendency in our profession to find new brooms in profusion, and to attempt to sweep away old knowledge in our enthusiasm for the new. For some children and adults, functional communication may be a high goal indeed. For others, it should be a step on the way to more adequate language. Nor, it seems to me, is communication disorder fully contained within pragmatics. Voice disorders, fluency failure, peculiarities of expressive style, as well as old fashioned misarticulations are not neatly folded into a formal pragmatic system. Successful communication involves more than the transmission of information. It involves access to the rich nuances language affords. We have criticized ourselves for looking at language too narrowly in terms of syntax and semantics. We must not make the same error in our rush to pragmatics.

## ADDENDUM

I would like to address one last issue that pertains to an earlier chapter. Terry Wertz described a series of studies that were designed to demonstrate that "therapy works" with aphasics, and I argued, perhaps too vigorously, that there is little value in research of that sort. "Does therapy work?" is the wrong question. I would like to suggest why I believe it to be the wrong question for research. First, I do recognize that there are strong pressures placed on our profession to justify its existence. This is the accountability monster, a good idea gone bad. Some years ago similar pressures were placed on ASHA to justify the expenditure of funds to support therapy for children in the schools. I was one of a group of persons who were called together to design a study that would finally convince legislators that our profession produces results. We began seriously, and naively, to design a master study, to be supported by the association, to make our case. Ultimately, nothing happened. As the study began to take shape, it collapsed because of its sheer impracticality. I am now even more convinced that that was the wrong kind of question to put to a research test.

I obviously don't mean that we shouldn't do research about therapy. The research must be designed, however, so that we can learn something that is potentially useful. Research that is designed to placate cynical critics has little chance of generating much that will be useful. When we started planning that earlier study to demonstrate the utility of articulation therapy, we began using familiar experimental models. There would be an experimental group and a control group. The control group would be untreated (an ethical problem) and the experimental group would be given the therapy. The groups would be equated at first and would be tested, perhaps on several occasions, during and after some period of therapy. A familiar experimental design. But then the questions surfaced. Which children? And which therapy? For how long? How was progress to be measured? Where would the children be located? On which dimensions in addition to therapy would the control and experimental groups be matched? What would be done to ensure that parents or teachers would not interfere with the study by providing instruction to the control group? It soon became evident that by the time we had controlled or accounted for relevant variables, it would be impossible to design a satisfactory experiment that would demonstrate in any convincing way that "therapy works."

I start with the assumption that therapy works. I can't imagine an experiment that would convince me otherwise. What I want to learn is which therapy, for which client, delivered by whom, in what schedule, over what period of time, and so forth. I want to ask questions that will teach me about the therapy process, and these turn out to be more modest, though no less complex in form. It is inconceivable to me that we could ever conclude that therapy, in general, doesn't work. It may not work quickly, and the gains may not be great, but the question of how much improvement justifies the enterprise is a social and ethical one, not an empiric one. McLean recalled for us an era in which therapists were actively discouraged from working with retarded children. Such an attitude now seems unthinkable. There is no question that retarded children can be helped, though in that former era the gains were not considered worth the effort. How do we determine the amount of gain that would qualify as an affirmative answer to the question "Does therapy work?" If an aphasic makes no appreciable gains but is prevented from slipping further into social isolation over a period of months or years, has therapy worked? If one method fails to achieve positive results, does that mean that no therapy would work? When gains are minimal isn't it more plausible that the therapy was not appropriate for those particular clients, or was terminated too soon, or that the measures of improvement were imprecise, or that we should have started therapy sooner, or later?

On the other hand, if we design a study that shows therapy works, but no more, we will have learned little that we didn't already know in the bones of our profession. Therapy questions should be framed so as to teach us about the implications of a theory of behavior or the disorder under question, or about the particular therapy approach we are using. It seems to me that we should start with some methods that we have reason to believe, through logical analysis, intuition, and clinical experience, have some probability of success, and then go about testing variations of these methods. At the very least, we should be comparing different methods and trying to match them up with subject variables that may interact with different approaches to therapy. Even better, I think, is to study parametric variations on a particular method. An infinite number of questions can be asked about the therapy process. They should be posed, I think, in a way that will add to the store of knowledge about the disorder in question, test the implications of a model or theory, or provide data about the methods we are using. Demonstration is also important, as is convincing the public of the value of our enterprise, but these should not be confused with research. There is a need to educate the users or consumers about the worth of our endeavors, but I don't think that broad questions that ask whether therapy works are efficient as ways of learning about the therapy enterprise or as a means for educating the public.

# PART VII

# EVALUATING PROGRAM EFFECTIVENESS

# 15

# PROGRAM EVALUATION FOR SPEECH AND HEARING SERVICES

*TERIS K. SCHERY*
*MARK W. LIPSEY*

Program evaluation has become a routine fact of life in many human service settings. Though still a relatively new concept to the speech, language, and hearing professional, it is increasingly being championed as an essential endeavor for them as well (Jones and Healey, 1976; Killen and Myklebust, 1980; Laney, 1982; Rees and colleagues, 1967; Snyder, 1980). The most immediate inducement has been increased requirements for systematic information on client services from external funding sources at the state and federal levels. As costs of therapy services have risen (along with everything else in the economy), federal and state tax revenues have not kept pace amid increasing resistance from taxpayers. This has produced pressure for speech and hearing professionals to justify clinical practice and its effectiveness.

The ASHA national office has laid important groundwork for a widespread program evaluation effort with the successful Professional Standards Review Organization (PSRO) workshops, which responded to practitioners' needs for systematizing service information and establishing "peer reviewed" standards for hospital and clinic programs. The Child Services Review System (CSRS) workshops introduced many of those concepts

to school personnel faced with the accountability demands of Public Law 94–142. The recently published information system, Comprehensive Assessment and Service Evaluation (CASE) was also developed to systematize data collection in speech and hearing programs. Program evaluation, however, has many faces, and a broader framework is needed to define its application to speech and hearing programs. Our purpose in this chapter is to review some of the constructive reasons why program evaluation should be undertaken and to provide some practical guidelines for the endeavor.

## WHAT PURPOSES CAN PROGRAM EVALUATION SERVE?

The broad function of program evaluation, in contrast, say, to basic research, is to provide information for decision-making (Weiss, 1972). A properly conducted program evaluation should yield information with implications for action. The major domains within which program information is needed concern: (1) accountability, (2) program premises, (3) management and administration, and (4) planning. Each of these requires brief explanation.

## ACCOUNTABILITY

If any profession is to avoid being perceived, in George Bernard Shaw's terms, as "a conspiracy against the laity," it must be open and accountable to its various constituencies. Accountability issues are perhaps the most familiar to the average speech pathologist. In most school and clinic settings "accountability" is interpreted as having readily accessible and complete records of clients served, along with a justifiable rationale (usually formal testing) to document their need for service. This level of accountability is usually aimed at fullfilling requirements for external funding agents, such as third party payment sources and state departments of education. We need to be aware, however, that there are potentially many constituencies with an interest in a program, and that each has somewhat different things for which it wants a program to "account."

Top policy makers, such as state and federal legislators, need information that will help them address broad issues: Does the program serve a real need? Should it be continued or dropped? Are there other approaches to the problem that are more worthy of support? The foremost current example of this level of scrutiny is the recent Department of Education evaluation report on PL 94-142 to the United States Congress, which may influence special education funding for years (1980).

Program administrators have a somewhat different set of concerns. Their interest is in knowing how to justify the organizational and financial arrangements through which the service is delivered and, indeed, how to demonstrate the efficacy of the service itself. Here, for example, issues such as staff to client ratios, effectiveness of paraprofessional aids, the usefulness of parent counseling programs, and so forth may require documentation.

A third constituency for program evaluation outcomes is the clinician, representing the clinical profession. A service oriented profession has a vested interest in assuring that the specialized services in which it trades are provided according to professional standards and in a manner that serves the needs and protects the rights of its clientele. This constituency has a right to know what treatment standards operate in a program, how they are supervised and maintained, and what new approaches the program might contribute to the profession as a whole.

Academicians and researchers in our profession would also like speech and hearing programs to be accountable. Their interest is in knowing that state of the art models and theoretic perspectives are being applied. In addition, the need for continuous research on treatment and its effects makes demands on programs. Speech and language programs have some responsibility to serve as field laboratories for researching questions on theory and method in the treatment of communication disorders.

The general public also has a stake in program accountability. As parents of school children, relatives of the geriatric population, and especially as taxpayers, the public is appropriately concerned that their money be wisely spent so that individuals requiring speech and language intervention are served as efficiently and cost-effectively as possible.

In recent years another constituency has become increasingly aware of its right to demand accountable programs—the clients themselves. Backed by federal legislation to protect children's and parents' rights to decide on the nature and extent of special educational services, parents of language disordered children are demanding evidence of "appropriate" intervention efforts. School-aged clients must now have an Individualized Educational Plan (IEP) with target objectives agreed upon by both the client (or parent) and the speech and language professional. This development has had perhaps the most pervasive influence on the procedures of clinicians working with children; lamentations about the paperwork required can be heard at any gathering of public school clinicians.

The legitimate claims of these various groups for accountability must be met if the speech and hearing profession is to retain credibility in an era when all human services are coming under increased scrutiny.

Program evaluation can provide essential information for responding to those claims. The speech and hearing professional who becomes involved in program evaluation for "accountability" reasons, however, must be careful to ask, "accountable to whom and for what?" Recognizing the perspective from which each constituency defines "accountable" will facilitate the design of an evaluation that is appropriate to the context and genuinely useful to the decisions and actions that must be taken as the profession and the programs evolve.

## PROGRAM PREMISES

Any profession that delivers services to the public necessarily bases those services on a series of premises, many of which are simply assumed rather than proven. For example, a physician assumes that medical treatment is as effective when dispensed in his or her office as it would be in the patient's home, though that belief has never been subjected to rigorous testing. Similarly, speech pathologists have had to make assumptions, often without proof, about the nature of their goals, clinical strategies, and projected impact. Improvement in professional services often comes about by questioning those assumptions and experimenting with alternatives. Program evaluation, well conducted, can contribute to this process. It can test the premises upon which the treatment model relies and demonstrate their validity or challenge the profession to adopt still better clinical procedures and models. Some of our assumptions are so basic that we have come to regard them as articles of faith. So, for example, we might paraphrase Gallagher (1981) and consider our reaction to such assumptions as the following:

1. Speech pathologists with master's degrees can deliver services more effectively and efficiently to language handicapped children and adults than can personnel without any special professional training. Can we prove that?

2. Special learning environments, such as resource rooms, special classes, and individual therapy, facilitate a child's acquisition of communicative skills better than the undifferentiated standard educational program. Can we prove that?

3. Special equipment and technology can provide additional learning efficiency for certain kinds of language handicapped adults and children. Can we prove that?

4. Clinical procedures or language programs designed to meet the specific needs of language disordered children help them learn communication skills more effectively than general stimulation from the regular social environment. Can we prove that?

Assumptions of this sort help determine the program model under which schools and clinics operate. Increasingly we are being called upon to demonstrate the validity of these assumptions because they are what justify the extra costs incurred for our services in school, hospital, and clinic settings. Program evaluation procedures can help us make our operating assumptions explicit and substantiate their reasonableness or suggest areas for change. Viewed in this framework, program evaluation becomes a challenge and an opportunity rather than a threat.

## MANAGEMENT AND ADMINISTRATION

Imagine trying to walk around without getting any feedback from your own sensory system about the movement of your body and its interaction with the environment. Your movemnts would be uncoordinated and uncontrolled; you would lurch around and be unable to set course toward any goal. The sensory system of a human services program is its management information system. Without good feedback about the details of program operation and its interaction with clientele, no program can be effectively managed. Good program evaluation must therefore not only look at program *outcome* but at program *process*. The process component of evaluation reports, on an ongoing basis, the status of the key operations and activities that constitute the program. Program evaluation is in part a management information system in support of effective program administration. Anderson (1976) reviewed the types of program process issues that might be covered in a comprehensive program evaluation:

**Access.** Are services reaching the target population? For instance, where are referrals originating? What kinds of cases are coming into the program? What proportion of appointments are broken? Are students in learning disabilities classes receiving language therapy to a greater or lesser extent than English as a Second Language (ESL) students?

**Equity.** Are services allocated in a fair and reasonable manner? For example, do all clients have equal opportunity to receive appropriate services? Are all elementary schools in the district assigned the equivalent speech therapy coverage based on need? Are some severely retarded children systematically being denied speech and language services because they do not meet criteria for "language disordered" classrooms or resource centers?

**Efficiency.** Can programs be improved to provide equivalent or better services at lower cost? Are supervised paraprofessional aids cost-effective additions to a hospital clinic staff? How many clinic supervisors are required to oversee a given number of student clinicians?

Introducing organized systems for feeding back information about a program's functioning to decision-makers is a practical and useful, if not necessarily glamorous, purpose of program evaluation. It is surprising how many speech and language programs are operating without such information systems. Single-person or very small programs may get by with the director's "clinical hunches" on such issues, but with larger programs and increasingly tight budgets comes the need for professional management as well as professional services.

### PLANNING

The use of program evaluation for planning purposes is tied both to providing management information and to testing program assumptions. A successful program is one that can foresee trends and needs and can formulate policies and strategies to maximize its own adaptation to such developments. By having a system in place for aggregating descriptive information on the program, an administrator can use the cumulative archive to discover trends that might affect the program's future. For example, California school speech and hearing clinicians recently noted a shift in their caseloads toward more severely handicapped students as a result of the return of many mildly handicapped children to regular classrooms under the PL 94-142 mandate for the least restrictive environment. At the same time, parent participation in selecting therapy goals through the IEP increased demand for language remediation for severely afflicted populations. With these trends identified, school supervisors scheduled staff training programs on such topics as augmentative communication techniques, sign language training, and preverbal communication skills to serve this changing clientele better.

Another use of program evaluation for planning is a logical outgrowth of the evaluation of treatment models. If a program is conscientious in its assessment of the effectiveness of its service, it will discover many ways to improve that service. For example, if parent support groups are shown to be an effective component of a program for treating preschool language disordered children, staff might begin to plan how to expand that component in their existing programs, perhaps by rotating some staff schedules to evenings so that parents can attend, allocating funds for transportation, child care services, and so forth.

### DEVELOPING A PROGRAM EVALUATION

A comprehensive program evaluation capable of fulfilling the various functions listed above will deal with two general issues. First, it will investigate the treatment model itself and its alternatives, including, possibly, no treatment at all. By treatment model we mean the set of cause and effect relations that make up the actual therapeutic interaction with a client. For example, a treatment may be predicated on a relationship between building comprehension skills and consequent improvement in productive language skills. Improvement in comprehension, in turn, may depend upon a client's ability to attend to the therapist. We might liken treatment to the administration of a drug, for example, penicillin. The treatment model, then, is the mechanism by which the drug is supposed to work, namely entering the bloodstream and poisoning alien bacteria. A good program evaluation must ask if in fact the delivered treatment actually produces the desired results and, if so, by what mechanism.

The second matter with which a comprehensive program evaluation will be concerned is the service delivery system. This refers to the various organized program activities, staff, and financial arrangements that provide for the identification and intake of clients, the delivery of treatment to them, and the maintenance of the service organization itself. Note that effective service delivery and effective treatment are not the same thing. A good treatment can be poorly delivered and an excellent service delivery system can provide a weak or even harmful treatment. From the point of view of the communicatively handicapped client, both effective treatment and effective delivery of that treatment are needed. One facet of program evaluation must provide information about these organizational matters.

Table 15–1  SAMPLE TOPICS FOR A COMPREHENSIVE PROGRAM EVALUATION

| Evaluation Issue | Program Aspect: | |
| --- | --- | --- |
| | CLINICAL TREATMENT | SERVICE DELIVERY |
| IMPLEMENTATION | Does a specifiable treatment model exist? Are there operating procedures defined for the treatment regimen? Are clients actually receiving treatment? | Is there an organization in place with adequate staff and budget? Are there procedures for identifying, recruiting, and enrolling clients? Are there clients coming through the program? |
| PROCESS | What clients are receiving treatment? On what schedule and over what time? Does the treatment as delivered actually fulfill the treatment plan? What are the activities of staff, family, other program components, and so on in support of treatment? | Are appropriate clients coming into the program? From where? Do all eligible clients have access to service? Are there delays, attrition or waiting lists for service? What do services cost? What are the key staff activities in support of service delivery? |
| OUTCOME | What effects or changes do clients experience which result from treatment? Does treatment affect other areas of functioning besides language? Does treatment have any indirect or unintended side effects on clients? | How many clients receive full service? What proportion receive less? What amount and type of service is delivered? How satisfied are clients with service? How many clients return for additional service? How widely is service distributed in the target client group? |

For both the treatment and the service delivery there are three broad issues that a comprehensive program evaluation attempts to address: Is it fully and appropriately implemented? How thorough and efficient is the process through which the results are supposed to be achieved? What is the outcome? Table 15–1 depicts the matrix that these issues form and illustrates the type of question that is pertinent to each cell.

## IMPLEMENTATION

Implementation issues have to do with whether there is a treatment or service delivery system in place and what sort of a treatment or system it is. An implemented program or treatment should have a definable structure that can be identified and documented. For the service delivery system this refers primarily to the existence of an organizational entity but also to the provisions for obtaining and enrolling clients. A well-implemented service delivery is based on an explicit and appropriate identification of potential clients, effective recruiting of those clients, accessibility of the program to them, an adequate screening process prior to intake, a prescribed procedure for providing service, and arrangements for maintaining contact while service is provided.

Implementation issues regarding the treatment, on the other hand, primarily have to do with whether or not there is an explicit treatment regimen in place that can be justified on the basis of a specifiable conceptual model. The treatment model should describe the key components of treatment, the process through which they take effect, and the effects they are expected to produce. An important related issue here is the strength of the treatment (Sechrest and Redner, 1979). A good treatment model will provide a framework that permits some judgment to be made about the intensity of treatment required to deal with a particular client problem. Implementation of the model requires, in addition, the establishment of routine procedures for providing the prescribed treatment.

**Process.** Process questions overlap implementation issues and have to do with the procedures and activities that constitute the treatment or the delivery system in everyday operation. For a treatment, this boils down to the question of the integrity with which the treatment plan is followed in actual application. For example, if the treatment plan called for a clinician to reinforce students verbally each time a verbalization was initiated, process monitoring would ascertain the extent to which that was actually done in the therapy setting. For the broader service delivery issues, process refers to such matters as the cost effectiveness of the service, the allocation of staff time, the number and type of clients served per unit of time, client waiting time before beginning service, and so forth.

**Outcome.** Outcome issues, of course, deal with the final results of the service and treatment process. The outcome of service delivery is measured in terms of the number and proportion of clients from the eligible pool to whom completed service is provided, that is, number of clients identified, number served, amount and types of service received, attrition rate during service, and so on. The outcome of treatment has to do with the actual effects the client experienced. Treatment outcomes may include not only improved communication skills, but also such things as better social functioning, higher achievement test scores, increased motivation, self-esteem, functional life skills, and so forth.

This general description is necessarily sketchy. As a practical matter, designing a comprehensive evaluation for a language intervention program requires that each cell of the matrix in Table 15–1 be filled with specific questions pertinent to the particular program that is to be evaluated. With those questions as a framework, various indicators and measures that can provide data to answer the evaluation questions are defined. A research design is formulated to specify when, where, and from whom those measures are to be obtained—some regularly, some only occasionally. Finally, a reporting format is developed to pull all the resulting information together in a form that can be readily interpreted by the various constituencies with interest in the program.

## WHAT ELSE IS NEEDED?

At this point the speech and hearing professional might well say, "Okay, I believe that program evaluation is necessary and I understand your generalities about how it is done. But we already engage in extensive testing of our clients, we maintain detailed case files, and we do a massive amount of paperwork preparing reports for external funding sources, accountants, third party payers, and so on ad infinitum. Don't we already have enough data available on our services and service delivery to constitute adequate program evaluation?" Unfortunately, the answer is probably no. Though some of the data collected for other purposes can be pressed into service for program evaluation, much of it cannot. Unless a program has specifically tailored its information collecting activities to the needs of program evaluation, the result is likely to fall far short of what is required. Since this is an important point, we will illustrate it more concretely by describing the data available in a typical school program and assessing the limitations of that data for program evaluation purposes.

The Los Angeles County Schools language disorders program is probably fairly representative of the kinds of situations speech pathologists in schools and many clinics face when they initiate program level research. This large public school program has operated self-contained classes for language disordered children for ten years. During that time it has grown from a single classroom to over 300 classes spread across the entire Los Angeles basin. At the beginning of the program the staff designed a standard test battery and set of procedures for gathering parent information. In addition to the usual need to maintain information for student files, the staff wanted to collect data that would permit them to look at the program and the children's progress critically. Thus they routinely collected and accumulated a variety of information beyond that necessary for minimal client files and for state and federal mandates.

Somehow the time for staff to collate and analyze all this information could never be spared from overbusy schedules and the constant demands for service to language handicapped children. This experience provides our first lesson: Adequate staff time must be allocated if "data" are going to turned into "evaluation." Eventually, as a separate research project, one of the authors undertook to organize and analyze the data (Schery, 1980). In the course of conducting that study a great deal was learned about the limitations of a data collection planned chiefly for program purposes when it is adapted to program evaluation purposes. To illustrate the importance of designing the data collection specifically for program evaluation, we will highlight the major problems.

**Choice of Test Instruments.** The tests that had been selected for use with the children in the Los Angeles County program were chosen primarily on the basis of their relevance to diagnosis, namely determining whether the children qualified as language disordered. The importance of screening at intake for this sort of clinical program requires a test battery able to substantiate the children's initial eligibility for service (California Education Code Title 5 regulations). The expectation was that these same tests (listed in Table 15–2) could be readministered on an annual basis and used to document change or growth in language, that is, to assess the amount of progress made by the students. Standardized psychometric tests such as those selected are very responsive to individual differences in children's language performance—that is the task for which they are primarily developed and it makes them quite appropriate for use in diagnosis. The stability and reliability that make these tests effective measures of indi-

Table 15–2  TESTS AND MEASURES
USED IN THE LOS ANGELES COUNTY
LANGUAGE DISORDERS PROGRAM

RECEPTIVE
  Peabody Picture Vocabulary Test
  Northwestern Syntax Screening Test/
    Receptive
  ITPA Auditory Reception
  DTLA Oral Directions

Expressive
  Northwestern Syntax Screening Test/
    Expressive
  ITPA Verbal Expression
  ITPA Manual Expression
  ITPA Grammatic Closure
  Mean Utterance Length from Spontaneous
    Language Sample

Combined
  ITPA Auditory Association
  DTLA Orientation
  DTLA Verbal Opposites
  DTLA Related Syllables
  Elicited Imitation Sentences

Memory
  ITPA Auditory Memory
  ITPA Visual Memory
  DTLA Unrelated Syllables

Production Ability
  Oral Motor Skills Ratings
  Articulation Ratings

Academic
  Reading
  Math
  Spelling

Note: ITPA = Illinois Test of Psycholinguistic
Ability; DTLA = Detroit Test of Learning Aptitude

vidual differences, however, reduce their
sensitivity to change in the performance of
the students tested (Carver, 1974; Schery,
1981). Criterion referenced tests would be
more appropriate as a sensitive change
measure. Thus the overriding importance
of the diagnostic issue in selecting these
tests was working against their ability to
document gain or growth in the pupils once
they entered the program. As instruments
to separate impaired students from "normal" students, they were effective; as
treatment assessment instruments, they
were limited.

Parenthetically, a factor analysis of the
measures in this diagnostic battery showed
a very large overlap among the tests (approximately 57 percent shared variance).
This suggested that the battery of measures, which took a minimum of 3 hours to
administer, was yielding highly redundant
information. Staff time could have been
used more effectively and the purposes of
treatment evaluation better served with a
wider range of measures, including not
only measures that were sensitive to language gain but measures on other aspects
of growth in addition to language. An easy
method for assessing the uniqueness of entries in a test battery is to do simple prod-
uct-moment correlations among the tests
(see Schery, 1981). In summary, the
speech and language clinician who wishes
to document outcomes of intervention
should be careful to use tests designed to
be sensitive to gain. Most standard psychometric batteries are not.

Missing Follow-up Data.  Although
the diagnostic intake evaluations were almost uniformly complete, as time went on
in the retesting schedule fewer program
records were maintained at the same level
of thoroughness. For example, the child or
the clinician might have been ill the day of
scheduled testing and the test was never
rescheduled. Clerical errors also occurred;
occasionally a test was actually administered and someone failed to record the
result on the proper form. Such oversights
are to be expected in any operating program, even one that is conscientiously attempting to maintain complete records.
For program evaluation purposes, however, failure to retest at the scheduled time
seriously erodes the treatment assessment
data, since that assessment depends heavily on post-test information to evaluate
progress.

An additional problem was truncation
of the test battery at retest time in some
nonuniform way. For example, one year
two clinicians omitted the ITPA in re-evaluations, while another diagnostician elected to include it but dropped out the more
informal measures of MLU, oral motor rating, and sentence imitation. Such shifting
of tests was especially likely for students
around 8 to 10 years of age, when many of

the standardized tests were no longer appropriately normed. Staff frequently substituted other measures that seemed more age appropriate for these older students (such as the Detroit Test of Learning Abilities) or used extrapolated norms. Clinicians' biases about what tests were useful also changed from time to time. When such changes were not implemented in a systematic fashion, the consequence was a great deal of missing information (or information that could not be used). The result of these various factors was that the longer a child was in the program, the less likely he was to have consistent, systematic test-retest data on the same battery of measures. This made little difference to routine program operation, but it was very demaging to the quality of the data for program evaluation purposes.

**Nonuniformity of Measures.** Since the Los Angeles County program was so large (covering over 4000 square miles) and operated in 4 distinct geographic areas, care had to be taken to keep 4 separate programs from developing. The supervisory staff were aware of this tendency and met weekly to establish and review policies and procedures. Despite such efforts, there were still problems. Certain psychologists had strong preferences for one nonverbal intelligence test over another, so several had to be allowed. There was substantial variation in the data recorded by teachers from the different program sites regarding their intervention efforts. In some areas, teachers wrote long narrative reports about each child's progress; elsewhere they relied on checklists and rating sheets. Even within a single school there was often little uniformity. From teacher to teacher, from year to year, the format and the content of what was recorded changed, making it virtually impossible to reconstruct what had taken place in the classrooms. What percentage of time was devoted to programmed language drill? What initial approach to reading was utilized? What reading materials? What amount of time was spent in group language experiences? How much additional work was sent home? Questions such as these were unanswerable for the majority of children

without laborious extraction from a widely diverse set of materials. It is just this information, however, that is essential to documenting and assessing the *process* component of the treatment within a program evaluation.

**Limited Range of Outcome Measures.** Since the Los Angeles County program was devoted to treatment of language disorders, the measures selected to index student progress naturally emphasized speech and language performance. There was nothing inappropriate about giving that outcome issue central priority, but it proved very limited for program evaluation purposes. A full assessment of the effects of intervention must consider other outcome issues as well, such as academic achievement in nonlinguistic areas, social and pragmatic communication skills, peer relations with normal children, family support and attitudes, motivation, self-esteem, functional life skills, and so forth. By and large, these issues were not salient to program staff when the testing material was selected, and consequently the range of outcome variables that could be addressed was relatively narrow.

A significant percentage of children entering the language disorders program over the period that the archive was maintained left the program from two to five years after admission because they no longer qualified based on language scores and teachers' ratings of progress. Unfortunately, the only program record of this tranistion was a final staff recommendation for subsequent placement (regular class, traditional speech therapy, tutoring or resource room service, private school placement, and so on). There was no provision made for following up to see if the recommended placement was in fact carried out, nor to determine how successful the child was in this "next environment" (Vincent and colleagues, 1980). Such subsequent tracking would have provided important information on long-range effects of the program and allowed staff to verify conclusions about the behaviors that led to "success" outside the program context. Ideally, the range of outcome measures should encompass effects that extend into wider ranging environments or environments subsequent to the immediate program.

**Treatment Process Issues.** In a broader evaluative context, another shortcoming of the range of available measures quickly became apparent as the program data were analyzed. Virtually all the systematic information in the files pertained to the child's performance or activities and not to the treatment received, that is, the performance and activities of the teachers, aides, and so on. The staff had placed such an emphasis on gathering clinical and psychometric data about the children that they had neglected to include systematic records of what they did to the children in their attempts to improve language performance. Also missing was any description of the various contextual features that surrounded the treatment for any child, for example, listing of the child's teachers and their backgrounds, amount of aid time, distance of the program from the home school, time spent on the bus, changes in classrooms and peer groups, number of field trips, contacts with support personnel (nurses, counselors, psychologists, and program specialists), parent attendance at meetings and teacher conferences, and so forth. Although some of this information had of course been recorded in one or another form during the program's operation, it had not been routinely included in the central files and over time had become nothing more than summary statistics on truancy, transportation reimbursement costs, and payroll records. By restricting the information so narrowly to the children and their performance on tests, the program had limited the kinds of potentially important information that could be considered when trying to discern what made a difference in how these children learned.

**Service Delivery Issues.** Thus far we have examined the program's data collection only as it pertained to treatment issues. In a large program such as Los Angeles County operated, an adequate program evaluation would require a great quantity of systematic ongoing information about the service delivery—the process and outcomes of the operations and activities that provided for the orderly identi-

fication of these children, distribution of services, costs, and general logistics of program operation. In Los Angeles County the program administrators were in fact concerned with such service delivery issues as the appropriateness of the qualifying disorder (especially as distinct from bilingual language performances, since Los Angeles County has a large Hispanic population), existence of waiting lists for placement (this was made illegal by PL 94–142), maintaining teacher-child ratios at a level to assure maximum funding, and calculating the best geographic locations for classrooms to minimize busing for children. The only data routinely gathered and reviewed relevant to service delivery issues, however, were attendance (ADA records are the basis upon which costs are reimbursed by the state), number of referrals waiting to be processed, number of openings in classes, and the number of miles the children were bused (for which the program was also reimbursed by the state). The State Department of Education maintained such records as the average cost per pupil for programs throughout the state, but there was no system for identifying the actual per pupil costs within the Los Angeles County program. This very minimal information is hardly adequate either as an effective management information system for program administration or for broader program evaluation purposes.

The kind of information that should have been routinely generated on service delivery issues, and its value, are illustrated by the retrospective summaries that we were able to create by digging into the archives and patching data together from diverse sources. We learned, for example, that in the 92 school districts that had contracted or were eligible for service by this program, the referral rate was highly uneven. Some districts had never referred a child. Other districts accounted for substantially more than their proportional number of referrals. There had been no way of monitoring this on an ongoing basis despite the potential implications such a pattern had for the equitable distribution of resources. Had this information been available in a timely way, it might have been possible to determine what was happening to the language disordered children in the nonreferring districts.

Another example involves the proportion of children in the program who came from bilingual Spanish-English homes. The overall percentage was 17 percent, a figure that closely approximated census figures for the bilingual population in the districts represented. The program administrators were greatly relieved—they had been concerned that some classes were disproportionately bilingual. For program evaluation purposes there should be a mechanism for routinely obtaining such information short of the massive combing of the records involved in the retrospective research study that finally extracted the figures.

As data were tabulated in this retrospective study, other useful service delivery information emerged which should have been available all along. The relative productivity of various diagnostic teams became apparent; there was notable variation in the number of referrals processed. The tracking of program continuity (or discontinuity) was sharply highlighted by one child who had attended eight different classes in three and one-half years in the program (during expansion phases, new classrooms were being added every few weeks and children and teaching staff often were reassigned and regrouped). It was possible to calculate the percentage of children who had required additional service, such as dental care or remedial physical education. Such figures could help in projecting staff needs for the future. Figures documenting the low percentage of appropriate referrals from some districts suggested the need for clearer communication to district personnel on the nature of the program and the kinds of children it served.

Like the Los Angeles County program, many schools and clinics may have some of the information needed to examine issues such as these buried in their records. Unless it is carefully organized and systematically obtained, however, it takes a massive effort to extract, analyze, and interpret it for program evaluation purposes.

If we are correct that the Los Angeles County language disorders program is representative in its maintenance of treatment and service data (and in fact we would judge it well above average), then the limitations we have discussed will also be typical of other programs. Though a great deal of information was recorded in various forms, it was not done as part of a deliberate, carefully constructed program evaluation plan. As a result, the available data had relatively little use for program evaluation purposes. Much of it was not systematically nor consistently reported, the range of measures was limited in various ways, client performance data were overemphasized relative to treatment process and service delivery data, and there was no integrated format that permitted ready analysis and interpretation of what was available. We have to conclude that few programs will already have in place data systems that are adequate for comprehensive program evaluation. It is likely to take some deliberate effort to establish good evaluation in the typical communication disorders program.

## CURRENT PRACTICE IN PROGRAM EVALUATION

We do not know of a single evaluation of a speech and language program that can be considered comprehensive in the terms described in this chapter. Indeed, there are surprisingly few studies of any sort that present themselves as program level research (Gallagher, 1981; Laney, 1982). These circumstances make it difficult to cite a good example from readily accessible literature which can serve as a model for speech and hearing professionals who wish to develop an evaluation plan for their own program.

Of the studies in the language intervention literature most pertinent to the topic of program evaluation, the most frequent is the clinical study in which a specific therapeutic intervention is assessed in terms of its remedial effects on one or more clients selected for research purposes (Leonard, 1981). These studies contribute to understanding the efficacy of treatment, an important aspect of program evaluation. Yet within that domain, many of these studies have a limited scope that restricts their applicability to program evaluation issues. The nature of those limitations is instructive, especially when contrasted with what is desirable for a full assessment of the treatment model in a program evaluation context.

Many of the clinical studies, for example, assess a specific clinical *techinque* rather than a broader treatment regimen. By technique, we mean such things as modeling (Courtright and Courtright, 1976), elicited imitation (Schwartz and Daly, 1978), telephone assignments (Vaughn, 1976), sign language input (Benaroya and colleagues, 1979), auditory perception training (Boise City Independent School District, 1974), and parent training effects (Bricker and Casuso, 1979). A full treatment regimen might be comprised of many such techniques, and its overall effects could be somewhat different from the effects of any single technique in isolation. In addition, assessment of a full treatment regimen would raise questions about the actual extent to which any technique was applied under program (not research) circumstances and the nature of the clients to whom it was applied. A treatment assessment should also address the question of the generality of the results—how long they last, the range of clients to which they apply, and whether or not they continue outside the research setting. Too many clinical studies leave these questions unexamined (Leonard, 1981).

A somewhat broader approach is represented by studies that compare entire treatment alternatives, for example, an in-class program versus traditional speech and language services (Cooper and colleagues, 1979; Weiss, 1980) or a self-contained special education classroom versus mainstreaming in a regular classroom (Forbes, 1980; Gottlieb, 1981; Jones and colleagues, 1978). This comparison encompasses all the variability of the clients and the intervention techniques characteristic of each treatment under reasonably typical circumstances. With adequate documenta-

tion of the treatment model, events, and clientele represented in each of these treatment "packages," this type of research does provide useful data for assessing the direct intervention facet of the programs they represent.

Whatever the approach, most studies of the efficacy of treatment for language disorders focus on outcome variables that have to do with specialized language performance. Certainly this is appropriate for the purposes of those studies, but from a program evaluation perspective there are other important outcome issues that also require attention. Zigler and Balla (1982) argue that the full range of functioning of the client is at issue—social competence, family relationships, motivation, physical well-being, and personality, as well as language performance. Speech and language pathologists may have sold themselves short by not including some measures of "impact" that go beyond standardized language tests. In addition, good program evaluation must be sensitive to unintended outcomes and side effects that were not expected to result from the treatment. For example, in a competitive classroom setting a child may gain in language proficiency but suffer in self-esteem.

Thus to adapt the established tradition of clinical studies in language intervention to the purposes of program evaluation, the enterprise must be broadened in several important ways. "Treatments" should be assessed in the form of representative packages of activities, procedures, and organizational context and not as isolated techniques. Within that treatment package, separate documentation should be obtained on the treatment plan or concept and the strength and integrity—that is, completeness—of the actual implementation. Outcome variables should span the spectrum of relevant client behaviors and be measured in ways that allow the generality, duration, and robustness of the effects to be determined.

The other facet of a comprehensive program evaluation, assessment of the service delivery system, is not so well represented in the speech and hearing literature as is research on clinical treatment. The importance of this facet has been well recognized, however. Sirotnik and Oakes (1981), for example, argue straightforwardly that outcome indicators have little value or meaning without an understanding of the organizational context in which they take place. The best available representatives of this perspective are those studies that have concerned themselves with assessing such things as the cost of clinical or school services (Hartman, 1981; Work, 1975) and consumer satisfaction with clinical services (Evans, 1980).

A full service delivery assessment would operate in the same spirit as these studies but would attempt more systematic and comprehensive coverage of the various functions that a service organization must perform. One way to depict the scope of such a study is to lay out a chart that shows every significant interaction between the client and the language intervention program beginning at a point prior to referral to the program and ending after the service and all follow-up contacts are complete. A full service delivery study would obtain information about the events and alternatives at each major point on that chart. That information would be combined with organizational information such as costs, staffing patterns, and procedures as they relate to those key interactions. The result would be a full description of the service delivery process in sufficient detail for its strengths and weaknesses to be discovered.

In a language intervention program of any size and complexity, getting together a full-scale evaluation responsive to both treatment efficacy and service delivery issues is clearly no trivial undertaking. It may be sensible to begin on a less ambitious scale, but begin we must if we are serious about having well-managed, effective intervention programs that can withstand scrutiny by both critics and advocates.

## REFERENCES

Anderson S, Ball S, Murphy R, et al: *Encyclopedia of Educational Evaluation*. San Francisco: Jossey-Bass, 1976

Benaroya S, Wesley S, Ogilvie L, Klein L, Clark E: Sign language and multisensory input training of children with communication and related developmental disorders: Phase II. J Aut Develop Dis 9(2):219–221, 1979

Boise City Independent School District, Idaho: Auditory perceptual and language development training program. Final Project Report, 1969–1972. Bureau of Elementary and Secondary Education, Idaho State Department of Education, Boise, Idaho, 1974

Bricker D, Casuso V: Family involvement: A critical component of early intervention. Excep Child 46(2):108–116, 1979

Carver R: Two dimensions of tests: Psychometric and edumetric. Am Psychol 29:512–518, 1974

Cooper J, Moodley M, Reynell J: The developmental language programme: Results from a five year study. Brit J Dis Commun 14: 57–69, 1979

Courtright J, Courtright I: Imitative modeling as a theoretical base for instructing language-disordered children. J Speech Hear Res 19:655–663, 1976

Evans R: Monitoring consumer satisfaction with cleft lip and palate services. Poster Session, ASHA Convention, Detroit, Michigan, 1980

Forbes D: Mainstreaming and preschool children: Effects on social behavior of the handicapped and the non-handicapped. Paper presented to Conference on Mainstreaming and Preschool Education, Cambridge, Massachusetts, October 1980

Gallagher J: Days of reckoning—days of opportunity: The 1981 statemen's roundtable. Invited address to Council of Exceptional Children, Dallas, Texas, April 1981. Available as ERIC Exceptional Child Education Report, Reston, Virginia

Gottlieb J: Mainstreaming: Fulfilling the promise? Am J Ment Defic 86(2):115–126, 1981

Hartman W: Estimating the costs of educating handicapped children: A resource-cost model approach, summary report. Educ Eval Policy Anal 3(4):33–47, 1981

Jones R, Gottlieb J, Guskin S, Yoshida R: Evaluating mainstreaming programs: Models, caveates, considerations and guidelines. Excep Child 44:588–601, 1978

Jones S, Healy W: Essentials of program planning, development, management and evaluation. Rockville, Maryland: ASHA, 1976

Killen J, Myklebust H: Evaluation in special education: A computer-based approach. J Learn Dis 13(8):35–39, 1980

Laney M: Research and evaluation in the public schools. Lang Speech Hear Serv Schools 13(1):53–60, 1982

Leonard L: Facilitating linguistic skills in children with specific language impairment. Appl Psycholing 2(2):89–118, 1981

Rees M, et al: An evaluation of speech and hearing problems in the schools: Research problems and capabilities of a research center for resolving issues pertaining to school programs. Rockville, Maryland: ASHA, 1967

Schery T: Correlates of language development in language disordered children: An archival study. Dissertation, Claremont Graduate School, 1980

Schery T: Selecting assessment strategies for language disordered children. Topics Lang Dis 1(3): 59–73, 1981

Schwartz A, Daly D: Elicited imitation in language assessment: A tool for formulating and evaluating treatment programs. J Commun Dis 11(1): 25–35, 1978

Sechrest L, Redner R: Strength and integrity of treatment in evaluation studies. Criminal Justice Evaluation Reports, Washington, DC:LEAA, 1979

Second Annual Report to Congress on the Implementation of Public Law 94-142: The Education for all Handicapped Children Act. Washington, DC: U.S. Department of Education, 1980

Sirotnik K, Oakes J: A contextual appraisal system for schools: Medicine or madness? Educ Leader 39(3):165–173, 1981

Snope T, Duran J, Dublinski S: C.A.S.E. Information System (Comprehensive Assessment and Service Evaluation). Developmental Learning Materials, 1981

Snyder L: Have we prepared the language disordered child for school? Topics Lang Dis 1(1):29–45, 1980

Vaughn G: Tel-communicology: Healthcare delivery system for persons with communicative disorders. J Am Speech Hear Assoc 18(1):13–17, 1976

Vincent L, Salisbury C, Walter G, Brown P, Gruenewald L, Powers M: Program evaluation and curriculum development in early childhood special education. In Sailor W, Wilcox B, Brown L (eds): *Methods of Instruction for Severely Handicapped Students*. Baltimore: Paul H. Brooks, 1980

Weiss C: *Evaluation Research: Methods of Assessing Program Effectiveness*. Englewood Cliffs, NJ: Prentice-Hall, 1972

Weiss R: Efficacy of INREAL intervention for preschool and kindergarten language handicapped and bilingual (Spanish) children. Handicapped Children's Early Education Program, Project Director's Report, Washington, DC, December 1980

Work R, et al: Accountability in a school speech and language program: Part J: Cost accounting. In *Speech, Language and Hearing Services in the Schools*. 6(1): 7–13, 1975.

Zigler E, Balla D: Selecting outcome variables in evaluations of early childhood special education programs. Topics Early Child Spec Educ, 1(4):11–22, 1982

# 16

## GENERALIZATION ACROSS SETTINGS: LANGUAGE INTERVENTION WITH CHILDREN

*JANIS M. COSTELLO*

There are essentially no examples in the literature of careful evaluation of the long-term effects of language treatment on children. Some general descriptions have been provided by Hall and Tomblin (1978), who gained information regarding 18 language impaired subjects 13 to 30 years following their language treatment, and by Weiner (1974), who tested a 16-year-old language delayed youth who had been receiving language treatment irregularly since age 4. Neither of these reports offered very positive findings regarding the effects of previous language treatment, but neither could offer systematic evaluation of that treatment or its components.

The ultimate assessment of the effectiveness of a given treatment or educational endeavor seems to be in whether the new behaviors it generates within a child's repertoire are used appropriately (or at all) outside the treatment environment (in the child's natural environment), and whether those behaviors are maintained over time. Thus, in an effort to address the issue of the evaluation of program effectiveness, this chapter describes the state of our knowledge regarding generalization across settings. That is, if we turn our attention to understanding what is known (or hypoth-

esized) regarding principles and procedures for producing behavior change that spreads beyond the confines of the clinician's office, then we will be taking the first step toward designing language treatment for children that will pass muster when we later evaluate its long-term effectiveness.

In reference to generalization and language intervention, Siegel and Spradlin (1978) have stated:

The therapist or teacher who trains speech or language makes the assumption that his efforts will have an effect on the child's communication outside the training sessions, otherwise, there would be no reason to engage in the training since it is usually an artificial intervention into the child's life, with no inherent value. (p. 389)

Current literature on language treatment is replete with statements that would support this view. Current literature on language treatment is also, however, conspicuously lacking in data to support this view. It seems the topic of generalization has become like the weather: Everybody talks about it, but no one does anything about it. In fact, out of something like 32 language treatment studies conducted in the last 18 years which were recently (and excellently) reviewed by Leonard (1981), only 5 studies even measured for the occurrence of generalization, let alone tried to study how to make it occur. There is more research on this process going on outside the area of language, but the same relative skimpiness of data exists there as well.

## GENERALIZATION: DEFINITIONS AND STATUS OF RESEARCH

Before we go further, let's define the varieties of generalization and pinpoint the version that is going to be concentrated on in this chapter. Drabman, Hammer, and Rosenbaum (1979) have described 16 varieties of generalization, yet the definition of Stokes and Baer (1977) is probably clearer. Their review of the generalization research in the applied behavior modification literature will serve as the framework for a portion of this chapter. They describe generalization as follows:

. . . the occurrence of relevant behavior under different, nontraining conditions (i.e., across subjects, settings, people, behaviors, and/or time) without the scheduling of the same events in those conditions as had been scheduled in the training conditions. Thus generalization may be claimed when no extratraining manipulations are needed for extratraining changes; or may be claimed when some extra manipulations are necessary, but their cost or extent is clearly less than that of the direct intervention. Generalization will not be claimed when similar events are necessary for similar effects across conditions. (p. 350)

In this chapter some of the literature on *generalization across settings* (also referred to as extratreatment, extratherapy, or extraclinic generalization) will be discussed and reviewed. This is the kind of generalization that occurs when a response that has been learned under one set of conditions subsequently occurs in a different setting and in the presence of stimuli that were not present during training, including the absence of reinforcement. For our purposes, we will be concentrating typically on language responses taught in some kind of a treatment setting and the

generalization of those responses to the child's natural environment. Because setting generalization refers to behavior occurring in the presence of novel (antecedent) stimuli, it is one kind of *stimulus generalization*.

Stimulus generalization (but not setting generalization) also occurs, for example, when a child who has been taught to say "ball" to a particular picture of a ball also says "ball" to a variety of other pictures of balls and to some real balls, or even to the written word ball. The newly learned response is emitted to novel stimuli of the same class which were not present during the original learning sessions. This could be referred to as *generalization within a stimulus class*.

Another kind of generalization is *generalization across behaviors* (or responses). *Response generalization* occurs when the effects of learning a particular behavior during treatment spread to other behaviors of the learner. Behavioral covariation is an illustration of this kind of generalization. For example, a formerly nonverbal mentally retarded child who has learned to say "hi" when persons approach might continue not only to give that greeting, but might also become more social in other ways, such as waving, smiling, and touching others when they approach. This is response generalization.

The response class that is demonstrated during response generalization may be more topographically bound than this example, however. When we teach a child correct articulation of the /s/ phoneme in a core of 20 words, we expect that the /s/ will be articulated correctly in nontreatment words as well. But we also know, because of the phenomenon of coarticulation, that each /s/ is produced a bit differently than /s/ in isolation or /s/ preceded and followed by different sounds. Therefore, the fact that we can teach a child 20 /s/ words and that child is thereby able to produce hundreds of others that weren't directly practiced, is due partially to response generalization. A similar form of generalization across behaviors occurs when a simple response is taught to the learner, who then becomes able to produce more complex versions of the response. When a child has been taught to use the present progressive verb in utterances ("Mommy washing") and then is noted to produce sentences such as "Daddy coming home" and "Baby is crying," this kind of generalization across response complexities has occurred.

A third variety of generalization, probably the most important for language and other kinds of sophisticated learning, is combined *stimulus-response generalization*. That is, when several stimuli that were not present during training can evoke responses within a response class, stimulus-response generalization has occurred. An excellent example of this phenomenon found in the language learning literature is in an early study by Guess, Sailor, Rutherford, and Baer (1968) in which mentally retarded subjects learned to produce nouns with the plural morphemes /s/ or /z/ appropriately added or omitted in response to either groups of objects or single objects. The subjects were trained on a small group of singular and plural items and quickly acquired the ability to label items appropriately on which they had not received instruction. This form of complex discrimination learning is the behaviorist's operational definition of conceptual behavior. That is, *concept formation* is demonstrated when a person generalizes among stimuli that are similar along some dimension, and discriminates between that stimulus class and other sets of stimuli (Whaley and Mallott, 1971). When this behavioral pattern is observed for language responses, researchers refer to this as a behavioral definition of the generative or productive use of language. Further, demonstrations of the generative use of language responses learned in treatment abound in the behavioral language intervention literature (for example, Baer and Guess, 1973; Bennett and Ling, 1972; Garcia, Guess, Byrnes, 1973; Gray and Ryan, 1973; Hegde and Gierut, 1979; Lutzker and Sherman, 1974; Schumaker and Sherman, 1970; Smeets and Striefel, 1976; Wheeler and Sulzer, 1970).

A fourth phenomenon referred to by some writers is *generalization across time*.

This phenomenon provides a demonstration of the longevity of behavior, either in the original teaching setting or in settings beyond, following withdrawal of the treatment contingencies. Some writers (for example, Ingham, 1981; Koegel and Rincover, 1977) have used the term *maintenance* to refer to this phenomenon of the durability of behavior over time. Maintenance can also be considered an active process—one in which procedures are designed and instigated to assure that a newly acquired behavior remains in the learner's repertoire. When reading the maintenance literature, therefore, one must determine whether the writer is referring to maintenance as a passive process wherein measurements are made periodically following the termination of instruction and behavior is shown to have lingered (or disappeared), or whether the writer is referring to the active process of instigating procedures directly for the purpose of maintaining the behavior in the learner's repertoire.

This differentiation between active and passive processes can also apply to generalization. That is, generalization can occur spontaneously as a by-product of treatment, and we need note it only by measuring the occurrence of the behavior of interest in settings outside of the treatment setting. However, as will be described in more detail below, where language learning and generalization across settings are concerned, such spontaneous generalization is not typically the case. Therefore, we have come to understand (passively if not actively) that generalization oftentimes must be (and can be) programmed and arranged if the newly acquired behavior is ever to occur in the natural environment. Since this manner of prodding the occurrence of the target behavior into the natural environment is technically not spontaneous generalization according to our definition, calling it such would seem to be a confusing misnomer. Therefore, it is suggested here that the term *transfer* be used to describe the process of planned or arranged generalization that is controlled by the clinician or experimenter and that is implemented when it has been observed that behavior has not spontaneously generalized to the natural environment following acquisition of a given behavior in the clinic setting. It may be that the last part of Stokes and Baer's (1977) generalization definition would better fit as transfer in this writer's definition, but it is difficult to tell exactly what they mean when they write that generalization will be credited " . . . when some extra manipulations are necessary, but their cost or extent is clearly less than that of the direct intervention" (p. 350).

Now that we see what is meant by the term(s) generalization, let's return to the observation that not much is being done to solve the problems that its absence provokes. That is, clinical observation and the experimental literature tell us that setting generalization, although expected and hoped for, often does not occur at the successful conclusion of language instruction designed to promote the acquisition of a particular response. This observation is frequently acknowledged, but, as noted above, appears not to have inspired much research. There seem to be some explanations, not the least of which is Ingham's (1981) comment that such often necessarily long-term studies don't add much to the thickness of a researcher's vita (since they take so much time to complete). Less cynically, Ingham and also Harris (1975) have pointed out the major technologic problems the researcher can encounter in attempts to measure truly spontaneous behavior in varieties of settings in a subject's natural environment. The added burden of controlling for reactivity of measurement by arranging for these measures to be obtained covertly can be overwhelming. Beyond these practical, but very powerful, considerations, Ingham (1981) has touched upon what is perhaps another major reason clinical scientists have stayed away from generalization research:

. . . the origins of this situation may really reside in the method used to train clinical researchers. For, quite apart from the difficulties of clinical research, the researcher's training is usually designed to regard any distance between an independent and dependent variable (treatment and outcome) as a yawning gap

which is filled with nothing but threats to the validity of an experiment: the greater the gap, the greater the source of terror to the researcher as well as error in research. (p. 180)

Another excuse for our not conducting generalization studies of language learning—an excuse that was legitimate several years ago—is that generalization of treatment effects cannot be assessed without first having treatment effects. In recent years our clinical experience and the experimental clinical literature have clearly shown that, from a variety of theoretic persuasions, we are now able to establish improved language skills in the repertoires of language deficient children of all types (for example, Bricker, 1972; Guess, Sailor, Baer, 1978; Lee, Koenigsknecht, Mulhern, 1975; Miller and Yoder, 1972, 1974; Waryas and Stremel-Campbell, 1978). So, it seems that now the time has come. We are in need of experimental analyses of generalization and methods to facilitate its occurrence.

## STIMULUS CONTROL: THE RECIPROCAL OF GENERALIZATION

Generalization is the opposite of discrimination, or stimulus control. When it is observed that a particular response is regularly evoked by a particular stimulus or set of stimuli, that response is referred to as being under stimulus control. Imitative responses, for example, are under the control of imitative stimuli; persons who have learned to follow instructions, and do so when an instruction is given, are under instructional (stimulus) control; a driver going to Santa Barbara from Los Angeles, who exits the San Diego freeway when the sign says "101 North" is under stimulus control. All of these are discriminated behaviors, as are essentially all learned behaviors. Each of us has thousands of responses in our behavioral repertoires, but we emit them at different and particular times according to the signals presented by the environment. Nearly all of our behavior, including and especially our language behavior, is thus under stimulus control. Further, those stimuli that precede behavior and signal its occurrence (referred to technically as discriminative stimuli or $S^Ds$) acquire stimulus control by being present during reinforcement of the responses they eventually come to evoke. Thus the principle of reinforcement remains at the center of learning, even for behavior under stimulus control (although the reinforcers may not always be observable because they may be occurring on a thin reinforcement schedule).

When behavior has been learned according to some specified and satisfactory criterion in the environment where the language instruction is administered, and when that same behavior subsequently does not occur in the natural environment, there must be a logical reason. One explanation could be that, without reinforcement, the response extinguishes. Even for behavior taught under a continuous reinforcement schedule, however, extinction usually is a gradual process, so we could expect the behavior would last long enough for us to observe its occurrence in the natural environment if it were, in fact, going to appear there. (See Koegel and Rincover [1977] for an excellent discussion and experiment dealing with the separation of generalization and maintenance phenomena.) Another hypothesis that could explain why the newly acquired behavior doesn't generalize might be stimulus control. It is likely that the learner does not emit the new language response(s) in a natural environment because the stimuli that have become $S^Ds$ for that response are not present in the natural environment.

A description of the typical language treatment environment contrasted to the typical natural environment is instructive. This contrast has been well described by Hart and Rogers-Warren (1978) and by Spradlin and Siegel (1982), but it is so familiar to most of us that we could easily provide this description ourselves. In the clinic setting the adult's language to the child is generally brief and highly structured, while in the natural environment it is considerably more varied in topic, length of utterance, and amount. In the clinic the

clinician presents models for the child to imitate that are designed to be precisely at the child's level of ability and to which the child's attention is carefully directed. In the natural environment any utterance of another person has the potential for serving as a model for the child, but such utterances are not controlled in their quality or style, and the child may or may not attend to them as models. In the clinic reinforcement for appropriate responding is generally dense, immediate, salient, artificial, and supplied by the clinician. In the natural environment we speculate that reinforcement for language responses occurs on an intermittent schedule, is sometimes not very immediate, is sometimes very subtle, and is rarely a piece of candy and a verbal, "Good boy!" In the clinic the demand on the child to produce language is high and responding is ideally very frequent, while in the natural environment the child may not be required to respond frequently and long periods of silence may be quite appropriate (and even appreciated). In concert with this, the clinic setting will provide many and obvious opportunities for the child to respond with language, while in the natrual environment there may be fewer such opportunities and they may be difficult for the child to recognize. Regarding the direct teaching of language, in the clinic such teaching is generally conducted systematically on the basis of a known rationale, but for short periods of time; while in the natural environment language teaching is more intuitive and sporadic but can take place at any time or location and in the presence of any stimuli.

Further, the nature of the language teaching that goes on in these two environments is typically quite different in terms of the behaviors targeted. In the clinic we have commonly selected labeling, describing, and somewhat contrived requests, and have paid special attention to syntactic forms and structure, while the natural environment may attend less to those variables (particularly form) and be more responsive to the communicative function or intent of a child's utterance. One last and very obvious difference between the two environments is that the clinical setting is usually a small room in a big building; and the clinician, his or her materials, and some stark furniture are often the only other things present. The major contrast that this presents to the natural environment is obvious.

This view of the clinical versus the natural environment led Spradlin and Siegel (1982) to respond, in rather an understatement that

. . . whatever it is that the child learns during these sessions, the conditions calling for those particular language forms are unlikely to occur in his home environment. The variables that motivate and control communication outside of the laboratory will scarcely have been approached during the training sessions. That is, the responses that have been taught may have only the barest topographical similarity to the responses that are to be generalized. (p. 4)

We could also add that the context in which those responses have been learned, that is, the stimuli that have been discriminative and have come to exert stimulus control over those responses during clinic treatment, are also likely not to be part of the natural environment. Given the picture presented above, it seems surprising that we have been surprised that setting generalization, from the clinic to the natural environment, has not occurred. According to a stimulus control model, we should be more surprised when it does occur!

## SETTING GENERALIZATION: POTENTIAL SOLUTIONS WITHIN THE CLINIC SETTING

Now that the problems have been more clearly described, it is possible to begin looking for solutions. Stokes and Baer (1977) did just this when they combed the behavior modification literature looking for occasions when measurements of setting generalization had been made. When such were found, and when generalization had occurred, they attempted to extract the processes that appeared to be responsible. In their article, which is already a classic, they induced nine processes that appear,

on the basis of empirical findings, to have the potential to facilitate generalization of behavior across settings. These processes (plus some of this writer's own ideas) are described below with illustrations from the language (or other) literature whenever such could be found.

In general, Stokes and Baer (1977) have described a variety of procedures that would be implemented *within the clinical setting* and might, in various ways, generate behavior that would more readily meld into the natural environment. It seems obvious that, in spite of the problems stimulus control presents for the continued use of a separate clinic-teaching setting, there are also many reasons for trying to retain it. Primarily, it offers a controlled and quiet environment where the clinician does not have to compete with distractions and can systematically introduce variables into the teaching setting as they become appropriate to the child's level of learning. It seems that some clinicians and researchers continue to believe that new behavior, especially one as complex as language, must be first established in this laboratory-like setting where extraneous variables can be controlled and targeted language responses can be systematically and progressively established. Continuing to conduct treatment in this restricted environment is also convenient and efficient for the clinician in terms of the logistics of arranging time and stimulus materials. We would all probably agree that if language can be taught effectively (as measured by the occurrence of generalization across settings) and economically (as measured at least by the expenditure of treatment and personnel time), conducting language treatment in a restricted clinic setting would be our first choice. Let's turn, then, to an overview of the procedures that might make this feasible.

## *TRAIN SUFFICIENT EXEMPLARS*

One of the most important procedures for facilitating generalization, advocated both by Siegel and Spradlin (1978) and by

Carr (1980) in their reviews of generalization, is the use of a considerable number of exemplars during language training. For example, when teaching syntax to a child, it is not enough for the child to learn to imitate one sentence each of five different syntactic structures. Such a child is left knowing how to say five sentences, but not how to generate novel sentences using any of those forms. He has not, therefore, learned a very large or useful body of language to help him get along in the natural environment, nor has he had the opportunity to learn a rule that would allow him to generate new utterances on his own. It appears that learning responses to a small and exclusive batch of $S^D$s promotes a limited and restrictive repertoire of responses. However, learning a class of responses to a variety of similar and related stimuli appears to promote generative use of the newly learned responses. Multiple exemplars are selected according to the stimulus dimensions along which one wants generalization to occur. Where setting generalization has been concerned, the multiple exemplars have most often been teachers and settings.

Three examples of this procedure were found in the language treatment literature, the first study conducted by Garcia (1974) with two severely retarded imitative subjects who learned a "conversational sequence" evoked by a picture. After a full response chain was learned to a given picture, subjects' responses were probed by the experimenter in the treatment setting, by a second experimenter talking with each subject in his or her bedroom, and by a third experimenter who met with the subjects in another room in the institution. In one kind of probe, the subjects were presented with ten new pictures to which to respond. No reinforcement was available. In the second kind of probe, treatment trials were shifted to a VR 3 schedule of reinforcement and new probe pictures were inserted during nonreinforced trials that were intermixed with reinforced trials on the previously trained pictures. Garcia refers to this as a generalization *training* procedure, although it is often used as a generalization *measure* in treatment research. In

this study it was found that the subjects did not respond correctly to new items, even in the teaching environment in the presence of the original experimenter, until response to the novel stimuli was bolstered by being intermixed with stimuli and responses that had already received training and were being concurrently reinforced. Even then, there was no generalization to the second and third experimenters in their respective testing environments. Next, the same teaching procedure was conducted by the second experimenter in her separate setting. Once again generalization, even in her presence, did not occur until the test trials were interspersed among reinforced treatment trials. At this time, however, responding in the presence of the third experimenter also improved (only during the interspersed task), thus showing spontaneous generalization to a third experimenter and setting. In this case, training on two exemplars (setting-experimenter combinations) was sufficient to begin the process of setting generalization in at least a limited fashion.

Handleman (1979) taught four autistic boys verbal responses to sets of common questions. Language treatment was conducted in two different kinds of settings: a restricted setting, much like the typical clinic setting, and a multiple-natural setting wherein the clinician and child moved through a mapped area of the clinic, stopping here and there and conducting treatment trials. Mothers measured the children's responses to trained and untrained questions at home in both a restricted setting (sitting at the kitchen table) and a multiple-natural setting (at various locations around the home). It was found that responses generalized to the home setting at a higher degree following the multiple-natural treatment. In this case, then, the multiple exemplars were different locations or settings, and this produced improved generalization to yet another setting as well as another experimenter (home and mother, respectively).

Stokes, Baer, and Jackson (1974) studied a nonverbal communicative response in four mentally retarded youngsters by teaching them to wave a greeting when they were approached by another person. As the response was being trained, each subject was probed sporadically throughout the day by anywhere from 4 to 14 different persons. The results demonstrated that each subject had to have training from two different teachers before the greeting response would generalize to persons who were not present during training. The authors also anecdotally noted broader setting generalization as well, as the greeting response generalized to the institution dining room and other locations within and outside of the institution, such as city streets and parks.

When one is using the techniques of training sufficient exemplars, one should be constantly measuring for generalization so that when sufficient exemplars have been introduced, training can be discontinued. It is not clear from the research thus far conducted whether this procedure facilitates stimulus control by expanding the items in the stimulus class until generalization occurs across new items in that class, or if the behavior generalizes simply as a function of added treatment trials.

## PROGRAM COMMON (ANTECEDENT) STIMULI

This is another procedure described by Stokes and Baer (1977). The underlying principle is that the treatment environment and the natural environment should be made more similar by having them both contain common stimuli. For the most part, researchers are advocating the use of stimuli in the clinic setting which occur in the natural environment. If these stimuli acquire stimulus control over the newly learned language responses in the teaching setting, then, when those stimuli occur naturally in the child's extraclinic environment, the appropriate responses should be evoked. It sounds logical and relatively simple, but that doesn't turn out to be quite the case.

Despite a rather thorough reading of the language literature, this writer has yet to find any research that pinpoints the salient stimuli that should and do evoke language responses from young children. Further, we know very little about the precise process of stimulus control and exactly what accounts for a neutral stimulus turning into a discriminative stimulus. We cannot predict for a given child whether or not generalization will occur or what stimuli will be responsible for evoking a new response in a nontreatment environment. Attempts at demonstrating stimulus generalization gradients, spoken of so eloquently in the animal literature, have failed with humans (Mowrer, 1971; Fahey, 1972; Costello and Bosler, 1976). Events that we refer to as stimuli for human behaviors are seldom single-dimension variables that can be quantified, controlled, and altered precisely according to their physical specifications, let alone their functional specifications. Even in the relatively controlled setting of the treatment environment, responses are acquired in the presence of a multitude of complicated, multidimensional stimuli. Pictures, objects, clinician verbalizations, and other clinical stimuli are presented by the clinician in the hope that they will act as $S^D$s to evoke the desired language response. They vie for the child's attention with the stimulus properties of the clinic room, the particular furniture present, the presence of a clinician (who is short, tall, male, female, with or without glasses, wearing certain clothing, showing certain facial expressions, using varieties of intonation), and so on. This does not even begin to tap the number of observable stimuli present in the treatment environment. Add internalized, unobservable $S^D$s that may also influence the child's responding, such as his state of deprivation for the available reinforcers, his interest in the (both relevant and irrelevant) stimulus variables, his desire to please the clinician, his fatigue, his boredom, and so on. Now compare this with the complexity of the stimulus dimensions that abound in the natural environment and are even more multidimensional. Language-evoking stimuli are embedded in the physical context, the social context, the child's intentions, the child's comprehension of the context, the language responses available to him, and myriad other dimensions of stimuli that occur subtly and simultaneously. What is it that the clinician should select from the natural environment to include in language treatment in the clinical setting? Although we can make some relatively reasonable guesses, we have no empirical data to guide us at this point.

An excellent, albeit extreme, example that demonstrates our naïveté regarding stimulus control is found in a study by Rincover and Koegel (1975). They taught ten autistic children simple discriminated responses to a strenuous learning criterion, and then tested these responses for generalization in an extratreatment setting (the lawn beside the lagoon outside of the treatment room). Four children showed no generalization across settings. They then proceeded to conduct an experimental analysis of stimulus control. For each child they were able to discover an incidental stimulus (incidental because it was not intended by the experimenters to be the $S^D$ that would evoke the child's response) that did, in fact, evoke correct responses in the extratreatment environment. One child, for example, during generalization testing, did not respond correctly to the presence of the previously presented picture, to the presence of the clinician who had taught him his correct response in the clinic, to returning to the treatment room and standing inside the door with the clinician and the other treatment stimuli present, or to the sight of the previously used positive reinforcer. He did respond correctly in the extratreatment environment, however, when the table and chairs from the clinic room were brought onto the lawn! Now that's stimulus control, but who would have predicted it?

Nonetheless, the procedure of using stimuli from the natural environment in the treatment setting has been espoused by Carr (1980) and is at the heart of the incidental teaching procedure described by Hart, Rogers-Warren, Risley, and their colleagues (Hart, 1981; Hart and Risley, 1968, 1974, 1975, 1980; Hart and Rogers-Warren, 1978). (Their description of milieu therapy will be addressed later in this chapter.)

The literature reviewed by this author produced only one example of this principle of using antecedent stimuli common to the natural environment during language treatment. (A special case of this procedure, the use of parents as clinicians, will be discussed separately.) Welch and Pear (1980) evaluated naming responses evoked by real objects in comparison with photographs of those objects and object pictures. They found that real objects were best at producing naming responses that generalized to the real objects in the natural environment for three of their four retarded children. (The fourth child showed no generalization.)

## PROGRAM COMMON (CONSEQUENT) STIMULI

Thus far we have been discussing the use in the treatment setting of *antecedent* stimuli from the natural environment. In an attempt to program common stimuli, it is also possible to select *consequent* stimuli (primarily positive reinforcers) from the natural environment and utilize them in the clinic setting. Although this has been advocated by Siegel and Spradlin (1982) in their recent discussion of generalization practices, essentially no experimental data are available to assess the helpfulness of this procedure in facilitating generalization across settings. The rationale is appealing, but it may be overly simplistic. As was true regarding antecedent stimuli, we know little of the events that act as reinforcers for language responses of children in their natural environments. Although there has been speculation, it has not yet led to empirical study. Inherent in the concept that the crux of language is its function or use (see, for example, Bates, 1976; Hart, 1981; Premack, 1970, 1971; Skinner, 1957) is the inference that the social-communication environment contains and controls events (reinforcers) that serve to shape and maintain this language use (and probably content and form as well). Skinner (1957) speculated on the nature of those reinforcers for various classes of language responses. Other writers have attempted to define classes of utterances by their assumed function (for example, Dore, 1977) rather than attempting to observe, specify or manipulate potential reinforcers (Hart, 1981).

Language treatment that attempts to utilize reinforcement integral to the natural environment is exemplified in the milieu therapy described by Hart (1981) and Hart and Rogers-Warren (1978) and discussed in the next section. There are no data-based studies in the literature yet which apply this procedure of using natural reinforcers. One study that is related to the issue was conducted by Williams, Koegel, and Egel (1981). While working with autistic children, they evaluated two different kinds of reinforcers: typically used food reinforcers (*arbitrary* reinforcers) and reinforcers that occurred as a natural part of the response, such as when opening a container was reinforced by finding a food reinforcer inside (referred to as *functional* reinforcers). The responses taught to the subjects and the stimuli used as reinforcers remained constant across the two conditions. The results demonstrated that responses followed by functional reinforcers were acquired more rapidly and maintained with the subsequent use of arbitrary reinforcers. The generalization of these behaviors to nontreatment settings was not studied.

Although there is a paucity of applied research examining the application of natural reinforcers, there are droves of examples in which the "naturalness" premise has been ignored. For example, a child who is learning to ask questions in a particular syntactic form might regard a picture and say, "What is the boy doing?" Oftentimes the clinician responds to this question by popping a piece of candy in the child's mouth and saying, "Good!" rather than answering the question with a description of the actions of the boy in the picture. Harris (1975) lists stimuli that have been provided as reinforcers in research on language treatment with nonverbal children: food, food plus praise, colored lights, tokens, music, physical contact, games, and play with a tape recorder. Although these stimuli were probably functional in producing increased rates of targeted language behaviors, most of them won't occur as consequences for language responses in the natural environment. Some would argue, however, that whatever the consequences for language in the natural environment, those consequences have not been functional or sufficient for the language deficient child (or he wouldn't be language deficient). Some of our research might be directed at ways to make naturally occurring potential reinforcers into stimuli that are as powerful as the artificial ones that have been used in much of our clinic-based language intervention.

## SELECT FUNCTIONAL RESPONSES

Stokes and Baer (1977) refer to this procedure as "introduce to natural maintaining contingencies." They describe it in the following manner:

Perhaps the most dependable of all generalization programming mechanisms is one that hardly deserves the name: the transfer of behavior control from the teacher-experimenter to stable, natural contingencies that can be trusted to operate in the environment to which the subject will return or already occupies. To a considerable extent, this goal is accomplished by choosing behaviors to teach that normally will meet maintaining reinforcement after the teaching. (p. 353)

This principle is currently addressed by researchers such as Hart and Rogers-Warren (1978), whose approach to the selection of target behaviors for language treatment follows currently popular pragmatics literature. They and many others writing about language today advocate selection of responses according to the function they serve. It is suggested that the function of language is the most salient and basic dimension of the response for the language learner and that content and form follow function. These architects of language intervention suggest that when language responses selected for treatment have immediate use for the child in the natural environment, generalization of those responses will be highly likely. Further, the language learning child will then be able to become part of the social interaction that is at the crux of communication, because he or she will quickly learn that language produces effects and exerts control.

To facilitate the acquisition of functional responses a group of researchers have described a process they refer to as *milieu therapy* (Hart and Rogers-Warren, 1978; Warren, Rogers-Warren, Baer, and Guess, 1980). Language instruction is conducted in the preschool setting, and naturally occurring opportunities to evoke and reinforce language (with appropriate and natural antecedent and consequent stimuli) are utilized as they occur. The teacher's goals are to create opportunities for language to be emitted; to prompt, model, or somehow evoke functional utterances; and to make sure that language use is reinforced by the natural contingencies of the environment, such as receiving the item asked for or maintaining a social, communicative interaction. Although these authors have not yet published data on the setting generalization produced by this procedure, it is certainly another process that seems logical and fruitful for further exploration.

MacDonald and Blott (1974) and Mac-Donald, Blott, Gordon, Spiegel, and Hartmann (1974) have described a program that incorporates some of this philosophy as well. The target behaviors they have selected to teach young language learners are based upon Brown's (1973) interpretation of Piaget's theories regarding language in the first 18 months. The selected language responses are word combinations that represent semantic relations first described by Schlesinger (1971) and also discussed by Bloom and Lahey (1978). Not only are children taught responses that express the earliest semantic relations acquired by normally developing children, they are taught these responses in both a clinic-type task and in natural contexts. That is, each session contains time allotted to teaching language responses through imitation, during conversation, and during

play. The data reported for this procedure (MacDonald, Blott, Gordon, Spiegel, and Hartmann, 1974) indicate that, in comparison with a no-treatment control group, it is successful in producing utterances of greater length (MLU) and complexity, especially for the particular utterance types taught by the program. Setting generalization data, however, have not been reported.

Two other reports address, from a theoretic perspective, the nature of the responses selected for language treatment. Both Holland (1975) and Lahey and Bloom (1977) describe the items that would be theoretically appropriate for a language deficient child's first lexicon. In similar fashion, they both suggest selecting responses that would be useful and meaningful to the child while fitting appropriately into the contexts of natural speaking settings. Neither article directly addresses the issue of generalization from the treatment setting to the natural environment, but both are relevant to this process by their strong push for selecting responses that would be used by the child and that would put his language into the communicative context and thus into contact with the natural consequences that would maintain those utterances.

Another response property considered mandatory by Lahey and Bloom (1977) is the selection of responses that would help the child learn the regularities that govern his language performance across content, form, and use dimensions. As discussed earlier in this chapter, a prerequisite for expanded language use is the child's acquisition of generative responding. If the child were unable to utilize his language repertoire to generate novel responses that fit the occasion, language use would not have the opportunity to come under adequate stimulus control or to come into contact with the reinforcing contingencies of the environment. Warren and colleagues (1980) have even gone so far as to say that setting generalization will not and cannot occur until this level of generalization (conceptualization of language rules) has occurred.

## TRAIN LOOSELY

The treatment described by Holland (1975) and also by the authors of milieu therapy (Hart and Rogers-Warren, 1978; Warren, Rogers-Warren, Baer, Guess, 1980) might meet with the requirements of Stokes and Baer's (1977) procedure described as training loosely. Language treatment is often designed in a narrow and rigid manner so that only certain responses are allowed, only certain discriminative stimuli are utilized, only certain reinforcers are presented, and only at certain times. When this is the case, differences between the treatment setting and the natural environment are spotlighted rather than muted. As Stokes and Baer describe, teaching designed loosely would promote a range of language responses that could be produced to varying types of stimuli with an accompanying range of consequences presented on varying schedules. Rather than design treatment that routinely searches out and removes any variables that might be meddlesome or incidental to the treatment, treatment that purports to train loosely would allow or even encourage the presence of such events. Thus the child would have the opportunity to learn to separate stimuli that should come to acquire stimulus control over their behavior from those that should be ignored. Siegel and Spradlin (1978) point this out as a way to teach the child ". . . to use the language response in the appropriate situation regardless of what other noncritical factors may be present or absent in the situation" (p. 391). In the typical language intervention design, the child has little opportunity to make such discriminations, although they are much needed in the natural environment.

As reasonable as this process sounds, however, Stokes and Baer (1977) were unable to find examples of it in the behavior modification literature. This should come as no shock. It is a description of the kind of treatment that would make most behavioral scientists quite nervous! It suggests little control over the nature, form, and complexity of the response, little influence exerted by the clinician, and little pos-

sibility for systematically measuring the behavior or experimentally assessing the functional relationships that might be occurring. It does seem to describe, however, what many clinicians have come to know as "play therapy," and may at least provide some rationale for such treatment. It seems actually to be the ultimate extension of the previously described principle of programming common stimuli.

This writer could also find no examples of this procedure in the empirically based language treatment literature. However, a related study that seemed to draw at least partially on the "train loosely" logic was one conducted by Dunlap and Koegel (1980) wherein two styles of treatment were compared in regard to the study of maintenance of learned behaviors among autistic children. In the constant condition, children were administered typical treatment tasks in which they were asked to emit the same response repeatedly as the task was presented over and over again for many trials. Subsequent tasks were introduced and practiced in the same repetitious manner. Reinforcement was provided for correct responses. (All of the behaviors had been previously learned by the subjects.) In the varied condition, the same number of different tasks was introduced for each subject. In this case, however, each consecutive trial was a different task requiring a different response and evoked by a different $S^D$ than the previous trial. The data not only indicated the maintenance of correct responding was considerably higher during the varied condition, but that children appeared more happy and motivated during these activities. They were not confused by the frequent change of task requirements but were alert and actively responding during this condition. Although this is far from the "loose" training described by Stokes and Baer, it does illustrate that stimulus and response variation is not incompatible with learning.

## MAKE CONTINGENCIES INDISCRIMINABLE

One of the characteristics of the natural environment is that it is often difficult for observers to determine what stimuli may be acting as reinforcers for a given behavior, because there may be no obvious consequence of a given response. For example, the child speaks and no one pays much attention. Or the events that immediately follow an utterance don't appear, intuitively, to offer much reinforcing value, such as when the child asks a question and the mother responds with an unrelated comment. Stokes and Baer (1977) have suggested that contingencies in the natural environment may also be indiscriminable to the child and that mirroring that condition in the clinical environment might be another way to make the treatment setting more like the natural environment and thus promote generalization across settings.

The most obvious procedure for making contingencies (the relationship between the response and its controlling reinforcer) indiscriminable is the use of intermittent reinforcement. It has been suggested that the reason intermittent reinforcement produces high response rates and resistance to extinction in learners is its quality of keeping the subject from being able to discriminate reinforcement delivery. There is no clear $S^D$ that signals to the subjects when to respond, so they just keep on responding consistently and frequently. Both Carr (1980) and Koegel and Rincover (1977) have stated that intermittent reinforcement should be considered a maintenance strategy rather than a generalization strategy. For purposes of this discussion, however, generalization and maintenance go hand in hand, since generalized language responses that are not maintained in the child's repertoire are of no value. (It is, however, important to understand that generalization and maintenance may require different technologies and that they should be considered separate, but related, entities.)

In Garcia's (1974) study that taught a verbal "conversational" chain to two mentally retarded subjects, maintaining their responses on a VR 3 schedule of reinforcement did not produce setting generalization. However, it may have maintained responding at a high enough rate to allow

testing for generalization which required evoking the response several times without accompanying reinforcement. This may not, however, have been the case, since no generalization was observed during the task that required the subjects to respond consecutively to ten new items. It is not clear whether the subjects emitted ten incorrect responses, thus displaying a lack of generalization, or simply failed to respond to all ten items, thus displaying a lack of maintenance.

Koegel and Rincover (1977), in the context of discussing the relative roles of maintenance and generalization, evaluated the maintenance of (nonlanguage) behavior for autistic subjects who had acquired behavior on different schedules of reinforcement (crf, FR 2, or FR 5). Subjects whose behavior had been on FR 5 schedules maintained correct responding indefinitely when the contingencies were removed, which was not the case for the remaining children.

In the same study, Koegel and Rincover also evaluated the use of delayed (but contingent) reinforcement as another method of making contingencies indiscriminable. In their method they presented the previously contingent positive reinforcer noncontingently, that is, never immediately following a correct response. For the first few presentations, responding would increase following this contingent delivery of the reinforcer. In this case, the reinforcer appeared to be acting as an $S^D$ and evoking responses by its presence. However, after several noncontingent presentations of the reinforcing stimulus, it finally lost its function and responses extinguished. Fowler and Baer (1981) also applied delayed reinforcement contingencies to (nonlanguage) behavior in a nursery school setting. Reinforcement was contingent upon the occurrence of particular responses in the morning, but was not delivered until the afternoon. The procedure was modestly successful at producing generalization to a second setting, but did not appear to be as powerful in promoting generalization as other techniques that have been described. It should also be noted that neither intermittent nor delayed reinforcement contingencies would be very efficient during the establishment of new behavior. Their value, if they have any in terms of generalization, would be in arranging such contingencies in the treatment setting after the new response had been well established in the subject's repertoire.

## MEDIATE GENERALIZATION

This set of techniques described by Stokes and Baer (1977) has been untapped by the applied language research. It centers on teaching the child responses that mediate or serve to induce the targeted response into the child's repertoire. Language itself, in terms of self-instruction, has been suggested as a potentially powerful mediating response that persons could learn in order to facilitate the occurrence of other behaviors. Mediating generalization is most often discussed in the context of self-control procedures. Rosenbaum and Drabman (1979) and O'Leary and Dubey (1979) have described a large body of research centered around teaching children self-control tactics, such as self-recording, self-evaluation of responses, setting one's own behavioral goals, and so on. None of these studies has involved language learning, but they suggest a potentially powerful set of tools for promoting generalization (or transfer); for if children become their own teachers, they never escape the treatment environment and teaching-learning could, in theory, be continuous.

Owen (1981), in an overview of research on procedures that generate and maintain life-style changes, described the cognitive components of self-control procedures that appear, with adults at least, to be important in producing behavior change. These theories suggest that a person's belief in his ability to control and change his own behavior and thus to have a ". . . sense of generalized personal efficacy . . ." (Owen, 1981) is an important component in self-control strategies.

No language studies using self-control procedures could be found. However, Johnston and Johnston (1972) gave chil-

dren who were learning articulation the opportunity to count their own correct responses and reinforced them for doing so. This procedure was effective in increasing the percentage of correct response, but it did not promote generalization of that correct responding to a second setting that was similar in many dimensions to the teaching setting. The children did not even take their counters with them to the second environment!

In another articulation study, Costello, Howard-Burger, and Graves (unpublished manuscript) taught misarticulating youngsters to judge the quality of their articulatory responses as correct or incorrect. Articulation learning occurred under this condition. Although generalization to the natural environment was reported only anecdotally, it appeared that such self-evaluation strategies might be successful in producing transfer of newly learned behavior beyond the confines of the treatment setting. (Note that this procedure is referred to here as a transfer, rather than a generalization, strategy.)

## INCREASE RESPONSE RATES

Hart (1981) has pointed out that children's language behavior will not come into contact with the maintaining consequences in the environment if the children do not produce enough language to withstand the intermittent, delayed, and subtle nature of those reinforcers. She has suggested, therefore, that high rates of language responding be established in language learning children so that their behavior is resistant to extinction in the natural environment. Although she does not specify how this should be done, the most common method of establishing high response rates is the use of intermittent reinforcement as discussed above (although here its use is suggested for a very different reason). If this tactic were to prove successful in promoting generalization of behavior to an extratreatment environment, one would wonder whether it was because of the use of intermittent reinforcement during extended treatment trials or simply because of the added practice afforded by those extra trials.

## TEACH GENERALIZED IMITATION

Both Harris (1975) and Hart (1981) have pointed out the efficacy of teaching children to become imitators. If a child were able to acquire new language responses through observing others, the language models that occur spontaneously and continually in the natural environment could become salient stimuli to the young child. Baer, Peterson, and Sherman (1968) were among the first to illustrate the durability of behaviors contained in an imitative response class. As long as some of the members of the class are occasionally reinforced, other imitative responses will continue to be emitted even without being reinforced. This would seem to be a necessary qualification for language behavior in the natural environment.

Hart (1981) goes on to suggest that imitation training would be most productive if it were combined with peer modeling. Although no data regarding generalization across settings have been provided yet, other authors have demonstrated peer modeling to be a fruitful technique for promoting language learning (Leonard, 1975; Courtright and Courtright, 1976, 1979).

## TRAIN "TO GENERALIZE"

This technique, described by Stokes and Baer (1977), suggests that the child be directly taught to generalize essentially through being reinforced every time a new response is generated in the presence of new stimuli. That is, generalized responses are differentially reinforced. This technique is probably included in some of the previously described tactics, such as training loosely and training sufficient exemplars, but no specific examples of it were found in the language intervention literature.

## TRAIN AND HOPE

A remaining generalization technique noted by Stokes and Baer (1977) was given the forlorn name of train and hope. However, incorporation into the treatment design of one or more of the ten procedures described above should lend more hope to the effectiveness of clinic-based language intervention where issues of setting generalization are concerned. It should be obvious from the preceding review that, although a wide range of within-clinic considerations has been suggested, there is little empirical evidence regarding their actual effectiveness as promoters of generalization, especially in the course of language intervention. That simply indicates that clinical researchers interested in setting generalization have a busy agenda ahead.

There are, however, a few studies that appear to have generated small amounts of setting generalization following the train and hope model. That is, each study describes a set of treatment procedures utilized to establish a new language response in subjects' repertoires. This acquisition phase was then followed by some variety of measurement for the occurrence of the language response outside of the treatment setting.

Martin (1975) used imitation training and social reinforcement to teach appropriate use of color and size adjectives to two severely retarded children. Generalization testing was conducted in a different setting and with a new experimenter on novel pictures. Generalization was easily obtained. The variables responsible for such an unusual effect were not speculated upon by the author, but could have been at least partially a result of the fact that the generalization task was the same as the treatment task (programming common stimuli, this time from the treatment setting into the natural environment rather than the reverse, which has been described above). Hegde, Noll, and Pecora (1979) also showed generalization of several syntactic forms to a nontreatment environment when the generalization task (with new stimuli) was the same as the treatment task.

In this case, the generalization environment was the home and the new experimenter was the subject's mother.

Hester and Hendrickson (1977) taught language delayed children to describe various agent-action-object relationships within a five-element syntactic form. Generalization was measured through observation of the children's language behavior during free play in their classroom. Generalization was produced for both lexical and syntactic forms, and the authors speculated that this was because of the functional nature of the language responses trained.

## SETTING GENERALIZATION: POTENTIAL SOLUTIONS OUTSIDE THE CLINIC SETTING

### SEQUENTIAL MODIFICATION

We have yet to look outside the treatment setting for procedures that might facilitate the occurrence of new language behavior beyond the clinic environment. Stokes and Baer (1977) provide yet one more technique that moves somewhat in this direction. Sequential modification occurs when the treatment environment is systematically extended from one location to another and another and another until spontaneous generalization to nontreatment environments has occurred. This process is rather like training sufficient exemplars when the exemplars are different settings. The various settings can be located within a broad treatment environment or can extend into the natural environment: a first step outside the clinic. Harris (1975) points out that sequential modification may be a necessary procedure, especially for mentally retarded subjects who typically have problems selecting relevant $S^D$s to which to respond.

In a study reviewed earlier as an example of training sufficient exemplars, Handleman (1979) compared the setting generalization effects of language training that occurred in a restricted, clinic-like setting at school versus treatment that was administered progressively throughout different locations within the school. It was found that generalization to the home setting was more likely to occur following the second, "multiple-natural" condition—an example of sequential modification. Garcia's (1974) study, noted earlier as an example of training sufficient exemplars, could also be considered sequential modification. Mentally retarded subjects were treated first by the experimenter in one setting, and then by a second experimenter in a second setting. Sequential instruction in two different settings was necessary before modest generalization to a third experimenter and setting was displayed. Also reported earlier was a study by Welch and Pear (1980) which described generalization of naming responses to the natural environment when clinic training utilized real objects as opposed to pictures or photographs. One subject displayed no generalization until the naming lessons with real objects as stimuli were conducted in two other treatment settings, thus sequential modification.

Rubin and Stolz (1974) added a variation to this procedure by conducting training (teaching a mentally retarded subject correct pronoun use among other verbal behaviors) in the institution throughout the day and in varieties of settings. The institution represented the natural environment for this subject. Initial training had been conducted in a clinic-like environment, but no setting generalization occurred until the treatment had been moved to the natural environment and spread throughout the day. Since both of these changes in the way of teaching was conducted occurred at the same time, one cannot determine whether the more influential variable was the extended practice in a variety of *different settings* or in *natural settings*. In the previous studies applying sequential modification, all of the added treatment conditions occurred within the broad confines of the unnatural, treatment environment. Rubin and Stolz added natural environmental settings to this formula.

Another example that could be considered sequential modification and that utilized the natural environment is the work of Mulac and Tomlinson (1977). Three groups of children were studied. One group received syntax instruction on the Monterey Language Programs (Gray and Ryan, 1973); one group received this syntax treatment followed by treatment administered by the mother in the home; the third (control) group received articulation instruction. More than 20 days following the termination of all treatment the children's conversational use of the target syntactic forms was assessed by the experimenter in a clinic playroom and by the mother at home. The subjects who had received added treatment through the transfer program administered by their mothers showed greater setting generalization. Of course, in all of these examples of sequential modification, one must ask whether it was the expanded stimulus control accomplished by moving the treatment from place to place which facilitated generalization, or whether it was simply the extra number of training trials this procedure afforded subjects. Would they have learned better, and generalized just as well, if the added trials had been conducted in the original treatment setting? This variable has not been controlled in any of the experiments utilizing sequential modification noted by this writer.

Among all of the techniques described as potential promoters of setting generalization, sequential modification appears to be the most consistently effective. Even with severely retarded subjects, the number of settings in which treatment was successively administered was not often very large (two to three settings). One might wonder, then, why more researchers and clinicians have not incorporated this technique into their treatment design and arranged for concurrent, as opposed to sequential, modification from the beginning. That is, why haven't we simply arranged for language treatment to occur simultaneously in two or three different settings, thus expanding stimulus control and making it more difficult for the subject to discriminate between treatment and nontreatment environments? Carr (1980) has pointed out the expense in terms of time and personnel that must be expanded to

use this technique. It is possible that most persons are willing to train and hope first, and then move to sequential modification if setting generalization does not spontaneously occur as a function of the training procedures. In an effort to save time and money, they would prefer not to do anything that would not have been necessary in the first place. However, the record appears to indicate rather clearly that language instruction as it is typically constructed will not produce much setting generalization without the addition of procedures designed specifically for that purpose.

It might also be pointed out here that sequential modification, especially when one or more of the added treatment settings are in the natural environment, might better be referred to as a transfer, rather than a generalization, strategy. It is a procedure designed to facilitate occurrence of newly learned responses in the natural environment by treating those behaviors directly in the natural environment.

## ADJUNCTIVE MILIEU THERAPY

A bigger step into the natural environment, and another technique that could be referred to as a transfer procedure, is the model referred to as milieu therapy and described by Hart and Rogers-Warren (1978) and Warren and colleagues (1980). In this model it is proposed that language intervention begin in the controlled clinic setting and then be extended to the extraclinic environment. The extraclinic treatment is then considered an adjunct to the clinic-based treatment. In this way the advantage of laboratory-like control can be exerted over the relevant variables so that targeted language responses could, in theory, be more easily established. This is also the setting in which the professional language clinician—equipped with needed sophisticated language-building knowledge and techniques—operates most conveniently. (It could be assumed that some or all of the within-clinic generalization facilitating techniques described in the previous discussion would be incorporated into this clinic-based language intervention design. In fact, Owen [1981] has suggested that the concurrent use of a range of such techniques is the most effective way of producing setting generalization, even though it wreaks havoc with our attempts at experimental analysis of generalization producing variables.)

Following the establishment of an appropriate, useful, and adequately extensive repertoire of language responses in the clinic setting, the next step in this model would be to extend language intervention activities to the natural environment in ways that would promote the occurrence of language responses by the child and then assure their maintenance.

The milieu therapy described earlier (Hart and Rogers-Warren, 1978; Warren and colleagues, 1980) is conducted in the preschool setting and is designed to function in this manner—as an adjunct to concurrent or previously completed clinic-based language instruction (although it is not difficult to visualize children for whom the milieu therapy alone would be sufficient language intervention). These authors outline three major objectives of this treatment. The first is to provide opportunities and reasons for language to be used by the child. They point out that such opportunities for language responses in-children in the natural environment may be fewer and more subtle than we appreciate, and Spradlin and Siegel (1982) concur in this opinion.

This point was well illustrated in an experiment conducted by Halle, Marshall, and Spradlin (1979). They observed that mentally retarded institutionalized children were using little language in daily activities, evening mealtime being one example. They found that by simply withholding the children's food trays until they asked for them (inserting a 15-second delay between the time the child walked up to the person who handed out trays and the time the tray was handed to the child), an opportunity for language was provided and was used by the children (initially with the help of promting). Further, application of this technique at other times (sequential modi-

fication) served to evoke language responses from the children in other settings (for example, lunchtime).

Adults and children with normal language use who frequent the natural environment of the language deficient child may be glibly talking nonstop, so that the child has little opportunity to insert his newly learned responses. Further, these responses may not yet be under the stimulus control of the natural environment's many and varied evoking stimuli, so the child may not recognize occasions when language could be appropriately used. Providing these opportunities, and making them salient, are important responsibilities of persons in the natural environment.

Also in relation to response-evoking stimuli in the natural environment, Spradlin and Siegel (1982) point out that this environment may not hold many appropriate language models for the child. Although some research would indicate that adults, parents in particular, intuitively adjust their language to the level appropriate for the child, this may not always be the case. Further, it is not clear that this kind of language functions as the best language model for language deficient children. Rogers-Warren and Warren (1980) have described a "mand-model-reinforce" tactic that can be used to incorporate both opportunities for language responses and appropriate language models for children. During incidental teaching (Hart and Risley, 1968, 1974, 1975, 1980), the teacher pinpoints a moment in the child's ongoing activity that would be conducive to a language response and then asks the child for such a response. For example, noticing the child looking at an assortment of toys aligned on a shelf, the teacher might ask, "What would you like to play with?" Having presented the mand, he or she awaits the child's response (Halle and colleagues, 1979). If none is forthcoming, or if the response is less than the teacher knows the child to be capable of, he or she models the kind of response that would be appropriate, perhaps even directly requesting repetition. Then, when an appropriate response is uttered by the child, the teacher provides prompt and natural reinforcement by awarding the desired toy (and possibly repeating or expanding the child's utterance in the process).

In the manner described above, the preschool teacher in milieu therapy is also addressing the second principle advocated by these authors: make language functional. If language responses are prompted from the child at times when such responses are particularly useful, the child can begin to learn the power and function of language. The third part of the equation, arranging reinforcement for the occurrence of language responses, is also illustrated in this example. The milieu therapy, or incidental teaching model, stresses incorporation of the kinds of events that are (theoretically) the natural reinforcers for communicative behaviors. The careful use of reinforcement serves the dual function of increasing the frequency of language usage as well as bringing language under appropriate stimulus control.

## ADJUNCTIVE HOME INTERVENTION

It should be obvious that the milieu therapy model could also be applied by parents of language deficient children in the children's home environment. Although the principles are relatively logical and simple, their actual application requires practice, judgment, and some knowledge of language development and treatment principles. These skills could, however, be taught to parents by having them participate in the language intervention setting in the clinic or preschool, or by having the clinician assist parents in learning these techniques in their home. MacDonald, Blott, Gordon, Spiegel, and Hartmann (1974) describe the incorporation of parents into their language training program, which was described earlier. The parents are trained alongside the clinician in the clinic setting and then continue the use of the language intervention activities in their home. Although no data have been presented regarding the role of the parent in the success of this language instruction

(or of its generalization effects), the logic of such procedures is compelling.

The importance of the natural environment, most particularly the home environment, to the maintenance of acquired language skills in language deficient children has been most poignantly presented in the report of Lovaas, Koegel, Simmons, and Long (1973). They reported follow-up information on autistic children who had received language (and other) instruction through the research program at UCLA. Subsequently some children returned to their homes and families, while others were institutionalized. The follow-up data clearly discriminated between these two groups and against the children who had remained institutionalized. The first group of children had maintained, and even continued to expand, the behavioral repertoires they had been taught, while the latter group essentially lost it all. This sad commentary should serve to remind us that if we have not clearly demonstrated that setting generalization has occurred following language intervention, and that the newly acquired language behaviors and the natural environment will be mutually supportive, then our responsibilities where language intervention is concerned have yet to be completed.

## PARENTS AS PRIMARY TREATMENT AGENTS

A major departure from all of the models of language treatment and generalization facilitation described above is an attempt to get the jump on generalization by arranging language treatment to occur exclusively in the natural environment. Maybe this can be done by training parents to be the primary treatment agents for their children. Parents in our society have been delegated the principle responsibility for their children's development and well-being, and thus language training should be their responsibility. Since this process essentially embraces all of the individual techniques described thus far, its potential as a successful language intervention strategy is quite good. If language intervention were conducted by parents, it could occur in any setting and at any time (sequential modification). Since there would be no separate treatment and nontreatment environments, the problems presented when a child discriminates between those two kinds of settings would be negated, as would the need to program common stimuli, make contingencies indiscriminable, mediate generalization, or specifically train the child "to generalize." Because language intervention would be occurring during a wide range of activities and in the myriad contexts that exist in the natural environment, training on a sufficient number of exemplars would be a natural outgrowth of this process, as would the use of evoking and consequent stimuli found naturally in the environment. Language utterances from the child could easily come under natural maintaining contingencies, and the entire process would probably illustrate the loose training philosophy. High rates of functional, useful language utterances could be a by-product of this kind of treatment. Parents could provide numerous opportunities for the child to respond, each response activating relevant parts of the treatment system.

On the other hand, in circumstances in which more powerful procedures or more intensive intervention are required to influence the child's language performance positively, special techniques from the laboratory could be instituted for as long as they were needed. For example, more obvious or direct reinforcers might be introduced to the home setting, or reinforcement schedules might be intensified. Imitation and modeling might be inserted for some intensive training on a particular aspect of language performance. When they had served their purpose, these contrived and artificial variables would be phased out and the natural environment would again be just that.

This writer was unable to find any examples of this kind of exclusively home-based language intervention reported in the literature. In a related study, however, Costello and Bosler (1976) taught parents of misarticulating children to administer a treatment program to correct phenome misarticulations. No part of the treatment was conducted by a professional clinician or held in a traditional treatment setting. The entire program was administered by mothers to their children at home. Generalization of correct articulation to a nontreatment environment was measured in four different settings in the university speech and hearing clinic at different stages during the parent-administered articulation instruction. Generalization from the treatment (home) to the nontreatment setting was pervasive.

Koegel and his colleagues (Koegel, Schreibman, Britten, Burke, and O'Neill, 1982; Koegel, Schreibman, Johnson, O'Neill, and Dunlap, in press) have for some time been in the business of training parents to be the primary treatment agents for their autistic children. In comparisons of the effectiveness of matched parent treatment and direct clinic intervention, these authors have reported unqualified success for the children whose parents have been their teachers. These children have improved at least as much as their clinic-treated controls in areas of appropriate play, appropriate speech and language, and social nonverbal behavior, and have shown substantial reductions in tantrums, self-stimulation, noncooperation, and psychotic speech. Further, children who were trained by their parents generalized these behavior improvements to the nontreatment clinic setting in their mothers' presence and, in fact, performed much better in the presence of their mothers than did the children whose training had been clinic-bound. These results were maintained during unstructured home observations. Children who had been trained at home displayed much better behavior at home than the children who had received 255 hours of professional treatment (which was highly successful in producing in-clinic behavior change). The investment of professional time with these children and their parents was only 25 to 30 hours—the time required to teach the parents the principles and skills of behavior management and to ensure that these skills would generalize across the many child behaviors that parents had to deal with. Beyond these impressive results, it turned out that the parents who were the primary treatment agents for their children had more leisure time than the parents whose children were being treated by professional clinicians!

In their latest article on language training philosophies and strategies, Spradlin and Siegel (1982) appear to advocate such parent-directed, home-based language treatment whenever it is deemed feasible. Although they ultimately express reservations about the possibilities for children's language learning in the natural environment, they write:

The problem of generalization raises the question of the best environment in which to carry out language instruction. There are strong arguments to support the teaching of language in a home environment. In theory at least, homes provide the opportunity for children to learn the useful functions of language; to name and request, describe, relate, influence, and all of the other uses of language. Moreover, once language is learned in the home environment, there need be no extreme concern about the durability of these skills, since the environment presents numerous occasions for language to occur and ample reinforcement when it does. Generalization should be less of a problem, since the children are acquiring language skills in the environment in which the skills are most useful. It is tempting to conclude that the home is the best setting for language instruction. By the same logic, parents may be the best teachers, since they have the most frequent and consistent access to the child, are involved in the widest variety of communication situations, and control innumerable reinforcers. . . .

It might seem that problems in generalization would be solved by moving the responsibility for teaching from the clinician to the parent, and from the clinic to the home. (p. 3)

It certainly appears that these views are worthy of systematic pursuit.

## CONCLUSIONS

The most pervasive conclusion provoked by this report on language training and setting generalization must be that we have more ideas and hypotheses and hunches than we have data. For us as a profession, and for the language deficient children we serve, it is time to put up or shut up. It is time for empirical answers to empirical questions.

## REFERENCES

Baer DM, Guess D: Teaching productive noun suffixes to severely retarded children. Am J Ment Defic 77:498–505, 1973

Baer DM, Peterson RF, Sherman JA: The development of imitation by reinforcing behavioral similarity to a model. J Exper Anal Behav 10: 405–416, 1968

Bates E: *Language and Context*. New York: Academic Press, 1976

Bennett CW, Ling D: Teaching a complex verbal response to a hearing impaired girl. J Appl Behav Anal 5:321–328, 1972

Bloom L, Lahey M: *Language Development and Language Disorders*. New York: John Wiley & Sons, 1978

Bricker WA: A systematic approach to language training. In Schiefelbusch RL (ed): *Language of the Mentally Retarded*. Baltimore: University Park Press, 1972

Brown R: *A First Language: The Early Stages*. Cambridge: Harvard University Press, 1973

Carr EG: Generalization of treatment effects following educational intervention with autistic children and youth. In Wilcox B, Thompson A (eds): *Critical Issues in Educating Autistic Children and Youth*. Washington, D.C.: U.S. Department of Education, Office of Special Education, 1980

Costello JM, Bosler S: Generalization and articulation instruction. J Speech Hear Dis 41:359–373, 1976

Costello JM, Howard-Burger L, Graves GA: Auditory discrimination and functional disorders of articulation. Unpublished manuscript

Courtright JA, Courtright IC: Imitative modeling as theoretical base for instructing language-disordered children. J Speech Hear Res 19:655–663, 1976

Courtright JA, Courtright IC: Imitative modeling as a language intervention strategy: The effects of two mediating variables. J Speech Hear Res 22:389–402, 1979

Dore J: Children's ilocutionary acts. In Freedle RO (ed): *Discourse Production and Comprehension*. Norwood, NJ: Ablex, 1977

Drabman RS, Hammer D, Rosenbaum MS: Assessing generalization in behavior modification with children. The generalization map. Behav Assess 1: 1979

Dunlap G, Koegel RL: Motivating autistic children through stimulus variation. J Appl Behav Anal 13:619–627, 1980

Fahey R: Comment on transfer of training in articulation. Letter to the Editor. J Speech Hear Dis 37:424, 1972

Fowler SA, Baer DM: "Do I have to be good all day?" The timing of delayed reinforcement as a factor in generalization. J Appl Behav Anal 14:13–24, 1981

Garcia E: The training and generalization of a conversational speech form in nonverbal retardates. J Appl Behav Anal 7:137–149, 1974

Garcia E, Guess D, Byrnes J: Development of syntax in a retarded girl using procedures of imitation, reinforcement and modeling. J Appl Behav Anal 6:299–310, 1973

Gray BB, Ryan BP: *A Language Program for the Nonlanguage Child*. Champaign, Ill: Research Press, 1973

Guess D, Sailor W, Baer DM: Children with limited language. In Schiefelbusch RL (ed): *Language Intervention Strategies*. Baltimore: University Park Press, 1978

Guess D, Sailor W, Rutherford G, Baer DM: An experimental analysis of linguistic development: The productive use of the plural morpheme. J Appl Behav Anal 1:297–306, 1968

Hall, P, Tomblin J: A follow-up study of children with articulation and language disorders. J Speech Hear Dis 43:227–241, 1978

Halle JW, Marshall AM, Spradlin JE: Time delay: A technique to increase language use and facilitate generalization in retarded children. J Appl Behav Anal 12:431–440, 1979

Handleman JS: Generalization by autistic-type children of verbal responses across settings. J Appl Behav Anal 12:273–284, 1979

Harris SL: Teaching language to nonverbal children—with emphasis on problems of generalization. Psycholog Bull 82:562–580, 1975

Hart B: Pragmatics: How language is used. Analy Interven Develop Dis 1:299–313, 1981

Hart B, Risley T: Establishing the use of descriptive adjectives in the spontaneous speech of disadvantaged preschool children. J Appl Behav Anal 1:109–120, 1968

Hart B, Risley T: Using preschool materials to modify the language of disadvantaged children. J Appl Behav Anal 7:243–256, 1974

Hart B, Risley T: Incidental teaching of language in the preschool. J Appl Behav Anal 8:411–420, 1975

Hart B, Risley T: In vivo language intervention: Unanticipated general effects. J Appl Behav Anal 13:407–432, 1980

Hart B, Rogers-Warren A: A milieu approach to language teaching. In Schiefelbusch RL (ed): *Language Intervention Strategies*. Baltimore: University Park Press, 1978

Hegde M, Gierut J: The operant training and generalization of pronouns and a verb form in a language delayed child. J Commun Dis 12:23–34, 1979

Hegde M, Noll M, Pecora R: A study of some factors affecting generalization of language training. J Speech Hear Dis 44:301–320, 1979

Hester P, Hendrickson J: Training functional expressive language: The acquisition and generalization of five-element syntactic responses. J Appl Behav Anal 10:316, 1977

Holland AL: Language therapy for children: Some thoughts on context and content. J Speech Hear Dis 40:514–523, 1975

Ingham RJ: Evaluation and maintenance in stuttering treatment: A search for ecstasy with nothing but agony. In Boberg E (ed): *Maintenance of Fluency*. New York: Elsevier, 1981

Johnston JM, Johnston GT: Modification of consonant speech-sound articulation in young children. J Appl Behav Anal 5:233–246, 1972

Koegel RL, Rincover A: Research on the difference between generalization and maintenance in extra-therapy responding. J Appl Behav Anal 10:1–12, 1977

Koegel RL, Schreibman L, Britten KR, Burke JC, O'Neill RE: A comparison of parent training to direct child treatment. In Koegel RL, Rincover A, Egel AL (eds): *Educating and Understanding Autistic Children*. San Diego: College Hill Press, 1982

Koegel RL, Shreibman L, Johnson J, O'Neill RE, Dunlap G: Collateral effects of parent-training on families with autistic children. In Dangel RF, Polster RA (eds): *Behavioral Parent-Training: Issues in Research and Practice*. New York: Guilford Press, in press

Lahey M, Bloom L: Planning a first lexicon: Which words to teach first. J Speech Hear Dis 43:340–350, 1977

Lee L, Koenigsknecht R, Mulhern S: *Interactive Language Development Teaching*. Evanston, IL: Northwestern University Press, 1975

Leonard LB: Modeling as a clinical procedure in language training. Lang Speech Hear Serv Schools 6:72–85, 1975

Leonard LB: Facilitating linguistic skills in children with specific language impairment. Appl Psycholing 2:89–118, 1981

Lovaas OI, Koegel RL, Simmons JQ, Long JS: Some generalization and follow-up measures on autistic children in behavior therapy. J Appl Behav Anal 6:131–166, 1973

Lutzker JR, Sherman JA: Producing generative sentence usage by imitation and reinforcement procedures. J Appl Behav Anal 7:447–460, 1974

MacDonald JD, Blott JP: Environmental language intervention: The rationale for a diagnostic and training strategy through rules, context and generalization. J Speech Hear Dis 39:244–256, 1974

MacDonald JD, Blott JP, Gordon K, Spiegel B, Hartmann M: An experimental parent-assisted treatment program for preschool language-delayed children. J Speech Hear Dis 39:395–415, 1974

Martin JA: Generalizing the use of descriptive adjectives through modeling. J Appl Behav Anal 8:203–209, 1975

Miller J, Yoder D: A syntax teaching program. In McLean J, Yoder D, Schiefelbusch RL (eds): *Language Intervention with the Retarded*. Baltimore: University Park Press, 1972

Miller J, Yoder D: An ontogenetic language teaching strategy for retarded children. In Schiefelbusch RL, Lloyd LL (eds): *Language Perspectives—Ac-*

*quisition, Retardation, and Intervention*. Baltimore: University Park Press, 1974

Mowrer DE: Transfer of training in articulation therapy. J Speech Hear Dis 36:427–446, 1971

Mulac A, Tomlinson C: Generalization of an operant remediation program for syntax with language-delayed children. J Commun Dis 10:231–244, 1977

O'Leary SG, Dubey DR: Applications of self-control procedures by children: A review. J Appl Behav Anal 12:449–466, 1979

Owen N: Facilitating maintenance of behavior change. In Boberg E (ed): *Maintenance of Fluency*. New York: Elsevier, 1981

Premack D: A functional analysis of language. J Exper Anal Behav 14:107–125, 1970

Premack D: Language in chimpanzee? Science 172:808–822, 1971

Rincover A, Koegel RL: Setting generality and stimulus control in autisic children. J Appl Behav Anal 8:235–246, 1975

Rogers-Warren A, Warren SF: Mands for verbalization: Facilitating the display of newly trained language in children. Behav Mod 4:361–382, 1980

Rosenbaum MS, Drabman RS: Self-control training in the classroom: A review and critique. J Appl Behav Anal 12:456–485, 1979

Rubin BK, Stolz SB: Generalization of self-referent speech established in a retarded adolescent by operant procedures. Behav Ther 5:93–106, 1974

Schlesinger IM: Production of utterances and language acquisition. In Slobin DI (ed): *The ontogenesis of grammar*. New York: Academic Press, 1971

Schumaker J, Sherman JA: Training generative verb usage by imitation and reinforcement procedures. J Appl Behav Anal 3:273–287, 1970

Siegel GM, Spradlin JE: Programming for language and communication therapy. In Schiefelbusch RL (ed): *Language Intervention Strategies*. Baltimore: University Park Press, 1978

Skinner BF: *Verbal Behavior*. New York: Appleton-Century-Crofts, 1957

Smeets PM, Striefel S: Training the generative usage of article-noun responses in severely retarded males. J Ment Defic Res 20:121–127, 1976

Spradlin JE, Siegel GM: Language training in natural and clinical environments. J Speech Hear Dis 47:2–6, 1982

Stokes TF, Baer DM: An implicit technology of generalization. J Appl Behav Anal 10:349–367, 1977

Stokes TF, Baer DM, Jackson RL: Programming generalization of a greeting response in four retarded children. J Appl Behav Anal 7:599–610, 1974

Warren SF, Rogers-Warren A, Baer DM, Guess D: The assessment and facilitation of language generalization. In Sailor W, Wilcox B, Brown L (eds): *Methods of Instruction for Severely Handicapped Students*. Baltimore: Brooks, 1980

Waryas CL, Stremel-Campbell K: Grammatical training for the language-delayed child—a new perspective. In Schiefelbusch RL (ed): *Language Intervention Strategies*. Baltimore: University Park Press, 1978

Weiner P: A language-delayed child at adolescence. J Speech Hear Dis 39:202–212, 1974

Welch SJ, Pear JJ: Generalization of naming responses to objects in the natural environment as a function of stimulus modality with retarded children. J Appl Behav Anal 13:629–643, 1980

Whaley DL, Mallott RW: *Elementary principles of behavior*. New York: Appleton-Century-Crofts, 1971

Wheeler A, Sulzer B: Operant training and generalization of a verbal response form in a speech deficient child. J Appl Behav Anal 3:139–146, 1970

Williams JA, Koegel RL, Egel AL: Response-reinforcer relationships and improved learning in autistic children. J Appl Behav Anal 14:53–60, 1981

# DISCUSSION: PART VII: EVALUATING PROGRAM EFFECTIVENESS

*LEIJA V. MCREYNOLDS*

The term evaluation has a number of meanings ranging from "interpretation" to "ascertaining the worth of." The broad nature of the definitions is reflected in Chapters 15 and 16.

## SETTING GENERALIZATION

In Chapter 16 Costello chose to discuss evaluation in terms of treatment effectiveness as represented by generalization of the target behavior to settings outside the treatment environment. She didn't speak directly to the how or why of evaluation, choosing to direct her remarks to the importance of arranging and organizing events and simuli in such a way as to facilitate generalization when it is desired in treatment. Thus my discussion of her chapter is not directed to what she had to say about methodology for evaluation of treatment, but rather to the topic she addressed and its relationship to evaluation. My remarks on Costello's chapter are somewhat limited because the topic was covered and presented comprehensively.

The variables presented by Costello were also described by authors who examined the applied behavior literature, as she noted. Although the identified variables were not found in the language intervention literature, they appeared to Costello to constitute principles that can be applied to any behavior, including language. As she noted, it is important to us to identify variables in training that will facilitate or enhance generalization. Without generalization we cannot make claims about treatment effectiveness. Edicts to train loosely, to train a sufficient number of exemplars, to program common stimuli in the training and generalization setting are practical and logical, representing variables that can readily be investigated in a controlled fashion. That the appropriate evaluations have not been conducted is, as she indicated, not surprising. We have conducted few evaluations of language treatment variables and even fewer evaluations of variables influencing language generalization, but she told us about that.

It's all right, for example, to propose that training be conducted in the natural environment, and by mothers, but until we know that the procedures we are using, or training mothers to use, are the most effective ones, we should be reluctant to encourage their use by anyone. Not only should we check out the procedures we use for training language behaviors, but having done that, we should proceed to evaluate these same treatment variables in regard to their influence on generalization of the language behaviors.

It seems to me that most of the variables discussed by Costello are particularly suitable for experimental evaluations. They could be explored in group designs in which two groups are used. The design could be a treatment-no-treatment one or, more appropriately, two groups receiving two different treatments for comparison purposes. Although group designs have been traditionally used as the primary method for research in speech pathology and audiology, many clinical researchers recognize the problems encountered when groups are required for experimental purposes. The problem is probably more severe in research involving disordered populations than it is in studies using normal individuals. That problem, of course, is the need to obtain a sufficient number of clients to fulfill the requirements for a statistical treatment of data. It is difficult to obtain a sufficient number of disordered clients to form groups, and when a no-treatment group is part of the design, we are reluctant to withhold treatment from clients in need of it. This lack of subjects may be one of the most important reasons for absence of treatment research in speech language pathology.

Fortunately, group designs for treatment research have now been supplemented with single subject experimental designs. (Hersen and Barlow, 1976; McReynolds and Kearns, 1982). The designs are appropriate for studies of treatment variables when the subject population is small, and particularly suitable for addressing the issue of generalization. Investigators have reported a number of advantages to use of single subject designs. These include the fact that the subject serves as his own control in that all conditions of the experiment are administered to him. With the appropriate single subject design no subject need go without treatment. Another advantage is that the designs are time-series designs in which behavior is monitored as it gradually changes during treatment and nontreatment. This constant and continuous surveillance enables the experimenter to document, with data, the moment by moment changes in the target behavior. Therefore the re-

search is both process and product research providing an in-depth study of the behavior from the start of treatment to the finish, and the effectiveness of the procedure throughout.

Flexibility is another plus in single subject designs. We frequently deplore the variability found in clients with the same disorder. Homogeneous groups are difficult to find. Single subject designs are flexible enough to allow modifications when variability is encountered to enable us to seek out the source or sources of variability.

The point is that we have available to us the tools to conduct controlled evaluations of our treatment effectiveness and variables which will facilitate generalization, not only to other settings, but to other individuals and behaviors related to the target behavior. We have not done so, as Costello pointed out. There is no literature on generalization research in language intervention. To identify promising variables she was forced to examine generalization research on behaviors other than language.

## PROGRAM EVALUATION

Teris Schery and Mark Lipsey's chapter addressed the issue of evaluation directly. They proposed that we conduct evaluations of entire programs, not only treatment programs but the delivery systems through which the interventions are administered. I agree with their sentiments, but with qualifications. They indicated that it probably isn't feasible or realistic to expect to conduct controlled, experimental research when evaluations are conducted in the "real world," and this may be correct. If so, we need to make some decisions. Should large-scale evaluations be initiated before we have accumulated data in a controlled manner in evaluations of single components within a program? How much confidence can we place in results from uncontrolled studies as opposed to results from well-controlled ones? Schery and Lipsey mentioned some of the problems encountered in the large-scale evaluation conducted in the Los Angeles schools, and indicated that this may not be the best approach. The task of evaluation is not an easy one, nor can it be a short one, primarily because there are so many factors and components needing evaluation and so many constituencies demanding evidence of effectiveness.

I have been thinking of these evaluations and how they can be accomplished most efficiently so that the information obtained is reliable, valid, and useful; information we can offer with confidence to support our programs and to modify and upgrade our services when necessary. After reading Schery and Lipsey's chapter I selected three issues they mentioned: issues I think we need to consider and make decisions about when we undertake evaluations. There are undoubtedly, other factors to consider, but these three seem important at the present time. I will pose the issues and present my views and suggestions for each individually.

The three questions are:

1. Should we initiate large scale evaluations immediately, or design evaluations that progress from specifics to large scale evaluations?

2. Should the sequence in which components are evaluated be prioritized?

3. Should we shift more emphasis to training skills needed to *evaluate* programs from skills needed to *administer* programs in training students and staff?

## Progression in Evaluation

At the extreme ends of a continuum, we have two approaches to program evaluation: (1) We can plan a large-scale evaluation in which data are collected on all components simultaneously, from all facets of the treatment program and delivery services, somewhat along the lines of the Los Angeles project described by Schery and Lipsey and the VA project reported by Wertz and colleagues; or (2) we can start small and gradually increase the scope of our evaluation. That is, we can examine one aspect of a program and when the results are obtained shift to examination of another aspect, then the two together, and so on.

The decision, of course, rests on determination of which approach will, in the long run, provide us with the best information. Naturally, there are advantages and disadvantages to both approaches.

One of the advantages in a large scale, simultaneous evaluation is that information can be obtained in a short time—short in comparison to a gradual approach, that is. If we choose to evalute single components and wait for results from that evaluation before starting evaluation of another, the entire program evaluation can take a considerable amount of time. An evaluation providing data from all components simultaneously could involve several years, but it would probably still take less time than a gradual evaluation.

Another advantage of a large-scale evaluation is that it probably provides a more realistic picture of the entire program because, as is frequently pointed out, the way in which individual components function when examined in isolation from the whole does not accurately reflect their function in a total program. The component in isolation may provide unrealistic evidence in comparison to evidence of its function as a component of a treatment program. And, as Schery and Lipsey pointed out, the natural setting, where many variables are operating, is different from a setting where confounding variables are controlled. Therefore, to obtain a more realistic evaluation of the function of a specific component in a complete and complex program, it is better to evaluate it in the context of that program.

Another reason for embarking on a large-scale evaluation is the opportunity for obtaining data. That is, if it is an ongoing program and the population is available, it is tempting to measure all aspects of the operation. We are reluctant to ignore data when it seems to be there to be recorded. The argument is that data are being generated, it would be a shame to ignore the data, so why not keep a record of all aspects, or as many as possible?

There are several advantages of a gradual approach to evaluation, although they are not all equally supported by empiric evidence. By gradual I mean starting small and gradually broadening the scope of the evaluation: starting with a specific component, adding another and another until the entire operation is ready for examination.

Perhaps one of the principal advantages is that a gradual approach can give us valuable insights that help us prevent occurrence of a problem more than once. If we encounter a problem in investigation of the first specific component, and without a doubt we will, we can circumvent that problem in designing evaluation of the next component and controlling for the influence of the same or a similar confounding variable.

It is easier to pose empiric questions, amenable to examination, when a specific component is to be explored, than it is when a large-scale, multiple-component operation is to be examined, and statement of purpose is important. If stated specifically enough it is possible to use operational definitions that allow accurate measurements and procedures to be developed to answer the question.

If one day we simply decide that we need to start recording data, without carefully specifying what question or questions the data are to answer, we may end with data too vague to be relevant. I believe that it is of the utmost importance to specify as precisely as possible what questions are to be explored. If the purpose is stated clearly, the rest of the components in the evaluation can be defined more readily. This means that the question cannot be broadly stated. For example, "Is the service delivery efficient" or "Is the treatment effective?" are poorly and broadly stated questions. Rather, it is necessary to specify which aspect or aspects of the service delivery is to be evaluated and what is meant by "efficient," and so on. Although it is not unusual for individuals and groups to define their purpose in broad terms and to record a variety of data, good scientific methodology requires a carefully thought out reason for gathering data to ensure that appropriate data are collected. This specificity is particularly important in program evaluations, because programs are complex entities in which a great number of

events are taking place. It is difficult, in such situations, to control the urge to keep records of all activities in the hope that something useful will show up. Such a shotgun approach may be a waste of time or provide nebulous data.

A carefully posed question helps generate operational definitions of events to be measured and/or recorded. It can also define the boundaries of the evaluations and the components to be evaluated, and this is important. The more operational the procedures and events, the more objective the measurements can be made, and the closer the units of measurement are to the events to be evaluated. Thus clearly posed questions and operational definitions facilitate obtaining believable data directly related to the purpose stated. I think this can best be done by not trying to gather data on all parts of a program at once.

There is some empiric evidence that a shotgun, large-scale approach may not always yield useful information. I'm referring to the Menninger Foundation project (Kernberg, 1973) as an example. It was started in 1954 and completed in 1973. It involved live, unaltered, minimally controlled, unmanipulated therapeutic environments in which the day to day activities of the clinicians and patients were not disturbed. The study involved 38 clinicians, 10 consultants, and 42 patients. Multiple patient characteristics were correlated with numerous treatment variables, which were identified through records kept by the clinicians on a daily basis. Analysis of the results showed that the study was very complex and the data difficult to interpret. Findings from different aspects of the program contradicted each other. Although the project was recognized as a nice attempt to evaluate treatment, it was difficult to attribute significance to the results because of the uncontrolled nature of the study. Clinicians changed, data were lost, patients changed, and so forth, so it was difficult to isolate or distinguish variables or procedures that were relevant from those that weren't. A large, uncontrolled study such as the Menninger project resembles a case study that is useful for descriptive purposes but that does not allow statements concerning treatment effectiveness or which parts of the treatment were necessary.

Problems of large scale evaluations were also described by Schery and Lipsey in their discussion of the Los Angeles school project. When many components are evaluated, many people need to be involved and coordinated for the effort. This means that there is a greater likelihood of confounding. Confounding may occur because people forget to record data, change the procedures, leave their jobs, or find the activity unmotivating and uninteresting and therefore keep inaccurate, sloppy records or neglect to keep any records. When a great deal of data is collected, there is a greater chance that some will be lost, misrecorded, inaccurate, and so forth.

In my opinion these kinds of confounds might be prevented if evaluations were planned to proceed from the specific to the general. By starting small, evaluations can be planned as carefully controlled ones. As the evaluation of one component proceeds, procedural and measurement problems are identified. Necessary changes for evaluation of the next component could be made which would result in a more efficient evaluation because confounding would be identified and controlled. Thus, with each component evaluation, the efficiency of the process would be increased and the data could be viewed as relatively stable. As each component is evaluated, it is combined with previously evaluated components until the entire program is brought together for evaluation.

Cost is another advantage in conducting a gradually programmed approach to evaluation of a complex program. It is less costly to plan and conduct an evaluation of a single component than it is to conduct an overall evaluation of many components. But what is more relevant is that it is less costly to find and eliminate confounding variables from a single component study than it is to make changes in a large-scale study. Think of it this way: If a confounding variable (or variables) is operating, the entire program is confounded when a large-scale evaluation is taking place, but only a small part of the entire program is affected if specific component evaluation is confounded. Changes can be made so that the confound does not influence results of the next component evaluation. If an entire program is confounded, results are not applicable and the cost of the entire evaluation is lost.

The most important criterion for deciding whether to initiate a large-scale total program evaluation at once, or to approach the evaluation piecemeal, is the usefulness of the data obtained by the approaches. The scientific value of the data would probably be greater in the gradual approach to evaluation. But Wertz and Schery can give us an informed opinion—I hope they will. The VA study was large scale, and since the next study has already started, I assume the investigators feel comfortable with such designs.

### Prioritizing Evaluation Sequences

Where should evaluation begin when there are many components to evaluate? Should the delivery service be made effective first, or should the treatment program be evaluated before examining the means by which treatment is delivered? Should both be evaluated simultaneously? If one or the other is selected, should the entire program undergo evaluation at one time, or should specific components of each be evaluated one at a time in a sequence of evaluations?

I've already answered the last question partially, stating that I believe it is scientifically more sound to conduct individual evaluations of variables and components before undertaking evaluations of a complete program. I am not against large-scale studies—the question is, when should they be initiated?

As to the first question, one could ask if it is more useful to develop excellent ways for administering and executing treatment programs before developing excellent intervention programs. A case can be made for either one, but if a choice is necessary, it seems more important to demonstrate that effective and efficient treatments are available to be administered before examining how the treatments are to fit into a system most efficiently. For both the staff conducting treatments and the staff planning the framework within which the treatments are to be presented, it seems more motivating and useful if a carefully evaluated program, whose effectiveness is supported by empiric evidence, is available before evaluating the way in which it is best presented.

However, if a gradual approach to evaluation is planned, a choice between evaluating treatment programs or delivery services may not be necessary. A single component of each aspect of the complex program could be started in evaluation simultaneously. This option is more possible if a gradual approach to evaluation is planned than it is if a large-scale, full program evaluation is conducted.

I also feel more comfortable with a gradual, one variable at a time approach to evaluation of either the delivery service or the treatment program. For example, in the service delivery operation, perhaps evaluation could begin with an examination of the referral sources, followed by examination of the information in each referral source entry. Systems for organizing the information could be examined next, and so on. When these evaluations are completed, the entire referral source system and information contained within would have been examined critically. The next step might be to compare the present system with another promising one to determine if the system should be retained as is, or modified in some way to make it more efficient. If modified, data could be collected which would identify the factors contributing to the added efficiency. As data on individual components are fed into the evaluation process, they are combined with each other to form a larger component for evaluation. Eventually the entire delivery system can be evaluated and compared with others for efficiency and effectiveness.

The gradual, sequential approach to evaluation may be more important to examination of treatment programs than to delivery of services. It can be done. Johnston and Pennypacker (1980) have described how the time-out procedure was developed and confirmed as an important

treatment variable in behavior disorders and noted that the procedure worked well in treatment packages.

Briefly, the research on time-out started with animal studies. Later, individual applied researchers conducted studies of time-out across populations, across behaviors, across situations and settings. The individual studies progressively began to explore different forms of time-out, again with replications across subjects, settings, individuals, and behaviors. The data accumulated until they formed a cohesive body of support for the efficacy of the procedure. Time-out was established as an effective treatment variable and was therefore incorporated into treatment programs in institutions, schools, clinics, and so on. Incorporation into treatment programs consisting of other variables that had been similarly evaluated over time demonstrated that it worked efficiently in treatment packages. Johnston and Pennypacker (1980) estimated that the process of establishing time-out as a reliable behavior treatment variable took approximately 16 years and numerous investigations. But it can be included in treatment programs with confidence because the evidence to support it is strong and durable. My point is that we need to think about all the variables involved and prioritize their study. Systematic research is essential.

Do we have the patience to conduct a number of experiments and to explore novel forms of a promising treatment variable, with a sufficient number of replications both direct and systematic, until the treatment can be recommended with few misgivings? We have not yet done so in speech and language, but it would be exciting if that were to happen. It seems idealistic but worth thinking about.

I know the objections to the approach I've suggested. It is time-consuming, and after all individual components have been identified and combined into a treatment package, it is possible that the treatment as a package will have an entirely different effect from the effect expected when each variable was explored individually—but that would be valuable information too. I think the critical question is not how much time, but rather what will provide us with data with which we can be most comfortable and in which we have the most confidence because it is scientifically sound.

## Shift in Training Emphasis

My discussion is directed to those of us in academic programs involved with students in formal coursework and clinical practicum. But it could apply to others who direct or interact with other clinicians and their staff. I'm not proposing that we neglect training our undergraduate and graduate students in the skills necessary to treat clients. They need to know how to administer treatments, and to know the treatments that are available. But it seems we spend much time in training them *how to do it*, and much less time in training them to *question* the treatments.

Oh, we may tell them to be critical and to question, or speculate, but do we spend much of our academic and practicum time in showing them how to question, or how to go about evaluating the treatments we train them to administer? If we are frank with ourselves, many of us will have to admit that we neglect this aspect of student or staff training.

Yet, this seems to me to be the most important of the three factors I've discussed. I refer, of course, to developing in our students a scientific attitude, an attitude of empiricism, a desire to examine treatment variables, compare treatments, for the purpose of obtaining objective evidence to support their clinical activities. Not only can we encourage them and teach them the skills of scientific inquiry—we can act as models for the endeavor.

We can plan excellent evaluations, well controlled and designed, but if the staff who are to conduct the evaluations are uninterested and unmotivated, the evaluations will probably be inadequate and inaccurate. We cannot rely on ourselves to do all the evaluations, we must involve others. Those others should see the necessity, the desirability of evaluations and how they can improve delivery of services and treatment of clients, for the burden of carrying out the evaluations will lie heavily on their shoulders.

For this purpose, I think it would be helpful if we devote more time and effort to instilling in our students and staff a scientific attitude, and train them well in the scientific method. A part of the clinical practicum could be devoted to training skills that would enable the students to design evaluation procedures and to see the importance of evaluation. These skills would later be available to us when we begin to develop evaluations in clinical and school settings.

## Descriptive Evidence

The most effective kind of evaluation is one in which a functional relationship is sought between the program, or component of a program, and the product outcome, or results. It is most effective because it provides information directly related to how useful the component is to the entire operation. It consists, of course, of an experimentally based evaluation.

This is not always possible, however, and may not even be desirable in the beginning, as noted by Schery and Lipsey. Perhaps a better start would be gathering or demanding some descriptive information on the treatments offered and the administrative aspects of the operation. I've thought of two categories of descriptive evidence that can be either gathered or demanded.

We might examine the rationale on which a treatment or delivery service is based. For example, was the treatment developed from a research base, a data base, or from opinions? Are the experientially derived procedures substantiated by objective information? If the foundation consists mostly of authoritarian concepts and little objective data, we might decide to wait for a treatment with a more solid base, or collect objective data before administering it. The less data, perhaps the more cautious we should be about administering a treatment program. Before we wholeheartedly adopt treatment programs offered to us by program developers, as consumers I think we should require information on how the program was developed. It would not be inappropriate for us to demand objective data to support the efficacy of a treatment from those who would encourage us to use it. I wish that we could somehow convince program developers that their treatments will be more acceptable if supported by objective data.

It is also possible to request presentation of actuarial data. That is perhaps the least difficult to obtain. Although it doesn't provide information on the effectiveness or efficiency of either the treatment or delivery service, it does provide information in regard to the kind of clients treated, the behaviors treated, and the settings in which the treatments have been applied.

It is possible to study actuarial data to examine their quality and quantity. Such examination can indicate to clinicians, teachers, and administrators whether only a small number of clients with narrowly defined problems have been successfully trained with the program, or if the treatment is applicable to a wide range of problems. For instance, is a language program successful in teaching only naming, or is it also useful for training syntactic and morphologic structures? Is the program best suited to treating adults, or only preschoolers? Has the program been applied in schools, to groups, in hospitals? Actuarial data, though descriptive in nature, can give us some idea of the scope of a treatment program.

My solutions to evaluation are not simple. Rather, they require long-term commitments from our profession, and a certain degree of doggedness and determination. Successful evaluations depend on the realization by our professionals of the importance of supporting our activities with scientific evidence.

## General Discussion

The need for evaluation was not an issue here; the need was acknowledged. At issue were the behaviors to be explored, the antecedent and consequent events, and the stimuli that should be identified for evaluation. Discussion centered around the behavioral model within which Costello had presented the variables ifluencing setting generalization.

The behavioral paradigm was thought to be too restricted and reductionistic in terms of the antecedent and consequent stimuli that effect language acquisition and intervention in the natural environment and the clinical milieu. More is taking place than can be observed, it was contended, and a behavioral model does not capture all the complexities involved in the social interactions that occur elsewhere and in the clinic.

Costello agreed that we have not yet identified all the antecedent and consequent events acting upon clients and influencing their language input and output. In fact, we have hardly begun to do so, particularly in regard to language intervention. We need to expand our exploration and our model to encompass the many variables that remain unidentified.

There was a hint in the discussion that some of the relevant variables may not be observable, at least not if the behavioral model is used to seek them. Possibly we should look to other models that will provide us with information inaccessible through a behavioral paradigm.

An important point was made that there are indeed many variables inaccessible to us now, but that doesn't necessarily mean they should remain inaccessible. It is up to us to find ways to define these variables, to develop appropriate and accurate measurement systems so that data directly related to these variables can be obtained in a carefully specified manner, in the natural environment as well as in the laboratory. This need extends not only to the client's language behavior but also to the social environment in which it occurs. All variables influencing the client's behavior should be considered.

I feel that some of the participants may have had a somewhat limited definition of the behavioral model or paradigm. In my view, the model does not place restrictions on the kinds of antecedent and consequent events to be included. Instead, any stimulus event or behavior can be included. The only restriction is that the variable or behavior be defined in such a way that it can be measured accurately and that the data represent directly what is being measured. Other than that, all variables can fit into the model. If a variable is not defined and cannot be measured, it cannot be scientifically verified and therefore cannot be supported by scientific evidence.

Perhaps the model we use for investigating language and intervention variables is less important than our need to design appropriate tools for measuring whatever we need to learn about. We can talk about the efficacy and efficiency, the success of our treatments, only when we have accurate data to present as evidence. Otherwise, we present opinions, not facts, and opinions can be readily ignored.

## REFERENCES

Hersen M, Barlow DH: *Single Case Experimental Designs*. New York: Pergamon Press, 1976

Johnston JM, Pennypacker HS: *Strategies and Tactics of Human Behavioral Research*. Hillsdale, NJ: Lawrence Erlbaum Associates, 1980

Kernberg OF: Summary and conclusions of psychotherapy and psychoanalysis. Final report of the Menninger Foundation's psychotherapy research project. *Int J Psychiat* 11:62–77, 1973

McReynolds LV, Kearns K: *Single Subject Experimental Designs in Communication Disorders*. Baltimore: University Park Press, 1982

# PART VIII

# THE CHARGE TO
# THE LANGUAGE
# PROFESSIONAL

# 17

# LANGUAGE INTERVENTION WITH CHILDREN

*NORMA S. REES*

This chapter covers my personal view of history as it applies to language intervention, as well as a few of my particular concerns.

The charge to the language professional working with children is probably no different today from what it always has been: to understand enough about language, its acquisition in normally developing children, and its manifestations in children who do not develop language normally to be able to identify goals, invent teaching procedures, and develop measurements that will elucidate our decisions about which goals apply to which children and when we have reached them. If the charge hasn't really changed, however, other factors have changed considerably. For one thing, the very concept of the language professional is new, something we didn't used to have at all. Aside from a few somewhat isolated instances, the goals and techniques of language intervention were not part of our professional currency until fairly recently. If I were to write a book about that period, I would title it *Language in the Closet*, because in those days many of us did what we now call language intervention but under some other rubric. I recall, for example, something called "delayed speech," which, in my practicum training, was a phenomenon manifested by a small group of young children who didn't talk or didn't talk much (at one point we

had two groups going, the Delayed Speech Group and the Advanced Delayed Speech Group). We played language-oriented games like Object Lotto with them and hoped for the best. Then there was the preschool deaf child with whom we did activities mysteriously called auditory training and speech reading, but all the time it was really language teaching. The notion of language intervention with children came out of the closet, I think, with the advent of a diagnostic entity called childhood aphasia, a term that came into popularity in the 1960s but that now seems to have gone out of style. In short, one of the new factors affecting the charge to the language professional is that today we believe there are children with language disorders (or impairments or deficits) and that there is a group of professionals whose business it is to do something about it.

A second significant factor characterizing the current scene is the explosion of information about language and language acquisition. To continue the autobiographic theme, as a student in speech pathology and audiology about all I knew about normal language development, apart from the order of phoneme acquisition, was that the first word (beginning the stage known as true speech) came after a period of babbling, and that after a while the child began to speak in sentences that got longer and more complex with increasing age.

About language itself I learned very little after high school classes in grammar and composition. That the situation is quite otherwise today is obvious, but it can be highlighted by a look at the "substantive areas in language acquisition" that speech-language pathology training programs provide, according to a survey by Muma, Pierce, and Muma (1981). The twelve "principles" of language acquisition most frequently mentioned by the respondents were the following:

1. Inflections: vocabulary, over-generalization, appropriate
2. One word, many referents; one referent, many words
3. Brown's five stages
4. Sequences: semantic functions
5. Brown's 14 morphemes
6. New words, old functions; new functions, old words
7. Sequences: syntactic systems
8. Knowledge and use (competence-performance)
9. Under-/overextensions
10. Pointing/naming
11. Performatives
12. Individual strategies

These items, taken from a much longer list, represent a rather mixed bag but nevertheless dramatically indicate the range and depth of current knowledge that the language professional is expected to have—and to keep up with, as new information arrives almost daily in such journals as *The Journal of Child Language, Discourse Processes, Applied Psycholinguistics,* and *First Language,* not to mention new books and the more familiar journals in speech and hearing, linguistics, and psychology.

To return to the point I started with, while the basic charge to the language professional has not altered over time, the most significant differences today are the language professional him or herself and the knowledge he or she is expected to have. Let us take another look at the growth of knowledge and the way it has affected the work of the language professional dealing with children.

Three periods in the growth of knowledge about language and language acquisi-

tion suggest themselves. The first period I have already alluded to: When we didn't even know enough to call it language, things were pretty simple for the pre-historic language professional. We had no tests and very few materials. We cut pictures out of magazines and bought Golden Books and toys and board games that stimulated talking and helped to teach vocabulary. In fact, vocabulary teaching was pretty much the major activity; color names were very big, as were animals, vehicles, and "community helpers" (postmen, firemen, and so forth).

When, in the 1960s, we began to learn about morphology, syntax, and semantics, things became very exciting for the language professional but still simple. We were able to set specific and clear goals for language intervention based on growing knowledge about language structures and age- and stage-related information about the acquisition of these structures in normal children. We developed programs for teaching is-verbing, wh-questions, and the agent-action relation. Some of us were attracted by Charles Osgood's model of language as interpreted by the Illinois Test of Psycholinguistic Abilities (Kirk, McCarthy, Kirk, 1968) and used it as a framework for measuring and training the discrete abilities that were supposed to add up to language. In spite of the hectic proliferation of tests and language training programs, in retrospect the task of the language professional seems to have been simple during this period because it was quite easy to decide what "behavior" was the immediate goal of intervention, and we were very clever at inventing procedures for establishing and shaping that behavior.

Things started getting rough for the language professional when it became apparent that morphology plus syntax plus semantics does not equal language and that the ITPA framework of discrete psycholinguistic abilities does not add up to a language user. Partly our dissatisfaction with the outcomes of the early language training programs, but more importantly our continually growing knowledge about the object itself—language as acquired and used by real people in real contexts—produced new ideas and expectations about language intervention. In addition to information about language structure (and I haven't even mentioned phonology), we were hearing about perception, neurolinguistics, cognitive development, social development, reading, pragmatics, and learning, and becoming uncomfortably aware that all these considerations are involved in the acquisition and use of language. The current state of affairs may truly be described as one in which the systems are overloaded; our problem in this period is to make sense out of the stream of information and translate it into principles and procedures of language intervention. We may update and restate the charge to the language professional accordingly: to find a way to integrate the available information about language and language-related factors and incorporate it into professional roles and practices. To climb down from this level of abstraction, let us consider some of the difficult issues we have to resolve. The review that follows is an attempt to highlight some matters of interest to me and is not to be viewed as an exhaustive survey of research and applied problems. I also attempt, insofar as possible, to avoid covering ground dealt with in other chapters.

## WHAT ARE THE PROPER GOALS OF LANGUAGE INTERVENTION WITH CHILDREN?

This issue might be restated as, What do we want children to be able to do? It seems obvious that if we were certain of the answer to this question we would know what we would like to be able to measure with respect to the child's language behavior and we would also know how to set the objectives of language intervention programs for individual children. Instead, it seems to me that clinical goals are often determined by the availability, attractiveness, or popularity of published tests and materials, as well as by certain buzzwords such as "transaction," "information processing," "referential communication," "mean length of utterance," "speech acts,"

and so forth. Moreover, because of yet another buzzword, "accountability," we are sometimes led to identify behavioral goals primarily because we know how to measure those behaviors with pretest/post-test assessment instruments, a state of affairs that always reminds me of the woman who lost her earring in the bedroom but was looking for it in the kitchen, explaining to her puzzled friend that "the light is better in here."

Lacking a coherent, integrated account of language and language acquisition, it is easy for the language professional to confuse means with ends. To illustrate, as a clinical goal, identifying the ability to repeat seven digits in the order presented rests on the assumption that a child who cannot perform this task will be unable to understand or produce sentences that are seven words (or is it morphemes?) in length. This is doubtless a strange enough assumption anyhow but the point I wish to make here is that the digit-repetition skill easily becomes an end in itself, and the more significant objective of sentence comprehension and production may never be directly addressed at all. An analogy may be taken from the sadder-but-wiser file I compiled as a former clinical director. One summer I hired a clinician who reported to me at the end of the six-week session about several children with rather routine articulation deficits that each had achieved the goal of being able to produce /p/, /b/, and /m/ in isolation. As a more timely example, now that pragmatics is part of everybody's orientation I find that clinicians sometimes spend a great deal of attention on referential communication to the neglect of other areas of functional communication. In short, we are so busy breaking down the whole into sets of manageable parts and identifiable subskills or prerequisite abilities and seizing something that we think we know how to do that we sometimes lose track of what it is all for.

To the question, What are the proper goals of language intervention with children? I propose the following answer.

The proper goals of language intervention with children are to provide them with the knowledge of language structures pertinent to their own language community and the conventional means and the ready inclination to put this knowledge to use in interpersonal communication as well as in thinking, learning, and problem-solving, insofar as the child's capacity and resources will allow. Where "conventional means" cannot apply or can apply only in limited ways, as in the case of children with severe physical, mental, or emotional handicaps, alternate structures and/or alternate means must be sought.

## WHAT ARE THE LIMITS OF LANGUAGE INTERVENTION?

Another way to put this question is, How can the language professional be certain that he or she is working on language and not something else altogether? Clinicians may, in some cases, regard their primary responsibility as teaching the structures of complete grammatical sentences; an example is Lee, Koenigsknecht, and Mulhern's *Interactive Language Development Teaching* (1975) in which the clinician is supposed to elicit "target responses" in the form of complete sentences, directing the child to "tell me the whole thing." Now, if the clinician decides to accept elliptical utterances as responses, is that language intervention or is it something different? To extend the question, is the clinician responsible for teaching code-switching ability, or is language intervention limited to a single standard form of the language? Pressing this issue still further, the clinician may be uncertain whether he or she is responsible for teaching the child when to keep quiet and when to say what, or whether responsibilities are limited to teaching the child the "what" on the assumption that the "when" will take care of itself or is somebody else's job (the classroom teacher? the family?). In short, are the social conventions of the use of language part of language intervention?

Similarly, we may question the place of written language in language intervention. Should the language professional teach reading and writing, or is that outside the limits of language intervention with children? My own point of view is that language is language, and so the language professional not only deals with oral language but also written language, sign language, and other augmentative systems. The problem with who teaches reading and writing is primarily political, not scientific, and secondarily (but importantly) a matter of whether the clinician has the requisite preparation for work in this area. But although I've answered the question of written language to my own satisfaction, it turns out to be a trick question, because if language is language, then perhaps the language professional is also responsible for teaching mathematical symbols and computer language to children who have difficulty with these school subjects. Moreover, the assertion that language is language may suggest to us that language intervention should include teaching English as a second language. Indeed, there are no simple answers—but I will venture one anyway.

To the question, What are the limits of language intervention? I propose this answer.

Everything that pertains to the child's use of language in his ordinary circumstances is potentially included in language intervention. The practical limits are set by (1) the child's own capacities, (2) the clinician's skills and knowledge, (3) the regulations about who may do what in school or clinical settings, and (4) the resources available to meet the child's needs.

## WHERE DOES COGNITION FIT IN?

A restatement of this question might be, If a particular level of cognitive development is a prerequisite for language development, what is the language clinician supposed to do about it? Certainly the viewpoint that the development of cognitive structures underlies language acquisition has influenced clinical thinking, at least since Bloom (1970) reported on children's early development of basic grammatical relations, stating that "the emergence of syntactic structures in their speech depended on the prior development of the cognitive organization of experience that is coded by language" (p. 228). With particular regard to children with language disorders, Morehead and Ingram's (1973) related conclusion was that these children "may have a specific cognitive deficit in all aspects of representational behavior which, according to Piaget, includes language" (p. 344). A view of the relationship between the development of cognitive structure and the development of language more like that of Bloom led Westby (1980), for example, to assert that "the assessment of a child's language should include the assessment of cognitive level" (p. 154). If the assessment reveals that the child's level of cognitive development is at or below the level of language development, Westby states that "it is unlikely that speech-language remediation would result in significant changes in the child's communication abilities." Moreover, if the clinician decides to work with such a child, "remediation should provide experiences to facilitate development of the cognitive sensorimotor or preoperational symbolic abilities rather than emphasizing language skills" (p. 161). The task, as seen by Westby, is to get the child's cognitive attainments to a point in advance of his language abilities so that language remediation will have something to hang on to.

Westby's recommendations illustrate this issue very well, and her own viewpoint about where cognition fits in is perfectly clear. The problem for the language professional seems to have two parts: (1) Is remediation of cognitive deficits part of language intervention? and (2) is the relationship between cognitive development and language development a simple one-way street after all?

The way I put the first part of the question suggests that cognition and language are different, if related, notions and that we could decide to deal with one, or the other, or both, or neither. Certainly the way Westby wrote about the subject fits this mode of thinking. However, recall that I also quoted Morehead and Ingram as including language as part of representational behavior. The distinction made by Westby and others is based on a view of

language remediation that focuses on "semantic concepts and syntactic structures" as the objects to be taught. Earlier, however, I proposed the broadest possible approaches to questions about the goals and limits of language intervention, and from such a standpoint the distinction between cognitive training and language training is difficult to maintain. When the language clinician engages the 2-year-old child in the activity of stacking blocks to build a tower, then knocking the tower down to start the process again, talking about it all the time, is the objective to facilitate cognitive development or language development? It seems to me that the obvious answer is both. The emphasis on cognitive development has had a positive effect in reminding language professionals that acquiring grammatical structures does not occur in a vacuum, and has served as a useful antidote to the programmed instruction consisting solely of steps toward particular linguistic structures, but it may have had a negative effect as well in persuading clinicians that cognitive attainments must be attended to first and independently of language. When I hear or read about clinicians using this approach I imagine them going about cognitive teaching with adhesive tape over their mouths to avoid contaminating the session with language.

The second part of the question I posed was, Is the relation between cognitive development and language development a simple one-way street? Putting the problem this way, of course, indicates that I believe it is not. There is instead good reason to believe that the child's growing mastery over language affects his cognitive growth as well. Bowerman (1976), for example, argues that nonlinguistic experience and sensorimotor growth are insufficient to account for the way children organize their perceptions into "conceptual chunks" that may be symbolized by linguistic units, and that language the child hears plays a role in this development. Schlesinger (1977) also points out that the child's learning of linguistic meanings is language learning, not merely cognitive learning, because the world's many languages make more distinctions than the universal cognitive structures in child development can account for; accordingly, Schlesinger concludes that "the child comes to perceive his environment in terms of the meaning relations expressed in his language" (p. 95). If language development can play a role in cognitive development, the one-way street is the wrong model.

To the question, Where does cognition fit in? I propose this answer: Everywhere.

I remember a talk by Paula Menyuk in which she called the question of the relation between cognitive development and language development a nonissue, because they arise together and interact all along the way. I can't put it any better.

## WHERE DOES PERCEPTION FIT IN?

The restatement of this question might well be, What is this business of auditory processing, and what does it have to do with language? Having already delivered myself of a lengthy comment on that subject (Rees, 1981), here it seems appropriate merely to point out that, while no one doubts that perceptual processing is an inevitable part of the full account of the operation of comprehending spoken (and written) language, the evidence for a separable auditory processing factor to be measured and remediated in language intervention programs is dubious. The language professional, regrettably, is faced with a veritable barrage of tests and remedial programs based on the assumption that auditory processing is a function composed of a set of component skills (auditory memory, auditory discrimination, auditory temporal ordering, blending, and closure) affecting a continuum of operations ranging from identification of nonlinguistic sounds to the comprehension of spoken discourse. The debt this kind of thinking owes to the Osgood-type model of language underlying the ITPA and its incompatibility with general linguistic and psycholinguistic theory is seldom acknowledged; here is a prime example of the challenge to the language

professional for integrating knowledge from various sources.

What auditory processing in the clinical sense has to do with language is a still unresolved question. There is, in fact, no good reason to assert that a specific skill, such as phonetic discrimination, is a prerequisite for language learning, and therefore remedial programs aimed to improve children's phonetic discrimination are not likely to benefit the larger goals of language intervention. The syndrome that has become known as "central auditory dysfunction" (Willeford, 1978) or "auditory perceptual disorders" (Manning, Johnston, Beasley, 1977) is offered as an explanation for affected children's difficulty with language as well as for the difficulty that language-normal children have with academic learning, but these authors offer no account of what these skills, or the lack of them, have to do with language learning or language use.

A better perspective on the role of perception in language learning may be found in the integrative reviews by Studdert-Kennedy (1976). Speech perception itself is a complex operation that goes beyond auditory skills to include the more specifically linguistic skills based on the listener's knowledge of the speech production capacities of his physiologic system, as well as the speech sound system of his language, or what Liberman and associates (1967) term "perception in the speech mode." Moreover, Studdert-Kennedy calls attention to the interaction of many levels of linguistic analysis on the actual processing of spoken utterances: auditory, phonetic, phonological, lexical, syntactic, and semantic. Today we would want to add the pragmatic, to recognize the role played by expectations of what kind of thing one is about to hear in the decision the listener makes about what he does hear.

Although auditory processing has been a hobby-horse of mine for some time, I have no scruples about including it here, because it furnishes such an excellent case for my claim that today's most important charge to the language professional is to integrate available knowledge and relate it to professional practice. To the question,

Where does perception fit in? I propose this answer.

Perception is part of a complex set of operations that interact with one another in the processing of spoken and written language; it is as much the result of knowing one's language as a prerequisite ability for learning the language.

To return to the theme of this chapter, an answer to the question of the challenge to the language professional can be stated thus: It is to reach reasoned conclusions about what language intervention is; who should perform it; how, when, and where; and to find reasoned ways to identify need for change and strategies to meet those needs. We can also add this to the challenge: To find appropriate objectives for language intervention. In my view, the only reasonable way to approach the questions of what, when, where, and how is to operate from the best possible basis of knowledge about language and its use in communication, learning, and development. There are also other factors that—while not insignificant—are quite different. For example, definitional matters, such as:

1. What is the distinction between "language intervention" and "language stimulation"?

2. What is the distinction between "language intervention" and "language teaching"?

3. Who is a language delayed child and how is he different from a language disordered or a language different child?

There are also a number of political questions, such as:

1. Who should deal with written language?

2. Who should teach English as a second language?

3. How can we get into a position where we can do our jobs with maximal autonomy?

We can even address some philosophic questions, such as:

1. Should the goal always be "normal" performance?

2. Should everybody wind up with the same skills and level of ability (should everybody talk the same)?

3. How much attention is it necessary to give to accountability and program evaluation?

There are problems I think can best be called methodological, such as:

1. Can clinical procedures and outcomes properly be described in behavioral terms?

2. What kinds of research will tell us most about the effectiveness of our intervention procedures?

Now these are legitimate questions, serious questions, interesting questions—but I believe that they are peripheral to our most significant needs. The real growth over the last three decades has been in our knowledge about language, *not* in our solutions to the definitional, political, philosophical, or methodological questions. Indeed, many of what I call peripheral questions are not about language intervention at all but about, for example, social values and social institutions, and many of them have not altered much since before language came out of the closet. The questions of who we shall serve and how much, for example, are answered in different ways as the social climate and economic resources fluctuate; but these questions, while worthy, are not questions about language intervention. They are important professional questions, but they are by no means unique to the language professional.

I started out, therefore, with a bias, and I am relieved to say that I ended with the same bias (change being painful). The challenge to the language professional is language itself. The central questions facing the language professional are the ones that relate to the goals and objectives of language intervention: finding out what these ought to be and then determining the place to start and identifying the necessary steps along the path. The problem remains one of acquiring and integrating knowledge about language, its acquisition, and its use by real live language users in real environments. Moreover, this knowledge is crucial for dealing with the methodological, philosophical, and political questions that I seemed to dismiss a while ago. How, for example, can one create an appropriate design for program evaluation without defining the desired outcome? How can we approach a question like whether the outcome should be "normal" performance until we know what normal performance consists of? Finally, how could we become autonomous professionals unless the content of our professional activity is clear and defensible?

## CONCLUSION

I have selected four issues to illustrate the kinds of challenges presented to the language professional by the knowledge base itself, much complicated by the fashions and politics of professional practice. Many other issues might be found to extend the list and emphasize the need for integration and perspective. In a sense what I have been saying is that knowledge is a burden, but I hope you will agree that the burden is exciting and stimulating, and a welcome substitute for the bliss of ignorance. Over the years one of the lessons I have learned is that every answer produces new questions. The challenge to the language professional will be to keep asking questions, trying out answers, and asking some more.

## *REFERENCES*

Bloom L: *Language Development: Form and Function in Emerging Grammars*. Cambridge, Mass: M.I.T. Press, 1970

Bowerman M: Semantic factors in the acquisition of rules for and use of sentence construction. In Morehead, DM and Morehead AE (eds): *Normal and Deficient Child Language*. Baltimore: University Park Press, 1976

Kirk S, McCarthy J, Kirk W: *Illinois Test of Psycholinguistic Abilities*, rev ed. Urbana: University of Illinois Press, 1968

Lee LL, Koenigsknecht RA, Mulhern S: *Interactive Language Development Teaching*. Evanston, Ill: Northwestern University Press, 1975

Liberman AM, Cooper FS, Shankweiler DP, Studdert-Kennedy M: Perception in the speech mode. Psychol Rev 74:431–461, 1967

Manning WH, Johnston KL, Beasley DS: The performance of children with auditory perceptual disorders on a time-compressed speech discrimination measure. J Speech Hear Dis 42:77–84, 1977

Morehead DM, Ingram D: The development of base syntax in normal and linguistically deviant children. J Speech Hear Res 16:330–352, 1973

Muma JR, Pierce S, Muma DL: Language training in speech-language pathology: Substantive domains. Paper read at the American Speech-Language-Hearing Association Meeting, Los Angeles, 1981

Rees NS: Saying more than we know: Is auditory processing disorder a meaningful concept? In Keith RW (ed): *Central Auditory and Language Disorders in Children*. Houston: College-Hill Press, 1981

Schlesinger IM: *Production and Comprehension of Utterances*. Hillsdale, NJ: Lawrence Erlbaum Associates, 1977

Studdert-Kennedy M: Speech perception. In Lass NJ (ed): *Contemporary Issues in Experimental Phonetics*. New York: Academic Press, 1976

Westby C: Assessment of cognitive and language abilities through play. Language Speech Hear Serv Schools 11:154–163, 1980

Willeford JA: Sentence tests of central auditory dysfunction. In Katz J (ed): *Handbook of Clinical Audiology*, 2nd ed. Baltimore: Williams & Wilkins, 1978

# 18

# SOME CHALLENGES FOR CLINICAL APHASIOLOGISTS

*JOHN C. ROSENBEK*

This chapter originally was to contain a set of charges to clinical aphasiologists, a prospect that occasioned some reluctance on the part of its author. Charges are duties imposed by authority. The only duty that clinical aphasiologists have is the same one they have had for generations: to treat aphasic people and their families with the greatest respect and the best existing methods. To repeat that charge seemed an insignificant task. The word "challenge," on the other hand, allows a certain freedom. Readers are free to ignore challenges, and the author is free to be an iconoclast rather than an authority.

The challenges which follow are tendentious. They reflect one person's view of what aphasiology and aphasiologists should be and do. Other writers with different biases would have listed different ones. Hopefully, as a result of reading these, they will.

## RESEARCH

Clinical aphasiology is developing a data base, but researchers, clinicians, and clinical researchers need never fear that all the questions will soon be answered. There is a perennial need for both basic and clinical research.

## BASIC RESEARCH

Clinical aphasiologists need to encourage basic research or research designed to describe normal or abnormal speech-language processes without regard for diagnostic or treatment implications (Netsell, 1982). To say it another way, they need to encourage research that probes what is predictable without worrying about how that predictability may help. Aphasiologists who ignore or squelch such research are purblind. They should not even demand that reports of basic research include a paragraph of "clinical implications." Eventually, clinicians and their patients will profit from basic research, and the gains will almost inevitably be as great and sometimes even greater than those from applied or clinical research. Clinical research merely applies the known; basic research probes the unknown.

## CLINICAL RESEARCH

To encourage and value basic research, however, is not to discourage or devalue applied or clinical research. Clinicians need to continue contributing a literature of their own. This literature should be based on the systematic study of both groups and single cases. Fortunately, we

317

already have several group studies of aphasia treatment's efficacy, and others are underway. Some of the major contributions of the group studies have been to silence some of aphasiology's detractors; to dilute, if only a little, the vitriolic attacks of others; and to convert still others to aphasiology's side. In this volume Wertz has reviewed these and other contributions made by group studies.

For a clinician trying to learn more about aphasia treatment techniques, however, group studies are a bit like a fly fisherman's waders. They keep his feet dry, but they do not improve his ability to tie a fly, pick his fishing hole, cast, or avoid dangerous stretches of water. For example, we are told by Wertz and his colleagues (1981) that their treatment was "traditional, individual stimulus-response type treatment of speech and language deficits in all communicative modalities" (p. 582). Two paragraphs are devoted to fleshing out this description. Basso, Capitani, and Vignolo (1979) say their rehabilitation was "based on two clinically observable facts and on one theoretical hypothesis" (p. 192). From their four-paragraph discussion of these, an experienced clinician can infer but not confirm what the specific techniques might have been. These comments are not intended to be critical. Researchers reporting group studies are forced to assume that readers already know what traditional methods are or where to look for them. Other crucial topics, such as the influence of type of aphasia, patient age, and timing of therapy on recovery compete for space in their articles.

Now consider how much more can be learned about technique from a single-case design like that described by Simmons (1978). In a program dubbed "giving each word the finger," she had an apraxic talker raise a finger (as if he were counting) in accompaniment to each word of sentence-length utterances. The result was a clinically significant improvement in speech. Her treatment steps and a rationale for them are included. We should replicate her treatment to see if it works for others, and we can because she was free to emphasize technique in her report of the experiment. Simmons' study demonstrates another strength of single-case designs: They bring research within each clinician's reach. Simmons treats for a living. The single-case design allows her to tell us about her day.

General guidelines for design are readily available (Hersen and Barlow, 1976), and soon a book on the topic written exclusively for speech, language, and hearing clinicians will appear (McReynolds and Kearns, 1982). Armed with these books, a colleague or two, a specific question about a specific technique or techniques, and a treatable patient, one is ready to try clinical research. And the research is publishable if it is well done. The charge that a scientifically sound article is nice but that the writer's N was too small is now recognized by journal editors for what it is: benighted.

## CHALLENGING TREATMENT'S SHIBBOLETHS

Aphasia treatment is fueled by a variety of untested tenets. Clinicians need to challenge these tenets in public because aphasic speakers are challenging them everyday in the privacy of clinics.

### TREATMENT DOES NO HARM

Many of us assume that treatment, if done by caring, intelligent clinicians never does harm. But treatment can wound. Those wounds may not weep, but they are real nonetheless. A patient in treatment can be wounded by being set off from his peers. A patient can be hurt by his failures, by the exposure of his deficits, and by the appearance of the activities and devices that we employ to help him. Even globally aphasic men and women thumb through magazines and show intense interest in the clock as they await meals and treatment. They, like their less seriously involved peers, want to appear normal. Much of treatment destroys that appearance. Before a clinician shatters a patient's facade, he or she must feel sure of being able to help the speaker rebuild something more real.

## PATIENTS WANT TREATMENT

Speech pathologists are taught that speech-language gives humans the edge over nonhumans and is essential to the quality of life. That lesson in turn has lead many clinicians to use the presence of a speech-language deficit as the most important (and sometimes the only) criterion for deciding to treat. It can be suggested, on the other hand, that a communication disorder is only a weak criterion for deciding to begin or continue treatment with an aphasic person. Many aphasic persons do not feel the need to *talk* and many more do not even feel the need to *communicate* beyond what time of day, routine, and a few grunts can tell. Many aphasic persons want to leave the hospital once they can walk independently or with minimal standby assistance. Sometimes fishing, walking, and even sitting are better than becoming a better communicator. Once a person decides he wants to be a fisherman rather than a patient, the clinician is obligated to give him his freedom and perhaps a bobber or two.

## THE TOUGH PART IS GETTING STARTED

Aphasiologists are often taught that planning treatment's first steps requires the greatest clinical acumen, but it can be argued that ending treatment is often infinitely tougher, because "cure" is a siren's song that beguiles clinicians to treat until they have tried every method in the literature at least once, regardless of its appropriateness or of the aphasic speaker's reaction. Sometimes our blindness even causes us to become part of the symptomatology: The patient has difficulty with two-step commands, has anomia, and goes to therapy three times a week. Many an aphasic speaker may show an interest in protracted treatment primarily because of not wanting to hurt "that nice therapist's feelings." Such benevolent victims must breathe easier once their clinicians finally suggest a termination or even a tapering of treat-

ment. Perhaps one difference between a consummate and an average clinician is that the former prepares for the end of treatment simultaneously with planning its beginning. Another difference is that the superior clinician knows it is time to quit even before the patient does. One has to be superior to be better than the patients one treats.

## TREAT THE WHOLE PERSON

Aphasiologists are taught to treat the whole person, because aphasia is a disorder not only of language but of the whole being. Perhaps. And perhaps we hinder as much as we help when we stop listening and begin advising. Many people, even brain damaged ones, are resilient. They are capable of solving or enduring their problems. Their ways may not be our ways, but heaven help a society dominated by clinicians' values. Clinicians think all problems have solutions; patients know and accept that some do not. The challenge is for clinicians to do less—sometimes.

## ORGANIZE TREATMENT INTO HIERARCHIES

Aphasiologists are told to use hierarchies for moving their patients toward volitional communication. Some patients, however, are unable to respond to one or more of these hierarchies because the activities that constitute them, while they may seem logical to the normal clinician who arranged them, are not at all logically ordered in the patient's eyes. Easy activities for nonaphasic speakers may be hard for aphasic ones. Activities that a normal clinician assumes are hierarchically ordered may be separate and unrelated for some aphasic speakers. Imitation is especially interesting in this context. It may be that imitation is very different neurophysiologically from spontaneous speech, especially for the aphasic speaker. If so, "follow the leader" treatment may be doomed not only for poor imitators, such as conduction aphasic speakers, but even for good imitators, such as transcortical motor aphasic speakers. Imitation then may not be the first step toward anything. Many other apparently simple activities may not be either.

## ESCHEW DRILLS

Clinical aphasiologists are told that drill is to be eschewed; that systematic stimulation is salutary and sufficient. Stimulation is probably good enough for acutely aphasic speakers, especially if physiologic recovery is occurring. Chronic speakers, however, may need drill, especially if the goal is to help them *communicate better* rather than *merely communicate*. For example, if the chronic aphasic person's trouble is with reading, and if diagnosis reveals a pattern of difficulty, that person may profit from drill of what is hard. The same is true in writing, speaking, gesturing, and even understanding.

Naming drills are almost universally maligned. It is argued that not since Adam was told to name the animals has a person had to supply names for things. Brookshire (1978) is one of many who warns against naming drills. We (Rosenbek, Green, Flynn, Wertz, Collins, 1977) have some data suggesting that a naming drill does occasionally help and that sometimes the benefit can be substantial (Rosenbeck, Collins, Donahue, Wurzman, in preparation). We drilled the naming of a 42-year-old victim of a gunshot wound whose residuals after 2 years were mild aphasia across all language modalities and a significant naming impairment. Not only did he learn names, but the learning generalized to untreated words and to other kinds of communicative performance as measured by a battery of speech-language and neuropsychologic tests.

## EMPHASIZE COMMUNICATION

We are instructed to emphasize communication rather than correctness. Hol-

land (1977) reminds us that aphasic persons communicate better than they talk, and she and others have defended pragmatics rather than programming in treatment. Emphasizing communication has heuristic and humanistic appeal, but in our experience mild and moderately impaired people who agree to stay in treatment are as interested in correctness as in getting their points across. We say "Yeah! I understand." They reply, "Yeah, but was it right?"

Clinical aphasiologists need to know about the relative efficacy of pragmatic and programming treatments and the hybrids like PACE (Davis and Wilcox, 1981) that combine elements of both. Some of us can be most pragmatic when we are having the least success helping the speaker. When he cannot change, we feel that we and the rest of his environment must. Changing listeners and environments, however, is different from changing speakers. It may be as good, but we need data.

## USE STRENGTHS TO IMPROVE WEAKNESS

A paper called "Wrinkled Feet" (Rosenbek, 1979) contained an evaluation of the traditional view in aphasia therapeutics that the clinician can use strengths to improve weaknesses. In our experience, the things the patient can do are often *dissociated* from the things he cannot and, therefore, of no use as deblockers or facilitators of impaired abilities. A variety of dissociations in aphasia are possible. Hier and Mohr (1977) have described a subtype of Wernicke's aphasia in which written and oral naming are dissociated, with written naming being superior to oral naming. We have knowingly treated two such patients. Their easily improved written naming had no influence on their spoken naming: They learned to write hundreds of words they could not learn to say. Similarly, gesturing may be dissociated from speaking. We have twice tried to deblock speaking by pairing it with gesturing. Both patients had severe Wernicke's aphasia and neither became better talkers, although both became better gesturers. This is not to say that deblocking by preceding something the patient cannot do with something he can is inevitably feckless. It is not. Neither will it ineluctably succeed. Clinical experiments may help us identify who can be deblocked and who cannot.

## ABANDONING THE PATIENT TO TREATMENT

Darley (1979) says, "We do not depend upon sentiment or intuition in declaring that therapy works. It works so well that every neurologist, psychiatrist, and speech-language pathologist responsible for patient management should refuse to accede to a plan that abandons the patient to neglect" (p. 629). Nor should we abandon every patient to treatment. Some deserve to be spared. The patient's attitude about treatment is the best criterion for deciding whom to spare. If a person is reluctant to enter treatment, but if that reluctance is more indicative of general depression (see Chapter 6) than of animosity toward speech treatment, counseling and support can be provided. If the person then comes to accept treatment, it can begin. If not, the clinician's only choice is to send him off with a blessing and the clinic phone number.

Severe and chronic aphasic speakers deserve special consideration. The kindest thing for some severely affected patients, especially if they show even mild resistance, is to allow them to go home for six months, follow their progress, and offer them treatment if they evolve into Broca's or some other more treatable aphasic type. Also, we should be especially careful about suggesting treatment for chronic aphasic speakers, reagrdless of severity, who have adjusted to their disabilities. Treatment may disturb them without improving them. A new nursing home contract is not a criterion for initiating treatment with chronic aphasic men and women, regardless of the severity of their condition.

## DEFINITION AND NOSOLOGY

Clinical aphasiology is relatively new, but aphasia has been described and studied for centuries (see Chapter 8). It may seem peculiar, then, to issue challenges about definition and classification at this late date. One person's "peculiar," however, is another's "mandatory." We must settle on the best available definition of aphasia and on the most clinically useful classification of people with it, because our failure to do so is affecting our clinical practice.

## DEFINITION OF APHASIA

Benson's book (1979) is entitled *Aphasia, Alexia, and Agraphia*. The implication is that aphasia involves listening and speaking but not reading and writing, although Benson admittedly seems to ignore this implication in the text. Damasio (1981) excludes other activities. He writes that ". . . aphasia relates exclusively to a disturbance in verbal language as opposed to other forms of language, for example, the language of gestures or of facial expression" (p. 52). Traditional aphasiologists handle definition somewhat differently. Darley (1982) joins Schuell, Jenkins, and Jiménez-Pabón (1964) in defining aphasia as a unitary disorder involving all aspects of language processing. They would argue, and Darley does, that a syndrome such as alexia without agraphia is not an aphasia, because deficits in auditory comprehension and oral language do not accompany the poor reading. Darely also excludes alexia without agraphia, and presumably other syndromes, from the aphasias on the basis of diagnosis ex juvantibus, which is to say diagnosis based on response to treatment. He says: "Patients with this disorder [alexia without agraphia] are not benefited by the general language stimulation that aphasic patients require" (p. 41). Alexia without agraphia is not aphasia because it does not respond to the same kind of treatment. Benson and Damasio's decisions about what is and what is not aphasia seem somewhat arbitrary. Darley's decisions seem less so. All, regardless of their real or apparent arbitrariness, raise interesting issues. On one hand, we are to exclude from aphasia coexisting deficits in reading and writing. On the other, we are to exclude reading and writing deficits unless they coexist with impaired auditory comprehension and speaking.

Darley's treatment hypothesis and others like it need to be tested. We have too few published studies in which alexia without agraphia has been treated (Wertz and colleagues, 1979) to know if he is right to exclude it from the aphasias. As we try to rule other syndromes, such as transcortical motor aphasia and alexia *with* agraphia, in or out, we have an even more basic problem: We have too little agreement on what is appropriate aphasia treatment. If we can agree on what is appropriate, it may be that we can eventually reclassify the aphasias and other speech-language deficits on the basis of their reaction to treatment.

## ON CLASSIFICATION SYSTEMS

Darley (1982) says that we ought to talk about *aphasia without adjectives*. He posits that differences among aphasic speakers can be explained on the basis of coexisting conditions, such as apraxia of speech, and because of differences in severity and duration of symptoms at the time of testing. Perhaps. We feel that adjectives such as global, transcortical motor, and some of the rest are helpful because they suggest differences in symptoms, localization, prognosis and treatment. Of course, not all adjectives are equally suggestive. However, the danger in treating aphasia without adjectives is that we are tempted to treat aphasic persons without regard for their differences. We may be tempted, for example, to begin every program with auditory stimulation. Adjectives are as likely to highlight differences as to conceal them.

## HELP FOR THE LEFT HEMISPHERE

Benson (1979) says that "for almost every right-handed and for many left-handed adults, the left hemisphere subserves all or most of the functions of language" (p. 7). Communication, however, requires contributions from other cortical and subcortical structures. These structures and their contributions are attracting an increasing number of researchers.

### THE RIGHT HEMISPHERE

Remember when the right hemisphere was the minor hemisphere? It is now fighting for equality with the left. Researchers are studying its contributions to communication (Hécaen, 1978), speculating on its importance to recovery from (or with) aphasia (Moscovitch, 1976), and trying to develop treatment plans to activate it during aphasia treatment (West, 1978; Myers, 1980). Some clinicians (Myers, in press) are developing methods for treating the communication deficits resulting from its damage. Fortunately, these plans go beyond merely placing a purple braid at the left margin of the patient's lap board.

### SUBCORTICAL MECHANISMS AND SYNDROMES

The contribution of subcortical structures to normal speech-language performance is being studied (Ojemann, 1975). As might be predicted, a variety of subcortical aphasic syndromes are also being discussed (Benson, 1979), although the number and distinctiveness of these are being debated (Benson, 1979; Alexander and LoVerme, 1980). The *clinical payoff* for recognizing the importance of subcortical structures to communication and of being able to diagnose subcortical aphasias may be a better prediction of how well individual patients will do. The *research payoff* may be that aphasiologists can contribute even further to knowledge about language's organization in the central nervous system.

## KEEPING UP

Aphasiologists increasingly have more prestige in the medical community. To retain it they will need to keep up not only with developments in aphasiology but in other fields as well. Two of the most important are linguistics and neuroradiology.

## *LINGUISTICS*

Linguists are trying to understand language's organization in the brain and the mechanism responsible for differences among aphasic syndromes. They are also studying aphasia for what it might reveal about normal speech-language function. Berndt and Caramazza's discussion of Broca's aphasia (1980) and Marin, Saffran, and Schwartz's study of dissociations in aphasia (1976) are examples of linguistic contributions that give clinicians clues about why selected aphasic syndromes appear as they do. These and similar studies provide insights about the proper focus of treatment for certain aphasic types and hypotheses about why certain procedures fail while others succeed. They simultaneously provide researchers with hypotheses about normal language function.

## *NEURORADIOLOGY*

Developments in neuroradiology are equally exciting and helpful (Oldendorf, 1981). First, transmission computed tomography (CT) has improved neuroradiology's ability to localize the site of structural lesions associated with various patterns of neurologic deficit. A more recent technologic advance, positron emission tomography (PET), is contributing more on the functional as opposed to the merely structural locus of lesions. While the data are only now coming in, it appears that functional lesions as revealed by PET are more extensive than structural ones revealed by CT (Hanson and colleagues, 1981). For example, lesions causing aphasia may involve more subcortical structures than originally thought. If this is true, we eventually will be forced to revise traditional concepts of localization in aphasia. PET and measurements of regional cerebral blood flow (rCBF) (Lassen, Ingvar, Skinhøj, 1978) may also expand our knowledge of the functional organization of *normal* cortical and subcortical structures. As a result, in the next decade we will no doubt have to learn a new set of notions about the neural substrates of speech and language. None of these developments dooms the clinical aphasiologist's function as a localizer of lesions, or as a contributor to knowledge of normal brain function. Instead, they dictate that the clinician make even more careful observations for correlation with constantly improving site of lesion and functional organization data.

## FEELINGS

A final challenge concerns the way you feel as professional speech pathologists. Feelings are as important to how clinicians perform as they are to how aphasic speakers do. Therefore a few words about confidence, pride, and laughter seem warranted.

Clinical aphasiologists (or some of us) lack confidence for a number of reasons, the foremost being that we have been asked some hard questions about our worth. It is important to remember that aphasiology is not being picked on when its methods are assailed or when it is challenged to prove its worth. Peer review is a fact of life in a medical setting; so are professional jealousies. Anonymity is the only protection against review and rancor; fortunately, we have never been anonymous. Besides, challenge has spurred us on. We might not have documented our worth so sedulously if we had not been challenged.

Clinical aphasiologists, however, have not had to turn exclusively to the review of others for their discomfort. We have questioned our worth because we realize that considerably less than 100 percent of the patients referred to us get better as a result of our treatment. The challenge is: Do not be shaken. *No* specialty does better. A portion of patients are unchanged by visiting *any* appropriate specialist. A portion get better without any specific treatment. A portion get better while under the specialist's care but not because of anything specific the specialist has done. One in three or one in four gets better because of something the specialist does. We can be proud of helping one in four or one in three. Presumably only the gods do more.

I think aphasiologists also question the intellectual demands of clinical, especially therapeutic, activity. Sharing a room with a patient twice daily is no more boring than much of dentistry, dermatology, thoracic surgery, or any other health care activity. Nor is it less professional. Why so many speech pathologists flee the clinic for administration is baffling. It is as if some people who have graduated from the American Speech-Language-Hearing Association's programs treat professional, clinical activities as externships that are to be gotten through—and beyond. Balderdash. Most of the *best* people we know would rather touch people than paper. They are proud to be clinicians.

The last challenge is to smile. Mencken (Dorsey, 1980) may be laughter's best advocate, for it was he who said, "A horse laugh is worth a thousand syllogisms." Norman Cousins (1979) brought laughter to medicine. In *Anatomy of an Illness* (1979) he says, "I made the joyous discovery that ten minutes of genuine belly laughter had an anesthetic effect and would give me at least two hours of pain-free sleep (p. 39). Cousins overcame severe disease in large measure because of his own efforts, including his calculated effort to laugh. And LaPointe has brought laughter to speech pathology. Perhaps too many of us are afraid that grinning betrays a lack of dedication, or that real scientists only laugh after the work is all done. Laughter is not only good medicine, it is good clinical science.

## REFERENCES

Alexander MP, LoVerme SR: Aphasia after left hemispheric intracerebral hemorrhage. Neurol 30:1193–1202, 1980

Basso A, Capitani E, Vignolo LA: Influence of rehabilitation on language skills in aphasic patients. Arch Neurol 36:190–196, 1979

Benson DF: *Aphasia, Alexia, and Agraphia.* New York: Churchill Livingstone, 1979.

Berndt RS, Caramazza A: A redefinition of the syndrome of Broca's aphasia: Implications for a neuropsychological model of language. Appl Psycholing 1:225–278, 1980

Brookshire RH: *An Introduction to Aphasia,* 2nd ed. Minneapolis: BRK Publishers, 1978

Cousins N: *Anatomy of an Illness as Perceived by the Patient: Reflections on Healing and Regeneration.* New York: Norton Press, 1979

Damasio A: The nature of aphasia: Signs and syndromes. In Sarno MT (ed): *Acquired Aphasia.* New York: Academic Press, 1981

Darley FL: Treat or neglect? ASHA 21:628–631, 1979

Darley FL: *Aphasia.* Philadelphia: WB Saunders Co, 1982

Davis GA, Wilcox MJ: Incorporating parameters of natural conversation in aphasia treatment. In Chapey R (ed): *Language Intervention Strategies in Adult Aphasia.* Baltimore: Williams & Wilkins, 1981, pp. 169–193

Dorsey J: *On Mencken.* New York: Alfred A. Knopf, 1980

Hanson, WR, Metter EJ, Kuhl DE, Phelps ME, Wasterlain CG: Regional Cerebral metabolism in aphasia (18 FDG PECT). Paper presented to the American Speech-Language-Hearing Association, Los Angeles, California, 1981

Hécaen, H: Right hemisphere contributions to language functions. In Buser PA, Rougeul-Buser A (eds): *Cerebral Correlates of Conscious Experience.* Amsterdam: North-Holland Publishing Co, 1978, pp 199–214

Hersen M, Barlow DH: *Single-case Experimental Designs: Strategies for Studying Behavior Change.* New York: Pergamon Press, 1976

Hier DB, Mohr JP: Incongrous oral and written naming. Evidence for a subdivision of the syndrome of Wernicke's aphasia. Brain Lang 4:115–126, 1977

Holland AL: Some practical considerations in aphasia rehabilitation. In Sullivan M, Kommers MS (eds): *Rationale for Adult Aphasia Therapy.* Omaha: University of Nebraska Medical Center, 1977, pp 167–180

Lassen NA, Ingvar DH, Skinhøj E: Brain function and blood flow. Sci Am 239:62–71, 1978

Marin OSM, Saffran EM, Schwartz MF: Dissociations of language in aphasia: Implications for normal function. Ann NY Acad Sci 280:868–884, 1976

McReynolds LV, Kearns KP: *Single-Subject Experimental Designs in Communicative Disorders.* Baltimore: University Park Press, 1982

Moscovitch M: On the representation of language in the right hemisphere of right-handed people. Brain Lang 3:47–71, 1976

Myers PS: Visual imagery in aphasia treatment: A new look. In Brookshire RH (ed): *Clinical Aphasiology: Conference Proceedings, 1980*. Minneapolis: BRK Publishers, 1980, pp 68–77

Myers PS: Right hemisphere communication disorders. In Perkins WH (ed): *Current Therapy of Communication Disorders*. New York: Thieme-Stratton Inc, in press

Netsell R: Personal communication, 1982

Ojemann GA: Subcortical language mechanisms. In Whitaker J. Whitaker HA (eds): *Studies in Neurolinguistics*, volume 2. New York: Academic Press, 1975, pp 103–138

Oldendorf WH: Nuclear medicine in clinical neurology: An update. Ann Neurol 10:207–213, 1981

Rosenbek, JC: Wrinkled feet. In Brookshire RH (ed): *Clinical Aphasiology: Proceedings of the Conference, 1979*. Minneapolis: BRK Publishers, 1979, pp 163–175.

Rosenbeck JC, Collins, M, Donahue E, Wurzman L: Treating dysnomia with drill: What's this? In preparation

Rosenbek JC, Green EF, Flynn M, Wertz RT, Collins M. Anomia: A clinical experiment. In Brookshire RH (ed): *Clinical Aphasiology: Conference Proceedings, 1977*. Minneapolis: BRK Publishers, 1977, pp 103–111

Schuell H, Jenkins JJ, Jiménez-Pabón E, *Aphasia in Adults*. New York: Harper and Row, Publishers, 1964.

Simmons NN: Finger counting as an intersystemic reorganizer in apraxia of speech. In Brookshire RH (ed): *Clinical Aphasiology: Conference Proceedings, 1978*. Minneapolis: BRK Publishers, 1978, pp 174–179

Wertz RT, Collins MJ, Weiss D, Kurtzke JF, Friden T, Brookshire RH, Pierce J, Holtzapple P, Hubbard DJ, Porch BE, West JA, Davis L, Matovitch V, Morley GK, Resurreccion E: Veterans Administration cooperative study on aphasia: A comparison of individual and group treatment. J Speech Hear Res 24:580–594, 1981

Wertz RT, Flynn M, Green EF, Rosenbek JC, Collins MJ: Alexia without agraphia: Some considerations for patient management. Aphasia Apraxia Agnosia 1:26–31 1979

West JF: Heightening the action imagery of materials used in aphasia treatment. In Brookshire RH (ed): *Clinical Aphasiology: Conference Proceedings, 1978*. Minneapolis: BRK Publishers, 1978, pp 201–211

# AN OUTSIDER'S VIEW
# OF LANGUAGE INTERVENTION

*PAUL FLETCHER*

It would not be possible to provide here a judicious and considered summary that would do justice to the complexity of the issues addressed in this book. Instead this chapter addresses what appear to be some key issues and directions. Inevitably the choice of topics will reflect the author's interests and prejudices. Nevertheless there should be some common ground— we do after all speak (roughly) the same language, and face common problems.

## LANGUAGE AS COMMUNICATION

One of the main themes in this volume concerns communication. A number of chapters have referred to, or urged, communication, or the inculcation of communication skills, as a crucial goal of intervention. There is a sense in which this is a laudable shift of emphasis in intervention programming. A stress on language as a means for social interaction, rather than as simply a set of sentences generated by an abstract grammar, is a healthy emphasis for a discipline concerned with language behavior in the broadest sense. Even if these two views are not ultimately incompatible (since appropriate language use requires at least control of sentences with well-formed internal structure), broader based views of discourse structure, and the possible effect of this structure on aspects of the internal structure of sentences, are welcome.[*] What is crucial, however, is how this broader perspective is translated into effective intervention planning and implementation.

If the communicative emphasis means an approach to language which has at its heart a functional syntax, then this does not seem too radical a shift. It means that we recognize that structures can be put to a variety of uses—auxiliary initial sentences, for example, can be used to ask questions, or to make requests, or to issue imperatives, albeit indirectly. Or it means that we realize that the appropriate way to look at personal pronouns is not just as members of a closed grammatic category, but as referent identifiers in discourse. The recognition of the uses to which sentence-types or grammatic items can be put inevitably affects our assessment of a client's linguistic capabilities and our remediation techniques.

To take our first example, we might no longer be concerned to introduce *yes/no* questions as a grammatic category that the child or adult has to learn, but instead we might concentrate on *can-* and *will-* initial sentences as requests for permission and action respectively. The focus thus shifts

---

[*]For a number of papers relevant to this topic see Hickman (1980).

from a transformational relationship between declaratives and *yes/no* questions, with no regard for the auxiliaries that may exemplify this relationship, to specific auxiliary-initial structures tied to specific social contexts. Of course we need some decision procedure for the order in which these auxiliary-initial structures are to be learned, and we also have to face difficult questions about the characteristics of the dialogue in which we embed the target structures, and the nature of the extra-linguistic contexts to which they relate. In addition we must at some point grasp the nettle of generalization. That said, there seems little in this outline of the communicative approach to quarrel with. Language is seen as a flexible and creative instrument in which sentence structures are put to use in social interactive situations. The goal of intervention is the learning of this language by the client, and the clinician's role, among other things, is to provide the right conditions for learning[†]

There is, however, a more restricted sense in which "communicative," or "communication," in relation to language programming, has been used. Here giving the client communicative skills does not seem to mean providing him with the grammatic and lexic means to realize a range of communicative functions, but something more concrete: giving him specific lexic items and/or sentence tokens that are appropriate for situations or events in which (we judge) he finds himself in his daily life. So we construct a specific language for ordering food, or going to a football game, or buying a newspaper. There are two problems with this approach. First, the set of situations in which language may be used in daily life is practically limitless, and making an inventory or imagining the possibilities is going to keep the clinician wildly busy. Second, such an approach to communication runs the risk of inculcating stereotypic and ritualized responses—exactly the situation we want to avoid. It seems safer to assume that the myriad situations in which clients may find themselves will reflect a limited set of communicative functions, themselves realized by a predictable set of syntactic structures.

Now it is possible that we are setting up here a false dichotomy. It may be that the communicative functions versus concrete communication events distinction is actually a distinction of therapeutic strategy with respect to quite different client populations—language impaired versus severely mentally retarded, for example. But since the vogue term "communicative" can be construed in such quite different ways, with serious implications for the clinician, it is worth making the difference explicit.

## INTERVENTION AND LANGUAGE LEARNING

Another important point concerns the relationship between intervention and research in language learning. Often the gap between the two is wide. It is necessarily narrowed, however, when we speak of language intervention begin not so much teaching language skills, but rather creating the conditions in which language can take place. For this to be more than hand-waving, those doing the intervening need to be provided with detailed and up-to-date information about language learning and the variables that influence it. This is no easy matter, as the following case study may illustrate.

As Skinner (1976) observes, "A thoroughgoing developmentalism . . . almost denies the possibility of effective action." In attempting intervention with children, we implicitly deny this developmentalism. Paradoxically, we tend to use information from normal development for both assessment and intervention. If we are serious about "creating the conditions for learning" in intervention, then we do need to know how learning proceeds in the normal child, and what variables affect it; we also need to know if the learning process is very different in the language impaired child.

---

[†]This idea is not unique to the language intervention field—our colleagues in second language learning have been discussing it for some time. See, for example, Hughes (1982).

These are complex questions but recognizing their complexity is a considerable step in the direction of answering them.

About 9 years ago, a clinician I was working with showed me some spontaneous speech data from a language impaired child who was 4 years old at the time. One of the noticeable features of the data was an absence of auxiliary verbs, and temporal and aspectual markers—those features of English structure which I have referred to elsewhere as verb-forms (Fletcher, 1979): The clinician then asked for advice on organizing her remediation program to remedy this deficiency. My response was that I would examine the normal language development literature and let her know. (To the best of my knowledge she is still waiting!) At that time child language models, taking their cue from the transformational literature, were syntactic in orientation, and heavily concerned with rule-formation. Auxiliaries were of interest for their role in question formation, not for their temporal, modal, or other meanings. Examination of transcripts from normal children between the ages of 2.6 and 3.0 indicated, however, that the first auxiliaries that appear mostly occur in initial position in sentences, though there are some restricted appearances in declaratives, mostly as responses such as *I can*. At least to being with, then, the notion that this behavior reflects a *rule* of inversion finds little support in the data. The first auxiliaries that occur (and the only auxiliaries for some time) are *can* and *will*. These are used by child and mother in requests for action and permissions that relate to action, and indirect commands: "Can me go library now?" "Can me see my birthday cake?" "Will you eat your toast?" These are *yes/no* questions in form, but not function. *Yes/no* questions require affirmation or denial of their predicates by hearers. When the child does deny, as by replying "I willn't" to "Will you eat your toast?" this is a refusal of an indirect command. As far as the child is concerned, the so-called indirect functions of sentence-initial auxiliaries come first, and the utility of *can* and *will* for regulating aspects of mother and child joint activity goes some way towards explaining

why, of all the auxiliaries available in the language, these particular modals turn up first. In general, features of discourse structure and their social interactive role seem more plausible as explanations of the child's learning at this point than competence-based notions of rule acquisition. Support for this view comes from studies of the relationship between maternal language use and child language growth (Newport, Gleitman, and Gleitman, 1977; Furrow, Nelson, and Benedict, 1979). Both these studies show a significant positive correlation between sentence-initial auxiliary use by mothers and the development of these items by the child.

But we cannot always rely on input, or rather the structure of the discourse the child takes part in, as the explanation for a specific feature of the child's language learning. In an intensive study of a British English (henceforth BE) child, an idiosyncratic morphologic overgeneralization was noted (see Fletcher, 1981, for full details). Between the ages of 2.6 and 3.0 this child used forms like *maden, tippen, getten, spoilen, bringen, comen* to refer to past actions, in sentences like "Me maden that," "Now me tippen that over," "Her getten cold feet." These were not isolated instances. For a period of about six months the child preferred to mark with-*en*, for past time reference, those verbs in her vocabulary that ended with consonants. This is an unusual strategy, certainly, but explicable as an idiosyncratic example of the application of the young child's well-attested morphologic analysis mechanism to English (where -*en* forms in the mother's speech, like *broken, fallen* can refer to past events). We are aware, from other children learning English, as well as from children learning other languages morphologically richer than English, that children around 3 years of age can perform inflectional morphologic analyses with great facility, provided the inflectional systems are semantically transparent. This research seems to indicate that children come to language learning equipped with quite powerful mechanisms for extracting morphologic rules. The existence of the mechanism seems more important than the character of the input so far as this area of language learning is concerned. Past participles that are -en marked in English are few, yet the child we studied still performs the requisite morphologic analysis. Even if we consider *token* frequency, rather than type, we find no relationship between input frequency and the child's use of -en. The incidence of -en in the mother's speech does not provide a straightforward explanation for the child picking it up.

The interaction between the child's learning mechanisms and the structure of the language he is learning may not always be obvious. In particular, if there is a *lexic* dimension to grammatic learning, it may not be easy to pick up. As part of our studies of verb-forms, we have been looking at how children differentiate past and present perfect (*he finished* versus *he's finished*, or *he fell* versus *he's fallen*). These categories have formal and functional overlap, and so a priori might constitute an area of difficulty for children. Past tenses, particularly irregular past, turn up quite early (possibly before the age of 2.6) in conversation protocols. If we identify present perfects in terms of *have* plus past participle, then we find these forms turning up, for BE, at around age 3.0. Closer scrutiny reveals, however, that the occurrence of *have* is, initially and for some time, restricted to the "past participle" *got*. In other words we do not really have a category "present perfect" at all, but one lexic item with which *have* appears. So it is not that the BE child of 3.0 is differentiating present perfects from pasts, but rather that he is differentiating *have got* from past tenses. In BE *have got* refers only to present states, attributes, or possessions, unlike have plus other past participles. The "lexic exception" (Fodor and Smith, 1978) that *have got* constitutes is the norm for the child for some time. Eventually the lexic restriction on *have* is lifted, and it becomes possible to talk of a grammatic category "present perfect."

How would we sum up the relevance of all this for the aforementioned clinician and her intervention programming? We began by thinking of intervention as "creating the conditions for learning." But until we have a clear idea of what those conditions are, we will find it difficult to impose control and direction on the learning process. What is suggested here is that learning for the normal child is a lengthy process in which the nature of the language environment, the child's own language mechanisms, and the language being learned, all play a part. It is the job of the developmental linguist to try to specify, in detail, what the relative contributions of these variables might be. There is no reason to suppose that language learning for the language impaired child is any less involved. Microanalytic approaches and intensive longitudinal studies would thus seem to be a priority.

Finally, in the welter of linguistic detail, a significant point may have escaped you. It was a clinician who precipitated this series of studies into verb-forms by asking her question. There seems to be no good reason why clinicians should wait passively for so-called feeder disciplines like linguistics and psychology to provide them with information. Indeed, it is quite possible that if they do stand idly by, the right kind of information will never be available. Asking specific questions, on the other hand, will not only focus the theories and procedures of the developmental linguist to fit the clinician's requirements, but will serve to organize what is increasingly a disorganized discipline. This will tide us over until the day when the majority of speech-language pathologists are practitioners *and* scientists, who will provide their own answers to the questions they ask.

## REFERENCES

Fletcher P: The development of the verb phrase. In Fletcher P, Garman M (eds): *Language Acquisition: Studies in First Language Development.* Cambridge University Press, 1979

Fletcher P: Verb form development: Lexis or grammar? Paper presented at the Second International Child Language Congress, Vancouver, August, 1981

Fodor JD, Smith M: What kind of an exception is 'have got'? Ling Inquiry 9:45–65, 1978

Furrow D, Nelson K, Benedict H: Mothers' speech to children and syntactic development: Some simple relationships. J Child Lang 6:423–442, 1979

Hickman M (ed): *Proceedings of a Working Conference on the Social Foundations of Language and Thought*. Chicago: Center for Psychosocial Studies, University of Chicago, 1980

Hughes GA: Second Language learning and communicative language teaching. In Johnson K, Porter D (eds): *New Perspectives in Communicative Language Teaching*. New York: Academic Press, 1982

Newport E, Gleitman L, Gleitman H: Mother, I'd rather do it myself: Some effects and non-effects of maternal speech style. In Snow CE, Ferguson CA (eds): *Talking to Children: Language Input and Acquisition*. Cambridge: Cambridge University Press, 1977

Skinner BF: *Walden 2*, rev ed New York: Macmillan Publishing Co, Inc, 1976

Strevens P: Special purpose language-learning: A perspective. In Kinsella V (ed): *Language Teaching and Linguistics: Surveys*. Cambridge: Cambridge University Press, 1978

Wilkins DAW: Dangerous dichotomies in applied linguistics and language teaching. In Crystal D (ed): *Linguistic Controversies: Essays in Linguistic Theory and Practice in Honour of F.R. Palmer*. London: Edward Arnold, 1982

# INDEX